Religion C 234

LDS Marriage and Family Relations
Student Manual

Department of Church History/Doctrine
Brigham Young University

KENDALL/HUNT PUBLISHING COMPANY
4050 Westmark Drive   Dubuque, Iowa 52002

Contents

Text of LDS Proclamation

President Gordon B. Hinckley

General Relief Society Meeting, 23 September 1995

We, the First Presidency and the Council of the Twelve Apostles of The Church of Jesus Christ of Latter-day Saints, solemnly proclaim that marriage between a man and a woman is ordained of God and that the family is central to the Creator's plan for the eternal destiny of His children.

All human beings—male and female—are created in the image of God. Each is a beloved spirit son or daughter of heavenly parents, and, as such, each has a divine nature and destiny. Gender is an essential characteristic of individual premortal, mortal, and eternal identity and purpose.

In the premortal realm, spirit sons and daughters knew and worshiped God as their Eternal Father and accepted His plan by which His children could obtain a physical body and gain earthly experience to progress toward perfection and ultimately realize his or her divine destiny as an heir of eternal life. The divine plan of happiness enables family relationships to be perpetuated beyond the grave. Sacred ordinances and covenants available in holy temples make it possible for individuals to return to the presence of God and for families to be united eternally.

The first commandment that God gave to Adam and Eve pertained to their potential for parenthood as husband and wife. We declare that God's commandment for His children to multiply and replenish the Earth remains in force. We further declare that God has commanded that the sacred powers of procreation are to be employed only between man and woman, lawfully wedded as husband and wife.

We declare the means by which mortal life is created to be divinely appointed. We affirm the sanctity of life and of its importance in God's eternal plan.

Husband and wife have a solemn responsibility to love and care for each other and for their children. "Children are an heritage of the Lord" (Psalms 127:3). Parents have a sacred duty to rear their children in love and righteousness, to provide for their physical and spiritual needs, to teach them to love and serve one another, to observe the commandments of God and to be law-abiding citizens wherever they live. Husbands and wives—mothers and fathers—will be held accountable before God for the discharge of these obligations.

The family is ordained of God. Marriage between a man and woman is essential to His eternal plan. Children are entitled to birth within the bonds of matrimony, and to be reared by a father and a mother who honor marital vows with complete fidelity. Happiness in family life is most likely to be achieved when founded upon the teachings of the Lord Jesus Christ. Successful marriages and families are established and maintained on principles of faith, prayer, repentance, forgiveness, respect, love, compassion, work and wholesome recreational activities. By divine design, fathers are to preside over their families in love and righteousness and are responsible to provide the necessities of life and the protection of their families. Mothers are primarily responsible for the nurture of their children. In these sacred responsibilities, fathers and mothers are obligated to help one another as equal partners. Disability, death or other circumstances may necessitate individual adaptation. Extended families should lend support when needed.

We warn that individuals who violate covenants of chastity, who abuse spouse or offspring, or who fail to fulfill family responsibilities will one day stand accountable before God. Further, we warn that the disintegration of the family will bring upon the individuals, communities and nations the calamities foretold by ancient and modern prophets.

We call upon responsible citizens and officers of government everywhere to promote those measures designed to maintain and strengthen the family as the fundamental unit of society.

The Family

Elder Henry B. Eyring of the Quorum of the Twelve Apostles

The Ensign, February, 1998, pp. 10–18

 he family unit is fundamental not only to society and to the Church but to our hope for eternal life.

Since the restoration of the gospel of Jesus Christ through the Prophet Joseph Smith, The Church of Jesus Christ of Latter-day Saints has issued a proclamation only four times.[1] It had been more than 15 years since the previous one, which described the progress the Church had made in 150 years of its history. Thus, we can understand the importance our Heavenly Father places upon the family, the subject of the fifth and most recent proclamation, given on 23 September 1995.[2]

Because our Father loves his children, he will not leave us to guess about what matters most in this life concerning where our attention could bring happiness or our indifference could bring sadness. Sometimes he will tell a person such things directly, by inspiration. But he will, in addition, tell us these important matters through his servants. In the words of the prophet Amos, recorded long ago, "Surely the Lord God will do nothing, but he revealeth his secret unto his servants the prophets" (Amos 3:7). He does this so that even those who cannot feel inspiration can know, if they will only listen, that they have been told the truth and been warned.

The title of the proclamation on the family reads: "The Family: A Proclamation to the World—The First Presidency and Council of the Twelve Apostles of The Church of Jesus Christ of Latter-day Saints."

Three things about the title are worth our careful reflection. First, the subject: the family. Second, the audience, which is the whole world. And third, those proclaiming it are those we sustain as prophets, seers, and revelators. All this means that the family must be of tremendous importance to us, that whatever the proclamation says could help anyone in the world, and that the proclamation fits the Lord's promise when he said, "Whether by mine own voice or by the voice of my servants, it is the same" (D&C 1:38).

Before we examine the words of the proclamation, let us note that the proclamation's title tells us something about how to prepare for the words that follow. We can expect that God won't just tell us a few interesting things about the family; he will tell us what a family ought to be and why. Further, we know that our Heavenly Father and his Son, Jesus Christ, want us to become like them so that we can dwell with them forever in families. We know that from this simple statement of their intent: "This is my work and my glory— to bring to pass the immortality and eternal life of man" (Moses 1:39).

Eternal Life: A Destination within Reach

Eternal life means to become like the Father and to live in families in happiness and joy forever, so of course we know that what he wants for us will require help beyond our powers. And if we have feelings of inadequacy, they can make it easier for us to repent and to be ready to rely on the Lord's help. The fact that the proclamation is applicable to all the world—applicable to every person and government in it—gives us assurance that we need not be overwhelmed with our feelings of inadequacy. Whoever we are, however difficult our circumstances, we can know that what our Father requires of us if we are to qualify for the blessings

3

of eternal life will not be beyond our ability. What a young boy said long ago when he faced a seemingly impossible assignment is true: "I know that the Lord giveth no commandments unto the children of men, save he shall prepare a way for them that they may accomplish the thing which he commandeth them" (1 Ne. 3:7).

We may have to pray with faith to know what we are to do, and after obtaining such knowledge we must pray with a determination to obey. But we can know what to do and be sure that the way has been prepared for us by the Lord. As we read what the proclamation tells us about the family, we can expect—in fact, we must expect—impressions to come to our minds as to what we are to do. And we can be confident it is possible for us to do according to those impressions.

The proclamation begins this way:

> We, the First Presidency and the Council of the Twelve Apostles of The Church of Jesus Christ of Latter-day Saints, solemnly proclaim that marriage between a man and a woman is ordained of God and that the family is central to the Creator's plan for the eternal destiny of His children.

Let us try to imagine ourselves as little children hearing those words for the first time and believing they are true. This can be a useful attitude whenever we read or hear the word of God, because he has told us, "Verily I say unto you, Whosoever shall not receive the kingdom of God as a little child shall in no wise enter therein" (Luke 18:17).

A little child would feel safe hearing the words "marriage between a man and a woman is ordained of God." The child would know that the longing to have the love of both a father and a mother, distinct but somehow perfectly complementary, exists because such longing is part of the eternal pattern, the pattern of happiness. The child would also feel safer knowing that God will help the mother and father resolve differences and love each other, if only they would ask for his help and try. Prayers of children across the earth would go up to God, pleading for his help for parents and for families.

Now read in that same way, as if we were little children, the next words of the proclamation:

> All human beings—male and female—are created in the image of God. Each is a beloved spirit son or daughter of heavenly parents, and, as such, each has a divine nature and destiny. Gender is an essential characteristic of individual premortal, mortal, and eternal identity and purpose.
>
> In the premortal realm, spirit sons and daughters knew and worshiped God as their Eternal Father and accepted His plan by which His children could obtain a physical body and gain earthly experience to progress toward perfection and ultimately realize his or her divine destiny as an heir of eternal life. The divine plan of happiness enables family relationships to be perpetuated beyond the grave. Sacred ordinances and covenants available in holy temples make it possible for individuals to return to the presence of God and for families to be united eternally.

Understanding these truths ought to make it easier for us to feel like a little child, not just as we read the proclamation but throughout our lives, because we are children—but in what a family and of what Parents! We can picture ourselves as we were, for longer than we can imagine, sons and daughters associating in our heavenly home with Parents who knew and loved us. Also, we know that in the premortal world we were men or women with unique gifts because of our gender and that the opportunity to be married and to become one was necessary for us to have eternal happiness. But now that we are here we can picture ourselves home again with our Heavenly Parents in that wonderful place, not only as sons and daughters but as husbands and wives, fathers and mothers, grandfathers and grandmothers, grandsons and granddaughters, bound together forever in loving families.

With that picture before us we can never be tempted to think, "Maybe I wouldn't like eternal life. Maybe I would be just as happy in some other place in the life after death, for haven't I heard that even the lowest kingdoms are supposed to be more beautiful than anything we have here on earth?"

To counter such attitudes, we must have the goal of eternal life not just in our minds but in our hearts. What we want is eternal life in families. We don't just want it if that is what happens to work out, nor do we want something that might seem to be only approaching eternal life. We want eternal life, whatever its cost in effort, pain, and sacrifice. Thus, whenever we are tempted to make eternal life our hope instead of our determination, we might think of a building I saw recently.

I was in Boston, Massachusetts. For a little nostalgia, I walked up to the front of the boardinghouse I was living in when I met Kathleen, who is now my wife. That was a long time ago, so I expected to find the house in a dilapidated condition. But to my surprise, it was freshly painted and much renovated. I recalled the wonderful deal the owners gave their student renters. I had my own large room and bath, furniture and sheets provided, maid service, six big breakfasts and five wonderful dinners a week, all for the price of $21 a week. More than that, the meals were ample and prepared with such skill that, with some affection, we called our landlady "Ma Soper." I now realize that I didn't thank Mrs. Soper often enough, nor Mr. Soper and their daughter, since it must have been some burden to have 12 single men to dinner every weeknight.

Now, this old boardinghouse could have the most spacious rooms, the best service, and the finest boarders, but we wouldn't want to live there for more than a short while. It could be beautiful beyond our power to imagine, but still we wouldn't want to live there forever, single, if we have even the dimmest memory or the faintest vision of a family with beloved parents and children like the one from which we came to this earth and the one which is our destiny to form and to live in forever. There is only one place in heaven where there will be families—the highest degree of the celestial kingdom. That is where we will want to be.

A child hearing and believing the words of the proclamation regarding families united eternally would begin a lifetime of looking for a holy temple where ordinances and covenants perpetuate family relationships beyond the grave. The child also would begin striving to become worthy and preparing in other ways to attract a potential mate who also has become worthy of such ordinances. The words of the proclamation make it clear that to receive those blessings requires some sort of perfecting experiences. A child might not sense at first, but soon would learn, that making resolutions and trying harder can produce only faltering progress toward perfection. Additional help is needed.

Further, with age will come temptations to do things that create feelings of guilt. Every child will someday feel those pangs of conscience, as we all have. And those who feel that priceless sense of guilt and cannot shake it may despair, sensing that eternal life requires a progress toward perfection that seems increasingly beyond them. So you and I must resolve to always speak to people who don't yet know what we know about how perfection is produced. We will do that because we know that someday they will want what we want and will then realize that we were their brother or sister and that we knew the way to eternal life. It isn't hard to be a member missionary if you think of that future moment when they and we will see things as they really are.

The Sanctity of Human Life

Some other words in the proclamation will have special meaning for us, knowing what we know about eternal life. They are in the next two paragraphs:

> The first commandment that God gave to Adam and Eve pertained to their potential for parenthood as husband and wife. We declare that God's commandment for His children to multiply and replenish the earth remains in force. We further declare that God has commanded that the sacred powers of procreation are to be employed only between man and woman, lawfully wedded as husband and wife.
> We declare the means by which mortal life is created to be divinely appointed.
> We affirm the sanctity of life and of its importance in God's eternal plan.

Believing those words, a child could spot easily the mistakes in reasoning made by some adults. For instance, apparently wise and powerful people blame poverty and famine on there being too many people in some parts of the earth or in all the earth. With great passion they argue for limiting births, as if that would produce human happiness. A child believing the proclamation will know that cannot be so, even before hearing these words from the Lord through his prophet Joseph Smith:

> For the earth is full, and there is enough and to spare; yea, I prepared all things, and have given unto the children of men to be agents unto themselves (D&C 104:17).

A child could see that Heavenly Father would not command men and women to marry and to multiply and replenish the earth if the children they invited into mortality would deplete the earth. Since there is enough and to spare, the enemy of human happiness as well as the cause of poverty and starvation is not the birth of children.

It is the failure of people to do with the earth what God could teach them to do if only they would ask and then obey, for they are agents unto themselves.

We would also see that the commandment to be chaste, to employ the powers of procreation only as husband and wife, is not limiting but, rather, expanding and exalting. Children are the inheritance of the Lord to us in this life and also in eternity. Eternal life is not only to have forever our descendants from this life. It is also to have eternal increase. This is the description of what awaits those of us married as husband and wife in the temple by a servant of God with authority to offer us the sacred sealing ordinances. Here are the words of the Lord:

> It shall be done unto them in all things whatsoever my servant hath put upon them, in time, and through all eternity; and shall be of full force when they are out of the world; and they shall pass by the angels, and the gods, which are set there, to their exaltation and glory in all things, as hath been sealed upon their heads, which glory shall be a fulness and a continuation of the seeds forever and ever.
>
> Then shall they be gods, because they have no end; therefore shall they be from everlasting to everlasting (D&C 132:19–20).

Now you can see why our Father in Heaven puts such a high standard before us in using procreative powers, whose continuation is at the heart of eternal life. The Lord Jesus Christ has told us what eternal life is worth: "If you keep my commandments and endure to the end you shall have eternal life, which gift is the greatest of all the gifts of God" (D&C 14:7).

We can understand why our Heavenly Father commands us to reverence life and to cherish the powers that produce it as sacred. If we do not have those reverential feelings in this life, how could our Father give them to us in the eternities? Family life here is the schoolroom in which we prepare for family life there. And to give us the opportunity for family life there was and is the purpose of creation. That is why the coming of Elijah was described this way:

> And he shall plant in the hearts of the children the promises made to the fathers, and the hearts of the children shall turn to their fathers. If it were not so, the whole earth would be utterly wasted at his coming (JS-H 1:39).

For some of us, the test in the schoolroom of mortality will be to want marriage and children in this life with all our hearts but to have them delayed or denied. Even such sorrow can be turned into a blessing by a just and loving Father and his Son, Jesus Christ. No one who strives with full faith and heart for the blessings of eternal life will be denied. And how great will be the joy and how much deeper the appreciation then after enduring in patience and faith now.

Achieving Happiness in Family Life

The proclamation describes our schooling here for family life:

> Husband and wife have a solemn responsibility to love and care for each other and for their children. "Children are an heritage of the Lord" (Psalm 127:3). Parents

have a sacred duty to rear their children in love and righteousness, to provide for their physical and spiritual needs, to teach them to love and serve one another, to observe the commandments of God, and to be law-abiding citizens wherever they live. Husbands and wives—mothers and fathers—will be held accountable before God for the discharge of these obligations.

The family is ordained of God. Marriage between man and woman is essential to His eternal plan. Children are entitled to birth within the bonds of matrimony, and to be reared by a father and a mother who honor marital vows with complete fidelity. Happiness in family life is most likely to be achieved when founded upon the teachings of the Lord Jesus Christ. Successful marriages and families are established and maintained on principles of faith, prayer, repentance, forgiveness, respect, love, compassion, work, and wholesome recreational activities. By divine design, fathers are to preside over their families in love and righteousness and are responsible to provide the necessities of life and protection for their families. Mothers are primarily responsible for the nurture of their children. In these sacred responsibilities, fathers and mothers are obligated to help one another as equal partners. Disability, death, or other circumstances may necessitate individual adaptation. Extended families should lend support when needed.

Those two paragraphs are filled with practical applications. There are things we can start to do now that have to do with providing for the spiritual and physical needs of a family. There are things we can do now to prepare, long before the need, so we can be at peace, knowing we have done all we can.

To begin with, we can decide to plan for success, not failure. Statistics are thrown at us every day in an effort to try to persuade us that a family composed of a loving father and mother with children loved, taught, and cared for in the way the proclamation enjoins is supposedly going the way of the dinosaurs, toward extinction. You have enough evidence in your own families to know that righteous people sometimes have their families ripped apart by circumstances beyond their control. It takes courage and faith to plan for what God holds before you as the ideal rather than what might be forced upon you by circumstances.

Conversely, there are important ways in which planning for failure can make failure more likely and the ideal less so. Consider these twin commandments as an example: "Fathers are to . . . provide the necessities of life . . . for their families" and "mothers are primarily responsible for the nurture of their children." Knowing how hard that might be, a young man might choose a career on the basis of how much money he could make, even if it meant he couldn't be home enough to be an equal partner. By doing that, he has already decided he cannot hope to do what would be best. A young woman might prepare for a career incompatible with being primarily responsible for the nurture of her children because of the possibilities of not marrying, of not having children, or of being left alone to provide for them herself. Or she might fail to focus her education on the gospel and the useful knowledge of the world that nurturing a family would require, not realizing that the highest and best use she could make of her talents and her education would be in her home. Consequently, because a young man and woman had planned thus, they might make what is best for a family less likely to be obtained.

Surely they are both wise to worry about the physical needs of that future family. The costs of buying a home, compared to average salaries, seem to be rising and jobs harder to hold. But there are other ways the young man and the young woman could think about preparing to provide for that future family. Income is only one part of it. Have you noticed husbands and wives who feel pinched for lack of money choose for a solution ways to make their family income keep rising but soon find that the pinch is there whatever the income? There is an old formula which goes something like this: Income five dollars and expenses six dollars: misery. Income four dollars and expenses three dollars: happiness.

Whether the young man can provide and, after work, return home to his family at a reasonable hour, and whether the young woman can be there to nurture children, can depend as much on how they learn to spend as on how they learn to earn. President Brigham Young said it this way, speaking to us as much as he did to the people in his day: "If you wish to get rich, save what you get. A fool can earn money; but it takes

7

a wise man to save and dispose of it to his own advantage. Then go to work, and save everything, and make your own bonnets and clothing."[3]

In today's world, instead of telling young couples to make bonnets, President Young might suggest they think carefully about what they really need in cars, clothes, recreation, houses, vacations, and whatever they will someday try to provide for their children. And he might point out that the difference in cost between what the world says is necessary and what children really need could allow the margin in time that a father and a mother might need with their children in order to bring them home to their Heavenly Father.

Even the most frugal spending habits and the most careful planning for employment may not be enough to ensure success, but those things could be enough to allow us the peace that comes from knowing we did the best we could to provide and to nurture.

There is another way we could plan to succeed, despite the difficulties that might lie before us. The proclamation sets a high standard for us when it describes our obligation to teach our children. We are somehow to teach them so that they love one another and serve one another, keep the commandments, and are law-abiding citizens. If we think of good families who have not met that test, and few meet it without some degree of failure over a generation or two, we could lose heart.

We cannot control what others choose to do, and so we cannot force our children to heaven, but we can determine what we will do. And we can decide that we will do all we can to bring down the powers of heaven into that family we want so much to have forever.

A key for us is in the proclamation: "Happiness in family life is most likely to be achieved when founded upon the teachings of the Lord Jesus Christ."

What could make it more likely that people in a family would love and serve one another, observe the commandments of God, and obey the law? It is not simply teaching them the gospel. It is in their hearing the word of God and then trying it in faith. If they do, their natures will be changed in a way that produces the happiness they seek. From Mormon, these words describe exactly how that change is the natural fruit of living the gospel of Jesus Christ:

> And the first fruits of repentance is baptism; and baptism cometh by faith unto the fulfilling the commandments; and the fulfilling the commandments bringeth remission of sins;
> And the remission of sins bringeth meekness, and lowliness of heart; and because of meekness and lowliness of heart cometh the visitation of the Holy Ghost, which Comforter filleth with hope and perfect love, which love endureth by diligence unto prayer, until the end shall come, when all the saints shall dwell with God (Moro. 8:25–26).

When we prepare our children for baptism, if we do it well, we prepare them for the process that will bring the effects of the Atonement into their lives and the powers of heaven into our homes. Think of the change we all need. We need the Holy Ghost to fill us with hope and perfect love so that we can endure by diligence unto prayer. And then we can dwell forever with God in families. How can it come? By the simple promise Mormon described to his son, Moroni. Faith in Jesus Christ unto repentance and then baptism by those with authority lead to remission of sins. That produces meekness and lowliness of heart. And that in turn allows us to have the companionship of the Holy Ghost, which fills us with hope and perfect love.

Concerning this desired love and happiness, the proclamation is careful in what it promises: "Happiness in family life is most likely to be achieved when founded upon the teachings of the Lord Jesus Christ." My heart aches a little to know that many who read those words will be surrounded by those who do not know or who deny the teachings of Jesus Christ. They can only do their best. But they can know this: their placement in a family, however challenging, is known by a loving Heavenly Father. They can know that a way is prepared for them to do all that will be required to qualify for eternal life. They may not see how God could give them that gift, nor with whom they will share it. Yet the promise of the gospel of Jesus Christ is sure:

But learn that he who doeth the works of righteousness shall receive his reward, even peace in this world, and eternal life in the world to come.

I, the Lord, have spoken it, and the Spirit beareth record. Amen (D&C 59:23–24).

That peace will come from the assurance that the Atonement has worked in our lives and from the hope of eternal life that springs from that assurance.

The proclamation warns that for those who fail to respond to its truths the result will be more disastrous than simply lack of peace in this life or absence of happiness. Here is the prophetic warning and the call to action, with which the proclamation ends:

> We warn that individuals who violate covenants of chastity, who abuse spouse or offspring, or who fail to fulfill family responsibilities will one day stand accountable before God. Further, we warn that the disintegration of the family will bring upon individuals, communities, and nations the calamities foretold by ancient and modern prophets.
>
> We call upon responsible citizens and officers of government everywhere to promote those measures designed to maintain and strengthen the family as the fundamental unit of society.

The family unit is fundamental not only to society and to the Church but also to our hope for eternal life. We begin to practice in the family, the smaller unit, what will spread to the Church and to the society in which we live in this world, which will then be what we practice in families bound together forever by covenants and by faithfulness. We can start now to "promote those measures designed to maintain and strengthen the family." I pray that we will. I pray that you will ask, "Father, how can I prepare?" Tell him how much you want what he desires to give you. You will receive impressions, and if you act on them, I promise you the help of the powers of heaven.

I testify that our Heavenly Father lives, that we lived with him as spirits, and that we would be lonely living anywhere but with him in the world to come. I testify that Jesus Christ is our Savior, that by suffering for the sins of all of us he made possible the changes in you and me that can give us eternal life. I testify that the Holy Ghost can fill us with hope and with perfect love. And I testify that the sealing power restored to Joseph Smith and now held by President Gordon B. Hinckley can bind us in families and give us eternal life, if we do all that we can do in faith.

Notes

1. These proclamations are printed in full in Daniel H. Ludlow, ed., Encyclopedia of Mormonism, 5 vols. (1992), 3:1151–57.
2. See Ensign, Nov. 1995, 102.
3. Journal of Discourses, 11:301.

We Live in Two Different Worlds as Members of the Church

Adapted from **Richard Chidester**

Natural World

1. No God (or 3 in 1, spirit essence)
2. No devil
3. Man is mortal/temporal only
4. Evolution
5. Progress through education
6. No hereafter—eat, drink, be merry
7. No moral absolutes
8. Force/power to get things done
9. Salvation through achievement
10. Image/appearance
11. $$, materialism is primary
12. Charisma, personality
13. Communication, reason, logic
14. Normal to fight, diversity
15. Politicians/intellectuals
16. Sex, $, in-laws
17. Techniques, skills, will-power
18. Doing things, action lists
19. Hacking at the leaves
20. Government programs, dependence
21. Sue, take to court, use law to obtain justice

Spiritual World

1. Heavenly Father, Christ, Holy Ghost
2. 1/3 came here - 34 billion
3. Physical/spiritual/being
4. A child of God
5. Man is fallen, needs a Savior
6. Judgment/resurrection/accountability
7. Right/wrong to every question
8. Love/covenants
9. Salvation through Christ
10. Character
11. Concern for others' welfare
12. Kindness, charity, love
13. Christlike attributes
14. Contention is of the devil
15. Prophets/scriptures
16. Pride, selfishness, sin
17. Humility, principles/ordinances
18. Becoming Christlike
19. Hacking at the roots
20. Self-reliance, family, church
21. Brothers/sisters sons and daughters of God—Golden Rule

Marriage and Divorce

President Spencer W. Kimball

Brigham Young University Devotional, 7 September 1976

Through the years I have warned the youth of Zion against the sins and vices so prevalent in our society—those of sexual impurity and all of its many ugly approaches. I have spoken of immodesty in dress and actions as one of the softening processes of Lucifer.

I have spoken plainly, warning youth of the pitfalls of petting and of all the other perversions into which young men and young women sometimes fall. I endeavored, also, to give hope to those who might have stepped over the bounds of propriety, and I have outlined to them the path by which total repentance might bring them to forgiveness.

I have warned the youth against the many hazards of interfaith marriage, and with all the power I possessed, I warned young people to avoid the sorrows and disillusionments that come from marrying out of the Church and the unhappy situations which almost invariably result when a believer marries an unbelieving spouse. I have pointed out the demands of the Church upon its members in time, energy, and funds; the deepness of the spiritual ties which tighten after marriage and as the family comes; the antagonisms that naturally follow such mismating; the fact that these and many other reasons argue eloquently for marriage within the Church, where husband and wife have common backgrounds, common ideals and standards, common beliefs, hopes, and objectives, and, above all, where marriage may be eternalized through righteous entry into the holy temple.

Now I wish to follow these important principles with a discussion of family life. This topic is not new nor is it spectacular, but it is vital.

Marriage is relevant in every life, and family life is the basis of our existence. I make no apology for discussing this subject. The entertainer gives to the people that which they desire. But I, like Paul, am pressed in the spirit to warn and to strengthen. May I have the blessings of our Heavenly Father in my words.

The ugly dragon of divorce has entered into our social life. Little known to our grandparents and not even common among our parents, this cancer has come to be so common in our own day that nearly every family has been cursed by its destructive machinations. This is one of the principal tools of Satan to destroy faith, through breaking up happy homes and bringing frustration of life and distortion of thought.

Honorable, happy, and successful marriage is surely the principal goal of every normal person. One who would purposely or neglectfully void its serious implications is not only not normal but is frustrating his own program. There are a few people who marry for spite or marry for wealth or marry on the rebound after having been jilted. How distorted is the thinking of such a one!

Marriage is perhaps the most vital of all the decisions and has the most far-reaching effects, for it has to do not only with immediate happiness, but also with eternal joys. It affects not only the two people involved, but their families and particularly their children and their children's children down through the many generations. It is absolutely appalling how many children today are growing up in our society who do not have two parents, a father and a mother—and neither one is totally sufficient, if two could be had.

11

In selecting a companion for life and for eternity, certainly the most careful planning and thinking and praying and fasting should be done to be sure that of all the decisions, this one must not be wrong. In true marriage there must be a union of minds as well as of hearts. Emotions must not wholly determine decisions, but the mind and the heart, strengthened by fasting and prayer and serious consideration, will give one a maximum chance of marital happiness.

Marriage is not easy; it is not simple, as evidenced by the ever-mounting divorce rate. Exact figures astound us. The following ones come from Salt Lake County, which are probably somewhere near average. There were 832 marriages in a single month, and there were 414 divorces. That is half as many divorces as marriages. There were 365 temple marriages, and of the temple marriages about 10 percent were dissolved by divorce. This is substantially better than the average, but we are chagrined that there should be *any* divorce following a temple marriage.

We are grateful that this one survey reveals that about 90 percent of the temple marriages hold fast. Because of this, we recommend that people marry those who are of the same racial background generally, and of somewhat the same economic and social and educational background. Some of these are not an absolute necessity, but preferred; and above all, the same religious background, without question. In spite of the most favorable matings, the evil one still takes a monumental toll and is the cause for many broken homes and frustrated lives.

With all conditions as nearly ideal as possible, there are still people who terminate their marriages for the reason of "incompatibility." We see so many movies and television programs and read so much fiction and come in contact with so many society scandals that the people in general come to think of "marrying and giving in marriage," divorcing and remarrying, as the normal patterns.

The divorce itself does not constitute the entire evil, but the very acceptance of divorce as a cure is also a serious sin of this generation. Because a program or a pattern is universally accepted is not evidence that it is right. Marriage never was easy. It may never be. It brings with it sacrifice, sharing, and a demand for great selflessness.

Many of the TV and movie screen shows and stories of fiction end with marriage, and "they lived happily ever after." Since nearly all of us have experienced divorce among our close friends or relatives, we have come to realize that divorce is not a cure for difficulty, but is merely an escape, and a weak one. We have come to realize also that the mere performance of a ceremony does not bring happiness and a successful marriage. Happiness does not come by pressing a button, as does the electric light; happiness is a state of mind and comes from within. It must be earned. It cannot be purchased with money; it cannot be taken for nothing.

Some think of happiness as a glamorous life of ease, luxury, and constant thrills; but true marriage is based on a happiness which is more than that, one that comes from giving, serving, sharing, sacrificing, and selflessness. Two people coming from different backgrounds soon learn after the ceremony is performed that stark reality must be faced. There is no longer a life of fantasy or of make-believe; we must come out of the clouds and put our feet firmly on the earth. Responsibility must be assumed and new duties must be accepted. Some personal freedoms must be relinquished, and many adjustments, unselfish adjustments, must be made.

One comes to realize very soon after the marriage that the spouse has weaknesses not previously revealed or discovered. The virtues which were constantly magnified during courtship now grow relatively smaller, and the weaknesses that seemed so small and insignificant during courtship now grow to sizable proportions. The hour has come for understanding hearts, for self-appraisal, and for good common sense, reasoning, and planning. The habits of years now show themselves; the spouse may be stingy or prodigal, lazy or industrious, devout or irreligious, be kind and cooperative or petulant and cross, demanding or giving, egotistical or self-effacing. The in-law problem comes closer into focus, and the relationships of the spouses to them is again magnified.

Often there is an unwillingness to settle down and to assume the heavy responsibilities that immediately are there. Economy is reluctant to replace lavish living, and the young people seem often too eager "to keep up with the Joneses." There is often an unwillingness to make the necessary financial adjustments.

Young wives often demand that all the luxuries formerly enjoyed in the prosperous homes of their successful fathers be continued in their own homes. Some of them are quite willing to help earn that lavish living by continuing employment after marriage. They consequently leave the home, where their duty lies, to pursue professional or business pursuits, thus establishing an economy that becomes stabilized so that it becomes very difficult to yield toward the normal family life. With both spouses working, competition rather than co-operation enters the family. Two weary workers return home with taut nerves, individual pride, increased independence, and then misunderstandings arise. Little frictions pyramid into monumental ones. Frequently, spouses sinfully turn to old romances or take up new ones, and finally the seemingly inevitable break comes with a divorce, with its heartaches, bitterness, disillusionments, and always scars.

While marriage is difficult, and discordant and frustrated marriages are common, yet real, lasting happiness is possible, and marriage can be more an exultant ecstasy than the human mind can conceive. This is within the reach of every couple, every person. "Soulmates" are fiction and an illusion; and while every young man and young woman will seek with all diligence and prayerfulness to find a mate with whom life can be most compatible and beautiful, yet it is certain that almost any good man and any good woman can have happiness and a successful marriage if both are willing to pay the price.

There is a never-failing formula which will guarantee to every couple a happy and eternal marriage; but like all formulas, the principal ingredients must not be left out, reduced, or limited. The selection before courting and then the continued courting after the marriage process are equally important, but not more important than the marriage itself, the success of which depends upon the two individuals—not upon one, but upon two.

When a couple have commenced a marriage based upon reasonable standards, no combination of power can destroy that marriage except the power within either or both of the spouses themselves; and they must assume the responsibility generally. Other people and agencies may influence for good or bad. Financial, social, political, and other situations may seem to have a bearing. But the marriage depends first and always on the two spouses who can always make their marriage successful and happy if they are determined, unselfish, and righteous.

The formula is simple; the ingredients are few, though there are many amplifications of each.

First, there must be the proper approach toward marriage, which contemplates the selection of a spouse who reaches as nearly as possible the pinnacle of perfection in all the matters that are of importance to the individuals. Then those two parties must come to the altar in the temple realizing that they must work hard toward this successful joint living.

Second, there must be a great unselfishness, forgetting self and directing all of the family life and all pertaining thereunto to the good of the family, and subjugating self.

Third, there must be continued courtship and expressions of affection, kindness, and consideration to keep love alive and growing.

Fourth, there must be a complete living of the commandments of the Lord as defined in the gospel of Jesus Christ.

With these ingredients properly mixed and continually kept functioning, it is quite impossible for unhappiness to come, for misunderstandings to continue, or for breaks to occur. Divorce attorneys would need to transfer to other fields and divorce courts would be padlocked.

Two individuals approaching the marriage altar must realize that to attain the happy marriage which they hope for, they must know that marriage is not a legal cover-all. Rather, it means sacrifice, sharing, and even a reduction of some personal liberties. It means long, hard economizing. It means children who bring with them financial burdens, service burdens, care and worry burdens; but also it means the deepest and sweetest emotions of all.

Before marriage, each individual is quite free to go and come as he pleases, to organize and plan his life as it seems best, to make all decisions with self as the central point. Sweethearts should realize before they take the vows that each must accept literally and fully that the good of the little new family must always be superior to the good of either spouse. Each party must eliminate the "I" and the "my" and substitute therefore "we" and "our." Every decision must take into consideration that now two or more are affected by

13

it. As she approaches major decisions now, the wife will be concerned as to the effect they will have upon the parents, the children, the home, and their spiritual lives. The husband's choice of occupation, his social life, his friends, his every interest must now be considered in the light that he is only a part of a family, that the totalness of the group must be considered.

Every divorce is the result of selfishness on the part of one or the other or both parties to a marriage contract. Someone is thinking of self-comforts, conveniences, freedoms, luxuries, or ease. Sometimes the ceaseless pinpricking of an unhappy, discontented, and selfish spouse can finally add up to serious physical violence. Sometimes people are goaded to the point where they erringly feel justified in doing the things that are so wrong. Nothing, of course, justifies sin.

Sometimes the husband or the wife feels neglected, mistreated, and ignored until he or she wrongly feels justified in adding to errors. If each spouse submits to frequent self-analysis and measures his own imperfections by the yardstick of perfection and the Golden Rule, and if each spouse sets about to correct self in every deviation found by such analysis rather than to set about to correct the deviations in the other party, then transformation comes and happiness is the result. There are many pharisaic people who marry who should memorize the parable of the Savior in Luke—people who prate their own virtues and pile up their own qualities of goodness and put them on the scales against the weaknesses of the spouse. They say, "I fast twice a week; I give tithes of all I possess" (see Luke 18:9-14).

For every friction, there is a cause; and whenever there is unhappiness, each should search self to find the cause or at least that portion of the cause which originated in that self.

A marriage may not always be even and incident-less, but it can be one of great peace. A couple may have poverty, illness, disappointment, failures, and even death in the family, but even these will not rob them of their peace. The marriage can be successful so long as selfishness does not enter in. Troubles and problems will draw parents together into unbreakable unions if there is total unselfishness there. During the depression of the 1930s there was a definite drop in divorce. Poverty, failures, disappointment—they tied parents together. Adversity can cement relationships that prosperity can destroy.

The marriage that is based upon selfishness is almost certain to fail. The one who marries for wealth or the one who marries for prestige or social plane is certain to be disappointed. The one who marries to satisfy vanity and pride or who marries to spite or to show up another person is fooling only himself. But the one who marries to give happiness as well as receive it, to give service as well as to receive it, and who looks after the interests of the two and then the family as it comes will have a good chance that the marriage will be a happy one.

There are many people who do not find divorce attorneys and who do not end their marriages, but who have permitted their marriage to grow stale and weak and cheap. There are spouses who have fallen from the throne of adoration and worship and are in the low state of mere joint occupancy of the home, joint sitters at the table, joint possessors of certain things that cannot be easily divided. These people will do well to re-evaluate, to renew their courting, to express their affection, to acknowledge kindnesses, and to increase their consideration so their marriage can again become beautiful, sweet, and growing.

Love is like a flower, and, like the body, it needs constant feeding. The mortal body would soon be emaciated and die if there were not frequent feedings. The tender flower would wither and die without food and water. And so love, also, cannot be expected to last forever unless it is continually fed with portions of love, the manifestation of esteem and admiration, the expressions of gratitude, and the consideration of unselfishness.

Total unselfishness is sure to accomplish another factor in successful marriage. If one is forever seeking the interest, comforts, and happiness of the other, the love found in courtship and cemented in marriage will grow into mighty proportions. Many couples permit their marriages to become stale and their love to grow cold like old bread or worn-out jokes or cold gravy. Certainly the foods most vital for love are consideration, kindness, thoughtfulness, concern, expressions of affection, embraces of appreciation, admiration, pride, companionship, confidence, faith, partnership, equality, and dependence.

To be really happy in marriage, there must be a continued faithful observance of the commandments of the Lord. No one, single or married, was ever sublimely happy unless he was righteous. There are temporary satisfactions and camouflaged situations for the moment, but permanent, total happiness can come only through cleanliness and worthiness. One who has a pattern of religious life with deep religious convictions can never be happy in an inactive life. The conscience will continue to afflict, unless it has been seared, in which case the marriage is already in jeopardy. A stinging conscience can make life most unbearable. Inactivity is destructive to marriage, especially where the parties are inactive in varying degrees. Religious differences are the most trying and among the most unsolvable of all differences.

Marriage is ordained of God. It is not merely a social custom. Without proper and successful marriage, one will never be exalted. Read the words of your Lord, that it is right and proper to be married.

That being true, the thoughtful and intelligent Latter-day Saint will plan his life carefully to be sure there are no impediments placed in the way. To make one serious mistake, one may place in the way obstacles that may never be removed and that may block the way to eternal life and godhood—our ultimate destiny. If two people love the Lord more than their own lives, working together in total harmony with the gospel program as their basic structure, they are sure to have this great happiness. When a husband and wife go together frequently to the holy temple, kneel in prayer together in their home with their family, go hand in hand to their religious meetings, keep their lives wholly chaste, mentally and physically, so that their whole thoughts and desires and love are all centered in the one being, their companion, and both are working together for the upbuilding of the kingdom of God, then happiness is at its pinnacle.

Sometimes in marriage there are other cleavings, in spite of the fact that the Lord said: Thou shalt love thy wife with all thy heart, and shalt cleave unto her and none else" (D&C 42:22).

This means just as completely that "thou shalt love thy *husband* with all thy heart and shall cleave unto *him* and none else." Frequently, people continue to cleave unto their mothers and their fathers and their friends. Sometimes mothers will not relinquish the hold they have had upon their children, and husbands as well as wives return to their mothers and fathers for advice and counsel and to confide; whereas cleaving should be to the wife or husband in most things, and all intimacies should be kept in great secrecy and privacy from others.

Couples do well to immediately find their own home, separate and apart from that of the in-laws on either side. The home may be very modest and unpretentious, but still it is an independent domicile. Their married life should become independent of her folks and his folks. The couple love their parents more than ever; they cherish their counsel; they appreciate their association; but they must live their own lives, being governed by their own decisions, by their own prayerful considerations after they have received the counsel from those who should give it. To cleave does not mean merely to occupy the same home; it means to adhere closely, to stick together:

> Wherefore, it is lawful that . . . they twain shall be one flesh, and all this that the earth might answer the end of its creation;
> And that it might be filled with the measure of man, according to his creation before the world was made (D&C 49: 16-17).

Our own record is not pleasing. Of 31,037 marriages, our records say only 14,169 were in the temple for eternity. This is 46 percent. There were 7,556 members married out of the Church. This is terribly disturbing to us. This is 24 percent, which means that about 9,000, or 30 percent, apparently thought so little of themselves and their posterity that they married out of the temple, which could give them a key to eternal life. Is it possible they do not know or do not they not care?

Of course, most such people who marry out of the Church and temple do not weigh the matter sufficiently. The survey I mentioned disclosed the fact that only about one out of seven would be converted and baptized into the Church. This is a great loss. It means that in many cases there is not only a loss of the unbaptized spouse, but also of the children and even sometimes the other spouse.

We love those few who join the Church after marriage. We praise them and honor them, but the odds are against this happening. According to the figures given above, this means that nearly 6,500 of the new marriages may never find both parties finally joining the Church to make the family totally united. This grieves us very much. The total program of the Lord for the family cannot be enjoyed fully if the people are unequally yoked in marriage.

We call upon all youth to make such a serious, strong resolution to have a temple marriage that their determination will provide for them the rich promises of eternal marriage with its accompanying joys and happiness. This would please the Lord, who counts on each of us so heavily. He has said that eternal life can be had only in the way he has planned it.

> And a white stone is given to each of those who come into the celestial kingdom, whereon is a new name written, which no man knoweth save he that receiveth it. The new name is the key word (D&C 130:11).

It is the normal thing to marry. It was arranged by God in the beginning. One is not wholly normal who does not want to be married. Remember, ". . . neither is the man without the woman, neither the woman without the man, in the Lord" (1 Corinthians 11:11).

No one can reject this covenant of celestial marriage and reach the eternal kingdom of God. This is certain.

> In the celestial glory there are three heavens or degrees,
> And in order to obtain the highest, a man must enter into this order of the priesthood [meaning the new and everlasting covenant of marriage];
> And if he does not, he cannot obtain it.
> He may enter into the other, but that is the end of his kingdom (D&C 131:1-4).

> For behold, I reveal unto you a new and an everlasting covenant; and if ye abide not that covenant, then are ye damned (D&C 132:4).

And dammed means stopped in progress.

These are the words of the Lord. They were said directly to us. There is no question about them.

> And as pertaining to the new and everlasting covenant, it was instituted for the fulness of my glory; and he that receiveth a fulness thereof must and shall abide the law. . . .
> Therefore, when they are out of the world [after they have died] they neither marry nor are given in marriage; but are appointed angels in heaven; which angels are ministering servants, to minister for those who are worthy of a far more, and an exceeding, and an eternal weight of glory.
> For these angels did not abide my law; therefore, they cannot be enlarged, but remain separately and singly, without exaltation, in their saved condition, to all eternity; and from henceforth are not gods, but are angels to God forever and ever.
> Abraham received all things, whatsoever he received, by revelation and commandment, by my word, saith the Lord, and hath entered into his exaltation and sitteth upon his throne.
> Go ye, therefore, and do the works of Abraham; enter ye into my law and ye shall be saved (D&C 132:6, 16-17, 29, 32).

This is the word of the Lord. It is very, very serious, and there is nobody who should argue with the Lord. He made the earth; he made the people. He knows the conditions. He set the program, and we are not intelligent enough or smart enough to be able to argue him out of these important things. He knows what is right and true.

We ask each Latter-day Saint to think of these things. Be sure that your marriage is right. Be sure that your life is right. Be sure that your part of the marriage is carried forward properly.

Now I ask the Lord to bless you. These things worry us considerably because there are too many divorces and they are increasing. It has come to be a common thing to talk about divorce. The minute there is a little crisis or a little argument in the family, we talk about divorce, and we rush and see an attorney. This is not the way of the Lord. We should go back and adjust our problems and make our marriage compatible and sweet and blessed.

I pray the Lord will bless each one who faces decisions before marriage and after marriage. I ask his blessings upon each one of you and give you my testimony that this church is true and divine, in the name of Jesus Christ. Amen.

Marriage and the Scriptures

Matthew 19:1-12, Mark 10:1-12.

Commentary by **Bruce R. McConkie**

Doctrinal New Testament Commentary, Vol. 1, pp. 546-549, 604-608.

1. As here recorded, our Lord's teachings about marriage and divorce are fragmentary and incomplete. They can only be understood when considered in connection with the law of celestial marriage as such has been revealed anew in modern times. These same general principles governing eternal marriage were known to and understood by the disciples in Jesus' day and also, in part at least, by the Pharisees. But the accounts here preserved by both Matthew and Mark of the Master's discussion on marriage and divorce are so condensed and abbreviated that they do not give a clear picture of the problem. Modern scriptural exegetes (those who analyze Bible passages) need the same background and knowledge **possessed by those who engaged in the original discussion.** To have a correct understanding of the part marriage and divorce play in the divine scheme of things, at least the following principles must be known:

(1) Marriage and the family unit are the central part of the plan of progression and exaltation. All things center in and around the family unit in the eternal perspective. **Exaltation consists in the continuation of the family unit in eternity.** Those for whom the family unit continues have eternal life; all others have a lesser degree of salvation in the mansions that are prepared.

(2) There was an eternal family in heaven to which all men belonged even before the creation of this earth. God himself, a personal being in whose image man is created, was and is the Eternal Father. All men are his spirit children and lived with him in the pre-existent first estate.

(3) Celestial or eternal marriage is the gate to exaltation. To fill the full measure of his creation and obtain eternal life a man must enter into this order of matrimony and keep all of the covenants and obligations that go with it. If a couple is so sealed, the two persons become husband and wife in this life and continue in the same relationship in the world to come (D&C 131:1-4; 132).

(4) There are also lesser orders of marriage. Only the very elect qualify for celestial marriage. Others, even in the Church, are married by civil authority for the duration of their mortal lives only.

(5) Divorce is not part of the gospel plan no matter what kind of marriage is involved. But because men in practice do not always live in harmony with gospel standards, the Lord, permits divorce for one reason or another, depending upon the spiritual stability of the people involved. In ancient Israel men had power to divorce their wives for relatively insignificant reasons (Deut. 24:1-4). Under the most perfect conditions there would be no divorce permitted except where sex sin was involved. In this day divorces are permitted in accordance with **civil statutes**, and the divorced persons are permitted by the Church to marry again without the stain of immorality which under a higher system would attend such a course.

2. Matt. 19:3. Legal justification for divorce today varies from almost the mere whim of the parties on the one hand to adultery on the other, depending upon the laws of the state of nation involved. This same divergence of opinion existed among the Jews, and Jesus was being asked to decide one of the burning issues of the day.

3. "Among the questions of the day fiercely debated between the great rival schools of Hillel and Shammai, no one was more so than that of divorce. The school of Hillel contended that a man had a right to divorce his wife for any cause he might assign, if it were no more than his having ceased to love her, or his having seen one he liked better, or her having cooked a dinner badly. The school of Schammai, on the contrary, held that divorce could be issued only for the crime of adultery, and offenses against chastity. If it were possible to get Jesus to pronounce in favor of either school, the hostility of the other would be roused, and hence, it seemed a favorable chance for compromising him" (Geikie, vol. 2, pp. 347-348, cited in Talmage's *Jesus the Christ*, p. 484).

4. (vs. 4-6) As he so often did in answering their questions, Jesus simply went back to basic principles. He referred them to the marriage of Adam and Eve which occurred before death entered the world and while the first man and the first woman were still in the Garden of Eden. He cited the divine decree itself, thus making this first marriage a pattern for all others and said that God himself had joined the parties together, and that man, therefore, did not have power to tear them asunder. In other words, Jesus is here preaching a sermon on celestial marriage, marriage that is to last forever, in this life and in the next, marriage that does not countenance divorce, except, as he then amplified, when sex sin occurs.

5. Matt. 19:1-11; Mark 10:10-12. This strict law governing divorce was not given to the Pharisees, nor to the world in general, but to the disciples only, "in the house," at a later time as Mark explains. Further, Jesus expressly limited its application. All men could not live such a high standard; it applied only to those "to whom it is given." Earlier in his ministry the Master had given it to some of his Jewish disciples (Matt. 5:31-32), and after his resurrection he would yet give it to the Nephites (3 Ne. 31-32). Presumably it prevailed among them during the near two-hundred-year period following his ministry on the American continent. We can suppose it prevailed in the City of Enoch and that it will be the law during the millennium. **It may have been in force at various times and among various people, but the Church is not bound by it today. At this time divorces are permitted in the Church for a number of reasons other than sex immorality, and divorced persons are permitted to marry again and enjoy all of the blessings of the gospel. If every divorced person who remarried were guilty of adultery, the Church would be obligated to expel such from membership and to deny them the blessings of the gospel and the temple.**

6. (vs. 12) Some added background and additional information is needed to understand fully what is meant by this teaching about eunuchs. In the true Church and among normal people there is no place for the practice of celibacy. "Apparently those who made themselves eunuchs were men who in false pagan worship had deliberately mutilated themselves in the apostate notion that such would further their salvation. It is clear that such was not a true gospel requirement of any sort. There is no such thing in the gospel as willful emasculation; such a notion violates every true principle of procreation and celestial marriage" (*Mormon Doctrine*, p. 223).

7. Matt. 22:23-33, Luke 20:27-40. This colloquy between Jesus and his Sadducean detractors does not question or throw doubt, in proper cases, on the eternal verity that the family unit continues in the resurrection. Jesus had previously taught the eternal nature of the marriage union. "What therefore God (not man!) hath joined together, let not man put asunder." That is, when a marriage is performed by God's authority—not man's!—it is eternal.

8. Indeed, almost the whole Jewish nation believed that marriage was eternal, and that parents would beget children in the resurrection. Those few who did not believe that marriage continued after death—and among such were the Sadducees, who could not so believe because they denied the resurrection itself—were nonetheless fully aware that such was the prevailing religious view of the people generally. Without doubt Jesus, the apostles, the seventies, and the disciples generally had discussed this doctrine.

9. The Sadducean effort here is based on the assumption that Jesus and the Jews generally believe in marriage in heaven. They are using this commonly accepted concept to ridicule and belittle the fact of the resurrection itself. They are saying: "How absurd to believe in a resurrection (and therefore in the fact that there is marriage in heaven) when everybody knows that a woman who has had seven husbands could not have them all at once in the life to come." A most instructive passage showing that the Jews believed there should be marriage in heaven is found in Dummelow. "There was some division of opinion among the rabbis as to whether resurrection would be to a natural or to a supernatural (spiritual) life," he says. "A few took the spiritual view, e.g. Rabbi Raf is reported to have often said, 'In the world to come they shall neither eat, nor drink, nor beget children, nor trade. There is neither envy nor strife, but the just shall sit with crowns on their heads, and shall enjoy the splendor of the Divine Majesty.' But the majority inclined to a materialistic view of the resurrection. The pre-Christian book of Enoch says that the **righteous after the resurrection shall live so long that they shall beget thousands.** The received doctrine is laid down by Rabbi Saadia, who says, 'As the son of the widow of Sarepton, and the son of the Shunamite, **ate and drank, and doubtless married wives, so shall it be in the resurrection'; and by Maimonides, who says, 'Men after the resurrection will use meat and drink, and will beget children, because since the Wise Architect makes nothing in vain, it follows of necessity that the members of the body are not useless, but fulfill their functions.'** The point raised by the Sadducees was often debated by the Jewish doctors, who decided that '**a woman who married two husbands in this world is restored to the first in the next'**" (Dummelow, p. 698).

10. How much nearer the truth were these Jews, on this point, than are the modern professors of religion who suppose that family love, felicity, and unity cease simply because the spirit steps out of the body in what men call death! What then is the Master Teacher affirming by saying, "in the resurrection **they** neither marry, nor are given in marriage, but are as the angels of God in heaven"? He is not **denying** but **limiting** the prevailing concept that there will be marrying and giving in marriage in heaven. He is saying that as far as "they" (the Sadducees) are concerned, that as far as "they" (the children of this world) are concerned, the family unit does not and will not continue in the resurrection. Because he does not choose to cast his pearls before swine, and because the point at issue is not **marriage** but **resurrection** anyway, Jesus does not here amplify his teaching to explain that there is marrying and giving of marriage in heaven only for those who live the fulness of gospel law—a requirement which excludes **worldly** people.

11. In his reply Jesus is approaching the problem much as he did in revealing the same eternal principles to Joseph Smith in modern times. He first told the Prophet that all blessings come to men as a result of obedience; that all eternal covenants, marriage included, must be performed with his authority and approved by his Spirit; and that only those things continue "after the resurrection" which conform to his law. "Therefore" that is, in the light of these principles, he said, "if a man marry him a wife in the world, and he marry her not by me nor by my word, and he covenant with her so long as he is in the world and she with him, their covenant and marriage are not of force when they are dead, and when they are out of the world; therefore, they are not bound by any law when they are out of the world." What is this but marriage until death do us part? And who are the participating parties but the Sadducees, "the children of this world," the people who do not overcome the world by accepting and living the gospel? "Therefore, when the (those who will not, do not, or cannot live the law of eternal marriage) are out of the world they neither marry nor or given in marriage." That is, there is neither marrying nor giving in marriage in heaven for those to whom Jesus was speaking; for those who do not even believe in a resurrection, let alone all the other saving truths; for those who are unrighteous and ungodly; for those who live after the manner of the world; for the great masses of unrepentant mankind. All of these will fall short of gaining the fulness of reward hereafter. What is their state? They will not be "gods" and thus have exaltation; their inheritance will be in a lesser degree of glory. As Jesus said to the Sadducees, they "are as the angels of God in heaven," "for they are equal unto the angels." As he said, in more detail and with greater plainness to Joseph Smith, they "are appointed angels in heaven; which angels are worthy of a far more, and an exceeding, and an eternal weight of glory. For these angels did not abide my law; therefore, they cannot be enlarged, but remain separately and singly, without

exaltation, in their saved condition, to all eternity; and from henceforth are not gods, but are angels of God forever and ever" (D&C 132:5-17).

12. Thus, in the resurrection, the unmarried remain everlastingly as angels or servants, but the married gain exaltation and godhood. This latter group consists of those who enter into that "order of the priesthood" named "the new and everlasting covenant of marriage," and who then keep the terms and conditions of that eternal covenant (D&C 131:1-4). It consists also of those who lived on earth under circumstances which prevented them from making the covenant for themselves personally, but who would have done so had the opportunity been afforded. For all such, on the just and equitable principles of salvation and exaltation for the dead, the ordinances will be performed vicariously in the temples of God, so that no blessing will ever be denied to any worthy person. And for that matter, there is no revelation, either ancient or modern, which says there is neither marrying nor giving in marriage in heaven itself for righteous people. All that the revelations set forth is **that such is denied to the Sadducees and other worldly and ungodly people.**

13. Matt. 22:24: In ancient Israel a man was obliged to marry his brother's widow if she was childless. The "firstborn" then succeeded "in the name of his brother which is dead, that his name be not put out of Israel." **Such a law could operate only in a period when plural marriage was authorized by Deity.** Provision was made in the law for someone else to marry the widow in certain circumstances (Deut. 5:4-10). Interestingly, it was this law of marriage that enabled Boaz and Ruth, progenitors of our Lord, to become man and wife (Ruth 4).

14. (vs. 29) "They did not understand the principle of sealing for time and for all eternity; that what God hath joined together neither man nor death can put asunder (Matt. 19:6). They had wandered from that principle. It had fallen into disuse among them; they had ceased to understand it; and consequently they did not comprehend the truth; but Christ did. She could only be the wife in eternity of the man to whom she was united by the power of God for eternity, as well as for time; and Christ understood the principle, but he did not cast his pearls before the swine that tempted him" (Joseph F. Smith, *Gospel Doctrine,* 5th ed., p. 280).

15. (vs. 31-32) "You say Jehovah is the God of Abraham, Isaac, and Jacob, and at the same time claim there is no resurrection. But you know that God is not the God of the dead but of the living, and therefore Abraham, Isaac, and Jacob live and will rise in the resurrection; hence, your doctrine that life ceases with death is false." Or: "You believe there is a God; you deny there is a resurrection. Is God the God only of the dead? Is he a failure? Is there no purpose in creation? Or could it be that you have erred and that there is in reality a resurrection?"

16. (JST Mark 12:32). How can there be a God unless there is a resurrection? Why would God create men and then let them vanish into nothingness? To be God he must be the God of something, and the dead are nothing; hence, there are no dead, "for all live unto him," "for he raiseth them up out of their graves."

Divine Deterrent to Creeping Relativism

Robert L. Millet, Dean of Religious Education

The Apostle Paul prophesied of our day, and many of the elements of that prophecy are pathetically present in today's newspaper. "This know also," he wrote,

> that in the last days perilous times shall come. For men shall be lovers of their own selves, covetous, boasters, proud, blasphemers, disobedient to parents, unthankful, unholy, without natural affection, trucebreakers, false accusers, incontinent, fierce, despisers of those that are good, traitors, heady, highminded, lovers of pleasures more than lovers of God; having a form of godliness; but denying the power thereof: from such turn away.

Perhaps as an indication of the source of the problem in our day, Paul concluded that such souls would be "ever learning, and never able to come to the knowledge of the truth" (2 Timothy 3:1-7).

We live in the day of an information explosion, a time when raw knowledge is being processed and disseminated far faster than we can incorporate or inculcate. But we also live in a time of moral erosion, indicating clearly that our decency has not kept pace with our discoveries. As a world, and more particularly as a nation, we have drifted from our moral moorings, strayed from the faith of our fathers. That the decline in society is due to a moral decay is perhaps obvious to most of us. I desire, however, to take a step beyond that premise. I suggest that the lack of scriptural or theological literacy and the subsequent lack of doctrinal depth are at the heart of our problem. Very often what we believe and know affect what we do. I suggest that when men and women comprehend the great plan of happiness—the plan of salvation, the gospel—many begin to see themselves within that plan as a vital part of God's program. They then begin to govern their actions accordingly.

The Erosion

I would like now to discuss some key factors that have contributed to our doctrinal desensitization and thereby our moral decline. We could choose any number of things that have hacked away at the roots of our religious heritage, but I will focus on four: (1) the trivialization of religion; (2) the loss of a moral sense; (3) a denial of personal responsibility; and (4) stressing ethics over doctrine. In subsequent sections we will consider some solutions to our problem.

1. *The Trivialization of Religion.* Whereas a hundred years ago religion was central to the outlook of most Americans, we have in the last three decades become prey to a growing secularism, a worldview that seeks to make sense of life without reference to God or the divine. If there is no real purpose to life, no God, no system of salvation, no hope of a life beyond the grave, and no divine parameters by which to distinguish right from wrong—in short, if anything goes, then eventually everything goes.

In the early 1960s a strange and to some frightful sound was heard throughout the academic world of religious studies—the cry that "God is dead." Protestant, Roman Catholic, and even Jewish theologians spoke often of Godless theologies, Christless christs, and Christian atheism, phrases that at first blush seem meaningless and absurd. The essence of their rhetorical requiem was that God had died in the hearts of men and women, that "God (had) passed out of our existence and become a dead entity for us because we crowded him out of our consciousness in creating and worshiping idols of our own ethnic likenesses." (Gabriel Vahanian's views, as cited in Ice and Carey, eds., *The Death of God Debate,* p. 16). How strikingly similar are the words of the Lord concerning the state of things at the time of Joseph Smith's call:

> They seek not the Lord to establish his righteousness, but every man walketh in his own way, and after the image of his own god, whose image is in the likeness of the world, and whose substance is that of an idol, which waxeth old and shall perish in Babylon, even Babylon the great, which shall fall (D&C 1:16).

The Death of God movement, though not necessarily characteristic of the rank and file of the religious world (or even typical of the views or feelings of the average priest, minister, or rabbi), nevertheless symbolized a growing disease in society, a loss of confidence in religious life, and a gradual distancing from religious values and time-honored traditions. Though the pendulum would yet swing to the religious right during the 1970s with the rise of the Charismatic Movement and Christian Fundamentalism, yet the age of existential anguish, of moral malaise, of cynicism and skepticism and doubt would take its terrible toll. In recent times, where religion has not been rejected outright, it has been either ignored or in many cases trivialized. As Professor Stephen L. Carter has pointed out :

> one sees a trend in our political and legal cultures toward treating religious beliefs as arbitrary and unimportant, a trend supported by a rhetoric that implies that there is something wrong with religious devotion. More and more, our culture seems to take the position that believing deeply in the tenets of one's faith represents a kind of mystical irrationality, something that thoughtful, public-spirited American citizens would do better to avoid. . . . The consistent message of modern American society is that whenever the demands of one's religion conflict with what one has to do to get ahead, one is expected to ignore the religious demands and act . . . well. . . *rationally.*

"One good way," Carter points out,

> to end a conversation—or start an argument—is to tell a group of well-educated professionals that you hold a political position (preferably a controversial one, such as being against abortion or pornography) because it is required by your understanding of God's will. In the unlikely event that anyone hangs around to talk with you about it, the chances are that you will be challenged on the ground that you are intent on imposing your religious beliefs on other people. And in contemporary political and legal culture, nothing is worse" (*The Culture of Disbelief,* pp. 6-7, 13, 23, emphasis in original).

2. *The Loss of a Moral Sense.* Certain problems arise whenever people either deny or ignore absolute truths. One Protestant writer has stated:

> I believe that one of the prime reasons this generation is setting new records for dishonesty, disrespect, sexual promiscuity, violence, suicide, and other pathologies, is because they have lost their moral underpinnings; their foundational belief in morality and truth has been eroded. . . . At one time, our society, by and large, explained the universe, humanity, and the purpose of life from the Judeo-Christian tradition: a belief that truth existed, and everyone could know and understand it. A clear understanding of what was right and wrong gave society a moral standard by which to measure crime

and punishment, business ethics, community values, character, and social conduct. . . .

That has changed dramatically, however. Our children are being raised in a society that has largely rejected the notions of truth and morality, a society that has somewhere lost the ability to decide what is true and what is right. Truth has become a matter of taste; morality has been replaced by individual preference" (Josh McDowell, *Right from Wrong*, pp. 12-13).

"If modern man has taken seriously the main intellectual currents of the last century or so," Professor James Wilson has written,

> he would have found himself confronted by the need to make moral choices when the very possibility of making such choices had been denied. God is dead or silent, reason suspect or defective, nature meaningless or hostile. As a result, man is adrift on an uncharted sea, left to find his moral bearings with no compass and no pole star, and so able to do little more than utter personal preferences, bow to historical necessity, or accept social conventions.

Further,

> If the moral sense is the result of nothing more significant than a cultural or historical throw of the dice, then it will occur to some people . . . that they are free to do whatever they can get away with by practicing indulgent self-absorption or embracing an angry ideology (*The Moral Sense*, pp. 5, 9).

In the 1960s a second movement began to take shape—hand in hand with the Death of God Movement—one that has had its flowering in our own time. It was known as Situation Ethics or Ethical Relativism. Inspired by the writings of Bishop John A. T. Robinson and Professor Joseph Fletcher, this movement proposed that any moral system is too shallow to provide answers to all situations and that every man and woman must decide what is right. It was a time when all were told to open themselves to the "new morality."

> The sanctions of Sinai have lost their terrors, and people no longer accept the authority of Jesus even as a great moral teacher. Robbed of its supranatural supports, men find it difficult to take seriously a code of living that confessedly depended on them" (Robinson, *Honest to God*, p. 109; see also Fletcher, *Situation Ethics: The New Morality*, chapters 1 and 2).

Many of you will remember how common it was to hear young people spout off with "It's all relative" or the even more common dictum, "There are no absolutes" (a pretty absolute statement, it seems to me!). Though we hear fewer chants and may notice fewer crusades for ethical relativism at the end of this decade, the die is cast and what was once parlor conversation or even college colloquy is now applied theology.

We seem to be caught in a vicious cycle. Knowing and sensing the things of God tend to prevent (or at least slow down) profligate wickedness. We cannot, however, come to know the things of God while we are sinning, for the Spirit of Truth will have difficulty penetrating the barriers we have erected through disobedience. Thus the need to declare repentance, to set forth the great plan of happiness, to teach of things eternal, of the need to bring our lives and our lifestyles into harmony with the mind and will of the Almighty. We cannot, simply cannot, as a people and a Church be guilty of moving the standards, shifting the anchors, or diluting the doctrine (especially the hard doctrine) in order to enhance our public image. Indeed, if those called to be the salt of the earth—those who have come out of the world by covenant (D&C 101:39-40)—lose their savor, either by mixture or by contamination, wherewith shall the world be salted or the people be saved?

3. *A Denial of Personal Responsibility.* The growth of the behavioral sciences in the last century has been phenomenal. Humankind seems at least as eager to understand the behavior and motivation of men and

women as they are to understand light waves and black holes and the mysteries of DNA. The application of scientific principles to the study of human behavior—in an effort to formalize and objectify that study—has resulted in the superimposition of a cause-effect model on man and woman. Though it may be healthy and in some cases helpful to search for root causes, the cause-effect, stimulus-response model for understanding man will forevermore yield deficient and perhaps even perverse results, so long as we ignore the role of moral agency in that process. I say that, not only in regard to Behaviorism, but also any other system—Humanistic or Freudian—that attempts to define the cause of human behavior solely in terms of inner mechanisms, self-actualization, id or ego functions, or even genetic predisposition.

Our fascination with causes ancillary to human agency has led us to paint ourselves into a corner in today's world. "Whereas in the late nineteenth century," James Wilson has written,

> crime rates seem to have increased during periods of economic growth, in the last few decades they have often increased during such periods. Over the course of the last hundred years the world has experienced a shift from an era in which crime chiefly responded to material circumstances to one in which it responds to cultural ones. That shift has many causes, but one is the collapse in the legitimacy of what once was respectfully called middle-class morality but today is sneeringly referred to as 'middle-class values.'
>
> The moral relativism of the modern age,

Wilson continues,

> has probably contributed to the increase in crime rates, especially the increases that occur during prosperous times. It has done so by replacing the belief in personal responsibility with the notion of social causation and by supplying to those marginal persons at risk for crime a justification for doing what they might have done anyway (*The Moral Sense*, p. 10).

Add to this movement the gradual attack our society has made on guilt—the inner monitor by which we sense within ourselves that we have violated the laws of God or the norms of society—and we find ourselves in a precarious position. "That kind of thinking," one Protestant theologian has observed,

> has all but driven words like *sin, repentance, contrition, atonement, and redemption* out of public discourse. If no one is supposed to feel guilty, how could anyone be a sinner? Modern culture has the answer: people are *victims*. Victims are not responsible for what they do; they are casualties of what happens to them. So every human failing must be described in terms of how the perpetrator has been victimized (John MacArthur, *The Vanishing Conscience*, p. 21, emphasis in original).

To be sure, there are real victims in society—abused children or spouses, persons who suffer at the hands of racism or sexism—and they deserve our empathy, our support, and our zealous defense against such tragedies. My specific concern is with men and women who do wrong, who knowingly violate the laws of decency and morality, and then seek refuge behind the growing wall of victimization. For example,

- A man who was shot and paralyzed while committing a burglary in New York recovered damages from the store owner who shot him. His attorney told a jury the man was first of all a victim of society, driven to crime by economic disadvantages. Now, the lawyer said, he is a victim of the insensitivity of the man who shot him. Because of that man's callous disregard of the thief's plight as a victim, the poor criminal will be confined to a wheelchair for the rest of his life. He deserves some redress. The jury agreed. The store owner paid a large settlement. Several months later, the same man, still in his wheelchair, was arrested while committing another armed robbery.

- Bernard McCummings parlayed a similar victimism into wealth. After mugging and brutally beating an elderly New York man in the subway, McCummings was shot while fleeing the scene. Permanently paralyzed, he sued and won $4.8 million in compensation from the New York Transit Authority. The man he mugged, a cancer patient, is still paying doctor bills. McCummings, the mugger—whom the courts deemed the greater victim—is now a multi-millionaire.

- In two separate cases in England, a barmaid who stabbed another woman to death in a bar-room brawl, and a woman who angrily drove her car into her lover were both acquitted of murder after they claimed acute pre-menstrual syndrome (PMS) addled their thinking and caused them to act in ways they could not control. Both received therapy rather than punishment.

- A San Francisco city supervisor claimed he murdered a fellow supervisor and Mayor George Mascone because too much junk food—especially Hostess Twinkies—made him act irrationally. Thus the famous "Twinkie" defense was born. A lenient jury bought the line and produced a verdict of voluntary manslaughter rather than murder. They ruled that the junk food resulted in "diminished mental capacity," which mitigated the killer's guilt. He was out of prison before the mayor's next term would have been complete (Cited in MacArthur, *The Vanishing Conscience,* pp. 22-23).

In the words of one author, what we have here is

> a formula for social gridlock: the irresistible search for someone or something to blame colliding with the unmovable unwillingness to accept responsibility. Now enshrined in law and jurisprudence, victimism is reshaping the fabric of society, including employment policies, criminal justice, education, urban politics, and, in an increasingly Orwellian emphasis on 'sensitivity' in language. A community of interdependent citizens has been displaced by a society of resentful, competing, and self-interested individuals who have dressed their private annoyances in the garb of victimism (Charles Sykes, *A Nation of Victims,* p. 15).

4. *Stressing Ethics over Doctrine.* In the absence of the real thing—the fulness of the gospel—there are many ideas and movements that seek to occupy center stage. Among the more popular in today's world is a focus upon Jesus as loving teacher, guide, and moral leader. For some persons, Jesus stands as the preeminent example of kindness, the ultimate illustration of social and interpersonal graciousness and morality. A favorite text for this group is the Sermon on the Mount, while their highest aspiration is the call to live the Golden Rule. A Roman Catholic philosopher has observed: "According to the theological liberal, (the Sermon on the Mount] is the essence of Christianity, and Christ is the best of human teachers and examples . . . . Christianity is essentially ethics. What's missing here?" he asks.

> Simply, the essence of Christianity, which is *not* the Sermon on the Mount. When Christianity was proclaimed throughout the world, the proclamation (*kerygma*) was not "Love your enemies!" but "Christ is risen!" This was not a new *ideal* but a new *event*, that God became man, died, and rose for our salvation. Christianity is first of all not ideal but real, an event, news, the gospel, the "good news." The essence of Christianity is not Christianity; the essence of Christianity is Christ (Peter Kreeft, *Back to Virtue,* p. 83, emphasis in original).

For many, the doctrine of Christ has been replaced by the ethics of Jesus. Those who insist that ethics must be discussed or taught or enforced point toward the declining moral standards of our day, the increase of drug abuse or teenage pregnancy, the prevalence of our inhumanity to each other. They contend that if Christianity is to make a difference in the world, we must find ways to transform ethereal theology into religious practice in a decaying society. They thus promote a social gospel, a relevant religion. The problem with a social gospel is that it is inherently and forevermore deficient as far as engaging the real problems of human beings. It almost always focuses on symptoms rather than causes. Ethics is not the essence of the gospel. Ethics is not necessarily righteousness. The very word *ethics* has come to connote socially acceptable standards based on current consensus, as opposed to absolute truths based on God's eternal laws. Ethics is too often to virtue and righteousness what theology is to religion—a pale and wimpy substitute. Indeed, ethics without that virtue that comes through the cleansing powers of the Redeemer is like religion without God, at least the true and living God.

It's All Absolute

Let us begin with the certain assurance that we cannot solve spiritual maladies through temporal solutions. Our problem in the world today is a detachment from morality, and morality cannot, in the long run, be severed from religion. Religion is a most interesting word. It means literally "to tie back to." It is related to the word ligament, that which ties the bone to the muscle. Religion is thus that which ties us back to God and to sacred things. To define morality in terms of utility (what works) or in terms of consensus (what most people believe) is to fall short of what was, is, and is to be (D&C 93:24).

As we noted in the last chapter, some things are. They just are. Neither congressional decisions nor popular opinion changes absolute truth. All the people in the world but the Latter-day Saints may decide that abortion is humane, homosexuality is merely an alternative lifestyle, and assisted suicide is compassionate, but that does not change the fact that these matters are sinful and wrong and contrary to the great plan of the Eternal God. They cannot bring happiness. They cannot result in peace. Every religious body on the globe except the Latter-day Saints may conclude that God is a spirit, that he is uninvolved in the daily doings of men and women, and that men and women will prosper according to their genius and not through the divine assistance of a Savior. But such sentiments do not matter a snap of the finger in the eternal scheme of things, for what God is, does, and accomplishes among his children—through the mediation of his Beloved Son—is in the realm of absolute truths. These things we know from scripture, from modern prophets, and by personal revelation.

"We know instinctively," one Christian writer has observed,

> that some things are right and some things are wrong. Let (a young woman) discover, for example, that her soccer shoes were stolen from her school locker and she'll feel wronged. She would not argue that the thief is entitled to his opinion of right and wrong; she would appeal to an objective sense of justice because she would claim that she had suffered an injustice. In so doing, of course, she would appeal to a moral law that she believes everyone—not just herself—ought to follow (McDowell, *Right from Wrong*, p. 78).

That is to say, while many who yearn to speak of ethical relativism or situational ethics do so from their philosophical perch above the real world, those same persons expect others to treat them according to a model of truth and morality that reflects a more objective and absolute way of knowing what is right or wrong. If it is true that "There are no atheists in foxholes," then it is also true that "There are no relativists who expect to be treated relatively" (Cited by McDowell, *Right from Wrong*, p. 78).

The Foundation for Ethics

"It is one thing," Elder Bruce R. McConkie has written,

> to teach ethical principles, quite another to proclaim the great doctrinal verities, which are the foundation of true Christianity and out of which eternal salvation comes. True it is that salvation is limited to those in whose souls the ethical principles abound,

27

but true it is also that Christian ethics, in the full and saving sense, automatically become a part of the lives of those who first believe Christian doctrines.

In summary,

> It is only when gospel ethics are tied to gospel doctrines that they rest on a sure and enduring foundation and gain full operation in the lives of the saints (*A New Witness for the Articles of Faith*, pp. 699-700).

The Latter-day Saints are occasionally criticized for expending so much of the resources of the Church on missionary work or the construction of temples. Some indicate that the institutional Church should be more involved in leading or officially supporting this or that crusade, in laboring for this or that social cause. "Where is your charity?" they ask. "Of what avail are your noble theological principles?" they inquire. I agree with Bruce Hafen, who pointed out that

> The ultimate purpose of the gospel of Jesus Christ is to cause the sons and daughters of God to become as Christ is. Those who see religious purpose only in terms of ethical service in the relationship between man and fellowmen may miss that divinely ordained possibility. It is quite possible to render charitable—even Christian—service without developing deeply ingrained and permanent Christ-like character. Paul understood this when he warned against giving all one's goods to feed the poor without charity. . . . **While religious philosophies whose highest aim is social relevance may do much good, they will not ultimately lead people to achieve the highest religious purpose, which is to become as God and Christ are** (*The Broken Heart*, pp. 196-97, emphasis added).

The Master warned what would happen if we seek to be his but are not built upon his gospel. If our effort "be not built upon my gospel," he said,

> and is built upon the works of men, or upon the works of the devil, verily I say unto you they have joy in their works for a season, and by and by the end cometh, and they are hewn down and cast into the fire, from whence there is no return (3 Nephi 27:11).

The works of the devil obviously pertain to carnality and devilishness, what Paul called "the works of the flesh"—such sins as adultery, fornication, idolatry, witchcraft, hatred, strife, and heresy (Galatians 5:19-21). They bring pleasure and telestial titillation for a season, but they result inevitably in shrinkage of the soul, followed in time by bitter loneliness and that awful alienation from things of lasting worth. Indeed, "their works do follow them, for it is because of their works that they are hewn down" (3 Nephi 27:12).

God's work and glory is to bring to pass the immortality and eternal life of man (Moses 1:39). Our most noble work will be accomplished and our greatest glory and joy will come, to the degree that we are similarly occupied with this overarching objective. The "works of men" may refer to what we know as honorable endeavors, worthwhile efforts to improve man and society, but labors whose focus are not truly on the Lord or his work and glory. Political agendas, ethical concerns, and environmental issues, all works of men, are good and proper, and we should be involved in them to the degree that our time and circumstances allow. Noble enterprises bring a measure of personal satisfaction. Too often, however, the works of men bring glory to men. More often than not, the works of men hack away at the leaves of the inconsequential while ignoring the spiritual roots of attitudes and behavior.

The poignant message of the Savior is that happiness, meaning lasting joy, comes only to those who are built upon his gospel and whose works are really the Lord's works. So many people, as C. S. Lewis observed, seek to invent some sort of happiness for themselves outside God, apart from God. And out of that hopeless attempt has come nearly all that we call human history—money, poverty, ambition, war, prostitution, classes, slavery—the long terrible story of man trying to find something other than God which will make him happy.

The reason why it can never succeed is this. . . . **God designed the human machine to run on Himself. He Himself is the fuel our spirits were designed to burn, or the food our spirits were designed to feed on. There is no other. That is why it is just no good asking God to make us happy in our own way without bothering about religion. God cannot give us a happiness and peace apart from Himself**, because it is not there. There is no such thing (*Mere Christianity,* pp. 53-54, emphasis added).

Similarly, Elder Neal A. Maxwell pointed out that

Mankind has not had much success in keeping the second commandment by loving our neighbors as ourselves, without also keeping the first great commandment, loving God with all of our heart, might, mind, and strength. **Try as mankind may to achieve the brotherhood of man without the Fatherhood of God, it is cosmetic and does not last!** ("This Is a Special Institution," Inaugural Address at BYU-Hawaii; cited in *Profile Magazine,* December 1994, p. 9, emphasis added).

Getting Back to the Source

Let me propose what might be a rather typical discussion between an LDS parent and child:

Father: "Billy, is it wrong to steal?"
Son: "Yea, Dad, it's wrong to steal."
Father: "Why is it wrong?"
Son: "Because you taught us that it's wrong."
Father: "That's right, son, we did. But why did we teach you that?"
Son: "Because the Church teaches us that it's not right to steal."
Father: "Right again. But why does the Church teach that?"
(Then there is a long pause).
Son: "I don't know, Dad. Is it because Heavenly Father doesn't want us to steal?"
Father: "You're absolutely right, Billy. Heavenly Father does not want us to steal.
     Why doesn't he want us to steal?"
(This time there is a longer and even more uncomfortable pause).
Son: "I don't really know, Dad."

This fictional encounter highlights a problem we face in teaching one another (and especially our children) the principles of morality and decency. Notice that the PRECEPT of "Thou shalt not steal" is pretty clear in this young man's mind. He has been taught the commandments and is able to articulate what he understands. A little less clear is that which underlies the precept, namely the PRINCIPLE, in this case the principle of Honesty. Our young man knows what has been forbidden (to steal), and he senses that the major reasons it is forbidden is because his parents, his Church, and his Heavenly Father have condemned it. Now those are all fine sources for the precept and the principle, but are they the ultimate or absolute source? No, for beneath the principle is the PERSON of God. A vital part of the great plan of happiness is the nature and kind of Being we worship. Fundamental to the purpose of life and the hope for glory hereafter is the knowledge that has been revealed concerning God—his character, his perfections, his relationship to us, and, most important to this discussion, the knowledge that we can become as he is.

To complete our conversation,

> Father: "Billy, we are commanded not to steal [the Precept] because the Lord wants his people to be honest [the Principle]. He wants us to be honest because he is a God of truth [the Person]. We are sent to earth to strive as best we can to become as he is. Only as we become a people of truth can we ever hope to be like our Heavenly Father."

It is one thing to teach that honesty is the best policy (utility) or to teach that it is best to be honest because most people in society expect us to deal respectfully and responsibly with one another (consensus). Both utility and consensus have done much in the past to maintain some semblance of order in our world. But with changing times and the erosion of time-honored values, many look about hopelessly for a more solid and enduring foundation. That foundation is doctrinal; it is the foundation of faith and theology. Our children deserve answers to the hard question of WHY. And the only lasting and satisfying answer to why we do what we do or why we do not do other things is to be found in the great plan of happiness, in the understanding of God and man, in the clear statement of our eternal possibilities here and hereafter.

As a priesthood leader, I have had occasion to listen as young people confess major moral transgressions. I have asked about why the violation of the law of chastity is so serious. I have been interested as they have spoken of disappointing their parents, postponing temple marriage or missions, bearing children out of wedlock, and contracting deadly diseases—all of which, from the perspective of utility or consensus are darned good reasons to stay morally clean. But there is more to it, much more, and it is that added light and added knowledge that come from our divinely given doctrine to which we turn for the greatest preventative medicine against serious sin.

I learned something very valuable many years ago when my wife and I timidly approached the much dreaded but needed conversation about the facts of life with our oldest child. We sweat and we stewed for weeks. We read. We debated. We prepared charts and graphs and pictures of the human reproductive system; we went into the conversation with several books under our arms. We had also prayed earnestly for inspiration. We dove into the presentation and discovered to our surprise that it was going in a direction that neither my wife nor I had anticipated. For about an hour we spoke of the plan of salvation—of who we are, where we came from, why we are here, and where we are going when we die. We spoke of physical bodies and experiences and Satan and opposition and relationships and families and children and temples and covenants and ordinances and sealing powers. The Spirit of the Lord was present, and so we learned a great deal from what we said. I think my daughter did also. At the end of that most unusual hour, I asked: "Now, sweetheart, do you understand why it is so very important to stay morally clean?" She nodded.

It was not until many years later that I sensed the significance of a passage of scripture, one that President Boyd K. Packer has emphasized again and again. Speaking of the ancients, Alma said: "God gave unto them commandments, **after having made known unto them the plan of redemption**" (Alma 12:32, emphasis added). From the knowledge of the person of God, as well as the doctrines and principles that follow, come the precepts. President Packer explained to Church Educational System personnel:

> Young people wonder "why?"—Why are we commanded **to do** some things, and why are we commanded **not** to do other things? A knowledge of the plan of happiness, even in outline form, can give young minds a "why."
>
> A parent once angrily scolded a child for a serious mistake, saying, "Why on earth did you do such a thing?" The child answered, "If I'd had a Why, I wouldn't have done it."
>
> Providing your students [or, we might add, our children] with a collection of unrelated truths will hurt as much as it helps. Provide a basic feeling for the whole plan, even with just a few details, and it will help them ever so much more. Let them know what it's all about, then they will have the "why."
>
> Most of the difficult questions we face in the Church right now, and we could

list them—abortion and all the rest of them, all of the challenges of who holds the priesthood and who does not—cannot be answered without some knowledge of the plan as a background. . . .

You will not be with your students or your own children at the time of their temptations. At those dangerous moments they must depend on their own resources. If they can locate themselves within the framework of the gospel plan, they will be immensely strengthened.

The plan is worthy of repetition over and over again. Then the purpose of life, the reality of the Redeemer, and the reason for the commandments will stay with them.

Their gospel study, their life experiences, will add to an ever-growing witness of the Christ, of the Atonement, of the restoration of the gospel ("The Great Plan of Happiness," Seventeenth Annual CES Religious Educators' Symposium, 10 August 1993, p. 3).

Having said all this, I hasten to add that even with a knowledge of the great plan of happiness before them, men and women, boys and girls may choose to walk in the ways of the world and thus settle for less than what they could be. But I have a conviction that the proper teaching of the Father's plan will do much to hold on to those who are children of the covenant and heirs to the promises made to Abraham, Isaac, and Jacob. We will speak of the power of the covenant and the binding nature of temple blessings in the next chapter.

Conclusion

Let me conclude where I began—with the sobering prophecy of the Apostle Paul. You recall that he warned of such sins in the last days as pride, blasphemy, disrespect for parents, ingratitude, dishonesty, immorality, and perversion. Finally, he spoke of persons who are "ever learning, and never able to come to the knowledge of the truth." (2 Timothy 3:1-7). The visible disarray in our world is but symptomatic of the invisible decay, an evidence that our moral foundation is under attack. And should we be surprised? The Psalmist warned that "the wicked bend their bows; lo, they make ready their arrow upon the string, that they may privily shoot at the upright in heart, to destroy their foundation" (JST, Psalms 11:2).

Indeed, the Latter-day Saints boldly proclaim that "the knowledge of the truth" of which Paul wrote constitutes the sure foundation upon which true believers must build their houses of faith. It is worth noting that the Apostle Paul did not leave us without comfort or recourse. Later in that same chapter, he wrote to Timothy:

But evil men and seducers shall wax worse and worse, deceiving, and being deceived. But continue thou in the things which thou hast learned and hast been assured of, knowing of whom thou hast learned them; and that from a child **thou hast known the holy scriptures, which are able to make thee wise unto salvation through faith which is in Christ Jesus.** And all Scripture given by inspiration of God, is profitable for doctrine, for reproof, for correction, for instruction in righteousness: that the man of God may be perfect, thoroughly furnished unto all good works" (JST, 2 Timothy 3:13-17, emphasis added).

The scriptures. The word of God. The living oracles. The doctrines of salvation—these are the means by which we come to know the Precepts, the Principles, and the Person of God. They set forth what we must and must not do, as well as who we are and what we may become. Thus President Packer explained:

True doctrine, understood, changes attitudes and behavior. The study of the doctrines of the gospel will improve behavior quicker than a study of behavior will improve behavior. . . . That is why we stress so forcefully the study of the doctrines of the gospel'' (Conference Report, October 1986, p. 20).

There is a power, a supernal power that flows from us when we teach the great plan of happiness. There is peace, consummate peace that comes into our lives when we erect our divine domiciles on the foundation of doctrine and faith. Therein is our safety. Therein is our hope.

The Lord's Plan For Men And Women

President Spencer W. Kimball

Conference, June 27,1975

Our Heavenly Father has a plan for man's growth from infancy to godhood. It is not always an easy life, but it can be most rewarding, depending upon our attitude toward it.

Let us trace the plan of God. When Moses was the Lord's prophet, he had great visions and revelations. He saw back to the beginning and before the beginning of this earth.

So also did Abraham: "I am the Lord thy God," said the Creator to Abraham, ". . . I rule in the heavens above, and in the earth beneath, in all wisdom and prudence, over all the intelligences thine eyes have seen from the beginning" (Abr. 3:19, 21).

And the Lord, standing among these numerous premortal spirits, said,

> We will go down, for there is space there, and we will take of these materials,
> and we will make an earth whereon these may dwell;
> And we will prove them herewith, to see if they will do all things whatsoever the
> Lord their God shall command them (Abr. 3:24-25).
> And the Gods watched those things which they had ordered until they obeyed
> (Abr. 4:18).

Then came, in succession, the whales and fish and living creatures and the winged fowls. "And the Gods saw that they would be obeyed, and that their plan was good" (Abr. 4:21).

And with the waters filled with life and the air with winged creatures, the Gods said, "We will bless them, and cause them to be fiuitful and multiply" (Abr. 4:22).

And the fifth "time," generally spoken of as a day, was fulfilled.

Another time came and living creatures, cattle, creeping things, and beasts of every kind were brought forth: "and the Gods saw they would obey" (Abr. 4:25).

Now with the earth organized, they took counsel and said "Let us go down and form man in our image, after our likeness; and we will give them dominion. . . .

"So the Gods went down to organize man . . . male and female" (Abr. 4:26-27).

And now the plan was completed, and you and I and our numberless brothers and sisters would be given an opportunity, in a normal, natural way, to come to the earth and to enjoy its possibilities.

We are all the spirit children of God; we are his supreme creation; the earth and all that pertains to it is for the growth, development, and satisfaction of all mankind. And the Lord said,

> Verily I say, that inasmuch as ye [live the commandments], the fulness of the
> earth is yours, . . .
> Yea, all things which come of the earth, in the seasons thereof, are made for the
> benefit and the use of man, both to please the eye and to gladden the heart;
> Yea, for food and for raiment, for taste and for smell, to strengthen the body and
> to enliven the soul.

And it pleaseth God that he hath given all these things unto man; for unto this end were they made to be used (D&C 59:16, 18-20).

Now the plan was drawn, the program was set up, every detail was considered.

And the sixth "time" was numbered, and they planned as follows: "We will cause them [male and female] to be fruitful and multiply, and replenish the earth, and subdue it" (Abr. 4:28).

This was not an afterthought or a gradual development. This was carefully planned prior to the actual creation.

Then the day came when

> the Gods came down and formed these the generations of the heavens and of the earth.
> And the Gods formed man from the dust of the ground, and took his spirit (that is, the man's spirit), and put it into him; and breathed into his nostrils the breath of life, and man became a living soul (Abr. 5:4, 7).

Then "formed they a woman, and brought her unto the man" (Abr. 5:16).

This was also divinely planned.

And Adam rejoiced and said

> now she shall be called Woman. . . .
> Therefore shall a man leave his father and his mother, and shall cleave unto his wife, and they shall be one flesh (Abr. 5:17, 18).

The Gods had said, "Let us make an help meet for the man, for it is not good that the man should be alone, therefore we will form an help meet for him" (Abr. 5:14).

We have indicated that they, the Gods, had planned the creation and had formed all things, including man and woman, and life was given to all things. There was real purpose in what they had done.

> So God created man in his own image, in the image of God created he him; male and female created he them.
> And God blessed them, and God said unto them, Be fruitful, and multiply, and replenish the earth, and subdue it (Gen. 1:27-28).

And he could have said, "And God blessed them that they might multiply and replenish the earth, for in that comes a great blessing that many people are missing."

This is no accident that children would be born. This is a program carefully planned. The Lord could have provided some other way, but how could parents love and nurture their children in such a case?

The bodies of men and the bodies of women were created differently so they complemented each other, so that the union of the two would bring a conception which would bring a living soul into the world, one of those numerous, uncountable spirits that Abraham saw when the Lord had pulled back the curtains.

Now we must emphasize here that the Lord made man and woman, male and female to reproduce after their kind, and in the billions of unions there has continued to come a male or a female. Their bodies are still so formed that they will continue to the end of time in producing male or female, the spirit children of God.

And when the Gods had completed each of the "times" of creation, they had noted that they were obeyed — the word had been obeyed! The Gods said "it is good, very good," as they looked over their total world and plan.

This was the normal, proper way to preserve the total program, to bring souls into the world and to give them opportunities for growth.

Let no carnal mind decide in his or her feigned brilliance or pretended wisdom that a mistake was made. The whole program was intelligently organized to bring children into the world with love and filial inter-dependence. Had the superficial ideas of many mortals of today prevailed, the world, the human race, and all proper things would long ago have come to an end.

34

It was the Lord Jesus Christ himself who said to the Pharisees, during his early ministry: "Have ye not read, that he which made them at the beginning made them male and female," and no other kind? (Matt. 19:4).

And they were given the commandment that the man should cleave to his wife,

> and they twain shall be one flesh.
> Wherefore, they are no more twain, but one flesh; What therefore God hath joined together, let not man put asunder (Matt. 19:5-6).

And therein is a strong denunciation by our Lord against the evils of divorce and family disruption.

The union of the sexes, husband and wife (and only husband and wife), was for the principal purpose of bringing children into the world. Sexual experiences were never intended by the Lord to be a mere plaything or merely to satisfy passions and lusts. We know of no directive from the Lord that proper sexual experience between husbands and wives need be limited totally to the procreation of children, but we find much evidence from Adam until now that no provision was ever made by the Lord for indiscriminate sex.

Knowing the proper order of the Lord's plan, then, let there be no prostituting of this sacred program.

We have many people in the world today who, in their gigantic presumption, attempt to create a world based on Satan's plans, for Satan rejoices when evils are performed.

One prominent speaker said sex is not the use of something inherently bad, but can become the misuse of something inherently good.

Certainly it is not easy for the woman to bear the child in distress and discomfort, but still her desire should be to her husband, for he will preside over her. And surely it is not easy for the man who must provide for his family by the sweat of his face, but it is the true plan. (See Gen. 3:16-19.) Great blessings come from it.

In nearly every time in holy scripture where mankind is mentioned as having been created, the terms "male and female" are used. Moses said in the fifth chapter of Genesis: "In the day that God created man, in the likeness of God made he him" (Gen. 5: 1). And that is no idle thought either, that you and I are made in the image of God, to become gods and queens and kings eventually.

"Male and female created he them; and blessed them, and called their name Adam" (Gen. 5:2).

Adam was their name. And I suppose that the name Adam was the family surname, just as Kimball is my name and my wife's name.

When the woman was given to Adam, he called her name Eve "because she was the mother of all living" (Moses 4:26). She was the first. Adam and Eve were the progenitors of the race. They were the first father and mother, and all the children of mortality are the offspring of this couple.

Now, this man and this woman were sealed for eternity, God being the sealer. He gave to Adam his wife, Eve. He intended that all men should live worthy to have performed this ordinance of marriage for time and all eternity. The Lord has said that in order to obtain the highest of the three heavens or degrees of glory in the celestial kingdom,

> a man must enter into this order of the priesthood [meaning the new and everlasting covenant of marriage];
> And if he does not, he cannot obtain it (D&C 131:2-3).

This is the proper way.

There are some men who fail to marry through their own choice. They deprive themselves. There may be many women who also deprive themselves of blessings. There are others who have never married because they have had no opportunity. We know, of course, that the Lord will make ample provision and that no one will ever be condemned for something he or she could not have helped. This is the Lord's program.

But, concerning marriage and the roles of man and woman, let no man defy God or set aside his divine program.

For it is written, I will destroy the wisdom of the wise, and will bring to nothing the understanding of the prudent.

Where is the wise? where is the scribe? where is the disputer of this world? hath not God made foolish the wisdom of this world? (I Cor. 1: 19-20).

Why do some allow themselves to criticize—criticize God's plan? Why can't they accept their roles in life and be grateful for them?

Recently in a local paper appeared an article by a courageous woman who said,

The scriptures designate that a man's most important responsibility in life is to be the guide, the protector and provider for his wife and children. In the beginning when God created man and woman, he said to the woman, "thy desire shall be to thy husband, and he shall rule [but I like the word preside] over thee" (Gen. 3:16). The Apostle Paul reaffirmed this when he said, "the husband is the head of the wife, even as Christ is the head of the church" (Eph. 5:23).

This woman speaks of the so-called intellectuals who would change the plan of God. She seems to be one of those who believes that God knew what he was doing when he organized the family of man.

I sincerely hope that our Latter-day Saint girls and women, and men and boys, will drink deeply of the water of life and conform their lives to the beautiful and comprehensive roles the Lord assigned to them.

I hope we shall not attempt to perfect an already perfect plan, but seek with all our might, mind, and strength to perfect ourselves in the comprehensive program given to us. Because some of us have failed, certainly it would be unfair to place the blame upon the program. Let us control our attitudes, our activities, our total lives, that we may be heir to the rich and numerous blessings promised to us.

What God-given roles each of us could play in this great divine drama! What satisfying personal lives we can live! What beautiful families we can nurture and train! What a heavenly future is ours!

God lives. This I know. Jesus is the Christ and this I know. This is his program, and this I also know.

The Marriage Decision

President Spencer W. Kimball

Stockholm, Sweden Area Conference, August 1974; *The Ensign,* February 1975, pp. 2-6

As we approach you at this time and find you growing up in power and strength, we find ourselves wishing for you not quantities of gold, nor acres of land, nor houses of unsurpassed beauty, nor jewels that sparkle, nor plaudits of vulgar men, nor treasures of earth, but what a great father, David, wished for his son; and, more important, what a wise son wished for himself as he came to the day of his greatest opportunity. The father, King David, had prayed: "And give unto Solomon my son a perfect heart, to keep thy commandments, thy testimonies, and thy statues, and to do all these things. . . ." (I Chron. 29:19).

May we talk of marriage and your life in total? Marriage is a vital part of life.

The Lord has said: "Therefore shall a man leave his father and his mother, and shall cleave unto his wife: and they shall be one flesh" (Gen. 2:24). And then he carried forward, saying further: ". . . Multiply, and replenish the earth, and subdue it. . . ." (Gen. 1:28). Accordingly, the program for every normal man and every normal woman is laid out for them. And it is expected by the Lord that every normal man and woman will find a companion and have a marriage in which they and their children will live in joy and happiness.

Recently I met a young returned missionary who is 35 years old. He had been home from his mission for 14 years and yet he was little concerned about his bachelorhood, and laughed about it.

I shall feel sorry for this young man when the day comes that he faces the Great Judge at the throne and when the Lord asks this boy: "Where is your wife?" All of his excuses which he gave to his fellows on earth will seem very light and senseless when he answers the Judge. "I was very busy," or "I felt I should get my education first," or "I did not find the right girl"—such answers will be hollow and of little avail. He knew he was commanded to find a wife and marry her and make her happy. He knew it was his duty to become the father of children and provide a rich, full life for them as they grew up. He knew all this, yet postponed his responsibility. So we say to all youth regardless of what country is your home, and regardless of the customs in your country, your Heavenly Father expects you to marry for eternity and rear a good, strong family.

The Lord planned that men and women would find each other and have a happy family relationship, be true to each other, and remain clean and worthy.

The Lord could have organized his world without this propagation program; he could have filled the earth with physical human bodies in some other way than that which he designed, perhaps some incubator process, but it seems that merely filling the earth with human beings was not the great objective of our Lord, and therefore a father and a mother were designed to be given to every child that was born, and they should love and teach that child and prepare him to become like his Father in heaven, in righteousness and purity.

It was never intended by the Lord that a large portion of one's life should be spent in the unmarried state. At a reasonable time in life it was intended that each young man should find that young woman who is best for him, and she should find the young man who would be her best companion. Long-delayed marriages are certainly not approved of the Lord.

Even though many young people do not at this time have temples in their own communities, there are generally temples within a reasonable distance. In my youth the Saints went from 500 miles to 800 miles for their marriages.

It is our earnest hope that when you have done your proper courting, that you would plan your honeymoon so that you could go to one of these nearest temples to be sealed for all eternity so that your children will be permanently yours and that you will be permanently their parents and so that it will be an eternal marriage.

It would be our hope that your parents would train you from infancy to do odd chores, to earn some money, and to put it away for your missions and your marriages.

We hope that young people will be willing to sacrifice the pomp and show and pageantry of the civil weddings so that they and generally their parents with them can go to the holy temple for their marriages. Often the cost of a reception or a holiday or expensive gifts would more than pay for a temple wedding. When Sister Kimball and I were married, we had no ring nor costly reception. Eight years later I bought her a small diamond. She was content to wait until then.

Now is the time for you to plan good strong marriages and organize your programs and set your standards and solidify your determination to prepare for that married period of your lives which will be beautiful and rewarding.

Accordingly, my beloved young people, you should be serious minded. Life is not wholly for fun and frolic. It is a most serious business. You will do well to grow up as children, associating with both girls and boys for those first years. When you get in the teen-age years, your social associations should still be general acquaintance with both boys and girls. Any dating or pairing off in social contacts should be postponed until at least the age of 16 or older, and even then there should be much judgment used in selections and in the seriousness.

Young people should still limit the close contacts for several years, since the boy will be going on his mission when he is 19 years old. There should be limited contacts and certainly no approach to the intimate relationships involving sex. There must never be any sex of any kind prior to marriage.

Every boy should have been saving money for his mission and be free from any and all entanglements so he will be worthy. When he is returned from his mission at 21, he should feel free to begin to get acquainted and to date. When he has found the right young woman, there should be a proper temple marriage. One can have all the blessings if he is in control and takes the experiences in proper turn: first some limited social get-acquainted contacts, then his mission, then his courting, then his temple marriage and his schooling and his family, then his life's work. In any other sequence he could run into difficulty.

After marriage young wives should be occupied in bearing and rearing children. I know of no scriptures or authorities which authorize young wives to delay their families or to go to work to put their husbands through college. Young married couples can make their way and reach their educational heights, if they are determined.

Our young people should realize, as quoted from President J. Reuben Clark, Jr:

> There is some belief, too much I fear, that sex desire is planted in us solely for the pleasures of full gratification; that the begetting of children is only an unfortunate incident. The direct opposite is the fact. Sex desire was planted in us in order to be sure that bodies would be begotten to house the spirits; that pleasures of gratification of the desire is an incident, not the primary purpose of the desire.

And then he says further:

> As to sex in marriage, the necessary treatise on that for Latter-day Saints can be written in two sentences: Remember the prime purpose of sex desire is to beget children. Sex gratification must be had at that hazard. You husbands: be kind and considerate of your wives. They are not your property; they are not mere conveniences; they are your partners for time and eternity (Conference Report, General Priesthood Conference, October 1949, pp. 194-95).

As we talk about marriage, we remember, as Luke says: "Strive to enter in at the strait gate: for many, I say unto you, will seek to enter in, and shall not be able" (Luke 13:24).

Only through celestial marriage can one find the straight way, the narrow path. Eternal life cannot be had in any other way. The Lord was very specific and very definite in the matter of marriage. He said: "For this is a day of warning, and not a day of many words. For I, the Lord, am not to be mocked in the last days" (D&C 63:58).

The scriptures say that "God is not the God of the dead, but of the living" (Matt. 22:32).

There are no dead except those who have chosen to be dead as to the law, dead as to the benefits, dead as to the blessings, dead as to the eternal nature of the gift.

In our own day there are many people who form their own conclusions and do their own rationalizing and calculate and evaluate and develop their own opinions and "kick against the pricks," and close the door to their own opportunities.

Some time ago, in deep anguish, a mother came to see me. She was left alone. Her son and his wife met with an accident, leaving several small children. She came with many regrets and told me that the young victims of a plane crash had not been married in the temple. Both coming from good families, they had either ignored it or postponed it. They had lived the majority of their lifetime on the earth and still had not had this ordinance performed. This accident left them separated. The statement "till death do you part" left them single and their children orphans.

Of course, someone can have the work done in the temple for these young people after they have been dead a year, but will those young people accept the ordinances in death which were of such little consequence to them while they lived? And, more important than all else, do you think that God would be thusly mocked? He is the God of the living and not of the dead. He identified this ordinance as one to be done by the living themselves.

Have you ever realized that there is no magic in death, that ceasing to breathe does not make angels of careless people, does not make believers of disbelievers, does not bring faith where there was skepticism?

Have you ever studied carefully the parable of the ten virgins? Those who had prepared themselves for the blessings promised were ready, and those who were unprepared were cast out. Procrastination is a veritable thief

In the early days of the restored Church the Lord said much that should have been warning to the readers of the scriptures, but since they did not understand, the voice of the Lord came again.

Remember the Lord said:

> . . . If a man marry a wife, and make a covenant with her for time and all eternity, if that covenant is not by me or by my word . . . then it is not valid neither of force when they are out of the world, because they are not joined by me, saith the Lord, neither by my word; when they are out of the world it cannot be received there, because the angels and the gods are appointed there, by whom they cannot pass; they cannot, therefore, inherit my glory; for my house is a house of order, saith the Lord God (D&C 132:18).

The Lord makes clear that even the rewards to the angels are secondary to and inferior to the blessings of those "who are worthy of a far more, and an exceeding, and an eternal weight of glory" (D&C 132:16).

The Lord promises much to you young people who take care of this marriage in a proper way. He says: "And they shall pass by the angels, and the gods, which are set there, to their exaltation and glory in all things, as hath been sealed upon their heads. . ." (D&C 132:19).

Now this is not a matter of opinion; it matters little what you or I should think or argue. These are facts; the judges at the gates will know for certain the records, the spirit, and the true record. The Book of Life (See Rev. 20:12) will show the earthly activities of all of us.

I have repeated the provisions and the restrictions and the glories and the benefits, because we are all inclined to let them pass our notice like water down the river, but the Lord has repeated over and over as his message of the revelation came to Joseph Smith over and over, and as we read the scriptures over and over. He says: "Verily, verily, I say unto you, except ye abide my law ye cannot attain to this glory" (D&C 132:21). Can anything be more forthright and unequivocal than that? There is no room for argument or quibbling.

There will be a new spirit in Zion when the young women will say to their boyfriends, "If you cannot get a temple recommend, then I am not about to tie my life to you, even for mortality." And the young returned missionary boys will say to their girlfriends, "I am sorry, but as much as I love you, I will not marry out of the holy temple."

Let me note the brighter side. Some weeks ago I divided a stake. In the process of searching for a new president of each stake, I interviewed 29 men and found that all 29 had been sealed for eternity. They had 121 children, the average 4.3 children per family (or 6.3 persons per family). There was not a single divorce in the whole group; there were no broken homes in these 29 families. Every child of the 12 had two parents; neither death nor divorce had broken these homes. All of these 29 men were fairly well employed, fairly well housed; 43 of all the children were teenagers, but there were no serious problems among them, no drugs nor drinking nor smoking. Everyone was faithfully moving toward his exaltation.

And so we wonder why, with all these blessings and promises, that people will fail to marry correctly and thus waste their lives in a frozen wilderness that may never thaw. Why will any young person ever give a single thought to a marriage out of the temple and jeopardize those glories that are available? Why would a person with a temple marriage think of divorce, of breaking up a family, or of immoralities and infidelities? Why, oh why?

My beloved brothers and sisters, remember that I have explained these matters to you. Never can you say that I did not warn you. Our young people are wonderful, with rich, glorious promises. The Lord loves you, we love you, and we want you to do right and enjoy the blessings that come with righteous living.

We have confidence in you and promise you rich blessings and a happy life if you listen and study and pray and keep your life totally directed along the straight and narrow way outlined by our Lord, Jesus Christ.

Reluctant to Marry

Victor L. Brown, Jr.

Ensign, April 1992, pp. 44-47

Overcoming normal fears can help one prepare for eternal marriage.

There are many reasons why members of the Church are single. Some people are willing to marry and yearn for an opportunity to love, be loved, and begin a family. Some have been so badly wounded by such things as abuse in childhood or marital troubles ending in divorce that marriage or remarriage terrifies them. Others may lack the physical or mental health required to enter into marriage. But some quite simply are reluctant to do what is necessary to marry and establish a family. It is those members, struggling with normal fears and apprehensions, that I would like to address.

Since Joseph Smith, the Lord's prophets have encouraged loving and supportive marriage relationships. Our living prophet, President Ezra Taft Benson, has continued that admonition. To the single men in the Church, he counseled,

> Do not be caught up in materialism, one of the real plagues of our generation—that is, acquiring things, fast paced living, and securing career success in the single state. . . . Honorable marriage is more important than wealth, position, and status (*Ensign,* May, 1988, p. 53).

To the single sisters President Benson said,

> I would also caution you . . . not to become so independent and self-reliant that you decide marriage isn't worth it and you can do just as well on your own. Some of our sisters indicate that they do not want to consider marriage until after they have completed their degrees or pursed a career. This is not right. . . . Our priorities are right when we realize there is no higher calling than to be an honorable wife and mother (*Ensign,* Nov. 1988, p. 97).

What perplexes me as a stake president is that many of those who are reluctant to marry are active members of the Church and are decent, honorable men and women. They strive to live the gospel and follow the counsel of the prophet and other leaders. I believe their reluctance to marry often can be attributed to factors or attitudes that immobilize them. Among these factors are fear of marriage, other priorities, and lack of relationship skills. Consider them briefly.

Overcoming Fear of Marriage

We must face the fact that an entire generation has been raised on a diet of unhappy stories about marriage. The devastation of this cannot be overestimated. Most people who read the newspapers or watch television news are aware that a large percent of marriages fail. They are ever more aware of the ugliness of abuse and its innumerable victims. By the media-portrayed standards of the world, infidelity appears to be normal and fidelity rare.

However, not much attention has been paid to the other side of the issue; there are happy marriages and happy homes. In these marriages, devastating problems within marriage are the exception, not the rule. There have always been more husbands and wives who remain true to their marriage vows than those who stray. We would be prudent to remember that Satan is the father of lies. He has no scruples. There is no lie he will not foster, no harm he will not do. It is his method to use the media to spread the illusion that marriage is an obsolete, even undesirable institution.

Due to this influence, normal fears and apprehensions about marriage may be hard to overcome, but they can be. Individuals who recognize this as a problem can seek help—from friends, examples, Church leaders, and the Lord. Without exception, all individuals can pray, seek priesthood blessings, and study and live the gospel of Christ in dealing with obstacles.

Again, I recognize that a person may be suffering from wounds that create severe, abnormal fears. He or she can also seek help; sometimes professional help is needed. These individuals can also find help and comfort from friends, Church leaders, and the Lord as they strive to find healing peace.

Setting Correct Priorities

It may be a fine line that divides prudent preparation for marriage from worldly priorities that improperly delay marriage. Nevertheless, there is a line.

Priorities of money, education, career, and even "freedom to enjoy life" come perilously close to selfishness and pride. If a person's first goals are self-serving, he or she inevitably will be cautious about marrying, because to marry is to become other-serving.

This is what is so detrimental about misunderstanding what is meant by self-reliance. It is unwise to always delay marrying so one can reach a vocational or financial or emotional status of independence.

There are no such mortal conditions as perfect self-reliance, independence, and freedom from need. Even the richest, most educated, most emotionally secure person must, in the gospel plan, invest himself in the well-being of others, the ultimate investment being in the family, in order to bring about a sense of personal security and self-worth through personal contribution to the welfare of others.

Our Exemplar is Jesus Christ. He is perfectly educated, absolutely emotionally secure and is the owner of all creation. His highest priority, his work, his glory, is "to bring to pass the immortality and eternal life of man" (Moses 1:39). How does a follower of Christ justify priorities that are only self-focused when his Savior has the salvation of all mankind as his highest priority?

From self-focus grows an insidious priority. It is the priority of seeking the flawless mate. This is not the silly process of looking for a pretty face or muscular physique. It is the process of seeking or waiting for a complete, mature, fully formed potential mate to appear in one's life. Few things bode more ill for the future than these attitudes that prevent a man and woman who are in love from investing eternally in each other. Along with rearing children, the great adventure of marriage is to grow together. Among a person's highest priorities ought to be the exhilaration of investing in the growth of his or her beloved partner in eternal marriage.

Obviously, this is quite a different thing from entering into marriage with someone who will not revere the covenants and ordinances of the gospel and who has no love for the Savior. That type of union brings only the promise of sorrow and heartbreak.

Developing Relationship Skills

It is sometimes difficult to develop meaningful, sincere relationships, especially when we are often surrounded with negative examples or carry wounds from our own relationships. One formula I have found practical and useful is to divide all relationships into three types or phases; civil, affectionate, and intimate.

Understanding and identifying these phases enables a person to overcome paralyzing caution about marrying and also to establish and grow after marriage, as well as in other relationships.

Civil relationships are brief, formal, and purposeful. To be socially competent, each of us must know how to speak to, listen to, greet, and treat others with civility. In proper social conversation, a civil person does not look down at the floor or wander away while someone is speaking to him. Civility in the fellowship of the Saints means greeting strangers and making them welcome. It means listening to the sacrament meeting speaker instead of whispering to the person next to you. It includes inviting someone to sit with you in church or offering to pick them up for the fireside rather than merely notifying them of their opportunity to attend.

Affectionate relationships last longer, are more relaxed; their purpose is enjoyment. We linger with people for whom we feel affection. We are warmed by their interest in us and in our efforts. We exchange more detailed reports about each other. We telephone, write a note, or visit. Affectionate relationships may suggest an appropriate hug or an arm around the shoulder.

To overcome caution about marriage and move beyond civilities, a person needs to learn how to be appropriately affectionate. There are good things to read about affection in scripture, biographies of honorable people, and carefully selected "how-to" books. The *Ensign* is a practical resource for finding written guidance regarding gospel-based affectionate relationships between children of our Heavenly Father.

Observing people who live gospel standards is useful. But this is no passive exercise. Each of us needs practice. We need to bake cookies and drop them by; pick up the person not just for one fireside but for other activities; listen with interest, sometimes at length, as he or she tells you of a vacation, of the latest car repair disaster, or of deep feelings of the heart and soul. When we learn how to appropriately express affection by showing thoughtfulness of this kind, we gain the skills necessary for nurturing affectionate relationships.

We must understand that there is risk in moving beyond civil relationships. Some people will disappoint or even reject us. Yet we are protected when the motive of our affection was not to manipulate someone into liking us but rather to be their friend. As followers of Christ, we may brighten another's life, which makes us less susceptible to wounds. And if perchance we are wounded, we heal rapidly.

Out of experiencing many civil and some affectionate relationships, we may develop a few intimate relationships. These are more enduring, more intense, and bring more joy. They are also potentially heartbreaking because we risk and invest much more. Seeing intimate relationships break up evokes caution in us. And well it should, for such breakups cause severe pain.

Yet there is truth to be learned from such heartache. Destruction of intimate relationships in our lives can usually be traced back through specific events and attitudes. Lessons can be learned, behavior can be modified, and changes can be made.

Intimacy may include hand holding, even embracing, praying earnestly for the other person's welfare, shedding tears of joy and sorrow. Intimacy is no toy to be played with. It can exalt or crush. What makes this more powerful type of relationship manageable for us is Jesus Christ, his gospel, and its ordinances and covenants.

Knowing him and living by his example, we learn to trust and become trustworthy. Thereby we become not a threat to someone's tender heart but a protector. And should our heart be broken by betrayal, we have the Comforter, the Holy Ghost, who embraces us in the arms of godly love.

Within certain relationships we may experience all three phases. At first we are civil, speaking carefully, staying within constraints of time, controlling emotion. As we move into the affectionate phase, we become more emotionally open and we have a desire to be together more. When a relationship grows beyond affection, we yearn to be together, for to be apart is lonely. We think, speak, and act in ways that build and solidify the relationship, thus ensuring that we can continue to be together. When a person does not know how to nurture a relationship through all three phases, he or she can learn how by observing and doing.

There is no more intimidating decision in life than whether to marry. It is not abnormal to feel cautious about it. In fact, to be oblivious to its significance can lead to some amazing surprises. But the command and counsel of the Lord to "multiply and replenish the earth" and that "man is not without the woman nor woman without the man in the Lord'' should lead us all to do all we can to be worthy to fulfill the Lord's directions.

While there are usually reasons why a person is reluctant to marry, generally speaking, the solution is not to avoid marriage. That only denies a man or woman life's deepest enjoyments, and casts aside God's greatest gifts. Making the decision to marry may take courage. It usually takes faith. It always takes prayer. But it's a wonderful opportunity, when approved by the Spirit, to step forward and receive more of a loving Father's blessings.

Living Worthy of the Girl You Will Someday Marry

President Gordon B. Hinckley

Ensign, May 1998, pp. 49-51

A **week ago President Faust** and the Young Women general presidency spoke to the young women of the Church in this tabernacle.

As I looked at that gathering of beautiful young women the question moved through my mind, "Are we rearing a generation of young men worthy of them?"

Those girls are so fresh and vibrant. They are beautiful. They are bright. They are able, They are faithful. They are virtuous. They are true. They are simply wonderful and delightful young women.

And so tonight, in this great priesthood meeting I wish to speak to you young men, their counterpart. The title of my talk "Living Worthy of the Girl You Will Someday Marry."

The girl you marry will take a terrible chance on you. She will give her all to the young man she marries. He will largely determine the remainder of her life. She will even surrender her name to his name.

As Adam declared in the Garden of Eden: "This is now bone of my bones, and flesh of my flesh. . . .

"Therefore shall a man leave his father and his mother, and shall cleave unto his wife: and they shall be one flesh" (Gen. 2:23-24).

As members of The Church of Jesus Christ of Latter-day Saints, as young men holding the priesthood of God, you have a tremendous obligation toward the girl you marry. Perhaps you are not thinking much of that now. But the time isn't far away when you will think of it, and now is the time to prepare for that most important day of your lives when you take unto yourself a wife and companion equal with you before the Lord.

That obligation begins with absolute loyalty. As the old Church of England ceremony says, you will marry her "for richer or for poorer, in sickness and in health, for better or for worse." She will be yours and yours alone, regardless of the circumstances of your lives. You will be hers and hers alone. There can be eyes for none other. There must be absolute loyalty, undeviating loyalty one to another. Hopefully you will marry her forever, in the house of the Lord, under the authority of the everlasting priesthood. Through all the days of your lives, you must be as true one to another as the polar star.

The girl you marry can expect you to come to the marriage altar absolutely clean. She can expect you to be a young man of virtue in thought and word and deed.

I plead with you boys tonight to keep yourselves free from the stains of the world. You must not indulge in sleazy talk at school. You must not tell sultry jokes. You must not fool around with the Internet to find pornographic material. You must not dial a long-distance telephone number to listen to filth. You must not rent videos with pornography of any kind. This salacious stuff simply is not for you. Stay away from pornography as you would avoid a serious disease. It is as destructive. It can become habitual, and those who indulge in it get so they cannot leave it alone, It is addictive.

It is a five-billion-dollar business for those who produce it. They make it as titillating and attractive as they know how. It seduces and destroys its victims. It is everywhere. It is all about us. I plead with you young men not to get involved in its use, You simply cannot afford to.

The, girl you marry is worthy of a husband whose life has not been tainted by this ugly and corrosive material.

Look upon the Word of Wisdom as more than a commonplace thing. I regard it as the most remarkable document on health of which I know. It came to the Prophet Joseph Smith in 1833, when relatively little was known of dietary matters. Now the greater the scientific research, the more certain becomes the proof of Word of Wisdom principles. The evidence against tobacco is now overwhelming, yet we see a tremendous increase in its use by young men and women. The evidence against liquor is just as great.

To me it is an ironic thing that service stations offer beer sales. An individual can get as drunk on beer and be as dangerous on the road as he can on any other alcoholic substance. It is simply a matter of how much he drinks. How absolutely inconsistent it is for a service station, where you get gas so you can drive, to also sell beer that can cause you to drive "under the influence" and become a terrible menace on the highway.

Stay away from it. It will do you no good. It could do you irreparable harm. Suppose you drink and drive and cause the death of someone. You will never get over it as long as you live. It will haunt you night and day. The one simple thing to do is simply to not touch it.

Likewise, stay away from illegal drugs, They can absolutely destroy you. They will take away your powers of reason. They will enslave you in a vicious and terrible way, They will destroy your mind and your body. They will build within you such cravings that you will do anything to satisfy them.

Would any girl in her right mind ever wish to marry a young man who has a drug habit, who is the slave of alcohol, who is addicted to pornography?

Avoid profanity. It is all around you in school. Young people seem to pride themselves on using filthy and obscene language as well as indulging in profanity, taking the name of our Lord in vain. It becomes a vicious habit which, if indulged in while you are young, will find expression throughout your life. Who would wish to be married to a man whose speech is laden with fifth and profanity?

There is another serious thing to which many young men become addicted. This is anger. With the least provocation they explode into tantrums of uncontrolled rage. It is pitiful to see someone so weak. But even worse, they are prone to lose all sense of reason and do things which bring later regret.

We hear much these days of the phenomenon called road rage. Drivers become provoked over some small irritation, They fly into a rage, even resulting in murder. A life of regret follows.

As the writer of Proverbs has said, "He that is slow to anger is better than the mighty; and he that ruleth his spirit than he that taketh a city" (Prov, 16:32).

If you have a temper, now is the time to learn to control it. The more you do so while you are young, the more easily it will happen. Let no member of this Church ever lose control of himself in such an unnecessary and vicious manner. Let him bring to his marriage words of peace and composure.

I constantly deal with those cases of members of the Church who have been married in the temple and who later divorce and then apply for a cancellation of their temple sealing. When first married, they are full of great expectations, with a wonderful spirit of happiness. But the flower of love fades in an atmosphere of criticism and carping, of mean words and uncontrolled anger. Love flies out the window as contention enters. I repeat, my brethren, if any of you young men have trouble controlling your temper, I plead with you to begin the work of making that correction now. Otherwise you will bring only tears and sorrow into the homes which you will someday establish. Jacob, in the Book of Mormon, condemns his people for their wickedness in marriage. Says he. "Behold, ye have done greater iniquities than the Lamanites, our brethren. Ye have broken the hearts of your tender wives, and lost the confidence of your children, because of your bad examples before them; and the sobbings of their hearts ascend up to God against you. And because of the strictness of the word of God, which cometh down against you, many hearts died, pierced with deep wounds" (Jacob 2:35).

Work for an education. Got all the training that you can. The world will largely pay you what it thinks you are worth. Paul did not mince words when he wrote to Timothy, "But if any provide not for his own, and specially for those of his own house, he hath denied the faith, and is worse than an infidel" (I Tim. 5:8).

It is your primary obligation to provide for your family.

Your wife will be fortunate indeed if she does not have to go out and compete in the marketplace. She will be twice blessed if she is able to remain at home while you become the breadwinner of the family.

Education is the key to economic opportunity. The Lord has laid a mandate upon us as a people to acquire learning "by study, and also by faith." (D&C 109:14). It is likely that you will be a better provider if your mind and hands are trained to do something worthwhile in the society of which you will become a part.

Be modest in your wants. You do not need a big home with a big mortgage as you begin your lives together. You can and should avoid overwhelming debt. There is nothing that will cause greater tensions in marriage than grinding debt. which will make of you a slave to your creditors. You may have to borrow money to begin ownership of a home. But do not let it be so costly that it will preoccupy your thoughts day and night.

When I was married my wise father said to me, "Get a modest home and pay off the mortgage so that if economic storms should come, your wife and children will have a roof over their heads."

The girl who marries you will not wish to be married to a tightwad. Neither will she wish to be married to a spendthrift. She is entitled to know all about family finances. She will be your partner. Unless there is full and complete understanding between you and your wife on these matters, there likely will come misunderstandings and suspicions that will cause trouble that can lead to greater problems.

She will wish to be married to someone who loves her, who trusts her, who walks beside her, who is her very best friend and companion. She will wish to be married to someone who encourages her in her Church activity and in community activities which will help her to develop her talents and make a greater contribution to society. She will want to be married to someone who has a sense of service to others, who is disposed to contribute to the Church and to other good causes. She will wish to be married to someone who loves the Lord and seeks to do His will. It is well, therefore, that each of you young men plan to go on a mission, to give unselfishly to your Father in Heaven a tithe of your life to go forth with a spirit of total unselfishness to preach the gospel of peace to the world wherever you may he sent. If you are a good missionary, you will return home with the desire to continue to serve the Lord, to keep His commandments, and to do His will. Such behavior will add immeasurably to the happiness of your marriage.

As I have said, you will wish to be married in one place and one place only. That is the house of the Lord. You cannot give to your companion a greater gift than that of marriage in God's holy house under the protective wing of the sealing covenant of eternal marriage. There is no adequate substitute for it. There should be no other way for you.

Choose carefully and wisely. The girl you marry will be yours forever. You will love her and she will love you through thick and thin, through sunshine and storm. She will become the mother of your children. What greater thing in all this world can there be than to become the father of a precious child, a son or daughter of God, our Father in Heaven, for whom we are given the rights and responsibilities of mortal stewardship.

How precious a thing is a baby. How wonderful a thing is a child. What a marvelous thing is a family. Live worthy of becoming a father of whom your wife and children will be proud.

The Lord has ordained that we should marry, that we shall live together in love and peace and harmony, that we shall have children and rear them in His holy ways.

And so, my dear young men, you may not think seriously about it now. But the time will come when you will fall in love. It will occupy all of your thoughts and be the stuff of which your dreams are made. Make yourself worthy of the loveliest girl in all the world. Keep yourself worthy through all the days of your life. Be good and true and kind one to another. There is so much of bitterness in the world. There is so much of pain and sorrow that come of angry words. There is so much of tears that follow disloyalty. But there can be so much of happiness if there is an effort to please and an overwhelming desire to make comfortable and happy one's companion.

When all is said and done, this is what the gospel is about. The family is a creation of God. It is the basic creation. The way to strengthen the nation is to strengthen the homes of the people.

I am satisfied that if we would look for the virtues in one another and not the vices, there would be much more of happiness in the homes of our people. There would be far less of divorce, much less of infidelity, much less of anger and rancor and quarreling. There would be more of forgiveness, more of love, more of peace, more of happiness. This is as the Lord would have it.

Young men, now is the time to prepare for the future. And in that future for most of you is a beautiful young woman whose greatest desire is to bond with you in a relationship that is eternal and everlasting.

You will know no greater happiness than that found in your home. You will have no more serious obligation than that which you face in your home. The truest mark of your success in life will be the quality of your marriage.

God bless you, my dear young men. I could wish for you nothing more wonderful than the love, the absolute total love, of a companion of whom you are proud and worthy in every respect. This choice will be the most important of all the choices you make in your life. I pray that heaven may smile upon you in the choice you make, that you may be guided, that you may live without regret, in the name of Jesus Christ, amen.

To the Single Adult Brethren of the Church

President Ezra Taft Benson

Priesthood Session of General Conference on 2 April 1988

For some time I have wanted to speak directly to the great body of single adult brethren of the Church. Many of you have served full-time missions. Many of you are giving outstanding service in your wards and stakes.

To you single adult brethren, I want you to know of my great love for each of you. I have great expectations for you and a great hope in you. You have so much to contribute to the Lord and to the kingdom of God now and in the future. You may be twenty-seven years of age, or thirty, or possibly even older.

Examine Priorities

Just what are your priorities at this time in your life?

May I suggest for your careful consideration the counsel we give to returning missionaries. This counsel applies just as much to those who have been home for a while as to those who may not have served full-time missions for the Church.

Here are some of the priorities we pray that you single adult brethren will consider to be essential in your life.

First, continue to draw close to the Savior through private, sincere, heartfelt prayer. Remember always, "the effectual fervent prayer of a righteous man availeth much" (James 5:16).

"Feast upon the words of Christ" (2 Nephi 32:3) by consistently studying the scriptures every day and by following the counsel of the living prophets. Particularly make the study of the Book of Mormon a lifetime pursuit and daily sup from its pages.

Be an example in your Church activity—honor the Sabbath day, attend your meetings, observe the Word of Wisdom, pay your tithes and offerings, support your leaders, and otherwise keep the commandments. Serve cheerfully and gratefully in every calling you receive. Live worthy of a temple recommend and enjoy the sweet, sacred spirit that comes from frequent temple attendance.

Dress and groom yourself in a way that reflects your lifelong commitment to share the gospel with others.

Be thoughtful, loving, helpful, and appreciative of your family as you seek to deepen those eternal relationships.

In your dating and courting, fully maintain the standards of the Church. Be morally clean. "Let virtue garnish [your] thoughts unceasingly" (D&C 121:45).

Remember the counsel of Elder Bruce R. McConkie that "the most important single thing that any Latter-day Saint ever does in this world is to marry the *right* person in the *right* place by the *right* authority" (*Choose an Eternal Companion*, Brigham Young University Speeches of the Year, Provo, 3 May 1966, p. 2).

Understand that temple marriage is essential to your salvation and exaltation.

Carefully select practical and worthwhile goals and, in an organized way, work to reach them.

Apply yourself prayerfully and diligently to selecting and pursuing academic and vocational goals.

Share the gospel and your testimony with those who are not members of the Church or who are less active.

Improve your community by active participation and service. Remember in your civic responsibility that "the only thing necessary for the triumph of evil is for good men to do nothing" (Edmund Burke, in George Seldes, comp., *The Great Thoughts*, New York: Ballantine Books, 1985, p. 60). Do something meaningful in defense of your God-given freedom and liberty.

Remember that your entire life is a mission and that each new phase of it can be richly rewarding as you magnify your talents and take advantage of your opportunities.

The Importance of Celestial Marriage

May I now say an additional word about an eternal opportunity and responsibility to which I have referred earlier and which is of greatest importance to you. I am referring to celestial marriage.

Just a few weeks ago, I received a letter from two devoted parents, part of which reads as follows:

> Dear President Benson: We are concerned about what seems to be a growing problem—at least in this part of the Church familiar to us—that is, so many choice young men in the Church over the age of thirty who are still unmarried.
>
> We have sons thirty, thirty-one, and thirty-three in this situation. Many of our friends also are experiencing this same concern for unmarried sons and daughters.

Their letter continues:

> In our experience these are usually young men who have been on missions, are well educated, and are living the commandments (except this most important one). There does not appear to be a lack of choice young ladies in the same age bracket who could make suitable companions.
>
> It is most frustrating to us, as their parents, who sometimes feel we have failed in our parental teachings and guiding responsibilities.

My dear single adult brethren, *we* are also concerned. We want you to know that the position of the Church has never changed regarding the importance of celestial marriage. It is a commandment of God. The Lord's declaration in Genesis is still true: "And the Lord God said, It is not good that the man should be alone" (Genesis 2:18).

Do Not Risk Greatest Joys

To obtain a fulness of glory and exaltation in the celestial kingdom, one must enter into this holiest of ordinances.

Without marriage, the purposes of the Lord would be frustrated. Choice spirits would be withheld from the experience of mortality. And postponing marriage unduly often means limiting your posterity, and the time will come, brethren, when you will feel and know that loss.

I can assure you that the greatest responsibility and the greatest joys in life are centered in the family, honorable marriage, and rearing a righteous posterity. And the older you become, the less likely you are to marry, and then you may lose these eternal blessings altogether.

President Spencer W. Kimball recounted an experience he once had:

> Recently I met a young returned missionary who is 35 years old. He had been home from his mission for 14 years and yet he was little concerned about his bachelorhood, and laughed about it.

I shall feel sorry for this young man when the day comes that he faces the Great Judge at the throne and when the Lord asks this boy: "Where is your wife?" All of his excuses which he gave to his fellows on earth will seem very light and senseless when he answers the Judge. "I was very busy," or "I felt I should get my education first," or 'I did not find the right girl'—such answers will be hollow and of little avail. He knew he was commanded to find a wife and marry her and make her happy. He knew it was his duty to become the father of children and provide a rich, full life for them as they grew up. He knew all this, yet postponed his responsibility" ("The Marriage Decision," *Ensign*, Feb. 1975, p. 2).

Replace Fears with Faith

I realize that some of you brethren may have genuine fears regarding the real responsibilities that will be yours if you do marry. You are concerned about being able to support a wife and family and provide them with the necessities in these uncertain economic times. Those fears must be replaced with faith.

I assure you, brethren, that if you will be industrious, faithfully pay your tithes and offerings, and conscientiously keep the commandments, the Lord will sustain you. Yes, there will be sacrifices required, but you will grow from these and will be a better man for having met them.

Work hard educationally and in your vocation. Put your trust in the Lord, have faith, and it will work out. The Lord never gives a commandment without providing the means to accomplish it (see 1 Nephi 3:7).

Also, do not be caught up in materialism, one of the real plagues of our generation—that is, acquiring things, fast-paced living, and securing career success in the single state.

Honorable marriage is more important than wealth, position, and status. As husband and wife, you can achieve your life's goals together. As you sacrifice for each other and your children, the Lord will bless you, and your commitment to the Lord and your service in His kingdom will be enhanced.

Expectations of a Mate

Now, brethren, do not expect perfection in your choice of a mate. Do not be so particular that you overlook her most important qualities of having a strong testimony, living the principles of the gospel, loving home, wanting to be a mother in Zion, and supporting you in your priesthood responsibilities.

Of course, she should be attractive to you, but do not just date one girl after another for the sole pleasure of dating without seeking the Lord's confirmation in your choice of your eternal companion.

And one good yardstick as to whether a person might be the right one for you is this: in her presence, do you think your noblest thoughts, do you aspire to your finest deeds, do you wish you were better than you are?

God bless you single adult brethren of the Church. May your priorities be right. I have suggested some very important priorities this evening. May you seriously consider and ponder them.

Know, my good brethren, that I have spoken from my heart and by His Spirit because of my love and concern for you. It is what the Lord would have you hear today. With all my heart I echo the words of the prophet Lehi from the Book of Mormon, "Arise from the dust, my sons, and be men" (2 Nephi 1:21), in the name of Jesus Christ, amen.

To the Single Adult Sisters of the Church

President Ezra Taft Benson

Women's Meeting, 24 September, 1988

Single adult sisters throughout the Church, I want you to know of my deep love and appreciation for you—for your goodness, for your faithfulness, for your desire to serve the Lord with all your heart "that Christ's true light through [you] will shine, . . . his name to glorify."

We See Your Example and Service

We see so many of you living Christlike lives worthy of emulation and giving such dedicated service in the Church.

We see you leading the music in Primary and, because of your love and care, children's eyes lighting up as they sing the sweet songs of Zion.

We see you teaching by the Spirit classes in Relief Society, Young Women, Primary, and Sunday School with such excellent preparation and bearing testimony of gospel truths and touching others' lives.

We see many of you effectively working with our teenage girls, taking them to camp, directing roadshows, going to their dances, and being a great example and a real friend to them.

We see you serving full-time missions for the Lord with devotion and dedication and returning from the mission field with an even greater capacity to serve.

We see you in singles wards and resident wards reaching out to the less active, to the shy, to the troubled, reaching out to the widow, the shut-in, and the lonely and inviting all of them to come unto Christ.

We see wise bishops and stake presidents calling you single adult sisters to leadership responsibilities in wards and stakes.

We see you in the presidencies of Relief Society, Young Women, and Primary organizations, where your talents and abilities are being fully utilized.

We see you as a vital part of the mainstream body of the Church. We pray that the emphasis we naturally place on families will not make you feel less needed or less valuable to the Lord or to His Church. The sacred bonds of Church membership go far beyond marital status, age, or present circumstance. Your individual worth as a daughter of God transcends all.

Now, we also know you have special challenges and special needs. Be assured that we are aware of these.

Keep the Goal of Celestial Marriage

I would like to express the hope we all have for you, which is so real, that you will be exalted in the highest degree of glory in the celestial kingdom and that you will enter into the new and everlasting covenant of marriage.

Dear sisters, never lose sight of this sacred goal. Prayerfully prepare for it and live for it. Be married in the Lord's way. Temple marriage is a gospel ordinance of exaltation. Our Father in Heaven wants each of His daughters to have this eternal blessing.

Therefore, don't trifle away your happiness by involvement with someone who cannot take you worthily to the temple. Make a decision now that this is the place where you will marry. To leave that decision until a romantic involvement develops is to take a risk the importance of which you cannot now fully calculate.

And remember, you are not required to lower you standards in order to get a mate. Keep yourselves attractive, maintain high standards, maintain your self-respect. Do not engage in intimacies that bring heartache and sorrow. Place yourselves in a position to meet worthy men and be engaged in constructive activities.

But also, do not expect perfection in your choice of a mate. Do not be so concerned about his physical appearance and his bank account that you overlook his more important qualities. Of course, he should be attractive to you, and he should be able to financially provide for you. But, does he have a strong testimony? Does he live the principles of the gospel and magnify his priesthood? Is he active in his ward and stake? Does he love home and family, and will he be a faithful husband and a good father? These are qualities that really matter.

And I would also caution you single sisters not to become so independent and self-reliant that you decide marriage isn't worth it and you can do just as well on your own. Some of our sisters indicate that they do not want to consider marriage until after they have completed their degrees or pursued a career. This is not right. Certainly we want our single sisters to maximize their individual potential, to be well educated, and to do well at their present employment. You have much to contribute to society, to your community, and to your neighborhood. But we earnestly pray that our single sisters will desire honorable marriage in the temple to a worthy man and rear a righteous family, even though this may mean the sacrificing of degrees and careers. Our priorities are right when we realize there is no higher calling than to be an honorable wife and mother.

The Lord Knows and Loves You

I also recognize that not all women in the Church will have an opportunity for marriage and motherhood in mortality. But if those of you in this situation are worthy and endure faithfully, you can be assured of all blessings from a kind and loving Heavenly Father—and I emphasize all blessings.

I assure you that if you have to wait even until the next life to be blessed with a choice companion, God will surely compensate you. Time is numbered only to man. God has your eternal perspective in mind.

I also recognize that some of our sisters are widowed or divorced. My heart is drawn to you who are in these circumstances. The Brethren pray for you, and we feel a great obligation to see that your needs are met. Trust in the Lord. Be assured He lovedsyou and we love you.

If you are a single parent, make friends with others in similar situations and develop friendships with married couples. Counsel with your priesthood leaders. Let them know of your needs and wants. Single parenthood is understood by the Lord. He knows the special challenges that are yours. You are His daughters. He loves you and will bless and sustain you. This I know.

Learn, Progress, Serve

Now, to all the single adult sisters, regardless of your present situation:

Be faithful. Keep the commandments. Establish a deep and abiding relationship with the Lord Jesus Christ. Know that He is there—always there. Reach out to Him. He does answer prayers. He does bring peace. He does give hope. In the words of the

Psalmist: "He is my refuge and my fortress: . . . in him will I trust" (Ps. 91:2). Study carefully the life of the Savior. He is our great exemplar.

Make the scriptures your constant companion. Read daily from the Book of Mormon and receive of its strength and spiritual power.

Realize your personal self-worth. Never demean yourself. Realize the strength of your inner self and that, with God's help, you "can do all things through Christ which strengtheneth [you]" (Philip. 4:1). Life does not begin only upon marriage. There are important things for you to do right now.

Sister Eliza R. Snow declared: "There is no sister so isolated and her sphere so narrow but what she can do a great deal towards establishing the kingdom of God upon the earth." ("An Address," *Women's Exponent,* 15 Sept. 1873, p. 62.)

Become fully involved in the Church. Attend all your meetings and your single adult activities.

Reach out to others. Rather than turning inward, forget self and really serve others in your Church callings, in personal deeds of compassionate service, in unknown, unheralded personal acts of kindness.

If you really want to receive joy and happiness, then serve others with all your heart. Lift their burden, and your own burden will be lighter. Truly in the words of Jesus of Nazareth: "He that findeth his life shall lose it: and he that loseth his life for my sake, shall find it" (Matt. 10:39).

And always be improving yourself. Set personal achievement goals and stretch to accomplish them. Improve yourself physically, socially, mentally, and spiritually. Incorporate the splendid Pursuit of Excellence program into your life. Keep growing and learning and progressing and serving others.

Be Thankful for Blessings

And finally, my dear sisters be thankful to the Lord for your blessings. Think more about what you do have than what you don't have. Dwell upon the goodness of the Lord to you. Remember His words to the Prophet Joseph: "He who receiveth all things with thankfulness shall be made glorious; and the things of this earth shall be added unto him even an hundred fold, yea, more" (D&C 78:19). My humble desire for the wonderful single adult sisters of the Church is that you will receive all that the Father hath, "even an hundred fold, yea, more."

And I promise you that indeed you will. All of the blessings of our Father in Heaven will be yours if you continue faithful, if you are true, and if you serve Him and His children with all your heart, might, mind, and strength.

You are choice daughters of our Father in Heaven. You are jewels in His crown. Your virtue and purity make your price above rubies.

In the words of President David O. McKay, "A beautiful, modest gracious woman is creation's masterpiece. When to these virtues a woman possesses as guiding stars in her life righteousness and godliness and an irresistible impulse and desire to make others happy, no one will question if she be classed among those who are truly great" (*Gospel Ideals*, Salt Lake City: The Improvement Era, 1953, p. 449.)

God bless and sustain you always. I leave my blessings upon you wonderful sisters with love in my heart for you, and do so in the name of Jesus Christ, amen.

Revelation

Elder Dallin H. Oaks

BYU Devotional, 29 September 1981

I am going to speak this morning about revelation. Revelation is communication from God to man. It can occur in many different ways. Some prophets, like Moses and Joseph Smith, have talked with God face to face. Some persons have had personal communication with angels. Other revelations have come, as Elder James E. Talmage described it, "through the dreams of sleep or in the waking visions of the mind" *(Articles of Faith,* p. 229). In its more familiar forms, revelation or inspiration comes by means of words or thoughts communicated to the mind (D&C 8:23; Enos 1:10), by sudden enlightenment (D&C 6:14-15), by positive or negative feelings about proposed courses of action, or even by inspiring performances, as in the performing arts, the beautiful music we heard at the beginning of this devotional assembly being a notable example. As Elder Boyd K. Packer has stated, "Inspiration comes more as a feeling than as a sound" ("Prayers and Answers," *Ensign,* November 1979, p. 19).

Assuming you are familiar with these different forms of revelation or inspiration, I have chosen to discuss this subject in terms of a different classification—the purpose of the communication. I can identify eight different purposes served by communication from God: (1) to testify; (2) to prophesy; (3) to comfort; (4) to uplift; (5) to inform; (6) to restrain; (7) to confirm; and (8) to impel. I will describe each of these in that order, giving examples.

My purpose in suggesting this classification and in giving these examples is to persuade each of you to search your own experience and to conclude that you have already received revelations and that you can receive more revelations because communication from God to men and women is a reality. President Lorenzo Snow declared that it is "the grand privilege of every Latter-day Saint . . . to have the manifestations of the spirit every day of our lives" (*CR*, April 1899, p. 52). President Harold B. Lee taught:

> Every man has the privilege to exercise these gifts and these privileges in the conduct of his own affairs; in bringing up his children in the way they should go; in the management of his business, or whatever he does. It is his right to enjoy the spirit of revelation and of inspiration to do the right thing, to be wise and prudent, just and good, in everything that he does (*Stand Ye in Holy Places,* Salt Lake City: Deseret Book, 1974, pp. 141-42).

As I review the following eight purposes of revelation, I hope you will recognize the extent to which you have already received revelation or inspiration and resolve to cultivate this spiritual gift for more frequent use in the future.

Purposes of Revelation

1. The *testimony* or witness of the Holy Ghost that Jesus is the Christ and that the gospel is true is a revelation from God. When the apostle Peter affirmed that Jesus Christ was the Son of the living God, the Savior called him blessed, "for flesh and blood have not revealed it unto thee, but my Father which is in heaven"

(Matthew 16:17). This precious revelation can be part of the personal experience of every seeker after truth and, once received, becomes a pole star to guide in all the activities of life.

2. *Prophecy* is another purpose or function of revelation. Speaking under the influence of the Holy Ghost and within the limits of his or her stewardship, a person may be inspired to predict what will come to pass in the future. This is the office of the Prophet, Seer and Revelator, who prophesies for the Church, as Joseph Smith prophesied the Civil War (D&C 87) and foretold that the Saints would become a mighty people in the Rocky Mountains. Prophecy is part of the calling of a patriarch. Each of us is privileged to receive prophetic revelation illuminating future events in our lives, like a Church calling we are to receive. To cite another example, after our fifth child was born, my wife and I did not have any more children. After more than ten years, we concluded that our family would not be any larger, which grieved us. Then one day, while my wife was in the temple, the Spirit whispered to her that she would have another child. That prophetic revelation was fulfilled a year and a half later with the birth of our sixth child, for whom we had waited thirteen years.

3. A third purpose of revelation is to give *comfort.* Such a revelation came to the Prophet Joseph Smith in Liberty Jail. After many months in deplorable conditions, he cried out in agony and loneliness, pleading with the Lord to remember the persecuted Saints. The comforting answer came:

> My son, peace be unto thy soul; thine adversity and thine afflictions shall be but a
> small moment; And then, if thou endure it well, God shall exalt thee on high; thou
> shalt triumph over all thy foes (D&C 121:7-8).

In that same revelation the Lord declared that, no matter what tragedies or injustices should befall the Prophet, "Know thou, my son, that all these things shall give thee experience, and shall be for thy good" (D&C 122:7).

Each of us knows of other examples of revelations of comfort. Some have been comforted by visions of departed loved ones or by feeling their presence. The widow of a good friend told me how she had felt the presence of her departed husband, giving her assurance of his love and concern for her. Others have been comforted in adjusting to the loss of a job or a business advantage or even a marriage. A revelation of comfort can also come in connection with a blessing of the priesthood, either from the words spoken or from the feeling communicated in connection with the blessing.

Another type of comforting revelation is the assurance received that a sin has been forgiven. After praying fervently for an entire day and night, a Book of Mormon prophet recorded that he heard a voice, which said, "Thy sins are forgiven thee, and thou shalt be blessed."

"Wherefore," Enos wrote, "my guilt was swept away" (Enos 1:5-6; also see D&C 61:2). This assurance, which comes when a person has completed all the steps of repentance, gives assurance that the price has been paid, that God has heard the repentant sinner, and that his or her sins are forgiven. Alma described that moment as a time when he was no longer "harrowed up by the memory" of his sins.

> And oh, what joy, and what marvelous light I did behold; yea, my soul was filled
> with joy . . . there can be nothing so exquisite and sweet as was my joy (Alma, 36:19-21).

4. Closely related to the feeling of comfort is the fourth purpose or function of revelation, to *uplift.* At some time in our lives, each of us needs to be lifted up from a depression, from a sense of foreboding or inadequacy, or just from a plateau of spiritual mediocrity. Because it raises our spirits and helps us resist evil and seek good, I believe that the feeling of uplift that is communicated by reading the scriptures or by enjoying wholesome music, art, or literature is a distinct purpose of revelation.

5. The fifth purpose of revelation is to *inform.* This may consist of inspiration giving a person the words to speak on a particular occasion, such as in the blessings pronounced by a patriarch or in sermons or other words spoken under the influence of the Holy Ghost. The Lord commanded Joseph Smith and Sidney Rigdon to lift up their voices and speak the thoughts that he would put in their hearts,

> For it shall be given you in the very hour, yea, in the very moment, what ye shall say (D&C 100:5-6; see also 84:85; 124:97).

On some sacred occasions, information has been given by face-to-face conversations with heavenly personages, such as in the visions related in ancient and modem scriptures. In other circumstances, needed information is communicated by the quiet whisperings of the Spirit. A child loses a treasured possession, prays for help, and is inspired to find it; an adult has a problem at work, at home, or in genealogical research, prays, and is led to the information necessary to resolve it; a Church leader prays to know whom the Lord would have him call to fill a position, and the spirit whispers a name. In all of these examples—familiar to each of us—the Holy Ghost acts in his office as a teacher and revelator, communicating information and truths for the edification and guidance of the recipient.

Revelation from God serves all five of these purposes: testimony, prophecy, comfort, uplift, and information. I have spoken of them only briefly, giving examples principally from the scriptures. I will speak at greater length about the remaining three purposes of revelation, giving examples from my personal experience.

6. The sixth type or purpose of revelation is to *restrain* us from doing something. Thus, in the midst of a great sermon explaining the power of the Holy Ghost, Nephi suddenly declared, "And now I . . . cannot say more; the Spirit stoppeth mine utterance" (2 Nephi 32:7). The revelation that restrains is one of the most common forms of revelation. It often comes by surprise, when we have not asked for revelation or guidance on a particular subject. But if we are keeping the commandments of God and living in tune with his Spirit, a restraining force will steer us away from things we should not do.

One of my first experiences in being restrained by the Spirit came soon after I was called as a counselor in a stake presidency in Chicago. In one of our first presidency meetings, our stake president made a proposal that our new stake center be built in a particular location. I immediately saw four or five good reasons why that was the wrong location. When asked for my counsel, I opposed the proposal, giving each of those reasons. The stake president wisely proposed that each of us consider the matter prayerfully for another week and discuss it further in our next meeting. Almost perfunctorily I prayed about the subject and immediately received a strong impression that I was wrong, that I was standing in the way of the Lord's will, and that I should remove myself from opposition to it. Needless to say, I was restrained and promptly gave my approval to the proposed construction. Incidentally, the wisdom of constructing the stake center in that location was soon evident, even to me. My reasons to the contrary turned out to be shortsighted, and I was soon grateful to have been restrained from relying on them.

Several years ago I picked up the desk pen in my office at BYU to sign a paper that had been prepared for my signature, something I did at least a dozen times each day. That document committed the university to a particular course of action we had decided to follow. All the staff work had been done, and all appeared to be in order. But as I went to sign the document, I was filled with such negative thoughts and forebodings that I put it to one side and asked for the entire matter to be reviewed again. It was, and within a few days additional facts came to light which showed that the proposed course of action would have caused the university serious problems in the future.

On another occasion, the Spirit came to my assistance as I was editing a casebook on a legal subject. A casebook consists of several hundred court opinions, together with explanatory material and text written by the editor. My assistant and I had finished all of the work on the book, including the necessary research to assure that these court opinions had not been reversed or overruled. Just before sending it to the publisher, I was leafing through the manuscript, and a particular court opinion caught my attention. As I looked at it, I had a profoundly uneasy feeling. I asked my assistant to check that opinion again to see if everything was in order. He did and reported that it was. In a subsequent check of the completed manuscript, I was again stopped at that case, again with a great feeling of uneasiness. This time I went to the law library myself. There, in some newly received publications, I discovered that this case had just been reversed on appeal. If that opinion had been published in my casebook, it would have been a serious professional embarrassment. I was saved by the restraining power of revelation.

7. Seventh. A common way to seek revelation is to propose a particular course of action and then pray for inspiration to *confirm* it. The Lord explained the confirming type of revelation when Oliver Cowdery failed in his efforts to translate the Book of Mormon:

> Behold, you have not understood; you have supposed that I would give it unto you, when you took no thought save it was to ask me.
>
> But, behold, I say unto you, that you must study it out in your mind; then you must ask me if it be right, and if it is right I will cause that your bosom shall burn within you; therefore, you shall feel that it is right (D&C 9:7-8).

Similarly, the prophet Alma likens the word of God to a seed and tells persons studying the gospel that if they will give place for the seed to be planted in their hearts, the seed will enlarge their souls and enlighten their understanding and begin to be delicious to them (Alma 32). That feeling is the Holy Ghost's confirming revelation of the truth of the word.

When he spoke on the BYU campus some years ago on the subject "Agency or Inspiration," Elder Bruce R. McConkie stressed our responsibility to do all that we can before we seek a revelation. He gave a very personal example. When he set out to choose a companion for eternity, he did not go to the Lord and ask whom he ought to marry. "I went out and found the girl I wanted, " he said. "She suited me; . . . it just seemed . . . as though this ought to be. . . . [Then] all I did was pray to the Lord and ask for some guidance and direction in connection with the decision that I'd reached" *(Speeches of the Year,* 1972-73, Provo, Utah: Brigham Young University Press, 1973, p. 111).

Elder McConkie summarized his counsel on the balance between agency and inspiration in these sentences:

> We're expected to use the gifts and talents and abilities, the sense and judgment and agency with which we are endowed [p. 108]. . . . Implicit in asking in faith is the precedent requirement that we do everything in our power to accomplish the goal that we seek [P. 110]. . . . We're expected to do everything in our power that we can, and then to seek an answer from the Lord a confirming seal that we've reached the right conclusion [p. 113].

As a Regional Representative, I was privileged to work with four different members of the Council of the Twelve and with other General Authorities as they sought revelation in connection with the calling of stake presidents. All proceeded in the same manner. They interviewed persons residing in the stake—counselors in the stake presidency, members of the high council, bishops, and others who had gained special experience in Church administration—asking them questions and hearing their counsel. As these interviews were conducted, the servants of the Lord gave prayerful consideration to each person interviewed and mentioned. Finally, they reached a tentative decision on the new stake president. This proposal was then prayerfully submitted to the Lord. If it was confirmed, the call was issued. If it was not confirmed, or if they were restrained, that proposal was tabled, and the process continued until a new proposal was formed and confirming revelation was received.

Sometimes confirming and restraining revelations are combined. For example, during my service at BYU, I was invited to give a speech before a national association of attorneys. Because it would require many days to prepare, this was the kind of speaking invitation I had routinely declined. But as I began to dictate a letter declining this particular invitation, I felt restrained. I paused and reconsidered my action. I then considered how I might accept the invitation, and as I came to consider it in that light, I felt the confirming assurance of the Spirit and knew that this was what I must do. The speech that resulted, "A Private University Looks at Government Regulation," opened the door to a host of important opportunities. I was invited to repeat that same speech before several other nationally prominent groups. It was published in *Vital Speeches,* in a professional journal, and in several other periodicals and books, from which it was used as a leading statement of the private university's interest in freedom from government regulation. This speech led to BYU's being consulted by various church groups on the proper relationship between government and a church-related college. These consultations in turn contributed to the formation of a national organization of church-related colleges and universities that has provided a significant coalition to oppose unlawful or unwise government regulation. I have no doubt, as I look back on the event, that this speaking invitation I almost declined was one of those occasions when a seemingly insignificant act made a great deal of difference. Those are the times when it is vital for us to receive the guidance of the Lord, and those are the times when revelation will come to aid us if we hear and heed it.

8. The eighth purpose or type of revelation consists of those instances when the Spirit *impels* a person to action. This is not a case where a person proposes to take a particular action and the Spirit either restrains or confirms. This is a case where revelation comes when it is not being sought and impels some action not proposed. This type of revelation is obviously less common than other types but its rarity makes it all the more significant.

A scriptural example is recorded in the first book of Nephi. When Nephi was in Jerusalem to obtain the precious records from the treasury, the Spirit of the Lord directed him to kill Laban as he lay drunk in the street. This act was so far from Nephi's heart that he recoiled and wrestled with the Spirit, but he was again directed to slay Laban, and he finally followed that revelation (1 Nephi 4).

Students of Church history will recall Wilford Woodruff's account of an impression that came to him in the night telling him to move his carriage and mules away from a large tree. He did so, and his family and livestock were saved when the tree crashed to the ground in a tornado that struck 30 minutes later (see Matthias F. Cowley, *Wilford Woodruff: History of His Life and Labors,* Salt Lake City: Bookcraft, 1964, pp. 331-32).

As a young girl, my grandmother, Chasty Olsen Harris, had a similar experience. She was tending some children who were playing in a dry riverbed near their home in Castle Dale, Utah. Suddenly she heard a voice that called her by name and directed her to get the children out of the riverbed and up on the bank. It was a clear day, and there was no sign of rain. She saw no reason to heed the voice and continued to play. The voice spoke to her again, urgently. This time she heeded the warning. Quickly gathering the children, she made a run for the bank. Just as they reached it, an enormous wall of water, originating with a cloudburst in the mountains many miles away, swept down the canyon and roared across where the children had played. Except for this impelling revelation, she and the children would have been lost.

For nine years Professor Marvin Hill and I had worked on the book *Carthage Conspiracy,* which concerns the 1845 court trial of the murderers of Joseph Smith. We had several different sources of minutes on the trial, some bearing their authors's names and others unsigned. The fullest set of minutes was unsigned, but because we had located them in the Church Historian's Office, we were sure they were the minutes kept by George Watt, the Church's official scribe who was sent to record the proceedings of the trial. We so stated in seven drafts of our manuscript, and we analyzed all our sources on that assumption.

Finally, the book was completed, and within a few weeks the final manuscript would be sent to the publisher. As I sat in my office at BYU one Saturday afternoon, I felt impelled to go through a pile of unexamined books and pamphlets accumulated on the table behind my desk. At the very bottom of the pile of 50 or 60 publications, I found a printed catalog of the contents of the Wilford C. Wood Museum, which Professor LaMar Berrett, the author, had sent to me a year and a half earlier. As I quickly flipped through the pages of this catalog of Church history manuscripts, my eyes fell on a page describing the manuscript of the trial minutes we had attributed to George Watt. This catalog page told how Wilford Wood had purchased the original of that set of minutes in Illinois and had given the Church a typewritten version, the same version we had obtained from the Church Historian. We immediately visited the Wilford Wood Museum in Woods Cross, Utah, and obtained additional information which enabled us to determine that the minutes we had thought were the official Church source had been prepared by one of the lawyers for the defense. With this knowledge, we returned to the Church Historian's office and were able to locate for the first time George Watt's official and highly authentic set of minutes on the trial. This discovery saved us from a grievous error in the identification of one of our major sources and also permitted us to enrich the contents of our book significantly. The impression I received that day in my office was a cherished example of the way the Lord will help us in our righteous professional pursuits when we qualify for the impressions of his Spirit.

I had another choice experience with impelling revelation a few months after I began my service at BYU. As a new and inexperienced president, I had many problems to analyze and many decisions to reach. I was very dependent on the Lord. One day in October, I drove up Provo Canyon to ponder a particular problem. Although alone and without any interruption, I found myself unable to think of the problem at hand. Another pending issue I was not yet ready to consider kept thrusting itself into my mind: Should we modify BYU's academic calendar to complete the Fall Semester before Christmas? After ten or fifteen minutes of unsuccessful efforts to exclude thoughts of this subject, I finally realized what was happening. The issue of the calendar did not seem timely to me, and I was certainly not seeking any guidance on it, but the Spirit was vying to communicate with me on that subject. I immediately turned my full attention to that question and began to record my thoughts on a piece of paper. Within a few minutes, I had recorded the details of a three-semester calendar, with all of its powerful advantages. Hurrying back to the campus, I reviewed it with my colleagues and found them enthusiastic. A few days later the Board of Trustees approved our proposed new calendar, and we published its dates, barely in time to make them effective in the fall of 1972. Since that time, I have reread these words of the Prophet Joseph Smith and realized that I had the experience he described:

> A person may profit by noticing the first intimation of the spirit of revelation; for instance, when you feel pure intelligence flowing into you, it may give you sudden strokes of ideas . . . and thus by learning the Spirit of God and understanding it, you may grow into the principle of revelation (*Teachings*, p. 151).

Revelations Not Received

I have now described eight different purposes or types of revelation: (1) testifying, (2) prophesying, (3) comforting, (4) uplifting, (5) informing, (6) restraining, (7) confirming, and (8) impelling. Each of these refers to revelations that are received. Before concluding I will suggest a few ideas about revelations that are not received.

First, we should understand what can be called the principle of "stewardship in revelation." Our Heavenly Father's house is a house of order, where his servants are commanded to "act in the office in which [they are] appointed" (D&C 107:99). This principle applies to revelation. Only the president of the Church receives revelation to guide the entire Church. Only the stake president receives revelation for the special guidance of the stake. The person who receives revelation for the ward is the bishop. For a family, it is the priesthood leadership of the family. Leaders receive revelations for their own stewardships. Individuals can receive revelation to guide their own lives. But when one person purports to receive revelation for another person outside his or her own stewardship—such as a Church member who claims to have revelation to guide the entire Church or a person who claims to have a revelation to guide another person over whom he or she has no presiding authority according to the order of the Church—you can be sure that such revelations are not from the Lord. "These are counterfeit signals" (Boyd K. Packer, "Prayers and Answers," *Ensign*, November 1979, p. 20). Satan is a great deceiver, and he is the source of some of these spurious revelations. Others are simply imagined.

If a revelation is outside the limits of stewardship, you know it is not from the Lord, and you are not bound by it. I have heard of cases where a young man told a young woman she should marry him because he had received a revelation that she was to be his eternal companion. If this is a true revelation, it will be confirmed directly to the woman if she seeks to know. In the meantime, she is under no obligation to heed it. She should seek her own guidance and make up her own mind. The man can receive revelation to guide his own actions, but he cannot properly receive revelation to direct hers. She is outside his stewardship.

What about those times when we seek revelation and do not receive it? We do not always receive inspiration or revelation when we request it. Sometimes we are delayed in the receipt of revelation, and sometimes we are left to our own judgment. We cannot force spiritual things. It must be so. Our life's purpose to obtain experience and to develop faith would be frustrated if our Heavenly Father directed us in every act, even in every important act. We must make decisions and experience the consequences in order to develop self-reliance and faith.

Even in decisions we think very important, we sometimes receive no answers to our prayers. This does not mean that our prayers have not been heard. It only means that we have prayed about a decision which, for one reason or another, we should make without guidance by revelation. Perhaps we have asked for guidance in choosing between alternatives that are equally acceptable or equally unacceptable. I suggest that there is *not* a right and wrong to *every* question. To many questions, there are only two wrong answers or two right answers. Thus, a person who seeks guidance on which of two different ways he should pursue to get even with a person who has wronged him is not likely to receive a revelation. Neither is a person who seeks guidance on a choice he will never have to make because some future event will intervene, such as a third alternative that is clearly preferable. On one occasion, my wife and I prayed earnestly for guidance on a decision that seemed very important. No answer came. We were left to proceed on our own best judgment. We could not imagine why the Lord had not aided us with a confirming or restraining impression. But it was not long before we learned that we did not have to make a decision on that question because something else happened that made a decision unnecessary. The Lord would not guide us in a selection that made no difference.

No answer is likely to come to a person who seeks guidance in choosing between two alternatives that are equally acceptable to the Lord. Thus, there are times when we can serve productively in two different fields of labor. Either answer is right. Similarly, the Spirit of the Lord is not likely to give us revelations on matters that are trivial. I once heard a young woman in a testimony meeting praise the spirituality of her husband, indicating that he submitted every question to the Lord. She told how he accompanied her shopping and would not even choose between different brands of canned vegetables without making his selection a matter of prayer. That strikes me as improper. I believe the Lord expects us to use the intelligence and experience he has given us to make these kinds of choices. When a member asked the Prophet Joseph Smith for advice on a particular matter, the Prophet stated:

> It is a great thing to inquire at the hands of God, or to come into His presence:
> and we feel fearful to approach Him on subjects that are of little or no consequence
> (*Teachings,* p. 22).

Of course we are not always able to judge what is trivial. If a matter appears of little or no consequence, we can proceed on the basis of our own judgment. If the choice is important for reasons unknown to us, such as the speaking invitation I mentioned earlier or even a choice between two cans of vegetables when one contains a hidden poison, the Lord will intervene and give us guidance. When a choice will make a real difference in our lives—obvious or not—and when we are living in tune with the Spirit and seeking his guidance, we can be sure we will receive the guidance we need to attain our goal. The Lord will not leave us unassisted when a choice is important to our eternal welfare. I know that God lives and that revelation to his children is a reality. I pray that we will be worthy and willing, and that he will bless us to grow in this principle of revelation. I bear you my testimony of the truthfulness of the gospel, in the name of Jesus Christ. Amen.

Excerpts from "Circles of Exaltation"

President Spencer W. Kimball

1968, Talk to CES Teachers

We have had numerous surveys, small and large, and it seems that those who fill missions marry in the temple. Of course, there are exceptions to that rule, but it has been variously estimated by people who have made surveys that anywhere from 80 to 90 percent of all the young men and women who fill honorable missions and return in honor are eventually married in the temple. I believe that is conservative. We see exceptions to the rule constantly. There are those returned missionaries who go astray, who commit transgressions. There are the occasional ones who apostatize, but they are **so few** and **stand out like "sore thumbs,"** whereas the great masses who have filled honorable missions fit into the total picture and are not always noted. But if we could accept that even 90 percent of all the boys and girls who fill honorable missions are married in the temple, then we have something to work on as seminary teachers, haven't we?

We would be happy if we could get every boy and many young women to fill missions. (We send young women only when they are age 21 or more and have no immediate and proper prospect of a good Latter-day Saint marriage. We would not break up such a marriage, for the marriage is more important than the mission.) Whereas now we have maybe 30 to 40 percent of our young people marrying in the temple. If 90 percent of all those who fill missions marry in the temple, you can see that we would immediately multiply temple marriage by as much as 100 to 200 percent—and that, of course, furthers exaltation.

A mission is not just a casual thing—it is not an alternative program in the Church. **Neither is a mission a matter of choice any more than tithing is a choice, any more than sacrament meeting is a choice, any more than the Word of Wisdom is a choice**. Of course, we have our free agency, but the Lord has given us choices. We can do as we please. We can go on a mission or we can remain home. But every normal young man is as much obligated to go on a mission as he is to pay his tithing, attend his meetings, keep the Sabbath day holy, and keep his life spotless and clean. Can you accept that? If you can and if you give it great emphasis as you go back into the seminaries and institutes, you will have achieved much, because there are many **parents who think of a mission as some little satellite activity that would be nice to explore if it ever becomes convenient, but is not a necessity.**

In America, it is possible that practically every normal boy can go on a mission largely or totally with his own funds. Every Tuesday as we go over the applications for missions and read all the information about the applicant we check the funds that are available to them. When an application states that a young man has saved $3,000 for his mission, we all say, "Hallelujah! Wonderful!" When a boy has saved $1,000, that is wonderful, too. But when an application states that a boy will be totally supported by his ward or by his quorum or by a friend, then we think someone has failed—his parents first, of course, but also maybe a seminary teacher or an institute instructor has failed. They didn't make an impression. The boy was not planning for his mission all of his life as he should have been doing.

If every little boy is encouraged by his parents, bishop, home teachers, and others and is given little jobs to do with the understanding that part of every dollar which comes into his hands goes into his mission box, then we need not worry about his wondering whether to go on a mission or go to college. He will go to both. He will go one year to college and two years on a mission and then as many years as he wishes, to college afterward.

We are short on missionaries. The average stake that I visit has only between **25 percent to 40 percent of its eligible boys** on missions. That's all! Where are the other boys? Why do they not go on missions? I think there is **nothing basically wrong with the boys**, but I think that **we have not helped them catch the vision of this Church and its mission in the world**.

We must begin to think about our obligation rather than our convenience. The time, I think, has come when sacrifice must be an important element again in the Church. Remember the story of how Brigham Young and Heber C. Kimball went on their missions. Remember they were both ill. They were in poverty. Remember how Brigham Young fell down and could not get up, and Grandfather Heber C. Kimball went over and tried to lift him up but could not because he was so weak. So he called across the street to another brother and said, "Come on over here and help me get Brother Brigham up!" The next day both of them were on their missions. But we ofttimes must have everything ideal and perfect.

I tell you it is sad to realize that only a little over a third of all our boys and girls are marrying in the temple. What happens to the other two-thirds? Many of these marry out of the temple in civil ceremonies. A few of them occasionally convert their spouses—**maybe one out of six or seven**. We lose many! Thousands of members of the Church who could have been good members are in Los Angeles, Seattle, Denver, Houston, New York, and Philadelphia and now have no relationship whatsoever with the Church. Their **parents were members; their grandparents were stalwarts; their great-grandparents crossed the plains**. But they have been lost! Why? Because we overlooked many of these basic things. So the work is changing and we have a bigger world. The members of the Council of the Twelve probably travel more today in a single week than Peter and his associates traveled in their entire lives. Yet our responsibility is the same.

What a Mission Does for You

1. You learn that the *Church is TRUE!* As you begin a mission you begin a serious study of the scriptures, you teach others the plan of salvation which makes you appreciate the Restoration. As you come to understand the doctrines of men, you understand why there is so much skepticism and immorality in the world. The moorings are gone, the foundation cracked. The message we bear is sorely needed in the world.

2. You come to *love and appreciate our Heavenly Father* as your Father. He lives as does His Son Jesus Christ. The gospel now moves from the realm of theory to reality and practice. You learn that the Holy Ghost is very sensitive to righteous thoughts and behavior and you learn the joy of having Him as a constant companion.

3. The *scriptures* begin to make sense. Up until now, they seemed like a lot of words—but now take on meaning, and you are amazed that you understand them and love them! The Book of Mormon becomes a good friend. The Doctrine and Covenants contains powerful revelations from the Lord to Joseph Smith, and the Pearl of Great Price restores information lost from Genesis. You come to appreciate that the Bible is true—but that there are places where inspiration and a prophet's touch was needed to clarify understanding and omissions. You wish you could return to Seminary and this time you would listen and study harder.

4. You learn that *Satan i*s real, that he hates this Church and missionary work. He will do anything to get missionaries to fall and investigators to reject the truth.

5. *Companion relations* is one of the most important lessons of a mission. Getting along with another human being, a brother or sister, will prepare you for marriage, employment, and human relations. You will have a number of companions who will give you experience in dealing with a variety of personalities! You learn to share, to compromise, to give your opinion, and to provide leadership in a companionship.

6. You learn to *speak,* to *share your own ideas and thoughts,* to hear yourself think out loud and test your ideas to see what you really believe. You hear others explain and expound on basic doctrinal themes to solidify your own.

7. You learn to *get up* in the mornings, get going, and be productive.

8. You learn that *priestcraft* exists, that there are anti-Mormons and they are bitter in spirit. They have taken principles out of context and gone to great lengths to destroy this work.

9. You come to know that *Joseph Smith* is the Lord's Prophet of the latter days. Moroni was right—his name is had for good and evil in the world—but honest souls love what he restored.

10. *Service* is a great source of happiness. Giving of yourself to others reflects the spirit of the Master. Effective home teaching is desperately needed.

11. You will see the *humanness of mankind, missionaries, and members of the Church*, as well as yourself. The Church is made up of all kinds of personalities. There is room for everyone. You will now fervently pray that some personality types of which you have been critical in the past will accept the gospel.

12. You learn the *doctrines of the Church*, learn how to teach them simply and clearly to others. It is great preparation for Family Home Evening lessons (at least you know six discussions you could teach!)

13. You will learn *obedience* to common sense rules, the laws of the gospel, and that the Spirit is very sensitive to our obedience. Obedience truly is the first law of heaven.

14. You will *overcome selfishness*. The Book of Mormon teaches that anytime you have political freedom, leisure time, economic prosperity, and an abundance of material goods, there is danger in apathy and self-centeredness. You will learn that the Spirit of the Lord will not sustain contention, pride, gossip, arrogance, or unrighteousness.

15. For the first time in your life you will come to *know* that we have *Living Prophets*. General Conference will become important to you.

16. You will learn how to *manage your finances,* to cook, to keep a clean apartment. You will learn to write checks, balance a checkbook, and learn basic budgeting skills—in order to live on less than your income.

17. You learn *time management.* At the first of a mission time may pass slowly, but as skills and work ethic improve you will find time flies.

18. You will anticipate *receiving mail—"junk mail"—any kind!* Hearing from and corresponding with loved ones and friends while sharing your mission will build lasting relationships with others.

19. Your *family* will be more important than ever. You will gain a strong appreciation for your parents and a desire to see all of your family active in the Church.

20. You will learn to *work* and *work hard.* This training will be great for obtaining jobs, better grades in school and a lifetime of productivity.

21. You learn to *live away from home*—perhaps for the first time. You decide who you are, what you are on a mission for, and how to deal with your independence. The education you gain in the field is worth a college degree; it is the most important kind of learning you will need to be successful.

22. You learn the importance and need for *prayer*. Not just superficial "give me's", but a sincere outpouring of your heart to the only One who can help you at times. Pleading with Him in behalf of others is a great step forward in your own development of charity. There are many times when you will need to call on your Heavenly Father for help.

23. You will be trained to express your *feelings* for the gospel, investigators, for companions, which will help you learn to express to your spouse and children your love for them.

24. You *contribute* your talents in blessing others. You grow close to other missionaries in district and zone meetings and develop lifelong friendships. You will feel compassion for companions and others and desire to help others improve in their attributes and skills in human relations. Learning to love and bless people becomes a high priority. You see the heartbreak that comes from gossip and rumors.

25. You learn to *control thoughts*—to cast out of your mind ideas that are unworthy of you in your important calling. Carnal and base desires become offensive to you. You learn to hate sin, yet love the sinner.

26. You learn to *respect priesthood authority*. You watch others develop leadership skills, your own abilities blossom, and you are honored to serve with those who take positions of leadership in the mission.

27. You learn to *deal with discouragement*. Not everyone will join the church, and at times you will feel rejection (as did the Savior), and you will learn to rise above minor discouragement and to feel the Spirit of the Lord and the power of all church members who are pleading in prayer for your success.

28. Now we know why the Lord called *every young man* and many sisters to serve missions—and until you serve, you do not understand what He meant. You have to be there to learn the lessons. (Perhaps it was like that in the pre-mortal life. They tried to tell us what mortality was about, but you *have to be here* to experience it!) Life means so much more than it ever did before. Thank God for missions!

The Church Activity of Returned Missionaries of The Church of Jesus Christ of Latter-day Saints

Sent out from the office of the First Presidency (President Kimball) to all bishops and stake presidents.

A study was conducted among a statistically valid sample of returned missionaries who have been home for one, three, five and ten years. The study was conducted to determine to what extent returned missionaries are active (or inactive) in the Church. A secondary purpose was to identify major problems encountered upon returning home from the mission field and suggestions for dealing with those problems.

Major Findings

Temple Marriage: Of those missionaries who were married at the time of the survey, ninety-five percent had been married in the temple or subsequently sealed. Twenty-eight percent had not married and one percent were divorced and single.

Church Positions: Eighty-nine percent of the returned missionaries held a current Church position (including home teaching and visiting teaching) at the time of the survey.

Meeting Attendance: Ninety-seven percent of the returned missionaries reported that they are currently attending at least one sacrament meeting per month, and ninety-one percent are attending three or more times per month. Attendance at priesthood meeting and Sunday School was comparable.

Other Measures: Eighty-five percent of the respondents had a current temple recommend. Ninety-two percent claimed to be full tithe payers. Ninety-seven percent said they observe the Word of Wisdom. Eighty-nine percent reported that they pray at least a few times a week and seventy-five percent reported that they study the scriptures weekly or more frequently.

Problems/Adjustments: The major concerns of returning missionaries, according to the respondents, are (in order): (1) problems associated with dating, courtship, and marriage; (2) loss of routine and structure after the mission; (3) adjusting to family and friends; (4) homesickness for the mission field; (5) lack of a Church assignment; and (6) financial-employment problems.

Causes of Inactivity: The primary reasons why returned missionaries go inactive, in the opinion of the respondents, are (in order): (1) lack of a Church calling; (2) feeling that they have done their part and may take a "spiritual vacation"; (3) weak testimony or commitment; (4) depression, loneliness, feeling unimportant (5) worldly pressures; and (6) a critical attitude toward Church leaders and members.

Helping RM's: Suggestions from the respondents for helping returned missionaries adjust to post-mission life and remain active in the Church include (in order): (1) provide a meaningful Church assignment; (2) bishops and priesthood leaders conduct periodic follow-up interviews;

(3) have special seminars or classes to deal with adjustment problems; (4) set realistic, meaning-ful goals; and (5) continue with gospel study and meaningful prayer.

In summary, it appears that the great majority of returned missionaries are active in terms of attendance at Church meetings, possession of temple recommends, Church callings, observance of the Word of Wisdom, and payment of tithes. They also engage in prayer and scripture study, though in many cases the frequency of these activities **may be insufficient to maintain a high degree of spirituality.**

The findings from this study do not suggest that returned missionaries are falling away from the Church in great numbers. However, the loss of even a small percentage of the returned missionary force of the Church is a significant loss. And those who are "active" still need to be strengthened. Consequently, the welfare of returned missionaries should continue to be a matter of great concern to the Church.

Sisters Going on Missions/Returned Missionaries

Now I wish to say something to bishops and stake presidents concerning missionary service. It is a sensitive matter. There seems to be growing in the Church an idea that all young women as well as all young men should go on missions. We need some young women. They perform a remarkable work. They can get in homes where the elders cannot.

I confess that I have two granddaughters on missions. They are bright and beautiful young women. They are working hard and accomplishing much good. Speaking with their bishops and their parents, they made their own decisions to go. They did not tell me until they turned in their papers. I had nothing to do with their decision to go.

Now, having made that confession, I wish to say that the First Presidency and the Council of the Twelve are united in saying to our young sisters that they are not under obligation to go on missions. I hope I can say what I have to say in a way that will not be offensive to anyone. Young women should not feel that they have a duty comparable to that of young men. Some of them will very much wish to go. If so, they should counsel with their bishop as well as their parents. If the idea persists, the bishop will know what to do.

I say what had been said before, that missionary work is essentially a priesthood responsibility. As such, our young men must carry the major burden. This is their responsibility and their obligation.

We do not ask the young women to consider a mission as an essential part of their life's program. Over a period of many years, we have held the age level higher for them in an effort to keep the number going relatively small. Again to the Sisters I say that you will be as highly respected, you will be considered as being as much in the line of duty, your efforts will be as acceptable to the Lord and to the Church whether you go on a mission or do not go on a mission.

We constantly receive letters from young women asking why the age for sister missionaries is the same as it is for elders. We simply give them the reasons. We know that they are disappointed. We know that many have set their hearts on missions. We know that many of them wish this experience before they marry and go forward with their adult lives. I certainly do not wish to say or imply that their services are not wanted. I simply say that a mission is not necessary as a part of their lives (President Gordon B. Hinckley, *Conference Report,* October 1997:72-73).

Counseling Returning Missionaries Concerning Marriage

1. It is entirely appropriate and desirable that priesthood leaders counsel returning missionaries on the importance of continuing to live standards that will lead to celestial marriage. It is considered unwise, however, to recommend or imply that the missionary should be married within a specified time period following his release. Although the returned missionary should keep himself worthy and pointed toward marriage, the decision to marry is of such importance that it should be approached only after the most prayerful and careful consideration. During the post-mission period of social, emotional, and physical readjustment, and the

differing individual demands of employment and education, the returned missionary should not feel pressured by specific time constraints in approaching this very personal, sacred, and significant decision.

2. According to custom, men are expected to take the initiative in seeking marriage. That is why President Joseph F. Smith directed his prophetic pressure at men. He said, "No man who is marriageable is fully living his religion who remains unmarried," (Gospel Doctrine, Salt Lake City: Deseret Book Co., 1939, p. 275). We hear of some worthy LDS men in their thirties who are busy accumulating property and enjoying freedom from family responsibilities without any sense of urgency about marriage. Beware, brethren. You are deficient in a sacred duty.

Knowledge of the great plan of happiness also gives Latter-day Saints a distinctive attitude toward the bearing and nurturing of children (Dallin H. Oaks, "The Great Plan of Happiness," *Ensign,* November 1993, p. 75).

3. There is increasing evidence that some young women are being strongly encouraged to serve full-time missions. Though capable and effective, young women do not have the same responsibility to serve full-time missions as do young men who hold the priesthood. We are grateful that some desire to serve as full-time missionaries, but they should not be made to feel obligated to do so. A young woman should not be recommended for a mission if it would interfere with a specific marriage proposal (*Bulletin,* 1993, Vol. 2, p. 2).

Agency or Inspiration?

Elder Bruce R. McConkie

The New Era, January 1975

My wife and I were having a serious discussion recently in which we were counting our many blessings. We named a host of things that have come to us, because of the Church, because of our family, because of the glorious restoration of eternal truth that has taken place in this day; and then she climaxed the discussion by asking this question: "What's the greatest blessing that has ever come into your life?"

Without a moment's hesitation I said, "The greatest blessing that has ever come to me was on the thirteenth day of October in 1937 at 11:20 A.M. when I was privileged to kneel in the Salt Lake Temple at the Lord's altar and receive you as an eternal companion."

She said, "Well, you passed that test."

I believe that the most important single thing that any Latter-day Saint ever does in this world is to marry the right person, in the right place, by the right authority; and that then—when they have been so sealed by the power and authority that Elijah the prophet restored—the most important remaining thing that any Latter-day Saint can ever do is so to live that the terms and conditions of the covenant thus made will be binding and efficacious now and forever. And so I'd like, if properly guided, to make some suggestions that apply in all fields of choice—in all fields, at least all major fields, of activity—but that apply particularly to the matter of eternal marriage, singling that out as the one thing paramount above all others.

When we dwelt in the presence of God our Heavenly Father, we were endowed with agency. This gave us the opportunity, the privilege, to choose what we should do, to make a free, untrammeled choice. When father Adam was placed in the Garden of Eden he was given this same power, and we now possess it. We're expected to use the gifts and talents and abilities, the sense and judgement and agency with which we are endowed.

But on the other hand we're commanded to seek the Lord, to desire his Spirit, to get the spirit of revelation and inspiration in our lives. We come into the Church and a legal administrator places his hands upon our head and says, "Receive the Holy Ghost." This gives us the gift of the Holy Ghost, which is the right to the constant companionship of that member of the Godhead, based on faithfulness.

And so we're faced with two propositions. One is that we ought to be guided by the spirit of inspiration, the spirit of revelation. The other is that we're here under a direction to use our agency, to determine what we ought to do on our own; and we need to strike a fine balance between these two, if we're going to pursue a course that will give us joy, satisfaction, and peace in this life and lead to eternal reward in our Father's kingdom.

When we were with our Father in the preexistent sphere, he observed and studied us and he knew how we should respond to his laws when we were in his presence, when we had the knowledge that he was our Father and that the teaching presented to us came from him. We walked by sight. Now he's finding out how we'll respond when we walk by faith, when we're outside his presence and we have to rely on things other than the personal counsel that we once received from him.

I'd like to present three case studies, out of which, perhaps, we can draw some very realistic and sound conclusion as to what ought to be in our lives. I'll take these illustrations out of the revelations that the Lord has given us.

Case Study #1: "You have not understood" — You have to work hard — *w/ all your might, mind, & strength.*

Case study number one: There was a man named Oliver Cowdery. In the early days he operated as an amanuensis to the Prophet. He was the scribe. He wrote down the words that the Prophet dictated while the Spirit rested upon him in the translation processes (the Book of Mormon was then being translated). Brother Cowdery was relatively spiritually immature at that time, and he sought and desired to do something beyond his then present spiritual capacity. He wanted to translate. And so he importuned the Prophet, the Prophet took the matter up with the Lord, and they got a revelation. The Lord said, "Oliver Cowdery, verily, verily, I say into you, that assuredly as the Lord liveth, who is your God and Redeemer, even so surely shall you receive a knowledge of whatsoever things you shall ask in faith, with an honest heart, believing that you shall receive. . . ." And then one thing he might receive is defined as, " a knowledge concerning the engravings of old records, which are ancient, which contain those parts of my scripture of which has been spoken by the manifestation of my Spirit."

Having thus dealt with the specific problem, then the Lord revealed a principle that applies to it and all other like situations: "Yea, behold, I will tell you in your mind and in your heart, by the Holy Ghost, which shall come upon you and which shall dwell in your heart. Now, behold, this is the spirit of revelation" (D&C 8:1-3).

Oliver did what a good many of us would have done. He had the instructions I have read, and he assumed that they meant what they seemed on the surface to say, which was that if in faith he asked God, he'd have power to translate. But in his condition of relative spiritual immaturity, he hadn't yet learned what was involved in asking of God, or how to generate the kind of faith or do the specific thing that has to be done in order to get an answer to a prayer. And so he asked. And as you know, he failed; he was totally unable to translate. This caused some concern, I suppose, to him and the Prophet. The matter was referred back to the Lord, whose promise they had been attempting to conform to; and the answer came, the reason came, why he couldn't translate: "Behold, you have not understood; you have supposed that I would give it unto you, when you took no thought save it was to ask me" (D&C 9:7).

Now, seemingly, that's all he'd been instructed to do, to ask in faith; but implicit in asking in faith is the precedent requirement that we do everything in our power to accomplish the goal that we seek. We use every faculty and capacity and ability that we possess to bring about the eventuality that may be involved. This is translating the Book of Mormon, it's choosing a wife, it's choosing employment, it's doing any one of ten thousand important things that arise in our lives.

The Lord continued:

> I say unto you, that you must study it out in your mind; then you must ask me if it
> be right, and if it is right, I will cause that your bosom shall burn within you; therefore,
> you shall feel that it is right. But if it be not right you shall have no such feelings, but
> you shall have a stupor of thought that shall cause you to forget the thing which is
> wrong; therefore, you cannot write that which is sacred save it be given you from me
> (D&C 9:8-9).

How do you choose a wife? I've heard a lot of young people from Brigham Young University and elsewhere say, "I've got to get a feeling of inspiration. I've got to get some revelation. I've got to fast and pray and get the Lord to manifest to me whom I should marry." Well, maybe it will be a little shock to you, but never in my life did I ask the Lord whom I ought to marry. It never occurred to me to ask him. I went out and found the girl I wanted; she suited me; I evaluated and weighed the proposition, and it just seemed a hundred percent to me as though this ought to be. Now, if I'd done things perfectly, I'd have done some counseling with the Lord, which I didn't do; but all I did was pray to the Lord and ask for some guidance and direction in connection with the decision that I'd reached. A more perfect thing to have done would have been to counsel with him relative to the decision and get a spiritual confirmation that the conclusion, which I by my agency and faculties had arrived at, was the right one.

Case Study #2: "Why are you asking me?"

Do all that you can – and the Lord will pick up the slack; but mind you, ~~you~~ you must DO.

Now, case study number two: There was a man whose name is not preserved to us in the ancient record. He's known as the brother of Jared. From other sources, we know his name was Moriancumer. He was the spiritual leader, initially, of the Jaredite people. As they started their progress from the tower of Babel to their American promised land, he was the one who communed with the Lord to get the direction, the spiritual guidance that they as a people needed.

And some very interesting things occurred. They got to the waters that they were going to cross, and the Lord said to him, "Build some barges." But interestingly, the Lord didn't tell him how to build the barges. The brother of Jared had done it on a previous occasion; he didn't need instruction; he didn't need revelation to guide him. So he built the barges.

But this time they were going to be used under some peculiar and difficult circumstances, and he needed something more than was now present in them: he needed some air. And this was a problem that was beyond him. So he took that matter up with the Lord, and because it was totally beyond his capacity to solve, the Lord solved it for him and said, "Do thus and so and you'll have air."

But then the brother of Jared—having confidence because he was talking to the Lord, because he was communing and getting answers—asked another question: he asked for a solution to a problem that he should have figured out by himself and not taken up with the Lord. He said, "What will we do for light in the vessels?"

And the Lord talked to him about it a little and then he said this: "What will ye that I should do that ye may have light in your vessel?" (Ether 2:23) In effect, "What are you asking me for? This is something you should have solved." And he talked a little more, and he repeated in essence the question: "What will ye that I should prepare for you that ye may have light when ye are swallowed up in the depths of the sea?" (Ether 2:25) In other words, "Moriancumer, this is your problem. Why are you troubling me? I've given you agency; you are endowed with capacity and ability. Get out and solve the problem."

Well, the brother of Jared got the message. He went up into a mount called Shelem, and the record says he "did molten out of a rock sixteen small stones; and they were white and clear, even as transparent glass" (Ether 3:1).

Well, the brother of Jared took sixteen little crystals of some sort (he could hold all of them in his hands) up on the mount. The record says, "He did carry them in his hands upon the top of the mount" (Ether 3:1), and then he said in effect to the Lord, "Now this is what I hope you will do." You really don't tell the Lord what to do, but you get some inspiration, and then you talk the matter over with him. And so Moriancumer said to the Lord, "Touch these stones, O Lord, with thy finger, and prepare them that they may shine forth in darkness; and they shall shine forth unto us in the vessels which we have prepared, that we may have light while we shall cross the sea" (Ether 3:4).

And the Lord did what the brother of Jared asked, and this is the occasion when he then saw the finger of the Lord; and, while he was in tune, he received revelation that exceeded anything that any prophet had ever gained up to that moment. The Lord revealed more to him about his nature and personality than ever heretofore had come forth, and it all came about because he'd done everything that he could do and because he'd counseled with the Lord.

There's a fine balance between agency and inspiration. We're excited to do everything in our power and then to seek an answer from the Lord, a confirming seal that we've reached the right conclusion; and sometimes, happily, in addition, we get added truths and knowledge that we hadn't even supposed.

Case Study #3: "They shall counsel between themselves and me"

Now, case study number three. In the early history of the Church, the Lord commanded the Saints to assemble in a certain place in Missouri. The decree went forth: "Assemble." Specifically, the decree went forth, "Let the Presiding Bishop come here and do such and such." Now notice what happened. The Lord is talking:

> As I spake concerning my servant Edward Partridge, this land is the land of his residence, and those whom he has appointed for his counselors; and also the land of the residence of him whom I have appointed to keep my storehouse; Wherefore, let them bring their families to this land, [and here's the point] as they shall counsel between themselves and me (D&C 58:24-25).

You see, the Lord said "assemble" to Zion. The details and the arrangements, however, the *how* and the *when* and the *circumstances,* are to be determined by the agency of those who are called to assemble, but they are to counsel with the Lord. Now, when you counsel with the Lord, you talk something over. I bring my children in and we counsel on a problem. I don't tell them what ought to be; I say, "What do you think? What's your evaluation? What do you want to do in this situation? What's the best thing to do?" And they tell me what they think. and if I happen to have any wisdom or judgement on the matter, I express my views. The Lord has all wisdom, all knowledge, and all power; he knows how to govern and control and direct us in a perfect manner. He lets us determine what we should do, but he expects us to counsel with him.

Now, after the Lord had said this to the Presiding Bishopric of the Church, he gave the principle that governed in that situation, and it governs in all situations. And this is one of our glorious revealed truths. He said:

> For behold, it is not meet that I should command in all things; for he that is compelled in all things, the same is a slothful and not a wise servant; wherefore he receiveth no reward.
>
> Verily I say, men should be anxiously engaged in a good cause, and do many things of their own free will, and bring to pass much righteousness; For the power is in them, wherein they are agents unto themselves. And inasmuch as men do good they shall in nowise lose their reward.
>
> But he that doeth not anything until he is commanded, and receiveth a commandment with a doubtful heart, and keepeth it with slothfulness, the same is damned (D&C 58:26-29).

The Prophet Joseph Smith was asked, "How do you govern so great and diverse a people as the Latter-day Saints?"

He replied, "I teach them correct principles and they govern themselves."

Now, that's the order of heaven. That's how the Almighty operates. That's how the Church is supposed to operate. We're supposed to learn correct principles and then govern ourselves. We make our own choices, and then we present the matter to the Lord and get his approving, ratifying seal.

"Counsel with the Lord in all thy doings"

Those are the three case studies; let us come to the revealed conclusion. There was a man named Alma, a mighty and great prophet. He had a son named Helaman, who was a holy and righteous man, following the pattern that his father had set. And to Helaman, Alma said this: "O, remember, my son, and learn wisdom in thy youth; yea, learn in thy youth to keep the commandments of God. Yea, and cry unto God for all thy support" (Alma 37:35-36). Do you think, if you're counseled to pray to the Lord for support, both temporal and spiritual that that's all you have to do? The Lord's prayer says, "Give us this day our daily bread." Do you go out and sit down in the desert or on the mountain and pray with all the fervor you can possess, "Give us this day our daily bread," or do you go out and plant crops and raise herds and do everything that you can in your situation to accomplish the end result?

Continuing: "yea, let all thy doings be unto the Lord, and whithersoever thou goest let it be in the Lord; yea, let thy thoughts be directed unto the Lord; yea, let the affections of thy heart be placed upon the Lord forever" (Alma 37:36). Now note: "Counsel with the Lord in all thy doings, and he will direct thee for good" (Alma 37:37).

What was Oliver Cowdery's problem? "You took no thought save it was to ask . . . you must study it out in your mind" (D&C 9:7-8).

Well, do you want a wife? Do you want anything that's right and proper? You go to work, and you use the agency and power and ability that God has given you. You use every faculty, you get all the judgement that you can centered on the problem, you make up your own mind, and then, to be sure that you don't err, you counsel with the Lord. You talk it over. You say, "This is what I think; what do you think?" And if you get the calm, sweet surety that comes only from the Holy Spirit, you know you've reached the right conclusion; but if there's anxiety and uncertainty in your heart, then you'd better start over, because the Lord's hand is not in it, and you're not getting the ratifying seal that, as a member of the Church who has the gift of the Holy Ghost, you are entitled to receive.

". . . yea, when thou liest down at night lie down unto the Lord, that he may watch over you in your sleep, and when thou risest in the morning let thy heart be full of thanks unto God; and if ye do these things, ye shall be lifted up at the last day." (Alma 37:37). If you learn how to use the agency that God has given you, and if you try to make your own decisions, and if you reach conclusions that are sound and right, and if you counsel with the Lord and get his ratifying seal of approval upon the conclusions you've reached, then you've received revelation, for one thing; and for another thing, you're going to have the great reward of eternal life and be lifted up at the last day. We're not all equal by any means; some have one talent and capacity and some another. But if we use the talents we have, somehow we'll come out all right.

One Monday when we were celebrating Washington's birthday, I was down at my mother's sawing a log in the backyard. She came out to give me some direction and see how I was doing it, and she wasn't very pleased. She thought I ought to do it differently. She went back into the house and in a few minutes my younger brother arrived. She said to him, "I think you'd better go out in the backyard and give Bruce some help and see that he does this thing right" And then she said to him, "Bruce isn't very bright." Well, so I'm not. So I start where I am, and I go forward from there. I start using such talent as I have, and I begin to apply the principles of eternal truth to my life. I consult and counsel with the Lord in the process, and no matter where I am, the gospel takes me forward and onward and upward, and blessings flow to me that will ennoble and sanctify and improve me in this life and eventually give me glory and honor and dignity in the life to come.

We have the spirit of revelation

I think we've said enough; the principles are before us. Let me just do one thing more. Let me do, in effect, what my friend Alma would do. After he'd preached a sermon, he said, "And this is not all. Do ye not suppose that I know of these things myself?" (Alma 5:45). That is he'd given them the case studies, he'd quoted the revelations, he'd told them what was involved, and then he bore personal testimony. This is what we ought to do in the Church. We ought to learn how to teach by the power of the Spirit, so that when we get through talking about the gospel subjects we'll know whether what we'd be said is right, and we'll be in a position to bear testimony, not alone of the truth and divinity of the work, but also that the doctrine we proclaim and the everlasting truths we expound are right, that they are the mind and voice and will of the Lord. The glorious, wondrous thing about this work and about these doctrines is that they are true. There isn't anything in this world, no truth that we can conceive of, to compare with the truth that the work we're engaged in is true, that the Lord's hand is here. It's a literal fact that we have the gift and power of the Holy Ghost.

We have the spirit of revelation, the spirit of testimony, the spirit of prophecy. These things must be, or we're not in the Church and kingdom of God; we're not the Lord's people.

The fact is that we do have them; revelation works. Don't shy away from getting revelation. Joseph Smith said, "God hath not revealed anything to Joseph, but what he will make known unto the Twelve, and even the least Saint may know all things as fast as he is able to bear them" (*Teachings of the Prophet Joseph Smith*, p. 149). We're entitled to the spirit of revelation, but what I'm attempting to teach is that there's a how and procedure, and there are conditions precedent. It is our obligation to go to work on our problems and then counsel with the Lord and get the ratifying seal of the Holy Spirit on the conclusions that we've reached; and that ratifying seal is the spirit of revelation.

God grant us wisdom in these things. God grant us the courage and the ability to stand on our own feet and use our agency and abilities and capacities we possess; then let's be sufficiently humble and amenable to the Spirit, bow our will to his will, to get his ratifying, confirming seal of approval, to get in our lives in that way the spirit of revelation. And if we so do, there's no question about the rest; it's peace in this life; it's glory and honor and dignity in the life to come.

A True and Sufficient Love

Twelve Questions to Ask When You Are Thinking about Engagement

Burton C. Kelly

Printed in the *Ensign*, February 1979, pp. 47-49

When I first met Mike and Elaine, I knew right away that they meant a lot to each other. As they spoke to me in my office, I could also tell that they were a serious, concerned couple challenged by one of life's most important decisions. There was a trace of anxiety in their voices. "Yes, we love each other," they said, "but is our love true and sufficient for eternal marriage?" Both had asked this question, discussed it at some length, and prayed about it. Mike said he was relatively certain that Elaine was the one for him, but Elaine wasn't as sure. How was she to know? Elaine was afraid of making a mistake on this most important decision.

While they had come from relatively happy homes, both Mike and Elaine knew people with very unhappy marriages, among them some of their own close friends. These were people who had married, full of love, only to find marriage a most difficult state. One of Elaine's friends, married in the temple, had said, "I knew the day after my marriage that I had made a terrible mistake." A friend of Mike's had related how his wife had left him three weeks after their temple marriage and how they had later been divorced. Elaine therefore thought her qualms had substance. On the other hand, they both had friends who said, "My marriage is the greatest thing that has ever happened to me"; "I have never had any regrets about my marriage"; and "I thought we were in love when we got married, but now our love is so much greater there is no comparison."

In both the happy and sad experiences, their friends had felt at the time of marriage that they were doing the right thing. The Lord's statement to Oliver Cowdery was familiar to both of them: "Behold, you have not understood; you have supposed that I would give it unto you, when you took no thought save it was to ask me. But, behold, I say unto you, that you must study it out in your mind; then you must ask me if it be right, and if it is right I will cause that your bosom shall burn within you; therefore, you shall feel that it is right. But if it be not right you shall have no such feelings, but you shall have a stupor of thought that shall cause you to forget the thing which is wrong" (D&C 9:7-9).

They both agreed that the only way they could know for sure was to receive a confirmation from the Holy Ghost. Elaine asked, "How will I know that I have really studied it out adequately in my own mind? How can I know that I have really done my part so that I can approach the Lord, knowing he will tell me whether my decision is correct?"

I assured them that their question was a common one, faced by virtually all young couples at some time during their dating and courtship. I also commended them for their care in making the decision. I suggested that we consider the following twelve questions as guidelines for the answer:

1. Are you better people when you are with each other? Does each of you inspire the other to do his best in studies, jobs, church callings, and other significant responsibilities? Or do you both live below your standards and ideals when you are together? (President Spencer W. Kimball speaks of the motivation leading to sexual impurity as lust not love). Whether or not you bring out the best in each other was a favorite criterion of President McKay.

2. Does either of you want to date anyone else? If so, you are not yet prepared to give yourself fully to the other. You are not really prepared to live the commandment of the Lord: "Thou shalt love thy wife [husband] with all thy heart and shall cleave unto her [him] and none else" (D&C 42:22). The total commitment necessary in marriage is not possible as long as you are interested in dating someone else. This does not mean that you may not admire persons of the opposite sex or be impressed by them. But it does mean that you will not have a romantic interest in them.

3. Do you truly enjoy each other's company? Or do you just enjoy each other when you are doing things you like to do? A hallmark of true love is enjoying the companionship of the other person regardless of the particular activity of the moment. The joy need not come from the activity but just from being together and sharing with each other. The companionship of each other is the primary source of satisfaction, not the activity.

4. Do you feel better about yourself when you are with him or her? Do you feel like a person of true worth, a child of God? Few things in life have more impact on what we become than what we think of ourselves. Our concept of ourselves as persons of true worth and our identity as children of God are critical. Do you help one another to have more self-esteem, or do you tend to find fault with each other? It is certainly appropriate to encourage each other to improve, but this should be done in a spirit of love. If either of you tends to focus on the other's failings, your love for each other is in question. For as it says in the scriptures, "Charity [the pure love of Christ] suffereth long, and is kind, . . . envieth not, . . . is not puffed up, does not behave itself unseemly, . . . is not easily provoked, thinketh no evil; rejoiceth not in iniquity, . . . beareth all things, . . . hopeth all things, endureth all things" (1 Cor. 13:4-7). True love is actively creative—it leads to the discovery of successful methods of improving or contributing to the life of another.

5. Are his or her needs as important to you as your own? Do you each find yourself continually looking for appropriate ways to make the other happy? Or are you each seeking your own happiness and interests without first considering those of the other? True love "seeketh not her own" (1 Cor. 13:5).

6. Are you each free to be yourself when you are together or must you always be on guard? Do you need to hide what you really are? Or are you confident that you are fully accepted and loved? Unfortunately, our society sometimes encourages coyness, playing it cool, hiding part of ourselves from others—especially in a dating relationship. In a marriage relationship, however, each partner must be free to be himself. This does not mean that you must share everything; it means that you are free to share when the need arises. This freedom also means that each conscience is clear. If one of you has had a serious transgression in the past that you have not fully repented of, you are not prepared to enter marriage. You cannot truly accept another without fully accepting yourself. Nor can you fully give of yourself when the barrier of guilt exists.

7. Are you prepared to marry the family of your prospective mate? While you may think that you only marry one person, in a real sense, you marry into a whole family. The parents of your mate become the grandparents of your children. Do you each feel good about that—and the influence they will have on your children? Even when separated by wide distances, there is still significant involvement with each other's families. Do both of your families support you in your decision to get married and will they support you in future decisions? Unresolved conflicts with one or both sets of parents will place added strains on your relationship.

8. How do you each treat your own parents? Do you respect them as individuals and respect their position and authority? It is likely that you will treat each other the same way you each treat members of your own family.

9. How does each of you feel about the other being a parent of your children? Mike, will Elaine be the type of mother that you really wish for your children? And will you want your children to be like her—because they probably will be. Of course, Elaine, you will need to ask the same question about Mike as the father of your children. Are you each now, or are you becoming, the type of individuals that you would be happy to have your children become? Have you discussed your goals for parenthood? And do you both agree upon and accept the gospel plan of bringing children into your home?

10. Do you each accept the patriarchal order? For you, Elaine, is Mike the type of priesthood bearer that you really trust? Are you willing to counsel together in love, but if necessary, abide by his counsel in righteousness and follow him in a spirit of genuine willingness? Does Mike seek your opinion on issues involving both of you? Can you call upon him in full faith and confidence to give you a special blessing when you desire? Is Mike honoring his priesthood so that he will be able to bless your children in times of illness or other needs?

For Mike: Do you fully obey your priesthood leaders in all righteousness? Are you willing to set a model of obedience to them for Elaine and your future children? Do you love and respect her enough that you give careful consideration to her ideas and feelings and make all possible decisions together? Are you willing to follow her ideas when they seem more inspired and correct than your own? Once an issue has been carefully and prayerfully considered, does Elaine accept the final decision willingly—or rebel against it? Do you trust her to help your children learn to be obedient to your righteous direction by being a model for them? Does Elaine inspire you to be a righteous priesthood leader in your home?

11. What will your destiny together be? Your potential destiny is that of god and goddess. If each of you continues to progress as you are now, is godhood likely? Will your prospective mate help you to achieve that great destiny? Do you both accept the law of perfection and the principle of eternal progression? Does each of you see the other as becoming perfect? (If either sees the other as nearly perfect right now, perhaps you need to doff your rose colored glasses.) Is the destiny of godhood one that both of you have accepted and one that you want to help each other achieve? At this point you may be wondering if all of these criteria carry equal weight. Must all of them be answered in the affirmative for you to feel confident in your decision? My experiences with many couples suggest that they are all important. Most of them are more than important; they are critical. However, this does not mean that they are all equally important, and perhaps if one or two of them are not fully met, the deficit is not insurmountable. You will need to consider the risk and decide.

The final guideline, number twelve, is all-important: after carefully considering the foregoing questions and then reaching a decision have you had your decision confirmed by the Lord? For this final confirmation you should go to the Lord only after you have "studied it out in your own mind." You must keep in mind that even the Prophet "Joseph had to pray all the time, exercise faith, live his religion, and magnify his calling, to obtain the manifestations of the Lord, and to keep him steadfast in the faith" (*Journal of Discourses*, 2:257). One of the problems that many young people have in going to the Lord for confirmation is that they want the Lord to give them only the answer they want rather than his answer. To receive an answer, a person must approach the Lord with a truly open mind and a willingness to accept whatever the Lord says. With this attitude, you will be prepared to hear and heed the Lord's counsel.

You may be wondering how your decision will be confirmed by the Holy Ghost. Will there be some dramatic witness such as a dream, vision or voice? In some cases, yes, but in most, probably no. In addition to the "burning in the bosom" or the contrary "spirit of darkness," there are other indicators. In a revelation given to Hyrum Smith the Lord said, "Put your trust in that Spirit which leadeth to do good—yea, to do justly, to walk humbly, to judge righteously: and this is my Spirit. Verily, verily, I say unto you, I will impart unto you of my Spirit, *which shall enlighten your mind, which will fill your soul with joy*" (D&C 11:12-13; italics added). To Oliver Cowdery the Lord said, "Yea, behold, I will tell you in your mind and in your heart, by the Holy Ghost, which shall come upon you and shall dwell in your heart.

"Now behold, this is the spirit of revelation" (D&C 8:2-3). Further, to Oliver the Lord said,

"Behold, thou knowest that thou hast inquired of me and I did enlighten thy mind: and now I tell thee these things that thou mayest know that thou hast been enlightened by the Spirit of truth. . . .

"Verily, verily, I say unto you, if you desire a further witness, cast your mind upon the night that you cried unto me in your heart, that you might know concerning the truths of these things.

"*Did I not speak peace to your mind concerning the matter*? What greater witness can you have than from God?" (D&C 6:15, 22-23; italics added) Also, in the words of President Brigham Young, "Can men live so that they can have the serene, blessed, calm, soft, soothing Spirit of the Lord always to abide with them? Yes, they can. . . . Can women? They can" (*Journal of Discourses*, 5:169).

Yes, through careful pondering, studying, fasting, and praying, you each can come to know whether or not your love is true and sufficient to *enter* marriage. You can know whether or not you are making the right choice. You still need to remember, however, the words of Nephi: "After ye have gotten into this straight and narrow path, I would ask if all is done? Behold, I say unto you, Nay; for ye have not come thus far save it were by the word of Christ with unshaken faith in him. . . .

"Ye must press forward, . . . feasting upon the word of Christ, and endure to the end" (2 Nephi 31:19-20). You must continue to live by the guide lines which enabled you to make your initial decision. I know the Lord will bless you in making this most important decision as you do it according to his counsel.

Burton C. Kelly, a counselor/teacher at Brigham Young University and father of nine children, serves as a high councillor in the Orem Utah South Central Stake.

Women of the Church

President Gordon B. Hinckley, President of The Church of Jesus Christ of Latter-day Saints

Address given at the Sunday Morning Session, 166th Semiannual General Conference, October 6, 1996

Half, **possibly more than half**, of the adult members of the Church are women. It is to them that I wish particularly to speak this morning. I do so with the hope that the men will also hear.

First let me say to you sisters that you do not hold a second place in our Father's plan for the eternal happiness and well-being of His children. You are an absolutely essential part of that plan.

Without you the plan could not function. Without you the entire program would be frustrated. As I have said before from this pulpit, when the process of creation occurred, Jehovah, the Creator under instruction from His Father, first divided the light from the darkness, and then separated the land from the waters. There followed the creation of plant life, followed by the creation of animal life. Then came the creation of man and culminating that act of divinity came the crowning act, the creation of woman.

Each of you is a daughter of God, endowed with a divine birthright. You need no defense of that position.

As I go about from place to place I am interviewed by representatives of the media. Invariably they ask about the place of women in the Church. They do so in an almost accusatory tone, as if we denigrate and demean women. I invariably reply that I know of no other organization in all the world which affords women so many opportunities for development, for sociality, for the accomplishment of great good, for holding positions of leadership and responsibility.

I wish all of these reporters could have been in the Tabernacle a week ago Saturday when the General Relief Society Meeting was held. It was an inspiration to look into the faces of that vast gathering of daughters of God, women of faith and ability, women who know what life is about, and have something of a sense of the divinity of their creation. I wish they could have heard that great chorus of young women from Brigham Young University, who touched our hearts with the beauty of their singing. I wish they could have heard the stirring messages of the Relief Society General Presidency, each of whom spoke on a phase of the subject, Faith, Hope, and Charity.

What able people these women are. They express themselves with power and conviction and great persuasiveness. President Faust concluded that service with a wonderful talk.

If those reporters who are prone to raise this question could have sat in that vast congregation, they would have known, even without further inquiry, that there is strength and great capacity in the women of this Church. There is leadership and direction, a certain spirit of independence, and yet great satisfaction in being a part of this the Lord's kingdom, and of working hand in hand with the priesthood to move it forward.

Many of you are here today who were in that meeting. Today you are seated with your husbands, men whom you love and honor and respect, and who in turn love and honor and respect you. You know how fortunate you are to be married to a good man who is your companion in life and who will be your companion throughout eternity. Together, as you have served in many capacities and reared your families and provided for them, you have faced a variety of storms and come through them all with your heads held high. Most of you are mothers, and very many of you are grandmothers and even great-grandmothers.

You have walked the sometimes painful, sometimes joyous path of parenthood. You have walked hand in hand with God in the great process of bringing children into the world that they might experience this estate along the road of immortality and eternal life. It has not been easy rearing a family. Most of you have had to sacrifice and skimp and labor night and day. As I think of you and your circumstances I think of the words of Ann Campbell, who wrote as she looked upon her children: "You are the trip I did not take; You are the pearls I cannot buy; You are my blue Italian lake. You are my piece of foreign sky." ("*The Treasure Chest*," p. 34).

You sisters are the real builders of the nation wherever you live. For you have created homes of strength and peace and security. These become the very sinew of any nation.

Unfortunately a few of you may be married to men who are abusive. Some of them put on a fine face before the world during the day, and come home in the evening, set aside their self-discipline, and on the slightest provocation fly into outbursts of anger.

No man who engages in such evil and unbecoming behavior is worthy of the priesthood of God. No man who so conducts himself is worthy of the privileges of the House of the Lord. I regret that there are some men undeserving of the love of their wives and children. There are children who fear their fathers and wives who fear their husbands. If there be any such within the hearing of my voice, as a servant of the Lord I rebuke you and call you to repentance. Discipline yourselves. Master your temper. Most of the things that make you angry are of very small consequence. And what a terrible price you are paying for your anger. Ask the Lord to forgive you. Ask your wife to forgive you. Apologize to your children.

There are many women among us who are single. Generally, this is not of their own choice. Some have never had the opportunity to marry one with whom they would wish to spend eternity. To you single women who wish to be married I repeat what I recently said in a meeting for singles in this Tabernacle, "Do not give up hope. And do not give up trying. But do give up being obsessed with it." The chances are that if you forget about it and become anxiously engaged in other activities, the prospects will brighten immeasurably.

I believe that for most of us the best medicine for loneliness is work, service in behalf of others. I do not minimize your problems, but I do not hesitate to say that there are many others whose problems are more serious than are yours. Reach out to serve them, to help them, to encourage them. There are so many boys and girls who fail in school for want of a little personal attention and encouragement. There are so many elderly people who live in misery and loneliness and fear for whom a simple conversation would bring a measure of hope and happiness.

Included among the women of the Church are those who have lost their husbands through abandonment, divorce, and death. Great is our obligation to you. As the scriptures declare: "Pure religion and undefiled before God and the Father is this, To visit the fatherless and widows in their affliction, and to keep himself unspotted from the world" (James 1:27).

I received this letter from one who counts herself fortunate, and indeed fortunate she is. She writes:

> Although I have been raising our four boys as a single parent, . . . I am not alone. I have a wonderful "ward family" that has rallied around us. . .
>
> My Relief Society president has been there for me through my greatest hardships, encouraging my spiritual growth, personal prayer, and temple attendance.
>
> Our bishop has been generous in providing needed food and clothing and helped send two of the boys to camp. He has had interviews with all of us and given each of us blessings and needed encouragement. He has helped me to budget and do what I can to help my family.
>
> Our home teachers have come regularly and even gave the boys blessings as they started the new school year.
>
> Our stake president and his counselors have checked in on us on a regular basis, by taking time to visit with us at church, on the phone, or visiting our home.
>
> This church is true, and my boys and I are living proof that God loves us and that a "ward family" make all the difference.

Our priesthood leaders have been instrumental in keeping the boys active in church and in the Scouting program. (One) is an Eagle Scout and is receiving his fourth palm this week. (Another) is an Eagle with three palms. And (a third) has just turned in his Eagle papers this week. The youngest is a Webelos and loves Cub Scouts.

We are always met with loving hearts and warm handshakes. The Christ-like attitude of the stake and our ward has helped us through trials we never imagined possible.

Life has been hard. . . but we put on the whole armour of God as we kneel in family prayer each day, asking for help and guidance and sharing thanks for the blessings we have received. I pray daily for the constant companionship of the Holy Ghost to guide me as I raise these boys to be missionaries and encourage them to be true to the gospel and the priesthood they hold.

I am proud to say I am a member of The Church of Jesus Christ of Latter-day Saints. I know this church is true, I sustain my church leaders. We are doing well, and I thank everyone for their love, and prayers, and acceptance.

What a great letter that is. How much it says about the way this Church functions and should function throughout the world. I hope that every woman who finds herself in the kind of circumstances in which this woman lives, is similarly blessed with an understanding and helpful bishop, with a Relief Society president who knows how to assist her, with home teachers who know where their duty lies and how to fulfill it, and with a host of ward members who are helpful without being intrusive.

I have never met the woman whose letter I have read. Notwithstanding the cheerful attitude she conveys, I am sure there has been much of struggle and loneliness, and at times fear. I notice that she works to provide for her needs and the needs of her boys, who are in their teens. I assume her income is inadequate, because she indicates that the bishop has helped them with food and clothing.

Some years ago President Benson delivered a message to the women of the Church. He encouraged them to leave their employment and give their individual time to their children. I sustain the position which he took. Nevertheless, I recognize, as he recognized, that there are some women, it has become very many in fact, who have to work to provide for the needs of their families. To you I say, do the very best you can. I hope that if you are employed full time you are doing it to ensure that basic needs are met and not simply to indulge a taste for an elaborate home, fancy cars, and other luxuries. The greatest job that any mother will ever do will be in nurturing, teaching, lifting, encouraging, and rearing her children in righteousness and truth. None other can adequately take her place.

It is well-nigh impossible to be a full-time homemaker and a full-time employee. I know how some of you struggle with decisions concerning this matter.

I repeat, do the very best you can. You know your circumstances, and I know that you are deeply concerned for the welfare of your children. Each of you has a bishop who will counsel with you and assist you. If you feel you need to speak with an understanding woman, do not hesitate to get in touch with your Relief Society president.

To the mothers of this Church, every mother who is here today, I want to say that as the years pass, you will become increasingly grateful for that which you did in molding the lives of your children in the direction of righteousness and goodness, integrity and faith. That is most likely to happen if you can spend adequate time with them.

For you who are single parents I say that many hands stand ready to help you. The Lord is not unmindful of you. Neither is His church.

May He bless you, my beloved sisters who find yourselves in the situation of single parenthood. May you have health and strength and vitality to carry the heavy burden that is yours. May you have loving friends and associates to bear you up in your times of trial. You know the power of prayer as perhaps few others do. Many of you spend much time on your knees speaking with your Father in Heaven, with tears running down your cheeks. Please know that we also pray for you.

With all that you have to do, you are also asked to serve in the Church. Your bishop will not ask you to do anything that is beyond your capacity. And as you so serve a new dimension will be added to your life.

You will find new associations, stimulating associations. You will find friendship and sociality. You will grow in knowledge and understanding and wisdom, and in your capacity to do. You will become a better mother because of the service you give in the work of the Lord.

Now in conclusion, I wish to say a word to you older women, many of whom are widows. You are a great treasure. You have passed through the storms of life. You have weathered the challenges now facing your younger sisters. You are mature in wisdom, in understanding, in compassion, in love and service. There is a certain beauty that shines through your countenance. It is the beauty that comes of peace. There may still be struggle, but there is mature wisdom to meet it. There are health problems, but there is a certain composure concerning them. The bad memories of the past have largely been forgotten while the good memories return and bring sweet and satisfying enrichment to life.

You have learned to love the scriptures, and you read them. Your prayers for the most part are prayers of thanksgiving. Your greetings are words of kindness. Your friendship is a sturdy staff on which others may lean. What a resource you are to the women of The Church of Jesus Christ of Latter-day Saints. You love the Church, you accept its doctrine, you honor your place in its organization, you bring luster and strength and beauty to its congregations. How thankful we are to you. How much you are loved, respected, and honored.

I salute my own beloved companion. It will soon be sixty years that we walked from the Salt Lake Temple as husband and wife, with love for one another. That love has strengthened through the years. We have faced many problems during our years of marriage. Somehow, with the blessing of the Lord, we have survived them all.

It is becoming physically harder to stand tall and straight as we did in our younger years. No matter, we still have one another and we still stand together, even though we lean a little. And when the time for separation comes there will be much of sorrow, but there will also be the comfort that will come from the assurance that she is mine and I am hers for the eternity that lies ahead.

And so, my beloved sisters, please know how much we appreciate you. You bring a measure of wholeness to us. You have great strength. With dignity and tremendous ability you carry forward the remarkable programs of the Relief Society, the Young Women, and the Primary. You teach Sunday School. We walk at your side as your companions and your brethren with respect and love, with honor and great admiration. It was the Lord who designated that men in His church should hold the priesthood. It was He who has given you your capabilities to round out this great and marvelous organization, which is the church and kingdom of God. I bear testimony before the entire world of your worth, of your grace and goodness, of your remarkable abilities and tremendous contributions, and invoke the blessings of heaven upon you, in the name of the Lord Jesus Christ, amen.

Covenant Marriage

Elder Bruce C. Hafen

Address by Elder Bruce C. Hafen, 166th Semiannual General Conference, Saturday Afternoon Session, October 5, 1996

Three summers ago, I watched a new bride and groom, Tracy and Tom, emerge from a sacred temple. They laughed and held hands as family and friends gathered to take pictures. I saw happiness and promise in their faces as they greeted their reception guests, who celebrated publicly the creation of a new family. I wondered that night how long it would be until these two faced the opposition that tests every marriage. Only then would they discover whether their marriage was based on a contract or a covenant.

Another bride sighed blissfully on her wedding day, "Mom, I'm at the end of all my troubles!" "Yes," replied her mother, "but at which end?" When troubles come, the parties to a contractual marriage seek happiness by walking away. They marry to obtain benefits, and will stay only as long as they're receiving what they bargained for. But when troubles come to a covenant marriage, the husband and wife work them through. They marry to give and to grow, bound by covenants to each other, to the community, and to God. A contract companion gives 50 percent; a covenant companion gives 100 percent.

Marriage is by nature a covenant, not just a private contract one may cancel at will. Jesus taught about contractual attitudes when he described the "hireling," who performs his conditional promise of care only when he receives something in return. When the hireling "seeth the wolf coming," he "leaveth the sheep, and fleeth . . . because he careth not for the sheep." By contrast, the Savior said, "I am the good shepherd . . . and I lay down my life for the sheep." Many people today marry as hirelings. And when the wolf comes, they flee. This idea is wrong. It curses the earth, turning parents' hearts away from their children and from each other.

Before their marriage, Tom and Tracy received an eternal perspective on covenants and wolves. They learned through the story of Adam and Eve about life's purpose and how to return to God's presence through obedience and the atonement. Christ's life is the story of giving the atonement. The life of Adam and Eve is the story of receiving the atonement, which empowered them to overcome their separation from God and all opposition until they were eternally "at one," with the Lord, and with each other.

Without the Fall, Lehi taught, Adam and Eve would never have known opposition. And "they would have had no children; wherefore they would have remained in a state of innocence, having no joy, for they knew no misery. " Astute parents will see a little connection here—no children, no misery! But in the Garden, they could never know joy. So the Lord taught them they would live and bear children in sorrow, sweat, and thorns. Still, the ground was cursed "for their sake": their path of affliction also led to the joy of redemption and comprehension. That is why the husband and wife in a covenant marriage sustain and lift each other when the wolf comes. If Tom and Tracy had understood all this, perhaps they would have walked more slowly from the garden-like temple grounds, like Adam and Eve, arm in arm, into a harsh and lonely world.

And yet—marrying and raising children can yield the most valuable religious experiences of their lives. Covenant marriage requires a total leap of faith: they must keep their covenants without knowing what risks that may require of them. They must surrender unconditionally, obeying God and sacrificing for each other. Then will they discover what Alma called "incomprehensible joy."

Of course, some have no opportunity to marry. And some divorces are unavoidable. But the Lord will ultimately compensate those faithful ones who are denied mortal fulfillment.

Every marriage is tested repeatedly by three kinds of wolves. The first wolf is natural adversity. After asking God for years to give them a first child, David and Fran had a baby with a serious heart defect. Following a three week struggle, they buried their newborn son. Like Adam and Eve before them, they mourned together, brokenhearted, in faith before the Lord.

Second, the wolf of their own imperfections will test them. One woman told me through her tears how her husband's constant criticism finally destroyed not only their marriage but her entire sense of self-worth. He first complained about her cooking and house-cleaning, then about how she used her time, how she talked, looked, and reasoned. Eventually she felt utterly inept and dysfunctional. My heart ached for her, and for him.

Contrast her with a young woman who had very little self-confidence when she first married. Then her husband found so much to praise in her that she gradually began to believe she was a good person and that her opinions mattered. His belief in her rekindled her innate self-worth.

The third wolf is the excessive individualism that has spawned today's contractual attitudes. A 7 year-old girl came home from school crying, "Mom, don't I belong to you? Our teacher said today that nobody belongs to anybody—children don't belong to parents, husbands don't belong to wives. I am yours, aren't I, Mom?" Her mother held her close and whispered, "Of course you're mine and I'm yours, too." Surely marriage partners must respect one another's individual identity, and family member are neither slaves nor inanimate objects. But this teacher's fear, shared today by many, is that the bonds of kinship and marriage are not valuable ties that bind, but are, instead, sheer bondage. Ours is the age of the waning of belonging.

The adversary has long cultivated this overemphasis on personal autonomy, and now he feverishly exploits it. Our deepest God-given instinct is to run to the arms of those who need us and sustain us. But he drives us away from each other today, with wedges of distrust and suspicion. He exaggerates the need for having space, getting out, and being left alone. Some people believe him then wonder why they feel left alone.

And despite admirable exceptions, children in America's growing number of single parent families are far more at risk than children in two-parent families. The primary cause of today's general decline in today's child well-being is a remarkable "collapse of marriage."

Many people even wonder these days what marriage is. Should we prohibit same-sex marriage? Should divorce be more difficult to obtain? Some say these questions are not society's business, because marriage is a private contract. But as modern prophets recently proclaimed, marriage is ordained of God. Even secular marriage was historically a three-party covenant among a man, a woman, and the state.

Society has a huge interest in the outcome and the offspring of every marriage. So the public nature of marriage distinguishes it from all other relationships. Guests come to weddings, wrote Wendell Berry, because sweethearts "say their vows to the community as much as to one another," giving themselves not only to each other, but also to the common good "as no contract could ever join them."

When we observe the covenants we make at the altar of sacrifice, we discover hidden reservoirs of strength. I once said in exasperation to my wife, Marie, "The Lord placed Adam and Eve on the earth as full grown people. Why couldn't he have done that with this boy of ours, the one with the freckles and the unruly hair?" Marie said to me, "The Lord gave us that child to make Christians of us."

One night Marie exhausted herself for hours helping that child build a diorama of a Native American village on a cookie sheet. It was a test no hireling would have endured. At first he fought her efforts, but by bedtime, I saw him lay "his" diorama proudly on a counter. He started for his bed, then turned around, and ran back across the room and hugged his mother, grinning his fourth grade grin. Later I asked Marie in complete awe, "how did you do it?" She said, "I just made up my mind that I couldn't leave him, no matter what." Then she added: "I didn't know I had it in me." She discovered deep internal wellsprings of compassion, because the bonds of her covenants gave her strength to lay down her life for her sheep, even an hour at a time.

Now I return to Tom and Tracy, who this year discovered wellsprings of their own. Their second baby threatened to come too early to live. They might have made a hireling's convenient choice and gone on with their lives, letting a miscarriage occur. But because they tried to observe their covenants by sacrifice, active Tracy lay almost motionless at home for five weeks, then in a hospital bed for another five. Tom was with her virtually every hour when he wasn't working or sleeping. They prayed their child to earth. She is here, and she is theirs.

One night, Tracy lay in the hospital and wondered if how she felt was like the Savior might have felt. She felt like it was a privilege. She was a shepherd, not a hireling. She, like so many parents in Zion, are willing to lay down their lives for their sheep, even an hour and a day at a time. May we restore covenant marriage. May we find joy, even as Adam and Eve did. In the name of Jesus Christ, amen.

To Live the Great Plan of Happiness

Elder Richard G. Scott of the Quorum of the Twelve

Address given at the Sunday Afternoon Session, 166th Semiannual General Conference, *Ensign*, November 1996, pp. 73-75

Scriptures record: "**And I, God,** created man, . . . male and female created I them.[1] This was done spiritually in your pre-mortal existence when you lived in the presence of your Father in Heaven. Your gender existed before coming to earth. You elected to have his earth experience as part of His plan for you. The prophets call it, The plan of Mercy;"[2] "The Eternal Plan of Deliverance;"[3] "The Plan of Salvation;"[4] and, yes, "The Great Plan of Happiness."[5] You were taught this plan before you came to earth and there rejoiced in the privilege of participating in it.

Obedience to the plan is a requisite for full happiness in this life and a continuation of eternal joy beyond the veil. Essential to His plan of happiness is agency—the right of personal choice. Also fundamental is the holy privilege of procreation to be exercised within the commitment of legal marriage. Marriage between man and woman is essential to His eternal plan. The family is ordained of God.[6] As husband and wife, you have the responsibility to bear children and to nurture and train them spiritually, emotionally, and physically.[7]

Satan also has a plan. It is a cunning, evil, subtle plan of destruction.[8] It is his objective to take captive the children of Father in Heaven and with every possible means frustrate The Great Plan of Happiness.

Our Heavenly Father endowed His sons and daughters with unique traits specifically fitted for their individual responsibilities as they fulfill His plan. To follow His plan requires that you do those things He expects of you as a son or daughter, husband or wife. Those roles are different, but entirely compatible. In the Lord's plan, it takes two—a man and a woman—to form a whole. Indeed, a husband and wife are not two identical halves, but a wondrous, divinely determined combination of complementary capacities and characteristics.

Marriage allows these different characteristics to come together in oneness—in unity—to bless a husband and wife, their children and grandchildren. For the greatest happiness and productivity in life, both husband and wife, are needed. Their efforts interlock and are complementary. Each has individual traits that best fit the role the Lord has defined for happiness as a man or woman. When used as the Lord intends, those capacities allow a married couple to think, act, and rejoice as one—to face challenges together and overcome them as one—to grow in love and understanding and through temple ordinances to be bound together as one whole, eternally. That is the plan.

You can learn how to be more effective parents by studying the life of Adam and Eve. Adam was Michael who helped create the earth—a glorious, superb individual. Eve was his equal—a full, powerfully contributing partner. After they had partaken of the fruit, the Lord spoke with them. Their comments reveal some different characteristics of a man and woman. To Adam He said, "Hast thou eaten of the tree whereof I commanded thee that thou shouldst not eat . . . ?"[9] Now Adam's response was characteristic of a man who wants to be perceived as being as close to right as possible. Adam responded, "The woman thou gavest me and commandest that she should remain with me, she gave me of the fruit of the tree and I did eat."[10] And the Lord said unto Eve: "What is this thing which thou hast done?"[11] Eve's response was characteristic of a woman. Her answer was very simple and straight forward. "The serpent beguiled me, and I did eat."[12]

Later, "Adam blessed God and began to prophesy concerning all the families of the earth, saying: Blessed be the name of God, for because of. transgression my eyes are opened, and in this life I shall have joy, and again in the flesh I shall see God."[13] Adam was thinking about his responsibilities. He was trying to align his performance with the desires of the Lord. Eve said, "Were it not for our transgression we never should have had seed, and never should have known good and evil, and the joy of our redemption and the eternal life which God giveth unto all the obedient."[14] Eve's response was characteristic of a woman. She embraced all, wanted to make sure that everyone was considered. One response was not more correct than the other. The two perspectives resulted from the traits inherent in men and women. The Lord intends that we use those differences to fulfill his plan for happiness. By counseling together they arrived at a broader, more correct understanding of truth.

They worked together.[15] They obeyed the commandment to have children.[16] They knew The Plan of Happiness and followed it, even though at times it resulted in hardship and difficulty for them.

They were commanded: "Thou shalt repent and call upon God in the name of the Son forevermore."[17] And they did. Further, they taught their children The Plan of Happiness.[18] They worked together to overcome challenges[19] and "(They) ceased not to call up on God."[20]

Because Adam and Eve were obedient, the Holy Ghost led them. As husband and wife, you can receive direction in your lives by qualifying for the gift of the Holy Ghost through obedience to the teachings of the Savior.

Beware of the subtle ways Satan employs to take you from The Plan of God[21] and true happiness. One of Satan's most effective approaches is to demean the role of wife and mother in the home. This is an attack at the very heart of God's plan to foster love between husband and wife, and to nurture children in an atmosphere of understanding, peace and appreciation and support. Much of the violence that is rampant in the world today is the harvest of weakened homes. Government and social plans will not effectively correct that nor can the best efforts of schools and churches fully compensate for the absence of the tender care of a compassionate mother and wife in the home.

[margin note: wicked Traditions]

This morning President Hinckley spoke of the importance of women. Study this message. As a mother guided by the Lord, you weave a fabric of character in your children from threads of truth through careful instruction and worthy example. You imbue the traits of honesty. faith in God, duty, respect for others, self-confidence. the desire to contribute, to learn, to give, in your trusting children's minds and hearts. No day-care center can do that. It is your sacred right and privilege.

Of course, as a woman you can do exceptionally well in the work place, but is that the best use of your divinely appointed talents and feminine traits? As a husband, don't encourage your wife to go to work to help in your divinely appointed responsibility of providing resources if you can possibly help it. As the prophets have counseled: possible with the help of the Lord, as parents work together to keep mother in the home.[22] Your presence there will strengthen the self-confidence of your children and decrease the chance of emotional challenges. Moreover, as you teach truth by word and example, those children will come to understand who they are and what they can obtain as divine children of Father in Heaven.

I know I have been speaking of the ideal and you may be disturbed because your life may not now fit that mold. I promise you that through your obedience and continuing faith in Jesus Christ and your understanding of the whole Plan of Happiness, even if important parts of it aren't present in your life now, they will be yours in the Lord's due time. I also promise you that you can have significant growth and happiness now in your present circumstances. As a daughter or son of God, live whatever portion of the plan you can, the best you are able.

Your desire to be a wife and mother may not have its total fulfillment here, but it will in His time as you live in faith and obedience to merit it.[23] Don't be lured away from the Plan of Our God[24] to the ways of the world where motherhood is belittled, femininity is decried, and the divinely established role of a wife and mother is mocked. Let the world go its way. You follow the plan of the Lord for the greatest measure of true, eternal achievement, and the fullness of happiness. The lack of promised blessings for which you qualify will be fully rectified in this life or in the next.

I often interview strong priesthood leaders. When these men speak of their wives, it is with deep tenderness and obvious appreciation. Often, tears flow. Their comments include: "She is more spiritual, purer, and more committed than I. She is the strength of my life," or "I couldn't do it without her." As a woman, please don't judge how worthwhile and needed, and loved you are by our inept ability to express our true feelings. Your divinely conferred trait of giving of self without counting the cost leads you to underestimate your own worth.

I humbly thank our Father in Heaven for His daughters, you who were willing to come to earth to live under such uncertain circumstances. Most men could not handle the uncertainties you are asked to live with. Social customs require that you wait to be asked for marriage. You are expected to go with your husband wherever his employment or a call will take him. Your environment and neighborhood is determined by his ability to provide, meager or not. You place your life in the Lord's hands each time you bear a child. He makes no such sacrifice. The blessing of nurturing children and caring for a husband is often intermingled with many routine tasks. But you do all these things willingly because you are a woman. Generally you have no idea of how truly wonderful and capable you are, how very much appreciated and loved, or how desperately needed, for most men don't tell you as completely and as often as is needed.

How can you receive the greatest happiness and blessings from this earth experience?

- Learn the doctrinal foundation of The Great Plan of Happiness by studying the scriptures, pondering their content, and praying to understand them. Carefully study and use the Proclamation of the First Presidency and the Twelve on the Family.[25] It was inspired of the Lord.

- Listen to the voice of current and past prophets. Their declarations are inspired. You may verify that counsel in your own mind and heart as it applies to your special circumstances. Ask the Lord to confirm your choices and accept accountability for them. Obey the inner feelings that come as promptings from the Holy Ghost. Those feelings are engendered by your righteous thoughts and acts and your determination to seek the will of the Lord and to live it.

- When needed, seek counsel and guidance from parents and your priesthood leaders. A choice mother wrote: "How did the pioneer women . . . respond to the challenges of their day? They listened to their prophet's voice and followed him because they knew he spoke the will of the Lord. They met the challenges and reaped great blessings because of their faith and obedience. Their first priorities were not security, nice homes, or an easy life. No sacrifice was too great for them to make for their precious husbands and children."[26]

Obviously, I don't know what it feels like to be a woman, but I do know what it is to love one with all of my heart and soul. I constantly express to the Lord overflowing gratitude for the unending blessings that flow to our children and so abundantly to me from the life of one of His precious daughters. I want the happiness we have found together to be yours. The more closely you personally adhere to his plan for you on Earth, the greater will be your happiness, fulfillment and progress. The more qualified you will be to receive the rewards he had promised for obedience.

I so testify, for the Savior lives, and he loves you, in the name of Jesus Christ, amen.

Notes

1. Moses 2:27. See also Moses 2:28, Moses 3:5. James R. Clark, "Messages of the First Presidency" 4:303, James E. Talmage, "Millennial Star," 24 August 1922. p. 530.
2. Alma 42:15.
3. 2 Ne. 11: 5.
4. Moses 6:62.
5. Alma 42:8.
6. The Family. A Proclamation to the World. "Ensign," November 1996. p 102.
7. The Family: A Proclamation to the World. "Ensign," November 1996. p 102.

8. See 2 Ne. 9:2, 3, 5: Alma 2:45; Helaman 2:8; 3 Ne. 1: 16; D&C 10: 12, 23.

9. Moses 4:17.

10. Moses 4:18.

11. Moses 4:19.

12. Moses 4:19.

13. Moses 5:10.

14. Moses 5:11.

15. Moses 5:1.

16. Moses 5:2.

17. Moses 5:7-8.

18. Moses 5:12.

19. Moses 5:13.

20. Moses 5:16.

21. 2 Ne. 9:13.

22. Spencer W. Kimball, San Antonio Fireside, 3 December 1977, pp. 9-10.

23. Gordon B. Hinckley, in Conference Report, Apr. 1991, 94; or Ensign, May 1991, 71.

24. 2 Ne. 9:13.

25. The Family, a Proclamation to the World. "Ensign," November 1996, pg. 102.

26. Jeanene W. Scott. BYU Womens Conference. April 6, 1989, p. 1.

The Eternal Family

Elder Robert D. Hales of the Quorum of the Twelve

Address given at the Sunday Morning Session, 166th Semiannual General Conference, *Ensign*, November 1996, pp. 64-67

I **too wish to speak** to all those who would like to know about eternal families and how families can be forever.

One year ago The First Presidency and Quorum of the Twelve Apostles of The Church of Jesus Christ of Latter-day Saints issued a Proclamation to the World concerning The Family. It summarizes eternal gospel principles that have been taught since the beginning of recorded history, even before the earth was created.

The doctrine of the family begins with heavenly parents. Our highest aspiration is to be like them. The Apostle Paul taught that God is the father of our spirits (see Hebrews 12:9). From the Proclamation we read: "In the premortal realm, spirit sons and daughters knew and worshiped God as their Eternal Father and accepted His plan by which His children could obtain a physical body and gain earthly experience to progress toward perfection and ultimately realize his or her divine destiny as heir of eternal life." (The Family, A Proclamation to the World). The Proclamation also reiterates to the world that "Marriage between a man and a woman is ordained of God and . . . the family is central to the Creator's plan for the eternal destiny of His children" (Family Proclamation). From the earliest beginnings, God established the family and made it eternal. Adam and Eve were sealed in marriage for time and all eternity: "And thus all things were confirmed unto Adam, by an holy ordinance, and the Gospel preached, and a decree sent forth, that it should be in the world, until the end thereof, and thus it was . . . And Adam knew his wife, and she bare unto him sons and daughters, and they be (Moses 5:59; Moses 5:2).

The Savior himself spoke of this sacred marriage covenant and promise when He gave the authority to His disciples to bind in heaven sacred covenants made on earth. "And I will give unto thee the keys of the kingdom of heaven: and whatsoever thou shalt bind on earth shall be bound in heaven: and whatsoever thou shalt loose on earth shall be loosed in heaven" (Matthew 16:19). In this latter day the promise of eternal families was restored in 1829 when the powers of the Melchizedek priesthood were restored to the earth. Seven years later, in the Kirtland temple, the keys to perform the sealing ordinances were restored as recorded in the Doctrine and Covenants. "Elijah the prophet, who was taken to heaven without tasting death, stood before us, and said: Behold, the time has fully come, which was spoken of by the mouth of Malachi . . . the keys of this dispensation are committed into your hands" (D&C 110:13, 14, 16). With the restoration of these keys and priesthood authority comes the opportunity for all who are worthy to receive the blessings of eternal families. "Yea the hearts of thousands and tens of thousands shall greatly rejoice in consequence of the blessings which shall be poured out, and the endowment with which my servants have been endowed in this house" (D&C 110:9).

What is the promise of these sealings which are performed in the temples? The Lord outlines the promise and requirements in this sacred verse: "And again, verily I say unto you, if a man marry a wife by my word, which is my law, and by the new and everlasting covenant, and it is sealed unto them by the Holy Spirit of promise, by him who is anointed, unto whom I have appointed this power and the keys of this priesthood; and it shall be said unto them—Ye shall come forth in the first resurrection; and if it be after the first resurrection, in the next resurrection; and shall inherit thrones, kingdoms, principalities, and powers, dominions, all heights and depths—then shall it be written in the Lamb's Book of Life . . . and shall be of full force when they are out of the world: and they shall pass by the angels, and the gods, which are set there to their exaltation and glory in all things, as hath been sealed upon their heads, which glory shall be a fulness and a continuation of the seeds forever and ever (D&C 132:19).

As taught in this scripture, an eternal bond doesn't just happen as a result of the sealing covenants we make in the temple. How we conduct ourselves in this life will determine who we will be, and what we will be, for all the eternities to come. To receive the blessing of the sealing that our Heavenly Father has given us, we have to keep the commandments and conduct ourselves in such a way that our families will want to live with us in the eternities. The family relationships we have here on this earth are important, but they are much more important for their effect on our families for generations in mortality and throughout all eternity: By divine commandment, spouses are required to love each other above all others. The Lord clearly declares, "Thou shall love thy wife with all thy heart, and shalt cleave unto her and none else" (D&C 42:22).

The Proclamation states: "By divine design, fathers are to preside over their families in love and righteousness and are responsible to provide the necessities of life and protection for their families (See I Timothy 5:8). (By divine design,) mothers are primarily responsible for the nurture of their children" (Family Proclamation). By divine design, husband and wife are equal partners in their marriage and parental responsibilities. By direct commandment of God, "parents have a sacred duty . . . to teach (their children) to love and serve one another, to observe the commandments of God and to be law abiding citizens (in the countries where they reside)" (Family Proclamation; see Mosiah 4:14-15; D&C 68:25-28).

Because of the importance of the family to the eternal plan of happiness. Satan makes a major effort to destroy the sanctity of the family; demean the importance of the role of men and women; encourage moral uncleanliness and violations of the sacred law of chastity; and to discourage parents from placing the bearing and rearing of children as one of their highest priorities.

So fundamental is the family unit to the plan of salvation that God has declared a warning that those "individuals who violate the covenants of chastity, who abuse spouse or offspring, or who fail to fulfill family responsibilities will one day stand accountable before God (their maker). . . . The disintegration of the family will bring upon individuals, communities, and nations the calamities foretold by ancient and modern prophets" (Family Proclamation).

While our individual salvation is based on our individual obedience, it is equally important that we understand that we are each an important and integral part of a family and the highest blessings can be received only within an eternal family. When families are functioning as designed by God, the relationships found therein are the most valued of mortality. The plan of the Father is that family love and companionship will continue into the eternities. Being one in a family carries a great responsibility of caring, loving, lifting and strengthening each member of the family so that all can righteously endure to the end in mortality and dwell together throughout eternity. It is not enough just to save ourselves. It is equally important that parents, brothers, and sisters are saved in our families. If we return home alone to our Heavenly Father, we will be asked, "Where is the rest of the family?" This is why we teach that families are forever. The eternal nature of an individual becomes the eternal nature of the family.

The eternal nature of our body and our spirit is a question often pondered by those who live in mortality. All people who will ever live on earth are members of a human family and are eternal children of God, our loving Heavenly Father. After birth and tasting of death in mortality, all will be resurrected because of the Atonement of Jesus Christ, the Only Begotten Son of God the Father. Depending on our individual obedience to the laws, ordinances, and commandments of God, each mortal can have the blessing of attaining eternal life; that is, returning to live in the presence of their Heavenly Father and His son Jesus Christ, for all the eternities to come. Through making and keeping the sacred covenants found in the temple ordinances, individuals can return to the presence of God and will be reunited with their families eternally.

The home is where we are nurtured and where we prepare ourselves for living in mortality. It is also where we prepare ourselves for death and for immortality because of our belief and understanding that there is life after death, not only for the individual but also for the family.

Some of the greatest lessons of gospel principles about the eternal nature of the family are learned as we observe how members of the Church, when faced with adversity, apply gospel principles in their lives and in their homes. In the past year, I have witnessed the blessings of joy which come to those who honor and revere the gospel teachings of the eternal family during times of adversity in their lives.

A few months ago I had the opportunity of visiting a man who had been diagnosed with a terminal illness As a devoted priesthood holder, he was confronted by the realities of mortality. He found strength, however, in the example of the Savior who, in the Lord's Prayer, "After this manner therefore pray ye: . . . Thy will be done in earth, as it is in heaven" (Matthew 6:9-1). My friend took courage in knowing that, as Jesus was required to endure great pain and agony in the Garden of Gethsemane while completing the atoning sacrifice, He uttered the words, "O my Father, if this cup may not pass away from me, except I drink it, thy will be done" (Matthew 26:42).

My friend came to accept the phrase "Thy will be done" as he faced his own poignant trials and tribulations. As a faithful member of the Church, he was now confronted with some sobering concerns. Particularly touching were his questions, "Have I done all that I need to do to faithfully endure to the end? What will death be like? Will my family be prepared to stand in faith and be self-reliant when I am gone?"

We had the opportunity to discuss all of these questions. They are clearly answered in the doctrine as taught to us by our Savior. We discussed how he had spent his life striving to be faithful, to do what God asked of him, to be honest in his dealings with his fellow men, and to care for and love his family. Isn't that what is meant by enduring to the end? We talked about what happens immediately after death, about what God has taught us about the world of spirits. It is a place of paradise and happiness for those who have lived righteous lives. It is not something to fear.

After our conversation, he called together his wife and the extended family—children and grandchilren—to teach them again the doctrine of the Atonement that all will be resurrected. Everyone came to understand that just as the Lord has said, while there will be mourning at the temporary separation, there is no sorrow for those who die in the Lord (See Revelation 14: 13; D&C 42:46). His blessing promised him comfort and reassurance that all would be well, that he would not have pain. That he would have additional time to prepare his family for his departure—even that he would know the time of his departure. The family related to me that on the night before he passed away, he said he would go on the morrow. He passed away the next afternoon at peace with all of his family at his side. This is the solace and comfort that comes to us when we understand the gospel plan and know that families are forever.

Contrast these events with an incident which happened to me when I was a young man in my early twenties. While serving in the Air Force, one of the pilots in my squadron crashed on a training mission and was killed. I was assigned to accompany my fallen comrade on his final journey home to be buried in Brooklyn. I had the honor of standing by his family during the viewing and funeral services and representing our government in presenting the flag to his grieving widow at grave side. The funeral service was dark and dismal. No mention was made of his goodness or his accomplishments. His name was never mentioned. At the conclusion of the services, his widow turned to me and asked, "Bob, what is really going to happen to Don?" I was then able to give her the sweet doctrine of the resurrection and the reality that, if baptized and sealed in the temple for time and eternity, they could be together eternally. The clergyman standing next to her said, "That is the most beautiful doctrine I have ever heard."

The fullness of the gospel of Jesus Christ brings great comfort in the stressful times of mortality. It brings light where there is darkness and a calming influence where there is turmoil. It gives eternal hope where there is mortal despair. It is more than just beautiful doctrine. It is a reality in our lives that if we can be obedient and obtain the eternal rewards that God grants us, if we will draw nigh unto Him and embrace the eternal doctrine, we will be blessed.

Another incident that has touched my life recently happened when a young man with a terminal illness passed away. He knew that his illness would first take away his manual dexterity and his ability to walk. Then its progression would take his ability to speak: and finally his respiratory system would cease to function. But he also had faith that families are forever. With this knowledge, he spoke to each of his children and recorded video recordings for when he was gone. He produced recordings to be given to his sons and daughters at important, sacred occasions in their lives, such as baptisms, priesthood ordinations, and weddings. He spoke to them with the tender love of a father who knew that, while his family was forever, for a time he would not physically be able to be with them but spiritually would never leave their side.

The examples of faith shown by steadfast widows and widowers, along with that of their children, after the passing of a spouse or parent are an inspiration to all of us. Great lessons can be learned as we observe their faith and obedience as they strive to remain faithful so that they can once again be together as families through eternity.

The knowledge and understanding of the doctrine that God lives and Jesus is the Christ and that we have an opportunity to be resurrected and live in the presence of God the Father and His Son, Jesus Christ, makes it possible to endure otherwise tragic events. This doctrine brings a brightness of hope into an otherwise dark and dreary world. It answers the simple questions of where we came from, why we are here, and where we are going. These are truths that must be taught and practiced in our homes.

God lives. Jesus is the Christ. Through His Atonement, we will all have the opportunity of being resurrected. This is not just an individual blessing; it is much more than that. It is a blessing to each one of us and to our families. That we may be eternally grateful, that we can live in the presence of God the Eternal Father and His Son, Jesus Christ, that we may be together in the eternities to come, that we might understand the joy, and that we not only teach this doctrine but live true to it in our lives and in our families is my prayer in the name of Jesus Christ, amen.

Some Thoughts about the Priesthood

1. All Priesthood is Melchizedek, but there are **different portions** or **degrees** of it (Joseph Smith, *Teachings*, p. 180).

2. There are **three grand orders of priesthood** referred to here. 1st. The Melchizedek Priesthood. The 2nd Priesthood is **patriarchal authority. Go to and finish the temple, and God will fill it with power, and you will then receive more knowledge concerning this priesthood.** The 3rd is what is called the Levitical Priesthood [or Aaronic]. . . made without an oath; but the Priesthood of Melchizedex is by an oath and covenant (*ibid*, p. 322-23).

3. I do not care what office you hold in this Church—you may be an apostle, you may be a patriarch, a high priest, or anything else—you cannot receive the *fulness of the priesthood unless you go into the temple of the Lord and receive these ordinances of which the Prophet speaks. No man can get the fulness of the priesthood outside of the temple of the Lord.* . . . Do not think because somebody has a "higher" office in this Church than you have that you are barred from any blessings, because you can go into the temple and . . . have them sealed upon you as an elder in this Church, and then you have ALL that any man can get (JFS, *Doct. of Salv.* 3, pp. 131-133).

4. Now what was the **GOSPEL OF ABRAHAM** (restored by Elias)? It was the commission, the mission, the endowment and power, the message of salvation, given to Abraham. It was a divine promise that both in the world and out of the world his seed should continue "as innumerable as the stars; or, if ye were to count the sand upon the seashore ye could not number them." (D&C 132:30; Gen. 17; Abr. 2:1-12). Thus the gospel of Abraham restored by Elias] was one of Celestial marriage; it was a gospel or *commission to provide a lineage for the elect portion of the premortal spirits.* (*MD*, BRM, pp. 219-220).

5. Alma taught the great truth that **EVERY PERSON WHO HOLDS THE MELCHIZEDEK PRIESTHOOD WAS FOREORDAINED TO RECEIVE THAT HIGH AND HOLY ORDER IN THE PREMORTAL COUNCILS OF ETERNITY** (Alma 13:3-9). BRM, *MD*, p. 290.

6. The Lord has chosen a small number of choice spirits of [his] sons and daughters to inherit this earth, and **this company of choice spirits** have been kept in the spirit world for 6,000 years to come forth in the last days to stand in the flesh in this last Dispensation of the Fulness of Times, to **organize** the Kingdom of God upon the earth, to **build it up** and to **defend it** and to **receive the eternal and everlasting Priesthood** of God (Wilford Woodruff, quoted by Pres. Benson, *IE*, Aug. 1963:671).

7. Our young people are among the most blessed and favored of our Father's children. They are **the nobility of heaven, a choice and chosen generation** who have a divine destiny (think of our three-fold mission). Their spirits have been reserved to come forth in this day when the gospel is

on earth, and when the Lord needs **VALIANT SERVANTS** to carry on his great latter-day work. We have confidence in the young and rising generation in the Church and **PLEAD** with them *NOT TO FOLLOW THE FASHIONS AND CUSTOMS OF THE WORLD, NOT TO PARTAKE OF A SPIRIT OF REBELLION, NOT TO FORSAKE THE PATHS OF TRUTH AND VIRTUE* (JFS, *CR*, Apr. 1970:6).

8. (a couple) can enter an order of the priesthood named *the new and everlasting covenant of marriage* (see D&C 131:2), named also the *patriarchal order*, because of which order we can create for ourselves eternal family units of our own, patterned after the family of God our Heavenly Father (Bruce R. McConkie, *Ensign*, May, 1982:34).

9. Those who endure in perfect faith, who receive the Melchizedek Priesthood, and who gain the blessings of the temple (including celestial marriage) are eventually ordained *kings* and *priests*. These are offices given faithful holders of the Melchizedek Priesthood, and in them they will bear rule as exalted beings during the millennium and in eternity (*Mormon Doctrine*, p. 599).

10. If righteous men have power through the gospel and its crowning ordinance of celestial marriage to become kings and priests to rule in exaltation forever, it follows that the **women** by their side (without whom they cannot attain exaltation) will be queens and priestesses (Rev. 1:6; 5:10). Exaltation grows out of the eternal union of a man and his wife (*ibid*, p. 613).

11. We have great concern about the growing number of homes in the Church where the influence of a father is hardly felt. In more and more families the mother and children are left to carry out the father's duties as well as their own. Divorce, pursuit of wealth, and indifference to sacred things are only three of many reasons why fathers neglect the welfare of their families. *In this life a father is never released from his responsibility.* We call bishops, and they serve for a time and are released. Stake Presidents likewise are called, serve, and are released. But a father's calling *is an eternal calling if he lives worthily* (H. Burke Peterson, *Ensign*, Nov. 1977:87).

12. There is a warning: Despite that calling which is spoken of in the scriptures as "foreordination," we have another inspired declaration: "Behold, there are many called, but few are chosen . . ." (D&C 121:34). This suggests that even though we have our free agency here, there are many who were foreordained before the world was, to a greater state than *they have prepared themselves for here.* Even though they might have been among the noble and great from among whom the Father declared he would make his chosen leaders, they may fail of that calling here in mortality. Then the Lord poses this question: "And why are they not chosen?" (D&C 121:34). Two answers are given—first, "Because their hearts are set so much upon the things of this world . . ." And second, they "aspire to *the honors of men*" (D&C 121:35; Pres. Harold B. Lee, *CR*, Oct. 1973:7).

13. CAUTION: It is very important to understand that the three grand orders of priesthood are part of the Melchizedek Priesthood and First Presidency and Quorum of Twelve preside over all orders. **Many fundamentalists have confused this and assumed that the Patriarchal authority was higher or greater than that of the Melchizedek Priesthood. That is not so.** all three orders are appendages of the Melchizedek Priesthood.

What Our Temple Marriage Means to Us

Doug Brinley

1. We live gospel principles and keep our covenants with God and mutual promises to each other so that we will have the Spirit of the Lord with us to keep us soft and pliable. We know that obedience to true principles is the key to our happiness and success. We are committed to build an eternal kingdom with God as our partner.

2. We made a profound promise at marriage to work out problems that arise between us; we love and respect each other and will be Christ-like in our actions—patient, kind, charitable, loving, forgiving, understanding, etc. We treat each other in ways that build and strengthen each other so that we can attain to our tallest spiritual stature.

3. We have never been married before this life—this is our first-ever opportunity to create bodies for other spirit children; we know that our strengths **and** weaknesses will become more obvious after marriage, requiring patience, charity, and kindness on each other's part. We realize that dating was somewhat artificial—yet it proved that we can be Christ-like—and we realize that we must be patient with each other's background and family orientation which is undoubtedly different than ours. Neither of us came from the "true family."

4. We strengthen emotional bonds by sharing our inner feelings and ideas without put-downs and belittling one another. We pledge ourselves to learn all we can about each other's heart and feelings.

5. Our friendship allows us to communicate feelings and ideas about all aspects of our relationship. We know that we can improve in our communication, sensitivity, intimacy, love, appreciation, and improvements that can make our relationship better.

6. We know we have different perspectives on many things—that there is neither a "right" or "wrong" way to do most things. We counsel together and decide the "best" course of action and sustain our decisions.

7. We apologize freely when we offend, err, or misjudge. We pray together and for each other daily and express our gratitude to the Lord for our eternal sealing.

8. We will develop a healthy communication system to handle our differences so that each feels free to express his or her ideas without ridicule or rejection.

9. We live the law of chastity, conscious of each other's needs for love and affection. We will not use intimacy as a weapon to hurt or belittle each other.

10. We check in periodically to see how we are doing as partners—and willingly make any changes that will help us function more smoothly.

11. We parent our children together as partners, for we are both responsible for bringing them into the world. We understand that our children are the offspring of our Heavenly Parents, too and they are loan to us as a stewardship that has eternal implication.

12. It is easy to approach each other when we need help. We listen with attention and interest for we are eternal companions and there is much we need to share without fear of embarrassment or put-down.

13. We avoid sarcasm and criticism.

14. We are positive with each other—shaping and reinforcing the things we like so that the other knows what we like and how we like things to be done. We will be good teachers and humble students, for we know that there is much to learn from each other.

15. We know that our marriage can be no better than either of us is as a person. We will stay in shape physically, mentally, spiritually, emotionally, and be mutual therapists.

16. We know we model male and female roles for our children and we must not disappoint the Lord who has sent them to us to rear in his behalf. We know too, that their marriages will be greatly influenced by the kind of model we set for them.

17. We are tentative rather than dogmatic. After all, sometimes what seems to be a good idea may not turn out to be such, and we want to leave room for changing our minds.

18. We know that because Satan will never marry, he is determined to destroy our relationship. We avoid his temptations and deceptions to get us to break our covenants so that we can't be eternal companions. He wants each of us to be alone and separate as he is.

19. We have seen the damage that comes from divorce. The negative impact on children and on our society at large, is such that we want to contribute to the Lord's kingdom and set an example for others to follow. We will exercise our best efforts to keep our marriage strong and viable.

20. We will continue to date and court each other, never taking for granted our love and commitment. We will be pleasant, cheerful, and do all that we can to make of our home a Celestial unit of the Celestial Kingdom.

What I Hope You Will Teach Your Children about the Temple

President Ezra Taft Benson

Logan Temple Centennial, May 17, 1984

The last time I saw President Heber J. Grant was in the Church Administration Building when he was quite aged. President Grant's chauffeur had driven him to the Church Administration Building where the chauffeur called for another brother to help him assist President Grant, one on each arm, to his office.

I was just entering the glass door opposite the Lion House in the Church Administration Building as President Grant was coming toward the door. He said to the two brethren assisting him, "Isn't that Brother Benson coming?"

They replied, "Yes."

He said, "Come here. Come here, Brother Benson."

I walked over to him, and President Grant said, "Did I ever tell you about the mean trick Brigham Young played on your great-grandfather?"

I said, "No, President. I didn't know Brigham Young ever played a mean trick on anyone."

He responded, " Oh, yes, he did. I'll tell you about it."

I could see that these two brethren were practically holding President Grant up, so I said, "I'll come to the house some time. I'd like to hear it. "

He replied, "No, I'll tell you right here. These brethren can steady me while I tell you."

He said, "You know where Zion's Bank and ZCMI are over on the corner?"

I said, "Yes."

He continued, "Your great-grandfather built the finest home in Salt Lake City on that corner, with the exception of Brigham Young's home (which, of course, was the Lion House). He had it all finished. It was a beautiful home—two stories with a porch at both levels on both sides of the house. It had a white picket fence around it with fruit trees and ornamental trees and with a little stream running through the yard. He was all ready to move his families in from their log cabins when President Young called him into the office one day. 'Brother Benson,' he said, 'we would like you to go to Cache Valley and pioneer that area and preside over the Saints. We suggest you sell your home to Daniel H. Wells.'

"Now," President Grant said, "Daniel H. Wells was Brigham Young's counselor. Wasn't that a mean trick? Come on, brethren, let's go."

In all the years that I had attended the Benson reunions I had never heard that story. So I had it verified by the Church Historical Department, and they assured me that the facts were as President Grant related them. They told me they had a tintype picture of the old home.

Since that time, I have been most grateful for the so-called "mean trick" of President Young, because were it not for that, the Bensons would not have their roots in Cache Valley.

I love Cache Valley, and I love the Saints in the area. And I am most grateful to be here on this anniversary of the Logan Temple centennial. This beautiful temple has truly been a beacon of light to Cache Valley. If our children and their children are taught well, this edifice will continue to be a symbol of special significance.

The temple is an ever-present reminder that God intends the family to be eternal. How fitting it is for mothers and fathers to point to the temple and say to their children, "That is the place where we were married for eternity." By so doing, the ideal of temple marriage can be instilled within the minds and hearts of your children while they are very young.

I am grateful to the Lord that my temple memories extend back—even to young boyhood. I remember so well, as a little boy, coming in from the field and approaching the old farm house in Whitney, Idaho. I could hear my mother singing "Have I Done Any Good in the World Today?" (Hymns, no. 58)

I can still see her in my mind's eye bending over the ironing board with newspapers on the floor, ironing long strips of white cloth, with beads of perspiration on her forehead. When I asked her what she was doing, she said, "These are temple robes, my son. Your father and I are going to the temple at Logan."

Then she put the old flatiron on the stove, drew a chair close to mine, and told me about temple work— how important it is to be able to go to the temple and participate in the sacred ordinances performed there. She also expressed her fervent hope that some day her children and grandchildren and great grandchildren would have the opportunity to enjoy these priceless blessings.

These sweet memories about the spirit of temple work were a blessing in our farm home, our little rural ward of three hundred, and the old Oneida Stake. These memories have returned as I have performed the marriage of each of our children and grandchildren, my mother's grandchildren and great-grandchildren, under the influence of the Spirit in the House of the Lord.

These are choice memories to me, and I have often reflected on them. In the peace of these lovely temples, sometimes we find solutions to the serious problems of life. Under the influence of the Spirit, sometimes pure knowledge flows to us there. Temples are places of personal revelation. When I have been weighed down by a problem or a difficulty, I have gone to the House of the Lord with a prayer in my heart for answers. These answers have come in clear and unmistakable ways.

I would like to direct my remarks to you parents and grandparents. I would like to share with you what I would hope you would teach your children about the temple.

The temple is a sacred place, and the ordinances in the temple are of a sacred character. Because of its sacredness we are sometimes reluctant to say anything about the temple to our children and grandchildren.

As a consequence, many do not develop a real desire to go to the temple, or when they go there, they do so without much background to prepare them for the obligations and covenants they enter into.

I believe a proper understanding or background will immeasurably help prepare our youth for the temple. This understanding, I believe, will foster within them a desire to seek their priesthood blessings just as Abraham sought his.

When our Heavenly Father placed Adam and Eve on this earth, He did so with the purpose in mind of teaching them how to regain His presence. Our Father promised a Savior to redeem them from their fallen condition. He gave to them the plan of salvation and told them to teach their children faith in Jesus Christ and repentance. Further, Adam and his posterity were commanded by God to be baptized, to receive the Holy Ghost, and to enter into the order of the Son of God.

To enter into the order of the Son of God is the equivalent today of entering into the fullness of the Melchizedek Priesthood, which is only received in the House of the Lord.

Because Adam and Eve had complied with these requirements, God said to them, "Thou art after the order of him who was without beginning of days or end of years, from all eternity to all eternity (Moses 6:67).

Three years before Adam's death, a great event occurred. He took his son Seth, his grandson Enos, and other high priests who were his direct-line descendants, with others of his righteous posterity, into a valley called Adam-ondi-Ahman. There Adam gave to these righteous descendants his last blessing.

The Lord then appeared to them.

The vast congregation rose up and blessed Adam and called him Michael, the prince and archangel. The Lord himself declared Adam to be a prince forever over his own posterity.

Then Adam in his aged condition rose up and, being filled with the spirit of prophecy, predicted "whatsoever should befall his posterity unto the latest generation." All this is recorded in section 107 of the Doctrine and Covenants (verses 53-56).

The Prophet Joseph Smith said that Adam blessed his posterity because "he wanted to bring them into the presence of God (*Teachings of the Prophet Joseph Smith,* sel. Joseph Fielding Smith, Salt Lake City: Deseret Book Co., 1938, p. 159).

Here is an illuminating passage from Section 107 of the Doctrine and Covenants which tells us how Adam was able to bring himself and his righteous posterity into God's presence:

> The order of this priesthood was confirmed to be handed down from father to son, and rightly belongs to the literal descendants of the chosen seed, to whom the promises were made.
>
> This order was instituted in the days of Adam, and came down by lineage in [order] . . . that his posterity should be the *chosen of the Lord,* and that *they should be preserved unto the end of the earth* (D&C 107:4042; italics added).

How did Adam bring his descendants into the presence of the Lord?

The answer: Adam and his descendants entered into the priesthood order of God. Today we would say they went to the House of the Lord and received their blessings.

The order of priesthood spoken of in the scriptures is sometimes referred to as the patriarchal order because it came down from father to son.

But this order is otherwise described in modern revelation as an order of family government where a man and woman enter into a covenant with God—just as did Adam and Eve—to be sealed for eternity, to have posterity, and to do the will and work of God throughout their mortality.

If a couple are true to their covenants, they are entitled to the blessing of the highest degree of the celestial kingdom. These covenants today can only be entered into by going to the House of the Lord.

Adam followed this order and brought his posterity into the presence of God. He is the great example for us to follow.

Enoch followed this pattern and brought the Saints of his day into the presence of God.

Noah and his son Shem likewise followed the same pattern after the flood.

Abraham, a righteous servant of God, desiring as he said, "to be a greater follower of righteousness," sought for these same blessings. Speaking of the order of the priesthood, he said: "It was conferred upon me from the fathers; it came down from the fathers, from the beginning of time. . . even the right of the firstborn, or the first man, who is Adam, our first father, through the fathers unto me" (Abr. 1:2-3).

So Abraham declared: "I sought for mine appointment unto the Priesthood according to the appointment of God unto the fathers" (Abr. 1:4).

Moses taught this order of priesthood to his people and "sought diligently to sanctify his people that they might behold the face of God;

"But they hardened their hearts and could not endure his presence; therefore, the Lord in his wrath, for his anger was kindled against them, swore that they should not enter into his rest while in the wilderness, which rest is the fulness of his glory.

"Therefore, he took Moses out of their midst, and the Holy Priesthood also" (D&C 84:23-25).

We learn through the Joseph Smith Translation that the Lord further instructed Moses: "I will take away the priesthood out of their midst; *therefore my holy order,* and ordinances thereof" (JST Ex. 34: 1; italics added).

This higher priesthood, with its attendant ordinances, was taken from Israel till the time of Jesus Christ.

My purpose in citing this background is to illustrate that this order of priesthood has been on the earth since the beginning, and it is the only means by which we can one day see the face of God and live (See D&C 84:22).

Between Moses and Christ only certain prophets possessed the right to the higher priesthood and the blessings that could bring men into the presence of God. One of these prophets was Elijah.

Elijah held the keys of the sealing power and did many mighty miracles in his day. He had power to seal the heavens, raise the dead, relieve the drought-stricken land, and call down fire from heaven.

He was the last prophet to hold the keys of the priesthood, according to the Prophet Joseph Smith. He was subsequently translated and taken up into heaven without tasting death.

He, as a translated being, restored the keys of this priesthood to the Savior's chief Apostles—Peter, James, and John—on the Mount of Transfiguration. But within a generation, the Church was destroyed by a major apostasy, and the blessings of the priesthood were removed from the earth.

It took a new dispensation from heaven to restore this blessing to our day.

It is significant that the first revelation given in 1823, recorded as section 2 of the Doctrine and Covenants, gave this promise about the priesthood:

> Behold, I will reveal unto you the Priesthood, by the hand of Elijah the prophet,
> before the coming of the great and dreadful day of the Lord.
> And he shall plant in the hearts of the children the promises made to the fathers,
> and the hearts of the children shall turn to their fathers.
> If it were not so, the whole earth would be utterly wasted at his coming (D&C 2:13).

What priesthood was Elijah to reveal? John the Baptist restored the keys to the Aaronic Priesthood. Peter, James, and John restored the keys of the kingdom of God. Why send Elijah?

"Because he holds the keys of the authority to administer in *all the ordinances* of the priesthood, or the sealing power (*Teachings,* p. 172; italics added). So said the Prophet Joseph Smith!

The Prophet Joseph said further that these keys were "the revelations, ordinances, oracle, powers and endowments of the fulness *of the Melchizedek Priesthood* and of the kingdom of God on the earth (*Teachings,* p. 337; italics added).

Even though the Aaronic Priesthood and Melchizedek Priesthood had been restored to the earth, the Lord urged the Saints to build a temple to receive the keys by which this order of priesthood could be administered on the earth again, "for there [was] not a place found on earth that he may come to and restore again that which was lost . . . even *the fulness of the priesthood"* (D&C 124:28; italics added).

Again the Prophet Joseph said: "If a man gets a fullness of the priesthood of God he has to get it in the same way that Jesus Christ obtained it, and that was by keeping all the commandments and obeying all the ordinances of the house of the Lord" (*Teachings,* p. 308).

So the Kirtland Temple was completed at great sacrifice to the Saints.

Then, on 3 April 1836, the Lord Jesus Christ and three other heavenly beings appeared in this holy edifice. One of these heavenly messengers was Elijah, to whom the Lord said he had "committed the keys of the power of turning the hearts of the fathers to the children, and the hearts of the children to the fathers, that the whole earth may not be smitten with a curse" (D&C 27:9).

Elijah brought the keys of sealing powers—that power which *seals* their posterity to them endlessly, that which *seals* their forefathers to them all the way back to Adam. This is the power and order that Elijah revealed—that *same order* of priesthood which God gave to Adam and to all the ancient patriarchs which followed after him.

And this is why the Lord said to the Prophet Joseph Smith, "For verily I say unto you, the keys of the dispensation, which ye have received, have come down from the fathers, and last of all, being sent down from heaven unto you" (D&C 112:32).

In a later revelation the Lord explained:

> In the celestial glory there are three heavens or degrees;
> And in order to obtain the highest, a man must enter into *this order of the priesthood* [meaning the new and everlasting covenant of marriage];
> And if he does not, he cannot obtain it. He may enter into the other, but that is the end of his kingdom; he cannot have an increase (D&C 131:1-4; italics added).

When our children obey the Lord and go to the temple to receive their blessings and enter into the marriage covenant, they enter into the same *order of the priesthood* that God instituted in the very beginning with father Adam.

This order entitles them to the same blessings of Abraham, of whom the Lord said that he "hath entered into his exaltation and sitteth upon his throne" (D&C 132:29).

Then He significantly added: "This promise is yours also, because ye are of Abraham" (D&C 132:31).

So again I emphasize: This order of priesthood can only be entered into when we comply with all the commandments of God and seek the blessings of the fathers as did Abraham by going to our Father's house. They are received in no other place on this earth!

I hope you would teach this truth about the temple to your children and your grandchildren. Go to the temple—our Father's house—to receive the blessings of your fathers that you may be entitled to the highest blessings of the priesthood. "For without this no man can see the face of God, even the Father, and live" (D&C 84:22).

Our Father's house is a house of order. We go to *His* house to enter into that order of priesthood which will entitle us to all that the Father hath, if we are faithful. For as the Lord has revealed in modem times, Abraham's seed are "lawful heirs" to the priesthood (See D&C 86:8-11).

Now let me say something else to all who can worthily go to the House of the Lord. When you attend the temple and perform the ordinances that pertain to the House of the Lord, certain blessings will come to you:

- You will receive the spirit of Elijah, which will turn your hearts to your spouse, to your children, and to your forebears.

- You will love your family with a deeper love than you have loved before.

- Your hearts will be turned to your fathers and theirs to you.

- You will be endowed with power from on high as the Lord has promised.

- You will receive the key of the knowledge of God (See D&C 84:19). You will learn how you can be like Him. Even the power of godliness will be manifest to you (See D&C 84:20).

- You will be doing a great service to those who have passed to the other side of the veil in order that they might be "judged according to men in the flesh, but live according to God in the spirit" (D&C 138:34).

Such are the blessings of the temple and the blessings of frequently attending the temple.

So I say at this centennial commemoration of the Logan Temple: God bless Israel! God bless those of our forebears who constructed this holy edifice. God bless us to teach our children and our grandchildren what great blessings await them by going to the temple. God bless us to receive all the blessings revealed *by Elijah the prophet* so that our callings and election will be made sure.

I testify with all my soul to the truth of this message and pray that the God of Abraham, Isaac, and Jacob will bless modern Israel with the compelling desire to seek all the blessings of the fathers in the House of our Heavenly Father.

Temple Blessings and Applications

Carlos E. Asay, BYU Religion Faculty

March 6, 1998

When **Sister Asay and I** were called to serve in the Salt Lake Temple, President Gordon B. Hinckley instructed us to become advocates of temple activity and commanded us to speak about temple matters "at all times in all things, and in all places that (we) may be in . . . " (Mosiah 18:9).

We have been true to that charge, even though some have accused us of becoming overly-zealous in our work. Such accusations do not bother us. We would rather be true to a prophet's commission than to be acceptable to those who become tinged with guilt whenever the House of the Lord is mentioned.

Elder Dallin H. Oaks tells of a time when he attended a high priest group meeting without prior appointment or announcement. A rather surprised group leader greeted him at the door by saying, "Welcome, dear brother, our group is like all other groups of high priests in the Church. We would rather hear something interesting than something that is true. "

Unfortunately, there are some who call themselves saints that regard temple related subjects as dull and reserved only for the nearly-dead. Like the "spotted" high priest who greeted Elder Oaks, they want their ears tickled by news of BYU's improved athletic program or a discussion of some other wafer-thick, fringe-related gospel subject. They just don't feel comfortable discussing the weightier matters of the law and the place where "covenants, contracts, bonds, obligations, oaths, vows, performances, connections, associations, or expectations "become very meaningful (D&C 132:7).

Perhaps some of this shyness away from temples and the things that are really true is associated with ignorance or feelings of personal unworthiness. Perhaps some of this shyness is related to the way concepts of salvation and exaltation have been taught by parents, teachers, and church leaders. Perhaps some of this shyness is related to the fact that many church members only dip their toes in temple "waters" and never become deeply immersed in the work. And, perhaps this aversion to temples can be traced to a lack of understanding of personal applications and blessings. After all, we are human and most of us want to know, "What's in it for me?" Only a few have the faith of Father Adam and are able to make their temple offering by saying simply, I know not, save the Lord commanded me" (Moses 5:6).

I do, therefore, draw your attention to some of the blessings and personal applications of the temple. These blessings and personal applications will seem rather obvious to most, if not all, of you. However, I seriously question whether most of your students have pondered some of the "what's in it for me" thoughts that I desire to share. The list I have in mind is not complete—more could be added. Yet, my list of *six* blessings/applications is a beginning worthy of serious consideration.

The Blessings of an Examined Life

Only certified members are permitted to enter the House of the Lord. Such certification comes through searching interviews with priesthood leaders on an annual basis and the issuance of temple recommends.

This process provides us an opportunity to examine ourselves, whether we be in the faith, and to prove ourselves (see 2 Cor. 13:5). It involves a review of our lives with ordained servants of the Lord who can help us correct anything that is amiss.

President Boyd K. Packer writes:

> The interview for a temple recommend is conducted privately between the bishop and the Church member concerned. Here the member is asked searching questions about his personal conduct and worthiness and about his loyalty to the Church and its officers. The person must certify that he is morally clean and is keeping the Word of Wisdom, paying a full tithing, living in harmony with the teachings of the Church, and not maintaining any affiliation or sympathy with apostate groups (*The Holy Temple,* p. 53).

A few years ago, one member of our extended family made an appointment with her bishop for a temple recommend interview. On the appointed date she went to the bishop's office with high expectations of receiving encouragement and spiritual advice from her priesthood leader. Instead, the bishop met her at the door, handed her a signed recommend, and told her to obtain a second signature from a member of the stake presidency.

She left the bishop's office feeling that she had been short-changed or even cheated. He failed to ask her a single question; he said little or nothing about the temple; and, he missed a golden opportunity to teach someone who came ready and willing to learn.

Later, she went to the stake center where she was interviewed by a conscientious member of the stake presidency. The man invited her to sit down. He took the time to get acquainted. He asked all of the required questions and emphasized the importance of worshipping in the House of the Lord on a frequent basis. At the close of the conversation, he looked earnestly into the eyes of Aunt Karen and asked, "How many years has it been since you obtained your first temple recommend?"

Aunt Karen reflected a moment answered, "Almost twenty-five years."

Pausing briefly and allowing Aunt Karen to mull over her response, the stake president continued, "Are you twenty-five times better today than you were then?"

This thought-provoking inquiry caused Aunt Karen to do some serious soul-searching. She could not dismiss from her mind the words of her concerned priesthood leader. Over and over again she wondered, am I progressing in my life as I should be progressing? Do I serve in my Church-calling with a singleness of purpose? Am I walking so as to keep myself blameless before God (Alma 5:27).

I believe it was Socrates who said, "An unexamined life is not worth living." How blessed we are to belong to a church with temples and a program requiring annual examinations of our lives!

The Blessings of Participating in Perfect Pedagogy

Recently, I attended a stake conference on the University of Utah campus. The speaker who preceded me at the pulpit stated that the BYU was the Lord's University. Then, remembering where he was and realizing that he might be tarred and feathered if he didn't cushion his words, meekly added, "and so is the University of Utah."

I stood and corrected the speaker, saying that I respected both the BYU and U of U but that neither institution was the Lord's University. I stated that the Lord's University was the holy temple.

The final speaker, President Gordon B. Hinckley, acknowledged the differences of opinion shared by the other speakers and said, "Let me put the matter to rest—as President Asay has said, "The Temple is the Lord's University!"

Yes, the temple is the Lord's University. The campus is the sparkling building and its beautiful grounds; the professors are the ordinance workers and the Holy Spirit; the curriculum is the gospel of Jesus Christ; and the instructional approach involves cognitive, affective, and motor or skill learning.

Perfect teaching, like pure religion, involves knowing, feeling, and doing. It appeals to all of one's senses and results in an acquisition of knowledge, a stimulation of throbs in the heart, and actual participation in meaningful activities.

Elder John A. Widtsoe wrote:

> The wonderful pedagogy of the temple service, especially appealing to me as a professional teacher, carries with it evidence of the truth of temple work. We go to the temple to be informed and directed to be built up to be blessed. How is all this accomplished? *First* by the spoken word, through the lectures and conversation, just as we do in the class room, except with more elaborate care, *then* by the appeal to the eye by representations by living, moving beings; and by pictorial representations [and, we would now add, filmed presentations] in the wonderfully decorated rooms. . . . Meanwhile the recipients themselves, the candidates for blessings, engage actively in the temple service. . . . Altogether our temple worship follows a most excellent pedagogical system. I wish instruction were given so well in every school room throughout the land, for we would then teach with more effect than we now do. For these reasons, among many others, I've always felt that temple work is a direct evidence of the truth of the work reestablished by the Prophet Joseph Smith. It may be that the temple endowment and the other temple ordinances form the strongest available evidence of the divine inspiration of the Prophet Joseph Smith (*Temple Worship*, p. 59).

As the Apostle Paul taught in the temple: "all things (are) done unto edifying" (I Cor 14:26).

My task, your task, and the task of all who have tasted the living waters flowing from temple wells is to invite others to matriculate in the Lord's University and to benefit from perfect pedagogy.

The Blessings of being Perfected in an Understanding of our Ministries

In section 97 of the Doctrine and Covenants, reference is made to the temple as *"a place of thanksgiving for all saints"* and as *"a place of instruction for all those who are called to the work of the ministry in all their several callings and offices; that they may be perfected in the understanding of their ministry, in theory, in principle, and in doctrine, and in all things pertaining to the Kingdom of God on the earth* (D&C 97: 13-14).

When I was called to serve as a bishop nearly forty years ago, my stake president, James E. Faust, instructed me to read the handbooks, to pray about the calling, and to attend the temple where I might brood over my new responsibilities. He knew that I needed the instruction, spirit, comfort, and influence of the House of the Lord.

Members of the church, particularly young people, need to understand why missionaries are endowed before they begin their service. Experience has shown that endowed missionaries are much more dedicated and serve more effectively than those unendowed. This knowledge caused the Brethren to fly missionaries thousands of miles at great expense to receive their endowments when there were few temples in the world. Now that temples are more accessible to the saints, virtually all missionaries visit a temple and receive their endowments before entering a training center.

Each missionary should begin his mission with this prayer inscribed in his mind and written in his heart:

> And we ask thee, Holy Father, that thy servants may go forth from this house armed with thy power, and that thy name may be upon them, and thy glory be round about them, and thine angels have charge over them; And from this place they may bear exceedingly great and glorious tidings, in truth, unto the ends of the earth, that they may know that this is thy work, and that thou hast put forth thy hand, to fulfil that

which thou hast spoken by the mouths of the prophets, concerning the last days (D&C: 109:22-23)

I'm convinced that the work of the church would be accelerated —in both stride and pace—if church leaders encouraged members upon receipt of a calling to go to the temple to seek an understanding of their ministries.

The Blessings of the Holy Endowment

After nearly sixty years of temple going, President David O. McKay is reported to have said, "Now I *am beginning to understand the endowment.*" If it took that spiritual giant three score of years to understand the endowment, it will take us more than a visit or two to the temple to plumb the depths of this godly mystery.

The Holy Endowment has been defined in various ways. Joseph Smith said, *"You need an endowment . . . in order that you may be prepared and able to overcome all things"* (*History of the Church* 2:309).

Brigham Young's oft-quoted description reads:

> Your endowment is, to receive all those ordinances, in the House of the Lord, which are necessary for you, after you have departed this life, to enable you to walk back into the presence of the Father, passing the angels who stand as sentinels, being enabled to give them the key words, the signs and tokens, pertaining to the holy Priesthood, and gain your eternal exaltation in spite of earth and hell (*Journal of Discourses* 2:31).

James E. Talmage referred to the endowment as administered in modern temples as a *"course of instruction"*—a course which *"comprises instruction relating to the significance and sequence of past dispensations, and the importance of the present as the greatest and grandest era in human history"* (*The House of the Lord,* pp. 99-100).

"There are few, even temple workers," said David O. McKay, *"who comprehend the full meaning and power of the temple endowment."* He continued, *"Seen for what it is, it is the step-by-step ascent into the Eternal Presence"* (*Temple of the Ancient World,* p. 58). This step-by-step ascent is symbolized in the Salt Lake Temple as you proceed from room to room.

Boyd K. Packer wrote:

> To endow is to enrich, to give to another something long lasting and of much worth. The temple endowment ordinances enrich in three ways: (a) The one receiving the ordinance is given power from God. "Recipients are endowed with power from on high." (b) A recipient is also endowed with information and knowledge. "They receive an education relative to the Lord's purposes and plans" (*Mormon Doctrine* p. 277) (c) When sealed at the altar a person is the recipient of glorious blessings, powers, and honors as part of his endowment (*The Holy Temple* p. 153).

All of the above definitions of the holy endowment are correct. Each provides an insight worthy of our serious consideration. The endowment is a preparatory process, a course of instruction, a step-by-step ascent Godward, and an enriching gift of power, knowledge, and glorious blessings.

However, in addition to all that has been said, I regard the ordinances of the endowment as an **exchange of love** between God, Our Father, and us. We know that *"God so loved the world, that he gave his only begotten Son, that whosoever believeth in him should not perish, but have everlasting life"* (John 3:16). We also know that the Only Begotten Son, even Jesus the Christ, *"so loved the world that he gave his own life, that as many as would believe might become the sons of God "* (D & C:34:3). Thus, every commandment, every ordinance, every covenant, every law, every *"thou shalt,"* every *"thou shalt not,"* and every teaching received from Our Father in Heaven and His Son, Our Savior—especially those received in the House of the Lord—is an expression of divine love

In the process of receiving the outpourings of love from Deity in the temple, we are invited to covenant that we will obey the laws, keep the commandments and live as we have been taught. Consequently, every covenant or promise we make with God is an expression of our love to him in return. Did not Jesus say, *"If ye love me, keep my commandments?"* (John 14:15). He might well have said, *"If ye love me covenant to keep my word for 'verily is the love of God perfected'"* (I John 2:5).

Yes, the endowment is an exchange of love—divine love. God loves us so he provides us words to live by. We love Him and His Son in return so we enter into covenants and go forward with promises to keep. If we are true to commitments made and the love professed, we draw claim upon blessings that assure us happiness in this life and the prospects of exaltation in the life to come.

The Blessing of Walking on the Bridge that Spans Heaven and Earth

Thornton Wilder said, *"There is a land of the living and the land of the dead, and the bridge is love."* President Gordon B. Hinckley adds, *"The temple is a bridge between heaven and earth."* So merging Wilder's and Hinckley's thoughts, we conclude: that the labor of love performed in the temple in behalf of both the living and the dead connects or bridges the two worlds—the worlds of the seen and unseen.

After all, the ordinances performed in the temple are for time and all eternity. They are also performed in the presence of God, angels, and mortal witnesses. Thus, it stands to reason, that people on both sides of the veil—a very thin veil—are invested in the work performed in the house of the Lord. As Dr. Hugh Nibley has stated: *"The main function of the temple is to supply a binding link between the worlds. Without that, it is nothing but a civic social center or a senior citizens' club"* (*Temples of the Ancient World*, p. 32).

A modern revelation includes these significant words, *"It is sufficient to know, in this case, that the earth will be smitten with a curse unless there is a welding link of some kind or other between the fathers and the children"* (*D&C.128:18*). The specific welding link referred to in this instance was baptism for the dead. However, there are other welding links between the generations, such as family histories, biographies, and all the ordinances of the temple. Unless we walk the temple bridge and do all within our power to bind ourselves to our fathers, our very perfection and salvation will be placed in jeopardy (see D&C 128:15)

We *"were set to be a light unto the world, and to be the saviors of men; and inasmuch as (we) are not the saviors of men, (we) are as salt that has lost its savor, and is thenceforth good for nothing but to be cast out and trodden under foot of men"* (D&C: 103:9-10). We maintain our **"savor"** best by keeping ourselves unspotted or unpolluted by the sins of the world. And, we become saviors of men by going to the temple and doing for others what they cannot do for themselves. King Benjamin asked, *"For how knoweth a man the master whom he has not served, and who is a stranger unto him, and is far from the thoughts and intents of his heart?"* (Mosiah 5:13). No one can really know and feel close to the Savior without becoming involved in saving services for others! No one can really save himself and others without participating in the exalting ordinance work performed in the House of the Lord or on the bridge that spans heaven and earth (See I Tim. 4:16)

A few weeks ago, a couple dressed in grubby clothes with three disheveled children tagging behind approached one of our recommend desk attendants and said, "We have been on a tour of Temple Square and we have learned that families may be sealed for time and all eternity in this place. We want to be sealed and become a forever family." When told that only worthy members of the church were permitted to enter the temple, the man became belligerent and created quite a scene. He demanded the right to claim his family blessings. In the end, security men were called to restrain the man and escort him outside.

It seems to me that there are many who hope for something beyond the grave, especially when they have loved ones whose association is held dear. Something inside of all men seems to yearn for a continuance of family relationships and a sociality of a never ending nature. All hope for that bridge between the two worlds—a bridge that many among us take for granted.

The Blessing of Taking Away From the Temple Precious Teachings, Feelings, and Resolves

One of our granddaughters, twelve years of age, asked my wife, "What does it mean to take out your endowment? Is that like taking out your appendix?"

Some wonder about the appropriateness of using the expression, "take out your endowment." Surely we don't want our little ones to think that we go to the temple to undergo some medical procedure. Nor do we want them to grow up thinking that something bizarre occurs within those high, grey walls. However, if you ponder carefully the expression and relate it to the stated purposes of the temple, it not only makes sense but provokes some edifying thoughts about worship and services rendered in the House of the Lord.

We go to the temple to receive sacred truths and to participate in saving, even exalting ordinances. But, if we do not take out or take away with us certain feelings, resolves, and desires related to those truths and ordinances, why receive them in the first place? Moreover, if we receive instructions and make covenants in the presence of heavenly beings and mortal witnesses, what happens to us when we fail to live according to promises made?

To receive and not take out or carry away with us the offerings of the temple not only results in a forfeiture of promised blessings but mocks God in the process.

More than Wet Hair!

Many of our youth and some adults come to the temple and perform baptisms for the dead. They participate in that cleansing ordinance which constitutes the gateway into the Kingdom of God (see 1 Nephi 31:17). Over and over again, they are immersed in the water as a short, yet very significant, ordinance is voiced.

The issue is: What happens to the proxies in the process of performing baptisms for the dead? Do they learn something and enjoy a personal spiritual experience? Or, do they just go away with wet hair?

I would hope that young and old alike who enter the baptistry would perform their services in good faith and go away—

- Realizing that sacred things must be guarded and that no one should be baptized unworthily (Mormon 9:29).

- Knowing that baptism is a rebirth and the gateway into the Kingdom of God (2 Nephi 31:17-20).

- Understanding the specific commitments related to baptism (Mosiah 18: 8-10).

- Believing that being born of the Spirit is essential and must follow the immersion in water (John 3:5).

- Understanding why Christ was baptized and why we must follow His example (2 Nephi 31:1-21).

These and other "take away" thoughts and feelings should be the reward of those who serve in the baptistry.

More than Beautiful Language!

All of the temple goers who have not previously been endowed and many others participate in initiatory ordinances, sometimes referred to as the washings and anointings. Such ordinances are administered in preparation of entering into the House of the Lord and the receipt of the Holy endowment.

But, the issue is: What happens to the participants in the process of this cleansing and blessing? Do they learn something in the process and enjoy a personal spiritual experience? Or, do they just go away having heard some beautiful language?

I would hope that those who receive the initiatory ordinances would go away—

- Having learned that no unclean thing or person should be allowed to enter the House of the Lord and receive sacred blessings (D&C 97:15-17; 94:9; 109:20; 110:8).

- Having understood that the body and spirit constitute the soul of man and that both body and spirit should be properly nourished and cared for (D&C 88:15; D&C 89).

- Having learned that the Spirit or spark of divinity within all of us should be allowed to call the cadence of our lives. Someone has written:

> How can a man have too much religion? . . . It is the one thing that availeth. A man is but a beast as he lives from day to day, eating and drinking, breathing and sleeping. It is only when he raises himself and concerns himself with the immortal spirit within him, that he becomes in very truth a man . . . how sad a thing it would be that the blood of the Redeemer should be spilled to no purpose (A. Conan Doyle, ''The White Company,'' . . . p. 181).

- Having remembered the promise that we will be made strong to meet the challenges of life and all other promises given.

Unless these and other truths are taken away with us we experience something akin to the dream of a night vision wherein a hungry man dreams that he eats but upon awakening finds his soul empty (see 2 Nephi 27:3).

More than an Unusual Dramatization!

Those who come to the temple and receive the endowment are exposed to "wonderful pedagogy." In the Salt Lake Temple, this instruction is not given by "slick professionals," nor is it a light entertaining presentation. But rather, it is a precious gift extended to us by a loving Father in Heaven.

The issue is: What happens to the patrons involved? Is the experience more than a time consuming process? Is it more than an unusual dramatization?

I would hope that those who come into the sacred precincts of the temple would have a spiritual experience and go away—

- Understanding that the endowment is an endowment of knowledge, spiritual power, and high resolve. Those who receive the endowment should "go forth . . . armed with (God's) power, and (with his) name . . . upon them, and (his) glory . . . round about them, and . . . angels (loving) charge over them" (D&C 109:22).

- Understanding that the endowment is a step-by-step ascent Godward, as President McKay has taught, providing we allow it to direct the course of our lives.

- Understanding that the endowment is an exchange of love. God gives us laws, commandments and teachings because he loves us. We covenant with him to obey divine laws in return because we love him (see John 14:15; John 5:3).

- Understanding that the endowment centers upon *teachings, covenants,* and *blessings;* and that it is surrounded by symbolism so that truth is revealed to the believers "line upon line, precept upon precept, here a little and there a little" (2 Nephi 28:30).

- Understanding that the endowment, if received in good faith and observed throughout our lives, will bring us happiness in this life and the prospects of eternal life hereafter.

In summary, I would hope that those who receive their endowments would go away with these words of the prophets ringing in their ears:

> There are few, even temple workers, who comprehend the full meaning and power of the temple endowment. Seen for what it is, it is the step-by-step ascent into the Eternal Presence . . . If our young people could but glimpse it, it would be the most powerful spiritual motivation of their lives (David O. McKay, as quoted in *Temples in the Ancient World,* p. 58).

> If you understood the ordinances of the house of the Lord, you would crawl on your hands and (knees) for thousands of miles in order to receive them (Spencer W. Kimball, as quoted in *Temples in the Ancient World,* p. 59).

More than Confessions of Love!

The individual or personal blessings of the temple are associated with baptism, initiatory ordinances, and the endowment. However, the family blessings of the temple are linked to the sealings of husbands and wives and children to parents. These sealings are referred to as the crowning blessings of the temple.

Yet, the issue is: What happens to those who kneel at the altars and exchange vows? Do they understand that they have participated in a solemn sacrament, made commitments of an eternal nature, and done something of great significance in the eyes of God? Or, do they go away with only the confessions of love ringing in their ears?

I would hope and pray that those who are married for time and eternity and those who participate in sealings would go away—

- Realizing that the new and everlasting covenant of marriage is requisite in obtaining the highest heaven or degree in the celestial glory (D&C 131: 1-3).

- Realizing that one who participates in celestial marriage must abide the conditions of that law in order to receive the promised blessings (D&C 132: 5-7). Those who are married in a celestial way should live celestially.

- Realizing that celestial marriage is really a triangular affair involving a man, a woman, and God. Therefore, the marriage partners are expect to live righteously and serve wilfully so that the Holy Spirit of Promise may abide with them.

- Realizing that those who are married and sealed together for eternity are expected to reverence one another and become sanctifying influences to one another. As the poet said: *"Me lift thee; and thee lift me; and we will both ascend together."*

- Realizing that the ultimate test of love is sacrifice. Thus, selfishness must be pushed aside and replaced by a love that is more willing to give than to receive.

How wonderful it would be if forever families were forever keeping the commandments and seeking to create a heaven on earth. Many times I have stated: No one should have to ask you "have you been married in the temple?" Your celestial covenant should be made obvious by the way you treat each other and by the Spirit that dwells in your home.

In addition to all the "take away" items mentioned relating to baptisms, initiatory ordinance, endowments, and sealings, there are some feelings and understandings of a general nature that should be mentioned. I refer to—

- The understanding that all things in the temple should be done unto edifying and done decently and in order (I Cor. 14:25, 40).

- The feeling that the temple is a place of holiness (D&C 109: 12-13).

- The feeling that the temple is a place of joy and beauty for those who seek to be Saviors on Mt. Zion (Obad. 1:27; D&C 128: 15-18).

- The understanding that the temple is a place to be revisited again and again.

President Boyd K. Packer has written: "What we gain from the temple will depend to a large degree on what we take to the temple in the way of humility and reverence and a desire to learn" (*The Holy Temple*, p. 42).

I would add: what we gain from the temple will depend to a large degree on what we resolve to take away with us when we leave its sanitary environment and go back into the world.

Perhaps it is unreasonable to expect temple patrons to take away from the temple all that I have mentioned in this paper. It certainly cannot be mastered and internalized in a visit or two. However, if we prepare ourselves and others to enter the Lord's University by seeking in advance an understanding of the doctrine related to temple ordinances, it is certain that we will learn more while there and go away with a greater desire to live as we have been taught.

God help us to take away from the temple all that has been mentioned in this paper and more—much more!

Conclusion

Many, many other blessings and personal applications related to the House of God could be cited. I have said little or nothing about—

- the blessing of becoming better acquainted with God and receiving a manifestation of the Son of Man (see D & C 109:5).

- the blessing of engaging in true worship and practicing pure religion.

- the blessing of putting on the full armor of God (See Eph. 6:13-18).

- the blessing of growing up in God, receiving a fullness of the Holy Ghost, becoming organized according to God's laws, and obtaining every needful thing (see D&C 109:15).

- the blessing of becoming more knowledgeable regarding the blessings of the Fathers (Abraham, Isaac, and Jacob). [Priesthood—Posterity—Prosperity—gospel—eternal lives]—And, many more!

On one occasion the Prophet Joseph Smith stated, *"The Church is not fully organized, in its proper order, and cannot be, until the Temple is completed, where places will be provided for the administration of the ordinances of the Priesthood"* (TJPJS, p. 224).

In the Seminar for New Temple Presidents and Matrons held in September, 1996, President Gordon B. Hinckley said, *"Without temples and temple activity we would have only half a church."*

If the above statements are true, and I believe that they are, then those who do not attend the temple and participate in temple ordinances, are not **"fully organized"** and are practicing a partial religion—not a pure or complete religion. Moreover, it could be added, those who practice a partial religion will not receive the full blessings of the gospel of Jesus Christ or the crowning blessings of the Holy Priesthood.

The question follows: What can priesthood leaders and parents and teachers do to inspire greater interest in the temple? In answer to this question, I propose these actions:

1. **Teach the doctrine.** Use the scriptures and the teachings of the prophets, living and dead, in helping people understand the need for temples and temple worship.

2. **Show the way.** Parents and leaders must lead others to the temple. It is one thing to command people to attend the temple. However, it is a far more virtuous thing to invite people to go with you to the temple.

3. **Create a temple environment within your home and church unit.** Everything done at home or at church should point people toward the temple. Talk of the temple, preach of the temple, write of the temple, and do all else to remind people of the blessings to be received in the House of the Lord.

4. **Speak more of the blessings and personal applications of the temple.** There is cause to speak about the duties and responsibilities of the members as pertaining to the temple. But, members also need to know how they may benefit individually and collectively by becoming involved in temple activities.

President Joseph Fielding Smith said:

These blessings insure to us, through our faithfulness, the pearl of great price the Lord has offered us, for these are the greatest blessings we can receive in this life. It is a wonderful thing to come into the Church, but you cannot receive an exaltation until you have made covenants in the house of the Lord and received the keys and authorities that are there bestowed and which cannot be given in any other place on the earth today (*Doctrines of Salvation,* comp. Bruce R. McConkie, 3 vols (Salt Lake City: Bookcraft, 1954 56) 2:253).

President Boyd K. Packer adds:

No work is more of a protection to this church than temple work and the genealogical research which supports it. No work is more spiritually refining. No work we do gives us more power. No work requires a higher standard of righteousness. . . . If we will accept the revelation concerning temple ordinance work, if we will enter into our covenants without reservation or apology, the Lord will protect us. We will receive inspiration sufficient for the challenges of life. . . . **So come to the temple—come and claim your blessings. It is a sacred work** (*The Holy Temple* p. 40).

On one occasion Alma prayed *"that the eyes of the people might be opened to see and know of the goodness and glory of God"* (Mosiah 27:22). I pray the same for you and those whom you teach. For it is through temple ordinances and worship that the full power of godliness is manifested unto men in the flesh (see D&C 84:20-21).

Marital Roles

Spouse
Kinship
Sexual
Parenting
Provider
Housekeeper
Religious
Recreation
Therapist

Where do you learn how to carry out these roles?
What if you didn't have a good model in your home?
How can you improve your role performances?
How do you change role expectations/scripts?
Role discrepancies—what are they?
How will you handle them?

Role Expectations
Role Performances
Role Discrepancies

How do you resolve?

1. Christlike traits
2. Student/teacher
3. Change role expectations
4. Change role performances
5. Compromise—core beliefs
6. Feedback—a better student/teacher
7. Be responsible—F. Burton Howard article

The Importance of a Good Marriage

Douglas E. Brinley

From the moment of birth into mortality to the time we are married in the temple, everything we have in the gospel system is to prepare and qualify us to enter that holy order of matrimony which makes us husband and wife in this life and in the world to come. Then from the moment we are sealed together by the power and authority of the holy priesthood—everything connected with revealed religion is designed to help us keep the terms and conditions of our marriage covenant, so that this covenant will have . . . force in the life to come.

Thus celestial marriage is the crowning ordinance of the gospel, the crowning ordinance of the house of the Lord. Thus the family unit is the **most important organization in time or in eternity**. We should have more interest in and concern for **our families than for anything else in life**. There is **nothing** in this world as important as the creation and perfection of family units (Bruce R. McConkie, *Improvement Era*, June 1970:43-44).

l. **Personal Happiness**. To be really happy in marriage, one must have a continued faithful observance of the commandments of the Lord. **No one, single or married, was ever sublimely happy unless he was righteous**. There are **temporary** satisfactions and camouflaged situations for the moment, but permanent, total happiness, can come only through cleanliness and worthiness. One who has a pattern of religious life with deep religious convictions can never be happy in an inactive life. . . If two people love the Lord more than their own lives and then love each other more than their own lives, working together in total harmony with the gospel program as their basic structure, they are sure to have this great happiness. When a husband and wife go together frequently to the holy temple, kneel in prayer together in their home with their family, go hand in hand to their religious meetings, keep their lives wholly chaste—mentally and physically—so that their whole thoughts and desires and loves are all centered in the one being—their companion—and both work for the upbuilding of the kingdom of God, **then happiness is at its pinnacle** (Pres. Spencer W. Kimball, *Marriage & Divorce*, p. 8).

2. **Companionship**. Some married couples live very superficially together. They communicate about routine matters, but do not share their deepest thoughts. They live almost separate lives under one roof (boardinghouses, I call them). They meet each other's elementary needs but never venture into what I call relationship-in-depth. . . . They simply live together on the basis of a **mutual exchange of services**. He "brings home the bacon," she takes care of the house; he takes care of the cars while she manages the children, etc. Based on a few such elementary exchanges, the marriage soon becomes dull and dreary. Such mediocre marriages are **very common in our culture**. Yet often these very people are tormented by the longing for a relationship that is richer, deeper, and more meaningful. They are **love-starved** and often they turn in other directions to seek what marriage has failed to give them. (Then we have to discipline them.) **Sharing life in depth with your spouse is the solution to most of our human problems** (David Mace, *Getting Ready for Marriage*, 1972:68).

3. **Theology**. Some will gain celestial bodies with all the powers of exaltation and eternal increase....In both of these (lower) kingdoms there will be changes in the bodies and limitations. They **will not have the power of increase**, neither the **power** or **nature** to live as husbands and wives, for this will be denied them and they **cannot increase. . . .** Some of the functions in the celestial body will not appear in the terrestrial body, neither in the telestial body, and the power of procreation will be removed (Joseph Fielding Smith, *Doctrines of Salvation*, pp. 287-288).

Could wicked and malicious beings, who have eradicated every feeling of love from their bosoms, be permitted to propagate their species, the offspring would partake of all the evil, wicked, and malicious nature of their parents. . . It is for **this reason** that God **will not permit** Satan and his followers to multiply; it is for this reason that God has ordained marriages for the righteous only; it is for this reason that God will put a final stop to the multiplication of the wicked after this life; it is for this reason that none but those who have kept the celestial law will be permitted to multiply after the resurrection; . . . for they alone are prepared to beget and bring forth (spirit) children (Orson Pratt, *JD*, 13:186).

4. **The Effect on Children**. An author once said, "The most important thing a father can do for his children is to love their mother." And I would add to that, "A woman happy with her husband is better for her children than a hundred books on child care" (Pres. Harold B. Lee, *BYU Speeches*, 1973:92).

We have great concern about the growing number of homes in the Church where the influence of a father is hardly felt. In more and more families the mother and children are left to carry out the father's duties as well as their own. **In this life a father is never released from his responsibility**. We call bishops, and they serve for a time and are released. Stake presidents likewise are called, serve, and are released. But a father's calling is **an eternal calling if he lives worthily** (H. Burke Peterson, *Ensign*, Nov. 1977, p. 87).

5. **Sexual Intimacy**. . . . The foundation of such relationships is **good relations** between husband and wife in **all other areas of the marriage**. It is difficult for a wife to give of herself spontaneously and freely if she is resentful and angry with her husband. Both must work to be respectful, courteous, loving with each other in all areas of their interaction so that they can give freely and without fear of being hurt in this most intimate of relationships. . . . Unproductive and unresolved conflict; lack of privacy; fear of being ridiculed, hurt, dominated, or used; fear of losing oneself to another; fatigue; in-law problems, business difficulties; and a lack of confidence in oneself or one's mate are among those things that most often hinder good sexual relationships (G. Hugh Allred, "How to Strengthen Your Marriage and Family," p. 255-56).

6. **Alternatives**. (There are none!) Many people there are, though, who do not find divorce attorneys and who do not end their marriages, but who have permitted their marriages to grow stale and weak and cheap. There are spouses who have fallen from the throne of adoration and worship and are in the low state of mere joint occupancy of the home, joint sitters at the table, joint possessors of certain things which cannot be easily divided. These people are on the path that leads to trouble. These people will do well to (1) re-evaluate (2) to renew their courting, (3) to express their affection, (4) to acknowledge kindnesses, and (5) to increase their consideration so their marriage again can become **beautiful**, **sweet**, and **growing**. Love is like a flower, and, like the body, it needs constant feeling. The tender flower would wither and die without food and water. And so love, also, cannot be expected to last forever unless it is continually fed with portions of love, the manifestation of esteem and admiration, the expressions of gratitude, and the consideration of unselfishness (Pres. Spencer W. Kimball, *Marriage & Divorce*, p. 7).

What God Hath Joined Together

President Gordon B. Hinckley, First Counselor in the First Presidency

General Conference, April 1991

T**en days ago, I had** a beautiful and touching experience in the Salt Lake Temple, the building immediately to the east of this tabernacle. There in that holy sanctuary I had the privilege of sealing in marriage, in two separate but consecutive ceremonies, two beautiful young women who are twins, each to a handsome and able young man of her choice. That evening, a double wedding reception was held where hundreds of friends came to express their love and good wishes.

Mothers often shed tears at a wedding ceremony. Sisters also, and sometimes fathers. Seldom do grandparents show any emotion. But these beautiful girls were my own granddaughters, and I must confess that this old grandfather choked up and had a difficult time. I don't understand why. Certainly it was a happy occasion, a fulfillment of dreams and prayers. Perhaps my tears were really an expression of joy and of gratitude to God for these lovely brides and their handsome young husbands. In sacred promises, they pledged their love and loyalty one to another for time and all eternity.

How wonderful a thing is marriage under the plan of our Eternal Father, a plan provided in His divine wisdom for the happiness and security of His children and the continuity of the race.

He is our Creator, and He designed marriage from the beginning. At the time of Eve's creation, Adam said, "This is now bone of my bones, and flesh of my flesh. . . .

Therefore shall a man leave his father and his mother, and shall cleave unto his wife: and they shall be one flesh" (Gen. 2:23-24).

Paul wrote to the Corinthian Saints, "Neither is the man without the woman, neither the woman without the man, in the Lord" (1 Cor. 11:11).

In modern revelation, the Lord has said, "And again, verily I say unto you, that whoso forbiddeth to marry is not ordained of God, for marriage is ordained of God unto man" (D&C 49:15).

President Joseph F. Smith once declared "that no man can be saved and exalted in the kingdom of God without the woman, and no woman can reach perfection and exaltation in the kingdom of God, alone. . . . God instituted marriage in the beginning. He made man in His own image and likeness, male and female, and in their creation it was designed that they should be united together in sacred bonds of marriage, and one is not perfect without the other" (*Conference Report*, April 1913, p. 118).

Surely no one reading the scriptures, both ancient and modern, can doubt the divine concept of marriage. The sweetest feelings of life, the most generous and satisfying impulses of the human heart, find expression in a marriage that stands pure and unsullied above the evil of the world.

Such a marriage, I believe, is the desire—the hoped-for, the longed-for, the prayed-for desire—of men and women everywhere.

While riding a plane some time ago, I picked up a copy of the *New York Magazine*. As I thumbed through it, I came to a section titled "Strictly Personals." I counted 159 advertisements placed by lonely men and women seeking partners. It was evident that those who had placed the ads had labored to cast themselves in the best light possible. I wish I had time to read some of them to you. You would enjoy them. There was nothing of an unseemly nature. It was easy to sense that behind these witty and clever descriptions was much of sadness and loneliness, a great desire to find an amiable companion with whom to walk the road of life.

My heart reaches out to those among us, especially our single sisters, who long for marriage and cannot seem to find it. Our Father in Heaven reserves for them every promised blessing. I have far less sympathy for the young men, who under the customs of our society, have the prerogative to take the initiative in these matters but in so many cases fail to do so. Strong words have been spoken to them in the past by Presidents of this church.

Marriage usually means children and family. Can a young mother, having given birth to her first child, doubt the divinity and the wonder and the miracle of it all? Can a young father, looking upon his newborn son or daughter, sense other than that this is a part of the design of the Almighty?

Of course, all in marriage is not bliss. Years ago I clipped these words from a column written by Jenkins Lloyd Jones:

> There seems to be a superstition among many thousands of our young who hold hands and smooch in the drive-ins that marriage is a cottage surrounded by perpetual hollyhocks to which a perpetually young and handsome husband comes home to a perpetually young and ravishing wife. When the hollyhocks wither and boredom and bills appear the divorce courts are jammed. . . .
>
> Anyone who imagines that bliss is normal is going to waste a lot of time running around and shouting that he has been robbed (Deseret News, 12 June 1973, p. A-4).

Stormy weather occasionally hits every household. Connected inevitably with the whole process is much of pain—physical, mental, and emotional. There is much of stress and struggle, of fear and worry. For most, there is the ever-haunting battle of economics. There seems never to be enough money to cover the needs of a family. Sickness strikes periodically. Accidents happen. The hand of death may reach in with dread stealth to take a precious one.

But all of this seems to be part of the processes of family life. Few indeed are those who get along without experiencing some of it. It has been so from the beginning. Cain quarreled with Abel and then did a terrible thing. How great must have been the grief in the hearts of their parents, Adam and Eve.

Absalom was the third son of David, a son favored and loved. David had given him a name which meant "father of peace." But he brought not peace—rather, anger and ambition and sorrow. He killed his brother and conspired against his father. In the midst of his evil actions, in his wicked pursuit for his father's throne, while riding a mule Absalom's head caught in the branches of an oak tree, and he was left hanging helpless. Joab, nephew of David and captain of the king's army, seizing the opportunity to get rid of this rebellious and traitorous son, pierced his heart with darts. He apparently felt he was doing a favor to the king.

But when David heard of his son's death, even though that son had conspired to destroy him, "the king was much moved, and went up to the chamber over the gate, and wept: and as he went, thus he said, O my son Absalom, my son, my son Absalom! would God I had died for thee, O Absalom, my son, my son! . . . [And] the king covered his face, and . . . cried" (2 Sam. 18:33; 19:4).

Through the history of the generations of man, the actions of rebellious children have been ladened with sorrow and heartbreak, but even when there has been rebellion, the strong cords of family life have reached out to encircle the rebellious one.

I know of no more beautiful story in all of literature than that told by the Master as recorded in the fifteenth chapter of Luke. It is the story of a heady and greedy son who demanded his inheritance, which he wasted until none was left. Penitent, he returned to his father, and his father, seeing him afar off, ran to him and embraced him and fell upon his neck and kissed him.

Some of you within the sound of my voice could recount family sorrows in your own experience. But among the greatest of tragedies, and I think the most common, is divorce. It has become as a great scourge. The most recent issue of the World Almanac says that in the United States during the twelve months ending with March 1990, an estimated 2,423,000 couples married. During this same period, an estimated 1,177,000 couples divorced (See The World Almanac and Book of Facts, 1991, New York: World Almanac, 1990, p. 834).

This means that in the United States almost one divorce occurred for every two marriages. Those are only figures written on the pages of a book. But behind them lies more of betrayal, more of sorrow, more of neglect and poverty and struggle than the human mind can imagine. Millions of those divorced in this nation are lonely, frustrated, insecure, and unhappy. Millions of single parents are struggling to rear families, carrying burdens beyond their capacity to handle. Millions of children are growing up in single family homes from which the parent, usually the mother, out of necessity, is absent much of the time. These "latch-key children" return from school each day to empty houses, where, in many cases, there is inadequate food and only the refuge of the television set. Not only are the children suffering, but all of society is paying a frightful price for their circumstances. As they grow older, the incidence of drugs increases among them. Vast numbers turn to criminal behavior. Inadequately trained, many are unemployed. Some aimlessly squander their lives. Millions have become the "flotsam and jetsam" of society, washed upon the shore by oceans of neglect, abuse, and frustration, helpless to correct their circumstances. *Time* magazine, discussing the problems of New York City, stated that the most serious is the breakdown of the family. Sixty percent of those in New York City public schools, totalling some 600,000, come from one-parent homes. Comparable studies would doubtless bring forth similar statistics for other large cities in America and most of the large cities of the world.

We are building and maintaining more prisons than we can afford. The costs are enormous, almost beyond comprehension.

In an alarming percentage of the cases of those who are warehoused in these facilities, there will be found in their background a broken home where a father abandoned his family and a mother struggled in vain to handle the overpowering odds against her.

Why all of these broken homes? What happens to marriages that begin with sincere love and a desire to be loyal and faithful and true one to another?

There is no simple answer. I acknowledge that. But it appears to me that there are some obvious reasons that account for a very high percentage of these problems. I say this out of experience in dealing with such tragedies. I find selfishness to be the root cause of most of it.

I am satisfied that a happy marriage is not so much a matter of romance as it is an anxious concern for the comfort and well-being of one's companion.

Selfishness so often is the basis of money problems, which are a very serious and real factor affecting the stability of family life. Selfishness is at the root of adultery, the breaking of solemn and sacred covenants to satisfy selfish lust. Selfishness is the antithesis of love. It is a cankering expression of greed. It destroys self-discipline. It obliterates loyalty. It tears up sacred covenants. It afflicts both men and women.

Too many who come to marriage have been coddled and spoiled and somehow led to feel that everything must be precisely right at all times, that life is a series of entertainments, that appetites are to be satisfied without regard to principle. How tragic the consequences of such hollow and unreasonable thinking!

Bitter consequences are seen in the lives of children who need but do not have a father who loves them, teaches them, protects them, and leads them along the path of life by example and precept. Let me recount for you something I heard about two years ago in this tabernacle. The occasion was a great gathering of single men and women. Elder Marion D. Hanks conducted a panel discussion. Included in that panel was an attractive and able young woman, divorced, the mother of seven children then ranging in ages from five to sixteen. She said that one evening she went across the street to deliver something to a neighbor. Listen to her words as I recall them:

> As I turned around to walk back home, I could see my house lighted up. I could hear echoes of my children as I had walked out of the door a few minutes earlier: "Mom, what are we going to have for dinner?" "Can you take me to the library?" "I have to get some poster paper tonight." Tired and weary, I looked at that house and saw the light on in each of the rooms. I thought of all of those children who were home waiting for me to come and meet their needs. My burdens felt very heavy on my shoulders.

I remember looking through tears toward the sky, and I said, "Oh, my Father, I just can't do it tonight. I'm too tired. I can't face it. I can't go home and take care of all those children alone. Could I just come to You and stay with You for just one night? I'll come back in the morning."

I didn't really hear the words of reply, but I heard them in my mind. The answer was, "No, little one, you can't come to me now. You would never wish to come back. But I can come to you."

There are so many, so very, very many, like that young mother. She recognizes a divine power available to her. She is fortunate enough to have some around to love her and help her, but very many do not have such help. In loneliness and desperation, watching their children drift toward drugs and crime and helpless to stop that drift, they weep and pray.

There is a remedy for all of this. It is not found in divorce. It is found in the gospel of the Son of God. He it was who said, "What therefore God hath joined together, let not man put asunder" (Matt. 19:6). The remedy for most marriage stress is not in divorce. It is in repentance. It is not in separation. It is in simple integrity that leads a man to square up his shoulders and meet his obligations. It is found in the Golden Rule.

Marriage is beautiful when beauty is looked for and cultivated. It can be ugly and uncomfortable when one is looking for faults and is blinded to virtue. As Edgar A. Guest once remarked, "It takes a heap o' livin' in a house t' make it home" ("Home," in Collected Verse of Edgar A. Guest, Chicago: Reilly and Lee Co. 1934, p. 12). That is true. I can show you throughout this church hundreds of thousands of families who make it work with love and peace, discipline and honesty, concern and unselfishness.

There must be recognition on the part of both husband and wife of the solemnity and sanctity of marriage and of the God-given design behind it.

There must be a willingness to overlook small faults, to forgive, and then to forget.

There must be a holding of one's tongue. Temper is a vicious and corrosive thing that destroys affection and casts out love.

There must be self-discipline that constrains against abuse of wife and children and self. There must be the Spirit of God, invited and worked for, nurtured and strengthened. There must be recognition of the fact that each is a child of God—father, mother, son, and daughter, each with a divine birthright—and also recognition of the fact that when we offend one of these, we offend our Father in Heaven.

There may be now and again a legitimate cause for divorce. I am not one to say that it is never justified. But I say without hesitation that this plague among us, which seems to be growing everywhere, is not of God, but rather is the work of the adversary of righteousness and peace and truth.

(Due to time constraints, the remainder of this talk was not given over the pulpit. President Hinckley has asked that it be included in his text).

You need not be his victims. You can rise above his wiles and entreaties. Get rid of the titillating entertainment, the pornography that leads to evil desires and reprehensible activity. Wives, look upon your husbands as your precious companions and live worthy of that association. Husbands, see in your wives your most valued asset in time or eternity, each a daughter of God, a partner with whom you can walk hand in hand, through sunshine and storm, through all the perils and triumphs of life. Parents, see in your children sons and daughters of your Father in Heaven, who will hold you accountable for them. Stand together as their guardians, their protectors, their guides, their anchors.

The strength of the nations lies in the homes of the people. God is the designer of the family. He intended that the greatest of happiness, the most satisfying aspects of life, the deepest joys should come in our associations together and our concerns one for another as fathers and mothers and children.

God bless the homes of our people. May He bless those homes that there may be loyal and true fathers, and good and wonderful mothers, and obedient and ambitious children reared in "the nurture and admonition of the Lord" (Enos 1:17), I humbly pray in the name of Jesus Christ, amen.

Live Up to Your Inheritance

President Gordon B. Hinckley

General Women's Meeting, 24 September 1983

My beloved sisters, it is a privilege and an honor to be with you.

I suppose this is the largest gathering of women ever convened in the history of the Church. The Tabernacle is filled to capacity. Additionally, women are assembled in over six hundred stake centers, and many others are watching in homes where television is available. As I have looked over this vast congregation, I have thought, "What a profitable day for the hairdressers!"

I know that many of you out there feel lonely at times. Some of you girls find that there are only two or three Latter-day Saints in the large schools which you attend. You women who work may find yourselves the only members of the Church at your places of employment. You who are widows and some who have been divorced may feel that you are alone. The numbers who are participating in this meeting tonight should give you the assurance that you are not alone. You are part of the greatest sorority or sisterhood on earth. It probably includes some two million women.

This vast congregation includes girls and women from the age of ten and up. I am happy for the inclusion of the ten-year-olds. Ten is a great age, a beautiful age, when a child who previously appeared to be all arms and legs and appetite seems to partake of a refining influence that brings with it beauty and grace. It is like blossoms in the spring that burst with the warmth of the sun. It is a time of awakening of mental and physical powers. It is the bridge season between childhood and youth.

Do you know that the great prophet-historian Mormon received his charge concerning the sacred records when he was only ten years of age? The book which we have today, this sacred and marvelous testament of Christ, resulted from Mormon's faithfulness in meeting that assignment. Never discount the importance of a ten-year-old.

"What are little girls made of? Sugar and spice, and everything nice." So goes the old nursery rhyme. But more importantly, they are the promise of the future. Through them, eventually, must filter the qualities of all of the earlier generations, which will become the bone and the tissue, the minds and the spirits, of the generations yet to be.

To you young girls I say with all of the strength and conviction I can muster, be sweet, be good, be strong and virtuous and wonderful. Somehow I feel that the Lord included you with those of whom he spoke when he said, "Except ye . . . become as little children, ye shall not enter into the kingdom of heaven" (Matt. 18:3). Channing Pollock, the gifted author and playwright, once wished, through one of his characters, that we might all be born old and gradually grow younger and ever more innocent until at death we have become as little children.

I next would like to say a few words to you young women, you who have crossed the threshold from childhood and early youth into the maturity of your later teens and early twenties. For you this must be a season for strength. It is a season that demands discipline of mind and of body. This is the season for preparation, and the Lord has said, "If ye are prepared ye shall not fear" (D&C 38:30).

It is a time for education. The world that lies ahead of you will be fiercely competitive. Now is the time to train yourselves for possible future responsibilities.

Education is a tradition that has come down from our early history. We believe in the training of our youth, girls as well as boys. Brigham Young once said, "We have sisters here who, if they had the privilege of studying, would make just as good mathematicians or accountants as any man" (Journal of Discourses, 13:61).

You have available to you tremendous opportunities for training your minds and your hands. You will wish for marriage and the companionship of a good husband. But none of us can foretell the future. Prepare yourselves for any eventuality. You need not go to a university if that is not your taste. There are wonderful technical colleges across the land which will hone your skills and assist you in qualifying yourselves for future responsibilities.

Hopefully, most of you will marry. But the training you have received will not have been in vain. It will be a blessing whether you be single or married.

Keep yourselves worthy of marriage. This is an age when strength is needed to retain that worthiness. Seldom if ever in the history of the world have we been so widely exposed to those seductive influences which lead to degradation, sin, and regret. The merchants of pornography and some designers of entertainment are as clever as hell itself with their beguiling wares. They would lead you into a trap that could eventually bring only sorrow, remorse, and heartache.

Said the Lord, "Let virtue garnish thy thoughts unceasingly." He then gave this promise: "Then shall thy confidence wax strong in the presence of God. . . ."

"The Holy Ghost shall be thy constant companion . . . ; thy dominion shall be an everlasting dominion, and without compulsory means it shall flow unto thee forever and ever" (D&C 121:45-46).

I paraphrase a few words of a statement made by the First Presidency more than forty years ago:

> How glorious is she who lives a chaste life. She walks unfearful in the full glare of the noonday sun, for she is without moral infirmity. She can be reached by no shafts of base calumny, for her armor is without flaw. Her virtue cannot be challenged by any just accuser, for she lives above reproach. Her cheek is never blotched with shame, for she is without hidden sin. She is honored and respected by all mankind, for she is beyond their censure. She is loved by the Lord, for she stands without blemish. The exaltations of eternities await her coming (See Message of the First Presidency, Heber J. Grant, J. Reuben Clark, Jr.; David O. McKay, 3 Oct. 1942).

Now if there be any here who have slipped, I hold out to you the assurance that there is forgiveness for the individual who truly repents. God will forgive those who acknowledge the error of their ways and who demonstrate by the goodness of their lives the sincerity of their repentance.

I should like now to say a few words to those of you who are married. I would hope that you may have been married in the house of the Lord. Our Father in Heaven, who loves his children, has provided for them a privilege beyond price, and that is the eternal sealing of the most precious of all relationships.

To you who have this priceless blessing, live worthy of it. Loyalty is of the very essence of your temple vows and covenants—loyalty to your companion, loyalty to your children, loyalty to God with whom you have made solemn covenant. He will not be mocked. Glorious and wonderful are the promises to those who keep their covenants and walk in obedience to his divine commandments. The sense of responsibility that comes therewith will sweeten marriage, will bring a sanctifying influence to the home, will make more precious the children who come of that union, and will give peace throughout the seasons of life and comfort in time of death.

I recognize that there are many in this vast congregation who have not had the opportunity of temple marriage, whose husbands may not be members of the Church or may not have qualified themselves to go to the house of the Lord. To you I wish to say, be patient, be prayerful. Stifle your tendency to criticize. Live the kind of life in your home that will cause your companion to see in you that goodness, that virtue, and that strength which come of the gospel.

I remember a family I knew fifty years ago. The wife was a devoted member of the Church. The husband was not a member. He smoked and drank. She hoped and she prayed. She lived for the day when his heart might be touched by the Spirit of the Lord. Years passed one after another into more than a decade. Her example was one of goodness and gladness and faith. After many years he began to soften. He saw what the Church did for her and for their children. He turned around. He humbled himself. He was baptized. He has since served as a quorum president and a bishop, as a missionary, and as a worker in the temple.

You have not failed until you have quit trying, and please remember that your example in your home will be a more persuasive sermon than will any other kind of preachment.

I salute most warmly and sincerely you dedicated and wonderful homemakers. I have only respect for the title "housewife."

I clipped this from the Wall Street Journal, titled "The Most Creative Job in the World":

> It involves taste, fashion, decorating, recreation, education, transportation, psychology, romance, cuisine, designing, literature, medicine, handicraft, art, horticulture, economics, government, community relations, pediatrics, geriatrics, entertainment, maintenance, purchasing, direct mail, law, accounting, religion, energy and management. Anyone who can handle all those has to be somebody special. She is. She's a homemaker (3 June 1983).

Now, a word to you who have not married. It would be a beautiful world if every girl had the privilege of marriage to a good man whom she could look upon with pride and gladness as her companion in time and eternity, hers alone to love and cherish, to respect and help.

But it does not always work out that way. There are some who, for reasons unexplainable, do not have the opportunity of marriage. To you I should like to say, don't spend your time and wear out your lives wandering about in the wasteland of self-pity. God has given you talents of one kind or another. He has given you the capacity to serve the needs of others and bless their lives with your kindness and concern. Reach out to someone in need. There are so very many out there. Add knowledge to knowledge. Refine your mind and skills in a chosen field of discipline. There are tremendous opportunities for you if you are prepared to take advantage of them. Nearly all of the honorable vocations of life are now open to women. Do not feel that because you are single God has forsaken you. The world needs you. The Church needs you. So very many people and causes need your strength and wisdom and talents.

Be prayerful, and do not lose hope. But do not become obsessed with ambition to find a companion. Your obsession likely will only make you less attractive, or it may cause a weakening of your standards. Live the very best life of which you are capable, and the Lord in his greater wisdom and in his eternal season will give you answer to your prayers.

To you women who find it necessary to work when you would rather be at home, may I speak briefly. I know that there are many of you who find yourselves in this situation. Some of you have been abandoned and are divorced, with children to care for. Some of you are widows with dependent families. I honor you and respect you for your integrity and spirit of self-reliance. I pray that the Lord will bless you with strength and great capacity, for you need both. You have the responsibilities of both breadwinner and homemaker. I know that it is difficult. I know that it is discouraging. I pray that the Lord will bless you with a special wisdom and the remarkable talent needed to provide your children with time and companionship and love and with that special direction which only a mother can give. I pray also that he will bless you with help, unstintingly given, from family, friends, and the Church, which will lift some of the burden from your shoulders and help you in your times of extremity.

We sense, at least in some small degree, the loneliness you must occasionally feel and the frustrations you must experience as you try to cope with problems that sometimes seem beyond your capacity to handle. Sometimes you need food for your tables, and we trust that bishops will be there to supply food and other goods and services under the great program which the Lord has provided in his Church. But we know that more often your greater need is for understanding and appreciation and companionship. We shall try a little harder to cultivate these virtues, and I urge you sisters who are in a position to do so to reach out with greater concern to those who find themselves in these less fortunate circumstances.

Now to others who work when it is not necessary and who, while doing so, leave children to the care of those who often are only poor substitutes, I offer a word of caution. Do not follow a practice which will bring you later regret. If the purpose of your daily employment is simply to get money for a boat or a fancy automobile or some other desirable but unnecessary thing, and in the process you lose the companionship of your children and the opportunity to rear them, you may find that you have lost the substance while grasping at the shadow.

In conclusion, I should like to say a word to all women of the Church. I know of no doctrine which states that we made a choice when we came to earth as to whether we wished to be male or female. That choice was made by our Father in Heaven in his infinite wisdom. I am satisfied that he loves his daughters as much as he loves his sons. President Harold B. Lee once remarked that priesthood is the power by which God works through us as men. I should like to add that motherhood is the means by which God carries forward his grand design of continuity of the race. Both priesthood and motherhood are essentials of the plan of the Lord.

Each complements the other. Each is needed by the other. God has created us male and female, each unique in his or her individual capacities and potential. The woman is the bearer and the nurturer of children. The man is the provider and protector. No legislation can alter the sexes. Legislation should provide equality of opportunity, equality of compensation, equality of political privilege. But any legislation which is designed to create neuter gender of that which God created male and female will bring more problems than benefits. Of that I am convinced.

I wish with all my heart we would spend less of our time talking about rights and more talking about responsibilities. God has given the women of this church a work to do in building his kingdom. That concerns all aspects of our great triad of responsibility—which is, first, to teach the gospel to the world; second, to strengthen the faith and build the happiness of the membership of the Church; and, third, to carry forward the great work of salvation for the dead.

This is a season for strength. I conclude with these stirring words of Moroni, written as he sealed his record to come forth in the dispensation of the fulness of times:

> Awake, and arise from the dust, O Jerusalem; yea, and put on thy beautiful garments, O daughter of Zion; and strengthen thy stakes and enlarge thy borders forever, that thou mayest no more be confounded, that the covenants of the Eternal Father which he hath made unto thee, O house of Israel, may be fulfilled.
>
> Yea, come unto Christ, and be perfected in him, and deny yourselves of all ungodliness (Moro. 10:31-32).

Put on thy beautiful garments, O daughters of Zion. Live up to the great and magnificent inheritance which the Lord God, your Father in Heaven, has provided for you. Rise above the dust of the world. Know that you are daughters of God, children with a divine birthright. Walk in the sun with your heads high, knowing that you are loved and honored, that you are a part of his kingdom, and that there is for you a great work to be done which cannot be left to others.

God be thanked for the wonderful women of this Church. May he plant in your hearts a sense of pride in your capacities and a conviction of truth which shall be as a rudder to keep you safe through every storm, I humbly pray in the name of Jesus Christ, amen.

Marriage

Elder Boyd K. Packer, of the Quorum of the Twelve Apostles

Ensign, May, 1981, pp. 13-15

The prophet Jacob foretold the destruction of a people because they were blind to ordinary things, "which blindness," he said, "came by looking beyond the mark" (Jacob 4:14).

We often seek for things we cannot seem to find when they are within easy reach—ordinary, obvious things.

I wish to talk about an ordinary word. I have tried for months—really tried—to find some way to hold this word up in such a way that you would be very impressed with what it means.

The word is *marriage*.

I have wished that I could set before you a finely carved chest, placing it where the light is just right. I would carefully unlatch it and reverently uncover the word—marriage.

Perhaps then you would see that it is priceless!

I cannot show it to you that way, so I will do the best I can using other ordinary words.

It is my purpose to endorse and to favor, to encourage and defend marriage.

Many regard it nowadays as being, at best, semiprecious, and by some it is thought to be worth nothing at all.

I have seen and heard, as you have seen and heard, the signals all about us, carefully orchestrated to convince us that marriage is out of date and in the way.

There is a practice, now quite prevalent, for unmarried couples to live together, a counterfeit of marriage. They suppose that they shall have all that marriage can offer without the obligations connected with it. They are wrong!

However much they hope to find in a relationship of that kind, they will lose more. Living together without marriage destroys something inside all who participate. Virtue, self-esteem, and refinement of character wither away.

Claiming that it will not happen does not prevent the loss; and these virtues, once lost, are not easily reclaimed.

To suppose that one day they may nonchalantly change their habits and immediately claim all that might have been theirs had they not made a mockery of marriage is to suppose something that will not be.

One day, when they come to themselves, they will reap disappointment.

One cannot degrade marriage without tarnishing other words as well, such words as *boy, girl, manhood, womanhood, husband, wife, father, mother, baby, children, family, home.*

Such words as *unselfishness* and *sacrifice* will then be tossed aside. Then self-respect will fade and love itself will not want to stay.

If you have been tempted to enter such a relationship or if you now live with another without marriage, leave! Withdraw from it! Run away from it! Do not continue with it! Or, if you can, make a marriage out of it.

Even a rickety marriage will serve good purpose as long as two people struggle to keep it from falling down around them.

And now a word of warning. One who destroys a marriage takes upon himself a very great responsibility indeed. Marriage is sacred!

To willfully destroy a marriage, either your own or that of another couple, is to offend our God. Such a thing will not be lightly considered in the judgments of the Almighty and in the eternal scheme of things will not easily be forgiven.

Do not threaten nor break up a marriage. Do not translate some disenchantment with your own marriage partner or an attraction for someone else into justification for any conduct that would destroy a marriage.

This **monumental transgression** frequently **places heavy burdens upon little children. They do not understand the selfish yearnings of unhappy adults who are willing to buy their own satisfaction at the expense of the innocent.**

God Himself decreed that the physical expression of love, that union of male and female which has power to generate life, is authorized only in marriage.

Marriage is the shelter where families are created. That society which puts low value on marriage sows the wind and, in time, will reap the whirlwind—and thereafter, unless they repent, bring upon themselves a holocaust!

Some think that every marriage must expect to end in unhappiness and divorce, with the hopes and dreams predestined to end in a broken, sad wreck of things.

Some marriages do bend, and some will break, but we must not, because of this, lose faith in marriage nor become afraid of it.

Broken marriages are not typical.

Remember that trouble attracts attention! We travel the highway with thousands of cars moving in either direction without paying much attention to any of them. But should an accident occur, we notice immediately.

If it happens again, we get the false impression that no one can go safely down the road.

One accident may make the front page, while a hundred million cars that safely pass are not regarded as worth mentioning.

Writers think that a happy, stable marriage does not have the dramatic appeal, the conflict worth featuring in a book or a play or a film. Therefore, we constantly hear about the ruined ones and we lose our perspective.

I believe in marriage. I believe it to be the ideal pattern for human living. I know it to be ordained of God. The restraints relating to it were designed to protect our happiness.

I do not know of any better time in all of the history of the world for a young couple who are of age and prepared and who are in love to think of marriage. There is no better time because it is your time.

I know that these are very troubled times. Troubles like we have now are very hard on marriages.

Do not lose faith in marriage. Not even if you have been through the unhappiness of a divorce and are surrounded with pieces of a marriage that has fallen apart.

If you have honored your vows and your partner did not do so, remember God is watching over us. One day, after all of the tomorrows have passed, there will be recompense. Those who have been moral and faithful to their covenants will be happy and those who have not will be otherwise.

Some marriages have broken up in spite of all that one partner could do to hold the marriage together. While there may be faults on both sides, I do not condemn the innocent one who suffers in spite of all that was desired and done to save the marriage.

And to you I say, **do not lose faith in marriage itself**. Do not let your disappointment leave you bitter or cynical or justify any conduct that is unworthy.

If you have had no opportunity for marriage or if you have lost your companion in death, keep your faith in marriage.

Some years ago an associate of mine lost his beloved wife. She died after a lingering illness, and he watched in helpless agony as the doctors withdrew all hope.

One day near the end she told him that when she was gone she wanted him to marry again and he was not to wait too long a time. He protested! The children were nearly grown and he would go the rest of the way alone.

She turned away and wept and said, "Have I been such a failure that after all our years together you would rather go unmarried? Have I been such a failure?"

In due time there came another, and their life together has reaffirmed his faith in marriage. And I have the feeling that his first beloved wife is deeply grateful to the second one, who filled the place that she could not keep.

Marriage is yet safe, with all its sweet fulfillment, with all its joy and love. In marriage all of the worthy yearnings of the human soul, all that is physical and emotional and spiritual, can be fulfilled.

Marriage is not without trials of many kinds. These tests forge virtue and strength. The tempering that comes in marriage and family life produces men and women who will someday be exalted.

God has ordained that life should have its beginning within the protecting shelter of marriage, conceived in a consummate expression of love and nurtured and fostered with that deeper love which is accompanied always by sacrifice.

Marriage offers fulfillment all the way through life—in youth and young love, the wedding and on the honeymoon, with the coming of little children and the nurturing of them. Then come the golden years when young ones leave the nest to build one of their own. The cycle then repeats itself, as God has decreed it should.

There is another dimension to marriage that we know of in the Church. It came by revelation. This glorious, supernal truth teaches us that marriage is meant to be eternal.

There are covenants we can make if we are willing, and bounds we can seal if we are worthy, that will keep marriage safe and intact beyond the veil of death.

The Lord has declared, "For behold, this is my work and my glory—to bring to pass the immortality and eternal life of man" (Moses 1:39).

The ultimate end of all activity in the Church is that a man and his wife and their children can be happy at home and that the family can continue through eternity. All Christian doctrine is formulated to protect the individual, the home, and the family.

These lines express something of the place of marriage in the eternal progress of man:

> We have within a burning flame,
> A light to kindle lights,
> The sacred fire of life itself
> Which is misused ignites
> A smold'ring, suffocating cloud
> Of sorrow and distress.
> When used by law this power brings forth
> A life, a family, happiness.
>
> Temptors from the darkest realm
> Seek to pervert this power
> In acts of wickedness and waste
> Until there comes the hour
> Of judgment and of recompense,
> When bitter tears are shed
> O'er power once held to foster life
> That now is gone and dead.
>
> I know this power to be a key,
> A very key to God's own plan
> Which brings to pass eternal life
> And immortality for man.
> And marriage is the crucible

Where elements of life combine,
Where mortal temples are conceived
Within that plan divine.

Then spirit offspring of our God
Can come through mortal birth
To have a choice, to face the test—
The purpose of our stay on earth.
Here good and evil stand alike
Before decision's sovereign nod.
Those who elect the righteous path
Will part the veil, return to God.

A gift from God, the plan provides
That mortal beings in humble strait
Be given power, supernal power,
To share their love and help create
A living child, a living soul,
Image of man, and of Deity.
How we regard this sacred gift
Will fix our course, our destiny!

Eternal love, eternal marriage, eternal increase! This ideal, which is new to many, when thoughtfully considered, can keep a marriage strong and safe. No relationship has more potential to exalt a man and a woman than the marriage covenant. No obligation in society or in the Church supersedes it in importance.

I thank God for marriage. I thank God for temples. I thank God for the glorious sealing power, that power which transcends all that we have been given, through which our marriages may become eternal. May we be worthy of this sacred gift, I pray in the name of Jesus Christ, amen.

For Time and All Eternity

Elder Boyd K. Packer

Conference Report, October 1993, pp. 27-32

The Great Plan of Happiness

Dear brethren and sisters, the scriptures and the teachings of the Apostles and prophets speak of us in premortal life as sons and daughters, spirit children of God.[1] Gender existed before, and did not begin at mortal birth.[2]

In the great council in heaven,[3] God's plan was presented:[4] the plan of salvation,[5] the plan of redemption,[6] the great plan of happiness.[7] The plan provides for a proving; all must choose between good and evil.[8] His plan provides for a Redeemer, an atonement, the Resurrection, and, if we obey, our return to the presence of God.

The adversary rebelled and adopted a plan of his own.[9] Those who followed him were denied the right to a mortal body.[10] Our presence here confirms that we sanctioned our Father's plan.[11]

The single purpose of Lucifer is to oppose the great plan of happiness, to corrupt the purest, most beautiful and appealing experiences of life: romance, love, marriage, and parenthood.[12] The specters of heartbreak and guilt[13] follow him about. Only repentance can heal what he hurts.

God's Plan Requires Marriage and Family

The plan of happiness requires the righteous union of male and female, man and woman, husband and wife.[14] Doctrines teach us how to respond to the compelling natural impulses which too often dominate how we behave.

A body patterned after the image of God was created for Adam,[15] and he was introduced into the Garden.[16] At first, Adam was alone. He held the priesthood,[17] but alone, he could not fulfill the purposes of his creation.[18]

No other man would do. Neither alone nor with other men could Adam progress. Nor could Eve with another woman. It was so then. It is so today.

Eve, an help meet, was created. Marriage was instituted,[19] for Adam was commanded to cleave unto his *wife* [not just to a *woman*] and "to none else."[20]

A choice, it might be said, was imposed upon Eve.[21] She should be praised for her decision. Then "Adam fell that men might be."[22]

Elder Orson F. Whitney described the Fall as having "a twofold direction—downward, yet forward. It brought man into the world and set his feet upon progression's highway."[23]

God blessed Adam and Eve "and said unto them: Be fruitful, and multiply."[24] And so the family was established.

God Values Men and Women Equally

There is nothing in the revelations which suggests that to be a man rather than to be a woman is preferred in the sight of God, or that He places a higher value on sons than on daughters.

All virtues listed in the scriptures—love, joy, peace, faith, godliness, charity—are shared by both men and women,[25] and the highest priesthood ordinance in mortality is given only to man and woman together.[26]

After the Fall, natural law had far-reaching sovereignty over mortal birth. There are what President J. Reuben Clark, Jr., called "pranks" of nature,[27] which cause a variety of abnormalities, deficiencies, and deformities. However unfair they seem to man's way of reasoning, they somehow suit the purposes of the Lord in the proving of mankind.

The following of every worthy instinct, the responding to every righteous urge, the consummating of every exalting human relationship are provided for and approved in the doctrines of the gospel of Jesus Christ and protected by commandments revealed to His church.

The Roles of Men and Women

Except Adam and Eve by nature be different from one another, they could not multiply and fill the earth.[28] The complementing differences are the very key to the plan of happiness.

Some roles are best suited to the masculine nature and others to the feminine nature. Both the scriptures and the patterns of nature place man as the protector, the provider.[29]

Those responsibilities of the priesthood, which have to do with the administration of the Church, of necessity function outside the home. By divine decree, they have been entrusted to men. It has been that way since the beginning, for the Lord revealed that "the order of this priesthood was confirmed to be handed down from father to son. . . . This order was instituted in the days of Adam."[30]

A man who holds the priesthood does not have an advantage over a woman in qualifying for exaltation. The woman, by her very nature, is also co-creator with God and the primary nurturer of the children. Virtues and attributes upon which perfection and exaltation depend come naturally to a woman and are refined through marriage and motherhood.

The priesthood is conferred only upon worthy men in order to conform to our Father's plan of happiness. With the laws of nature and the revealed word of God working in harmony, it simply works best that way.

The priesthood carries with it awesome responsibility.

> No power or influence *can* or ought to be maintained by virtue of the priesthood,
> only by persuasion, by long-suffering, by gentleness and meekness, and by love unfeigned; by kindness, and pure knowledge.[31]

Should a man "exercise control or dominion or compulsion . . . in any degree of unrighteousness,"[32] he violates "the oath and covenant which belongeth to the priesthood."[33] Then "the heavens withdraw themselves; the Spirit of the Lord is grieved."[34] Unless he repents he will lose his blessings.

While the different roles of man and woman are set forth in exalted celestial declarations, they are best demonstrated in the most practical, ordinary, down-to-earth experiences of family life.

Recently I heard a speaker in sacrament meeting complain that he could not understand why his grandchildren always spoke of going to *Grandma's* house, never to Grandpa's house. I solved that great mystery for him: Grandpas don't bake pies!

Natural and Spiritual Laws Are Eternal

Natural and spiritual laws which govern life were instituted from before the foundation of the world.[35] They are eternal, as are the consequences for either obeying or disobeying them. They are not based on social or political considerations. They cannot be changed. No pressure, no protest, no legislation can alter them.

Years ago I supervised the Indian seminaries. On a visit to a school at Albuquerque, the principal told me of an incident that happened in a first grade class.

During a lesson, a kitten wandered into the room and distracted the youngsters. It was brought to the front of the room so all could see it.

One youngster asked: "Is it a boy kitty or a girl kitty?"

The teacher, unprepared for that discussion, said, "It doesn't matter; it's just a kitten."

But the children persisted, and one little boy said, "I know how we can tell if it is a boy kitty or a girl kitty."

The teacher, cornered, said, "All right, you tell us how we can tell if it is a boy kitty or a girl kitty."

The boy answered, "We can vote on it!"

Some things cannot be changed. Doctrine cannot be changed.

"Principles which have been revealed," President Wilford Woodruff said,

> for the salvation and exaltation of the children of men . . . are principles you cannot annihilate. *They are principles that no combination of men [or women] can destroy.* They are principles that can never die. . . . They are beyond the reach of man to handle or to destroy. . . . It is not in the power of the whole world put together to destroy those principles. . . . Not one jot or tittle of these principles will ever be destroyed.[36]

During World War II, men were called away to fight. In the emergency, wives and mothers worldwide were drawn into the work force as never before. The most devastating effect of the war was on the family. It lingers to this generation.

Multiply and Replenish the Earth

In the October 1942 general conference, the First Presidency delivered a message to "the Saints in every land and clime," in which they said, "By virtue of the authority in us vested as the First Presidency of the Church, we warn our people."

And they said:

> Amongst His earliest commands to Adam and Eve, the Lord said: "Multiply and replenish the earth." He has repeated that command in our day. He has again revealed in this, the last dispensation, the principle of the eternity of the marriage covenant. . . .
>
> The Lord has told us that it is the duty of every husband and wife to obey the command given to Adam to multiply and replenish the earth, so that the legions of choice spirits waiting for their tabernacles of flesh may come here and move forward under God's great design to become perfect souls, for without these fleshly tabernacles they cannot progress to their God-planned destiny. Thus, every husband and wife should become a father and mother in Israel to children born under the holy, eternal covenant.
>
> By bringing these choice spirits to earth, each father and each mother assume towards the tabernacled spirit and towards the Lord Himself by having taken advantage of the opportunity He offered, an obligation of the most sacred kind, because the fate of that spirit in the eternities to come, the blessings or punishments which shall await it in the hereafter, depend, in great part, upon the care, the teachings, the training which the parents shall give to that spirit.
>
> No parent can escape that obligation and that responsibility, and for the proper meeting thereof, the Lord will hold us to a strict accountability. No loftier duty than this can be assumed by mortals.

Motherhood Is a Holy Calling

Speaking of mothers, the First Presidency said:

> Motherhood thus becomes a holy calling, a sacred dedication for carrying out the Lord's plans, a consecration of devotion to the uprearing and fostering, the nurturing in body, mind, and spirit, of those who kept their first estate and who come to this earth for their second estate "to see if they will do all things whatsoever the Lord their God shall command them" (Abraham 3:25). To lead them to keep their second estate is the work of motherhood, and "they who keep their second estate shall have glory added upon their heads for ever and ever" (op. cit.) [Abr. 3:6].
>
> This divine service of motherhood can be rendered only by mothers. It may not be passed to others. Nurses cannot do it; public nurseries cannot do it; hired help cannot do it—only mother, aided as much as may be by the loving hands of father, brothers, and sisters, can give the full needed measure of watchful care.

The First Presidency counseled that

> the mother who entrusts her child to the care of others, that she may do non-motherly work, whether for gold, for fame, or for civic service, should remember that "a child left to himself bringeth his mother to shame" (Prov. 29:15). In our day the Lord has said that unless parents teach their children the doctrines of the Church "the sin be upon the heads of the parents" (D&C 68:25).
>
> Motherhood is near to divinity. It is the highest, holiest service to be assumed by mankind. It places her who honors its holy calling and service next to the angels.[37]

That message and warning from the First Presidency is needed more, not less, today than when it was given. And no voice from any organization of the Church on any level of administration equals that of the First Presidency.[38]

Any soul who by nature or circumstance is not afforded the blessing of marriage and parenthood or who innocently must act alone in rearing children, working to support them will not be denied in the eternities any blessing—provided they keep the commandments.[39]As President Lorenzo Snow promised: "That is sure and positive."[40]

Parable of the Treasure and Keys

I close with a parable.

Once a man received as his inheritance two keys. The first key, he was told, would open a vault which he must protect at all cost. The second key was to a safe within the vault which contained a priceless treasure. He was to open this safe and freely use the precious things which were stored therein. He was warned that many would seek to rob him of his inheritance. He was promised that if he used the treasure worthily, it would be replenished and never be diminished, not in all eternity. He would be tested. If he used it to benefit others, his own blessings and joy would increase.

The man went alone to the vault. His first key opened the door. He tried to unlock the treasure with the other key, but he could not, for there were two locks on the safe. His key alone would not open it. No matter how he tried, he could not open it. He was puzzled. He had been given the keys. He knew the treasure was rightfully his. He had obeyed instructions, but he could not open the safe.

In due time, there came a woman into the vault. She, too, held a key. It was noticeably different from the key he held. Her key fit the other lock. It humbled him to learn that he could not obtain his rightful inheritance without her.

They made a covenant that together they would open the treasure and, as instructed, he would watch over the vault and protect it; she would watch over the treasure. She was not concerned that, as guardian of the vault, he held two keys, for his full purpose was to see that she was safe as she watched over that which was most precious to them both. Together they opened the safe and partook of their inheritance. They rejoiced for, as promised, it replenished itself.

With great joy they found that they could pass the treasure on to their children; each could receive a full measure, undiminished to the last generation.

Perhaps some few of their posterity would not find a companion who possessed the complementary key, or one worthy and willing to keep the covenants relating to the treasure. Nevertheless, if they kept the commandments, they would not be denied even the smallest blessing.

Because some tempted them to misuse their treasure, they were careful to teach their children about keys and covenants.

There came, in due time, among their posterity some few who were deceived or jealous or selfish because one was given two keys and another only one. "Why," the selfish ones reasoned, "cannot the treasure be mine alone to use as I desire?"

Some tried to reshape the key they had been given to resemble the other key. Perhaps, they thought, it would then fit both locks. And so it was that the safe was closed to them. Their reshaped keys were useless, and their inheritance was lost.

Those who received the treasure with gratitude and obeyed the laws concerning it knew joy without bounds through time and all eternity.

I bear witness of our Father's plan for happiness, and bear testimony in the name of Him who wrought the Atonement, that it might be, in the name of Jesus Christ, amen.

Notes

1. See D&C 76:24; see also Numbers 16:22; Hebrews 12:9.
2. See D&C 132:63; First Presidency, "Origin of Man" (November 1909), in James R. Clark, comp., *Messages of the First Presidency of The Church of Jesus Christ of Latter-day Saints*, 6 vols. (Salt Lake City: Bookcraft, 1965-75), 4:203; see also Spencer W. Kimball, "The Blessings and Responsibilities of Womanhood," *Ensign*, March 1976, p. 71; Gordon B. Hinckley, *Ensign*, Nov. 1983, p. 83.
3. See *Teachings of the Prophet Joseph Smith*, sel. Joseph Fielding Smith (Salt Lake City: Deseret Book Co., 1938), pp. 348-49, 357, 365.
4. See Abraham 3:24-27.
5. See Jarom 1:2; Alma 24:14; 42:5; Moses 6:62.
6. See Jacob 6:8; Alma 12:25-36; 17:16; 18:39; 22:13-14; 39:18; 42:11, 13.
7. Alma 42:8.
8. See Alma 42:2-5.
9. See 2 Nephi 9:28; Alma 12:4, 5; Helaman 2:8; 3 Ne. 1:16; D&C 10:12, 23; Moses 4:3.
10. See *Teachings of the Prophet Joseph Smith*, pp. 181, 297.
11. See *Teachings of the Prophet Joseph Smith*, p. 181.
12. See 2 Nephi 2:18; 28:20.
13. See Alma 39:5; Moroni 9:9.
14. See D&C 130:2; 131:2; 1 Cor. 11:11; Ephesians 5:31.
15. See Moses 6:8-9.
16. See Moses 3:8.
17. See Moses 6:67.
18. See Moses 3:18.
19. See Moses 3:23-24.
20. D&C 42:22; emphasis added.
21. See Moses 4:7-12.
22. 2 Nephi 2:25.
23. *Cowley and Whitney on Doctrine*, comp. Forace Green (Salt Lake City: Bookcraft, 1963), p. 287.

24. Moses 2:28; see also Genesis 1:28; 9:1.
25. See Gaatians. 5:22-23; D&C 4:5-6; Alma 7:23-24.
26. See D&C 131:2.
27. See "Our Wives and Our Mothers in the Eternal Plan," (address given in general Relief Society conference, 3 October 1946), in *J. Reuben Clark: Selected Papers on Religion, Education, and Youth*, ed. David H. Yarn, Jr. (Provo, Utah: Brigham Young University Press, 1984), p. 62.
28. See Genesis 1:28, note 28c.
29. See D&C 75:28; 1 Timothy 5:8.
30. D&C 107:40-41; see also D&C 84:14-16.
31. D&C 121:41-42; italics added.
32. D&C 121:37.
33. D&C 84:39.
34. D&C 121:37.
35. See *Teachings of the Prophet Joseph Smith*, pp. 308, 367.
36. In *Journal of Discourses*, 22:342; italiacs added.
37. In Conference Report, October 1942, pp. 7, 11-12.
38. See D&C 107:8-9, 22, 91.
39. See D&C 137:7-9.
40. "Discourse by President Lorenzo Snow," *Millennial Star*, 31 August 1899, p. 547.

Covenants

Elder Boyd K. Packer, of the Quorum of the Twelve Apostles

Ensign, November 1990, pp. 84-86

It was an experience to hear President Joseph Fielding Smith pray. Even when he was past ninety he would pray that he would "keep his covenants and obligations and endure to the end." The word covenant is the subject of my message.

The Lord told the ancients, "With thee will I establish my covenant" (Gen. 6:18). He told the Nephites, "Ye are the children of the covenant" (3 Ne. 20:26). And he described the restored gospel as the "new and . . . everlasting covenant" (D&C 22:1). Every Latter-day Saint is under covenant. Baptism is a covenant; so is the sacrament. Through it we renew the covenant of baptism and commit to "always remember him and keep his commandments" (D&C 20:77).

Three Dangerous Life-Styles

My message is to you who are tempted either to promote, to enter, or to remain in a life-style which violates your covenants and will one day bring sorrow to you and to those who love you.

Growing numbers of people now campaign to make spiritually dangerous life-styles legal and socially acceptable. Among them are abortion, the gay-lesbian movement, and drug addiction. They are debated in forums and seminars, in classes, in conversations, in conventions, and in courts all over the world. The social and political aspects of them are in the press every day.

Moral and Spiritual

The point I make is simply this: there is a MORAL and SPIRITUAL side to these issues which is universally ignored. For Latter-day Saints, morality is one component which must not be missing when these issues are considered—otherwise sacred covenants are at risk! Keep your covenants and you will be safe. Break them and you will not.

The commandments found in the scriptures, both the positive counsel and the "shalt nots," form the letter of the law. There is also the spirit of the law. We are responsible for both.

Some challenge us to show where the scriptures specifically forbid abortion or a gay-lesbian or drug-centered life-style. "If they are so wrong," they ask, "why don't the scriptures tell us so in 'letter of the law' plainness?" These issues are not ignored in the revelations. The scriptures are generally positive rather than negative in their themes, and it is a mistake to assume that anything not specifically prohibited in the 'letter of the law' is somehow approved of the Lord. All the Lord approves is not detailed in the scriptures, neither is all that is forbidden. The Word of Wisdom, for instance, makes no specific warning against taking arsenic. Surely we don't need a revelation to tell us that!

The Lord said, "It is not meet that I should command in all things; for he that is compelled in all things, the same is a slothful and not a wise servant" (D&C 58:26). The prophets told us in the Book of Mormon that "men are instructed sufficiently that they know good from evil" (2 Ne. 2:5; see Hel. 14:31).

Life is meant to be a test to see if we will keep the commandments of God (See 2 Ne. 2:5). We are free to obey or to ignore the spirit and the letter of the law. But the agency granted to man is a moral agency (See D&C 101:78). We are not free to break our covenants and escape the consequences.

The laws of God are ordained to make us happy. Happiness cannot coexist with immorality: the prophet Alma told us in profound simplicity that "wickedness never was happiness" (Alma 41:10).

Right of Choice

Always when these destructive life-styles are debated, "individual right of choice" is invoked as though it were the one sovereign virtue. That could only be true if there were but one of us. The rights of any individual bump up against the rights of another. And the simple truth is that we cannot be happy, nor saved, nor exalted, without one another.

Tolerance

The word tolerance is also invoked as though it overrules everything else. Tolerance may be a virtue, but it is not the commanding one. There is a difference between what one is and what one does. What one is may deserve unlimited tolerance; what one does, only a measured amount. A virtue when pressed to the extreme may turn into a vice. Unreasonable devotion to an ideal, without considering the practical application of it, ruins the ideal itself.

Abortion

Nowhere is the right of choice defended with more vigor than with abortion. Having chosen to act, and a conception having occurred, it cannot then be unchosen. But there are still choices; always a best one.

Sometimes the covenant of marriage has been broken; more often none was made. In or out of marriage, abortion is not an individual choice. At a minimum, three lives are involved.

The scriptures tell us: "Thou shalt not . . . kill, nor do anything like unto it" (D&C 59:6).

Except where the wicked crime of incest or rape was involved, or where competent medical authorities certify that the life of the mother is in jeopardy, or that a severely defective fetus cannot survive birth, abortion is clearly a "thou shalt not." Even in these very exceptional cases, much sober prayer is required to make the right choice.

We face such sobering choices because we are the children of God.

Man Not Just an Animal

Little do we realize what we have brought upon ourselves when we have allowed our children to be taught that man is only an advanced animal. We have compounded the mistake by neglecting to teach moral and spiritual values. Moral laws do not apply to animals for they have no agency. Where there is agency, where there is choice, moral laws must apply. We cannot, absolutely cannot, have it both ways.

When our youth are taught that they are but animals, they feel free, even compelled, to respond to every urge and impulse. We should not be so puzzled at what is happening to society. We have sown the wind, and now we inherit the whirlwind. The chickens, so the saying goes, are now coming home to roost.

Gay and Lesbian Rights

Several publications are now being circulated about the Church which defend and promote gay or lesbian conduct. They wrest the scriptures attempting to prove that these impulses are inborn, cannot be overcome, and should not be resisted; and therefore, such conduct has a morality of its own. They quote

137

scriptures to justify perverted acts between consenting adults. That same logic would justify incest or the molesting of little children of either gender. Neither the letter nor the spirit of moral law condones any such conduct.

I hope none of our young people will be foolish enough to accept those sources as authority for what the scriptures mean. Paul, speaking on this very subject, condemned those "who changed the truth of God into a lie, and worshipped and served the creature more than the Creator" (Rom. 1:25). In that same reference the word covenant breakers is used for the only time in scripture (See Rom. 1:31).

Some choose to reject the scriptures out of hand and forsake their covenants. But they cannot choose to avoid the consequences. That choice is not theirs or ours or anybody's.

All of us are subject to feelings and impulses. Some are worthy and some of them are not; some of them are natural and some of them are not. We are to control them, meaning we are to direct them according to the moral law.

The legitimate union of the sexes is a law of God. The sacred covenants made by husband and wife with God protect the worthy expression of those feelings and impulses which are vital to the continuation of the race and essential to a happy family life. Illicit or perverted conduct leads without exception to disappointment, suffering, to tragedy.

Local Priesthood Leaders

We receive letters pleading for help, asking why should some be tormented by desires which lead toward addiction or perversion. They seek desperately for some logical explanation as to why they should have a compelling attraction, even a predisposition, toward things that are destructive and forbidden.

Why, they ask, does this happen to me? It is not fair! They suppose that it is not fair that others are not afflicted with the same temptations. They write that their bishop could not answer the "why," nor could he nullify their addiction or erase the tendency.

We are sometimes told that leaders in the Church do not really understand these problems. Perhaps we don't. There are many "whys" for which we just do not have simple answers. But we do understand temptation, each of us, from personal experience. Nobody is free from temptations of one kind or another. That is the test of life. That is part of our mortal probation. Temptation of some kind goes with the territory.

What we do know is where these temptations will lead. We have watched these life-styles play themselves out in many lives. We have seen the end of the road you are tempted to follow. It is not likely that a bishop can tell you what causes these conditions or why you are afflicted, nor can he erase the temptation. But he can tell you what is right and what is wrong. If you know right from wrong, you have a place to begin. That is the point at which individual choice becomes operative. That is the point at which repentance and forgiveness can exert great spiritual power.

I believe that most people are drawn into a life of drug addiction or perversion or submit to an abortion without really realizing how morally and spiritually dangerous they are.

A Tempter

Perhaps the worst of all conditions which we can create for ourselves is to become a tempter and lead an innocent one into a life-style that is destructive. The tempter entices others to come out of a "closet," to violate covenants which they have made with God. He promises emancipation and exhilaration without saying that such a course may be spiritually fatal.

A tempter will claim that such impulses cannot be changed and should not be resisted. Can you think of anything the adversary would rather have us believe?

The Lord warned, "Whosoever shall offend one of these little ones that believe in me, it is better for him that a millstone were hanged about his neck, and he were cast into the sea" (Mark 9:42).

Support Groups

There are support groups of many kinds which seek to fortify those struggling to withdraw from drug addiction or to master other temptations. On the other hand, there are organizations which do just the opposite. They justify immoral conduct and bind the chains of addiction or perversion ever tighter. Do not affiliate with such an organization. If you have already, withdraw from it.

Spirit of Sympathy and Love

Now, in a spirit of sympathy and love, I speak to you who may be struggling against temptations for which there is no moral expression. Some have resisted temptation but never seem to be free from it. Do not yield! Cultivate the spiritual strength to resist—all of your life, if need be.

Some are tortured by thoughts of covenants already forsaken and sometimes think of suicide. Suicide is no solution at all. Do not even think of it. The very fact that you are so disturbed marks you as a spiritually sensitive soul for whom there is great hope.

You may wonder why God does not seem to hear your pleading prayers and erase these temptations. When you know the gospel plan, you will understand that the conditions of our mortal probation require that we be left to choose. That test is the purpose of life. While these addictions may have devoured, for a time, your sense of morality or quenched the spirit within you, it is never too late.

You may not be able, simply by choice, to free yourself at once from unworthy feelings. You can choose to give up the immoral expression of them.

The suffering you endure from resisting or from leaving a life-style of addiction or perversion is not a hundredth part of that suffered by your parents, your spouse or your children, if you give up. Theirs is an innocent suffering because they love you. To keep resisting or to withdraw from such a life-style is an act of genuine unselfishness, a sacrifice you place on the altar of obedience. It will bring enormous spiritual rewards.

Remember that agency, that freedom of choice that you demanded when you forsook your covenants? That same agency can now be drawn upon to exert a great spiritual power of redemption.

The love we offer may be a tough love, but it is of the purest kind; and we have more to offer than our love. We can teach you of the cleansing power of repentance. If covenants have been broken, however hard it may be, they may be reinstated, and you can be forgiven. Even for abortion? Yes, even that!

"Come now, and let us reason together, saith the Lord: though your sins be as scarlet, they shall be as white as snow; though they be red like crimson, they shall be as wool" (Isa. 1:18).

God bless you who are struggling to resist or to free yourself from these terrible temptations that now sweep across the world, and from which we are not free in the Church. Bless those who love you and sustain you. There is great cleansing power in the priesthood. There is great cleansing power in the Church. It is a gospel of repentance. He is our Redeemer. Of him I bear witness—Jesus Christ the son of God, the Only Begotten of the Father, who sacrificed himself that we might be clean. And of him I bear witness, in the name of Jesus Christ, amen.

Scriptures from Elder Packer's Talk on Covenants

1. Genesis 13:13
   But the men of Sodom were wicked and sinners before the Lord exceedingly (footnote 13-b TG homosexuality).
2. Genesis 18:20-22
   And the Lord said, Because the cry of Sodom and Gomorrah is great, and because their sin is very grievous (footnote 20b TG homosexuality).
3. Genesis 19:5
   And they called unto Lot, and said unto him, Where are the men which came in to thee this night? bring them out unto us, that we may know them (footnote 5a — 'know' is used both in Hebrew

and English in this kind of context as a euphemism in place of a sexual word, as in 'Adam knew his wife and she conceived' (Genesis 4:1).

4. Genesis 19:9-15 (JST)

5. Leviticus 18:22, 29

Thou shalt not lie with mankind, as with womankind: it is abomination; For whosoever shall commit any of these abominations, even the souls that commit them shall be cut off from among their people.

6. Leviticus 20:13

If a man also lie with mankind, as he lieth with a woman, both of them have committed an abomination; they shall surely be put to death; their blood shall be upon them.

7. Deuteronomy 23:17

There shall be no whore of the daughters of Israel, nor a sodomite of the sons of Israel (footnote 17b, Hebrew: a professional male or female prostitute, or cultist; TG Homosexuality).

8. Romans 1:24-27

Wherefore God also gave them up to uncleanness through the lusts of their own hearts, to dishonour their own bodies between themselves;

Who changed the truth of God into a lie, and worshiped and served the creature more than the Creator, who is blessed for ever. Amen.

For this cause God gave them up unto vile affections: for even their women did change the natural use into that which is against nature;

And likewise also the men, leaving the natural use of the woman, burned in their lust one toward another; men with men working that which is unseemly, and receiving in themselves that recompense of their error which was meet.

9. I Corinthians 6:9

Know ye not that the unrighteous shall not inherit the kingdom of God? Be not deceived: neither fornicators, nor idolaters, nor adulterers, nor effeminate, nor abusers of themselves with mankind; (footnotes 9e &f, catamites, male homosexuals).

10. 1 Timothy 1:9-10

Knowing this, that the law is not made for a righteous man, but for the lawless and disobedient, for the ungodly and for sinners, for unholy and profane, for murders of fathers and murderers of mothers, for manslayers,

For whoremongers, for them that defile themselves with mankind, for menstealers, for liars, for perjured persons, and if there be any other thing that is contrary to sound doctrine; (footnotes 10b & c, homosexuals, homosexuality).

President Kimball Speaks Out on Morality

President Spencer W. Kimball

Ensign, November 1980, pp. 94-98

My beloved brothers and sisters, while this is a grave responsibility, and not an easy one, I am eager to discuss with you some matters of importance.

I love youth. I rejoice when they grow up clean and stalwart and tall. I sorrow with them when they have misfortunes and remorse and troubles.

Numerous disasters have occurred in mid-ocean by collisions of ships, sometimes with icebergs, and numerous people have gone to watery graves. I believe you young people are wholesome and basically good and sound; but you, too, are traveling oceans which to you are at least partially uncharted, where there are shoals and rocks and icebergs and other vessels, and where great disasters can come unless warnings are heeded.

A couple of years ago as my jet plane soared in the air gaining altitude, the voice of the stewardess came clearly over the loudspeaker: "We are moving into a storm area. We shall skirt the danger, but there may be some turbulence. Be sure your seat belts are securely fastened."

And, as a leader of the Church and in a measure being responsible for youth and their well-being, I raise my voice to say to you: "You are in a hazardous area and period. Tighten your belts, hold on, and you can survive the turbulence."

I have interviewed thousands of young people and many seem to flounder. Some give excuses for their efforts and indulge in unwarranted rationalizations. I hope I may be able to clarify at least in some areas the stand of the God of heaven and his church on some vital issues.

First, let us pause to remind ourselves that we are the spiritual children of God, and that we are his supreme creation. In each of us there is the potentiality to become a God—pure, holy, true, influential, powerful, independent of earthly forces. We learn from the scriptures that we each have eternal existence, that we were in the beginning with God (see Abr. 3:22). That understanding gives to us a unique sense of man's dignity.

But there are false teachers everywhere, using speech and pornographic literature, magazines, radio, TV, street talk—spreading damnable heresies which break down moral standards, and this to gratify the lust of the flesh.

Lucifer in his diabolical scheming deceives the unwary and uses every tool at his command. Seldom does one go to a convention, a club meeting, a party, or a social gathering without hearing vulgarity, obscenity, and suggestive stories.

Peter cautioned us: "Be sober, be vigilant; because your adversary the devil, as a roaring lion, walketh about, seeking whom he may devour" (1 Pet. 5:8).

And the Savior said that the very elect would be deceived by Lucifer if it were possible. He will use his logic to confuse and his rationalizations to destroy. He will shade meanings, open doors an inch at a time, and lead from purest white through all the shades of gray to the darkest black.

So I wish today to help define meanings of words and acts for you young people, to fortify you against error, anguish, pain, and sorrow.

Necking, Petting, Fornication

I will begin with a true story. The characters are real. He was well proportioned and, like King David, "ruddy, and withal of a beautiful countenance, and goodly to look to" (1 Sam. 16:12).

With him at his side was a lovely girl, slight of frame and beautiful of face and form. It was obvious that they loved one another, for as they sat together across the desk from me, he reached quietly for her hand and there were meaningful glances.

The melodious voice was hesitant and a bit choked with emotion as he introduced his girl friend, and there was pleading in their eyes. "We are in difficulty, Brother Kimball," he said. "We have broken the law of chastity. We prayed and fasted and agonized and finally came to the conclusion that we must try to make adjustments.

"That junior prom date was a turning point. It started out a very special one. But as I see it now, it turned out to be a tragic one, the beginning of our troubles. When I saw her coming downstairs that night, I thought no girl was ever so beautiful and so sweet. We danced through the evening; and then when we sat in the car, long and silently afterward, my thoughts became unruly as we became more and more intimate.

"Neither of us dreamed what was happening to us," he continued, "but all the elements were there to break down resistance. We did not notice time—the hours passed. The simple kisses we had often exchanged gradually developed into petting. We stopped at that. But there were other nights—the bars were down. We loved each other so much that we convinced ourselves that it was not so wrong merely to pet since we sort of belonged to one another anyway. Where we ended one night became the starting point for the next night, and we continued on and on, until finally it happened—almost as though we could not control ourselve—we had intercourse. We had even talked about it and agreed that whatever else we did we would not go that far. And then when it was late—so late—so everlastingly late—we woke up to the meaning of what we had done."

Immorality does not begin in adultery or perversion. It begins with little indiscretions like sex thoughts, sex discussions, passionate kissing, petting and such, growing with every exercise. The small indiscretion seems powerless compared to the sturdy body, the strong mind, the sweet spirit of youth who give way to the first temptation. But soon the strong has become weak, the master the slave, spiritual growth curtailed. But if the first unrighteous act is never given root, the tree will grow to beautiful maturity and the youthful life will grow toward God, our Father.

"Can we be forgiven, Brother Kimball?" the young couple asked.

"Yes," I replied, "the Lord and his church can and will forgive, but not easily. The way of the transgressor is hard. It always has been and it always will be. The Lord said: 'I tell thee, thou shalt not depart thence, till thou hast paid the very last mite'" (Luke 12:59).

But I went on to tell them that in his goodness he provided for us a way to forgiveness. One may do-as he pleases, but he cannot evade responsibility. He may break laws, but he cannot avoid penalties. One gets by with nothing. God is just. Paul said, "Be not deceived; God is not mocked; for whatsoever a man sowed, that shall he also reap" (Gal. 6:7).

Serious as is the sin of fornication (sexual intercourse by the unmarried), there is forgiveness upon condition of total repentance. But first one must come to a realization of the seriousness of his sin. Since the beginning there has been in the world a wide range of sins. Many of them involve harm to others, but every sin is against ourselves and God, for sins limit our progress, curtail our development, and estrange us from good people, good influences, and from our Lord.

The early apostles and prophets mention numerous sins that were reprehensible to them. Many of them were sexual sins—adultery, being without natural affection, lustfulness, infidelity, incontinence, filthy communications, impurity, inordinate affection, fornication. They included all sexual relations outside marriage—petting, sex perversion, masturbation, and preoccupation with sex in one's thoughts and talking. Included are every hidden and secret sin and all unholy and impure thoughts and practices. One of the worst of these is incest. The dictionary defines incest as "sexual intercourse between persons so closely related that they are forbidden by law to marry." The spirituality of one's life may be severely, and sometimes irreparably, damaged by such an ugly sin. The First Presidency and the Quorum of the Twelve have determined that the penalty for incest shall be excommunication. Also, one excommunicated for incest shall not be baptized again into the Church without the written permission of the First Presidency.

Conscience tells the individual when he is entering forbidden worlds, and it continues to prick until silenced by the will or by sin's repetition.

Can anyone truthfully say he did not know such things were wrong? These unholy practices, whatever may be their unmentionable names with all their approaches and numerous manifestations, are condemned by the Lord and his church. Some may be more heinous than others, but all are sin, in spite of statements to the contrary of those who falsely pretend to know. The Lord's prophets declare they are not right.

The world may have its norm; the Church has a different one. It may be considered normal by the people of the world to use tobacco; the Church's standard is a higher plane where smoking is not done. The world's norm may permit men and women social drinking; the Lord's church lifts its people to a norm of total abstinence. The world may countenance premarital sex experiences, but the Lord and his church condemn in no uncertain terms any and every sex relationship outside of marriage.

Paul lashed out against these unholy evidences of the vulgar mind and of uncontrolled passion and desire:

"Wherefore God also gave them up to uncleanness through the lusts of their own hearts, to dishonour their own bodies between themselves" (Rom. 1:24).

Since courtship is prelude to marriage and encourages close associations, many have convinced themselves that intimacies are legitimate—a part of the courting process. Many have cast off bridle and harness and have relaxed the restraints. Instead of remaining in the field of simple expressions of affection, some have turned themselves loose to fondling, often called "necking," with its intimate contacts and its passionate kissing. Necking is the younger member of this unholy family. Its bigger sister is called "petting." When the intimacies have reached this stage, they are surely the sins condemned by the Savior:

"Ye have heard that it was said by them of old time, Thou shalt not commit adultery:

"But I say unto you, That whosoever looketh on a woman to lust after her hath committed adultery with her already in his heart" (Man. 5:27-28).

Who would say that he or she who pets has not become lustful, has not become passionate? Is it not this most abominable practice that God rebuked in his modern reiteration of the Ten Commandments: "Thou shalt not steal; neither commit adultery, nor kill, nor do anything like unto it" (D&C 59:6).

What, may I ask you, is like unto adultery if it is not petting? Did not the Lord recognize that this heinous sin is but the devil's softening process for the final acts of adultery or fornication? Can a person in the light of the Lord's scriptures pursue the path of petting with clear conscience? Can anyone convince himself that this is not deep sin?

We must repeat what we have said many times: Fornication with all its big and little brothers and sisters was evil and wholly condemned by the Lord in Adam's day, in Moses' day, in Paul's day, and in our own day. The Church has no tolerance for any kind of perversions. The Lord has indicated his lack of tolerance, stating:

"For I the Lord cannot look upon sin with the least degree of allowance" (D&C 1:31).

When the scriptures are so plain, how can anyone justify immoralities and call them love? Is black white? Is evil good? Is purity filthiness?

That the Church's stand on morality may be understood, we declare firmly and unalterably, it is not an outworn garment, faded, old-fashioned, and threadbare. God is the same yesterday, today, and forever, and his covenants and doctrines are immutable; and when the sun grows cold and the stars no longer shine, the law of chastity will still be basic in God's world and in the Lord's church. Old values are upheld by the Church not because they are old, but rather because through the ages they have proved right. It will always be the rule.

Dating Standards

In order to avoid difficulty and possible temptation, I suggest again the following standard. Any dating or pairing off in social contacts should be postponed until at least the age of 16 or older, and even then there should still be much judgment used in selections and in the seriousness. Young people should still limit the close contacts for several years, since the boy will be going on his mission when he is 19 years old.

Dating and especially steady dating in the early teens is most hazardous. It distorts the whole picture of life. It deprives you of worthwhile and rich experiences; it limits friendships; it reduces the acquaintances which can be so valuable in selecting a partner for time and eternity.

There is definitely a time for the dance, for travel, for associations, for the date, and even for the steady date that will culminate in the romance which will take young people to the holy temple for eternal marriage. But it is the timing that is so vital. It is wrong to do even the right things at the wrong time in the wrong place under the wrong circumstances.

I believe the youth of Zion want to hear the clear and unmistakable tones of the trumpet, and it is my hope that I can play the tune with accuracy and precision so that no honest person will ever be confused. I hope fervently that I am making clear the position of the Lord and his church on these unmentionable practices.

Self-abuse

Masturbation, a rather common indiscretion, is not approved of the Lord nor of his church, regardless of what may have been said by others. whose "norms" are lower. Latter-day Saints are urged to avoid this practice. Anyone fettered by this weakness should abandon the habit before he goes on a mission or receives the holy priesthood or goes in the temple for his blessings.

Sometimes masturbation is the introduction to the more serious sins of exhibitionism and the gross sin of homosexuality. We would avoid mentioning these unholy terms and these reprehensible practices were it not for the fact that we have a responsibility to the youth of Zion that they be not deceived by those who would call bad good, and black white.

Homosexuality

The unholy transgression of homosexuality is either rapidly growing or tolerance is giving it wider publicity. If one has such desires and tendencies, he overcomes them the same as if he had the urge toward petting or fornication or adultery. The Lord condemns and forbids this practice with a vigor equal to his condemnation of adultery and other such sex acts. And the Church will excommunicate as readily any unrepentant addict.

Again, contrary to the belief and statement of many people, this sin, like fornication, is overcomable and forgivable, but again, only upon a deep and abiding repentance, which means total abandonment and complete transformation of thought and act. The fact that some governments and some churches and numerous corrupted individuals have tried to reduce such behavior from criminal offense to personal privilege does not change the nature nor the seriousness of the practice. Good men, wise men, God-fearing men everywhere still denounce the practice as being unworthy of sons and daughters of God; and Christ's church denounces it and condemns it so long as men and women have bodies which can be defiled.

James said: "A double minded man is unstable in all his ways.

"Blessed is the man that endureth temptation: for when he is tried, he shall receive the crown of life, which the Lord hath promised to them that love him.

"Let no man say when he is tempted, I am tempted of God: for God cannot be tempted with evil, neither tempteth he any man:

"But every man is tempted, when he is drawn away of his own lust, and enticed.

"Then when lust hath conceived, it bringeth forth sin: and sin, when it is finished, bringeth forth death.

"Do not err, my beloved brethren" (James 1:8, 12-16).

This heinous homosexual sin is of the ages. Many cities and civilizations have gone out of existence because of it. It was present in Israel's wandering days, tolerated by the Greeks, and found in the baths of corrupt Rome.

This is a most unpleasant subject to dwell upon, but I am pressed to speak of it boldly so that no youth in the Church will ever have any question in his mind as to the illicit and diabolical nature of this perverse program. Again, Lucifer deceives and prompts logic and rationalization which will destroy men and women and make them servants of Satan forever. Paul told Timothy:

"For the time will come when they will not endure sound doctrine; but after their own lusts shall they heap to themselves teachers, having itching ears;

"And they shall turn away their ears from the truth, and shall be turned unto fables" (2 Tim. 4:3-4; see also Moses 5:50-55).

"God made me that way," some say, as they rationalize and excuse themselves for their perversions. "I can't help it, " they add. This is blasphemy. Is man not made in the image of God, and does he think God to be "that way"? Man is responsible for his own sins. It is possible that he may rationalize and excuse himself until the groove is so deep he cannot get out without great difficulty, but this he can do. Temptations come to all people. The difference between the reprobate and the worthy person is generally that one yielded and the other resisted. It is true that one's background may make the decision and accomplishment easier or more difficult, but if one is mentally alert, he can still control his future. That is the gospel message—personal responsibility.

And now, my dear brothers and sisters, I have spoken frankly and boldly against the sins of the day. Even though I dislike such a subject, I believe it necessary to warn the youth against the onslaught of the arch tempter who, with his army of emissaries and all the tools at his command, would destroy all the youth of Zion, largely through deception, misrepresentation, and lies.

"Be wise in the days of your probation," said Mormon, "strip yourselves of all uncleanness; ask not, that ye may consume it on your lusts, but ask with a firmness unshaken, that ye will yield to no temptation, but that ye will serve the true and living God" (Morm. 9:28).

Repentance

Beloved youth, for those of you who have erred, the Lord and his church can forgive. The image of a loving, forgiving God comes through clearly to those who read and understand the scriptures. Since he is our Father, he naturally desires to raise us up, not to push us down, to help us live, not to bring about our spiritual death.

Repentance seems to fall into five steps:

1. **Sorrow for sin**. To be sorry for our sin we must know something of its serious implications. When fully convicted, we condition our minds to follow such processes as will rid us of the effects of the sin. We are sorry. We are willing to make amends, pay penalties, to suffer even to excommunication if necessary.

2. **Abandonment of sin**. It is best when one discontinues his error because of his realization of the gravity of his sin and when he is willing to comply with the laws of God. The thief may abandon his evil in prison, but true repentance would have him forsake it before his arrest and return his booty without enforcement. The sex offender who voluntarily ceases his unholy practices is headed toward forgiveness. Alma said, "Blessed are they who humble themselves without being compelled to be humble" (Al. 32:16).

The discontinuance must be a permanent one. True repentance does not permit repetition. The Lord revealed this to the Prophet Joseph Smith concerning repentance: "By this ye may know if a man repenteth of his sins—behold, he will confess them and forsake them" (D&C 58:43).

3. **Confession of sin**. The confession of sin is an important element in repentance. Many offenders have seemed to feel that a few prayers to the Lord were sufficient. They have thus justified themselves in hiding their sins.

✴ "He that covereth his sins shall not prosper: but whoso confesseth and forsaketh them shall have mercy" (Prov. 28:13).

Especially grave efforts such as sexual sins shall be confessed to the bishop as well as to the Lord. There are two remissions which one might wish to have. First, the forgiveness from the Lord, and second, the forgiveness of the Lord's church through its leaders. As soon as one has an inner conviction of his sins, he should go to the Lord in "mighty prayer" as did Enos and never cease his supplications until he shall, like Enos, receive the assurance that his sins have been forgiven by the Lord. It is unthinkable that God absolves serious sins upon a few requests. He is likely to wait until there has been long, sustained repentance as evidenced by a willingness to comply with all his other requirements. Next, the offender should seek the forgiveness of the Church through his bishop. No priest or elder is authorized to thus act for the Church. The Lord has a consistent, orderly plan. Every soul in stakes is given a bishop who, by the very order of his calling and his ordination, is a "judge in Israel." The bishop is our best earthly friend. He will hear the problems, judge the seriousness, then determine the degree of repentance and decide if it warrants an eventual forgiveness. He does this as the earthly representative of God—the master physician, the master psychologist, the master psychiatrist. If repentance is sufficient he may waive penalties, which is tantamount to forgiveness. The bishop claims no authority to absolve sins, but he does share the burden, waive penalties, relieve tension and strain; and he may assure a continuance of activity. He will keep the whole matter most confidential.

4. **Restitution for sin**. When one is humble in sorrow, has unconditionally abandoned the evil, and confessed to those assigned by the Lord, he should next restore insofar as possible that which was damaged. If he burglarized, he should return to the rightful owner that which was stolen. Perhaps one reason murder is unforgivable is that having taken a life, the murderer cannot restore it. Restitution in full is not possible. Also, having robbed one of virtue, it is impossible to give it back.

However, the truly repentant soul will usually find things which can be done to restore to some extent. The true spirit of repentance demands this. Ezekiel taught, "If the wicked . . . give again that he had robbed, walk in the statutes of life, without committing iniquity; he shall surely live" (Ezek. 33:15).

Moses taught, "If a man shall steal an ox or a sheep, . . . he shall restore five oxen for an ox, and four sheep for a sheep" (Exo. 22:1).

A pleading sinner must also forgive all people of all offenses committeth against himself. The Lord is under no obligation to forgive us unless our hearts are fully purged of all hate, bitterness, and accusations against all others.

5. **Do the will of the Father**. I received many birthday cards for my 83rd birthday in March of 1978. One was bound in a book and had 4,700 autographs of youth who had signed the book. There were many others also, and other thousands of signatures. They were pledging their lives with such statements as the following:

"Dear President Spencer W. Kimball:

"As a member of our world, I pledge to you and with the Lord to lengthen my stride, to quicken my pace, to stretch my soul in the work of the Lord.

"I promise to pay my tithing faithfully and regularly all my life.

"I promise to you and the Lord to live the Word of Wisdom, even though temptations arise. No tobacco, liquor, tea, coffee, or drugs will I ever touch.

"I promise to remember my nightly and morning prayers. I shall never forget the Lord nor his rich promises, his protecting care, and his rich blessings.

"I promise above all that I will keep my life clean and unspotted from the numerous insidious temptations. There will never be any approach to immorality of any nature.

"I pledge that I shall lengthen my stride in the reading and absorbing of the scriptures and other good books.

"I pledge sincerely that I will quicken my pace in my love of my fellowman and work together with them in achieving righteousness.

"I will stretch my soul to understand all of the commandments of the Lord and live them with great precision and care and love."

Now, brothers and sisters, you are sweet and wonderful, and we are proud of you, proud of the records you make, proud of the devotion you show, proud of the sacrifice you make. I tell you, we love you. How we pray for you every meeting we hold, every night and morning in our homes, and every night in our bedrooms; we pray for you that you will keep yourselves clean. Clean—we mean clean from beginning to end. Free from all the ugly things the world is pushing upon us—the drugs, and drinking, and smoking, the vulgarity, the pornography—all those things you don't need to participate in. You must not give yourselves to them.

Put on the full armor of God. Attend to your personal and family prayers and family devotions; keep holy the Sabbath; live strictly the Word of Wisdom; attend to all family duties; and above all, keep your life clean and free from all unholy and impure thoughts and actions. Avoid all associations which degrade and lower the high, righteous standards set up for us. Then your life will sail smoothly and peace and joy will surround you.

The Law of Chastity

President Ezra Taft Benson

BYU Devotional, Tuesday, October 13, 1987

In this dispensation the Lord reiterated the commandment given at Sinai when He said, "Thou shalt not . . . commit adultery, . . . *nor do anything like unto it*" (D&C 59:6; emphasis added). From the beginning of time, the Lord has set a clear and unmistakable standard of sexual purity. It always has been, it is now, and it always will be the same. That standard is the law of chastity. It is the same for all—it is the same for men and women; it is the same for old and young; it is the same for rich and poor.

In the Book of Mormon, the prophet Jacob tells us that the Lord delights in the chastity of His children (see Jacob 2:28). Do you hear that, my brothers and sisters? The Lord is not just pleased when we are chaste. He *delights* in chastity. Mormon taught the same thing to his son, Moroni, when he wrote that chastity and virtue are "most dear and precious above all things" (Moroni 9:9).

My dear brothers and sisters, the law of chastity is a principle of eternal significance. We must not be swayed by the many voices of the world. We must listen to the voice of the Lord and then determine that we will set our feet irrevocably upon the path He has marked.

Reaping the Consequences

The world is already beginning to reap the consequences of its abandonment of any standards of morality. As just one example, recently the secretary of the Department of Health and Human Services in the United States warned that if a cure for AIDS is not quickly found, it could become a worldwide epidemic that "will dwarf such earlier medical disasters as the Black Plague, smallpox and typhoid" ("HHS Chief Says AIDS Will Dwarf the Plague," *Salt Lake Tribune*, 30 January 1987, p. A-1).

As the world seeks solutions for this disease, which began primarily through widespread homosexuality, people look everywhere but to the law of the Lord. There are numerous agencies, both public and private, trying to combat AIDS. They seek increased funding for research. They sponsor programs of education and information. They write bills aimed at protecting the innocent from infection. They set up treatment programs for those who have already become infected. These are important and necessary programs, and we commend those efforts. But why is it we rarely hear anyone calling for a return to chastity, for a commitment to virtue and fidelity?

I recognize that most people fall into sexual sin in a misguided attempt to fulfill basic human needs. We all have a need to feel loved and worthwhile. We all seek to have joy and happiness in our lives. Knowing this, Satan often lures people into immorality by playing on their basic needs. He promises pleasure, happiness, and fulfillment.

But this is, of course, a deception. As the writer of Proverbs says: "Whoso committeth adultery with a woman lacketh understanding: he that doeth it destroyeth his own soul" (Proverbs 6:32). Samuel the Lamanite taught the same thing when he said, "Ye have sought for happiness in doing iniquity, which thing is contrary to the nature of . . . righteousness" (Helaman 13:38). Alma said it more simply: "Wickedness never was happiness" (Alma 41:10).

Do not be misled by Satan's lies. There is no lasting happiness in immorality. There is no joy to be found in breaking the law of chastity. Just the opposite is true. There may be momentary pleasure. For a time it may seem like everything is wonderful. But quickly the relationship will sour. Guilt and shame set in. We become fearful that our sins will be discovered. We must sneak and hide, lie and cheat. Love begins to die. Bitterness, jealousy, anger, and even hate begin to grow. All of these are the natural results of sin and transgression.

On the other hand, when we obey the law of chastity and keep ourselves morally clean, we will experience the blessings of increased love and peace, greater trust and respect for our marital partners, deeper commitment to each other, and, therefore, a deep and significant sense of joy and happiness.

We must not be misled into thinking these sins are minor, or that consequences are not that serious. One of the most sobering statements about being unchaste is that of Alma to his son Corianton: "Know ye not, my son," he said, "that these things are an abomination in the sight of the Lord; yea, *most abominable above all sins* save it be the shedding of innocent blood or denying the Holy Ghost?" (Alma 39:5; emphasis added). Very few of us will ever be guilty of murder or of the sin against the Holy Ghost. But the law of chastity is frequently broken, and yet it stands next to these other sins in seriousness in the eyes of the Lord.

My beloved brothers and sisters, are we living in accordance with these scriptures? Do we clearly understand the seriousness of sexual sins? Do we constantly stress the blessings that come from obedience to this law? I say again, as have all the prophets before me, there is one standard of virtue and chastity, and all are expected to adhere to it. What the Lord says unto one, He says unto all: "Ye must practise virtue and holiness before me continually" (D&C 46:33).

Six Steps to Prepare and Prevent

There is an old saying that states: It is better to prepare and prevent than it is to repair and repent. How true that is of the law of chastity. The first line of defense in keeping ourselves morally clean is to prepare ourselves to resist temptation and prevent ourselves from falling into sin.

For those who are pure and chaste, may I give six steps that are steps of preparation and prevention, steps that will insure that you never fall into this transgression:

1. **Decide now to be chaste**. The decision to be chaste and virtuous need only be made once. Make that decision now and let it be so firm and with such deep commitment that it can never be shaken. Don't wait until you are alone in a parked car or caught in a compromising situation to decide to be chaste. Decide now!

2. **Control your thoughts**. No one steps into immorality in an instant. The first seeds of immorality are always sown in the mind. When we allow our thoughts to linger on lewd or immoral things, the first step on the road to immorality has been taken. I especially warn you against the evils of pornography. Again and again we hear from those caught in deep sin that often the first step on their road to transgression began with pornographic materials. The Savior taught that even when a man looks upon a woman to lust after her, or in other words, when he lets his thoughts begin to get out of control, he has already committed adultery with her in his heart (see Matthew 5:28, D&C 63:16).

3. **Always pray for the power to resist temptation**. Temptation will come to all of us. It will take many forms and appear in many disguises, but the Lord has given us the key for resisting it. He said to the Prophet Joseph: "Pray always, that you may come off conqueror; yea, that you may conquer Satan, and that you may escape the hands of the servants of Satan that do uphold his work" (D&C 10:5). It should be part of our daily prayers to ask the Lord for constant strength to resist temptations, especially temptations that involve the law of chastity.

4. **If you are married, avoid flirtations of any kind**. Sometimes we hear of a married man going to lunch with his secretary or other women in the office. Men and women who are married sometimes flirt with and tease members of the opposite sex. So-called harmless meetings are arranged or inordinate amounts of time are spent together. In all of these cases, people rationalize by saying that these are natural expressions of friendship. But what may appear to be harmless teasing or simply having a little fun with someone of the opposite sex can easily lead to more serious involvement and eventual infidelity. A good question to ask ourselves is this: Would my spouse be pleased if he or she knew I was doing this? Would a wife be pleased to know that her husband lunches alone with his secretary? Would a husband be pleased if he saw his wife flirting and being coy with another man? My beloved brothers and sisters, this is what Paul meant when he said: "Abstain from all appearance of evil" (1 Thessalonians 5:22).

5. **If you are married, avoid being alone with members of the opposite sex whenever possible**. Many of the tragedies of immorality begin when a man and woman are alone in the office or at church or driving in a car. At first there may be no intent or even thought of sin. But the circumstances provide a fertile seedbed for temptation. One thing leads to another, and very quickly tragedy may result. It is so much easier to avoid such circumstances from the start so that temptation gets no chance for nourishment.

6. **For those who are single and dating members of the opposite sex, carefully plan positive and constructive activities so that you are not left to yourselves with nothing to do but share physical affection.** Once again this is the principle of filling one's life with the positive so that the negative has no chance to thrive. When young people are left to themselves for long periods of time with no specific planned activities, often they turn to necking and petting to fill the empty hours.

Five Steps to Repair and Repent

But I realize that there may be some, even now within the sound of my voice, for whom the counsel to prepare and prevent is too late. You may already be deeply entangled in serious sin. If this is the case, there is no choice now but to repair your lives and repent of your sins. To you I would suggest five important things you can do to come back to a state of moral purity.

1. **Flee immediately from any situation you are in that is either causing you to sin or that may cause you to sin.** When Joseph of Egypt was entrapped by Potiphar's wife alone in the house, it would have been easy for Joseph to have rationalized. After all, he had not encouraged her. After all, he was her servant. After all, it would hurt her feelings if he refused. Had Joseph stood there and rationalized, he could easily have fallen. There is a great lesson in how he did respond. The scripture says, "And he left his garment in her hand, *and fled, and got him out*" (Genesis 39:12; emphasis added). He fled and got himself out. My beloved brothers and sisters, if you are currently in a situation where your moral purity is being or could be compromised, follow Joseph's example. Flee from it and get yourself out. You cannot linger in sin and expect to have success in repentance.

2. **Plead with the Lord for the power to overcome.** One of Satan's most effective strategies with those he has lured into sin is to whisper in their ears that they are not worthy to pray. He will tell you that Heavenly Father is so displeased with you that He will never hear your prayers. This is a lie, and he says it to deceive us. The power of sin is great. If we are to extricate ourselves from it, especially serious sin, we must have a power greater than ourselves. No one is more anxious to help you flee from sin than your Father in Heaven. Go to

Him. Acknowledge your sin, confess your shame and your guilt, and then plead with Him for help. He has the power to help you triumph.

3.   **Let your priesthood leaders help you resolve the transgression and come back into full fellowship with the Lord.** Certain sins are of such gravity that they put our standing in the Church in jeopardy. Sexual sins are among those of such seriousness (see D&C 42:24). Full repentance of such sins requires that we not only confess our sins and resolve them with the Lord, but that we also do so with the Church. This is done through appropriate priesthood leaders. The bishops and stake presidents have been appointed by revelation to serve as watchmen over the Church and as judges in Israel. While only the Lord can forgive sins, the priesthood leaders play a critical role in the process of repentance. Even if we are disfellow-shipped or excommunicated, it is a beginning step in the process of repentance, and the sooner one begins, the sooner one can find the sweet peace and joy that come with the mir-acle of forgiveness.

4.   **Drink from the divine fountain and fill your lives with positive sources of power.** It is not enough simply to try to resist evil or empty our lives of sin. We must also fill our lives with righteousness. We must engage in activities that bring spiritual power. I speak of such activities as immersing ourselves in the scriptures. There is a power that flows into our lives when we read and study the scriptures on a daily basis that cannot be found in any other way. Daily prayer is another source of great power. Fasting for specific strength or special blessings can strengthen us beyond our normal ability. Christian service, church attendance, service in the kingdom—all can add to our storehouse of strength and power. We must do more than simply remove the negative influences from our lives. We must replace them with righteous activities that fill us with the strength and determination to live as we should.

5.   **Remember that through proper repentance you can become clean again.** Moroni taught that "despair cometh because of iniquity" (Moroni 10:22). Those who are caught in immor-ality may be experiencing the devastating effects of despair. But there is an alternative. For those who pay the price required by true repentance, the promise is sure. You can be clean again. The despair can be lifted. The sweet peace of forgiveness will flow into your lives.

Finding Joy

The words of the Lord through Isaiah are sure: "Come now, and let us reason together, saith the Lord: though your sins be as scarlet, they shall be as white as snow; though they be red like crimson, they shall be as wool" (Isaiah 1:18).

And in this dispensation the Lord spoke with equal clarity when He said, "Behold, he who has re-pented of his sins, the same is forgiven, and I, the Lord, remember them no more" (D&C 58:42).

As I said earlier, when it comes to the law of chastity, it is better to prepare and prevent than it is to re-pair and repent.

My beloved brothers and sisters in the gospel, our Heavenly Father desires nothing for us but to be happy. He tells us only those things that will bring us joy. And one of the surest principles given by God to help us find that joy is the law of chastity.

I pray with all my heart that you will consider most solemnly the joyful consequences of keeping this law and the tragic consequences of violating it. And I do this in the name of our Savior, Jesus Christ. Amen.

Making the Right Choices

Elder Richard G. Scott

Ensign, November 1994, pp. 37-39

Present tonight are many young men who hold the priesthood of God.[1] Some of you look forward to being a missionary when you are older. Others are planning to go soon; still others have completed missions and are seeking an eternal companion. I am sobered by the realization that some of you will not reach these worthy goals because of other choices you are making now.

I am grateful this is a private priesthood meeting, for I have felt impressed to treat sensitive yet important matters. While they apply to all present, I particularly want to talk with you young men. I will speak as though you and I were alone in a private interview and no one else can hear us. My purpose is to help you learn how to make the right choices. That will help you develop strong feelings of self-worth. You will have confidence to do right and overcome strong negative peer pressure and bad influences.

As a young boy, I felt that some things that I heard discussed by others at school about private parts of the body were wrong. Yet, I wasn't really sure how wrong or why they were wrong. You may have similar feelings. Since in tonight's setting you cannot ask me anything, I will use some of the confidential questions most frequently asked by youth I have met across the world. I will answer them by what I have learned from the scriptures and the prophets. You then will have clear standards from which to make choices. I pray that as we talk the Holy Ghost will let you feel the truth of what is said. I know that as you listen and think of how our interview applies to you, there will come impressions regarding what to do about it in your own life.

Question: Could you give us some help about resisting peer pressure? Why do some people do things that are wrong, then brag about how much fun they are having? When I don't participate, they make me feel stupid because I won't do it.

Answer: You can't please God without upsetting Satan, so you will get pressure from those he tempts to do wrong. Individuals who do wrong want you to join them because they feel more comfortable in what they are doing when others do it also. They may also want to take advantage of you. It is natural to want to be accepted by peers, to be part of a group—some even join gangs because of that desire to belong, but they lose their freedom, and some lose their lives. One of the hardest things for you to recognize is how truly strong you already are and how others silently respect you. We have great confidence in you. You don't need to compromise your standards to be accepted by good friends. The more obedient you are, the more you stand for true principles, the more the Lord can help you overcome temptation?[2] You can also help others because they will feel your strength. Let them know about your standards by consistently living them. Answer questions about your principles when you are asked, but avoid being preachy. I know from personal experience that works.

No one intends to make serious mistakes. They come when you compromise your standards to be more accepted by others. You be the strong one. You be the leader. Choose good friends and resist peer pressure together.

Question: How do we keep bad thoughts from entering our minds, and what do we do when they come?

Answer: Some bad thoughts come by themselves. Others come because we invite them by what we look at and listen to?[3] Talking about or looking at immodest pictures of a woman's body can stimulate powerful emotions. It will tempt you to watch improper videocassettes or movies. These things surround you, but you must not participate in them. Work at keeping your thoughts clean by thinking of something good.[4] The mind can think of only one thing at a time. Use that fact to crowd out ugly thoughts.[5] Above all, don't feed thoughts by reading or watching things that are wrong. If you don't control your thoughts, Satan will keep tempting you until you eventually act them out.[6]

Question: Why is the law of chastity so important? Why is sex before marriage wrong?

Answer: Fundamental to the great plan of happiness and central to the teachings of the Savior is the family. A new family begins when a man and a woman make sacred marriage vows and are legally bound together to become husband and wife, father and mother. The perfect beginning is through sealing in the temple. With marriage they commit the best of themselves to be absolutely loyal to each other and to invite children to be nurtured and taught. The father assumes his role as provider and protector, the mother her role as the heart of the home, with her tender, loving, nurturing influence. Together they strive to instill in themselves and their children principles such as prayer, obedience, love, giving of oneself, and the quest for knowledge.

Within the enduring covenant of marriage, the Lord permits husband and wife the expression of the sacred procreative powers in all their loveliness and beauty within the bounds He has set.[7] One purpose of this private, sacred, intimate experience is to provide the physical bodies for the spirits Father in Heaven wants to experience mortality. Another reason for these powerful and beautiful feelings of love is to bind husband and wife together in loyalty, fidelity, consideration of each other, and common purpose.

However, those intimate acts are forbidden by the Lord outside the enduring commitment of marriage because they undermine His purposes.[8] Within the sacred covenant of marriage, such relationships are according to His plan. When experienced any other way they are against His will. They cause serious emotional and spiritual harm. Even though participants do not realize that is happening now, they will later. Sexual immorality creates a barrier to the influence of the Holy Spirit with all its uplifting, enlightening, and empowering capabilities. It causes powerful physical and emotional stimulation. In time that creates an unquenchable appetite that drives the offender to even more serious sin. It engenders selfishness and can produce aggressive acts such as brutality, abortion, sexual abuse, and violent crime. Such stimulation can lead to acts of homosexuality, and they are evil and absolutely wrong.[9]

Sexual transgression would defile the priesthood you now hold, sap your spiritual strength, undermine your faith in Jesus Christ, and frustrate your ability to serve Him. Consistent, willing obedience increases your confidence and ability. It produces character that allows you to face difficult challenges and overcome them. It qualifies you to receive inspiration and power from the Lord.[10]

Question: They always tell us we shouldn't become sexually involved, but they never tell us the limits. What are they?

Answer: Any sexual intimacy outside of the bonds of marriage—I mean any intentional contact with the sacred, private parts of another's body, with or without clothing—is a sin and is forbidden by God. It is also a transgression to intentionally stimulate these emotions within your own body.[11] Satan tempts one to believe that there are allowable levels of physical contact between consenting individuals who seek the powerful stimulation of emotions they produce, and if kept within bounds, no harm will result. As a witness of Jesus Christ, I testify that is absolutely false. Satan particularly seeks to tempt one who has lived a pure, clean life to experiment through magazines, videocassettes, or movies with powerful images of a woman's body. He wants to stimulate appetite to cause experimentation that quickly results in intimacies and defilement. Powerful habits are formed which are difficult to break. Mental and emotional scars result.

When you are mature enough to plan seriously for marriage, keep your expressions of feelings to those that are comfortable in the presence of your parents.[12] To help you keep these sacred commandments, make a covenant with the Lord that you will obey them. Decide what you will do and will not do. When temptation comes, do not change your standards. Do not abandon them when circumstances seem to justify an exception. That is Satan's way to hurt you by making it seem that sometimes God's law does not apply. There are no exceptions.

Question: Before you are married, how far is too far to go if it is with your girlfriend?

Answer: Before marriage there can be no sexual contact with a girlfriend, fiancée or anyone else, period.[13] While a commandment, that standard is for your happiness. That's why the Church counsels you to go in groups and not to date while you are young. Later, as you prepare for marriage, remember that true love elevates, protects, respects, and enriches another. It motivates you to make sacrifices for the girl you love. Satan would promote counterfeit love, which is really lust. That is driven by hunger to satisfy personal appetite. Protect the one you love by controlling your emotions to the limits set by the Lord. You know how to be clean. We trust you to do it.

Question: How do you go about repenting after a sexual sin is committed? What sins should you tell the bishop?

Answer: All of the sexual transgressions we have discussed require sincere repentance with the participation of the bishop. Should you have done any of this, repent now. It is wrong to violate these commandments of the Lord. It is worse to do nothing about it. Sin is like cancer in the body. It will never heal itself. It will become worse unless cured through repentance. Your parents can help strengthen you. Then you can become clean and pure by repentance under the guidance of the bishop. He may seem to be busy or unavailable. Tell him you are in trouble and need help. He will listen.

A youth in serious trouble said:

> I have done things that I knew were bad. I have been taught they were ever since
> I can remember. I know repentance is a great gift; without it I would be lost. But I'm
> not ready to repent of my sins, yet I know when I am ready I can.

How tragic. The thought of intentionally committing serious sin and repenting later is perilously wrong. Never do that.[14] Many start that journey of intentional transgression and never make it back. Premeditated sin has greater penalties and is harder to overcome. If there is sin, repent now—while you can.

I pray that as we have talked you have had feelings to do better.[15] You hold the priesthood of God. That is a sacred responsibility,[16] and also a singular privilege.[17] You will be fortified in your determination to live righteously as you study the scriptures, especially the Book of Mormon. Listen to your parents, leaders, and the prophet we have sustained today. Have faith in the Savior. He will help you.[18] Remember He said, "I the Lord, am bound when ye do what I say; but when ye do not what I say, ye have no promise."[19]

Please stay morally clean. The Lord will make that possible as you do your part with all your strenght.[20] Jesus Christ lives, and He loves you. He will help you as you do your part. In the name of Jesus Christ, amen.

Notes

1. See *Discourses of Wilford Woodruff,* sel. G. Homer Durham (Salt Lake City: Bookcraft, 1946), p. 64; see also *Millennial Star,* 51(1889):657.
2. See I Corinthians 10:13.
3. See H. Burke Peterson, *Ensign,* November 1993, pp. 42-44.
4. See *Teachings of Ezra Taft Benson* (Salt Lake City: Bookcraft, 1988), pp. 278,445-46.
5. See Boyd K. Packer, *Ensign,* January 1974, p. 27.

6. See Thomas S. Monson, *Ensign,* November 1990, p. 47; see also Robert L. Simpson, *Ensign,* January 1973, p. 112.
7. See Spencer W. Kimball, *Ensign,* May 1974, p. 7.
8. See Boyd K. Packer, *Ensign,* July 1972, pp. 111-13.
9. See Spencer W. Kimball, *Ensign,* November 1980, pp. 97-98.
10. See D&C 43:9, 15-16.
11. See Spencer W. Kimball, *Ensign,* November 1974, p. 8; November 1977, p. 6; November 1980, p. 97.
12. See *Teachings of Ezra Taft Benson,* pp. 283-84.
13. See *The Teachings of Spencer W. Kimball,* ed. Edward L. Kimball (Salt Lake City: Bookcraft, 1982), pp. 65, 176-77.
14. *Teachings of Ezra Taft Benson*, pp. 70-72.
15. See D&C 64:33-34.
16. See D&C 84:35-39. See also Spencer W. Kimball, *The Miracle of Forgiveness* (Salt Lake City: Bookcraft, 1969), pp. 124-25.
17. See *The Teachings of Spencer W. Kimball, p.* 494.
18. See Moroni 10:32.
19. D&C 82:10.
20. See 3 Nephi 18:20.

The Brilliant Morning of Forgiveness

President Boyd K. Packer

Ensign, November 1995, pp. 18-21

In April of 1847, Brigham Young led the first company of pioneers out of Winter Quarters. At that same time, sixteen hundred miles to the west the pathetic survivors of the Donner Party straggled down the slopes of the Sierra Nevada Mountains into the Sacramento Valley.

They had spent the ferocious winter trapped in the snowdrifts below the summit. That any survived the days and weeks and months of starvation and indescribable suffering is almost beyond belief.

Among them was fifteen-year-old John Breen. On the night of April 24, he walked into Johnson's Ranch. Years later John wrote:

> It was long after dark when we got to Johnson's Ranch, so the first time I saw it was early in the morning. The weather was fine, the ground was covered with green grass, the birds were singing from the tops of the trees, and the journey was over. I could scarcely believe that I was alive.
>
> The scene that I saw that morning seems to be photographed on my mind. Most of the incidents are gone from memory, but I can always see the camp near Johnson's Ranch.[1]

At first I was very puzzled by his statement that "most of the incidents are gone from memory." How could long months of incredible suffering and sorrow ever be gone from his mind? How could that brutal dark winter be replaced with one brilliant morning?

On further reflection, I decided it was not puzzling at all. I have seen something similar happen to people I have known. I have seen one who has spent a long winter of guilt and spiritual starvation emerge into the morning of forgiveness.

When morning came, they learned this:

> Behold, he who has repented of his sins, the same is forgiven, and I, the Lord, remember them no more.[2]
>
> *I, even I, am* he that blotteth out thy transgressions for mine own sake, and will not remember thy sins.[3]
>
> I will forgive their iniquity, and I will remember their sin no more.[4]
>
> For I will be merciful to their unrighteousness, and their sins and their iniquities will I remember no more.[5]

When the prophet Alma was young, he spent such a time *"racked,"* as he said, *"with eternal torment,* [his] soul . . . *harrowed up to the greatest degree.*[6]

He even thought, *"Oh. . . that I could be banished and become extinct both soul and body.'*[7]

But his mind caught hold of a thought. When he nurtured the thought and acted upon it, the morning of forgiveness came, and he said:

I could remember my pains no more; yea, I was harrowed up by the memory of my sins no more.

And oh, what joy, and what marvelous light I did behold; yea, my soul was filled with joy as exceeding as was my pain![8]

Letters come from those who have made tragic mistakes. They ask, "Can I *ever* be forgiven?" The answer is *yes!*

The gospel teaches us that relief from torment and guilt can be earned through repentance. Save for those few who defect to perdition after having known a fulness there is no habit, no addiction, no rebellion, no transgression, no offense exempted from the promise of complete forgiveness.

"Come now, and let us reason together, saith the Lord: though your sins be as scarlet, they shall be as white as snow; though they be red like crimson, they shall be as wool." That is, Isaiah continued, "if ye be willing and obedient."[9]

Even that grace of God promised in the scriptures comes only "after all we can do."[10]

You may tell yourself that your transgressions are not spiritually illegal. That will not work; neither will rebellion, nor anger, nor joking about them. You cannot do that. And you don't have to do it.

There is a way back. It will not help if, out of tender regard for your feelings, I avoid telling you about the hard part.

John Breen did not come to that morning at Johnson's Ranch simply by desiring it. He wallowed and clawed his way up over the pass, suffering every step of the way. But once he knew he would survive and the suffering would end, surely he did not complain at the ordeal. And he had help all the way down. He was with rescuers.

When an offense is minor, so simple a thing as an apology will satisfy the law. Most mistakes can be settled between us and the Lord, and that should be done speedily.[11] It requires a confession to Him, and whatever obvious repairs need to be made.

With sincere repentance as a pattern in our lives, measured by our willingness to "confess them and forsake them,"[12] the Lord has promised that we may "always *retain* a remission of [our] sins."[13]

Alma bluntly told his wayward son that "repentance could not come unto men except there were a punishment."[14]

The punishment may, for the most part, consist of the torment we inflict upon ourselves. It may be the loss of privilege or progress[15] (For further information see additional text in this endnote). We are punished *by* our sins, if not *for* them.

There are some transgressions which require a discipline which will bring about the relief that comes with the morning of forgiveness. If your mistakes have been grievous ones, go to your bishop. Like the rescuers who brought John Breen down from the mountaintops, bishops can guide you through the steps required to obtain forgiveness insofar as the Church is concerned. Each one of us must work out individually forgiveness from the Lord.

To earn forgiveness, one must make restitution. That means you give back what you have taken or ease the pain of those you have injured.

But sometimes you *cannot* give back what you have taken because you don't have it to give. If you have caused others to suffer unbearably—defiled someone's virtue, for example—it is not within your power to give it back.

There are times you cannot mend that which you have broken. Perhaps the offense was long ago, or the injured refuse your penance. Perhaps the damage was so severe that you cannot fix it no matter how desperately you want to.

Your repentance cannot be accepted unless there is a restitution. If you cannot undo what you have done, you are trapped. It is easy to understand how helpless and hopeless you then feel and why you might want to give up, just as Alma did.

The thought that rescued Alma, when he acted upon it, is this: Restoring what you cannot restore, healing the wound you cannot heal, fixing that which you broke and you cannot fix is the very purpose of the atonement of Christ.

When your desire is firm and you are willing to pay the "uttermost farthing,"[16] the law of restitution is suspended. Your obligation is transferred to the Lord. He will settle your accounts.

I repeat, save for the exception of the very few who defect to perdition, there is no habit, no addiction, no rebellion, no transgression, no apostasy, no crime exempted from the promise of complete forgiveness. That is the promise of the atonement of Christ.

How all can be repaired, we do not know. It may not all be accomplished in this life. We know from visions and visitations that the servants of the Lord continue the work of redemption beyond the veil.[17]

This knowledge should be as comforting to the innocent as it is to the guilty. I am thinking of parents who suffer unbearably for the mistakes of their wayward children and are losing hope.

Some members wonder why their priesthood leaders will not accept them just as they are and simply comfort them in what they call pure Christian love.

Pure Christian love, the love of Christ, does not presuppose approval of all conduct. Surely the ordinary experiences of parenthood teach that one can be consumed with love for another and yet be unable to approve unworthy conduct.

We cannot, as a church, approve unworthy conduct or accept into full fellowship individuals who live or who teach standards that are grossly in violation of that which the Lord requires of Latter-day Saints.

If we, out of sympathy, should approve unworthy conduct it might give present comfort to someone, but would not ultimately contribute to their happiness.[18]

In the most tender of sermons in the revelations on kindness and longsuffering, on meekness, gentleness on love unfeigned, the Lord instructs us to reprove "betimes with sharpness, when moved upon by the Holy Ghost; and then [show] forth afterwards an increase of love toward him whom thou hast reproved."[19]

The Lord provides ways to pay our debts to him. In one sense, we ourselves may participate in an atonement. When we are willing to restore to others that which we have not taken, or heal wounds that we did not inflict, or pay a debt that we did not incur, we are emulating His part in the Atonement.

So many live with accusing guilt when relief is ever at hand. So many are like the immigrant woman who skimped and saved and deprived herself, until by selling all of her possessions, she bought a steerage-class ticket to America.

She rationed out the meager provisions she was able to bring with her. Even so, they were gone early in the voyage. When others went for their meals, she stayed below deck—determined to suffer through it. Finally, on the last day, she must, she thought, afford one meal to give her strength for the journey yet ahead. When she asked what the meal would cost, she was told that all of her meals had been included in the price of her ticket.

That great morning of forgiveness may not come at once. Do not give up if at first you fail. Often the most difficult part of repentance is to forgive yourself. Discouragement is part of that test. Do not give up. That brilliant morning will come.

Then "the peace of God, which passeth . . . understanding" comes into your life once again.[20] Then you, like Him, will remember your sins no more. How will you know? You will know![21]

Some years ago I was in Washington, D.C., with President Harold B. Lee. Early one morning he called me to come into his hotel room. He was sitting in his robe reading *Gospel Doctrine* by President Joseph F. Smith, and he said,

> Listen to this!
> Jesus had not finished his work when his body was slain, neither did he finish it after his resurrection from the dead; although he had accomplished the purpose for which he then came to the earth, he had not fulfilled all his work. And when will he? Not until he has redeemed and saved every son and daughter of our father Adam that have been or ever will be born upon this earth to the end of time, except the sons of perdition. That is his mission. We will not finish our work until we have saved ourselves, and then not until we shall have saved all depending upon us; for we are to become saviors upon Mount Zion, as well as Christ. We are called to this mission.[22]

"There is never a time," the Prophet Joseph Smith taught, "when the spirit is too old to approach God. *All are within the reach of pardoning mercy, who have not committed the unpardonable sin.*"[23]

And so we pray, and we fast, and we plead, and we implore. We love those *who* wander, and we never give up hope.

I bear witness of Christ and of the power of His atonement. And I know that

> his anger kindleth against the wicked; they repent and in a moment it is turned away, and they are in his favor, and he giveth them life; therefore, weeping may endure for a night, but joy cometh in the morning.[24]

In the name of Jesus Christ, amen.

Notes

1. John Breen, "Pioneer Memoirs," unpublished, as quoted on "The Americanization of Utah," PBS television broadcast.
2. D&C 58:42.
3. Isaiah 43:25; emphasis added.
4. Jeremiah 31:34.
5. Hebrews 8:12; see also Hebrews 10:17.
6. Alma 36:12; emphasis added.
7. Alma 36:15; emphasis added.
8. Alma 36:19-20.
9. Isaiah 1: 18-19.
10. 2 Nephi 25:23.
11. See D&C 109:21.
12. D&C 58:43; see also Ezekiel 18:21-24, 31-32.
13. Mosiah 4:12; emphasis added.
14. Alma 42:16.
15. Forgiveness will come eventually to all repentant souls who have not committed the unpardonable sin (see Matthew 12:31). Forgiveness does not, however, necessarily assure exaltation, as is the case with David (see D&C 132:38-39; see also Psalm 16:10; Acts 2:25-27; *Teachings of the Prophet Joseph Smith,* p. 339).
16. See Matthew 5:25-26.
17. See D&C 138.
18. See *Teachings of the Prophet Joseph Smith,* pp. 256-57.
19. D&C 121:43.
20. Philippians 4:7.
21. See Mosiah 4:1-3.
22. Joseph F. Smith, *Gospel Doctrine,* 5th ed., Salt Lake City: Deseret Book Co., 1939, p. 442; emphasis added.
23. *Teachings of the Prophet Joseph Smith,* p. 191; emphasis added.
24. JST, Psalm 30:5; see also D&C 61:20.

Chastity

Elder Robert D. Hales, *Ensign*, May 1990, p. 40.

We are here at priesthood meeting this evening to learn those things which are necessary to prepare us to be strong and dedicated priesthood holders. We are preparing ourselves to take on higher laws and covenants such as obedience, sacrifice, service, chastity, and consecration of our time and talents. Why do we do this? We should learn this before we go to the temple, brethren, because afterwards it will help each of us to be valiant missionaries, caring eternal companions, and devoted fathers. We are preparing to return with honor to the presence of our Heavenly Father along with our entire families.

Elder M. Russell Ballard, *Ensign*, November 1990, p. 35.

We are aware that the youth of the Church are growing up in a world that is plagued with teenage moral misconduct. We also know that sexual sin has increased tremendously during the past twenty years. Far too many of the youth, particularly American youth, have violated the law of chastity before they reach the age of nineteen. Unfortunately, the youth of the Church are not immune. For this reason, I want to assure you young men that your leaders know of the challenges you face in today's society. However, we have confidence that you can develop the strength and integrity to surmount these challenges and live for the blessings that are promised to those who remain morally clean. I emphasize that you do not need to be caught in the trap of being immoral—not one of you, ever. Each one of you must look into the future to understand the consequences of your actions, both good and bad. The cartoon character Ziggy said it this way: "Our future is shaped by our past . . . so be very careful what you do in your past!"

Elder M. Russell Ballard, *Ensign*, November 1990, p. 36.

The youth told me that a clean conscience improves their self-esteem. Their relationships with others are better, and they enjoy a very positive acceptance. In fact, some of them said they have lots more fun because of their high standards. They never have to worry about the dreaded diseases that often follow those who transgress the law of chastity.

Elder Joseph B. Wirthlin, *Ensign,* November 1991, p. 17.

Obedience to the law of chastity would diminish cries for abortion and would go a long way toward controlling sexually transmitted disease. Total fidelity in marriage would eliminate a major cause of divorce, with its consequent pain and sadness inflicted especially upon innocent children.

Elder Richard G. Scott, *Ensign,* November 1991, p. 85.

Not all our prayers will be answered as we wish. It is not always easy to know the will of the Lord, yet there are some things we can be certain of. He will never ask us to do anything that is not completely in harmony with His teachings. We cannot count on help if we are immoral or otherwise deliberately disobedient unless we sincerely repent. One who prays to know if another is to be the eternal companion while violating in any degree the law of chastity has little hope of receiving confirmation without repentance.

President Gordon B. Hinckley, *Ensign,* November 1993, p. 59.

What is happening is simply an ugly expression of the declining values of our society. Those who are concerned with the problem advocate more legal regulation, large appropriations for increased police forces, tax increases to build additional jails and prisons. These may be needed to deal with the present problems. They may help in the near term. But they will be only as a bandage too small for the sore. They may help in taking care of the fruits, but they will not get at the roots. In searching for remedies, we speak of a greater work that must be done in our schools. But educators have largely abdicated their responsibility for teaching values. The Church is looked to—this and all other churches. I am grateful for what the Pope recently said in Denver in warning against moral pitfalls. I am pleased to note that the Baptists have begun a campaign for chastity. We as a church are doing much, very much, and I think we are accomplishing much. But it is not enough.

Elder Dallin H. Oaks, *Ensign,* November 1993, p. 74.

The power to create mortal life is the most exalted power God has given his children. Its use was mandated in the first commandment, but another important commandment was given to forbid its misuse. The emphasis we place on the law of chastity is explained by our understanding of the purpose of our procreative powers in the accomplishment of God's plan.

Elder Joseph B. Wirthlin, *Ensign,* May 1994, p. 40.

I plead with you young brethren of the priesthood to live above the curse of immorality that is plaguing the earth. Rise above the squalor of pornography, obscenity, and filth. Be virtuous and chaste. Uphold your young sisters in the gospel by respecting their budding womanhood and protecting their virtue. Always conduct yourselves according to the commandments of God when you are with them. You want your girlfriends to remain clean and pure. Just as you surely would protect the chastity of your own sister in your family, likewise protect the virtue of your sisters in God's family.

Elder Richard G. Scott, *Ensign,* Nov. 1994, p. 38

Question: Why is the law of chastity so important? Why is sex before marriage wrong?

Answer: Fundamental to the great plan of happiness and central to the teachings of the Savior is the family. A new family begins when a man and woman make sacred marriage vows and are legally bound together to become husband and wife, father and mother. The perfect beginning is through sealing in the temple. With marriage they commit the best of themselves to be absolutely loyal to each other and to invite children to be nurtured and taught. The father assumes his role as provider and protector, the mother her role as the heart of the home, with her tender, loving, nurturing influence. Together they strive to instill in themselves and their children principles such as prayer, obedience, love, giving of oneself, and the quest for knowledge.

Within the enduring covenant of marriage, the Lord permits husband and wife the expression of the sacred procreative powers in all their loveliness and beauty within the bounds He has set. One purpose of this private, sacred, intimate experience is to provide the physical bodies for the spirits Father in Heaven wants to experience mortality. Another reason for these powerful and beautiful feelings of love is to bind husband and wife together in loyalty, fidelity, consideration of each other, and common purpose.

However, those intimate acts are forbidden by the Lord outside the enduring commitment of marriage because they undermine His purposes. Within the sacred covenant of marriage, such relationships are according to His plan. When experienced any other way, they are against His will. They cause serious emotional and spiritual harm. Even though participants do not realize that is happening now, they will later. Sexual immorality creates a barrier to the influence of the Holy Spirit with all its uplifting, enlightening, and empowering capabilities. It causes powerful physical and emotional stimulation. In time that creates an unquenchable appetite that drives the offender to ever more serious sin. It engenders selfishness and can produce aggressive acts such as brutality, abortion, sexual abuse, and violent crime. Such stimulation can lead to acts of homosexuality, and they are evil and absolutely wrong.

President Ezra Taft Benson, "Chastity," BYU Devotional, 13 October 1987, *BYU Speeches of the Year,* 1987-80, p. 50.

I recognize that most people fall into sexual sin in a misguided attempt to fulfill basic human needs. We all have a need to feel loved and worthwhile. We all seek to have joy and happiness in our lives. Knowing this, Satan often lures people into immorality by playing on their basic needs. He promises pleasure, happiness, and fulfillment.

If you are married, avoid flirtations of any kind. Sometimes we hear of a married man going to lunch with his secretary or other women in the office. Men and women who are married sometimes flirt with and tease members of the opposite sex. So-called harmless meetings are arranged or inordinate amounts of time are spent together. In all of these cases, people rationalize by saying that these are natural expressions of friendship. But what may appear to be harmless teasing or simply having a little fun with someone of the opposite sex can easily lead to more serious involvement and eventual infidelity. A good question to ask ourselves is this: Would my spouse be pleased if he or she knew I was doing this? Would a wife be pleased to know that her husband lunches alone with his secretary? Would a husband be pleased if he saw his wife flirting and being coy with another man? My beloved brothers and sisters, this is what Paul meant when he said: "Abstain from all appearance of evil" (1 Thessalonians 5:22).

If you are married, avoid being alone with members of the opposite sex whenever possible. Many of the tragedies of immorality begin when a man and woman are alone in the office or at church or driving in a car. At first there may be no intent or even thought of sin. But the circumstances provide a fertile seedbed for temptation. One thing leads to another, and very quickly tragedy may result. It is so much easier to avoid such circumstances from the start so that temptation gets no chance for nourishment.

For those who are single and dating members of the opposite sex, carefully plan positive and constructive activities so that you are not left to yourselves with nothing to do but share physical affection. Once again this is the principle of filling one's life with the positive so that the negative has no chance to thrive. When young people are left to themselves for long periods of time with no specific planned activities, often they turn to necking and petting to fill the empty hours.

Beware of Pride

President Ezra Taft Benson

April Conference Report, 1989, pp. 3-7

My beloved brethren and sisters, I rejoice to be with you in another glorious general conference of the Church. How grateful I am for the love, prayers, and service of the devoted members of the Church throughout the world.

May I commend you faithful Saints who are striving to flood the earth and your lives with the Book of Mormon. Not only must we move forward in a monumental manner more copies of the Book of Mormon, but we must move boldly forward into our own lives and throughout the earth more of its marvelous messages.

This sacred volume was written for us—for our day. Its scriptures are to be likened unto ourselves (See I Ne. 19:23).

The Doctrine and Covenants tells us that the Book of Mormon is the "record of a fallen people." (D&C 20:9). Why did they fall? This is one of the major messages of the Book of Mormon. Mormon gives the answer in the closing chapters of the book in these words: "Behold, the pride of this nation, or the people of the Nephites, hath proven their destruction" (Moro. 8:27). And then, lest we miss that momentous Book of Mormon message from that fallen people, the Lord warns us in the Doctrine and Covenants, "Beware of pride, lest ye become as the Nephites of old" (D&C 38:39).

I earnestly seek an interest in your faith and prayers as I strive to bring forth light on this Book of Mormon message—the sin of pride. This message has been weighing heavily on my soul for some time. I know the Lord wants this message delivered now.

In the premortal council, it was pride that felled Lucifer, "a son of the morning" (2 Ne. 24:12-15; see also D&C 76:25-27; Moses 4:3). At the end of this world, when God cleanses the earth by fire, the proud will be burned as stubble and the meek shall inherit the earth (See 3 Ne. 12:5, 25:1; D&C 29:9; JS-H 1:37; Mal. 4:1).

Three times in the Doctrine and Covenants the Lord uses the phrase "beware of pride," including a warning to the second elder of the Church, Oliver Cowdery, and to Emma Smith, the wife of the Prophet (D&C 23:1; see also 25:14; 38:39).

Pride is a very misunderstood sin, and many are sinning in ignorance (See Mosiah 3:11; 3 Ne. 6:18). In the scriptures there is no such thing as righteous pride—it is always considered a sin. Therefore, no matter how the world uses the term, we must understand how God uses the term so we can understand the language of holy writ and profit thereby (See 2 Ne. 4:15; Mosiah 1:3-7; Alma 5:61).

Most of us think of pride as self-centeredness, conceit, boastfulness, arrogance, or haughtiness. All of these are elements of the sin, but the heart, or core, is still missing.

The central feature of pride is enmity—enmity toward God and enmity toward our fellowmen. *Enmity* means "hatred toward, hostility to, or a state of opposition." It is the power by which Satan wishes to reign over us.

Pride is essentially competitive in nature. We pit our will against God's. When we direct our pride toward God, it is the spirit of "my will and not thine be done." As Paul said, they "seek their own, not the things which are Jesus Christ's" (Phillip. 2:21).

Our will in competition to God's will allows desires, appetites, and passions to go unbridled (See Alma 38:12; 3 Ne. 12:30).

The proud cannot accept the authority of God giving direction to their lives (See Hel. 12:6). They pit their perceptions of truth against God's great knowledge, their abilities versus God's priesthood power, their accomplishments against His mighty works.

Our enmity toward God takes on many labels, such as rebellion, hard-heartedness, stiff-neckedness, unrepentant, puffed up, easily offended, and sign seekers. The proud wish God would agree with them. They aren't interested in changing their opinions to agree with God's.

Another major portion of this very prevalent sin of pride is enmity toward our fellowmen. We are tempted daily to elevate ourselves above others and diminish them (See Hel. 6:17; D&C 58:41).

The proud make every man their adversary by pitting their intellects, opinions, works, wealth, talents, or any other worldly measuring device against others. In the words of C. S. Lewis: "Pride gets no pleasure out of having something, only out of having more of it than the next man. . . . It is the comparison that makes you proud: the pleasure of being above the rest. Once the element of competition has gone, pride has gone" (*Mere Christianity,* New York: Macmillan, 1952, pp. 109-10).

In the pre-earthly council, Lucifer placed his proposal in competition with the Father's plan as advocated by Jesus Christ (See Moses 4:13). He wished to be honored above all others (See 2 Ne. 24:13). In short, his prideful desire was to dethrone God (See D&C 29:36; 76:28).

The scriptures abound with evidences of the severe consequences of the sin of pride to individuals, groups, cities, and nations. "Pride goeth before destruction" (Prov. 16:18). It destroyed the Nephite nation and the city of Sodom (See Moro. 8:27; Ezek. 16:49-50).

It was through pride that Christ was crucified. The Pharisees were wroth because Jesus claimed to be the Son of God, which was a threat to their position, and so they plotted His death (See John 11:53).

Saul became an enemy to David through pride. He was jealous because the crowds of Israelite women were singing that "Saul hath slain his thousands, and David his ten thousands" (1 Sam. 18:6-8).

The proud stand more in fear of men's judgment than of God's judgment (See D&C 3:6-7; 30:12; 60:2). "What will men think of me?" weighs heavier than "What will God think of me?"

King Noah was about to free the prophet Abinadi, but an appeal to his pride by his wicked priests sent Abinadi to the flames (See Mosiah 17:11-12). Herod sorrowed at the request of his wife to behead John the Baptist. But his prideful desire to look good to "them which sat with him at meat" caused him to kill John (Matt. 14:9; see also Mark 6:26).

Fear of men's judgment manifests itself in competition for men's approval. The proud love "the praise of men more than the praise of God" (John 12:42-43). Our motives for the things we do are where the sin is manifest. Jesus said He did "always those things" that pleased God (John 8:29). Would we not do well to have the pleasing of God as our motive rather than to try to elevate ourselves above our brother and outdo another?

Some prideful people are not so concerned as to whether their wages meet their needs as they are that their wages are more than someone else's. Their reward is being a cut above the rest. This is the enmity of pride.

When pride has a hold on our hearts, we lose our independence of the world and deliver our freedoms to the bondage of men's judgment. The world shouts louder than the whisperings of the Holy Ghost. The reasoning of men overrides the revelations of God, and the proud let go of the iron rod (See I Ne. 8:19-28; 11:25; 15:23-24).

Pride is a sin that can readily be seen in others but is rarely admitted in ourselves. Most of us consider pride to be a sin of those on the top, such as the rich and the learned, looking down at the rest of us (See 2 Ne. 9:42). There is, however, a far more common ailment among us—and that is pride from the bottom looking up. It is manifest in so many ways, such as faultfinding, gossiping, backbiting, murmuring, living beyond our means, envying, coveting, withholding gratitude and praise that might lift another, and being unforgiving and jealous.

Disobedience is essentially a prideful power struggle against someone in authority over us. It can be a parent, a priesthood leader, a teacher, or ultimately God. A proud person hates the fact that someone is above him. He thinks this lowers his position.

Selfishness is one of the more common faces of pride. "How everything affects me" is the center of all that matters—self-conceit, self-pity, worldly self-fulfillment, self-gratification, and self-seeking.

Pride results in secret combinations which are built up to get power, gain, and glory of the world (See Hel. 7:5; Ether 8:9, 16, 22-23; Moses 5:31). This fruit of the sin of pride, namely secret combinations, brought down both the Jaredite and the Nephite civilizations and has been and will yet be the cause of the fall of many nations (See Ether 8:18-25).

Another face of pride is contention. Arguments, fights, unrighteous dominion, generation gaps, divorces, spouse abuse, riots, and disturbances all fall into this category of pride.

Contention in our families drives the Spirit of the Lord away. It also drives many of our family members away. Contention ranges from a hostile spoken word to worldwide conflicts. The scriptures tell us that "only by pride cometh contention" (Prov. 13:10; see also Prov. 28:25).

The scriptures testify that the proud are easily offended and hold grudges (See I Ne. 16:13). They withhold forgiveness to keep another in their debt and to justify their injured feelings.

The proud do not receive counsel or correction easily (See Prov. 15:10; Amos 5:10). Defensiveness is used by them to justify and rationalize their frailties and failures (See Matt. 3:9; John 6:30-59).

The proud depend upon the world to tell them whether they have value or not. Their self-esteem is determined by where they are judged to be on the ladders of worldly success. They feel worthwhile as individuals if the numbers beneath them in achievement, talent, beauty, or intellect are large enough. Pride is ugly. It says, "If you succeed, I am a failure."

If we love God, do His will, and fear His judgment more than men's, we will have self-esteem.

Pride is a damning sin in the true sense of that word. It limits or stops progression (See Alma 12: 10-11). The proud are not easily taught (See 1 Ne. 15:3, 7-11). They won't change their minds to accept truths, because to do so implies they have been wrong.

Pride adversely affects all our relationships—our relationship with God and His servants, between husband and wife, parent and child, employer and employee, teacher and student, and all mankind. Our degree of pride determines how we treat our God and our brothers and sisters. Christ wants to lift us to where He is. Do we desire to do the same for others?

Pride fades our feelings of sonship to God and brotherhood to man. It separates and divides us by "ranks," according to our "riches" and our "chances for learning" (3 Ne. 6:12). Unity is impossible for a proud people, and unless we are one we are not the Lord's (See Mosiah 18:21; D&C 38:27; 105:2-4; Moses 7:18).

Think of what pride has cost us in the past and what it is now costing us in our own lives, our families, and the Church.

Think of the repentance that could take place with lives changed, marriages preserved, and homes strengthened, if pride did not keep us from confessing our sins and forsaking them (See D&C 58:43).

Think of the many who are less active members of the Church because they were offended and their pride will not allow them to forgive or fully sup at the Lord's table.

Think of the tens of thousands of additional young men and couples who could be on missions except for the pride that keeps them from yielding their hearts unto God (See Alma 10:6; Hel. 3:34-35).

Think how temple work would increase if the time spent in this godly service were more important than the many prideful pursuits that compete for our time.

Pride affects all of us at various times and in various degrees. Now you can see why the building in Lehi's dream that represents the pride of the world was large and spacious and great was the multitude that did enter into it (See 1 Ne. 8:26, 33; 11:35-36).

Pride is the universal sin, the great vice. Yes, pride is the universal sin, the great vice.

The antidote for pride is humility—meekness, submissiveness (See Alma 7:23). It is the broken heart and contrite spirit (See 3 Ne. 9:20, 12:19; D&C 20:37, 59:8; Ps. 34:18; Isa. 57:15, 66:2). As Rudyard Kipling put it so well:

> The tumult and the shouting dies;
> The captains and the kings depart.
> Still stands thine ancient sacrifice,
> An humble and a contrite heart.
> Lord God of Hosts, be with us yet,
> Lest we forget, lest we forget.
> (Hymns, 1985, no. 80).

God will have a humble people. Either we can choose to be humble or we can be compelled to be humble. Alma said, "Blessed are they who humble themselves without being compelled to be humble" (Alma 32:16).

Let us choose to be humble.

We can choose to humble ourselves by conquering enmity toward our brothers and sisters, esteeming them as ourselves, and lifting them as high or higher than we are (See D&C 38:24; 81:5; 84:106).

We can choose to humble ourselves by receiving counsel and chastisement (See Jacob 4:10; Hel. 15:3; D&C 63:55; 101:4-5; 108:1; 124:61, 84; 136:31; Prov. 9:8).

We can choose to humble ourselves by forgiving those who have offended us (See 3 Ne. 13: 11, 14; D&C 64:10).

We can choose to humble ourselves by rendering selfless service (See Mosiah 2:16-17).

We can choose to humble ourselves by going on missions and preaching the word that can humble others (See Alma 4:19; 31:5; 48:20).

We can choose to humble ourselves by getting to the temple more frequently.

We can choose to humble ourselves by confessing and forsaking our sins and being born of God (See D&C 58:43; Mosiah 27:25-26; Alma 5:7-14, 49).

We can choose to humble ourselves by loving God, submitting our will to His, and putting Him first in our lives (See 3 Ne. 11:11; 13:33; Moro. 10:32).

Let us choose to be humble. We can do it. I know we can.

My dear brethren and sisters, we must prepare to redeem Zion. It was essentially the sin of pride that kept us from establishing Zion in the days of the Prophet Joseph Smith. It was the same sin of pride that bought consecration to an end among the Nephites (See 4 Ne. 1:24-25).

Pride is the great stumbling block to Zion. I repeat: Pride is the great stumbling block to Zion.

We must cleanse the inner vessel by conquering pride (See Alma 6:2-4: Matt. 23:25-26).

We must yield "to the enticings of the Holy Spirit," put off the prideful "natural man," become "a saint through the atonement of Christ the Lord," and become "as a child, submissive, meek, humble" (Mosiah 3:19; see also Ama 13:28).

That we may do so and go on to fulfill our divine destiny is my fervent prayer in the name of Jesus Christ, amen.

Our Moral Environment

Elder Boyd K. Packer

April 1992, General Conference Address, *Ensign*, May 1992, pp. 66-68

I have been a General Authority for over thirty years, and a member of the Quorum of the Twelve Apostles for twenty-two. During those years, I have interviewed I don't know how many, surely thousands, of members of the Church and have talked with them in intimate terms of their worthiness, their sorrow, and their happiness. I only mention that in the hope that the credential of experience may persuade you to consider matters which have us deeply worried.

Moral Environment

Today I speak to members of the Church as an environmentalist. My message is not on the physical but on the moral and spiritual environment in which we must raise our families. As we test the moral environment, we find the pollution index is spiraling upward. The Book of Mormon depicts humanity struggling through a "mist of darkness" and defines the darkness as the "temptations of the devil" (1 Ne. 8:23; 12:17). So dense was that moral pollution that many followed "strange roads" and "fell away into forbidden paths and were lost" (See 1 Ne. 8:23-32). The deliberate pollution of the fountain of life now clouds our moral environment. The gift of mortal life and the capacity to kindle other lives is a supernal blessing. Its worth is incalculable!

The Spiritual Environment

The rapid, sweeping deterioration of values is characterized by a preoccupation—even an obsession—with the procreative act. Abstinence before marriage and fidelity within it are openly scoffed at—marriage and parenthood ridiculed as burdensome, unnecessary. Modesty, a virtue of a refined individual or society, is all but gone.

The Tempter

The adversary is jealous toward all who have the power to beget life. He cannot beget life; he is impotent. He and those who followed him were cast out and forfeited the right to a mortal body. His angels even begged to inhabit the bodies of swine (See Matt. 8:31). And the revelations tell us that "he seeketh that all men might be miserable like unto himself" (2 Ne. 2:27). With ever fewer exceptions, what we see and read and hear have the mating act as a central theme. Censorship is forced offstage as a violation of individual freedom. That which should be absolutely private is disrobed and acted out center stage. In the shadows backstage are addiction, pornography, perversion, infidelity, abortion, and—the saddest of them all—incest and molestation. In company with them now is a plague of biblical proportion. And all of them are on the increase.

Society excuses itself from responsibility except for teaching the physical process of reproduction to children in school to prevent pregnancy and disease and providing teenagers with devices which are supposed to protect them from both. When any effort is made to include values in these courses, basic universal values, not just values of the Church, but of civilization, of society itself, the protest arises, "You are imposing religion upon us, infringing upon our freedom."

Freedom to Choose

While we pass laws to reduce pollution of the earth, any proposal to protect the moral and spiritual environment is shouted down and marched against as infringing upon liberty, agency, freedom, the right to choose. Interesting how one virtue, when given exaggerated or fanatical emphasis, can be used to batter down another, with freedom, a virtue, invoked to protect vice. Those determined to transgress see any regulation of their life-style as interfering with their agency and seek to have their actions condoned by making them legal. People who are otherwise sensible say, "I do not intend to indulge, but I vote for freedom of choice for those who do."

Flawed Argument

Regardless of how lofty and moral the "pro-choice" argument sounds, it is badly flawed. With that same logic one could argue that all traffic signs and barriers which keep the careless from danger should be pulled down on the theory that each individual must be free to choose how close to the edge he will go.

No Free Agency

The phrase "free agency" does not appear in scripture. The only agency spoken of there is moral agency, "which," the Lord said, "I have given unto him, that every man may be accountable for his own sins in the day of judgment" (D&C 101:78).

Heeding the Warning

And the Lord warned members of his church, "Let not that which I have appointed be polluted by mine enemies, by the consent of those who call themselves after my name: For this is a very sore and grievous sin against me, and against my people" (D&C 101:97-98).

Because the laws of man, by and large, do not raise moral issues, we are taught to honor, sustain, and obey the law (see A of F 1:12), and that "he that keepeth the laws of God hath no need to break the laws of the land" (D&C 58:21).

The Right to Speak Out

When a moral issue does arise, it is the responsibility of the leaders of the Church to speak out. Gambling, for instance, certainly is a moral issue. Life is a moral issue. When morality is involved, we have both the right and the obligation to raise a warning voice. We do not as a church speak on political issues unless morality is involved. In thirty years and thousands of interviews, I have never once asked a member of the Church what political party they belonged to.

Physical and Moral Laws

There are both moral and physical laws "irrevocably decreed in heaven before the foundations of this world" (D&C 130:20) which man cannot overrule. For instance, do you think a vote to repeal the law of gravity would do any good? Suppose a law decreed that all children would be taken from their parents and raised by the state. Such a law would be wicked but probably could be enforced. Such things have been done before.

But suppose an article of that law stated, "Within fifteen days the mother will cease all emotional ties to her child." That provision is absolutely unenforceable. No matter how severe the penalty or the number of enforcers, it is absolutely unenforceable because it contravenes both natural and moral law.

No matter if fifteen weeks or months or fifteen years were allowed, it cannot be enforced! It may work with animals, but "all flesh," the scriptures teach, "is not the same flesh: but there is one kind of flesh of men, another flesh of beasts" (1 Cor. 15:39). It cannot be made to work with human mothers. Never!

A man-made law against nature would be as impossible to defend as a law annulling love between mother and child would be impossible to enforce!

Children of God

No greater ideal has been revealed than the supernal truth that we are the children of God, and we differ, by virtue of our creation, from all other living things (See Moses 6:8-10, 22, 59).

The Evil Idea

No idea has been more destructive of happiness, no philosophy has produced more sorrow, more heartbreak and mischief; no idea has done more to destroy the family than the idea that we are not the offspring of God, only advanced animals, compelled to yield to every carnal urge. Animals are not subject to moral law. Nevertheless, while by and large they are promiscuous in responding to their mating instincts, their mating rituals have set patterns and have rigid limitations. For instance, animals do not pair up with their own gender to satisfy their mating instincts. Nor are these instincts expressed in the molestation of their offspring.

The source of life is now relegated to the level of unwed pleasure, bought and sold and even defiled in satanic rituals. Children of God can willfully surrender to their carnal nature and, without remorse, defy the laws of morality and degrade themselves even below the beasts.

Most Abominable

If we pollute our fountains of life, there will be penalties "exquisite" and "hard to bear" (see D&C 19:15), more than all of the physical pleasure ever could be worth. Alma told his son Corianton, "Know ye not, my son, that these things are an abomination in the sight of the Lord; yea, most abominable above all sins save it be the shedding of innocent blood or denying the Holy Ghost?" (Alma 39:5).

The code for moral law is found in the scriptures, stated as simply as, "Wickedness never was happiness" (Alma 41:10). The scriptures speak in general terms, leaving us free to apply the principles of the gospel to meet the infinite variety of life. But when they say "thou shalt not," we had better pay attention.

The only legitimate employment of the power of procreation is between husband and wife, man and woman, who have been legally and lawfully married. Anything else violates the commandments of God. From Alma, "If ye speak against it, it matters not, for the word of God must be fulfilled" (Alma 5:58).

The Measure of a Successful Parent

It is a great challenge to raise a family in the darkening mists of our moral environment. We emphasize that the greatest work you will do will be within the walls of your home (see Harold B. Lee, *Ensign*, July 1973, p. 98), and that "no other success can compensate for failure in the home" (David O. McKay, Improvement Era, June 1964, p. 445).

The measure of our success as parents, however, will not rest solely on how our children turn out. That judgment would be just only if we could raise our families in a perfectly moral environment, and that now is not possible. It is not uncommon for responsible parents to lose one of their children, for a time, to influences over which they have no control. They agonize over rebellious sons or daughters. They are puzzled over why they are so helpless when they have tried so hard to do what they should.

It is my conviction that those wicked influences one day will be overruled. "The Prophet Joseph Smith declared—and he never taught a more comforting doctrine—that the eternal sealings of faithful parents and the divine promises made to them for valiant service in the Cause of Truth, would save not only themselves, but likewise their posterity. Though some of the sheep may wander, the eye of the Shepherd is upon them, and sooner or later they will feel the tentacles of Divine Providence reaching out after them and drawing them back to the fold. Either in this life or the life to come, they will return. They will have to pay their debt to justice; they will suffer for their sins; and may tread a thorny path; but if it leads them at last, like the penitent Prodigal, to a loving and forgiving father's heart and home, the painful experience will not have been in vain. Pray for your careless and disobedient children; hold on to them with your faith. Hope on, trust on, till you see the salvation of God" (Orson F. Whitney, in Conference Report, Apr. 1929, p. 110).

We cannot overemphasize the value of temple marriage, the binding ties of the sealing ordinance, and the standards of worthiness required of them. When parents keep the covenants they have made at the altar of the temple, their children will be forever bound to them. President Brigham Young said:

"Let the father and mother, who are members of this Church and Kingdom, take a righteous course, and strive with all their might never to do a wrong, but to do good all their lives; if they have one child or one hundred children, if they conduct themselves towards them as they should, binding them to the Lord by their faith and prayers, I care not where those children go, they are bound up to their parents by an everlasting tie, and no power of earth or hell can separate them from their parents in eternity; they will return again to the fountain from whence they sprang" (Doctrines of Salvation, comp. Bruce R. McConkie, 3 vols., Joseph Fielding Smith, 2:90-91).

Repentance

In the battle of life, the adversary takes enormous numbers of prisoners, and many who know of no way to escape and are pressed into his service. Every soul confined to a concentration camp of sin and guilt has a key to the gate. The adversary cannot hold them if they know how to use it. The key is labeled Repentance. The twin principles of repentance and forgiveness exceed in strength the awesome power of the adversary.

I know of no sins connected with the moral standard for which we cannot be forgiven. I do not exempt abortion. The formula is stated in forty words:

"Behold, he who has repented of his sins, the same is forgiven, and I, the Lord, remember them no more.

"By this ye may know if a man repenteth of his sins—behold, he will confess them and forsake them" (D&C 58:42-43).

I Will Remember Your Sins No More

However long and painful the process of repentance, the Lord has said, "This is the covenant . . . I will make with them. . . . I will put my laws into their hearts, and in their minds will I write them;

"And their sins and iniquities will I remember no more" (Heb. 10:16-17).

Civilizations, like Sodom and Gomorrah, destroyed themselves by disobedience to the laws of morality. "For the Spirit of the Lord will not always strive with man. And when the Spirit ceaseth to strive with man then cometh speedy destruction" (2 Ne. 26:11; see also Gen. 6:3; Ether 2:15; D&C 1:33; Moses 8:17).

God grant that we will come to our senses and protect our moral environment from this mist of darkness which deepens day by day. The fate of all humanity hangs precariously in the balance. And may we have the protection of Him who is our Father and our God, and may we merit the love and blessings of His Son, our Redeemer, in whose name, even the name of Jesus Christ, I bear witness, amen.

Why Stay Morally Clean

Elder Boyd K. Packer, Quorum of the Twelve

Ensign, July 1972, pp. 111-113

Surely all of us have been conscious of the fact that there has been a very powerful Spirit with us in this session this morning. Few times, I suppose, have I desired so much for the sustaining power of the Spirit as I discuss a very delicate and difficult subject.

Why Stay Morally Clean

There are many young people in our audience today. It is to them, particularly to the teenagers, that I speak. The subject should be of great interest to you—why stay morally clean.

I approach the subject with deepest reverence. This may surprise some, for this subject is the most talked about, sung about, and joked about of any subject. Almost always it is talked about immodestly.

I intend to sustain modesty, not to offend it, as I venture to speak on this most delicate subject.

Young people, my message is of very deep importance to you. It concerns your future happiness. Some things that I say may be new to you who have not read the scriptures.

Plan for Mortal Life

In the beginning, prior to your mortal birth, you lived with our Heavenly Father. He is real. He actually lives. There are those living upon the earth who bear witness of His existence. We have heard His servants do so in this session. He lives, and I bear testimony of it.

He knew you there. Because He loved you He was anxious for your happiness and for your eternal growth. He wanted you to be able to choose freely and to grow through the power of correct choice, so that you may become much as He is. To achieve this it was necessary for us to leave His presence. Something like going away to school. A plan was presented and each agreed to leave the presence of our Heavenly Father to experience life in mortality.

Two great things were in store for us as we came into this world. One, we would receive a mortal body, created in the image of God. Through it, by proper control, we might achieve eternal life and happiness. Two, we would be tried and tested in such a way that we could grow in strength and in spiritual power.

Now this first purpose is wonderfully important, for this body given us will be resurrected and will serve us through the eternities.

Under the accepted plan, Adam and Eve were sent to the earth as our first parents. They could prepare physical bodies for the first spirits to be introduced into this life.

Power of Creation

There was provided in our bodies—and this is sacred—a power of creation, a light, so to speak, that has the power to kindle other lights. This gift was to be used only within the sacred bonds of marriage.

Through the exercise of this power of creation, a mortal body may be conceived, a spirit enter into it, and a new soul born into this life.

This power is good. It can create and sustain family life, and it is in family life that we find the fountains of happiness. It is given to virtually every individual who is born into mortality. It is a sacred and significant power, and I repeat, my young friends, that this power is good.

You who are teenagers, like every other son and daughter of Adam and Eve, have this power within you.

The power of creation—or may we say procreation—is not just an incidental part of the plan: it is essential to it. Without it the plan could not proceed. The misuse of it may disrupt the plan.

Use of Creative Power

Much of the happiness that may come to you in this life will depend on how you use this sacred power of creation. The fact that you young men can become fathers and that you young women can become mothers is of utmost importance to you.

As this power develops within you, it will prompt you in the search for a companion and empower you to love and to hold him.

I repeat, this power to act in the creation of life is sacred. You can some day have a family of your own. Through the exercise of this power you can invite children to live with you—little boys and little girls who will be your very own—created in a way in your own image. You can establish a home, a dominion of power and influence and opportunity. This carries with it great responsibility.

This creative power carries with it strong desires and urges. You have felt them already in the changing of your attitudes and your interests.

Strong and Constant Feelings

As you move into your teens, almost of a sudden a boy or a girl becomes something new and intensely interesting. You will notice the changing of form and feature in your own body and in others. You will experience the early whispering of physical desire.

It was necessary that this power of creation have at least two dimensions: One, it must be strong, and two, it must be more or less constant.

This power must be strong, for most men by nature seek adventure. Except for the compelling persuasion of these feelings, men would be reluctant to accept the responsibility of sustaining a home and a family. This power must be constant too, for it becomes a binding tie in family life.

You are old enough, I think, to look around you in the animal kingdom. You soon realize that where this power of creation is a fleeting thing, where it expresses itself only in season, there is no family life.

It is through this power that life continues. A world full of trials and fears and disappointments can be changed into a kingdom of hope and joy and happiness. Each time a child is born, the world somehow is renewed in innocence.

Importance of Marriage

Again I want to tell you young people that this power within you is good. It is a gift from God our Father. In the righteous exercise of it, as in nothing else, we may come close to Him.

We can have, in a small way, much that our Father in Heaven has as He governs us, His children. No greater school or testing place can be imagined.

Is it any wonder then, that in the Church marriage is so sacred and so important? Can you understand why your marriage which releases these powers of creation for your use should be the most carefully planned, the most solemnly considered step in your life? Ought we to consider it unusual that the Lord directed that temples be constructed for the purpose of performing marriage ceremonies?

Enticements of Evil One

Now there are other things that I will tell you as a warning. In the beginning there was one among us who rebelled at the plan of our Heavenly Father. He vowed to destroy and to disrupt the plan.

He was prevented from having a mortal body and was cast out—limited forever from establishing a kingdom of his own. He became satanically jealous. He knows that this power of creation is not just incident to the plan, but a key to it.

He knows that if he can entice you to use this power prematurely, to use it too soon, or to misuse it in any way, you may well lose your opportunities for eternal progression.

He is an actual being from the unseen world. He has great power. He will use it to persuade you to transgress those laws set up to protect the sacred powers of creation.

Changed Tactics

In former times he was too cunning to confront one with an open invitation to be immoral. But rather, sneakingly and quietly he would tempt young and old alike to think loosely of these sacred powers of creation. To bring down to a vulgar or to a common level that which is sacred and beautiful.

His tactics have changed now. He describes it as only an appetite to be satisfied. He teaches that there are no attendant responsibilities to the use of this power. Pleasure, he will tell you, is its sole purpose.

His devilish invitations appear on billboards. They are coined into jokes and written into the lyrics of songs. They are acted out on television and at theaters. They will stare at you now from most magazines. There are magazines—you know the word, pornography—open, wicked persuasions to pervert and misuse this sacred power.

You grow up in a society where before you is the constant invitation to tamper with these sacred powers.

Words of Counsel

I want to counsel you, and I want you to remember these words.

Do not let anyone at all touch or handle your body, not anyone. Those who tell you otherwise proselyte you to share their guilt. We teach you to maintain your innocence.

Turn away from any who would persuade you to experiment with these life-giving powers.

That such indulgence is widely accepted in society today is not enough! For both parties to willingly consent to such indulgence is not enough!

To imagine that it is a normal expression of affection is not enough to make it right.

The only righteous use of this sacred power is within the covenant of marriage.

Never misuse these sacred powers.

And now, my young friends, I must tell you soberly and seriously that God has declared in unmistakable language that misery and sorrow will follow the violation of the laws of chastity. "Wickedness never was happiness" (Alma 41:10).

These laws were set up to guide all of His children in the use of this gift.

He does not have to be spiteful or vengeful in order that punishment will come from the breaking of the moral code. The laws are established of themselves.

Crowning glory awaits you if you live worthily. The loss of the crown may well be punishment enough. Often, very often, we are punished as much by our sins as we are for them.

Cleansing Power

I am sure that within the sound of my voice there is more than one young person who already has fallen into transgression. Some of you young people, I am sure, almost innocent of any intent but persuaded by the enticements and the temptations, already have misused this power.

Know then, my young friends, that there is a great cleansing power. And know that you can be clean.

If you are outside of the Church the covenant of baptism itself represents, among other things, a washing and a cleansing.

For those of you inside the Church there is a way, not entirely painless, but certainly possible. You can stand clean and spotless before Him. Guilt will be gone, and you can be at peace. Go to your bishop. He holds the key to this cleansing power.

Righteous Family Life

Then one day you can know the full and righteous expression of these powers and the attendant happiness and joy in righteous family life. In due time, within the bonds of the marriage covenant, you can yield yourselves to those sacred expressions of love which have as their fulfillment the generation of life itself.

Someday you will hold a little boy or a little girl in your arms and know that two of you have acted in partnership with our Heavenly Father in the creation of life. Because the youngster belongs to you, you may then come to love someone more than you love yourself.

This experience can come, insofar as I know, only through having children of your own or perhaps through fostering children born of another and yet drawn close into family covenants.

Some of you may not experience the blessings of marriage. Protect nonetheless these sacred powers of creation, for there is a great power of compensation that may well apply to you.

Meaning of Fatherhood

Through this loving one more than you love yourself, you become truly Christian. Then you know, as few others know, what the word father means when it is spoken of in the scriptures. You may then feel something of the love and concern that He has for us.

It should have great meaning that of all the titles of respect and honor and admiration that could be given Him, that God Himself, He who is the highest of all, chose to be addressed simply as Father.

Key to Happiness

Protect and guard your gift. Your actual happiness is at stake. Eternal family life, now only in your anticipations and dreams, can be achieved because our Heavenly Father has bestowed this choicest gift of all upon you—this power of creation. It is the very key to happiness. Hold this gift as sacred and pure. Use it only as the Lord has directed.

My young friends, there is much happiness and joy to be found in this life. I can testify of that.

I picture you with a companion whom you love and who loves you. I picture you at the marriage altar, entering into covenants which are sacred. I picture you in a home where love has its fulfillment. I picture you with little children about you and see your love growing with them.

I cannot frame this picture. I would not if I could. For it has no bounds. Your happiness will have no ends if you obey His laws.

I pray God's blessings upon you, our youth. May our Heavenly Father watch over you and sustain you that in the expression of this sacred gift you may draw close to Him. He lives. He is our Father. Of this I bear witness in the name of Jesus Christ, amen.

The Importance of Teaching Each Other in Marriage

1.   When persons manifest the least kindness and love to me, O what power it has over my mind, while the opposite course has a tendency to harrow up all the harsh feelings and depress the human mind (*Teachings of the Prophet Joseph Smith*, p. 240).

2.   . . . beware of self-righteousness, and be limited in the estimate of your own virtues, and not think yourselves more righteous than others; you must enlarge your souls towards each other, if you would do like Jesus, and carry our fellow-creatures to Abraham's bosom. He said he had manifested long-suffering, forbearance and patience towards the Church, and also to his enemies; and we must bear with each other's failings, as an indulgent parent bears with the foibles of his children. . . . As you increase in innocence and virtue, as you increase in goodness, let your hearts expand, let them be enlarged towards others; you must be long-suffering, and bear with the faults and errors of mankind. . . . Let this [Relief Society] teach women how to behave towards their husbands, to treat them with mildness and affection. When a man is borne down with trouble, when he is perplexed with care and difficulty, if he can meet with mildness, it will calm down his soul and soothe his feelings; when the mind is going to despair, it needs a solace of affection and kindness (*Ibid*, p. 228).

Critical Transitions in Marriage

As husbands and wives go through the life cycle together there are a number of challenges/crises/faith promoting/challenging experiences they face together to provide an opportunity to strengthen or weaken their relationship and commitment. They include:

1. Transition to marriage from singleness—time/friends/possessions/allegiance

2. Sexual, financial, in-law, schooling, schedules, commitment—challenges

3. Parenthood

4. Teenagers

5. Employment—gain/loss, moving/disruption of family

6. Aging parents

7. Death of parents

8. Middle age—perspectives on life

9. Female Menopause/male viropause

10. Changes in physical and mental functioning

11. Life-threatening diseases/accidents

12. Retirement

13. Advanced age

14. Widow/widower

All Married Couples have Differences

Chuck & Barb Snyder

Incompatibility: Grounds for a Great Marriage, pp. 15-33

She likes butter. He likes margarine.

She is a low-energy person. He is a high-energy person

She is relationship-oriented. He is goal-oriented.

She is left-handed. He is right-handed.

She is practical. He is a dreamer.

She likes the toilet paper roll to roll toward her. He doesn't care which way it rolls.

She likes to listen to soft violin music. He likes to listen to loud country music.

She has a difficult time making decisions. He makes them easily.

She likes a variety of foods. He likes the same old standbys.

She came from a loud family in which everyone shouted at each other. He came from a quiet family in which hardly anyone ever raised a voice.

She wants to resolve conflict immediately. He wants to wait awhile.

She wants to talk when she is angry. He doesn't want to talk when either of them is angry.

She believes stoplights are ordained of God to bring order into our lives. He believes stoplights are tools of Satan to disrupt his life.

She is a perfectionist. He is disorderly.

She keeps a clean desk. He has a roll top.

She likes one or two pets. He likes several.

She is a saver. He is a spender.

She is a planner. He is impulsive.

She asks for directions when she get lost. He feels that asking for directions is a sign of weakness.

She feels comfortable taking things back to the store when they aren't exactly what she wants. He stores them in the garage.

She likes to take her time. He is always in a hurry.

She does one thing at a time to conclusion. He likes to do many things at once.

She hates paperwork. He handles paperwork easily.

She smashes bugs in the house and kills spiders. He carefully takes them outside to safety.

Mending Our Marriage

Ensign, Oct. 1996, pp. 44-51

Asked about his concerns regarding Church members, President Gordon B. Hinckley replied, "I am concerned about family life in the Church. We have wonderful people, but we have too many whose families are falling apart. It is a matter of serious concern. I think it is my most serious concern" (*Church News,* 24 June 1995, 6).

Some Latter-day Saints enjoy a close union with their spouse while others try valiantly to keep their marriage together in the face of challenges or long-lasting trials. The *Ensign* recently asked members who at some point in their past had contemplated divorce how they were able to reject the idea of divorce and use gospel principles to improve their marriages. Of course, knowing what to do—even in cases where divorce is the answer—is vital, and the key is to be guided by the Holy Ghost.

In the following responses, even when one spouse was in need of serious change or repentance before the marriage could be saved, his or her partner was often led on a parallel journey that also resulted in refinement of character. Thus their trials, though different, eventually led to spiritual growth and unity in their marriage. It is hoped that others will benefit from seeing the spiritual patterns that led to healing solutions for these couples. Their responses follow the text introducing each topic.

Physical Abuse

Physical abuse often is in the news today. There is very little ever said in the press about finding healing solutions, yet such solutions can occur, especially when righteous principles are applied One husband, deeply distressed over his own behavior wrote:

My bishop greeted me warmly. He looked deep into my eyes and asked, "How is your marriage, Brother Moore*?"

It had been almost a year since I last sat with our bishop in a temple recommend interview. On that earlier occasion I had cast off an unbearable burden: I had confessed to having been abusive to my companion. Through tears I recounted the problems in our marriage and how I had responded to them in ways that were emotionally and physically abusive to my wife. My bitterness was profound, and our marital problems left me with little hope of finding any answers.

The irony of my failing marriage was that both my wife and I had come from strong Latter-day Saint homes, had a testimony of the truthfulness of the gospel, and had served in ward and stake callings. Our inability to get along seemed inconsistent with all that we knew about gospel living. I wondered if my wife and I could ever live together peaceably. But with two children, how could we divorce?

The bishop had counseled me for some time. The following week my wife and I traveled several hours to attend the temple. After the session, we sat in the celestial room side by side and talked. Tears coursed down our cheeks as the sorrow, the hurts, the pain and anguish of five turbulent years of marriage weighed

---

*Name has been changed.

upon us. We realized that we did love each other, but our inability to resolve conflict amicably kept us from *feeling* loved. Knowing that Father in Heaven wanted to help and would guide me, I wanted to try to change. I told my wife that I would give our marriage six more months and that during that time I would make every effort to better our relationship.

During the months that followed, I referred frequently to words I penned in my day-planner that helped me take a Christlike approach to solving our problems: "Do all I can possibly do to make my marriage succeed—*never criticize*; nurture a communicative atmosphere; pray specifically together."

Initially these goals seemed almost impossible to meet. Yet, applying these principles day after day, week after week brought about a perceptible change in the atmosphere of our home. My focus turned from blaming my wife to applying the resources of the gospel in my own life. I awakened to the power of the Atonement—that it was very personal, very applicable to my life. I found myself becoming more tolerant, less inclined to criticize, and more willing to listen.

For the first time in our marriage I was able to pray with my wife over very specific issues we had been unable to resolve alone. By opening my heart to the influence of the Spirit, my eyes were opened to just how much I could do as priesthood holder, father, and husband. Learning correct principles helped, but learning how to apply them has been the ongoing challenge.

Thus, a year after our experience in the temple I sat again with my bishop and responded to his query with a smile. "We're making progress. By staying focused on what *I* can do, on honoring the priesthood, on improving *my* relationship with the Lord, I have found that I am better able to take responsibility for my own emotional and spiritual feelings in my relationship with my wife."—**From California**

Financial Problems

Finances are often listed as a leading reason for couples divorcing and can indeed place great pressures on them, as this sister explains:

I was married in the temple to the man I love. But over the years my husband's inability to provide for our needs responsibly brought great hardship to our family. Our situation worsened until we went without many things, including running water or a phone, for long periods of time. Many good friends suggested I seek a divorce.

I had determined early in my marriage to stay spiritually in tune enough to know Heavenly Father's will for me. I worried about our children and struggled about whether to go to work. When in private moments of sheer frustration I considered divorce, I would pray. Always the answer came. My husband needed time to grow and make his mistakes and learn from them. I was to stay home to raise the children and be patient, loving, and supportive of his efforts in spite of the hardships.

This was not easy to accept. Sometimes I would feel great anger well up inside me because of the things we had to do without and the constant broken promises and financial chaos that plagued us. On some occasions I literally felt the Holy Ghost quelling my anger and giving me great peace so that I could endure. I knew then how much Father in Heaven cared about us.

As many years passed, I learned important lessons. I realized I couldn't do my husband's growing for him. I had to do my own. I came to rely on spiritual blessings and to focus less on material things. I learned to get by on what my husband could provide. I became an expert gardener and cook. Because we had no running water, I learned to can garden produce and to do laundry with rainwater. Since we lived in the woods, I studied about plants and animals. In short, I learned how to survive with very little, and these experiences, though difficult, gave me a new perspective about life and an appreciation for even small blessings.

Although I considered my husband's problems to be the source of my greatest trials, I found they also served in the end to bring both of us along separate and personal pathways to Jesus Christ. Those pathways have finally converged, and today we are stable, both financially and in our relationship as a couple. I'm thankful I relied on guidance from the Spirit and not the advice of friends. I'm humbled to realize the magnitude of Heavenly Father's love for me. —**From Missouri**

Substance Abuse

Some spouses face the challenge to keep the marriage relationship intact, sometimes for years, while their spouse deals with serious weaknesses, such as alcoholism. Such problems often consume most of the resources available to the marriage, and spouses are left with heavy burdens and little help. Yet many people feel impressed to stay. The wife of an alcoholic explains:

It was obvious after just a few weeks of my marriage that it wasn't going to be easy. Though my husband was a member of the Church, he was also a heavy drinker and smoker. But inside I said to myself that I could always divorce him if we couldn't make it work. With his heavy alcohol consumption, I found it very hard to communicate with him in any important area. During the more difficult times I was ready to throw my hands in the air and say, "I quit!" I even went looking at apartments and talked with attorneys.

But early on I also went to my Heavenly Father. I asked repeatedly for help in getting out of this awful relationship. Each time the answer that came to me was to stick it out. Sometimes the answer came as a feeling, or from my bishop's counsel, or by scripture study. One day's prayer brought me to the realization that I couldn't change this man; I could only change myself. Over the years many new insights came.

A bishop counseled me to work toward going to the temple. Line upon line I began working toward that goal. My husband had to write a letter of support so that I could go through the temple without him. He wrote a beautiful letter of love. My stake president promised me that if I would attend the temple regularly my husband would see the gospel through my eyes. Things did begin to improve, but there had been so many problems that I still considered divorce.

One day we hit a crisis. I had had it and decided the time had come to leave him. Sensing I meant it, my husband put down his can of beer and asked if we could try counseling again. I prayed quickly to know what to do and felt, once more, that we should try again. My husband committed to stop drinking if I would commit to stop considering divorce as an option.

To do this, we sold our home and moved to a new area for a new start. My husband replaced alcohol with jogging. But he still struggled to fill the void in his life. One day he heard an inner voice telling him to read the Book of Mormon. He started reading it and received a witness of the truth of it. With that, he set a goal to stop smoking too. When he had done this, he set a new goal for priesthood advancement, then for temple marriage.

On our 14th wedding anniversary we were finally married in the temple! I am so thankful my Heavenly Father has taught me patience and charity and has shown me that divorce was not the way to solve my problems. Although it took many years, we are so happy now. Our love has grown beyond what I could ever have foreseen. **—From Utah**

Health Problems

While drug and alcohol abuse severely test any marriage, so do other kinds of unexpected and unwanted problems, such as the severe health problems that nearly derailed this relationship:

My husband and I were married five years ago. He has been diabetic since the age of 11 but had few problems except when his blood sugar dropped. About six months after we were married, he was diagnosed with diabetic retinopathy and had laser surgery in both eyes. During the next few months he had several episodes with low blood sugar, requiring trips to the emergency room. He was also very moody.

During that first year I was frightened and wondered what I had gotten myself into. Sometimes I felt he must be faking it, and part of me just wanted to escape. I told him I thought I needed to leave. I had many conversations with my Heavenly Father (as did my husband too), and the message came to me that we didn't get married to get a divorce and that my husband wasn't trying to fake anything. Through the Spirit I was reminded that I need not endure this setback alone.

Our first child was born a strong and healthy girl. One night my husband got up to feed her, but the crying went on and on. I finally went to see what was wrong. He was holding her, but his low blood sugar prevented him from realizing he wasn't feeding her. I took the baby and the bottle and fed her. I was very stressed and lashed out at him, "Why don't you take care of yourself?" We constantly fought, or so it seemed.

In the next few years the pressure on our marriage increased. His name went on a kidney transplant waiting list, and he was sick so much that he lost his job. More complications developed, and he was in and out of the hospital often. We turned to Heavenly Father often in prayer. This wasn't the kind of life I had hoped for and dreamed about. Recently he suffered a near-fatal heart attack. It was a very scary time for all of us.

We wouldn't' have chosen to endure these things, and we can't say we have endured with flying colors. But we are still plugging along the best we can. What carried us through have been basic principles of gospel living: prayer, scripture study, and fasting. As we apply gospel principles in our lives, we are better able to cope with stress. Heavenly Father makes our challenges easier to bear. Slowly we have realized that we are committed to each other, that we love each other _no matter what,_ and that our Heavenly Father wants us to work things out together as best we can. The teachings of the Church have given us strength and hope to keep trying. **—From Arizona**

Immorality

Immorality is one of the most difficult transgressions for a spouse to deal with, but when repentance is part of the process, there is also hope for the marriage:

My husband seemed to lose his way and drifted into Word of Wisdom problems, then into worse things. Some 18 years ago, tired, worn out with the stress of alcohol, immorality, and other problems, I wanted to end the marriage. I went to my Heavenly Father in prayer.

Yet I felt through the Spirit that I should stay and keep our home together. The next day at church as I took the sacrament I felt a great sense of peace and love as the Spirit bore witness again that I was making the right choice.

There was no immediate reformation, but rather a gradual change took place over some 15 years. While he worked on his problems, I also had lessons to learn. I felt impressed to be humble and recognize that I too had sins. I was to express love and respect for my husband daily and concentrate in his good qualities. I was taught Christlike principles of forgiveness and prayed daily for him. Finally, I was impressed that I needed to set aside time, even if it was a sacrifice to do so, to be with him and build up the relationship. These answers always came as I earnestly sought Heavenly Father's guidance through prayer, faith, and scripture study.

After many years, the day finally came that he went in to see the bishop and confessed his immorality and other sins. He knew I would stand behind him through whatever action needed to be taken. We would face the future together.

I shall ever treasure the time he finally stood in the bishop's office, tears coursing down his cheeks, holding a temple recommend. We felt then the great love Heavenly Father and the Savior have for us. The sweetness of forgiveness was ours! Measured against eternity, my 18 years of waiting was but a moment.
—From Alberta, Canada

Mounting Pressures

Other kinds of pressures can also seriously impact marriages if those marriages are not securely rooted:

My husband and I had been married 10 months when our son was born. I thought that all of my dreams had come true, but within three months we were watching our little son have seizures. This was the start of a four-year struggle for his life that ended with his death and his newborn sister being diagnosed with the same disease. This all brought many pressures into our marriage.

During that first year we heard that 85 percent of the parents of seriously physically disabled children divorce. We made a decision not to consider that as an option. Instead we prayed and read scriptures daily.

Nevertheless, the struggles we coped with were draining. Pressures stemming from our son's illness were pulling us apart. I wanted to spend most of my time with my small son while my husband buried himself in activity—anything to keep busy. I thought he was indifferent; he thought I was hovering too much over our son. We fought almost daily. I was miserable and didn't think our marriage could last.

Then I felt the hand of Heavenly Father guide me, through a friend, to hear a talk about charity in marriage. The speaker suggested being charitable toward your spouse for just one month. I knew it would never work with *my* husband! But because I wasn't going to let it be my fault if we got a divorce, I determined to stop nagging and fighting with my husband for the next four weeks, which I did.

I turned to the scriptures and read about charity in Moroni 7. I learned that charity belongs more in marriage than anywhere else. As I changed, my husband began to change too. After the month was over, my husband was a different person!

Those weeks marked the beginning of a journey toward better times. During the months ahead we had to learn to be patient with each other. We both were grieving, and we realized we were doing so in different ways. Understanding increased as we prayed together, asking for the Spirit to guide us, and as we talked about what was happening to us individually and as a couple. We decided we both needed to be more diligent in extending kindness to each other. At last we came to understand that the challenges associated with our son's illness should not be allowed to threaten our marriage. Our son's illness was not the problem; our responses to it were. A gospel perspective makes all the difference. I learned that Heavenly Father, who knows us both, believes in our ability to make it together. How could I give up? —**From Utah**

Depression

Depression is a serious concern in some marriages. Because depression changes a person's view of the world, communication becomes difficult and problem solving a challenge. One husband explains his journey through the ordeal:

After having been married for over 10 years, I began suffering from depression. The onset consisted of occasional depressive episodes, the total emptiness of which cannot be described. I did not know what was wrong with me and fought to maintain my equilibrium while I tried to figure it out.

My wife found me increasingly difficult to live with. I thought she lacked understanding and sympathy. Our relationship quickly deteriorated into days of not speaking to each other, an incessant chain of arguments and faultfinding, strained public performances, and a desperate clinging to anything that offered respite and solace. For me, that was prayer. Suddenly, more than ever, I needed help.

I pleaded with Father in Heaven not only for healing but also for guidance on how to show my wife the error of her ways. I was distressed that she should choose this time in life to become impossible to live with, right when I had my hands full of my own fight for sanity.

After months of struggle, I finally concluded that we should get a divorce. Because I was miserable, I sought for and expected the Lord's approval of such a decision. Instead, I was vividly reminded that it had been revealed to me clearly and unforgettably to marry and be sealed to my wife. I had an unmistakable feeling of being loved by my Father in Heaven, and that warm feeling enabled me to carry on again.

After nearly three years of fighting the steady deterioration of my mental health, I finally realized I might have something physically wrong and sought professional help. Happily, a daily medicine has eliminated most of my depressive anxieties. As I healed, I began to experience normal moods again, and my wife and I initiated a return to creating and experiencing the loving relationship we'd had before.

Had I not considered the Lord the author and owner of my marriage covenant, I would have thrown it all away. I shudder to think how close I came to that each time I look at my wonderful wife and children and at the happiness we now enjoy. —**From Washington State**

Temptation to Give Up

Certainly one common approach of the adversary is to simply tempt people to quit. Persistent thoughts of divorce plague many people even in the absence of serious conflict:

My husband and I come from strong Latter-day Saint families. We were taught about the sacred nature of the temple and temple marriage and felt we were adequately prepared as to what those covenants meant. We prayed together as a family, studied our scriptures, attended the temple frequently, held callings, and spent as much quality time with our children as possible. It seemed we were doing everything we should be doing. Yet neither of us was truly happy.

We started talking about giving up. It was just causal nonsense at first, but soon the talk of ending our marriage became more and more frequent in our disagreements. Finally, one night we had another dispute that led to a long night of discussion. *What were we doing wrong?* Everything seemed in place, yet happiness eluded us. Eventually the question became *What are we doing to strengthen ourselves as a couple?* The answer was suddenly very clear. We had done little over the last few years to build our own personal relationship with each other. Did we want to start now?

The next morning as we looked at our three beautiful children who were entrusted to our care, who looked to us for love and stability and whose future happiness depended to a large extent on our decision, our eyes were suddenly opened. We owed it to them to make our marriage work.

We put the children to bed early that night and opened the latest conference issue of the *Ensign* and read, "Many church leaders and marriage counselors indicate that they have not seen one marriage in serious trouble where the couple was still praying together daily" (Joe J. Christensen, *Ensign,* May 1995, 64). While we had participated faithfully in family prayer, we had neglected praying together as a couple. From that night on we began praying together to seek help specifically in rebuilding our marriage.

As we did this, we became more spiritually in tune with each other and more open to the workings of the Spirit in solving our problems. Together we decided that divorce would no longer be a choice and that we wouldn't use it as a threat when we had disagreements. Instead, we had to become serious about finding solutions to our problems. As our attitude changed, we found that hurt feelings, pride, angry voices, and other negative behaviors softened because of the increased workings of the Spirit in our home. We are so grateful for the pure and simple power of prayer that has enabled us to continue striving for an eternal marriage. **—From Ontario, Canada**

Patience and Forgiveness

Because so many marital challenges involve a needed change of heart, repentance, and sometimes careful rebuilding of the relationship, partners who wait patiently through the process are a great strength and blessing to their spouses:

What helped me most was my husband's forgiveness and kindness. Because of the gospel, the healing of repentance, and a husband who was willing to put aside his own suffering because of my sin and to show forth full forgiveness and support, and especially because of Jesus Christ atoning for me, we were able to weather this challenge together.

How I love the gospel, Heavenly Father, and our Savior! How I love my righteous husband. How I value my second chance! **—From Colorado**

Guided Aright

In each of the above reports, one or both spouses prayed for spiritual guidance that they might be led to receive appropriate instruction, comfort, or guidance to carry them through difficult times. Obtaining such guidance is vital to the process of deciding how to best deal with marital problems.

President Gordon B. Hinckley has stated: "There may be now and again a legitimate cause for divorce. I am not one to say that it is never justified. But I say without hesitation that this plague among us, which seems to be growing everywhere, is not of God, but rather is the work of the adversary of righteousness and peace and truth.

"You need not be its victims" (*Ensign*, May 1991, 74).

Although for some couples it may take years to overcome causes of marital unhappiness while for others the challenges may tax the limits of their ability to endure and lead to divorce, the efforts to do one's best and apply gospel principles are both required and worth the necessary sacrifices. Indeed, obedience to the principles of righteous living has its own rewards (see D&C 58:2-4), such as spiritual strength and freedom from regret. Thus fortified for having drawn closer to the Lord, he will guide us aright in our trials (see D&C 88: 63-64).

Marriage and Divorce

Elder David B. Haight

Ensign, May 1984, pp. 12-14

I pray for the companionship of the Holy Spirit, that my remarks will be in harmony with revealed truth and will be received and understood by that same heavenly influence.

For more than twenty-five years we have witnessed an unending assault on the traditional family. Sacred values of human goodness, discipline, and love and honor for God our Eternal Father have been challenged.

A new self-centered generation has made the family a prime target of continuing belittlement. Marriage is downgraded or shunned, parenthood degraded and avoided. These, with other disturbing influences, have resulted in a torrent of evil temptations for so-called instant gratification and the demeaning of marriage and the sacred roles of wife and mother.

Unfortunately, there are many good human beings who would live differently, but they do not know of God's eternal plan for His children. We learn from the scriptures that the divine intent is that marriage is to be an eternal union with enduring family relationships throughout eternity.

Scripture reveals that, after the earth was developed, God created man in His own image and gave him dominion over the earth. By the side of man stood the woman, sharing with him the divinely bestowed honor and dignity of supremacy over all other creations. God said, "It is not good that the man should be alone; I will make him an help meet for him" (Gen. 2:18).

"In the image of God created he him; male and female created he them" (Gen. 1:27).

The Lord also instructed, "Therefore shall a man leave his father and his mother, and shall cleave unto his wife: and they shall be one flesh" (Gen. 2:24), thereby giving sanction to the union of male and female in authorized marriage, which is heaven-planned for the creation of mortal bodies.

The earliest recorded commandment to Adam and Eve was to "be fruitful, and multiply, and replenish the earth" (Gen. 1:28).

We regard children as gifts from God, committed to our care for loving, nurturing, and careful training.

The Lord also instructed, "And they shall also teach their children to pray, and to walk uprightly before the Lord" (D&C 68:28).

They are not to be mistreated or abused, for, with their parents, they are part of a family with the potential of eternal relationship.

President Spencer W. Kimball explained:

> The Lord organized the whole program in the beginning with a father who procreates, provides, and loves and directs, and a mother who conceives and bears and nurtures and feeds and trains. The Lord could have organized it otherwise but chose to have a unit with responsibility and purposeful associations where children train and discipline each other and come to love, honor, and appreciate each other. The family is the great plan of life as conceived and organized by our Father in Heaven (*Ensign,* July 1973, p. 15).

Marriage was meant to be and can be a loving, binding, and harmonious relationship between a husband and wife.

As we contemplate our Lord's declaration to Moses, "This is my work and my glory—to bring to pass the immortality and eternal life of man" (Moses 1:39), we reflect with sadness upon the present serious trend of families and homes being torn apart through divorce.

It would seem that a major underlying cause of divorce is in not understanding that marriage and families are God-given and God-ordained. If we understood the full meaning we would have less divorce and its attendant unhappiness. Couples would plan for a happy marriage relationship based on divine instruction. If couples understood from the beginning of their romance that their marriage relationship could be blessed with promises and conditions extending into the eternities, divorce would not even be a considered alternative when difficulties arise. The current philosophy—get a divorce if it doesn't work out—handicaps a marriage from the beginning.

The ever-increasing rise in divorce is ample evidence of how acceptable divorce has become—how quick and easy to obtain—divorce is tragic and painful, not only at the outset, but also in the years to come.

Divorce can never really be final. How can mothers and fathers really divorce themselves from their own flesh and blood children, or from the memories of days and years of shared experiences which have become part of their very lives.

Divorce rarely occurs without immense emotional, social, and financial upheaval. Most people underestimate the alienation, bitterness, disruption, and frustration between a divorcing couple, and among their children, friends, and relatives. Some never adjust to the resulting emotional consequences.

Perhaps most tragic of all is that more than 60 percent of all divorces involve children under eighteen years of age. Children of divorce all too often have a higher delinquency rate and less self-confidence, and tend to be more promiscuous and themselves more likely to have unhappy marriages.

Considering the enormous importance of marriage, it is rather astonishing that we don't make better preparation for success. Usually, young couples date for a few months or for a year or two, enjoying romance and getting acquainted, and then get married. Once married, they soon learn that romance must blend with spiritual beliefs, in-law relationships, money issues, and serious discussions involving ethics, children, and the running of a home.

Too many people are inadequately prepared for this lofty responsibility.

> People go to college for years to prepare for a vocation or profession . . . not
> [nearly] as . . . rewarding [or as important] as marriage (See Lowell S. Bennion, "Conference on Utah Families," Salt Lake Tribune, 6 April 1980, p. F-9).

Serious transgressions, as well as injured lives that sometimes are revealed in bishop's offices, all too frequently make it clear that husband and wife relationships deserve a great deal more prayerful attention than many are giving it. Fewer marriages would get in trouble, and more would be happier, if couples visited a warm-hearted bishop who might suggest ways of avoiding pitfalls, and encourage husbands and wives to thoughtfully use self-discipline and needed restraint and develop the loving attribute of unselfishness.

A few years ago, President Harold B. Lee received this letter from a married woman:

> When we thought that the end was here and that there was only one thing to do
> and that was to get a divorce, we had been told that we should counsel with our bishop.
> At first . . . we hesitated, because he was just a young man. . . . But he was our bishop
> so we went to see him. We poured out our soul to our young bishop. He sat and listened silently, and when we ran out of conversation he said, simply, "Well, my wife
> and I, we had problems, too, and we learned how to solve them." That is all . . . he
> said. But you know there was something that happened as a result of that young
> bishop's statement. We walked out of there and we said, "Well, if they can solve their
> problems, what is the matter with us?" (*Ensign*, Jan. 1974, p. 100).

A prominent producer recently stated:

> In movies and on television there is . . . reluctance to deal with marriage, . . . [except as] a comic turn or in soap operas. We prefer to stress . . . [sexual involvement] and leave [alone] . . . the happily-ever-after, . . . as in children's fairy stories (Karl E. Meyer, in The Wife of Your Youth, Palos Heights, Illinois: n.p., 1977).

Our concern is not just that media producers and writers don't portray happy, fruitful marriage, but that many married couples don't take their marriages seriously enough to work at them, protect them, nurture them, cultivate them day in and day out, week in and week out, year long, quarter-century long, half-a-century long, forever.

Middle-age divorce is particularly stressing, as it indicates that mature people, who are the backbone of our society, are not working carefully enough to preserve their marriages. Divorces granted to people over forty-five have increased at an alarming rate. When middle-aged people even consider breaking up their marriage—a couple who may have reared their children, who possibly have grandchildren—and now decide to go their separate ways, they need to realize that every divorce is the result of selfishness on the part of one or both.

In Malachi we read:

> The Lord hath been witness between thee and the wife of thy youth, against whom thou hast dealt treacherously: yet is she thy companion, and the wife of thy covenant.
>
> . . . Therefore take heed to your spirit, and let none deal treacherously against the wife of his youth (Mal. 2:14-15).

Marriage is a covenant. Two of the Ten Commandments deal directly with preserving the sanctity of marriage: "Thou shalt not commit adultery," and "Thou shalt not covet thy neighbour's wife" (Ex. 20:14, 17).

Jesus magnified the law against adultery: "But I say unto you, That whosoever looketh on a woman to lust after her hath committed adultery with her already in his heart" (Matt. 5:28). The ideal marriage is the faithfulness of a man and a woman to each other, a faithfulness that began when each had chosen the other. In Proverbs we read, "Let thy fountain be blessed: and rejoice with the wife of thy youth" (Prov. 5:18). Let her affection fill you at all times with delight, and be infatuated always with her love (See Prov. 5:19).

It is a privilege indeed to live our life with the wife of our youth, to enjoy the golden years together—neither objecting to the wrinkles nor the gray hair—but to continue acquiring a depth of love, oneness, and wisdom which can be shared with each other now and throughout all eternity. Marriage is sustained by faith and knowledge of its divine establishment, and is sustained daily by the energy of love. A wise man explained,

> When the satisfaction or the security of another person becomes as significant to one as one's own satisfaction and security then the state of love exists (Harry Stack Sullivan, Concepts of Modern Psychiatry 2d ed., New York: W. W. Norton and Co., 1961, p. 42).

A strong, shared conviction that there is something eternally precious about a marriage relationship builds faith to resist evil. Marriage should be beautiful and fulfilling, with joy beyond our fondest dreams, for "neither is the man without the woman, neither the woman without the man, in the Lord" (1 Cor. 11:1).

Latter-day Saints need not divorce—there are solutions to marriage problems. If, as husband and wife, you are having serious misunderstandings or if you feel some strain or tension building up in your marriage, you should humbly get on your knees together and ask God our Father, with a sincere heart and real intent, to lift the darkness that is over your relationship, that you may receive the needed light, see your errors, repent of your wrongs, forgive each other, and receive each unto yourselves as you did in the beginning. I solemnly assure you that God lives and will answer your humble pleas, for he has said, "Ye shall ask whatsoever you will in the name of Jesus and it shall be done" (D&C 50:29).

In the name of Jesus Christ, amen.

President James E. Faust on Marriage and Family

Ensign, May 1991, p. 68

The denial of our own sins, of our own selfishness, of our own weakness is like a crown of thorns which keeps us from moving up one more step in personal growth. Perhaps worse than sin is the denial of sin. If we deny that we are sinners, how can we ever be forgiven? How can the atonement of Jesus work in our lives if there is no repentance? If we do not promptly remove the slivers of sin and the thorns of carnal temptation, how can the Lord ever heal our souls? The Savior said, "Repent of your sins, and be converted, that I may heal you" (3 Ne. 9:13). It is most difficult for us to pray for those who hate us, who despitefully use us, who persecute us. By failing to take this vital extra step, however, we fail to remove some of the festering briars in our souls. Extending forgiveness, love, and understanding for perceived shortcomings and weaknesses in our wives, husbands, children, and associates makes it much easier to say, "God be merciful to me a sinner" (Luke 18:13).

Ensign, November 1977, p. 10

There are no simple, easy answers to the challenging and complex questions of happiness in marriage. There are also many supposed reasons for divorce. Among them are the serious problems of selfishness, immaturity, lack of commitment, inadequate communication, unfaithfulness; and all of the rest, which are obvious and well known.

Ensign, May 1993, p. 37

Perhaps we regard the power bestowed by Elijah as something associated only with formal ordinances performed in sacred places. But these ordinances become dynamic and productive of good only as they reveal themselves in our daily lives. Malachi said that the power of Elijah would turn the hearts of the fathers and the children to each other. The heart is the seat of the emotions and a conduit for revelation (See Mal. 4:5-6). This sealing power thus reveals itself in family relationships, in attributes and virtues developed in a nurturing environment, and in loving service. These are the cords that bind families together, and the priesthood advances their development. In imperceptible but real ways, the "doctrine of the priesthood shall distil upon thy soul [and thy home] as the dews from heaven" (D&C 121:45).

Ensign, November 1977, p. 10

In my experience there is another reason which seems not so obvious but which precedes and laces through all of the others, it is the lack of a constant enrichment in marriage, it is an absence of that something extra which makes it precious, special, and wonderful, when it is also drudgery, difficult, and dull.

Ensign, **November 1993, p. 38-39**

How should those who bear the priesthood treat their wives and the other women in their family? Our wives need to be cherished. They need to hear their husbands call them blessed, and the children need to hear their fathers generously praise their mothers (see Prov. 31:28). The Lord values his daughters just as much as he does his sons. In marriage, neither is superior; each has a different primary and divine responsibility. Chief among these different responsibilities for wives is the calling of motherhood. I firmly believe that our dear faithful sisters enjoy a special spiritual enrichment which is inherent in their natures.

Just Cause for Divorce

President James E. Faust

What then, might be "just cause" for breaking the covenants of marriage? Over a lifetime of dealing with human problems, I have struggled to understand what might be considered "just cause" for breaking of covenants. I confess I do not claim the wisdom nor authority to definitively state what is "just cause." Only the parties to the marriage can determine this. They must bear the responsibility for the train of consequences which inevitably follows if these covenants are not honored. In my opinion, "just cause" should be nothing less serious than a **prolonged and apparently irredeemable relationship which is destructive of a person's dignity as a human being.**

Surely it is not simply "mental distress" or "personality differences" or having "grown apart" or having "fallen out of love." This is especially so where there are children (James E. Faust, April 1993, Conference Report, p. 46).

Solving Emotional Problems in the Lord's Own Way

Elder Boyd K. Packer

Ensign, May 1978:91-93

Our bishops face increasing calls to counsel members with problems that have more to do with emotional needs than with the need for food or clothing or shelter. My message, therefore, is to the subject: **solving emotional problems in the Lord's own way**. Fortunately, the principles of temporal welfare apply to emotional problems as well. The Church was two years old when the Lord revealed that "the idler shall not have place in the church, except he repent and mend his ways" (D&C 75:29). The Church handbook states:

> [We must] earnestly teach and urge Church members to be self-sustaining to the full extent of their powers. No true Latter-day Saint will. . . **voluntarily shift from himself the burden of his own support. So long as he can, under the inspiration of the Almighty and with his own labors, he will supply himself with the necessities of life.**

Caring for Material Needs

We have succeeded fairly well in teaching Latter-day Saints that they should take care of their own material needs and then contribute to the welfare of those who cannot provide for themselves. If a member is unable to sustain himself, **then he is to call upon his own family, and then upon the Church, in that order, and not upon the government at all**. We have counseled bishops and stake presidents to be very careful to avoid abuses in the welfare program. When people are able but unwilling to take care of themselves, we are responsible to employ the dictum of the Lord that the idler shall not eat the bread of the laborer (See D&C 42:42).

The simple rule has been to take care of one's self. This couplet of truth has been something of a model: "Eat it up, wear it out, make it do, or do without." When the Church welfare program was first announced in 1936, the First Presidency said:

> Our primary purpose was to set up, in so far as it might be possible, a system under which the curse of idleness would be done away with, the evils of a dole abolished, and independence, industry, thrift and self-respect be once more established amongst our people. The aim of the Church is to help people help themselves (Conference Report, October 1936, p. 3).

A Self-help System

It is a self-help system, not a quick handout system. It requires a careful inventory of all personal and family resources, all of which must be committed before anything is added from the outside. It is not an unkind or an unfeeling bishop who requires a member to work to the fullest extent he can for what he receives from Church welfare. There should not be the slightest embarrassment for any member to be assisted by the Church. Provided, that is, that he has contributed all that he can. President Romney has emphasized,

> To care for people on any other basis is to do them more harm than good. The purpose of Church welfare is not to relieve [a Church member] from taking care of himself (Conference Report. October 1974, p. 166).

The principle of self-reliance or personal independence is fundamental to the happy life. In too many places, in too many ways, we are getting away from it.

Spiritual and Emotional Self-Reliance

The substance of what I want to say is this: The same principle—self-reliance—has application to the spiritual and to the emotional. We have been taught to store a year's supply of food, clothing, and, if possible, fuel—at home. There has been no attempt to set up storerooms in every chapel. We know that in the crunch our members may not be able to get to the chapel for supplies. **Can we not see that the same principle applies to inspiration and revelation, the solving of problems, to counsel, and to guidance? We need to have a source of it stored in every home, not just in the bishop's office**. If we do not do that, we are quite as threatened spiritually as we should be were we to assume that the Church should supply all material needs. Unless we use care, we are on the verge of doing to ourselves emotionally (and, therefore, spiritually) what we have been working so hard for generations to avoid materially.

The "Counselitis" Epidemic

We seem to be developing an epidemic of counselitis which drains spiritual strength from the Church, much like the common cold drains more strength out of humanity than any other disease. That, some may assume, is not serious. It is very serious! On one hand, we counsel bishops to avoid abuses in welfare help. On the other hand, some bishops dole out counsel and advice without considering **that the member should solve the problem himself**. There are many chronic cases, individuals who endlessly seek counsel but do not follow the counsel that is given. I have, on occasions, included in an interview this question: "You have come to me for advice. After we have carefully considered your problem, is it your intention to follow the counsel that I will give you?" This comes as a considerable surprise to them. They had never thought of that. Usually they then commit themselves to follow counsel.

The Greatest Therapy

It is easier then to show them how to help themselves, and more than that, how to help others. **That is the greatest therapy**. Speaking figuratively, many a bishop keeps on the corner of his desk a large stack of order forms for emotional relief. When someone comes with a problem, the bishop, unfortunately, without a question, passes them out, without stopping to think what he is doing to his people. **We have become very anxious over the amount of counseling that we seem to need in the Church. Our members are becoming dependent. We must not set up a network of counseling services without at the same time emphasizing the principle of emotional self-reliance and individual independence**. If we lose our emotional and spiritual independence, our self-reliance, we can be weakened quite as much, perhaps even more, than when we become dependent materially. If we are not careful, we can lose the power of individual revelation. What the Lord said to Oliver Cowdery has meaning for all of us.

> Behold, you have not understood; you have supposed that I would give it unto you, when you took no thought save it was to ask me.
> But, behold, I say unto you, that you must study it out in your mind, then you must

ask me if it be right, and if it is right I will cause that your bosom shall burn within
you; therefore, you shall feel that it is right.

But if it be not right you shall have no such feelings, but you shall have a stupor
of thought that shall cause you to forget the thing which is wrong (D & C 9:7-9).

Spiritual independence and self-reliance is a sustaining power in the Church. If we rob the members of that how can they get revelation for themselves? How will they know there is a prophet of God? How can they get answers to prayers? How can they know for sure for themselves? It is not an unfeeling bishop who requires those coming to him for counsel to exhaust every personal and family resource before helping them. Bishops, be careful with your "emotional order forms." Do not pass them out without having analyzed carefully the individual resources.

Follow Proper Channels

Teach our members to follow proper channels in solving problems. It is not unusual for some to "shop around" to get advice from friends and neighbors, from every direction, and then choose what they think is the best of it. That is a mistake. Some want to start with psychologists, with professional counselors, or to go directly to the General Authorities to begin with. The problems may need that kind of attention but only after every personal, and family, and every local resource has been exhausted. We mentioned that when a member has used all of his own resources there should be no embarrassment in receiving welfare assistance. That principle holds true with emotional assistance as well. There may be a time when deep-seated emotional problems need more help than can be given by the family, the bishop, or the stake president. In order to help with the very difficult problems, the Church has established some counseling services in areas where our membership is large (Only for those that come through proper channels).

The first category includes those services that ordinarily require a license from the local, state, or national government. The licensed services include: adoptions; the care of unwed mothers; the foster care of children; and, the Indian Placement Program. In July of 1977 the First Presidency issued a letter giving some instruction and caution to priesthood leaders, with reference to licensed services. Our purpose here will be to review principles that apply to the services offered under the heading clinical. Clinical services are offered (again, through proper channels only) in three successive steps:

First: consultation, wherein a priesthood leader consults with an LDS Social Services representative about a member with serious problems. Only the priesthood leader meets with the member. **The next step** is evaluation, wherein **a priesthood leader and the member** meet together with an LDS Social Services practitioner to evaluate the problem. Ordinarily this is one meeting only. Thereafter, the priesthood leader continues to help the member. In difficult and persistent cases, there is therapy. The member (and, when possible, the bishop) meets with an LDS Social Services practitioner for counseling. The bishop gives continuing help after termination of these sessions.

Bishops and stake presidents can exemplify self-reliance by resolving these problems locally. *Ultimately it is the member who must solve them.* **Bishops, you must not abdicate your responsibility to anyone—not to professionals, even to those employed by Church Social Services.** They would be the first to tell you so. You have a power to soothe and to sanctify and to heal that others are not given.

The Key of Forgiveness

Sometimes what a member needs is forgiveness—you have a key to that. If you find a case where professional help is justified, be very careful. There are some spiritually destructive techniques used in the field of counseling. When you entrust your members to others, do not let them be subject to these things. Solve problems in the Lord's way. Some counselors want to delve deeper than is emotionally or spiritually healthy. They sometimes want to draw out and analyze and take apart and dissect. While a certain amount of catharsis may be healthy, overmuch of it can be degenerating. It is seldom as easy to put something back together as it is to take it apart. By probing too deeply, or talking endlessly about some problems, we can fool-ishly cause the very thing we are trying to prevent. You probably know about the parents who said,

> Now, children, while we are gone, whatever you do, don't take the stool and go into the pantry and climb up to the second shelf and move the cracker box and get that sack of beans and put one up your nose, will you?

There is a lesson there.

Now, a bishop may ask, justifiably, "How in the world can I ever accomplish my job as bishop and still counsel those who really need it?" One stake president said to me: "Bishops don't have enough time to counsel. With the load we're putting on them, we're killing our bishops off." While there's some truth in that, I sometimes think it's a case of suicide.

The Role of a Bishop

Our study of the role of the bishop indicates that most bishops spend time ineffectively as program ad-ministrators. The influence of a bishop on a ward is more positive when he functions as a presiding officer, rather than getting so heavily involved in all of the program details. It is usually in program administration, with all of the meetings, training activities, etc., that the bishop spends too much time. Bishops, leave that to your counselors and the priesthood leaders and auxiliary leaders. [Some] problems. . ., for instance, can be solved by the home teacher and the quorum leaders. Trust them. Let go of it. And you will then be free to do the things that will make the most difference, counseling those who really need it—in the Lord's own way.

Two letters have gone to the field. The one was a two-thirds reduction in the number of personal priest-hood interviews required on all levels. The other was a shifting of major administrative meetings from weekly and monthly to monthly and quarterly. We have every hope that other relief will be filtering down through channels. In the meantime, bishop, you are in charge. Get the administrative and training part of your work in such efficient operation that you will have time to counsel your people.

Bishops, keep constantly in mind that fathers are responsible to preside over their families. Sometimes, with all good intentions, we require so much of both the children and the father that he is not able to do so. If my boy needs counseling, bishop, it should be my responsibility first, and yours second. If my boy needs rec-reation, bishop, I should provide it first, and you second. If my boy needs correction, that should be my re-sponsibility first, and yours second. If I am failing as a father, help me first, and my children second. Do not be too quick to take over from me the job of raising my children. Do not be too quick to counsel them and solve all of the problems. Get me involved. It is my ministry.

The Philosophy of Instant Gratification

We live in a day when the adversary stresses on every hand the philosophy of instant gratification. We seem to demand instant everything, including instant solutions to our problems. We are indoctrinated that somehow we should always be instantly emotionally comfortable. When that is not so, some become anx-ious—and all too frequently seek relief from counseling, from analysis, and even from medication. It was meant to be that life would be a challenge. To suffer some anxiety, some depression, some disappointment, even some failure is normal. Teach our members that if they have a good, miserable day once in a while, or several in a row, to stand steady and face them. Things will straighten out.

There is great purpose in our struggle in life. There is great meaning in these words entitled "The Les-son."

> Yes, my fretting, frowning child,
> I could cross the room to you more easily.

But I've already learned to walk,
So I make you come to me.

Let go now—there! You see?
Oh, remember this simple lesson child,
And when in later years you cry out with tight fists and tears

"Oh, help me God—please."
Just listen and you'll hear a silent voice
"I would, child, I would. But it's you, not I,
Who needs to try Godhood.

> (Carol Lynn Pearson, "The Lesson," *Beginnings*, New York: Doubleday and Co. 1975, p. 18).

Bishop, those who come to you are children of God. Counsel them in the Lord's own way. Teach them to ponder it in their minds, then to pray over their problems.

The Therapy of Reading the Scriptures

Remember that soothing, calming effect of reading the scriptures. Next time you are where they are read, notice how things settle down. Sense the feeling of peace and security that comes. Now, from the Book of Mormon, this closing thought: The prophet Alma faced a weightier problem than you, bishop, will likely see in your ministry. Like you, he felt uncertain; and he went to Mosiah. Mosiah wisely turned the problem back to him, saying:

> Behold, I judge them not; therefore I deliver them into thy hands to be judged.
> And now the spirit of Alma was again troubled; and he went and inquired of the Lord what he should do concerning this matter, for he feared that he should do wrong in the sight of God.
> And it came to pass that after he had poured out his whole soul to God, the voice of the Lord came to him (Mosiah 26:12-14).

That voice will speak to you, bishop. That is your privilege. I bear witness of that, for I know that He lives. May God bless you, bishop, the inspired judge in Israel, and those who come to you, as you counsel them in the Lord's own way. In the name of Jesus Christ, Amen.

Marital Satisfaction/Success/Happiness

Susan Blumel

7 **30 Studies between 1928-88**: 60 years of research on marital success. Factors from attractiveness of the partners to a wife's employment have all been explored. Here are some of the major ones:

1. Childhood environment—affects success in marriage

2. Children of divorced parents are more open to divorce

3. Adjustment during engagement→marital success—able to adjust in marriage

4. Verbally expressing affection, positive regard, warmth, empathy, and supporting each other

5. Attitudes of cooperation and consideration

6. Communication skills, controlled expression of hostility, joint-problem solving, and decision-making capabilities, along with the ability to compromise

7. Common likes/dislikes—socio-emotional status, similar religious beliefs and values

8. Emotional stability, maturity, responsibility, internal focus of control, high self esteem

9. Spend time together (positive)

10. Commitment to each other, to marriage, to fidelity

11. High degree of sexual satisfaction

12. Similar role expectations—toward equality

13. Both want children

14. High religiosity

15. Wife's employment approved by both spouses and choice is involved

16. Income, increased savings, agreement on expenditures

17. Education, higher age at marriage, and mutual service

Divorce Variables

1. Infidelity

2. Violent behavior, high conflict, manipulative communication, low compromise

3. Low income—$$ problems

4. Low educational levels, low SES

5. Wife employment necessary because of low income

6. Early marital ages

7. Low Commitment

8. Low religiosity

9. Lack of time together

10. Difference in values, SES, age, religiosity, race

11. No children or "too many" too fast

12. Extensive premarital sex, pre-marital pregnancy, premarital conflict

13. Live in urban areas

14. Emotional immaturity or problems

15. Brief dating prior to marriage

16. Loss of love and respect for mate, low expression of affection or respect

Principal Conclusion

Focus on self rather than focus on companion's happiness; interested in companion's feelings and interests—what I call the therapeutic role of marriage.

From AMCAP survey: 28 problem areas in marriage:

1. Communication

2. Unrealistic expectations of marriage or spouse

3. Demonstration of affection

4. Lack of loving feelings

5. Sex

6. Power struggles

7. Decision making/problem solving

8. Money management/finances

9. Value conflicts

10. Role conflicts

11. Children

12. Serious individual problems

13. Premarital/extra-marital affairs

14. Household management

15. In-laws/relatives

16. Jealousy

17. Employment/job

18. Recreation/leisure time

19. Alcoholism
21. Problems related to previous marriage
21. Psychosomatic problems
22. Friends
23. Substance addiction
24. Personal habits/appearance
25. Physical abuse
26. Religious differences
27. Health problems/physical handicap
28. Incest

Our Solemn Responsibilities

President Gordon B. Hinckley

Ensign, November 1991, pp. 49-52

A husband who domineers his wife, who demeans and humiliates her . . . not only injures her, but he also belittles himself.

Brethren, we have had an excellent meeting. Much has been spoken worthy of remembrance and application in our lives. I endorse and commend to you what the Brethren have said. I hope that every man and boy, wherever you may be, may leave this meeting tonight with a greater desire and a stronger resolution to live more worthy of the divine priesthood which each of us holds.

I speak to you in a somewhat personal tone, not to boast but by way of testimony and in a spirit of gratitude.

This conference marks two personal anniversaries for me. Thirty years ago at the October conference I was sustained a member of the council of the Twelve Apostles. Ten years ago I was sustained as a counselor in the First Presidency. I am deeply grateful to you and your families for your sustaining hands and hearts and prayers. Thank you. I confess I have never felt adequate to these tremendous callings. I suppose that every man and woman in this Church has those feelings in whatever office or calling he or she may be asked to serve.

I received a letter the other day from a grandson serving a mission in Poland. He is laboring with Elder Neuenschwander in an area where they are trying to open the work. It is difficult. He wrote, "I am president of a branch with four members, and I feel so inadequate."

I need not remind any of you, even you who are deacons, that it is an awesome thing to be clothed with the holy priesthood and to have the responsibility, great or small, to assist God our Eternal Father in bringing to pass the immortality and eternal life of His sons and daughters of all generations. No one of us can comprehend the magnitude and full meaning of that responsibility. But with our limited knowledge, we know we must be faithful and diligent in carrying forward our duty.

Remarkable and miraculous things happen when we do so. May I remind you of the rich and wonderful fruits of your labors over a period of years. I hesitate to use statistics, but these represent the results of your service and the mighty blessings of the Lord.

In the thirty years since I was ordained an Apostle, the membership of the Church has grown from 1,800,000 to a present estimated membership of 8,040,000, or an increase of 441 percent.

The number of stakes has grown from 345 to 1,817. That represents a 527 percent increase. Admittedly, we are creating smaller stakes and more of them in an effort to improve efficiency of administration. Nonetheless, in the time during which many of us have served, we have seen a miracle.

I have seen in the season of my apostleship the corps of full-time missionaries grow from 10,000 to approximately 45,000, for an increase of 425 percent, with a comparable growth in missions from 67 to 267, or a 398 percent growth.

Now, these are statistics, not particularly interesting in table form, but tremendously significant in the lives of millions of the sons and daughters of God our Eternal Father who live in 135 nations and territories scattered across the earth where the Church is established.

When I think of these things, I feel like standing and shouting hallelujah. But more appropriately, I feel to kneel and say in humility, thanks be to God and His beloved Son, our Redeemer, for the growth of this Their work, and thanks be to my brothers and sisters, young and old, you who have been faithful and diligent in your duty in causing this to happen. This has been a joyful thing to observe.

But during these ten years that I have served in the Presidency, I have also experienced much of sorrow. It is out of this experience that I wish to speak a little further. For a full decade now I have participated in the task of sitting in judgment on the worthiness of those who plead to come back into the Church after having been excommunicated. In every case there had been a serious violation of Church standards of conduct. In most cases there had been adultery, and in the majority of cases, husbands were the offenders. Disciplinary action had been taken against them. As months passed they longed for what they previously had. A spirit of repentance came into their hearts.

As one of these men said to me: "I really never understood nor appreciated the gift of the Holy Ghost until it was taken from me."

I have spoken on three or four occasions to the women of the Church during the past ten years. I have received in response to these various talks a substantial number of letters. I have kept some of them in a file marked "Unhappy Women."

These letters have come from many areas. But they are all written in the same tone. I wish to read you a portion of one of them which was received only last week. The writer has granted me permission to do so. I will not disclose any names.

Said she,

> I met my husband when he was a freshman. He was from a very active family with many years of service in the Church. He was so enthused about serving a mission. I thought we shared the gospel as our most important value in this life. We both enjoyed music and nature and had a high priority on gaining knowledge. We dated a few months, easily fell in love, and wrote to one another while he served an honorable mission. When he came back home, he got back into school and we were married in the Salt Lake Temple. We followed the counsel of Church leaders and began our family. I had been attending [the university] on an Honors at Entrance scholarship, but I became pregnant and sick and left school to devote my time and energy to my husband and infant son.
>
> For the next eighteen years I supported my husband while he finished school, got some work experience, and started his own business. We both served in leadership positions in the Church and community. We had five wonderful children. I taught the children the gospel, how to work, how to serve, how to communicate, and how to play the piano. I baked bread; canned peaches, apples, tomatoes; sewed dresses and quilts; cleaned house; and tended my flowers and vegetables. In many ways it seemed that we were an ideal family. Our relationship was sometimes sweet and sometimes difficult. Things were never perfect, because I am not a perfect woman and he is not a perfect man, but many things were good. I did not expect perfection, I just kept trying.
>
> Then came the crash. About a year ago he decided that he never loved me and that our marriage was a mistake from the beginning. He was convinced that there was nothing in our relationship for him. He filed for divorce and moved out. "Wait," I kept saying. "Oh, no. Stop! Don't do this. Why are you leaving? What is wrong? Please, talk to me. Look at our children. What of all our dreams? Remember our covenants. No, No! Divorce is not the answer." He would not hear me. I thought I would die.
>
> Now I am a single parent. What an enormous load of heartache, pain, and loneliness are behind that statement. It explains so much trauma and so much anger from my teenage sons. It explains so many tears from my little girls. It explains so many sleepless nights, so many family demands and needs. Why am I in this mess? What did I choose wrong? How will I ever get through school? How will I get through

this week? Where is my husband? Where is the father of my children? I join the ranks of tired women whose husbands leave them. I have no money, no job. I have children to care for, bills to pay, and not much hope.

I do not know if her former husband may be in this audience somewhere. If he is listening I may receive from him a letter justifying what he has done. I know there are two sides to every issue. But somehow, I cannot understand how a man who holds the holy priesthood and who has entered into sacred and binding covenants before the Lord could justify abandoning his responsibilities for his wife of eighteen years and the five children who exist because of him, and of whose flesh and blood and heritage they have partaken.

The problem is not new. I suppose it is as old as the human race. Certainly it existed among the Nephites. Jacob, son of Nephi, speaking as a prophet to his people, declared:

> For behold, I, the Lord, have seen the sorrow, and heard the mourning of the daughters of my people in the land of Jerusalem, yea, and in all the lands of my people, because of the wickedness and abominations of their husbands. . . .
> Ye have broken the hearts of your tender wives, and lost the confidence of your children, because of your bad examples before them; and the sobbings of their hearts ascend up to God against you (Jacob 2:31, 35).

Permit me to read from another letter. Said the writer:

> My husband is a good man with many outstanding qualities and character traits, but underneath it all there is a strong streak of authoritarianism . . . His volatile temper flares up often enough to remind me of all the potential ugliness of which he is capable.
> President Hinckley, . . . please remind the brethren that the physical and verbal abuse of women is INEXCUSABLE, NEVER ACCEPTABLE, AND A COWARDLY WAY OF DEALING WITH DIFFERENCES, especially and particularly despicable if the abuser is a priesthood holder.

Now, I believe that most marriages in the Church are happy, that both husbands and wives in those marriages experience a sense of security and love, of mutual dependence, and an equal sharing of burdens. I am confident that the children in those homes, at least in the vast majority of them, are growing up with a sense of peace and security, knowing that they are appreciated and loved by both of their parents, who, they feel, love one another. But I am confident, my brethren, that there is enough of the opposite to justify what I am saying.

Who can calculate the wounds inflicted, their depth and pain, by harsh and mean words spoken in anger? How pitiful a sight is a man who is strong in many ways but who loses all control of himself when some little thing, usually of no significant consequence, disturbs his equanimity. In every marriage there are, of course, occasional differences. But I find no justification for tempers that explode on the slightest provocation.

Said the writer of Proverbs: "Wrath is cruel, and anger is outrageous" (Prov. 27:4).

A violent temper is such a terrible, corrosive thing. And the tragedy is that it accomplishes no good; it only feeds evil with resentment and rebellion and pain. To any man or boy within the sound of my voice who has trouble controlling his tongue, may I suggest that you plead with the Lord for the strength to overcome your weakness, that you apologize to those you have offended, and that you marshal within yourselves the power to discipline your tongue.

To the boys who are here, may I suggest that you watch your temper, now, in these formative years of your life. As Brother Haight has reminded you, this is the season to develop the power and capacity to discipline yourselves. You may think it is the macho thing to flare up in anger and swear and profane the name of the Lord. It is not the macho thing. It is an indication of weakness. Anger is not an expression of strength. It is an indication of one's inability to control his thoughts, words, his emotions. Of course it is easy to get angry. When the weakness of anger takes over, the strength of reason leaves. Cultivate within yourselves the mighty power of self-discipline.

Now I move to another corrosive element that afflicts all too many marriages. It is interesting to me that two of the ten commandments deal with this—"Thou shalt not commit adultery" and "Thou shalt not covet" (Ex. 20:14, 17). Ted Koppel, moderator of ABC's "Nightline" program, is reported as saying the following to a group of students at Duke University concerning slogans that were proposed to reduce drugs and immorality:

> We have actually convinced ourselves that slogans will save us. . . But the answer is NO! Not because it isn't cool or smart or because you might end up in jail or dying in an AIDS ward, but NO because it is wrong, because we have spent 5,000 years as a race of rational human beings, trying to drag ourselves out of the primeval slime by searching for truth and moral absolutes. In its purest form, truth is not a polite tap on the shoulder. It is a howling reproach. What Moses brought down from Mount Sinai were not The Ten Suggestions.

Think about that for a moment. What Moses brought down were Ten Commandments, written by the finger of Jehovah on tablets of stone for the salvation and safety, for the security and happiness of the children of Israel, and for all of the generations which were to come after them.

Altogether too many men, leaving their wives at home in the morning and going to work, where they find attractively dressed and attractively made-up young women, regard themselves as young and handsome, and as an irresistible catch. They complain that their wives do not look the same as they did twenty years ago when they married them. To which I say, Who would, after living with you for twenty years?

The tragedy is that some men are ensnared by their own foolishness and their own weakness. They throw to the wind the most sacred and solemn of covenants, entered into in the house of the Lord and sealed under the authority of the holy priesthood. They set aside their wives who have been faithful, who have loved and cared for them, who have struggled with them in times of poverty, only to be discarded in times of affluence. They have left their children fatherless. They have avoided with every kind of artifice the payment of court-mandated alimony and child support.

Do I sound harsh and negative? Yes, I feel that way, as I deal with case after case and have done so over a period of time. Wrote Paul: "But if any provide not for his own, and specially for those of his own house, he hath denied the faith, and is worse than an infidel" (1 Tim. 5:8). In that same epistle, he said to Timothy: "Keep thyself pure" (v. 22).

Now I recognize that there may be some few cases where conditions of the marriage are totally intolerable. But these cases are in the minority. And even in these cases, where a marriage has been undertaken and children are brought into the world, there is a responsibility, binding and with accountability before God, to provide care for those for whose lives the father is responsible.

The complaint of a husband, after eighteen years of marriage and five children, that he no longer loves his wife is, in my judgment, a feeble excuse for the violation of covenants made before God and also the evasion of the responsibilities that are the very strength of the society of which we are a part. The finding of fault with consequent divorce is usually preceded by a long period in which little mistakes are spoken of in harsh and angry language, where tiny molehills of difference grow into great mountains of conflict. I am satisfied that the more unkindly a wife is treated, the less attractive she becomes. She loses pride in herself. She develops a feeling of worthlessness. Of course it shows.

A husband who domineers his wife, who demeans and humiliates her, and who makes officious demands upon her not only injures her, but he also belittles himself. And in many cases, he plants a pattern of future similar behavior in his sons.

My brethren, you who have had conferred upon you the priesthood of God, you know, as I know, that there is no enduring happiness, that there is no lasting peace in the heart, no tranquility in the home, without the companionship of a good woman. Our wives are not our inferiors.

Some men who are evidently unable to gain respect by the goodness of their lives, use as justification for their actions the statement that Eve was told that Adam should rule over her. How much sadness, how much tragedy, how much heartbreak has been caused through centuries of time by weak men who have used that as a scriptural warrant for atrocious behavior! They do not recognize that the same account indicates that Eve was given as a helpmeet to Adam. The facts are that they stood side by side in the garden. They were expelled from the garden together, and they worked together, side by side, in gaining their bread by the sweat of their brows.

Now, brethren, I know I have spoken of a minority. But the depth of the tragedy which afflicts that minority, and particularly the victims of that minority, has impelled me to say what I have said. There is an old adage that says: "If the shoe fits, wear it."

What I have spoken I have said with a desire to be helpful and, in some cases, in the spirit of a rebuke followed by an increase of love toward those whom I may have rebuked.

How beautiful is the marriage of a young man and a young woman who begin their lives together kneeling at the altar in the house of the Lord, pledging their love and loyalty one to another for time and all eternity. When children come into that home, they are nurtured and cared for, loved and blessed with the feeling that their father loves their mother. In that environment they find peace and strength and security. Watching their father, they develop respect for women. They are taught self-control and self-discipline, which bring the strength to avoid later tragedy.

The years pass. The children eventually leave the home, one by one. And the father and the mother are again alone. But they have each other to talk with, to depend on, to nurture, to encourage, and to bless. There comes the autumn of life and a looking back with satisfaction and gladness. Through all of the years there has been loyalty, one to the other. There has been deference and courtesy. Now there is a certain mellowness, a softening, an effect that partakes of a hallowed relationship. They realize that death may come any time, usually to one first with a separation of a season brief or lengthy. But they know also that because their companionship was sealed under the authority of the eternal priesthood and they have lived worthy of the blessings, there will be a reunion sweet and certain.

Brethren, this is the way our Father in Heaven would have it. This is the Lord's way. He has so indicated. His prophets have spoken of it.

It takes effort. It takes self-control. It takes unselfishness. It requires the true essence of love, which is an anxious concern for the well-being and happiness of one's companion. I could wish nothing better for all of you than this, and I pray that this may be your individual blessing, in the name of Jesus Christ, amen.

Areas of Change in Our Marriage

Adapted from unknown source by **Douglas E. Brinley**

In every relationship there are behaviors about which one or both partners would like changes. These particular behaviors may occur either too often or not often enough. For example, a partner may be dissatisfied because the other only takes out the garbage once a week. The change wanted in this case would be that the behavior occur *more often*. On the other hand, one might be dissatisfied because he thought his spouse spent too much time cleaning up the house (and not enough time with him/her); in this case—the change wanted would be that this behavior occur *less often*.

The following areas of behavior have to do with relationships—their being strengthened or weakened by the quantity or quality of behavior occurring. As you read each item, decide whether you are satisfied with the performance of your spouse. If you are—check the column marked with 0. If not—indicate the direction of change you would like—either more or less of that particular behavior and how strongly you desire change. If you feel it is a *major* item in your marriage—check that column.

I would like my husband/wife to:	Much Less -3	Less -2	Some-what less -1	About Right 0	Some-what More +1	More +2	Much More +3	Major Item
1. Manage money better								
2. Spend more time with me								
3. Have meals ready on time								
4. Strike/choke/push family members								
5. Initiate discussions with me								
6. Take me out dinner/play/movie, etc.								
7. Get together with his/her relatives								
8. Spend quality time with children								
9. Work late								
10. Initiate sexual intimacy with me								
11. Help with housework								
12. Argue								
13. Discipline children								
14. Allow me time to myself								
15. Agree to do things I like								
16. Give praise to me/children								
17. Express feelings/emotions calmly								
18. Enjoy my friends								
19. Listen to my thoughts/feelings								
20. Be patient with my faults								
21. Help in planning our time								
22. Come to meals on time								
23. Attend Church								
24. Express affection/non-sexual actions								
25. Watch TV								

	Much Less -3	Less -2	Some-what Less -1	About Right 0	Some-what More +1	More +2	Much More +3	Major Item
26. Swear/vulgar language								
27. View R-rated/pornographic movies								
28. Understand my ideas on modesty								
29. Vary sexual techniques								
30. Frequency of sexual relations								
31. Understand my weight problem								
32. Understand my family background								
33. Use of telephone								
34. Sensitivity to personal hygiene								
35. Talk about ex-spouse								
36. Enjoy being a parent								
37. See the need to fix things								
38. Eliminate clutter								
39. Lead out in our family								
40. Initiate FHE/Family Prayer/Scripture								
41. Take active part in teaching children								
42. Temper displayed								
43. Display moodiness/depression								
44. Display sarcasm, criticism								
45. Participate in athletics/exercise								
46. Spend individual time with children								
47. Spend time with my relatives/family								
48. Spend time on phone with family								
49. Time with the family versus work time								
50. Allow me time to relax/think/play								
51. Follow-up on ideas and joint plans								
52. Read good books/church books								
53. Take care of car								
54. Initiate social activities								
55. Think about and plan career change								
56. Use of computer/typewriter								
57. Bringing work home (ext. of office)								
58. Interest in children's homework								
59. Be romantic								
60. Really listen before judging/speaking								
61. Tidiness/cleanliness of home/bathroom								
62. Taste in clothing/makeup								
63. Initiate family activities								
64. Clean up after cooking/fixing/repair								
65. A positive influence in the home								
66. Talking to others about our problems								
67. Host/Hostess skills								
68.								
69.								
70.								

Remember that this type of feedback is designed to improve the quality of our marriages. Of course we don't like negative feedback, but how else can we "repent"—meaning that we stop or start, increase or decrease those things that are causing some "glitches" in our marital relations. Those items where there is some need to make some changes need to be discussed in all "faith, virtue, knowledge, temperance, patience, brotherly kindness, godliness, charity, humility, diligence (D&C 4:6). Use this list to strengthen and improve your skills as a marriage partner. There are many more items that could be added—perhaps you two could think of a few more that pertain to you and your relationship.

Shouldering Responsibility

Elder F. Burton Howard

April Conference Report, 1991, pp. 13-16

. . . **U**nwillingness to accept the responsibility for and consequences of one's actions is an all too common condition in today's world. Who has not heard of the drunken driver who sues his host for allowing him to get drunk, or of the accident victim who claims damages from the physician who tries to help him? Perpetrators of the most heinous crimes often plead guilty by reason of insanity or claim that they are victims of society's ills. The homeless blame alcohol. Alcoholics blame genetic deficiencies. Abusers and adulterers blame the broken homes of their childhood. And there are enough who agree with them to ensure that no one need feel terribly guilty for long if they don't want to.

The habit of shifting the burden of guilt onto someone else, while perhaps understandable in a secular setting, has more serious consequences in a spiritual one. There, too, it has an ancient but not honorable tradition.

Cain blamed God when his sacrifice was not accepted. "I was wroth," he said, "for his offering thou didst accept and not mine" (Moses 5:38).

Laman and Lemuel blamed Nephi for nearly all their troubles (see 1 Nephi 16:35-38). Pilate blamed the Jews when he condoned the crucifixion of the Savior, in whom he found "no fault" (Luke 23:4; see also Matthew 27:24).

Even the very elite have sometimes succumbed to the temptation to blame others for their disobedience or their failure to receive blessings. Aaron blamed the children of Israel when Moses charged him with bringing a great sin upon them by making a molten calf (see Exodus 32:19-24). And Martha may have blamed Mary for depriving her of the Savior's presence on that indelible day in Bethany (see Luke 10:40).

Today the practice continues. We hear at every hand phrases such as "My wife just doesn't understand me," "Loosen up—everybody does it," or "It wasn't really my fault." The second great commandment (see Matthew 22:35-40) is breached routinely by those who say, "He started it" or "She deserved it." Teens and adults alike jokingly attempt to justify behavioral lapses by saying. "The devil made me do it."

When faced with the consequences of transgression, rather than looking to ourselves as the source of the discomfort which always accompanies sin, many of us tend to blame someone else. Rather than getting out of a vicious and senseless circle, we fault our neighbor for our pain and try to pass it on. But to repent we must leave the circle.

The first step in the repentance process has always been simply to recognize that we have done wrong. If we are so hedged about by pride, rationalization, machismo, or a misdirected sense of self-esteem as to prevent us from ever admitting that we are part of the problem, we are in trouble. We then may not even know of our need to repent. We will have no idea whether the Lord is pleased with us or not and may become "past feeling" (1 Nephi 17:45). But all men, everywhere, must repent (see 3 Nephi 11:32). To fail to do so is to perish (see Luke 13:3; Helaman 7:28).

To excuse misconduct by blaming others is presumptuous at best and is fatally flawed with regard to spiritual things, for "we believe that men will be punished for their own sins, and not for Adam's transgression" (Articles of Faith 1:2). This means not only that we will not be punished for what Adam did in the Garden, but also that we cannot excuse our own behavior by pointing a finger to Adam or anyone else. The real danger in failing to accept responsibility for our own actions is that unless we do, we may never even enter on the strait and narrow path. Misconduct that does not require repentance may be pleasant at first, but it will not be for long. And it will never lead us to eternal life.

Just as foolish as believing that we can "pass it on" is the idea that the satisfaction of being in the circle, whatever that may be, can somehow excuse any wrongs committed there. This notion is widely shared and is most often expressed by the phrase, "The end justifies the means." Such a belief, if left undisturbed and unchecked, can also impede the repentance process and cheat us out of exaltation.

Those who teach it are almost always attempting to excuse the use of improper or questionable means. Such people seem to be saying. "My purpose was to do good or to be happy; therefore, any little lie, or misrepresentation, or lapse of integrity, or violation of law along the way is justified."

In certain circumstances, some say it is okay to conceal the truth, to dig just a small pit for an adversary, to pursue an advantage of some kind—such as superior knowledge or position—against another. "This is just common practice," or "I'm just looking after Number One," they say. "All's fair in love and war," or "That's the way the ball bounces," they say. But if the means which prompt the saying of these things are wrong, no amount of rationalization or verbal whitewash can ever make them right. To those who believe otherwise, Nephi said,

> Yea, and there shall be many which shall teach after this manner, false and vain
> and foolish doctrines, and shall be puffed up in their hearts, and shall seek deep to hide
> their counsels from the Lord (2 Nephi 28:9).

Some seek to justify their actions by quoting scripture. They often cite Nephi's killing of Laban as an example of the need to violate a law to accomplish a greater good and to prevent a nation from dwindling in unbelief. But they forget that Nephi twice refused to follow the promptings of the Spirit. In the end, he agreed to break the commandment only when he was convinced that "the Lord slayeth the wicked to bring forth his righteous purposes" (1 Nephi 4:13) and also (I believe) when he knew that the penalty for shedding blood had been lifted, in that one exceptional case, by Him whose right it is to fix and waive penalties.

The truth is that we are judged by the means we employ and not by the ends we may hope to obtain. It will do us little good at the last day to respond to the Great Judge, "I know I was not all I could have been, but my heart was in the right place."

In fact, there is danger in focusing merely on ends. To some who did, the Savior said:

> Many will say to me in that day: Lord, Lord, have we not prophesied in thy
> name, and in thy name have cast out devils, and in thy name done many wonderful
> works?
> And then will I profess unto them: I never knew you; depart from me, ye that
> work iniquity (3 Nephi 14:22-23).

The war in heaven was essentially about the means by which the plan of salvation would be implemented. It forever established the principle that even for the greatest of all ends, eternal life, the means are critical. It should be obvious to all thinking Latter-day Saints that the wrong means can never attain that objective.

The danger in thinking that the end justifies the means lies in making a judgment we have no right to make. Who are we to say that the Lord will pardon wickedness done to attain a perceived "greater good." Even if the goal is good, it would be a personal calamity to look beyond the mark and fail to repent of the wrong we do along the way.

Of course we have the right to strive for happiness. But as we do we should pause every now and then and look to ourselves. We should remember that "wickedness never was happiness" (Alma 41:10). And the sweet peace the gospel brings never comes at all when we justify our misconduct or blame others for our unhappiness. But there is a way out. We need only remember a pointless, irresponsible childhood game, and quietly walk away. Face up, quit, get out, confess, apologize, admit the harm we have done, and just plain walk away.

There are so many important things for us to do in mortality. There is not much time to waste on games. We must obtain essential ordinances. We must enter into and keep sacred covenants. We are to "live by every word which proceedeth forth out of the mouth of God" (D&C 98:11). We must love and serve one another. We are to be proved in all things (see D&C 98:14). Even little things like means. There will be trials. There will likely be other circles we will have to leave. How we respond to all of this will turn out to be the real measure of our salvation.

So to those, including myself, who from time to time have said, "I am not at fault—I was compelled by circumstances to do what I did," I say, "That may be so, but there is grave danger here. If there is any doubt at all, let us simply repent." For, in the words of Job, "If I justify myself, mine own mouth shall condemn me: if I say, I am perfect, it shall also prove me perverse" (Job 9:20).

And to those who say, "I may have done a little wrong, but my purpose was good and I believe God will justify my behavior," my response is, "Maybe so, but don't count on it." For in the 137th section of the Doctrine and Covenants, verse 9, we read,

"For I, the Lord, will judge all men according to their works, according to the desire of their hearts."

May the Lord bless us to see ourselves as we really are and to repent as needs be, I pray in the name of Jesus Christ, amen.

Being a Righteous Husband and Father

President Howard W. Hunter

General Conference, October 1994, *Ensign*, November 1994, pp. 49-51

My dear brethren of the priesthood, I consider it a privilege to meet with you this evening in this general priesthood meeting. The priesthood is the greatest brotherhood on the earth. I feel great strength in seeing your faithfulness and feeling your love and sustaining vote. We are particularly grateful to have so many of our Aaronic Priesthood brethren here with their fathers or advisers.

The subject of my address this evening will be more particularly directed to the husbands and fathers. All of you who hold the Aaronic Priesthood will soon arrive at the years of marriage and fatherhood. Therefore, what I say tonight has application to all present.

I wish to speak of the relationship that a man holding the priesthood should have with his wife and children. With a knowledge of the plan of salvation as a foundation, a man who holds the priesthood looks upon marriage as a sacred privilege and obligation. It is not good for man nor for woman to be alone. Man is not complete without woman. Neither can fill the measure of their creation without the other (see 1 Cor. 11:11; Moses 3:18). Marriage between a man and a woman is ordained of God (see D&C 49:15-17). Only through the new and everlasting covenant of marriage can they realize the fulness of eternal blessings (see D&C 131:1-4; 132:15-19). As a matter of priesthood responsibility, a man, under normal circumstances, should not unduly postpone marriage. Brethren, the Lord has spoken plainly on this matter. It is your sacred and solemn responsibility to follow his counsel and the words of his prophets.

The prophets of the past have spoken also of those who may not have opportunity to marry in this life. President Lorenzo Snow said:

> There is no Latter-day Saint who dies after having lived a faithful life who will lose anything because of having failed to do certain things when opportunities were not furnished him or her. In other words, if a young man or a young woman has no opportunity of getting married, and they live faithful lives up to the time of their death, they will have all the blessings, exaltation, and glory that any man or woman will have who had this opportunity and improved it. That is sure and positive" (*The Teachings of Lorenzo Snow*, comp. Clyde J. Williams, Salt Lake City: Bookcraft, 1984, p. 138).

I believe President Snow's statement to be true.

A man who holds the priesthood shows perfect moral fidelity to his wife and gives her no reason to doubt his faithfulness. A husband is to love his wife with all his heart and cleave unto her and none else (see D&C 42:22-26). President Spencer W. Kimball explained:

"The words *none else* eliminate everyone and everything. The spouse then becomes pre-eminent in the life of the husband or wife and neither social life nor occupational life nor political life nor any other interest nor person nor thing shall ever take precedence over the companion spouse" (*The Miracle of Forgiveness*, Salt Lake City: Bookcraft, 1969, p. 250).

The Lord forbids and his church condemns any and every intimate relationship outside of marriage. Infidelity on the part of a man breaks the heart of his wife and loses her confidence and the confidence of his children (see Jacob 2:35).

Be faithful in your marriage covenants in thought, word, and deed. Pornography, flirtations, and unwholesome fantasies erode one's character and strike at the foundation of a happy marriage. Unity and trust within a marriage are thereby destroyed. One who does not control his thoughts and thus commits adultery in his heart, if he does not repent, shall not have the Spirit, but shall deny the faith and shall fear (see D&C 42:23; 63:16).

A man who holds the priesthood has reverence for motherhood. Mothers are given a sacred privilege to "bear the souls of men; for herein is the work of [the] Father continued, that he may be glorified" (D&C 132:63).

The First Presidency has said: "Motherhood is near to divinity. It is the highest, holiest service to be assumed by mankind" (in James R. Clarke, comp., *Messages of the First Presidency*, 6 vols., Salt Lake City: Bookcraft, 1965-75, 6:178). The priesthood cannot work out its destiny, nor can God's purposes be fulfilled, without our helpmates. Mothers perform a labor the priesthood cannot do. For this gift of life, the priesthood should have love unbounded for the mothers of their children.

Honor your wife's unique and divinely appointed role as a mother in Israel and her special capacity to bear and nurture children. We are under divine commandment to multiply and replenish the earth and to bring up our children and grandchildren in light and truth (see Moses 2:28; D&C 93:40). You share, as a loving partner, the care of the children. Help her to manage and keep up your home. Help teach, train, and discipline your children.

You should express regularly to your wife and children your reverence and respect for her. Indeed, one of the greatest things a father can do for his children is to love their mother.

A man who holds the priesthood regards the family as ordained of God. Your leadership of the family is your most important and sacred responsibility. The family is the most important unit in time and in eternity and, as such, transcends every other interest in life.

We reiterate what was stated by President David O. McKay: "No other success [in life] can compensate for failure in the home" (David O. McKay quoting J. E. McCulloch, "Home, the Savior of Civilization," in Conference Report, Apr. 1935, p. 116) and President Harold B. Lee: "The most important of the Lord's work you and I will ever do will be within the walls of our own homes" (Harold B. Lee, *Stand Ye in Holy Places*, Salt Lake City: Deseret Book Co., 1974, p. 255). Effective family leadership, brethren, requires both quantity and quality time. The teaching and governance of the family must not be left to your wife alone, to society, to school, or even the Church.

A man who holds the priesthood accepts his wife as a partner in the leadership of the home and family with full knowledge of and full participation in all decisions relating thereto. Of necessity there must be in the Church and in the home a presiding officer (see D&C 107:21). By divine appointment, the responsibility to preside in the home rests upon the priesthood holder (see Moses 4:22). The Lord intended that the wife be a helpmeet for man (*meet* means equal)—that is, a companion equal and necessary in full partnership. Presiding in righteousness necessitates a shared responsibility between husband and wife; together you act with knowledge and participation in all family matters. For a man to operate independent of or without regard to the feelings and counsel of his wife in governing the family is to exercise unrighteous dominion.

Keep yourselves above any domineering or unworthy behavior in the tender, intimate relationship between husband and wife. Because marriage is ordained of God, the intimate relationship between husbands and wives is good and honorable in the eyes of God. He has commanded that they be one flesh and that they multiply and replenish the earth (see Moses 2:28; 3:24). You are to love your wife as Christ loved the Church and gave himself for it (see Eph. 5:25-31).

Tenderness and respect—never selfishness—must be the guiding principles in the intimate relationship between husband and wife. Each partner must be considerate and sensitive to the other's needs and desires. Any domineering, indecent, or uncontrolled behavior in the intimate relationship between husband and wife is condemned by the Lord.

Any man who abuses or demeans his wife physically or spiritually is guilty of grievous sin and in need of sincere and serious repentance. Differences should be worked out in love and kindness and with a spirit of mutual reconciliation. A man should always speak to his wife lovingly and kindly, treating her with the utmost respect. Marriage is like a tender flower, brethren, and must be nourished constantly with expressions of love and affection.

You who hold the priesthood must not be abusive in your relationship with children. Seek always to employ the principles of priesthood government set forth in the revelations (see D&C 93:40; 121:34-36, 41-45).

President George Albert Smith wisely counseled: "We should not lose our tempers and abuse one another. . . . Nobody ever abused anybody else when he had the spirit of the Lord. It is always when we have some other spirit" (in Conference Report, Oct. 1950, p. 8).

No man who has been ordained to the priesthood of God can with impunity abuse his wife or child. Sexual abuse of children has long been a cause for excommunication from the Church.

We encourage you, brethren, to remember that priesthood is a righteous authority only. Earn the respect and confidence of your children through your loving relationship with them. A righteous father protects his children with his time and presence in their social, educational, and spiritual activities and responsibilities. Tender expressions of love and affection toward children are as much the responsibility of the father as the mother. Tell your children you love them.

You who hold the priesthood have the responsibility, unless disabled, to provide temporal support for your wife and children. No man can shift the burden of responsibility to another, not even to his wife. The Lord has commanded that women and children have claim on their husbands and fathers for their maintenance (see D&C 83; 1 Tim. 5:8). President Ezra Taft Benson has stated that when a husband encourages or insists that his wife work out of the home for their convenience, "not only will the family suffer in such instances, . . . but [his] own spiritual growth and progression will be hampered" (*Ensign*, Nov., 1987, p. 49).

We urge you to do all in your power to allow your wife to remain in the home, caring for the children while you provide for the family the best you can. We further emphasize that men who abandon their family and fail to meet their responsibility to care for those they have fathered may find their eligibility for a temple recommend and their standing in the Church in jeopardy. In cases of divorce or separation, men must demonstrate that they are meeting family support payments mandated by law and obligated by the principles of the Church in order to qualify for the blessings of the Lord.

A man who holds the priesthood leads his family in Church participation so they will know the gospel and be under the protection of the covenants and ordinances. If you are to enjoy the blessings of the Lord, you must set your own homes in order. Together with your wife, you determine the spiritual climate of your home. Your first obligation is to get your own spiritual life in order through regular scriptural study and daily prayer. Secure and honor your priesthood and temple covenants; encourage your family to do the same.

Take seriously your responsibility to teach the gospel to your family through regular family home evening, family prayer, devotional and scripture-reading time, and other teaching moments. Give special emphasis to preparation for missionary service and temple marriage. As patriarch in the home, exercise your priesthood through performing the appropriate ordinances for your family and by giving blessings to your wife and children. Next to your own salvation, brethren, there is nothing so important to you as the salvation of your wife and children.

Brethren, I have spoken plainly to you regarding your responsibility as holders of the holy priesthood. If there are areas in your life where improvement may be needed, I encourage you to make this a matter of prayerful consideration.

I testify that this is what the Lord would have the brethren of the priesthood receive at this time. May you be blessed in your efforts to be righteous husbands and fathers, I pray as I bear solemn witness of the truthfulness of that which has been spoken this evening and do so in the name of the Lord Jesus Christ, amen.

Counsel to Husbands

Spencer W. Kimball, Conference Report, October 1979, pp. 71-72

The sisters in this dispensation include many of the most noble daughters of our Heavenly Father. . . .

Much of this special Church work will be judged by the way in which we serve and lead, in a Christ-like manner, the women of the Church who are in our homes. I say serve and lead because the headship of the man in the home is to be like the headship of Christ in the Church. Christ led by love, example, and self-less service. . . .

You wonderful stake presidents and bishops and your counselors and all of your brethren—please be especially thoughtful of the sisters who are, through no fault of their own, not presently given the blessing of being sealed for all eternity to a worthy man, so they do not inadvertently feel left out as we rightfully focus on family life. Do not regard their presence in your midst as a burden but as a blessing.

Ever bear in mind our special responsibilities to the widows, those who are divorced, others who are husbandless, and, in some cases, our young sisters who are fatherless. We simply cannot fulfill our responsi-bilities as men of God if we neglect the women of God. . . .

It is because we prize our women so greatly that we do not wish to have them drawn away into worldly paths. Most of them are strong and good and true, and they will be the more so when they are treated with love and respect and when their thoughts and feelings are valued and understood.

Our sisters do not wish to be indulged or to be treated condescendingly; they desire to be respected and revered as our sisters and our equals.

We shall all be judged and held accountable for how we carry out our various church assign-ments, and our mortal stewardship will get no more searching scrutiny than with regard to the way we have served and loved our families and our sisters and brothers of the church.

Harold B. Lee, *Ensign,* February 1972, p. 51

I have said many times to young couples at the marriage altar: Never let the tender intimacies of your married life become beastly. Let your thoughts smell of the sunshine. Let your words be wholesome and your association together be inspiring and uplifting, if you would keep alive the spirit of romance throughout your marriage together.

Dr. Henry Link, "Love, Marriage, and Children," Harold B. Lee, *Ibid.*

I am convinced that having a child is the final and strongest pledge of a couple's love for each other. It is an eloquent testimony that their marriage is a complete one. It lifts their marriage from the level of selfish love and physical pleasure to that of devotion centered around a new life. It makes self-sacrifice rather than self-indulgence their guiding principle. It represents the husband's faith in his ability to provide the neces-sary security, and it demonstrates the wife's confidence in his ability to do so. The net result is a spiritual se-curity which, more than any other power, helps to create material security as well.

In Harold B. Lee, *Ibid*, p. 50

Napoleon is quoted as having asked Madame Campan: "What is wanting in order that the youth of France will be well educated?" "Good mothers," was her reply. The Emperor was forcibly struck with this answer. "Here," he said, "is a system in one word—**mother**."

Discourses of Brigham Young, pp. 306-07, in Harold B. Lee, *Ibid.*

I fear some husbands have interpreted erroneously the statement that the husband is to be the head of the house and that his wife is to obey the law of her husband. Brigham Young's instruction to husbands was this: "Let the husband and father learn to bend his will to the will of his God, and then instruct his wives and children in this lesson of self-government by his example as well as by his precept."

Harold B. Lee, *Ibid.*, 53

A prominent speaker at a local service club dinner was quoted as saying this: "The nation has taken the wrong approach to many problems. We deal with the delinquent after he is a delinquent; the drug addict after he is an addict; the criminal after he is a criminal. We forget that we should work with our youngsters before these problems arise. There is no substitute for the family. This is where the children are brought up, where their habits are created; where they receive strength to face the world. The person who is against the 'establishment' is taking his problems out on the community because he has no communication with his parents." This man who was a prominent Puerto Rican official, concluded by saying, "The day we by-pass the family as the basic unit, we are going to be lost. In the typical family there is limited time between the parent and the child. This time should be well spent in commonly enjoyed activities."

N. Eldon Tanner, *Woman*, p. 4

After I had discussed business matters with some men one day, the conversation took on a more personal, informal note when one man said, "I have the most wonderful wife in the world." Another said "That's what you think. I think I have the best." A third man said, "Isn't it a great blessing to have a wife you love, who loves you, one who is a good mother and homemaker, who has high ideals, who believes in God and wants to help her family accept and live the teachings of the gospel of Jesus Christ?"

What woman could want any greater glory or tribute than that which comes form an appreciative and loving husband? The applause and homage of the world fade into insignificance when compared with the approbation of God and expressions of love and appreciation that come from the hearts and lips of those who are nearest and dearest to her. Now the point is—husband—are you saying those kinds of things to your wife, or just to other men, or not at all!!

Ibid., p. 11

Fathers, too, must assume their proper role and responsibility. Children need both parents. Fathers should assume with mothers the duties attendant upon the young children, the discipline and training of the older ones, and be a listening ear for those who need to discuss their problems or want guidance and counseling. Through love, establish a good relationship and line of communication with your children. . . .

It is unchristianlike, unfair, and displeasing to God for any husband or father to assume the role of dictator and adopt the attitude that he is superior in any way to his wife.

G. Homer Durham, *Ibid.*, p. 36

Man, as well as woman, has obligations to learn the difficult art of fatherhood in homemaking. This is not a task just for the woman. However, in altogether too many cases the role of fatherhood is one that is exercised in absentia, with infrequent moments when the father's intelligence and knowledge are applied to the deep concerns of family life.

Teachings of Spencer W. Kimball, p. 316

We have heard of men who have said to their wives, "I hold the priesthood and you've got to do what I say." Such a man should be tried for his membership. Certainly he should not be honored in his priesthood. We rule in love and understanding.

Priesthood & Church Government, p. 90

Unrighteous dominion: The Priesthood always presides and must, for the sake of order. The women of a congregation or auxiliary—many of them—may be wiser, far greater in mental powers, even greater in natural power of leadership than the men who preside over them. That signifies nothing. The Priesthood is not bestowed on the basis of mental power but is given to good men and they exercise it by right divine gift, called upon by the leaders of the Church. Woman has her gift of equal magnitude, and that is bestowed on the simple and weak as well as upon those who are great and strong.

Joseph Fielding Smith (??)

There is nothing in the teachings of the gospel which declares that men are superior to women. The Lord has given unto men the power of priesthood and sent them forth to labor in his service.

Teachings of Spencer W. Kimball, p. 316

In the beginning when God created man and the woman, he said to the woman, "Thy desire shall be to thy husband, and he shall rule [but I like the word *preside*] over thee."

H. Burke Peterson on "Unrighteous Dominion" July 1989

Ask yourself these questions:

1. Do I criticize family members more than I compliment them?

2. Do I insist that family members obey me because I am the father or husband and hold the priesthood?

3. Do I seek happiness more at work or somewhere other than in my home?

4. Do my children seem reluctant to talk to me about some of their feelings and concerns?

5. Do I attempt to guarantee my place of authority by physical discipline or punishment?

6. Do I find myself setting and enforcing numerous rules to control family members?

7. Do family members appear to be fearful of me?

8. Do I feel threatened by the notion of sharing with other family members the power and responsibility for decision making in the family?

9. Is my wife highly dependent on me and unable to make decisions for herself?

10. Does my wife complain that she has insufficient funds to manage the household because I control all the money?

11. Do I insist on being the main source of inspiration for each individual family member rather than teaching each child to listen to the Spirit?

12. Do I often feel angry and critical toward family members?

If the answer to any of these questions is yes, then we need to evaluate our relationship with our family members. We should then examine our relationship with the Lord. If a man feels a reduction or withdrawal of the Holy Ghost (manifested by contention, disunity, or rebellion), he may know that he is exercising unrighteous dominion.

Millennial Star 25:86 (July 18, 1844); Brigham Young in *LDS Prophets and D&C*, 4:531

Let the Saints cultivate a meek and quiet spirit, and all things shall in the end work together for your good.

Marriage and the Great Plan of Happiness

Elder Joe J. Christensen

April 1995 General Conference, May 1995, *Ensign*, pp. 64-66

We welcome and sustain our new First Presidency, Elder Eyring, and the newly called Seventies.

Barbara and I have been blessed with six children. Some years ago, when we had taken all of them to visit with their grandparents, my father said, "Joe, I think you and Barbara have started something you can't stop."

At this Easter season, we declare to all the world that Jesus is the Christ and that through his holy priesthood and its sealing power, marriages and families ideally need never stop, need never come to an end.

Today, I would like to speak to all of you about our marriages. Here are eight practical suggestions that, hopefully, may be of value in strengthening our marriages, now and in the future.

1. Remember the central importance of your marriage. Listen to these words from Elder Bruce R. McConkie on the importance of marriage in our Father in Heaven's "Great Plan of Happiness."

> From the moment of birth into mortality to the time we are married in the temple, everything we have in the whole gospel system is to prepare and qualify us to enter that holy order of matrimony which makes us husband and wife in this life and in the world to come. . . .
>
> There is nothing in this world as important as the creation and perfection of family units (McConkie, *Improvement Era*, June 1970, pp. 43-44).

2. Pray for the success of your marriage. Years ago, when it was common for a General Authority during a mission tour to interview all the missionaries, Elder Spencer W. Kimball, then a member of the Quorum of the Twelve, was visiting with an elder who was just about to finish his mission.

"When you get released, Elder, what are your plans?"

"Oh, I plan to go back to college," and then with a smile added, "then I hope to fall in love and get married."

Elder Kimball shared this wise counsel: "Well, don't just pray to marry the one you love. Instead, pray to love the one you marry."

We should pray to become more kind, courteous, humble, patient, forgiving, and especially, less selfish.

In order to recognize our personal problems or weaknesses which hinder us from being better marriage partners, we should come to the Lord in prayer and reap the benefits of this powerful Book of Mormon promise:

> If men come unto me I will show unto them their weakness. . . .
>
> For if they humble themselves before me, and have faith in me, then will I make weak things become strong unto them (Ether 12:27).

And so the need to pray. Many church leaders and marriage counselors indicate that they have not seen one marriage in serious trouble where the couple was still praying together daily. When problems arise and marriages are threatened, praying together as a couple may be the most important remedy.

3. Listen. Make the time to listen to your spouse; even schedule it regularly. Visit with each other and assess how you are doing as a marriage partner.

Brother Brent Barlow posed a question to a group of priesthood brethren: "How many of you would like to receive a revelation?" Every hand went up. He then suggested that they all go home and ask their wives how they could be better husbands. He added, ". . . I followed my own advice, and had a very informative discussion with (my wife) Susan for more than an hour that afternoon!" (ENSIGN, September 1992, p. 17). A conversation like that could be a revelation for any of us.

Have any of you brethren ever had your wife say something like I heard recently: "Joe, are you listening?" She wasn't the only one who wondered if I was listening. Some time ago, I was taking a nap and our little granddaughter Allison came and lifted up one of my eyelids and said, "Grandpa, are you in there?" We should be "in there" and responsive to our mate.

4. Avoid "ceaseless pinpricking." Don't be too critical of each other's faults. Recognize that none of us is perfect. We all have a long way to go to become as Christlike as our leaders have urged us to become.

"Ceaseless pinpricking" (as President Kimball called it) can deflate almost any marriage. Generally, each of us is painfully aware of our weaknesses, and we don't need frequent reminders. Few people have ever changed for the better as a result of constant criticism or nagging. If we are not careful, some of what we offer as constructive criticism is actually destructive.

At times it is better to leave some things unsaid. As a newlywed, Sister Lola Walters read in a magazine that in order to strengthen a marriage a couple should have regular, candid sharing sessions in which they would list any mannerisms they found to be annoying. She wrote:

> . . . We were to name five things we found annoying, and I started off. . . . I told him that I didn't like the way he ate grapefruit. He peeled it and ate it like an orange! Nobody else I knew ate grapefruit like that. Could a girl be expected to spend a lifetime, and even eternity, watching her husband eat grapefruit like an orange?. . .
>
> After I finished [with my five], it was his turn to tell the things he disliked about me. . . . [He] said, "Well, to tell the truth, I can't think of anything I don't like about you, Honey."
>
> Gasp.
>
> I quickly turned my back, because I didn't know how to explain the tears that had filled my eyes and were running down my face.
>
> Sister Walters concluded: "Whenever I hear of married couples being incompatible, I always wonder if they are suffering from what I now call the Grapefruit Syndrome" (*Ensign*, April 1993, p. 13).

Yes, at times, it is better to leave some things unsaid.

5. Keep your courtship alive. Make time to do things together—just the two of you. As important as it is to be with the children as a family, you need regular weekly time together. Scheduling it will let your children know that you feel that your marriage is so important that you need to nurture it. That takes commitment, planning, and scheduling.

It doesn't need to be costly. The time together is the most important element.

Once when my father-in-law was leaving the house after lunch to return to the field to work, my mother-in-law said, "Albert, you get right back in here and tell me you love me." He grinned and jokingly said, "Elsie, when we were married, I told you I loved you, and if that ever changes, I'll let you know."

It's hard to overuse the expression, "I love you." Use it daily.

6. Be quick to say, "I'm sorry." As hard as it is to form the words, be swift to say, "I apologize, and please forgive me," even though you are not the one who is totally at fault. True love is developed by those who are willing to readily admit personal mistakes and offenses.

When differences do arise, being able to discuss and resolve them is important, but there are instances when it is best to take a "timeout," biting your tongue and counting to ten or even a hundred is very important. And occasionally, even letting the sun go down on your wrath can help bring you back to the problem in the morning more rested, calm, and with a better chance for resolution.

Occasionally, we hear something like, "Why, we have been married for fifty years, and we have never had a difference of opinion." If that is literally the case, then one of the partners is overly dominated by the other or, as someone said, "is a stranger to the truth." Any intelligent couple will have differences of opinion. Our challenge is to be sure that we know how to resolve them. That is part of the process of making a good marriage better.

7. Learn to live within your means. Some of the most difficult challenges in marriage arise in the area of finances. "The American Bar Association. . . indicated that 89 percent of all divorces could be traced to quarrels and accusations over money" (*Ensign*, July 1975, p. 72). Be willing to postpone or forgo some purchases in order to stay within your budget. Pay your tithing first and avoid debt insofar as possible. Remember that spending $50 a month less than you receive equals happiness and spending $50 more equals misery. The time may have come to get out the scissors, your credit cards, and perform what Elder Holland called some "plastic surgery" (*Ensign*, June 1986, p. 30).

8. Be a true partner in home and family responsibilities. Don't be like the husband who sits around home expecting to be waited on, feeling that earning the living is his chore and that his wife alone is responsible for the house and taking care of the children. The task of caring for home and family is more than one person's responsibility.

Remember that you are in this partnership together. Barbara and I have discovered that we can make our bed every morning in less than a minute and it's done for the day. She says that she lets me do it to help me feel good about myself all day, and I guess there may be something to that.

Find time to study the scriptures together, and follow this sound counsel from President Kimball:

> . . . When a husband and wife go together frequently to the holy temple, kneel in prayer together in their home with their family, go hand in hand to their religious meetings, keep their lives wholly chaste, mentally and physically, . . . and both are working together for the upbuilding of the kingdom of God, then happiness is at its pinnacle (*Marriage and Divorce*, Salt Lake City: Deseret Book Co., 1976, p. 24).

In summary:

- Remember the central importance of your marriage.
- Pray for its success.
- Listen.
- Avoid "ceaseless pinpricking."
- Keep your courtship alive.
- Be quick to say, "I'm sorry."
- Learn to live within your means.
- Be a true partner in home and family responsibilities.

I testify that Jesus is the Christ. The tomb was empty on that third day, and ". . . as in Adam all die, even so in Christ shall all be made alive" (1 Cor. 15:22). Thus with gratitude for the sealing power within the restored gospel of Jesus Christ, we can confidently say with the poet, "I shall but love thee better after death" (Elizabeth Barrett Browning, "How Do I Love Thee?").

In the name of Jesus Christ, amen.

Of Souls, Symbols, and Sacraments

President Jeffrey R. Holland

BYU Devotional, 12 January 1988

$\mathbf{T}$**his responsibility to speak** to you never gets any easier for me. I think it gets more difficult as the years go by I grow a little older, the world and its litany of problems get a little more complex, and your hopes and dreams become evermore important to me the longer I am at BYU. Indeed, your growth and happiness and development in the life you are now living and in the life you will be living in the days and decades ahead are the central and most compelling motivation in my daily professional life. I care very much about you now and forever. Everything I know to do at BYU is being done with an eye toward who and what you are, and who and what you can become. The future of this world's history will be quite fully in your hands very soon—at least your portion of it will be—and an education at an institution sponsored and guided by The Church of Jesus Christ of Latter-day Saints is the greatest academic advantage I can imagine in preparation for such a serious and significant responsibility.

But that future, at least any qualitative aspect of it, must be vigorously fought for. It won't "just happen" to your advantage. Someone said once that the future is waiting to be seized, and if we do not grasp it firmly, then other hands, more determined and bloody than our own, will wrench it from us and follow a different course.

It is with an eye to that future—your future—and an awareness of this immense sense of responsibility I feel for you, that I approach this annual midyear devotional message. I always need the help and sustaining Spirit of the Lord to succeed at such times, but I especially feel the need for that spiritual help today.

Human Intimacy

My topic is that of human intimacy, a topic as sacred as any I know and more sacred than anything I have ever addressed from this podium. If I am not careful and you are not supportive, this subject can slide quickly from the sacred into the merely sensational, and I would be devastated if that happened. It would be better not to address the topic at all than to damage it with casualness or carelessness. Indeed, it is against such casualness and carelessness that I wish to speak. So I ask for your faith and your prayers and your respect.

You may feel this is a topic you hear addressed too frequently at this time in your life, but given the world in which we live, you may not be hearing it enough. All of the prophets, past and present, have spoken on it, and President Benson himself addressed this very subject in his annual message to this student body last fall.

I am thrilled that most of you are doing wonderfully well in the matter of personal purity. There isn't as worthy and faithful a group of university students anywhere else on the face of the earth. You are an inspiration to me. I acknowledge your devotion to the gospel and applaud it. Like Jacob of old, I would prefer for the sake of the innocent not to need to discuss such topics. But a few of you are not doing so well, and much of the world around us is not doing well at all.

The national press recently noted,

In America 3,000 adolescents become pregnant each day. A million a year. Four out of five are unmarried. More than half get abortions. "Babies having babies." [Babies] killing [babies] ("What's Gone Wrong with Teen Sex," *People*, 13 April 1987, p. 111).

That same national poll indicated nearly 60 percent of high school students in "mainstream" America had lost their virginity, and 80 percent of college students had. The *Wall Street Journal* (hardly in a class with the *National Enquirer*) recently wrote,

AIDS [appears to be reaching] plague[like] proportions. Even now it is claiming innocent victims: newborn babies and recipients of blood transfusions. It is only a matter of time before it becomes widespread among heterosexuals. . . .

AIDS should remind us that ours is a hostile world. . . . The more we pass ourselves around, the larger the likelihood of our picking something up. . . .

Whether on clinical or moral grounds, it seems clear that promiscuity has its price (*Wall Street Journal*, 21 May 1987, p. 28).

Of course, more widespread in our society than the indulgence of personal sexual activity are the printed and photographed descriptions of those who do. Of that lustful environment a contemporary observer says,

We live in an age in which voyeurism is no longer the side line of the solitary deviate, but rather a national pastime, fully institutionalized and [circularized] in the mass media (William F. May, quoted by Henry Fairlie, *The Seven Deadly Sins Today*, Notre Dame: University of Notre Dame Press, 1978, p. 178).

In fact, the rise of civilization seems, ironically enough, to have made actual or fantasized promiscuity a greater, not a lesser, problem. Edward Gibbon, the distinguished British historian of the eighteenth century who wrote one of the most intimidating works of history in our language (*The Decline and Fall of the Roman Empire*), said simply,

Although the progress of civilization has undoubtedly contributed to assuage the fiercer passions of human nature, it seems to have been less favourable to the virtue of chastity. . . . The refinements of life [seem to] corrupt, [even as] they polish the [relationship] of the sexes (Edward Gibbon, *The Decline and Fall of the Roman Empire*, vol. 40 of Great Books of the Western World, 1952, p. 92).

I do not wish us to spend this hour documenting social problems nor wringing our hands over the dangers that such outside influences may hold for us. As serious as such contemporary realities are, I wish to discuss this topic in quite a different way, discuss it specifically for Latter-day Saints—primarily young, unmarried Latter-day Saints, even those attending Brigham Young University. So I conspicuously set aside the horrors of AIDS and national statistics on illegitimate pregnancies and speak rather to a gospel-based view of personal purity.

Indeed, I wish to do something even a bit more difficult than listing the do's and don'ts of personal purity. I wish to speak, to the best of my ability, on why we should be clean, on why moral discipline is such a significant matter in God's eyes. I know that may sound presumptuous, but a philosopher once said, tell me sufficiently why a thing should be done, and I will move heaven and earth to do it. Hoping you will feel the same way as he and fully recognizing my limitations, I wish to try to give at least a partial answer to "Why be morally clean?" I will need first to pose briefly what I see as the doctrinal seriousness of the matter before then offering just three reasons for such seriousness.

The Significance and Sanctity

May I begin with half of a nine-line poem by Robert Frost. (The other half is worth a sermon also, but it will have to wait for another day.) Here are the first four lines of Frost's "Fire and Ice."

> Some say the world will end in fire,
> Some say in ice.
> From what I've tasted of desire
> I hold with those who favor fire.

A second, less poetic but more specific opinion is offered by the writer of Proverbs:

> Can a man take fire in his bosom, and his clothes not be burned?
> Can one go upon hot coals, and his feet not be burned? . . .
> But whoso committeth adultery with a woman lacketh understanding: he that doeth it destroyeth his own soul.
> A wound and dishonour shall he get; and his reproach shall not be wiped away (Proverbs 6:27-33).

In getting at the doctrinal seriousness, why is this matter of sexual relationships so severe that fire is almost always the metaphor, with passion pictured vividly in flames? What is there in the potentially hurtful heat of this that leaves one's soul—or perhaps the whole world, according to Frost—destroyed, if that flame is left unchecked and those passions unrestrained? What is there in all of this that prompts Alma to warn his son Corianton that sexual transgression is "an abomination in the sight of the Lord; yea, most abominable above all sins save it be the shedding of innocent blood or denying the Holy Ghost" (Alma 39:5)?

Setting aside sins against the Holy Ghost for a moment as a special category unto themselves, it is LDS doctrine that sexual transgression is second only to murder in the Lord's list of life's most serious sins. By assigning such rank to a physical appetite so conspicuously evident in all of us, what is God trying to tell us about its place in his plan for all men and women in mortality? I submit to you he is doing precisely that—commenting about the very plan of life itself. Clearly God's greatest concerns regarding mortality are how one gets into this world and how one gets out of it. These two most important issues in our very personal and carefully supervised progress are the two issues that he as our Creator and Father and Guide wishes most to reserve to himself. These are the two matters that he has repeatedly told us he wants us never to take illegally, illicitly, unfaithfully, without sanction.

As for the taking of life, we are generally quite responsible. Most people, it seems to me, readily sense the sanctity of life and as a rule do not run up to friends, put a loaded revolver to their heads, and cavalierly pull the trigger. Furthermore, when there is a click of the hammer rather than an explosion of lead, and a possible tragedy seems to have been averted, no one in such a circumstance would be so stupid as to sigh, "Oh, good. I didn't go all the way."

No, "all the way" or not, the insanity of such action with fatal powder and steel is obvious on the face of it. Such a person running about this campus with an arsenal of loaded handguns or military weaponry aimed at fellow students would be apprehended, prosecuted, and institutionalized if in fact such a lunatic would not himself have been killed in all the pandemonium. After such a fictitious moment of horror on this campus (and you are too young to remember my college years when the sniper wasn't fictitious, killing twelve of his fellow students at the University of Texas), we would undoubtedly sit in our dorms or classrooms with terror on our minds for many months to come, wondering how such a thing could possibly happen—especially here at BYU.

No, fortunately, in the case of how life is taken, I think we seem to be quite responsible. The seriousness of that does not often have to be spelled out, and not many sermons need to be devoted to it.

But in the significance and sanctity of giving life, some of us are not so responsible, and in the larger world swirling around us we find near-criminal irresponsibility. What would in the case of taking life bring absolute horror and demand grim justice, in the case of giving life brings dirty jokes and four-letter lyrics and crass carnality on the silver screen, home-owned or downtown.

Is such moral turpitude so wrong? That question has always been asked, usually by the guilty. "Such is the way of an adulterous woman; she eateth, and wipeth her mouth, and saith, I have done no wickedness" (Proverbs 30:20). No murder here. Well, maybe not. But sexual transgression? "He that doeth it destroyeth his own soul." Sounds near fatal to me.

So much for the doctrinal seriousness. Now, with a desire to prevent such painful moments, to avoid what Alma called the "inexpressible horror" of standing in the presence of God unworthily, and to permit the intimacy it is your right and privilege and delight to enjoy in marriage to be untainted by such crushing remorse and guilt—I wish to give those three reasons I mentioned earlier as to why I believe this is an issue of such magnitude and consequence.

The Doctrine of the Soul

First, we simply must understand the revealed, restored Latter-day Saint doctrine of the soul, and the high and inextricable part the body plays in that doctrine. One of the "plain and precious" truths restored to this dispensation is that "the spirit and the body are the soul of man" (D&C 88:15) and that when the spirit and body are separated, men and women "cannot receive a fulness of joy" (D&C 93:34). Certainly that suggests something of the reason why obtaining a body is so fundamentally important to the plan of salvation in the first place, why sin of any kind is such a serious matter (namely because its automatic consequence is death, the separation of the spirit from the body and the separation of the spirit and the body from God), and why the resurrection of the body is so central to the great abiding and eternal triumph of Christ's atonement. We do not have to be a herd of demonically possessed swine charging down the Gadarene slopes toward the sea to understand that a body is the great prize of mortal life, and that even a pig's will do for those frenzied spirits that rebelled, and to this day remain dispossessed, in their first, unembodied estate.

May I quote a 1913 sermon by Elder James E. Talmage on this doctrinal point:

> We have been taught . . . to look upon these bodies of ours as gifts from God. We Latter-day Saints do not regard the body as something to be condemned, something to be abhorred. . . . We regard [the body] as the sign of our royal birthright. . . . We recognize . . . that those who kept not their first estate . . . were denied that inestimable blessing. . . . We believe that these bodies . . . may be made, in very truth, the temple of the Holy Ghost. . . .
>
> It is peculiar to the theology of the Latter-day Saints that we regard the body as an essential part of the soul. Read your dictionaries, the lexicons, and encyclopedias, and you will find that nowhere [in Christianity], outside of the Church of Jesus Christ, is the solemn and eternal truth taught that the soul of man is the body and the spirit combined (Conference Report, October 1913, p. 117).

So partly in answer to why such seriousness, we answer that one toying with the God-given-and satanically coveted-body of another, toys with the very soul of that individual, toys with the central purpose and product of life, "the very key" to life, as Elder Boyd K. Packer once called it. In trivializing the soul of another (please include the word body there), we trivialize the Atonement that saved that soul and guaranteed its continued existence. And when one toys with the Son of Righteousness, the Day Star himself, one toys with white heat and a flame hotter and holier than the noonday sun. You cannot do so and not be burned. You cannot with impunity "crucify Christ afresh" (see Hebrews 6:6). Exploitation of the body (please include the word soul there) is, in the last analysis, an exploitation of him who is the Light and the Life of the world. Perhaps here Paul's warning to the Corinthians takes on newer, higher meaning:

> Now the body is not for fornication, but for the Lord; and the Lord for the body. . . .
> Know ye not that your bodies are the members of Christ? shall I then take the

members of Christ, and make them the members of an harlot? God forbid. . . .

Flee fornication. . . . He that committeth fornication sinneth against his own body. . .

. . . Know ye not that your body is the temple of the Holy Ghost which is in you, which ye have of God, and ye are not your own?

For ye are bought with a price: therefore glorify God in your body, and in your spirit, which are God's (1 Corinthians 6:13-20).

Our soul is what's at stake here—our spirit and our body. Paul understood that doctrine of the soul every bit as well as James E. Talmage did, because it is gospel truth. The purchase price for our fullness of joy—body and spirit eternally united—is the pure and innocent blood of the Savior of this world. We cannot then say in ignorance or defiance, "Well, it's my life," or worse yet, "It's my body." It is not. "Ye are not your own," Paul said. "Ye are bought with a price." So in answer to the question, "Why does God care so much about sexual transgression?" it is partly because of the precious gift offered by and through his Only Begotten Son to redeem the souls—bodies and spirits—we too often share and abuse in cheap and tawdry ways. Christ restored the very seeds of eternal lives (see D&C 132:19, 24), and we desecrate them at our peril. The first key reason for personal purity? Our very souls are involved and at stake.

A Symbol of Total Union

Second, may I suggest that human intimacy, that sacred, physical union ordained of God for a married couple, deals with a symbol that demands special sanctity. Such an act of love between a man and a woman is—certainly was ordained to be—a symbol of total union: union of their hearts, their hopes, their lives, their love, their family, their future, their everything. It is a symbol that we try to suggest in the temple with a word like seal. The Prophet Joseph Smith once said we perhaps ought to render such a sacred bond as "welding"—that those united in matrimony and eternal families are "welded" together, inseparable if you will, to withstand the temptations of the adversary and the afflictions of mortality (See D&C 128:18).

But such a total, virtually unbreakable union, such an unyielding commitment between a man and a woman, can only come with the proximity and permanence afforded in a marriage covenant, with the union of all that they possess—their very hearts and minds, all their days and all their dreams. They work together, they cry together, they enjoy Brahms and Beethoven and breakfast together, they sacrifice and save and live together for all the abundance that such a totally intimate life provides such a couple. And the external symbol of that union, the physical manifestation of what is a far deeper spiritual and metaphysical bonding, is the physical blending that is part of—indeed, a most beautiful and gratifying expression of—that larger, more complete union of eternal purpose and promise.

As delicate as it is to mention in such a setting, I nevertheless trust your maturity to understand that physiologically we are created as men and women to fit together in such a union. In this ultimate physical expression of one man and one woman they are as nearly and as literally "one" as two separate physical bodies can ever be. It is in that act of ultimate physical intimacy we most nearly fulfill the commandment of the Lord given to Adam and Eve, living symbols for all married couples, when he invited them to cleave unto one another only, and thus become "one flesh" (Genesis 2:24).

Obviously, such a commandment to these two, the first husband and wife of the human family, has unlimited implications—social, cultural, and religious as well as physical—but that is exactly my point. As all couples come to that moment of bonding in mortality, it is to be just such a complete union. That commandment cannot be fulfilled, and that symbolism of "one flesh" cannot be preserved, if we hastily and guiltily and surreptitiously share intimacy in a darkened corner of a darkened hour, then just as hastily and guiltily and surreptitiously retreat to our separate worlds—not to eat or live or cry or laugh together, not to do the laundry and the dishes and the homework, not to manage a budget and pay the bills and tend the children and plan together for the future. No, we cannot do that until we are truly one—united, bound, linked, tied, welded, sealed, married.

Can you see then the moral schizophrenia that comes from pretending we are one, sharing the physical symbols and physical intimacy of our union, but then fleeing, retreating, severing all such other aspects—and symbols—of what was meant to be a total obligation, only to unite again furtively some other night or, worse yet, furtively unite (and you can tell how cynically I use that word) with some other partner who is no more bound to us, no more one with us than the last was or than the one that will come next week or next month or next year or anytime before the binding commitments of marriage?

You must wait—you must wait until you can give everything, and you cannot give everything until you are at least legally and, for Latter-day Saint purposes, eternally pronounced as one. To give illicitly that which is not yours to give (remember—"you are not your own") and to give only part of that which cannot be followed with the gift of your whole heart and your whole life and your whole self is its own form of emotional Russian roulette. If you persist in sharing part without the whole, in pursuing satisfaction devoid of symbolism, in giving parts and pieces and inflamed fragments only, you run the terrible risk of such spiritual, psychic damage that you may undermine both your physical intimacy and your wholehearted devotion to a truer, later love. You may come to that moment of real love, of total union, only to discover to your horror that what you should have saved has been spent, and—mark my word—only God's grace can recover that piecemeal dissipation of your virtue.

A good Latter-day Saint friend, Dr. Victor L. Brown, Jr., has written of this issue:

> Fragmentation enables its users to counterfeit intimacy. . . .
>
> If we relate to each other in fragments, at best we miss full relationships. At worst, we manipulate and exploit others for our gratification. Sexual fragmentation can be particularly harmful because it gives powerful physiological rewards which, though illusory, can temporarily persuade us to overlook the serious deficits in the overall relationship. Two people may marry for physical gratification and then discover that the illusion of union collapses under the weight of intellectual, social, and spiritual incompatibilities. . . .
>
> Sexual fragmentation is particularly harmful because it is particularly deceptive. The intense human intimacy that should be enjoyed in and symbolized by sexual union is counterfeited by sensual episodes which suggest—but cannot deliver—acceptance, understanding, and love. Such encounters mistake the end for the means as lonely, desperate people seek a common denominator which will permit the easiest, quickest gratification (Victor L. Brown, Jr., *Human Intimacy: Illusion and Reality*, Salt Lake City, Utah: Parliament Publishers, 1981, pp. 5-6).

Listen to a far more biting observation by a non-Latter-day Saint regarding such acts devoid of both the soul and symbolism we have been discussing. He writes:

> Our sexuality has been animalized, stripped of the intricacy of feeling with which human beings have endowed it, leaving us to contemplate only the act, and to fear our impotence in it. It is this animalization from which the sexual manuals cannot escape, even when they try to do so, because they are reflections of it. They might [as well] be textbooks for veterinarians (Fairlie, *Seven Deadly Sins*, p. 182).

In this matter of counterfeit intimacy and deceptive gratification, I express particular caution to the men who hear this message. I have heard all my life that it is the young woman who has to assume the responsibility for controlling the limits of intimacy in courtship because a young man cannot. What an unacceptable response to such a serious issue! What kind of man is he, what priesthood or power or strength or self-control does this man have that lets him develop in society, grow to the age of mature accountability, perhaps even pursue a university education and prepare to affect the future of colleagues and kingdoms and the course of the world, but yet does not have the mental capacity or the moral will to say, "I will not do that thing"? No, this sorry drugstore psychology would have us say, "He just can't help himself. His glands have complete control over his life—his mind, his will, his entire future."

To say that a young woman in such a relationship has to bear her responsibility and that of the young man's too is the least fair assertion I can imagine. In most instances if there is sexual transgression, I lay the burden squarely on the shoulders of the young man—for our purposes probably a priesthood bearer—and that's where I believe God intended responsibility to be. In saying that I do not excuse young women who exercise no restraint and have not the character or conviction to demand intimacy only in its rightful role. I have had enough experience in Church callings to know that women as well as men can be predatory. But I refuse to buy some young man's feigned innocence who wants to sin and call it psychology.

Indeed, most tragically, it is the young woman who is most often the victim, it is the young woman who most often suffers the greater pain, it is the young woman who most often feels used and abused and terribly unclean. And for that imposed uncleanliness a man will pay, as surely as the sun sets and rivers run to the sea.

Note the prophet Jacob's straightforward language on this account in the Book of Mormon. After a bold confrontation on the subject of sexual transgression among the Nephites, he quotes Jehovah:

> For behold, I, the Lord, have seen the sorrow, and heard the mourning of the daughters of my people in the land. . . .
> And I will not suffer, saith the Lord of Hosts, that the cries of the fair daughters of this people . . . shall come up unto me against the men of my people, saith the Lord of Hosts. For they shall not lead away captive the daughters of my people because of their tenderness, save I shall visit them with a sore curse, even unto destruction (Jacob 2:31-33).

Don't be deceived and don't be destroyed. Unless such fire is controlled, your clothes and your future will be burned. And your world, short of painful and perfect repentance, will go up in flames. I give that to you on good word—I give it to you on God's word.

A Holy Sacrament

That leads me to my last reason, a third effort to say why. After soul and symbol, the word is sacrament, a term closely related to the other two. Sexual intimacy is not only a symbolic union between a man and a woman—the uniting of their very souls—but it is also symbolic of a union between mortals and deity, between otherwise ordinary and fallible humans uniting for a rare and special moment with God himself and all the powers by which he gives life in this wide universe of ours.

In this latter sense, human intimacy is a sacrament, a very special kind of symbol. For our purpose here today, a sacrament could be any one of a number of gestures or acts or ordinances that unite us with God and his limitless powers. We are imperfect and mortal; he is perfect and immortal. But from time to time—indeed, as often as is possible and appropriate—we find ways and go to places and create circumstances where we can unite symbolically with him, and in so doing gain access to his power. Those special moments of union with God are sacramental moments—such as kneeling at a marriage altar, or blessing a newborn baby, or partaking of the emblems of the Lord's supper. This latter ordinance is the one we in the Church have come to associate most traditionally with the word sacrament, though it is technically only one of many such moments when we formally take the hand of God and feel his divine power.

These are moments when we quite literally unite our will with God's will, our spirit with his spirit, where communion through the veil becomes very real. At such moments we not only acknowledge his divinity, but we quite literally take something of that divinity to ourselves. Such are the holy sacraments.

Now, once again, I know of no one who would, for example, rush into the middle of a sacramental service, grab the linen from the tables, throw the bread the full length of the room, tip the water trays onto the floor, and laughingly retreat from the building to await an opportunity to do the same thing at another worship service the next Sunday. No one within the sound of my voice would do that during one of the truly sacred moments of our religious worship. Nor would anyone here violate any of the other sacramental moments in our lives, those times when we consciously claim God's power and by invitation stand with him in privilege and principality.

But I wish to stress with you this morning, as my third of three reasons to be clean, that sexual union is also, in its own profound way, a very real sacrament of the highest order, a union not only of a man and a woman but very much the union of that man and woman with God. Indeed, if our definition of sacrament is that act of claiming and sharing and exercising God's own inestimable power, then I know of virtually no other divine privilege so routinely given to us all—women or men, ordained or unordained, Latter-day Saint or non-Latter-day Saint—than the miraculous and majestic power of transmitting life, the unspeakable, unfathomable, unbroken power of procreation. There are those special moments in your lives when the other, more formal ordinances of the gospel—the sacraments, if you will—allow you to feel the grace and grandeur of God's power. Many are one-time experiences (such as our own confirmation or our own marriage), and some are repeatable (such as administering to the sick or doing ordinance work for others in the temple). But I know of nothing so earth-shatteringly powerful and yet so universally and unstintingly given to us as the God-given power available in every one of us from our early teen years on to create a human body, that wonder of all wonders, a generically and spiritually unique being never seen before in the history of the world and never to be duplicated again in all the ages of eternity—a child, your child—with eyes and ears and fingers and toes and a future of unspeakable grandeur.

Imagine that, if you will. Veritable teenagers—and all of us for many decades thereafter—carrying daily, hourly, minute-to-minute, virtually every waking and sleeping moment of our lives, the power and the chemistry and the eternally transmitted seeds of life to grant someone else her second estate, someone else his next level of development in the divine plan of salvation. I submit to you that no power, priesthood or otherwise, is given by God so universally to so many with virtually no control over its use except self-control. And I submit to you that you will never be more like God at any other time in this life than when you are expressing that particular power. Of all the titles he has chosen for himself, Father is the one he declares, and Creation is his watchword—especially human creation, creation in his image. His glory isn't a mountain, as stunning as mountains are. It isn't in sea or sky or snow or sunrise, as beautiful as they all are. It isn't in art or technology, be that a concerto or computer. No, his glory—and his grief—is in his children. You and I, we are his prized possessions, and we are the earthly evidence, however inadequate, of what he truly is. Human life—that is the greatest of God's powers, the most mysterious and magnificent chemistry of it all—and you and I have been given it, but under the most serious and sacred of restrictions. You and I who can make neither mountain nor moonlight, not one raindrop nor a single rose—yet we have this greater gift in an absolutely unlimited way. And the only control placed on us is self-control—self-control born of respect for the divine sacramental power it is.

Surely God's trust in us to respect this future-forming gift is awesomely staggering. We who may not be able to repair a bicycle nor assemble an average jigsaw puzzle—yet with all our weaknesses and imperfections, we carry this procreative power that makes us very much like God in at least one grand and majestic way.

A Serious Matter

Souls. Symbols. Sacraments. Does any of this help you understand why human intimacy is such a serious matter? Why it is so right and rewarding and stunningly beautiful when it is within marriage and approved of God (not just "good" but "very good," he declared to Adam and Eve), and so blasphemously wrong—like unto murder—when it is outside such a covenant? It is my understanding that we park and pet and sleep over and sleep with at the peril of our very lives. Our penalty may not come on the precise day of our transgression, but it comes surely and certainly enough, and were it not for a merciful God and the treasured privilege of personal repentance, far too many would even now be feeling that hellish pain, which (like the passion we have been discussing) is also always described in the metaphor of fire. Someday, somewhere, sometime the morally unclean will, until they repent, pray like the rich man, wishing Lazarus to "dip . . . his finger in water, and cool my tongue; for I am tormented in this flame" (Luke 16:24).

Some say the world will end in fire,
Some say in ice.
From what I've tasted of desire
I hold with those who favor fire.

In closing, consider this from two students of civilization's long, instructive Story:

> No one man [or woman], however brilliant or well-informed, can come in one lifetime to such fullness of understanding as to safely judge and dismiss the customs or institutions of his society, for these are the wisdom of generations after centuries of experiment in the laboratory of history. A youth boiling with hormones will wonder why he should not give full freedom to his sexual desires; and if he is unchecked by custom, morals, or laws, he may ruin his life [or hers] before he matures sufficiently to understand that sex is a river of fire that must be banked and cooled by a hundred restraints if it is not to consume in chaos both the individual and the group (Will and Ariel Durant, *The Lessons of History*, New York: Simon and Schuster, 1968, pp. 35-36).

Or, in the more ecclesiastical words of James E. Talmage:

> It has been declared in the solemn word of revelation, that the spirit and the body constitute the soul of man; and, therefore, we should look upon this body as something that shall endure in the resurrected state, beyond the grave, something to be kept pure and holy. Be not afraid of soiling its hands; be not afraid of scars that may come to it if won in earnest effort, or [won] in honest fight, but beware of scars that disfigure, that have come to you in places where you ought not have gone, that have befallen you in unworthy undertakings [pursued where you ought not have been]; beware of the wounds of battles in which you have been fighting on the wrong side (Talmage, Conference Report, October 1913, p. 117).

I love you for wanting to be on the right side of the gospel of Jesus Christ. I express my pride in and appreciation for your faithfulness. As I said earlier, you are an absolute inspiration to me. I consider it the greatest of all professional privileges to be associated with you at this university at a time in your lives when you are finalizing what you believe and forging what your future will be.

If some few of you are feeling the "scars . . . that have come to you in places where you ought not have gone," I wish to extend to you the special peace and promise available through the atoning sacrifice of the Lord Jesus Christ. I testify of his love and of the restored gospel principles and ordinances which make that love available to us with all their cleansing and healing power. I testify of the power of these principles and ordinances, including complete and redeeming repentance, which are only fully realized in this the true and living church of the true and living God. That we may "come unto Christ" for the fullness of soul and symbol and sacrament he offers us, I pray in the name of Jesus Christ. Amen.

The Gospel and Romantic Love

Bruce C. Hafen

BYU Devotional, September 28, 1982

I **once heard President Holland** tell about a conversation he overheard between two freshmen women talking about their favorite subject. One of them said, "Do you believe in college marriage?" The other replied, "Well, yeah, if the colleges really love each other." I would like to believe that there are no two colleges anywhere who "love each other" more than BYU and Ricks. I am in love with both places and consider both as my home. I must admit I think it is a blessing to the BYU campus to have several thousand former Ricks students here. The blessings also flow the other way, as we at Ricks are continually assisted in many ways by our BYU friends. When you catch cold in Provo, we sneeze in Rexburg. When you itch, we scratch. Indeed, when your able academic vice-president, Jae Ballif, was given the title of "Provost" at the BYU campus, we immediately began to consider if our academic vice president should be called our "Rexburgst."

I'd like to say just a word about President Holland. For all his abundant gifts of personality and intellect, I think the core of Jeff Holland's soul is essentially spiritual. I believe the Lord has brought him here for a mission that is primarily spiritual in nature. He and Pat will bless this campus now and for years to come with their own unique blend of spiritual courage, insight, and devotion. Happily, the Lord has prepared the two of them in such a way that the intellectual life of this campus will only be made richer by the abundant brand of spiritual life the Hollands inspire.

Today's audience includes a few students who were at Ricks College earlier this year when I talked about "The Gospel and Romantic Love." I apologize to them because I am talking on that subject again today. I would add, however, that it is primarily because of the response of the Ricks students that I feel impressed to give this talk here. As I do so, I pray for inspiration, not only because of the importance and sensitivity of the subject, but also because of my great love and respect for the students of Brigham Young University.

Romantic Love

Elder Boyd K. Packer once said to a group of students on this campus:

> The powers awakened earlier in your life have been growing. You have been responding to them probably clumsily, but they now form themselves into a restlessness that cannot be ignored. You are old enough now to fall in love—not the puppy love of the elementary years, not the confused love of the teens, but the full-blown love of eligible men and women, newly matured, ready for life. I mean romantic love, with all the full intense meaning of the word, with all of the power and turbulence and frustration, the yearning, the retraining, and all of the peace and beauty and sublimity of love. No experience can be more beautiful, no power more compelling, more exquisite. Or,

227

if misused, no suffering is more excruciating than that connected with love (*Eternal Love,* BYU Fireside, 3 November 1963).

In approaching this topic, I feel I am walking on holy ground. This subject, delicate as it is, inspires my deepest reverence. The idea of romantic love, so commonplace that it is touched upon in virtually every book or movie or magazine, is also at the very center of the gospel of Jesus Christ. It is one of the greatest of God's laws that a man shall "leave his father and his mother, and shall cleave unto his wife: and they shall be one flesh" (Genesis 2:24). As Elder Packer put it, "Romantic love is not only a part of life, but literally a dominating influence of it. It is deeply and significantly religious. There is no abundant life without it. Indeed, the highest degree of the celestial kingdom is unobtainable in the absence of it."

The other side of this coin, of course, is represented by what Alma told his wayward son, Corianton, who had gone after the Lamanite harlot Isabel. He said to his son: "Know ye not . . . that these things are an abomination in the sight of the Lord; yea, most abominable above all sins save it be the shedding of innocent blood or denying the Holy Ghost?" (Alma 39:5).

I once saw, at close range, the face of a faithful father who had just learned that his handsome and promising young son had violated the law of chastity and that the boy's immature young girlfriend was pregnant. I'll never forget the look in that man's eyes as it dawned on him that his child of promise had willfully rejected what his parents had taught and what they wanted him to be. The father just sat in stunned silence, staring sadly at the rain outside his window in a grief that knew no comfort. As the tears ran freely down his face, he asked himself out loud: "Why? Why would he turn his back on all he knows to be right?" There came no answer but the gentle sound of the falling rain.

Why indeed? Why such a commandment? Sometimes we give as reasons for the law of chastity the risk of pregnancy or abortion, the possibility of an unwanted or embarrassing marriage, or the chance of a terrible venereal disease. With adultery, we talk about the damage of destroying an existing marriage or family. As serious as these things are, I'm not sure they are the fundamental reason for the Lord's having placed this commandment ahead of armed robbery, fraud, and kidnapping in the seriousness of sins. Think of it—unchastity is second only to murder. Perhaps there is a common element in those two things—chastity and murder. Both have to do with *life*, which touches upon the highest of divine powers. Murder involves the wrongful *taking* of life; sexual transgression may involve the wrongful *giving* of life, or the wrongful tampering with the sacred fountains of life-giving power. Perhaps we should not expect the reasons for this commandment to be fully understandable to our finite minds. So often with our deepest feelings of joy or testimony or gratitude, we may attempt to describe their meaning with words, but our words fail us when we try to plumb the depths of those precious things that are too sacred, too significant, and even too mysterious to be susceptible of quickly understood explanations. Why is nature so exquisitely beautiful and full of harmony? Why do our hearts respond to the sight of little children laughing? Why, especially, do our hearts respond to overflowing when those little children we see laughing before us are our very own children? All we know is that God himself has said, time after time, over all the generations of man, "Thou shalt love thy wife with all thy heart, and shalt cleave unto her and none else" (D&C 42:22), "Thou shalt not . . . commit adultery . . . nor do anything like unto it" (D&C 59:6).

Moral Revolution

I have been around enough to know that this is not the first time you have ever heard this subject mentioned from the pulpit. But I have also been around enough to know, especially recently, that no matter what you have heard and no matter how often, today we live in a world so completely soaked through with tragically wrong evil ideas about sex that you must be *warned*—in love and kindness, but warned —lest the moral sleeping sickness that has overcome this nation's atmosphere claim you into deadly slumber. There have always been violators of the moral code, but the last few years have witnessed in this country a staggering revolution in sexual attitudes. Our social norms apparently began to unravel during the unrest of the 1960s, among students to start with. Research shows that in the period from 1970 to 1975, the number of college

228

students who accept the practice of premarital sex grew from about 50 percent to nearly 90 percent (Katz and Cronin, "Sexuality and College Life," *Change,* February-March 1980, p. 44). College students are the most permissive of all groups, and they are your peer group. You cannot help being influenced by their general attitudes.

It would be of no help to you, by the way, to seek counsel about sexual norms in America from a typical professional therapist. The American Psychiatric Association recently voted to remove homosexuality from its list of disorders, even though one study pointed out by our own Allen Bergin showed that 50 percent of the male homosexuals surveyed in one American city had had at least 500 sexual partners and 28 percent of them had had 1,000 partners (See "Bringing the Restoration to the Academic World: Clinical Psychology as a Test Case," *BYU Studies* 19[1979]: 449, 464). If *that is* normal behavior, we've got problems. A representative of today's mainstream attitude among psychotherapists recently wrote in a professional journal that most people in his field believe "that human disturbance is largely associated with and springs from absolutistic thinking—from dogmatism, inflexibility, and that [being extremely religious] is essentially emotional disturbance" (Ellis, "Psychotherapy and Religious Values," *Journal of Consulting and Clinical Psychology* 48[1980]: 635). In other words, the way to relieve one's guilt about an immoral life is to begin believing there is no such thing as an immoral life. Whatever you want to do is moral if you want to do it. This same psychologist expressed his concern about the mental stability of people who commit themselves to "unequivocal loyalty to any interpersonal commitments, especially marriage." You can imagine what this man and his professional associates would think of temple marriage. The same attitudes are springing up everywhere in other fields. I've done a lot of reading in my own field of law; I've read widely in the social sciences. It's now simply a fact that most of those who write and most of those who produce today's movies, TV programs, and popular music, as well as those who set the editorial policies of many national magazines, believe that sex outside of marriage is really quite harmless, if not rather healthy. I recently heard Mormon film-maker Kieth Merrill express his opinion that today's movie producers have no more hesitation about showing sexual acts on the screen than they do about showing people eating dinner.

Something deep within our national soul has gone wrong, brothers and sisters, and it cannot help but influence our attitudes and dull our normal senses in frightening ways. Twenty years ago, there was much public support for the things you and I believe in, despite some occasional straying from those principles. All that is different now. Now we are almost suffocated by a dense fog of sensuality. Kenneth Kolson has described this basic change in national attitude talking about *Playboy* magazine:

> While Playboy is much the same thing that it was during the 1950s, it is not exactly the same thing, and the difference is crucial. During the 50s, there was, of course, pornography. We used to get it at the newsstand from the old man with the black cigar who would produce it, literally, from "under-the-counter." Sometimes it would circulate through the boys' locker room—usually pictures of fat [women] with missing teeth. It was available, all right, but one came by it ["out behind the barn," so to speak]. But now that the Playboy philosophy has been declared innocent by the grand jury of public opinion, now that it "is involved in the mainstream of our culture and values," it is acquired, and consumed, as thoughtlessly as a pound of bologna. You pack Mildred and the kids in the station wagon, buzz down to the local drugstore, plunk your two bucks down on the counter, and bring home artful pictures of young women who have straight teeth, deep suntans, and college educations. Every one of them is a former cheerleader, a current jogger, concerned about ecology. Middle class. When you get home, you throw your copy on the coffee table promiscuously [alongside Time and Newsweek], a public pronouncement that you buy Playboy for the literature. It's true: the difference between the 50s and [today] is that we don't give pornography a second thought any more (*Chronicles of Culture*, September-October 1979, p. 18).

And that is exactly what has gone wrong. We don't give it a second thought. The attitude of acceptance here and what I've seen in Europe is so widespread that there is nothing to compare with it in the last several centuries, in any civilized society; not since Rome, not since Sodom and Gomorrah.

The enormous scope of the drift is what makes it so treacherous. Even as we are surrounded by abnormality, everything somehow seems so normal. As written by Pascal:

> When everything is moving at once, nothing appears to be moving, as on board ship. When everyone is moving towards depravity, no one seems to be moving, but if someone stops, he shows up the others who are rushing on, by acting as a fixed point (Blaise Pascal, *Pensées, Vol.* 33, Chicago: Encyclopaedia Britannica, Great Books of the Western World, 1952).

We—you and I—must be that fixed point.

The Bondage of Satan

I want you to know that it isn't easy for me to paint such an extreme picture. I am usually a pretty calm and reasonable guy. But on this particular subject of sexual morality, I honestly believe our society is within the grip of the evil one, even in the moment when so many Americans feel more "free" than ever before. There is a reason why the scriptures record the word *devilish* after the words *carnal* and *sensual*. We read in the Pearl of Great Price that "Satan came among them . . . and they loved Satan more than God. And men began from that time forth to be carnal, sensual, and devilish" (Moses 5:13). And then when Cain slew Abel, he said "I am free" (Moses 5:33). Cain was never more in bondage than when he said, "I am free." In exactly the same way, the American people have never been in greater moral bondage than in this time when they glory in being "free" to pursue pleasure in any form they fancy as if there will never be any tomorrow.

Can you see why the Brethren tell us to stay away from X and R-rated movies? Can you see why they plead with us to avoid drugs, alcohol, and vulgar music, and the other products of the carnal environment that now surrounds us almost as water surrounds the fish of the sea? These aren't trivial things, brothers and sisters. This isn't just a modern version of a fussy Victorian concern about bobby sox, social dancing, and driving over twenty miles an hour. This is not just coke and makeup and nylons for twelve-year-olds. If the H-bomb symbolizes our age, we are playing now not just with fire, but with nuclear power. The prince of darkness has dragged out the heavy artillery. He is no longer limited to arrows and swords and BB guns. Now he is Darth Vader, with laser guns, light speeds, and the death star. We are near the end of a fight to the finish, and no holds are barred.

Love Sacred and Holy

Let me talk now, on the other hand, about the more positive aspects of the law of chastity, because that part of the law is fundamental and important. Elder Packer said,

> Oh, youth, the requirements of the Church are the highway to love, with guardrails securely in place, with help along the way. How foolish is the youth who feels the Church is a fence around love to keep him out. How fortunate is the young person who follows the standards of the Church, even if just from sheer obedience or habit, for he will find rapture and a joy fulfilled.

I'd like to read a provocative statement about the positive side of the law of chastity from an English writer:

> Never was an age more sentimental, more devoid of real feeling, more exaggerated in false feeling, than our own. The [TV] and the film are mere counterfeit emotion

all the time, the current press and literature the same. People wallow in emotion: counterfeit emotion. They lap it up: they live in it and on it.

A young couple fall in counterfeit love, and fool themselves and each other completely. Counterfeit love is good cake but bad bread. It produces a fearful emotional indigestion. The peculiar hatred of people who have not loved one another, but who have pretended to, is one of the phenomena of our time.

[But] there is a profound instinct of fidelity in man, which is deeper and more powerful than his instinct of faithless promiscuity. The instinct of fidelity is perhaps the deepest instinct in the great complex we call sex. Where there is real sex there is the underlying passion for fidelity. The prostitute knows this, because she can only keep men who want the counterfeit: and these men she despises.

The [Chief Thinkers of our Generation] know nothing of [this]. To [them] all sex is infidelity and only infidelity is sex. Marriage is sexless, null. Sex is only manifested in infidelity, and the queen of sex is the Chief Prostitute. This is the teaching of the Chief Thinkers, and the vulgar public agrees with them. Sex is a thing you don't have except to be naughty with. Apart from infidelity and fornication, sex doesn't exist.

[However, the truth is that] the [Christian] Church created marriage by making it a sacrament, a sacrament of man and woman united in communion, never to be parted, except by death. And even when separated by death, still not freed from the marriage. Marriage, making one complete body out of two incomplete ones, and providing for the complex development of the man's soul and the woman's soul in unison, throughout a lifetime. Marriage sacred and inviolable, the great way of earthly fulfillment for man and woman, in unison.

This oneness, gradually accomplished through a lifetime of twoness, is [one of] the highest achievements of time or eternity. From it springs [the greatest of human creations]—children. It is the will of God, that he wishes this, this oneness to take place, fulfilled over a lifetime. The oneness of man and woman in marriage completes the universe, as far as humanity is concerned, completes the streaming of the sun and the flowing of the stars (D.H. Lawrence, *Essays on Sex Literature and Censorship,* New York: Twayne, 1953, p. 89).

Properly understood, then, the scriptures counsel us to be virtuous not because romantic love is bad, but precisely because romantic love is so good. It is not only good; it is pure, precious, even sacred and holy. For that reason, one of Satan's cheapest and dirtiest tricks is to make profane that which is sacred. Building on a metaphor from President Harold B. Lee, it is as though Satan holds up to the world a degraded image of sexual love suggested by imagining the drunken, boisterous laughter of filthy men in a brothel, located on some crowded, dusty highway of life, where the flower of fair womanhood is jeered at, dirtied, brutalized, and ultimately crushed with unclean hands. Meanwhile, far, far away from the madding crowd, high up in the cool protected valleys of tall mountains, grows the priceless flower of virtue untarnished pure, and unsullied. It waits as a noble prize for those valiant few who are willing to climb to its heights by paying the price of patience, obedience, and a lifetime of devotion—an endless, unselfish loyalty to spouse and children.

Eight Steps

May I suggest now eight brief, practical steps for those who would one day be true sweethearts, based on a foundation of righteous living.

First, have reverence for the human body and the life-giving powers of that body. That basic attitude is what I have hoped to convey in most of what I have said today. Your body is a temple. It is sacred and holy. Have the same reverence for it that you have for any temple that seeks to be the dwelling place for the Spirit of the Lord. It is also the dwelling place of the seeds of human life, the nurturing of which, with your chosen companion, within the bounds set by God himself, is lovely, of good report, and praiseworthy.

Second, during the time of courtship, please be emotionally honest in the expression of affection. Sometimes you are not as careful as you might be about when, how, and to whom you express your feelings of affection. You must realize that the desire to express affection can be motivated by other things than true love. As Erich Fromm put it,

> Desire can be stimulated by the anxiety of aloneness, by the wish to conquer or be conquered, by vanity, by the wish to hurt or even to destroy, as much as it can be stimulated by love. It seems that sexual desire can easily blend with and be stimulated by any strong emotion, of which love is only one. Because sexual desire is in the minds of most people coupled with the idea of love, they are easily misled to conclude that they love each other when they want each other physically . . . [But] if [this] desire . . . is not stimulated by real love, . . . it . . . leaves strangers as far apart as they were before—sometimes it makes them ashamed of each other, or even makes them hate each other, because when the illusion has gone, they feel their estrangement even more markedly than before (*The Art of Loving,* New York: Harper and Row, 1956, pp. 45-46).

In short, save your kisses—you might need them some day. And when any of you—men or woman—are given entrance to the heart of a trusting young friend, you stand on holy ground. In such a place you must be honest with yourself—and with your friend—about love and the expression of its symbols.

Third, be friends first and sweethearts second. Lowell Bennion once said that relationships between young men and young women should be built like a pyramid. The base of the pyramid is friendship. And the ascending layers are built of things like time, understanding, respect, and restraint. Right at the top of the pyramid is a glittering little mystery called romance. And when weary travelers in the desert see that glitter on top of the pyramid from far off, they don't see what underlies the jewel to give it such prominence and hold it so high. Now, you don't have to be very smart to know that a pyramid won't stand up very long if you stand it on its point instead of its base. In other words, be friends first and sweethearts later, not the other way around. Otherwise, people who think they are sweethearts may discover they can't be very good friends, and by then it may be too late.

Fourth, develop the power of self-discipline and self-restraint. Please remember that nobody ever fell off a cliff who never went near one. You've got to be like Joseph, not like David. When Potiphar's wife tried to seduce him, the scripture says, Joseph "fled, and got him out" (Genesis 39:12). Joseph knew that it is wiser to avoid temptation than to resist it. King David, by contrast, somehow developed too much confidence in his own ability to handle temptation. He was tragically willing to flirt—flirt with evil, and it ultimately destroyed him. In your courtships, even when you feel there is a growing foundation of true love, show your profound respect for that love and the possibilities of your life together by restraining your passions. Please don't be deceived by the false notion that anything short of the sex act itself is acceptable conduct. That is a lie, not only because one step overpoweringly leads to another, but also because the handling of another's body is in an important sense part of the sexual act that is kept holy by the sanctuary of chastity. If ever you are in doubt about where the line is between love and lust, draw the line toward the side of love. Nobody ever fell off a cliff who never went near one.

Fifth, in your searching for the fulfillment of your romantic longings, live for the presence of the Holy Spirit, that you may have it as your constant guide. Don't date someone you already know you would not ever want to marry. If you should fall in love with someone you shouldn't marry, you can't expect the Lord to guide you away from that person after you are already emotionally committed. It is difficult enough to tune your spiritual receiver to the whisperings of heaven without jamming up the channel with the loud thunder of romantic emotion. The key to spiritual guidance is found in one word: worthiness. I won't take time to discuss it now but would urge you, if you want to do a little scripture study, to compare Doctrine and Covenants 63:16-17 with Doctrine and Covenants 121:45-46. You'll find something interesting there. Those who garnish their thoughts with virtue have the Spirit and have confidence in God's presence. Those who have lust in their hearts can't have the Spirit.

Sixth, avoid the habit of feeling sorry for yourself and don't worry excessively about those times when you feel socially unsuccessful. Everybody in the world doesn't have to marry you—it only takes one. I remember the experience of a choice young woman who had been very popular and successful in many ways in her hometown. She passed up two or three chances to get serious with young men, because she planned to attend college at a Church school, where she expected to find more promising opportunities. After she had been at that school for about six months without a date, however, she began to wonder if she had some loathsome disease. Seeing that experience through her eyes was very sobering for me about the risks we take in any large population center for LDS students, because sheer size and numbers can so easily cause people to make incredibly superficial judgments about others, in ways that emphasize appearance above far more important but less obvious factors.

The opportunities for developing friendships (as sometimes distinguished from having "dates") with members of the opposite sex are very plentiful at a place like BYU or Ricks. Often these relationships lead to more promising possibilities than does the big social whirl. It's also less expensive. In approaching these opportunities, remember: "Worry not that you are not well known. Seek to be worth knowing." The college-age years are a wonderful time in which to experience a variety of human relationships, to go places and do things, to read widely, to find yourself, to develop the roots of spiritual and emotional maturity. To gain this kind of ripeness and growth simply takes time, experience, and effort.

The discouragement you may feel as another empty Friday night rolls by is often a form of the insecurity we all encounter as we try to find ourselves. Without the apparent approval of your self-worth that comes through social success, you may begin to doubt whether your life is really worthwhile. That kind of self-doubt is only part of a larger problem that accompanies most of us, married or single, all the days of our lives. There are times when we wonder if the Lord loves us; we wonder if other people love us. And so we mistakenly seek the symbols of success—whether that is being popular or being rich or being famous within our own sphere. Sometimes you may let someone take improper liberties with you, or you may indulge yourself in some practice that seems to bring temporary relief but only makes you feel worse in the long run. Some even make poor marriage choices, just to show the world that *somebody* will have them.

Ultimately, however, only the Lord's approval of our lives really matters. If you seek to be worth knowing and seek to do his will, all the rest will take care of itself. Never forget that all things work together for good to them who love God (see Romans 8:28). Your time for marriage may not come until the autumn of your life and then, in Elder Packer's phrase: "be more precious for the waiting." Even if your time should not come in this life, the promises of eternal love are still yours in the Lord's view of time if only you are faithful.

Seventh, avoid at all costs, no matter what the circumstances, abortion and homosexuality. As serious as is fornication or adultery, you must understand that abortion and homosexuality are equally wrong and may be worse. Even persons who only assist others, much less pressure them, to have an abortion are in jeopardy of being denied the privilege of missionary service. They may also be called upon to face a Church court, at the peril of their membership in the Church.

Eighth, if through some unfortunate experience in your past, you have committed a moral transgression of the kind we have been talking about today, there is a way by which you may receive full forgiveness. There is no more glorious language in all scripture than the words of Isaiah, speaking as if it were by the voice of the Lord himself:

> Though your sins be as scarlet, they shall be white as snow; though they be red
> like crimson, they shall be as wool.
> If ye be willing and obedient, ye shall eat the good of the land (Isaiah 1:18-19).

The steps for the process of repentance are outlined in President Kimball's masterful book *The Miracle of Forgiveness.* If your transgressions are of the serious kind, you will need to see your bishop and voluntarily offer a full and complete confession. As frightening as that experience may seem to you, by this means you will find purpose and a peace of mind more hopeful and uplifting than you can now imagine. As you wonder how you might stand in the eyes of the Lord after such an experience, I commend to you the counsel of Elder Vaughn Featherstone, who talked in the October 1980 general conference about the repentance process for serious transgressions. The most memorable part of that candid and loving sermon was Elder Featherstone's expression of his attitude toward those who have had the courage and faith to confess their sins and even face Church discipline, if necessary. Because I so much share Elder Featherstone's feeling, I would like to quote a portion of his remarks:

> In Exodus 32, Moses had gone up to the mountain. The children of Israel had fashioned a golden calf with a graving tool. The people offered burnt offerings, and they sat down to eat, drink, and play; and there was great wickedness when Moses came down out of the mountain. He cast the tablets out of his hands, and they were broken; he burned the golden calf and caused the idolators to be slain.
>
> Then when the people had repented (and that is the key), Moses went back before the Lord and prayed, "Yet now, if thou wilt forgive their sin;—and if not, blot me, I pray thee, out of thy book which thou hast written" (Ex. 32:32).
>
> I have listened to possibly a thousand major transgressions; and each time after a truly repentant transgressor has left my office, I have either knelt or bowed my head in prayer and said, "Lord, forgive him or her, I pray thee. If not, blot my name also out of thy book. I do not want to be where they aren't, for they are some of the most Christike people I have ever met."
>
> Though their sins be as scarlet, they may become white as the driven snow (see Is. 1: 18) and the Lord has promised he would remember their sins no more (see D&C 58:42). ("Forgive Them, I Pray Thee," *Ensign,* November 1980, p. 31).

I guess one reason I appreciate Elder Featherstone's feelings so much is that those are also my feelings about you. That's why I am willing to take the risk today that maybe you think I'm being too serious. I'm willing to take that chance because I don't want to be where the students of Ricks College and Brigham Young University are not.

For all that I have said by way of warning about the social conditions of the day or the limits we must place on ourselves, I'd like you to remember that the teachings of the gospel about romantic love are full of hope and peace and joy of the most uplifting and everlasting kind. I will always remember my straight-arrow friend that I met here in Provo who told me he took his fiance to the bishop for a recommend to be married before they had ever experienced *any* physical dimension to their relationship—and I mean any! After the regular interview, the wise bishop asked them, "Well, do you feel the spark when you hold each other close?" My friend was perplexed. "The spark?" The bishop tried to explain, but my friend was having trouble catching on. So the bishop *assigned* them to take one week to see if they had "the spark" in their relationship. He knew they'd figure it out and still remain worthy. As my friend told me this story, I couldn't help asking, "Well, what did you find out?" He blushed a little bit, and then he said, "Well, we finally fulfilled the assignment. " They learned the same thing that I have learned, about being sweethearts on the foundation of everlasting friendship and love. I testify to you with all my heart that the commandments of God are designed for our ultimate happiness, and that being sweethearts in the way the Lord intended it is worth waiting for, in the name of Jesus Christ. Amen.

Improving Sexual Communication in Marriage

Douglas E. Brinley

Toward a Celestial Marriage, pp. 139-146

What are some guidelines we can follow to improve our sexual relationships in marriage? First, whether we are newly married or have years of experience, we need to know that this relationship requires **patience**, **understanding**, and **a willingness to communicate** together about this sacred aspect of our marriage. It will require frequent **monitoring**. There must be a sharing of our own sexual feelings, preferences, and responses. Sexual intimacy is a new venture for brides and grooms who will need to cooperate, assist, and provide gentle, clear instruction to each other. We must be good teachers and humble students. As the life cycle adds years, the complexities of our lives and physical changes may affect our sexual responses. Feelings and reactions may be different during pregnancy, after child-birth, or in our later years. Sexual interest is not always static. Aging may affect hormonal levels. We may need more time for sexual arousal, or more physical stimulation for arousal—but there is no reason why healthy individuals should not find satisfaction in their sexual relations **their entire lives**.

Secondly, it is clear that sexual fulfillment begins with the **quality of life in the non-sexual areas of marriage**. It is difficult for either spouse to give of himself or herself, freely and fully, without fear of being hurt when the companion is upset, angry, or moody. The sexual expression is a barometer of a couple's total marriage experience. Dating and courting—**in marriage**—are part of a life-long activity where romantic validation between partners is frequent and creative and sets the stage for heightened sexual pleasure and intimacy.

Third, in general, men have a greater sexual "drive" (since a climax is more predictable for them than for a wife and and therefore sexual release may become an important goal). If that is true in your marriage (and in some it is not), it will require mutual understanding. A husband will need to exercise self-control, restraint, and charity in being sensitive to his wife's needs, desires, and interests. On the other hand, it is very validating to a husband when his wife initiates "love-making" frequently because she understands that to him, normally, love and sex are the same thing! **Charity must always be the ruling virtue for both**. Mutual consideration between spouses will allow each one to be comfortable in initiating intimacy and realizing there will be times when sexual relations are not preferable or desirable to either one.

Knowing that husbands are sexually aroused by erotic messages and that women enjoy a romantic approach is important. Of course, holding and touching, and genuine expressions of love and endearment, are important elements for both.

Fourth, both spouses should be aware that a number of factors may hinder their sexual satisfaction. If either one is unsympathetic to the pressures and worries of the spouse, or if physical factors interfere—weight, hygiene, poor technique—may detract from their responses. There will be times when neither spouse feels "sexy," or sexually aroused. Both will need to be mature enough to realize there are no performance standards, no one to please except each other. Both must share their own honest feelings about sexual pleasure realizing that respect and love for each may override personal preferences at times.

Fifth, because of strong pre-marital sexual standards and pre-marital abstinence, married couples may not be quite sure of how to be loving partners. Each must realize that the best source of help is the companion.

The spouse is the one who can best provide feedback and instruction on sexual technique. Some couples go for years without sharing how they would prefer to be loved. A sincere desire to learn and please each other, coupled with a sense of humor—neither one embarrassing the other—can do much to increase sexual fulfillment. Both must help each other to an arousal of sexual passion and be interested in the spouse's sexual satisfaction.

Marriage is not just for sex, of course, but sex is a profound means of expressing love and commitment. It is designed to be a physical, emotional, and spiritual union; hence a high form of "validation." Just as a good marriage increases sexual interest, so satisfactory sexual relations adds soul-binding emotional strength to the marriage. There are few ways as powerful as the sexual union of a man and woman that are so expressive of mutual love. By shutting out the world, a couple, in the intimacy and privacy of their own space, can renew their commitments. Feelings of love and appreciation, a willingness to cooperate, to share in the joys and challenges of mortality, to be therapeutic, are sown in the sacred union of a couple whose love is centered in charity and eternal covenants. Both can be raised to a greater level of spirituality by an act of love which expresses their emotional feelings so aptly. I have seen couples who have gone years without sharing sexual intimacy. What a tremendous loss it has been to their souls. How consoling, how refreshing, how relaxing and wholesome physical intimacy should be for marrieds who live in a world of stress and who are in need of frequent reassurance that they are desirable and loved by their eternal companion.

When we meet each other's sexual needs, trust is strengthened and our ability to function as a team increases. Our relationship is eternal. That means we can afford to be patient with our sexual feelings before marriage, and we can be patient with our sexual progress and the processes that will develop between the two of us. The media myth of the perfect (and instant) orgasm is just that—a myth. In many marriages it takes some time before we can establish the psychological and emotional climate where our expression of love for each other ripens and matures. So much stress in our society is put on the mechanics, techniques, and skills of sex that it is easy to see a sexual encounter as an athletic performance! Well, it's not a game and no one should be keeping score.

Another gentle reminder is that you're in this together. Nobody has a problem alone. If the husband is troubled with sexual arousal, that's a problem for both of you, not just him. If the wife, is unable to respond well sexually, that's a problem for both of you. The sexual relationship is part of the total relationship. The husband who snarls his way home through traffic, snaps when his wife asks, "How'd it go today?", growls because dinner is tardy, is not likely to find a warm reception when suddenly, at 10 o'clock, he turns off the news and sends out amorous signals!

Suggestions:

1. Acquire a vocabulary so that you can discuss intimacy comfortably—and often.

2. As you discover what pleases you and what you enjoy—share that with your spouse. It's your responsibility to assist your companion in meeting your needs—after all, you are the expert on you. You may wish that your partner could read your mind and your body—and eventually, in a good sexual relationship, you will be so in tune with each other that you may be able to, but that will probably come much later.

3. Learn what constitutes a good experience for your partner. It means that you must learn from your spouse about moods, timing, and what is relaxing, stimulating, and pleasurable. Both of you should be able to answer these questions: What situations make love-making the best experience for me? for you? What is really needed and wanted in the way of techniques for me? for you? What aspects of love-making are the most pleasurable for me? for you? What about frequency? environment? And even if I know what the answers have been in the past, how about **this** time. Phrases such as "I really enjoy it when you. . ." or "How do you feel about. . ." may help.

4. For "old marrieds" part of the process is realizing that a series of steps exist between the first physical touch and the most passionate embrace. What are those steps in your marriage? Some couples tend to skip these steps after they have been married for awhile and focus only on the final stages of sexual expression. Often the greatest tenderness and romance is expressed either before or after our love-making.

The Gospel Perspective on Morality

1. In the celestial glory there are three heavens or degrees; And in order to obtain the highest (degree), a man must enter into this order of the priesthood (meaning the new and everlasting covenant of marriage); and if he does not, he cannot obtain it (the highest degree). He may enter into the other, but that is the end of his kingdom; **he cannot have an increase** (D&C 131:1-4).

2. Except a man and his wife enter into an everlasting covenant and be married for eternity, while in this probation, by the power and authority of the Holy Priesthood, they will CEASE TO INCREASE WHEN THEY DIE: that is they will NOT HAVE ANY CHILDREN AFTER THE RESURRECTION. But those who are married by the power and authority of the priesthood in this life (and are faithful) continue to increase and have children in the celestial glory (Joseph Smith, *History of the Church,* 5:391).

3. The First Presidency explained:
   "The doctrine of this Church is that sexual sin—the illicit sexual relations of men and women—stands, in its enormity, next to MURDER. The Lord has drawn NO ESSENTIAL DISTINCTIONS BETWEEN FORNICATION AND ADULTERY AND HARLOTRY OR PROSTITUTION" (Roy W. Doxey, *Latter-day Prophets and the D&C*, 2:12). [They have now added incest.]

4. Could wicked and malicious beings, who have eradicated every feeling of love from their bosoms, be permitted to propagate their species, the offspring would partake of all the evil, wicked, and malicious nature of their parents. It is for this reason that God will not permit the fallen angels to multiply; it is for this reason that God has ordained marriages for the righteous only; it is for this reason that God will put a final stop to the MULTIPLICATION OF THE WICKED AFTER THIS LIFE: IT IS FOR THIS REASON THAT NONE BUT THOSE WHO HAVE KEPT THE CELESTIAL LAW WILL BE PERMITTED TO MULTIPLY AFTER THE RESURRECTION. . .FOR THEY ALONE ARE PREPARED TO BEGET AND BRING FORTH SUCH (SPIRIT) OFFSPRING (Orson Pratt. *The Seer*, pp. 156-7).

5. God . . . has ordained that the highest order and class of beings that should exist in the eternal worlds should exist in the capacity of husbands and wives, and they alone should have the privilege of propagating their species. . . . Now it is wise no doubt, in the Great Creator to thus limit this great and heavenly principle to those who have arrived or come to the highest state of exaltation. . . . Consequently, He does not entrust this privilege of multiplying spirits with the terrestrial or telestial, or the lower order of beings there, nor with angels. But why not? BECAUSE THEY HAVE NOT PROVED THEMSELVES WORTHY OF THIS GREAT PRIVILEGE (Orson Pratt, *Journal of Discourses*, 13:186).

6. Know ye not, my son, that these things (sexual transgressions) are an abomination in the sight of the Lord; yea, most abominable above all sins save it be the SHEDDING OF INNOCENT BLOOD OR DENYING THE HOLY GHOST (Alma 39:5).

7. If a man or woman who has been sealed to a spouse commits adultery, he or she cannot be sealed to the partner in the adultery **unless** authorized by the First Presidency.

8. It was at this time that I received from him (Joseph) the first idea of eternal family organization, and the eternal union of the sexes in those inexpressibly endearing relationships which none but the highly intellectual, the refined and pure in heart, know how to prize, and which are at the very foundation of everything worthy to be called happiness. It was from him that I learned that the wife of my bosom might be secured to me for time and all eternity; and that the refined sympathies and affections which endeared us to each other emanated from the fountain of divine eternal love (Parley P. Pratt, *Autobiography*, pp. 297-98).

9. So far as the stages of eternal progression and attainment have been made known through divine revelation, we are to understand **that only resurrected and glorified beings can become parents of spirit offspring. Only such exalted souls have reached maturity in the appointed course of eternal life; and these spirits born to them in the eternal worlds will pass in due sequence through the several stages or estates by which the glorified parents have attained exaltation** (First Presidency, 30 June 1916, *Messages of the First Presidency*, Clark, 5:34).

10. What do we mean by endless or eternal increase? We mean that through the righteousness and faithfulness of men and women who keep the commandments of God they will come forth with celestial bodies, fitted and prepared to enter into their great, high and eternal glory in the celestial kingdom of God, and unto them, through their preparation there will come children, who will be **spirit children**. I don't think that is very difficult to comprehend and understand. The nature of the offspring is determined by the nature of the substance that flows in the veins of the being. When blood flows in the veins of the being, the offspring will be what blood produces, which is tangible flesh and bone, but when that which flows in the veins is spirit matter (as in a resurrected being) a substance which is more refined and pure and glorious than blood, the offspring of such beings will be "spirit children" (*Melvin J. Ballard—Crusader for Righteousness*, p. 211).

Sexual Stewardship

1. We hope that our parents and leaders will not tolerate pornography. It is really garbage, but today is peddled as normal and satisfactory food. Many writers seem to take delight in polluting the atmosphere with it. We live in a culture which venerates the orgasm, trading wives, living together without the benefit of marriage, and similar craves. How low can humans plunge? It is sad that decent people are thrown into a filthy area of mental and spiritual pollution. We call upon all of our people to do all in their power to offset this ugly revolution (President. Kimball, Conference Report, Oct. 1974, p. 7).

2. The human body is the sacred home of the spirit child of God, and unwarranted tampering with or defilement of this sacred tabernacle can bring only remorse and regret. No indecent exposure or pornography or other aberrations to defile the mind and spirit. No fondling of bodies, one's own or that of others, and no sex between persons except in proper marriage relationships. This is positively prohibited by our Creator in all places, at all times, and we reaffirm it. EVEN IN MARRIAGE THERE CAN BE SOME EXCESSES AND DISTORTIONS. No amount of RATIONALIZATION to the contrary can satisfy a **disappointed Father in Heaven** (President Kimball, Conference Report, 1974, p. 8-9).

3. Libraries are loaded with books with shocking pictures, showing people how to totally satisfy their animal natures, but few books are found on self-control, of continence. With the theory that "life is for sex," every imagination of the minds of men devise ways to more completely get what they call "sexual fulfillment," which they DEMAND at the expense of all else—family, home, eternal life. There should be from press and lecture platform and pulpit deep and resounding voices urging man to rise above the carnal and rest his mind on things clean and sacred (President Kimball, Conference Report, April 1971, pp. 6-7).

4. Let us instruct young people who come to us, to know that a woman should be queen of her own body. The marriage covenant does not give the man the right to enslave her or to abuse her or to use her merely for

the gratification of his passion. Your marriage ceremony does not give you that right (President McKay, *Gospel Ideals*, p. 471).

5. Brethren, we who lead the Church are responsible to see that you are taught in plainness. I, therefore, must make reference to a matter that otherwise I would not present in a meeting such as this. There are evil and degrading practices which, in the world, are not only condoned but **encouraged**. Sometimes **married couples** in their intimate expression of love to one another are drawn into practices that are unholy, unworthy, and unnatural. We receive letters from time to time asking for a definition of "unnatural" or "unworthy." Brethren, you know the answer to that. If in doubt at all, do not do it. Surely no holder of the priesthood would feel worthy to accept advancement in the priesthood or sign his temple recommend if any impure practice were a part of his life (President. Tanner, Conference Report, October 1978; *Ensign,* November 1978, p. 42).

6. Even though sex can be an important and satisfactory part of married life we must remember that life is not designed just for sex. **Even marriage does not make proper certain extremes in sexual indulgence.** . . . Perhaps the Lord's condemnation included secret sexual sins in marriage when he said: "And those who are not pure and have said they were pure, shall be destroyed, saith the Lord God" (D&C 132:52). "The First Presidency has interpreted oral sex as constituting an unnatural, impure, or unholy practice" (Letter of January 5, 1982 to all Stake Presidents, Bishops).

7. If sex is considered as sacred to us as it should be, then it deserves that status both **before** and **after** the wedding ceremony. "Anything" does not go in marriage. Decency is as important for married people as for the unmarried. Perversions are perversions whenever indulged in, and the marriage ceremony cannot take away their stain. When indecency, indignity and unnatural practices are thrust upon a good woman by a lustful man, can she be blamed for resisting? Can any woman retain her self-respect or her regard for her husband if he insists upon and she submits to unnatural practices? It is the unnatural, the extreme and the indecent which sickens self-respecting women (Mark E. Petersen, *Marriage and Common Sense,* pp. 94-95).

9. If you study divorces, . . . you will find there are one, two, three, four reasons. Generally sex is the first. They did not get along sexually. They may not say that in the court. They may not even tell that to their attorneys, but that is the reason. Husband and wife . . . are authorized, in fact they are commanded, to have proper sex when they are properly married for time and eternity. That does not mean that we need to go to great extremes. That does not mean that a woman is the servant of the husband. It does not mean that any man has a right to demand sex anytime that he might want it. He should be reasonable and understanding and it should be a general program between the two, so they understand and everybody is happy about it (President Kimball, *Teachings,* p. 312).

10. If it is unnatural, you just don't do it. That is all, and all the family life should be kept clean and worthy and on a very high plane. There are some people who have said that behind the bedroom doors anything goes. That is not true and the Lord would not condone it (Spencer W. Kimball, *Teachings,* p. 312).

11. The world may have its norm; the Church has a different one. It may be considered normal by the people of the world to use tobacco; the Church's standard is a higher plane where smoking is not done. The world's norm may permit men and women social drinking; the Lord's church lifts its people to a norm of total abstinence. The world may countenance premarital sex experiences, but the Lord and his church condemn in no uncertain terms any and every sex relationship outside of marriage, and even indecent and uncontrolled ones within marriage. And so, though many self-styled authorities justify these practices as a normal release, the church condemns them and could not knowingly send such people, unrepentant, into the mission field or give them places of trust or positions of responsibility or temple privileges. Such unholy practices were condemned by ancient prophets and are today condemned by the Church.

Paul lashed out against these unholy evidences of the vulgar mind and of uncontrolled passion and desire: "Wherefore God also gave them up to uncleanness through the lusts of their own hearts, to dishonour their own bodies between themselves (Romans 1:24). (Spencer W. Kimball, *Faith Precedes the Miracle,* pp. 174-5).

12. Elder Packer at BYU "The Fountain of Life," March 1992.

I must include a caution to you who are married. A couple may be tempted to introduce things into your relationships which are unworthy. Do not, as the scriptures, warn, change the natural use into that which is against nature (Rom. 1:26). If you do, the tempter will drive a wedge between you.

If something unworthy has become part of your relationship, don't ever do it again! Now, what exactly do I mean by that? You know what I mean by that, and I will not respond to any questions about it.

They Twain Shall Be One

Thoughts on Intimacy in Marriage

Brent A. Barlow

Ensign, September, 1986, pp. 49-53

Several years ago when I was a young missionary and had just received a new companion, we met a Protestant minister who invited us in out of the cold. After exchanging points of view on various topics, he asked us, "And what is the Mormon attitude towards sexuality?"

I choked on my cup of hot chocolate, but my new companion seemed unmoved. "Well," said the minister after a moment of silence, "could you please tell me the Mormon philosophy toward sexuality?" I was tongue tied and believed my new companion knew next to nothing on the matter. However, when my companion realized that I didn't have an answer, he finally said, "Sir, we believe in it."

It has been more than twenty years since that time, and I have been asked the same question by numerous students, friends, professional people, and LDS members and nonmembers alike. And still, I haven't yet been able to come up with a better answer than the one given by my supposedly naive companion: "We believe in it."

We believe in it inasmuch as we know of the sorrow that comes from the inappropriate use of sexuality outside the realm of marriage. We are acutely aware of what the prophets, past and present, have warned in these matters. As Alma declared to his son Corianton, "Wickedness never was happiness" (Alma 41:10).

But we also believe in the good that can be derived from the appropriate use of intimacy in marriage. We are well aware of the joy and unity that can come to a married couple when this particular dimension of the marital relationship is nurtured.

Yet, in spite of the potentially joyful aspects of sexuality in marriage, for many it is a source of frustration and even contention. Indeed, the inability of married couples to intimately relate to each other is one of the major causes of divorce. President Spencer W. Kimball noted that even in our own church, "if you study the divorces, as we have had to do in these past years, you will find there are one, two, three, four reasons. Generally sex is the first. They did not get along sexually. They may not say that in court. They may not even tell that to their attorneys, but that is the reason" (*The Teachings of Spencer W. Kimball,* ed. Edward L. Kimball, Salt Lake City: Bookcraft, 1982, p. 312).

Why does something so beautiful sometimes become a source of so many problems? Part of the difficulty stems from mistaken ideas. Some people still believe that sexual intimacy is a necessary evil by which we have children. These people get an inaccurate view from parents who were too embarrassed to discuss such matters with their children or who were so concerned that their children live the law of chastity that they taught only the negative consequences of the improper use of intimacy.

Some develop inappropriate attitudes from mistaken interpretations of biblical verses. In Ephesians 5:22, for example, women are encouraged to "submit" to their husbands. Some have erroneously believed that this scripture means women are to submit or yield themselves to their husbands even if they do so unwillingly. Under these conditions, neither the thought nor the act does much to promote marital oneness.

In reality, however, sexuality is a beautiful power given to mankind from God. President Kimball has observed: "The Bible celebrates sex and its proper use, presenting it as God-created, God-ordained, God-blessed. It makes plain that God himself implanted the physical magnetism between the sexes for two reasons: for the propagation of the human race, and for the expression of that kind of love between man and wife that makes for true oneness. His commandment to the first man and woman to be 'one flesh' was as important as his command to 'be fruitful and multiply'" (Quoting Billy Graham, ENSIGN, May 104, p. 7).

It is also of interest to note that the word sex or *sexualiaty* does not appear in the scriptures. Rather, it is described in holy writ with the words *know* or *knew*. This idea of "knowing" or "becoming acquainted with" connotes a deeply satisfying aspect of married love.

To be able to know each other physically, couples need to talk together about the physical dimensions of their relationship. Partners who feel free to discuss finances, discipline, recreational activities, and so forth, often feel uncomfortable discussing this intimate subject. And they sometimes assume that their intimate relationship should just "naturally" work out and that to discuss it means something has gone wrong. This is simply not true. While these intimacies, because of their sacred nature, should not be discussed with friends or other relatives, it is totally appropriate to discuss them with a marriage partner.

In this regard Elder Hugh B. Brown has noted: "Many marriages have been wrecked on the dangerous rocks of ignorant and debased sex behavior, both before and after marriage. Gross ignorance on the part of newlyweds on the subject of the proper place and functioning of sex results in much unhappiness and many broken homes.

"Thousands of young people come to the marriage altar almost illiterate insofar as this basic and fundamental function is concerned. . . .

"If they who contemplate this most glorifying and intimate of all human relationships [marriage] would seek to qualify for its responsibilities, . . . if they would frankly discuss the delicate and sanctifying aspects of harmonious sex life which are involved in marriage, . . . much sorrow, heartbreak, and tragedy could be avoided" (*You and Your Marriage,* Salt Lake City: Bookcraft, 1960, pp. 22 23, 73).

Talking about this intimate relationship—including the emotional feelings that attend it can go a long way in strengthening a marriage.

Some problems in this aspect of marriage occur when one spouse or the other either unwisely limits its use or uses it inappropriately. Sexuality should be an integral part of loving and giving. Any use which doesn't include these feelings is improper.

In my work as a marriage counselor, I have found that there are some couples who feel that sexuality should be restricted to one dimension—reproduction. Yet President Kimball has said: "We know of no directive from the Lord that proper sexual experiences between husbands and wives need be limited totally to the procreation of children" (ENSIGN, Oct. 1975, p. 4). While creating children is an integral and beautiful aspect of marital intimacy, to use it only for that purpose is to deny its great potential as an expression of love, commitment, and unity.

On the other hand, there are couples who seem to feel that the only reason for sexuality is physical gratification. These people become so obsessed with the achievement of sensation that the emotion of love is all but forgotten. Still others use sexuality as a weapon or a bargaining tool. This is not only a misuse of a God-given privilege, it shows great selfishness on the part of one or both partners and makes sexuality a destructive rather than a unifying element in marriage.

Lack of information about men's and women's sexual expressions and feelings can also cause problems in marriage.

Some people cling to old stereotypes, mistakenly perceiving women as being less sexual than men. Not long ago I was invited to speak to a group of LDS married couples on the topic of sexuality in marriage. At the conclusion of my remarks one young wife asked, "Why is the sex drive so much stronger in men than in women?" I told the group I seriously questioned whether or not it was. For years it has been widely believed that men have the greater interest and drive towards sexual fulfillment. In addition, many women have been culturally conditioned to believe that their sexual inclinations are less than those of men and if they are not, they should be or something is supposedly wrong. But recent research indicates that the capacity for sexual response in women is just as great, and in some cases even greater, than that of males. Recognizing this can help both partners be more aware of and sensitive to the other's desires and expectations.

Sometimes the image of men and women shown in the media subtly and incorrectly influences our perception of sexuality. Seldom does the media present a balanced, mature, loving marital relationship. Men are often presented as strong, dashing heroes with little commitment and only one desire—sex. Women are portrayed as hopelessly romantic, pragmatically businesslike, or silly, who in any case have one function—that of satisfying man's one desire. Both of these narrow views deny the individuality of men and women. They ignore the fact that both are children of God, each with his or her own hopes, desires, talents, and emotions. When a husband and wife forget this truth and see the other as an object, sexuality can do little or nothing to promote intimacy.

Then there are, of course, physical or psychological problems which can damage this aspect of marriage. A husband or a wife who has been sexually abused for example, may have deep-seated emotional problems. In these cases, it would be appropriate to consult a bishop or qualified counselor for help. And a medical doctor may be able to help with physical problems.

One great problem in this, as in all other aspects of marriage, is selfishness. I doubt that there is any human relationship better than marriage to teach us the need for Christlike love—that unqualified and unconditional love that persuades us to think more of another than we think of ourselves. Yet few of us, even those of us in a seemingly good marriage, have learned to do this as well as we could or should. It's not always easy to put all other considerations aside and look to our companion to see what his or her needs are and then do our best to fulfill them. One young wife said that the problem isn't necessarily that husbands and wives don't know how to love each other, but that "people don't know how to love people." We tend to do for others what would make us happy if someone would do the same for us. And afterward we wonder why the other person isn't happy. One great key to success in marriage is to find out what would make our spouse happy and then to find joy in providing that happiness.

When we see sexuality as a vital part of marital harmony and happiness, it becomes more than something we simply give or receive. I like to think of it as something a husband and wife can share. It might be called a sexual guardianship.

In the parable of the talents, Jesus taught that we should improve on whatever has been entrusted to our care (See Matt. 25:14-30). And in marriage we are often given joint guardianships, such as children, fidelity, and the day-to-day maintenance of family members.

Examples of joint guardianships in marriage are found in the scriptures. In Moses, chapter five, we are given insights into what Adam and Eve did and were accountable for *together*. In verse one we read, "Adam began to till the earth, and to have dominion over all the beasts of the field.... And Eve, also, his wife, did labor with him." Thus, they shared the joint responsibility of work or labor. In sharing other dimensions of life, they also had sexual relationships and bore children *together* (v. 2); prayed and received inspiration *together* (v. 4); received commandments *together* (v. 5); taught their children *together* (v. 12); and mourned *together* (v. 27).

Paul implies a sexual responsibility when he says: "Let the husband render unto the wife due benevolence; and likewise also the wife unto the husband.

"The wife hath not power of her own body, but the husband: and likewise also the husband hath not power of his own body, but the wife " (I Cor. 7:3-4).

To me, this means that neither the husband nor the wife alone control the physical relationship, that both are diligent in their commitment to each other, and that both have a nurturing attitude toward the other. With that in mind, let's look at some of the ways husbands and wives can fulfill their part of this guardianship and better this dimension of their marriage.

To the Husband

A husband needs to spend time with his wife. The two need to have time together to share ideas, to grow and learn together, and to experience joy together. A wife is not going to be too excited about a husband who spends all his time at work, at church meetings, in hobbies that exclude her, or in front of the television or newspaper. A husband who always spends time in ways that exclude his wife communicates to her that she is not very important. Yet his wife should be the most important person in his life.

President Spencer W. Kimball, referring to Doctrine and Covenants 42:22 ("Thou shalt love thy wife with all thy heart, and shalt cleave unto her and none else"), said that "the words *none else* eliminate everyone and everything. The spouse then becomes preeminent in the life of the husband or wife and neither social life nor occupational life nor political life nor any other interest nor person nor thing shall ever take precedence over the companion spouse" (*Miracle of Forgiveness*, Salt Lake City: Bookcraft, 1969, p. 250).

If her husband places other things first and is unable to find time to develop intimacy in other parts of his relationship with his wife, she will probably not be very interested in sexual intimacy.

Similarly, a wife may not be interested if she feels her husband is unaware of or doesn't care about the seemingly small struggles of her life. One wife once commented to me that she wished her husband would "come home from work, look into my eyes, and ask me how I feel, how was my busy day, and then give me a kiss and a long hug." Most wives deeply appreciate little helps that show their husband is sensitive to their needs. Many have told me of the appreciation they feel when their husbands help around the house or care for the children after a long and hectic day. Other wives appreciate their husband's help when they are ill, pregnant, or overwhelmed with housework. Little things—thank yous, compliments, and I love yous are important. When these "little" elements are added to a marriage, sexuality becomes more meaningful and an expression of deep love. Without these "extras," sexual intimacy can become that which is ultimately satisfying to neither the husband nor the wife.

Wives also enjoy romance. The problem here is that sometimes husbands and wives have a different definition of romance. Many wives include in their definition the time they spend together doing things they are both interested in. They include expressions of love both verbal and written, or small gifts that have meaning for just the two of them. If the romance in marriage is limited to sexuality, wives may feel more exploited than loved.

One complaint that I have heard many times from wives is that there is little affection in their marriage. In a survey I conducted some time ago, I found that most wives put sexual satisfaction fairly high on their list of what they desired in marriage. But most wives ranked nonsexual intimacy even higher. Many told of the satisfaction they feel when they hold hands with their husbands, or sit close together while reading or watching television. A wife also appreciates her husband's concern for her in the sexual relationship itself.

As a husband learns to find out and meet his wife's various needs, the love in their marriage and all the expressions of that love will likely improve.

To the Wife

Perhaps the most important thing a wife can do to improve the sexual relationship in her marriage is to realize her husband is also a being with various needs, hopes, and aspirations. Unfortunately the media blatantly convey the idea that men want only one thing out of a relationship. To adopt this narrow view of men is to do them an injustice. Men, even those who may have mistaken ideas of marital relationships, are still children of God, and treating them as such can only help improve the relationship.

Many of the ideas that apply to husbands also apply to wives. Just as husbands need to find time for their wives, so wives need to find time for their husbands. Some wives spend most of their time at work, caring for the children, or cleaning house. When children are finally in bed at night and parents have a few moments away from them, wives often prefer doing "relaxing" things—watching TV, doing needlework, reading a book, talking on the phone—to spending time with their husbands. If their husbands want to be with them, they are often tired and emotionally unavailable. Men are not likely to appreciate or understand such actions. If the activities of the day really are so tiring that a woman has little time or energy left to develop her relationship with her husband, she or the couple together might examine her life carefully, to decide which things can be given up for the good of the most important relationship she will ever be involved in.

Men also appreciate affection. In some ways, when it comes to affection, men can be as romantic as women. A husband enjoys putting his arms around his wife or kissing her before leaving in the morning. These actions are not necessarily sexual; they are instead his romantic expression of the love he feels for her.

If these expressions of affection are continually met with "not now," he may feel that his wife is indifferent to the love they share. These expressions are to the husband what words of appreciation and kind deeds are to the wife. A wife who rejects them tells her husband she doesn't really care about him. On the other hand, when she stops for a quick hug or even better, initiates the affectionate action herself, she deepens the love between her and her husband.

When it comes to sexuality, some wives become very concerned about their "rights," often speaking of their "right" to say no and yes. But marriage is also a relationship of responsibility and opportunity. In marriage, both partners have the opportunity to give. I believe few wives realize the power they have to help keep their husbands near them physically, emotionally, and even spiritually. On the other hand, I also believe few wives sense the degree of frustration and alienation husbands feel when a wife ignores his needs and interests. I believe a wise and loving Heavenly Father has given a wife the ability to achieve oneness with her husband. The key is unselfishness.

Elder Parley P. Pratt once noted that "our natural affections are planted in us by the Spirit of God, for a wise purpose; and they are the very main springs of life and happiness—they are the cement of all virtuous and heavenly society.

"The fact is, God made man, male and female; he planted in their bosoms those affections which are calculated to promote their happiness and union" (Parker Pratt Robison, ed., *Writings of Parley Parker Pratt,* Salt Lake City: Deseret News Press, 1952, pp. 52-53). As husbands and wives learn to give of themselves and to understand each others' needs and desires, these affections will grow until they do indeed "promote their happiness and union."

I Have A Question

Homer Ellsworth

Ensign, August 1979, pp. 23-24

Is it our understanding that we are to propagate children as long and as frequently as the human body will permit? Is there not any kind of "gospel family-planning," for lack of a better way to say it?

Dr. Homer Ellsworth, gynecologist and former member of the Melchizedek Priesthood General Committee. I hear this type of question frequently from active and committed Latter-day Saint women who often ask questions that are outside my professional responsibilities. Here are some of the principles and attitudes I believe apply to this fundamental question, a question most couples ask themselves many times during their childbearing years.

I rejoice in our basic understanding of the plan of salvation, which teaches us that we come to earth for growth and maturity, and for testing. In that process we may marry and provide temporal bodies for our Heavenly Father's spirit children. That's basic, it seems to me. In contemplating this truth, I also take great delight in the Church's affirmative position that it is our blessing and joy, and our spiritual obligation, to bear children and to have a family. It impresses me that the positive is stressed as our goal.

I rejoice in our understanding that one of the most fundamental principles in the plan of salvation is free agency. The opportunity to make free agency choices is so important that our Heavenly Father was willing to withhold additional opportunities from a third of his children rather than deprive them of their right of choice. This principle of free agency is vital to the success of our probation. Many of the decisions we make involve the application of principles where precise yes-and-no answers are just not available in Church handbooks, meetings, or even the scriptures.

Our growth process, then, results from weighing the alternatives, studying the matter carefully, and seeking inspiration from the Lord. This, it seems to me, is at the heart of the gospel plan. It has always given me great joy and confidence to observe that in their administration of God's teachings, our inspired prophets do not seek to violate this general plan of individual agency, but operate within broad guidelines that provide considerable individual flexibility.

I recall a President of the Church, now deceased, who visited his daughter in the hospital following a miscarriage.

She was the mother of eight children and was in her early forties. She asked, "Father, may I quit now?" His response was, "Don't ask me. That decision is between you, your husband, and your Father in Heaven. If you two can face him with a good conscience and can say you have done the best you could, that you have really tried, then you may quit. But, that is between you and him. I have enough problems of my own to talk over with him when we meet!" So it is clear to me that the decisions regarding our children, when to have them, their number, and all related matters and questions can only be made after real discussion between the marriage partners and after prayer.

In this process of learning what is right for you at any particular time, I have always found it helpful to use a basic measuring stick: *Is it selfish?* I have concluded that most of our sins are really sins of selfishness. If you don't pay your tithing, selfishness is at the heart of it. If you commit adultery, selfishness is at the heart of it. If you are dishonest, selfishness is at the heart of it. I have noted that many times in the scriptures we observe the Lord chastising people because of their selfishness. Thus, on the family questions, if we limit our families because we are self-centered or materialistic, we will surely develop a character based on self-ishness. As the scriptures make clear, that is not a description of a celestial character. I have found that we really have to analyze ourselves to discover our motives. Sometimes superficial motivations and excuses show up when we do that.

But, on the other hand, we need not be afraid of studying the question from important angles—the physical or mental health of the mother and father, the parents' capacity to provide basic necessities, and so on. If for certain personal reasons a couple prayerfully decides that having another child immediately is unwise, the method of spacing children—discounting possible medical or physical effects—makes little difference. Abstinence, of course, is also a form of contraception, and like any other method it has side effects, some of which are harmful to the marriage relationship.

As a physician I am often required to treat social-emotional symptoms related to various aspects of living. In doing so I have always been impressed that our prophets past and present have never stipulated that bearing children was the sole function of the marriage relationship. Prophets have taught that physical intimacy is a strong force in strengthening the love bond in marriage, enhancing and reinforcing marital unity. Indeed, it is the rightful gift of God to the married. As the Apostle Paul says, "The wife hath not power of her own body, but the husband and likewise also the husband hath not power of his own body but the wife." Paul continues, "Depart ye not one from the other, except it be with consent for a time, that ye may give yourselves to fasting and prayer; and come together again, that Satan tempt you not for your incontinency" (I Cor. 7:45, JST). Abstinence in marriage, Paul says, can cause unnecessary temptations and tensions, which are certainly harmful side effects.

So, as to the number and spacing of children, and other related questions on this subject, such decisions are to be made by husband and wife righteously and empathetically communicating together and seeking the inspiration of the Lord. I believe that the prophets have given wise counsel when they advise couples to be considerate and plan carefully so that the mother's health will not be impaired. When this recommendation of the First Presidency is ignored or unknown or misinterpreted, heartache can result.

I know a couple who had seven children. The wife, who was afflicted with high blood pressure, had been advised by her physician that additional pregnancy was fraught with grave danger and should not be attempted. But the couple interpreted the teachings of their local priesthood leaders to mean that they should consider no contraceptive measures under any circumstances. She died from a stroke during the delivery of her eighth child.

As I meet other people and learn of their circumstances, I am continually inspired by the counsel of the First Presidency in the General Handbook of Instructions that the health of the mother and the well-being of the family should be considered. Thirty-four years as a practicing gynecologist and as an observer of Latter-day Saint families have taught me that not only the physical well-being but the emotional well-being must also be considered. Some parents are less subject to mood swings and depression and can more easily cope with the pressures of many children. Some parents have more help from their families and friends. Some are more effective parents than others, even when their desire and motivation are the same. In addition, parents do owe their children the necessities of life. The desire for luxuries, of course, would not be an appropriate determinant of family size; luxuries are just not a legitimate consideration. I think every inspired human heart can quickly determine what is a luxury and what is not.

In summary, it is clear to me that couples should not let the things that matter most be at the mercy of those that matter least. In searching for what is most important I believe that we are accountable not only for what we do but for why we do it. Thus, regarding family size, spacing of children, and attendant questions, we should desire to multiply and replenish the earth as the Lord commands us. In that process, Heavenly Father intends that we use the free agency he has given in charting a wise course for ourselves and our families. We gain the wisdom to chart that wise course through study, prayer, and listening to the still small voice within us.

The Father and the Family

Elder Boyd K. Packer

General Conference, April 1994, *Ensign*, May 1994, pp. 19-21

The family is safe within the Church. We are not in doubt as to the course we must follow. It was given in the beginning, and guidance from on high is renewed as need may be.

A family begins when a young man and woman are drawn to one another by an irresistible force of nature. They offer to one another that which distinguishes him as male and her as female, and they want, above all else, to find the one with whom they can completely express their love. They want to have children—to be a family.

These compelling forces of nature should not be resisted, only approached cautiously, protecting those life-generating powers until promises have been made to one another, covenants with the Lord, and a legal ceremony performed, witnessed, and recorded.

Then, and only then, as husband and wife, man and woman, may they join together in that expression of love through which life is created.

The ultimate purpose of every teaching, every activity in the Church is that parents and their children are happy at home, sealed in an eternal marriage, and linked to their generations.

The ultimate purpose of the adversary, who has "great wrath, because he knoweth that he hath but a short time," is to disrupt, disturb, and to destroy the home and the family. Like a ship without a rudder, without a compass, we drift from the family values which have anchored us in the past. Now we are caught in a current so strong that unless we correct our course, civilization as we know it will surely be wrecked to pieces.

Moral values are being neglected and prayer expelled from public schools on the pretext that moral teaching belongs to religion. At the same time, atheism, the secular religion, is admitted to class, and our youngsters are proselyted to a conduct without morality.

World leaders and court judges agree that the family must endure if we are to survive. At the same time, they use the words freedom and choice as tools to pry apart the safeguards of the past and loosen up the laws on marriage, abortion, and gender. In so doing, they promote the very things which threaten the family.

None of this is new. Jacob, the Book of Mormon prophet, told the people of Nephi:

> I . . . am weighed down with much more desire and anxiety for the welfare of your souls than I have hitherto been. . . .
>
> It grieveth me that I must use so much boldness of speech concerning you, before your wives and your children, many of whose feelings are exceedingly tender and chaste and delicate before God.

This crisis of the family is no surprise to the Church. We have certainly known what was coming.

I know of no better testimony that we are led by prophets than our preparation for this present emergency.

The scriptures speak of prophets as "watch[men] upon the tower" who see "the enemy while he [is] yet afar off" and who have "beheld also things which were not visible to the natural eye . . . [for] a seer hath the Lord raised up unto his people."

Thirty-three years ago the Brethren warned us of the disintegration of the family and told us to prepare. It was announced by the First Presidency and the Quorum of the Twelve Apostles that the Church would be restructured.

The weekly family home evening was introduced by the First Presidency, who said that "the home [is] the basis of a righteous life and . . . no other instrumentality can take its place nor fulfil its essential functions."

Parents are provided with excellent materials for teaching their children, with a promise that the faithful will be blessed.

While the doctrines and revealed organization remain unchanged, all agencies of the Church have been reshaped in their relationship to one another and to the home.

So sweeping were those changes that the entire curriculum of the Church was overhauled—based on scriptures, with excellent manuals for each course.

And years were spent preparing new editions of the Bible, the Book of Mormon, the Doctrine and Covenants, and the Pearl of Great Price. Except for correcting printing errors and adding three revelations to the Doctrine and Covenants, the scriptural text remains unchanged.

Cross-references and other helps were added to make the scriptures more accessible. In the Topical Guide, for instance, under the heading of "Jesus Christ" there are eighteen pages—small print, single-spaced—the most comprehensive compilation of scriptural references on the Lord that has ever been compiled in the history of the world.

The new editions of the scriptures are complete in English and Spanish, and work is now under way in dozens of languages.

We can only imagine where we would be if we were just now reacting to this terrible redefinition of the family. But that is not the case. We are not casting frantically about trying to decide what to do. We know what to do and what to teach.

The family is very much alive and well in the Church. Hundreds of thousands of happy families face life with an unwavering faith in the future.

The course we follow is not of our own making. The plan of salvation, the great plan of happiness, was revealed to us, and the prophets and Apostles continue to receive revelation as the Church and its members stand in need of more.

We, like Jacob, must teach "according to the strict commands of God," "notwithstanding the greatness of the task." Like Jacob, we also run the risk of enlarging "the wounds of those who are already wounded, instead of consoling and healing their wounds."

When we speak plainly of divorce, abuse, gender identity, contraception, abortion, parental neglect, we are thought by some to be way out of touch or to be uncaring. Some ask if we know how many we hurt when we speak plainly. Do we know of marriages in trouble, of the many who remain single, of single-parent families, of couples unable to have children, of parents with wayward children, or of those confused about gender? Do we know? Do we care?

Those who ask have no idea how much we care; you know little of the sleepless nights, of the endless hours of work, of prayer, of study, of travel—all for the happiness and redemption of mankind.

Because we do know and because we do care, we must teach the rules of happiness without dilution, apology, or avoidance. That is our calling.

I once learned a valuable lesson from a mission Relief Society president. In a conference, she announced some tightening up of procedures. A sister stood up and defiantly said, "Those rules can't apply to us! You don't understand us! We are an exception."

That wonderful Relief Society president replied, "Dear sister, we'd like not to take care of the exception first. We will establish the rule first, and then we'll see to the exception." Many times I have borrowed from her wisdom, grateful for what she taught me.

Now, following the example of Jacob, I speak to the men of the Church. Most of you are worthy fathers and husbands who do what you should do. But there are women whose hearts have been broken and children who are neglected, even abused.

If we are to help them, we must begin with the men. The next series of stake and regional conferences will be devoted to teaching the doctrines and principles of responsible and worthy manhood.

Some of you had no worthy example to follow and now visit the abuse or neglect of your own parents upon your wife and children.

Brethren, do you understand that we emphasize the teaching of the scriptures because they are the constant? From them we learn the purposes of life, the gifts of the Spirit. From them we learn about personal revelation, how to discern good from evil, truth from error. The scriptures provide the pattern and the basis for correct doctrine.

From doctrine, we learn principles of conduct, how to respond to problems of everyday living, even to failures, for they, too, are provided for in the doctrines.

If you understand the great plan of happiness and follow it, what goes on in the world will not determine your happiness. You will be tried, for that is part of the plan, but "thine afflictions shall be but a small moment; and then, if thou endure it well, God shall exalt thee on high."

Your responsibility as a father and a husband transcends any other interest in life. It is unthinkable that a Latter-day Saint man would cheat on his wife or abandon the children he has fathered, or neglect or abuse them.

The Lord has "commanded you to bring up your children in light and truth."

You are responsible, unless disabled, to provide temporal support for your wife and children. You are to devote, even sacrifice yourself, to the bringing up of your children in light and truth.

That requires perfect moral fidelity to your wife, with no reason ever for her to doubt your faithfulness.

Never should there be a domineering or unworthy behavior in the tender, intimate relationship between husband and wife.

Your wife is your partner in the leadership of the family and should have full knowledge of and full participation in all decisions relating to your home.

Lead your family to the Church, to the covenants and ordinances. We are trying to reduce the length and number of meetings and activities outside of the home.

I cannot express the depth of my devotion to my wife and children, their companions, and their children. I have learned more by far from them than they from me. That learning comes in ordinary experiences, the joy and the pain of everyday life.

I learned from a little boy the identity and value of a human soul. Some years ago, two of our little boys were wrestling on the rug. They had reached that pitch where laughter turns to tears. I worked a foot gently between them and lifted the older boy (then just four) to a sitting position on the rug, saying, "Hey, there, you monkeys, you'd better settle down."

He folded his little arms and looked at me with surprising seriousness. His little boy feelings had been hurt, and he protested, "I not a monkey, Daddy, I a person."

I was overwhelmed with love for him. I realized he was a child of God. How much I wanted him to be "a person"—one of eternal worth. From such ordinary experiences, I have learned to understand doctrine. "Children," truly, "are an heritage of the Lord."

The family is safe within the Church. We are not in doubt as to the course we must follow. It was given in the beginning, and guidance from on high is renewed as need may be.

As we continue on our course, these things will follow as night the day:

The distance between the Church and a world set on a course which we cannot follow will steadily increase.

Some will fall away into apostasy, break their covenants, and replace the plan of redemption with their own rules.

Across the world, those who now come by the tens of thousands will inevitably come as a flood to where the family is safe. Here they will worship the Father in the name of Christ, by the gift of the Holy

251

Ghost, and know that the gospel is the great plan of happiness, of redemption, of which I bear witness in the name of Jesus Christ, amen.

Notes

1. Rev. 12:12.
2. Jacob 2:3, 7; see vs. 1-13.
3. D&C 101:54; see vs. 45, 53-54; 2 Kgs. 9:17.
4. Moses 6:36; see also Mosiah 8:15-17.
5. In Conference Report, 6 Oct. 1961, p. 79; Improvement Era, Jan. 1962, p. 36.
6. See "Message from the First Presidency," Family Home Evening Resource Book, Salt Lake City: The Church of Jesus Christ of Latter-day Saints, 1983, p. iv.
7. Jacob 2:9-10.
8. See Jacob 2:35.
9. D&C 121:7-8.
10. D&C 93:40; see vs. 36-40.
11. See D&C 83:2.
12. See D&C 93:40.
13. See D&C 121:41-43.
14. Ps. 127:3.

Families and Fences

Elder Boyd K. Packer

Conference Report, October 1970, pp. 118-22

I come to this pulpit this Sabbath morning with a new obligation, anxious perhaps as never before for the sustaining influence of the Spirit of the Lord, for an interest in your faith and prayers for us here and for those who shall be listening, as I speak to the parents of wayward and lost children.

Sometime ago, a father, worried about a serious problem with his son, was heard to remark, "When he leaves and we don't know where he is, there's pain in our hearts, but when he's here there are times when he's a pain in the neck." It's about that pain in the heart that I want to speak. I speak to a very large audience, I fear.

Hardly is there a neighborhood without at least one mother whose last waking, anxious thoughts and prayers are for a son or a daughter wandering who knows where. Nor is there much distance between homes where an anxious father can hardly put in a day's work without being drawn within himself time after time, to wonder, "What have we done wrong? What can we do to get our child back?"

Even parents with the best intentions—some who have really tried—now know that heartache. Many parents have tried in every way to protect their children—only now to find they are losing one. For the home and the family are under attack. Ponder these words, if you will:

Profanity Nudity Immorality Divorce Pornography Addiction Violence Perversion. These words have taken on a new meaning in the last few years, haven't they?

You are within walking distance, at least within a few minutes' drive, of a theater in your own neighborhood. There will be shown, within the week, a film open to young and old alike that as recently as ten years ago would have been banned, the film confiscated, and the theater owner placed under indictment. But now it's there, and soon it will be seen at home on your television screens.

The apostle Paul prophesied to Timothy:

> This know also, that in the last days perilous times shall come.
> For men shall be lovers of their own selves, covetous, boasters, proud, blasphemers, disobedient to parents. . . (2 Tim. 3:12).

There is more to that scripture, but we stop on that phrase "disobedient to parents."

We have no desire to touch the subject that causes you so much pain, nor to condemn you as a failure. But you are failing, and that's what makes it hurt. If failure is to end, one must face squarely problems like this, however much it hurts.

A few years ago I was called in the wee hours of the morning to the side of my ailing mother, who was hospitalized for a series of tests.

"I'm going home," she said. "I'll not continue with these tests. I want you to take me home right now. I won't go through another day of this."

"But mother," I said, "you must go through with this. They have reason to believe that you have cancer, and if it is as they suppose, you have the worst kind."

There! It had been said. After all the evading, all the whispered conversations. After all the care never to say that word when she was around. It was out!

She sat quietly on her bed for a long time and then said, "Well, if that's what it is, that's what it is, and I'll fight it." Her Danish dander was up. And fight it she did, and winner she was.

Some may suppose she lost her battle to that disease, but she came away a glorious, successful winner. Her victory was assured when she faced the painful truth. Her courage began then.

Parents, can we first consider the most painful part of your problem? If you want to reclaim your son or daughter, why don't you leave off trying to alter your child just for a little while and concentrate on rolling. The changes must begin with you, not with your children.

You can't continue to do what you have been doing (even though you thought it was right) and expect to unproduce some behavior in your child, when your conduct was one of the things that produced it.

There! It's been said! After all the evading, all the concern for wayward children. After all the blaming of others, the care to be gentle with parents. It's out!

It's you, not the child, that needs immediate attention.

Now parents, there is substantial help for you if you will accept it. I add with emphasis that the help we propose is not easy, for the measures are equal to the seriousness of your problem. There is no patent medicine to effect an immediate cure.

And parents, if you seek for a cure that ignores faith and religious doctrine, you look for a cure where it never will be found. When we talk of religious principles and doctrines and quote scripture, interesting, isn't it, how many don't feel comfortable with talk like that. But when we talk about your problems with your family and offer a solution, then your interest is intense.

Know that you can't talk about one without talking about the other, and expect to solve your problems. Once parents know that there is a God and that we are his children, they can face problems like this and win.

If you are helpless, he is not.

If you are lost, he is not.

If you don't know what to do next, he knows.

It would take a miracle, you say? Well, if it takes a miracle, why not.

We urge you to move first on a course of prevention.

There is a poem entitled "The Fence or the Ambulance." It tells of efforts to provide an ambulance at the bottom of a cliff and concludes with these two verses:

> Then an old sage remarked: It's a marvel to me That people give far more attention To repairing results than to stopping the cause When they'd much better aim at prevention. Let us stop at its source all this mischief, cried he, Come neighbors and friends, let us rally; If the cliff we will fence, we might almost dispense With the ambulance down in the valley. Better guide well the young than reclaim them when old, For the voice of true wisdom is calling: 'To rescue the fallen is good, but 'tis best To prevent other people from falling.' Better close up the source of temptation and crime, Than deliver from dungeon or galley; Better put a strong fence round the top of the cliff, Than an ambulance down in the valley.
>
> —Joseph Malins

We prevent physical disease by immunization. This heart pain you are suffering perhaps might likewise have been prevented with very simple measures at one time. Fortunately the very steps necessary for prevention are the ones that will produce the healing. In other words, prevention is the best cure, even in advanced cases.

Now I would like to show you a very practical and a very powerful place to begin, both to protect your children and, in the case of one you are losing, to redeem him.

I have in my hands the publication Family Home Evenings. It is the seventh in a series and is available across the world in 17 languages. If you would go through it with me, you would find that this one is based on the New Testament. The theme is free agency. While it draws lessons from New Testament days, it does not content itself with them back then and there. It leaps across the centuries and concerns itself with you, and here and now.

It is well illustrated, much of it in full color, and has many meaningful activities for families with children of any age.

Here, for instance, is a crossword puzzle. And here on this colorful page is a game. Cut it out and make a spinner of cardboard, and the whole family can play. You'll find yourselves, depending on the moves you make, somewhere between "Heavenly Treasures" and "Earthly Pleasures."

Here is a lesson entitled "How Our Family Came to Be." ". . . Tell your children, it suggests, how you met, fell in love, and married. Be sure both parents participate, and illustrate your story with pictures and mementoes you have saved—the wedding dress, the announcements, wedding pictures. It might be a good idea to tape your narrative and keep it for your children to play to their children some day."

Let me list some of the other titles: "Our Family Government," "Learning to Worship," "Speaking Words of Purity," "Family Finances," "Parenthood, a Sacred Opportunity," "Respect for Authority," "The Value of Humor," "So You're Going to Move," "When the Unexpected Happens," "The Birth and Infancy of the Savior."

Here is one entitled "A Call to Be Free." That's the siren call your child is following, you know. This lesson includes a page of very official-looking colored certificates with instructions to "choose for each family member some activity he has not learned to do; then give each member a certificate . . . signed by the father: 'This certificate gives the owner permission to play a tune on the piano as a part of family home evening.'" (Of course, the child has never had piano lessons).

Other certificates may include (depending on the age of the child) "walking on one's hands, speaking in a foreign language, or painting an oil portrait." Then as each member says he cannot do the thing permitted, talk about why he is not free to do the thing he is permitted to do. The discussion will reveal that "each person must learn the laws that govern the development of an ability and then learn to obey those laws. Thus obedience leads to freedom."

Here, under special helps for families with small children, it suggests they put toy cars on the table top and feel free to run them anywhere they want and in any manner they like. Even little minds can see the results of this.

There is much more to this lesson and to all of these special lessons—subtle, powerful magnets that help to draw your child closer to the family circle.

I This program is designed for a family meeting to be held once a week. In the Church, Monday night has been designated and set aside, Churchwide, for families to be at home together. Instruction has recently gone out, from which I quote:

> Those responsible for priesthood and auxiliary programs, including temple activities, youth athletic activities, student activities, etc., should take notice of this decision in order that Monday night will be uniformly observed throughout the Church and the families be left free from Church activities so that they can meet together in the family home evening (Priesthood bulletin, September 1970).

With this program comes the promise from the prophets, the living prophets, that if parents will gather their children about them once a week and teach the gospel, those children in such families will not go astray.

Some of you outside the Church, and unfortunately many within, hope that you could take a manual like this without accepting fully the gospel of Jesus Christ, the responsibilities of Church membership, and the scriptures upon which it is based. You are permitted to do that (We could even give you a "certificate" to permit you to raise an ideal family). You still would not be free to do so without obeying the laws. To take a program like this without the gospel would have you act as one who obtained a needle to immunize a child against a fatal disease but rejected the serum to go in it that could save him.

Parents, it is past time for you to assume spiritual leadership of your family. If there is no substance to your present belief, then have the courage to seek the truth.

There is, living now, the finest generation of youth that ever walked the earth. You have seen some of them serving on missions. Perhaps you have turned them away. You ought to seek them out. If they are nothing else, they are adequate evidence that youth can live in honor. And there are tens of thousands of them who are literal saints—Latter-day Saints.

Now parents, I desire to inspire you with hope. You who have heartache, you must never give up. No matter how dark it gets or no matter how far away or how far down your son or daughter has fallen, you must never give up. Never, never, never. I desire to inspire you with hope.

> Soft as the voice of an angel, whispering a message unheard, Hope with a gentle persuasion whispers her comforting word. Wait till the darkness is over, wait till the coming of dawn, Hope for the sunshine tomorrow, after the shower is gone. Whispering hope, Oh how welcome thy voice. . . .

God bless you heartbroken parents. There is no pain so piercing as that caused by the loss of a child, nor joy so exquisite as the joy at his redemption.

I come to you now as one of the Twelve, each ordained as a special witness. I affirm to you that I have that witness. I know that God lives, that Jesus is the Christ. I know that though the world "seeth him not, neither knoweth him," that he lives. Heartbroken parents, lay claim upon his promise: "I will not leave you comfortless; I will come to you" (John 14:17-18). In the name of Jesus Christ. Amen.

To the Fathers in Israel

An Address Given by **President Ezra Taft Benson**

in the Priesthood Session of General Conference on 3 October 1987
Ensign, November 1987, pp. 48-51

My dear brethren, I am grateful to be here with you in this glorious assembly of the priesthood of God. I pray that the Spirit of the Lord will be with me and with you as I address you on a most vital subject. This evening I would like to speak to the fathers assembled here and throughout the Church about their sacred callings.

I hope you young men will also listen carefully, inasmuch as you are now preparing to become the future fathers of the Church.

Fathers, yours is an eternal calling from which you are never released. Callings in the Church, as important as they are, by their very nature are only for a period of time, and then an appropriate release takes place. But a father's calling is eternal, and its importance transcends time. It is a calling for both time and eternity.

President Harold B. Lee truly stated that "the most important of the Lord's work that you [fathers] will ever do will be the work you do within the walls of your own home. Home teaching, bishopric's work, and other Church duties are all important, but the most important work is within the walls of your home" (*Strengthening the Home*, [pamphlet, 1973], p. 7).

What, then, is a father's specific responsibility within the sacred walls of his home? May I suggest two basic responsibilities of every father in Israel.

Providing for Material Needs

First, you have a sacred responsibility to provide for the material needs of your family.

The Lord clearly defined the roles of providing for and rearing a righteous posterity. In the beginning, Adam, not Eve, was instructed to earn the bread by the sweat of his brow.

The Apostle Paul counsels husbands and fathers, "But if any provide not for his own, and specially for those of his own house, he hath denied the faith, and is worse than an infidel" (1 Timothy 5:8).

Early in the history of the restored Church, the Lord specifically charged men with the obligation to provide for their wives and family. In January of 1832 He said, "Verily I say unto you, that every man who is obliged to provide for his own family, let him provide, and he shall in nowise lose his crown" (D&C 75:28). Three months later the Lord said again, "Women have claim on their husbands for their maintenance, until their husbands are taken" (D&C 83:2). This is the divine right of a wife and mother. While she cares for and nourishes her children at home, her husband earns the living for the family, which makes this nourishing possible.

In a home where there is an able-bodied husband, he is expected to be the breadwinner. Sometimes we hear of husbands who, because of economic conditions, have lost their jobs and expect the wives to go out of the home and work, even though the husband is still capable of providing for his family. In these cases, we urge the husband to do all in his power to allow his wife to remain in the home caring for the children while he continues to provide for his family the best he can, even though the job he is able to secure may not be ideal and family budgeting may have to be tighter.

Also, the need for education or material things does not justify the postponing of children in order to keep the wife working as the breadwinner of the family.

Counsel of President Kimball

I remember the counsel of our beloved prophet Spencer W. Kimball to married students. He said: "I have told tens of thousands of young folks that when they marry they should not wait for children until they have finished their schooling and financial desires. . . . They should live together normally and let the children come. . . .

"I know of no scriptures," President Kimball continued, "where an authorization is given to young wives to withhold their families and go to work to put their husbands through school. There are thousands of husbands who have worked their own way through school and have reared families at the same time" ("Marriage Is Honorable," in *Speeches of the Year,* 1973, [Provo: Brigham Young University , 1974], p. 263).

A Mother's Role in the Home

Brethren of the priesthood, I continue to emphasize the importance of mothers staying home to nurture, care for, and train their children in the principles of righteousness.

As I travel throughout the Church, I feel that the great majority of Latter-day Saint mothers earnestly want to follow this counsel. But we know that sometimes the mother works outside of the home at the encouragement, or even insistence, of her husband. It is he who wants the items of convenience that the extra income can buy. Not only will the family suffer in such instances, brethren, but your own spiritual growth and progression will be hampered. I say to all of you, the Lord has charged men with the responsibility to provide for their families in such a way that the wife is allowed to fulfill her role as mother in the home.

Family Preparedness More Urgent Today

Fathers, another vital aspect of providing for the material needs of your family is the provision you should be making for your family in case of an emergency. Family preparedness has been a long-established welfare principle. It is even more urgent today. I ask you earnestly, have you provided for your family a year's supply of food, clothing, and, where possible, fuel? The revelation to produce and store food may be as essential to our temporal welfare today as boarding the ark was to the people in the days of Noah.

Also, are you living within your income and saving a little?

Are you honest with the Lord in the payment of your tithes? Living this divine law will bring both spiritual and material blessings.

Yes, brethren, as fathers in Israel you have a great responsibility to provide for the material needs of your family and to have the necessary provisions in case of emergency.

Providing Spiritual Leadership

Second, you have a sacred responsibility to provide spiritual leadership in your family.

In a pamphlet published some years ago by the Council of the Twelve, we said the following: "Fatherhood is leadership, the most important kind of leadership. It has always been so; it always will be so. Father, with the assistance and counsel and encouragement of your eternal companion, you preside in the home" (*Father, Consider Your Ways* [pamphlet, 1973], pp. 4-5).

However, along with that presiding position come important obligations. We sometimes hear accounts of men, even in the Church, who think that being head of the home somehow puts them in a superior role and allows them to dictate and make demands upon their family.

The Apostle Paul points out that "the husband is the head of the wife, *even as* Christ is the head of the church" (Ephesians 5:23; italics added). That is the model we are to follow in our role of presiding in the home. We do not find the Savior leading the Church with a harsh or unkind hand. We do not find the Savior treating His Church with disrespect or neglect. We do not find the Savior using force or coercion to accomplish His purposes. Nowhere do we find the Savior doing anything but that which edifies, uplifts, comforts, and exalts the Church. Brethren, I say to you with all soberness, He is the model we must follow as we take the spiritual lead in our families. Particularly is this true in your relationship with your wife.

Love Your wives

Here again the counsel from the Apostle Paul is most beautiful and to the point. He said simply, "Husbands, love your wives, even as Christ also loved the church" (Ephesians 5:25).

In latter-day revelation the Lord speaks again of this obligation. He said, "Thou shalt love thy wife with all thy heart, and shalt cleave unto her and none else" (D&C 42:22). To my knowledge there is only one other thing in all scripture that we are commanded to love with all our hearts, and that is God Himself. Think what that means!

This kind of love can be shown for your wives in so many ways. First and foremost, nothing except God Himself takes priority over your wife in your life—not work, not recreation, not hobbies. Your wife is your precious, eternal helpmate—your companion.

What does it mean to love someone with all your heart? It means to love with all your emotional feelings and with all your devotion. Surely when you love your wife with all your heart, you cannot demean her, criticize her, find fault with her, or abuse her by words, sullen behavior, or actions.

What does it mean to "cleave unto her"? It means to stay close to her, to be loyal and faithful to her, to communicate with her, and to express your love for her.

Love means being sensitive to her feelings and needs. She wants to be noticed and treasured. She wants to be told that you view her as lovely and attractive and important to you. Love means putting her welfare and self-esteem as a high priority in your life.

You should be grateful that she is the mother of your children and the queen of your home, grateful that she has chosen homemaking and motherhood—to bear, to nourish, to love, and to train your children—as the noblest calling of all.

Husbands, recognize your wife's intelligence and her ability to counsel with you as a real partner regarding family plans, family activities, and family budgeting. Don't be stingy with your time or with your means. Give her the opportunity to grow intellectually, emotionally, and socially as well as spiritually.

Remember, brethren, love can be nurtured and nourished by little tokens. Flowers on special occasions are wonderful, but so is your willingness to help with the dishes, change diapers, get up with a crying child in the night, and leave the television or the newspaper to help with the dinner. Those are the quiet ways we say "I love you" with our actions. They bring rich dividends for such little effort.

This kind of loving priesthood leadership applies to your children as well as to your wife.

A Father's role in the Home

Mothers play an important role as the heart of the home, but this in no way lessens the equally important role fathers should play, as head of the home, in nurturing, training, and loving their children.

As the patriarch in your home, you have a serious responsibility to assume leadership in working with your children. You must help create a home where the Spirit of the Lord can abide. Your place is to give direction to all family life. You should take an active part in establishing family rules and discipline.

259

Your homes should be havens of peace and joy for your family. Surely no child should fear his own father—especially a priesthood father. A father's duty is to make his home a place of happiness and joy. He cannot do this when there is bickering, quarreling, contention, or unrighteous behavior. The powerful effect of righteous fathers in setting an example, disciplining and training, nurturing and loving is vital to the spiritual welfare of his children.

Ten Ways to Give Spiritual Leadership

With love in my heart for the fathers in Israel, may I suggest ten specific ways that fathers can give spiritual leadership to their children:

1. Give father's blessings to your children. Baptize and confirm your children. Ordain your sons to the priesthood. These will become spiritual highlights in the lives of your children.

2. Personally direct family prayers, daily scripture reading, and weekly family home evenings. Your personal involvement will show your children how important these activities really are.

3. Whenever possible, attend Church meetings together as a family. Family worship under your leadership is vital to your children's spiritual welfare.

4. Go on daddy-daughter dates and father-and-sons' outings with your children. As a family, go on campouts and picnics, to ball games and recitals, to school programs, and so forth. Having Dad there makes all the difference.

5. Build traditions of family vacations and trips and outings. These memories will never be forgotten by your children.

6. Have regular one-on-one visits with your children. Let them talk about what they would like to. Teach them gospel principles. Teach them true values. Tell them you love them. Personal time with your children tells them where Dad puts his priorities.

7. Teach your children to work, and show them the value of working toward a worthy goal. Establishing mission funds and education funds for your children shows them what Dad considers to be important.

8. Encourage good music and art and literature in your homes. Homes that have a spirit of refinement and beauty will bless the lives of your children forever.

9. As distances allow, regularly attend the temple with your wife. Your children will then better understand the importance of temple marriage and temple vows and the eternal family unit.

10. Have your children see your joy and satisfaction in service to the Church. This can become contagious to them, so they, too, will want to serve in the Church and will love the kingdom.

Your Most Important Calling

Oh, husbands and fathers in Israel, you can do so much for the salvation and exaltation of your families! Your responsibilities are so important.

Remember your sacred calling as a father in Israel—your most important calling in time and eternity—a calling from which you will never be released.

May you always provide for the material needs of your family and, with your eternal companion at your side, may you fulfil your sacred responsibility to provide the spiritual leadership in your home.

To this end I pray, in the name of Jesus Christ, amen.

To the Mothers in Zion

An Address Given at a Fireside for Parents by **President Ezra Taft Benson**

of The Church of Jesus Christ of Latter-day Saints on 22 February 1987

I rejoice in the opportunity of being with you this evening.

I have been touched by the beautiful music and the splendid instructions we have received.

There is no theme I would rather speak to than home and family, for they are at the very heart of the gospel of Jesus Christ. The Church, in large part, exists for the salvation and exaltation of the family.

Tonight, at this fireside for parents, seeking the sweet inspiration of heaven I would like to speak directly to the mothers assembled here and throughout the Church, for you are, or should be, the very heart and soul of the family.

No More Noble Work

No more sacred word exists in secular or holy writ than that of mother. There is no more noble work than that of a good and God-fearing mother.

This evening I pay tribute to the mothers in Zion and pray with all my heart that what I have to say to you will be understood by the Spirit and will lift and bless your lives in your sacred callings as mothers.

President David O. McKay declared: "Motherhood is the greatest potential influence either for good or ill in human life. The mother's image is the first that stamps itself on the unwritten page of the young child's mind. It is her caress that first awakens a sense of security; her kiss, the first realization of affection; her sympathy and tenderness, the first assurance that there is love in the world" (*Gospel Ideals* [Salt Lake City: The Improvement Era, 1953], p. 452).

President McKay continues: 'Motherhood consists of three principal attributes or qualities: namely, (1) the power to bear, (2) the ability to rear, (3) the gift to love. . . .

This ability and willingness properly to rear children, the gift to love, and eagerness, yes, longing to express it in soul development, make motherhood the noblest office or calling in the world. She who can paint a masterpiece or write a book that will influence millions deserves the admiration and the plaudits of mankind; but she who rears successfully a family of healthy, beautiful sons and daughters, whose influence will be felt through generations to come, . . . deserves the highest honor that man can give, and the choicest blessings of God" (*Gospel Ideals*, pp. 453-54).

With all my heart I endorse the words of President McKay.

A Mother's Role Is God-ordained

In the eternal family, God established that fathers are to preside in the home. Fathers are to provide, to love, to teach, and to direct.

But a mother's role is also God-ordained. Mothers are to conceive, to bear, to nourish, to love, and to train. So declare the revelations.

In section 132 of the Doctrine and Covenants the Lord states that the opportunity and responsibility of wives is "to multiply and replenish the earth, according to my commandment, and to fulfil the promise which was given by my Father before the foundation of the world, and for their exaltation in the eternal worlds, that they may bear the souls of men; for herein is the work of my Father continued that he may be glorified" (D&C 132:63).

Husbands and Wives Are Co-creators

With this divine injunction, husbands and wives, as co-creators, should eagerly and prayerfully invite children into their homes. Then, as each child joins their family circle, they can gratefully exclaim, as did Hannah, "For this child I prayed; and the Lord hath given me my petition which I asked of him: Therefore also I have lent him to the Lord; as long as he liveth he shall be lent to the Lord" (1 Sam. 1:27-28).

Isn't that beautiful? A mother praying to bear a child and then giving him to the Lord.

I have always loved the words of Solomon: "Children are an heritage of the Lord and . . . happy is the man [and woman] that hath [their] quiver full of them" (Psalm 127:3-5).

I know of the special blessings of a large and happy family, for my dear parents had a quiver full of children. Being the oldest of eleven childrm I saw the principles of unselfishness, mutual consideration, loyalty to each other, and a host of other virtues developed in a large and wonderful family with my noble mother as the queen of that home.

Young mothers and fathers, with all my heart I counsel you not to postpone having your children, being co-creators with our Father in Heaven.

Do not use the reasoning of the world, such as, "We'll wait until we can better afford having children, until we are more secure, until John has completed his education, until he has a better-paying job, until we have a larger home, until we've obtained a few of the material conveniences," and on and on.

This is the reasoning of the world, and is not pleasing in the sight of God. Mothers who enjoy good health, have your children and have them early. And, husbands, always be considerate of your wives in the bearing of children.

Do not curtail the number of your children for personal or selfish reasons. Material possessions, social convenience, and so-called professional advantages are nothing compared to a righteous posterity. In the eternal perspective, children—not possessions, not position, not prestige—are our greatest jewels.

Brigham Young emphasized: "There are multitudes of pure and holy spirits waiting to take tabernacles, now what is our duty?—To prepare tabernacles for them; to take a course that will not tend to drive those spirits into the families of the wicked, where they will be trained in wickedness, debauchery, and every species of crime. It is the duty of every righteous man and woman to prepare tabernacles for all the spirits they can" (*Discourses of Brigham Young*, sel. John A. Widtsoe [Salt Lake City: Deseret Book Co., 1954], p. 197).

Yes, blessed is the husband and wife who have a family of children. The deepest joys and blessings in life are associated with family, parenthood, and sacrifice. To have those sweet spirits come into the home is worth practically any sacrifice.

Special Promises of God

We realize that some women, through no fault of their own, are not able to bear children. To these lovely sisters, every prophet of God has promised that they will be blessed with children in the eternities and that posterity will not be denied them.

Through pure faith, pleading prayers, fasting, and special priesthood blessings, many of these same lovely sisters, with their noble companions at their sides, have had miracles take place in their lives and have been blessed with children. Others have prayerfully chosen to adopt children, and to these wonderful couples we salute you for the sacrifices and love you have given to those children you have chosen to be your own.

Rearing Children the Lord's Way

Now, my dear mothers, knowing of your divine role to bear and rear children and bring them back to Him, how will you accomplish this in the Lord's way? I say the "Lord's way," because it is different from the world's way.

The Lord clearly defined the roles of mothers and fathers in providing for and rearing a righteous posterity. In the beginning, Adam—not Eve—was instructed to earn the bread by the sweat of his brow. Contrary to conventional wisdom, a mother's calling is in the home, not in the marketplace.

Again, in the Doctrine and Covenants, we read: "Women have claim on their husbands for their maintenance, until their husbands are taken" (D&C 83:2). This is the divine right of a wife and mother. She cares for and nourishes her children at home. Her husband earns the living for the family, which makes this nourishing possible. With that claim on their husbands for their financial support, the counsel of the Church has always been for mothers to spend their full time in the home in rearing and caring for their children.

We realize also that some of our choice sisters are widowed and divorced and that others find themselves in unusual circumstances where, out of necessity, they are required to work for a period of time. But these instances are the exception, not the rule.

In a home where there is an able-bodied husband, he is expected to be the breadwinner. Sometimes we hear of husbands who, because of economic conditions, have lost their jobs and expect their wives to go out of the home and work even though the husband is still capable of providing for his family. In these cases we urge the husband to do all in his power to allow his wife to remain in the home caring for the children while he continues to provide for his family the best he can, even though the job he is able to secure may not be ideal and family budgeting will have to be tighter.

Counsel of President Kimball

Our beloved prophet Spencer W. Kimball had much to say about the role of mothers in the home and their and callings and responsibilities. I am impressed tonight to share with you some of his inspired pronouncements. I fear that much of his counsel has gone unheeded, and families have suffered because of it. But I stand this evening as a second witness to the truthfulness of what President Spencer W. Kimball said. He spoke as a true prophet of God.

President Kimball declared: "Women are to take care of the family—the Lord has so stated—to be an assistant to the husband, to work with him, but not to earn the living, except in unusual circumstances. Men ought to be men indeed and earn the living under normal circumstances" (*Teachings of Spencer W. Kimball*, ed. Edward L. Kimball [Salt Lake City: Bookcraft, 1982], p. 318).

President Kimball continues: "Too many mothers work away from home to furnish sweaters and music lessons and trips and fun for their children. Too many women spend their time in socializing, in politicking, in public services when they should be home to teach and train and receive and love their children into security" (*Teachings of Spencer W. Kimball*, p. 319).

Remember the counsel of President Kimball to John and Mary—"Mary, you are to become a career woman in the greatest career on earth—that of homemaker, wife, and mother. It was never intended by the Lord that married women should compete with men in employment. They have a far greater and more important service to render (*Faith Precedes the Miracle* [Salt Lake City: Deseret Book Co., 1975], p. 128).

Again President Kimball speaks: The husband is expected to support his family and only in an emergency should a wife secure outside employment. Her place is in the home, to build the home into a heaven of delight.

"Numerous divorces can be traced directly to the day when the wife left the home and went out into the world into employment. Two incomes raise the standard of living beyond its norm. Two spouses working prevent the complete and proper home life, break into the family prayers, create an independence which is not cooperative, causes distortion, limits the family, and frustrates the children already born" (Fireside address, San Antonio, Texas, 3 Dec. 1977).

Finally, President Kimball counsels: "I beg of you, you who could and should he bearing and rearing a family, wives, come home from the typewriter, the laundry, the nursing, come home from the factory, the cafe. No career approaches in importance that of wife, homemaker, mother—cooking meals, washing dishes, making beds for one's precious husband and children. Come home, wives, to your husbands. Make home a heaven for them. Come home, wives, to your children, born and unborn. Wrap the motherly cloak about you and, unembarrassed, help in a major role to create the bodies for the immortal souls who anxiously await.

"When you have fully complemented your husband in home life and borne the children, growing up full of faith, integrity, responsibility, and goodness, then you have achieved your accomplishment supreme, without peer, and you will be the envy [of all] through time and eternity" (Fireside address, San Antonio, Texas).

President Kimball spoke the truth. His words are prophetic.

Ten Ways to Spend Time with Children

Mothers in Zion, your God-given roles are so vital to your own exaltation and to the salvation and exaltation of your family. A child needs a mother more than all the things money can buy. Spending time with your children is the greatest gift of all.

With love in my heart for the mothers in Zion, I would now like to suggest ten specific ways our mothers may spend effective time with their children.

Be at the Crossroads. First, take time to always be at the crossroads when your children are either coming or going—when they leave and return from school, when they leave and return from dates, when they bring friends home. Be there at the crossroads whether your children are six or sixteen. In Proverbs we read, "A child left to himself bringeth his mother to shame" (Proverbs 29:15). Among the greatest concerns in our society are the millions of latchkey children who come home daily to empty houses, unsupervised by working parents.

Be a Real Friend. Second, mothers, take time to be a real friend to your children. Listen to your children, really listen. Talk with them, laugh and joke with them, play with them, cry with them, hug them, honestly praise them. Yes, regularly spend unrushed one-on-one time with each child. Be a real friend to your children.

Read to Your Children. Third, mothers, take time to read to your children. Starting from the cradle, read to your sons and daughters. Remember what the poet said:

You may have tangible wealth untold;
Caskets of jewels and coffers of gold.
Richer than I you can never be—
I had a mother who read to me.   (Strickland Gillilan, "The Reading Mother.")

You will plant a love for good literature and a real love for the scriptures if you will read to your children regularly.

Pray with Your Children. Fourth, take time to pray with your children. Family prayers, under the direction of the father, should be held morning and night. Have your children feel of your faith as you call down the blessings of heaven upon them. Paraphrasing the words of James, "The . . . fervent prayer of a righteous [mother] availeth much" (James 5:16). Have your children participate in family and personal prayers, and rejoice in their sweet utterances to their Father in Heaven.

Have Weekly Home Evening. Fifth, take time to have a meaningful weekly home evening. With your husband presiding, participate in a spiritual and an uplifting home evening each week. Have your children actively involved. Teach them correct principles. Make this one of your great family traditions. Remember the marvelous promise made by President Joseph F. Smith when home evenings were first introduced to the Church: "If the Saints obey this counsel we promise that great blessings will result. Love at home and obedience to parents will increase. Faith will be developed in the hearts of the youth of IsraeL and they will gain power to combat the evil influence and temptations which beset them" (James R. Clark, comp., *Messages of the First Presidency of The Church of Jesus Christ of Latter-day Saints*, 6 vols. [Salt Lake City Bookcraft, 1965-75], 4:339). This wonderful promise is still in effect today.

Be Together at Mealtimes. Sixth, take time to be together at mealtimes as often as possible. This is a challenge as the children get older and lives get busier. But happy conversation, sharing of the day's plans and activities, and special teaching moments occur at mealtime because mothers and fathers and children work at it.

Read Scriptures Daily. Seventh, take time daily to read the scriptures together as a family. Individual scripture reading is important, but family scripture reading is vital. Reading the Book of Mormon together as a family will especially bring increased spirituality into your home and will give both parents and children the power to resist temptation and to have the Holy Ghost as their constant companion. I promise you that the Book of Mormon will change the lives of your family.

Do Things as a Family. Eighth, take time to do things together as a family. Make family outings and picnics and birthday celebrations and trips special times and memory builders. Whenever possible, attend, as a family, events where one of the family members is involved, such as a school play, a ball game, a talk, a recital. Attend church meetings together and sit together as a family when you can. Mothers who help families pray and play together will stay together and will bless children's lives forever.

Teach Your Children. Ninth, mothers, take time to teach your children. Catch the teaching moments. This can be done anytime during the day—at mealtime, in casual settings, or at special sit-down times together, at the foot of the bed at the end of the day, or during an early morning walk together. Mothers, you are your children's best teacher. Don't shift this precious responsibility to day-care centers or baby-sitters. A mother's love and prayerful concern for her children are her most important ingredients in teaching her own.

Teach children gospel principles. Teach them it pays to be good. Teach them there is no safety in sin. Teach them a love for the gospel of Jesus Christ and a testimony of its divinity.

Teach your sons and daughters modesty, and teach them to respect manhood and womanhood. Teach your children sexual purity, proper dating standards, temple marriage, missionary service, and the importance of accepting and magnifying Church callings.

Teach them a love for work and the value of a good education.

Teach them the importance of the right kind of entertainment, including appropriate movies and videos and music and books and magazines. Discuss the evils of pornography and drugs, and teach them the value of living the clean life.

Yes, mothers, teach your children the gospel in your own home, at your own fireside. This is the most effective teaching that your children will ever receive. This is the Lord's way of teaching. The Church cannot teach like you can. The school cannot. The day-care center cannot. But you can, and the Lord will sustain you. Your children will remember your teachings forever, and when they are old, they will not depart from them. They will call you blessed—their truly angel mother.

Mothers, this kind of heavenly, motherly teaching takes time—lots of time. It cannot be done effectively part-time. It must be done all the time in order to save and exalt your children. This is your divine calling.

Truly Love Your Children. Tenth and finally, mothers, take the time to truly love your children. A mother's unqualified love approaches Christlike love.

Here is a beautiful tribute by a son to his mother: "I don't remember much about her views of voting nor her social prestige; and what her ideas on child training, diet, and eugenics were, I cannot recall. The main thing that sifts back to me now through the thick undergrowth of years is that she loved me. She liked to lie on the grass with me and tell stories, or to run and hide with us children. She was always hugging me. And I liked it. She had a sunny face. To me it was like God, and all the beatitudes saints tell of Him. And sing! Of all the sensations pleasurable to my life nothing can compare with the rapture of crawling up into her lap and going to sleep while she swung to and fro in her rocking chair and sang. Thinking of this, I wonder if the woman of today, with all her tremendous notions and plans, realizes what an almighty factor she is in shaping of her child for weal or woe. I wonder if she realizes how much sheer love and attention count for in a child's life."

Mothers, your teenage children also need that same kind of love and attention. It seems easier for many mothers and fathers to express and show their love to their children when they are young, but more difficult when they are older. Work at this prayerfully. There need be no generation gap. And the key is love. Our young people need love and attention, not indulgence. They need empathy and understanding, not indifference from mothers and fathers. They need the parents' time. A mother's kindly teachings and her love for and confidence in a teenage son or daughter can literally save them from a wicked world.

Blessings of the Lord upon Parents

In closing, I would be remiss this evening if I did not express my love and eternal gratitude for my sweetheart and companion and the mother of our six children. Her devotion to motherhood has blessed me and our family beyond words of expression. She has been a marvelous mother, completely and happily devoting her life and her mission to her family. How grateful I am for Flora!

May I also express my gratitude to you fathers and husbands assembled this evening. We look to you to give righteous leadership in your home and families and, with your companions and the mothers of your children, to lead your families back to our Eternal Father.

Now God bless our wonderful mothers. We pray for you. We sustain you. We honor you as you bear, nourish, teach, and love for eternity. I promise you the blessings of heaven and "all that [the] Father hath" (see D&C 84:38) as you magnify the noblest calling of all—a mother in Zion. In the name of Jesus Christ, amen.

They Lied to Me about Life----
Life Is What You Are

Jaroldeen Edwards

Right after my first novel was published I was interviewed by a large East Coast newspaper for a feature article. The reporters came to my home in Connecticut on a Saturday morning. They were two attractive and sophisticated New York women who had graduated from a prestigious Ivy League school. Both had achieved considerable success in journalism.

The lead reporter was about 30, had been an editor of *Seventeen* magazine, had worked for several major publications, and was now a sought-after feature writer. She was dressed in the latest fashion and seemed the ultimately successful career woman.

I must confess that I was a little chagrined as the morning progressed. I was trying so hard to give the appearance of a professional writer, but every few minutes one of my children would pop into the living room with a problem or a question. My boys were playing a noisy game in the family room, the stereo was on in the basement play room, and the phone would not stop ringing. Neighborhood friends ran in and out of the doors, and finally, my 5-year-old (who had had enough of having to "stay out of the living room") came bouncing in with a smile and plunked herself down on my lap.

We finished the interview, which had taken about two hours, and the reporters got up to leave. The younger one asked if she could use my phone. As she left, the cool and sophisticated senior reporter walked over and sat down on the couch next to me.

"There's something I want to tell you," she said intensely.

I looked at her in surprise. Very slowly, she said, "I just want you to know that we were sold a lie."

"What do you mean?" I asked, totally puzzled.

"I mean, when I went to college they lied to us," she replied. "They told us we were brilliant, and that we had the obligation to seek success. We were told not to throw our lives away on husbands and children, but to go out into the world and to succeed. We were told that only through a professional career could we 'find ourselves' or live a worthwhile life.

"I just want you to know that this morning I have realized it was all a lie. I have come to know that a career is not a life—it is only something you do until you find a life. Life is what you are. I would like to tell you I would trade all my so-called worldly success for one day of living your life."

These and other incidents in my life have developed in me a strong, practical conviction that, whenever possible, it is of critical importance that a mother stays at home with her children (*Church News,* March 10, 1990, p. 8).

Mothers

1. . . . and I wish to say without equivocation that a woman will find greater satisfaction and joy and make a greater contribution to mankind by being a wise and worthy mother raising good children than she could make in any other vocation (President N. Eldon Tanner, *Woman,* 1979, p. 9).

2. It is of great concern to all who understand this glorious concept that Satan and his cohorts are using scientific arguments and nefarious propaganda to lure women away from their primary responsibilities as wives, mothers, and homemakers. We hear so much about emancipation, independence, sexual liberation, birth control, abortion, and other insidious propaganda belittling the role of motherhood, all of which is Satan's way of destroying woman, the home, and the family—the basic unit of society (*ibid,* p. 5).

3. Women, you are of great strength and support to the men in your lives, and they sometimes need your help most when they are least deserving. A man can have no greater incentive, no greater hope, no greater strength than to know that his mother, his sweetheart, or his wife has confidence in him and loves him. And a man should strive every day to live worthy of that love and confidence (*ibid*, p. 7).

4. A woman's basic role, whereby she fulfills the measure of her creation, is that of motherhood. If we are to clearly understand a woman's role as mother, we need to understand her place in God's eternal design.
    The stewardships assigned to man and woman are part of God's eternal plan to prepare us for godhood, and we cannot disregard them without risking our positions in that plan. Adam received his responsibility to be father of the human race and to wrest from the earth that which was needed for his family's temporal existence. Eve also received her responsibility; to bring sons and daughters into this world, to be "the mother of all living" (Moses 4:26). From the beginning woman was to stand by man's side, sharing with him the divinely bestowed honor, blessings, and responsibilities of governing that which the Lord entrusted to their care. The most precious treasures entrusted to them would be the children whom their Father would send (David B. Haight, *Woman,* p. 13-14).

5. Patience. . . is being pleasant when she feels otherwise. It is helping a youngster with school work when she could be relaxing at the end of a busy day. It is helping a child write a letter when she knows it will take much of her precious time for him to say all he has on his mind. It is looking for material for a Sunday School talk when she has her own lesson to prepare. It is keeping her voice calm and sweet when she feels neither calm nor sweet. Patience is doing many things every day that let her family know that they are the center of her life (*ibid*, l5).

6. It is the charge of mother to take these spirit children of our Heavenly Father and give them mortal bodies, and then to love, teach, and guide them back to him. He has trusted his choicest

possessions to her care and keeping. He has shown a great deal of love and faith in her. As a loving parent himself, he understands the struggles and achievements, the sorrows and joys. He will never leave us alone. He wants his children to turn to him, and he will extend as much help as is needed and will be accepted. The mother who prays frequently and fervently for herself and teaches her children to pray gains access to an unlimited reservoir of wisdom and strength (*ibid*, p. 17, See also the story he tells of President Kimball visiting homes during stake conference visits).

7. Others may clothe and feed and diaper the child, but no one can take the place of mother. That is reinforced by the story of the six-year-old who got lost in a grocery store. He began to call ''Martha, Martha.'' When the mother was found she said: ''Honey, you should not call me Martha, I am 'Mother' to you.'' To which the child responded, ''Yes, I know, but the store was full of mothers, and I wanted mine.'' He didn't want a substitute. . . .Thus, when a mother honors and magnifies her calling, she is preparing for the eternities. She is not only preparing her children for their eternal destiny, but she is also preparing herself to become a queen and a priestess forever (*ibid*. p. 9).

8. As the First Presidency have declared: ''Motherhood is near to divinity. It is the highest, holiest service to be assumed by mankind. It places her who honors its holy calling and service next to the angels'' (Conference Report, October l942 pp. 12-13).

9. G. Homer Durham: The influence of woman on mature man is an profoundly significant as her influence on children. All human beings are involved in each other's lives. It would appear from scripture, from history, and from observation, that women have a capacity to exercise unusual influence for the uplift of culture, character, morals, high ideals, and true religion.
I believe the greatest teaching role of woman is that of mother. My wife has been my most influential teacher as she has been a teacher and exemplar to our children. ...Using her body as the primal home for her unborn child, the woman teaches us the true example of total sacrifice through the care she takes with herself and the unborn child; her preparations in the home in joyful anticipation of its arrival; her months of discomfort and anxiety; her fulfilling daily responsibilities to her family and to others without complaint; her serenity in waiting and her glorious expectations. It is from her own mother's love and example that a daughter receives the desire, the hope, the courage, to become herself a mother (Rex D. Pinegar, *Woman*, p. 21-22).

10. President Jimmy Carter, in an address in the Salt Lake Tabernacle on Nov. 27, 1978, emphasized the tremendously important influence his home surroundings had on his life: ''My first church was my family,'' he stated. ''I first heard the Bible read in my family. I first heard prayer in my family. I learned about God within my family. My first school was my family; my first government was my family. There in an embryonic stage of growth, I began to perceive the world around me. And when I had questions, they were answered; when I had doubts they were resolved; when I had needs, they were met'' (*ibid*, p. 23).

11. As a wife, a woman fills another of her key teaching functions. It is my feeling that many accomplishments a man makes are the result of teachings received from his wife. From the determining of his diet to the development of his attitude toward life, a husband interacts with his wife. A man will usually strive to become everything the woman he loves desires him to be. . . . Bonnie (has) lifted me to a higher, more excellent level of performance of my duties (*ibid*, p. 27).

12. Some homes, like universities, have more competent, dedicated faculties than others. Universities are generally judged by the learning of their faculties and their competence in stimulating further learning. In the home woman is the most important ''faculty member''—taking the world as a whole, and measuring ''faculty competence'' in terms of the quality and quantity of time spent with the ''students'' (G. Homer Durham, *Woman*, p. 34).

13. Elder Durham quoting from Sister Kimball:

   1. The role of mother is the most exacting and difficult of all professions.

   2. A woman should, therefore, be skilled in child training, in psychology and sociology, in economics and management, in nutrition and nursing. She should seek a well-rounded education. . . .

   Speaking in practical terms Sister Kimball said: "I would hope that every girl and woman here has the desire and the ambition to qualify in two vocations—that of homemaking, and that of preparing to earn a living outside the home, if and when the occasion requires. An unmarried woman is always happier if she has a vocation in which she can be socially of service and financially independent." Speaking of married women, Sister Kimball noted that any married woman "may become a widow without warning. Property may vanish as readily as a husband may die. Thus, any woman may be under the necessity of earning her own living and helping to support dependent children." Also emphasized was the fact that the later years of a woman's life "should be viewed as a time that can be socially and professionally productive. . . The active woman cannot hold her hands. . ." (*Ensign*, March. 1977, pp. 58-59, reported by Durham in *Woman*, pp. 35-36).

14. No matter how competent the father, the breadth and depth of his knowledge, or his spiritual qualities, the primary influence in the lives of men and women is in the hands of woman. She is at the very heart of civilization. If the great educational institution known as home and family does not function, things turn for the worse. Where family prayer, family devotions, and well-spoken, polite, and courteous language are accompanied by study, learning, compassion, and love, society and civilization flourish. . . [quoting BY]: "I would not have them neglect to learn music and would encourage them to read history and the scriptures, to take up a newspaper, geography, and the other publications, and make themselves acquainted with the manners and customs of distant kingdoms and nations, with their laws, religion, geographical location on the face of the world, their climate, national productions, the extent of their commerce, and the nature of their political organization; in fine, let our boys and girls be thoroughly instructed in every useful branch of physical and mental education" (JD 9:189) (quoted in *Woman*, p. 37).

15. There may be some thoughtful, devoted women, and many others outside the realm of Church membership, who feel that the dual role of homemaking and liberal-vocational-professional education for women places too much emphasis upon the former and not enough upon the latter. To this it may be replied that, in the light of history, it is impossible to overemphasize the importance of what Sister Kimball described as "the most exacting and difficult of all professions," namely that of mother. Sister Kimball knows the learning required of lawyers, surgeons, engineers, architects, chemists; yet she lists motherhood as the most exacting and difficult (*ibid*, p. 38).

16. [after quoting Gen. 2:18]. Since it was "not good that the man should be alone" before he became subject to death through transgression, why should man assume it will be good to be alone when he is redeemed from the effects of the fall? If man needed a helpmeet before he was subject to death, he should need a helpmeet when his body is restored, through the resurrection, to its former state. . . . Why should men claim they separate at death if those same bodies of flesh and bone come forth from the grave? (LeGrand Richards, *Woman,* p. 41).

17. How can righteous men and women who have teamed together in the rearing of their children, and sacrificed for them and for each other, believe that the righteousness or justice of God would put an end to their association and companionship? God will not, if they are married for eternity by the priesthood of God. . . (*ibid*, p. 43).

   . . . Thus The Church of Jesus Christ of Latter-day Saints stands alone in teaching the doctrine of the eternal duration of the marriage covenant and family unit. How can anyone in whose heart

270

burns a true love for the wife of his bosom and for his own children do other than want to believe this doctrine? What could eternity offer to interest one unless he could enjoy it with those whom he has loved in mortality and with whom he has spent his life? (*ibid.* 44).

18. From Family Research Council, Gary L. Bauer, President 700 13th St. NW, Suite 500, Washington, DC 20005. From letter May 9, 1994: Abraham Lincoln once said, "The greatest book I ever read, you ask me? My mother." Abe was right, of course. Every day mothers give out hugs, wipe away tears, help children discover the joy of learning, instill values, pack lunches, make houses into homes, pass on faith and help sons and daughters become responsible citizens. A mother's role is truly one of the most important in the world.

19. Numerous mothers prefer the added luxuries of two incomes to the satisfactions of seeing children grow up in the fear of God (Spencer W. Kimball, Conference Report, October 1961, p. 31).

20. The greatest gift my mom ever gave to us kids was her enduring presence. My mother chose to stay home even though, financially, our family could really have used a second paycheck with no extravagance. Even as a child I was aware that we lived from paycheck to paycheck. Mom's presence in our home was indeed a sacrifice. She was always there, even when I didn't always think I wanted her to be. It used to bug me sometimes as a teenager when my mom would always wait up for us. Well, it only bothered me when I wanted to stay out past curfew or I was tempted to do something that I knew I couldn't feel comfortable doing and then go home and talk to my mom about it. And we all knew that is exactly what we had to do. When we got home, Mom wanted to talk: "How did it go? What did you do? Did he open doors for you?" She was sincerely interested in us and saw every moment with her children as a teaching moment. I didn't realize it then, but some of my greatest learning moments were at 1:00 a.m. on the living room couch with my mom after a bad date.

I remember my mom saying, "There is no such thing as quality time without quantity time. If you wanna be a good mom—the kind of mom that every child truly needs—you've gotta put in your hours." I have admired my mom so much for her long-suffering and enduring devotion to all of her children. With kids ranging from 24 years of age to 7, she refuses to abandon even the last of these for other interests, no matter how good or even deserving they may seem. Kids need their mom to be there when they get home from school, no matter how old they are.

The greatest aspect of my mother's example was her genuine love for her calling. She hated poopy diapers and dirty dishes just as much as anybody else, but she truly loved motherhood and instilled in all her daughters the desire to serve righteously as mothers in Zion as well. And for that I will be eternally grateful (Sarah Brown, February 1995, p. 234).

The Importance of Keeping Marriage Covenants

Spencer W. Kimball

Conference Report, October 1962, pp. 57-59

As **to the importance** of keeping covenants the Lord warned: "And as the covenant which they made unto me (as in a temple sealing) has been broken (through transgression), even so it has become void and of none effect. And woe **to him by whom this offense cometh**, for **it had been better for him that he had been drowned in the depth of the sea**. But blessed are they who have kept the (marriage) covenant and observed the commandment, for they shall obtain mercy (D&C 54:4-6). The Lord will not be mocked.

A man who has entered into sacred covenants in the house of the Lord to remain true to the marriage vow is a **traitor to that covenant** if he separates himself from his wife and family just because he has **permitted** himself to become **infatuated** with a pretty face and comely form of some young girl (or lady) who flattered him with a smile. Even though a loose interpretation of the law of the land would grant such a man a bill of divorce, I think he is **unworthy of a recommend** to have his second marriage solemnized in the temple (this is now the policy of the church: "If a member who has been sealed to a spouse commits adultery (or fornication), that member may not be sealed to the other person involved in the adultery" (Church Handbook).

And any woman who will **break up her home** because of some **selfish desire**, or who has been untrue to her husband, is also untrue to the covenants she has made in the house of the Lord. . . . For a couple who have basked in the sunshine of each other's love to stand by and see the clouds of misunderstanding and discord obscure the love-light of their lives is tragedy indeed. **In the darkness that follows**, the love sparkle in each other's eyes is obscured, and to try to restore it is [very difficult] (President David O. McKay, Conference Report, April 1969, p. 8).

Some let their marriages get stale and common. There are those married people who permit their eyes to wander and **their hearts to become vagrant, who think it is not improper to flirt a little, to share their hearts, and have desire for someone other than the wife or the husband, the Lord says** in no uncertain terms: "Thou shalt love thy wife with **all** thy heart, and shall cleave unto her and none else" (D&C 42:22).

And when the Lord says all thy heart, it allows for **no sharing nor depriving**. The words **none else** eliminate **everyone and everything**. The spouse then becomes pre-eminent in the life of the husband or wife, and neither social life nor **occupational life** nor political life nor any other interest nor person nor thing shall ever take precedence over the companion spouse. Marriage presupposes **total allegiance and total fidelity.** Each spouse takes the partner with the understanding that he or she gives self totally to the spouse, all the heart, strength, loyalty, honor, and affection with all dignity. Any **divergence is sin, any sharing the heart is transgression**.

In conclusion, I plead with all young people bound by marriage vows and covenants to make that marriage holy, keep it fresh, express affection meaningfully and sincerely and often. Husbands, **come home— body, spirit, mind, loyalties, interests, and affections, and love your companion into an holy and unbreakable relationship. Wives, come home with all your interests, fidelity, yearnings, loyalties, and affection, and working together make your home a blessed heaven**.

Home-breaking is **sin**, and any thought, act, or association which will tend to destroy another's home is a grievous transgression. A certain young woman was single and was therefore free to properly seek a mate, but she gave attention to and received attention from a married man. She was in transgression. She argued that his marriage was "already on the rocks" and the wife of her new boy friend did not understand him and that he was most unhappy at home, and he did not love his wife.

Regardless of the state of the married man, the young woman was in serious error to comfort him and listen to his disloyal castigation of his wife and to entertain him. The man was **in deep sin**. He was disloyal and unfaithful. So long as he is married to a woman, he is **duty bound to protect her and defend her** and the same responsibility is with his wife.

There are those who look with longing eyes, who want and desire and crave these romantic associations. So to desire to possess, to inordinately want and yearn for such, is to **covet**, and the Lord in powerful terms condemns it: "And again, I command thee that thou shalt not covet thy neighbor's wife; nor seek thy neighbor's life."

How powerful! The seventh and tenth commandments are interwoven into one great command which is awesome in its warning. To covet that which belongs to another is sin, and that sin begins when **hearts begin to entertain a glamorous interest in anyone else. There are many tragedies affecting spouses, children, and loved ones. Even though these "affairs" begin near-innocently, like an octopus the tentacles move gradually to strangle**. When dates or dinners or rides or other contacts begin, the abyss of tragedy opens wide its mouth. And, it has reached **deep iniquity when physical contacts of any nature have been indulged in**. Man's desires are fed and nurtured by the food-thoughts, be they degenerate or holy.

Many super-selfish folk think only of themselves when they begin to cross the lines of propriety in their romanticizing outside their homes; to those who ignore the innocent parents, the innocent spouse, and the innocent children, the scriptures are replete with warnings. Little do most of those who deviate think of the innocent bystanders until the heaviness of final guilt weighs down upon them. The Lord speaks again: "For behold, I, the Lord, have seen the sorrow, and heard the mourning of the daughters of my people. . . because of the wickedness and abominations of their husbands." "Ye have broken the hearts of your tender wives, and lost the confidence of your children, because of your bad example before them; and the sobbings of their hearts ascend up to God against you. . .many hearts died, pierced with deep wounds" (Jacob 2:31, 35) (President Kimball, Conference Report, October 1962, pp. 57-59).

Sins Against the Marriage Covenant

Tragedy of Broken homes

Throughout our land we see the tragedy of broken homes, fathers and mothers separated, children denied the natural affections. Children have a right to the blessings coming from this sacred union. They are entitled to the love and care of faithful parents, and the happiness and devotion which true worship brings.

When these blessings are lost, the whole community suffers and the integrity of government is weakened. It is a shame and a disgrace that so much evil is coming out of broken homes, and this comes largely because we have forgotten God and our obligations to serve and honor him. Truly we have much room for repentance and a return to the simple worship of true Christianity.

Divorce Not Part of Gospel Plan

If all mankind would live in strict obedience to the gospel, and in that love which is begotten by the Spirit of the Lord, all marriages would be eternal, divorce would be unknown. Divorce is not part of the gospel plan and has been introduced because of the hardness of heart and unbelief of the people.

When the Pharisees tempted Christ saying: "Is it lawful for a man to put away his wife for every cause, he answered them: "Have ye not read, that he which made them at the beginning made them male and female, and said, 'For this cause shall a man leave father and mother, and shall cleave to his wife; and they twain shall be one flesh? Wherefore they are no more twain, but one flesh.' What therefore God hath joined together, let not man put asunder." Then when they asked why Moses permitted divorce, the answer of the

Lord was: "Moses because of the hardness of your hearts suffered you to put away your wives; but from the beginning it was not so. Moreover, what God joins together is eternal."

Salvation Lost Through Divorce

There never could be a divorce in this Church **if the husband and wife were keeping the commandments of God.** Within the week, my attention was called to a case where a man and woman, married in the temple for time and all eternity, have tired of each other. They have reared a family. Now he wants to go his way, and she wants to go her way. But they want to be friends! There are no hard feelings between them. They have just got tired. They want a change.

Do they have the spirit of the gospel in their hearts? I say to you, no, or they would not be tired of each other. That could not follow. They got tired of living the principles of eternal truth. A man would not get tired of his wife, if he had the love of God in his heart! A woman would not get tired of her husband, **if she had in her heart the love of God, that first of all commandments. They could not do it!**

And then think of the children. Here you have a broken home. These people get a divorce, and then they want to get a cancellation, perhaps, of their sealing. They want to marry somebody else. And there you have a broken home. What is going to become of the parents? What is going to become of the children? Haven't the children any rights?

Disobedience Brings Divorce

When divorce comes to those who are married in the temple, it has come because they have **violated the covenants and the obligations** they have taken upon themselves to be true to each other, true to God, and true to the Church. If they will continue to live in that faithfulness, if they will have love in their hearts for each other, respect each other's rights and not one attempt to take an advantage unduly of the other but have the other consideration, there will be no failures.

And when a man and a woman are married in the temple for time and all eternity and then seek through the courts a separation, perhaps also to come to the President of the Church to get a cancellation, what have they done? Children likely have been born, and these children belong to God; they are his children, sent to that home with all the rights of protection from father and mother, guidance from father and mother, to be built up and strengthened in the faith, and to go into the heavens, into the celestial kingdom with the father and mother to sit with them in exaltation and glory.

But frequently a man and a woman cannot live together, many times because of some trivial thing that arises and they separate. What have they done to those children? They have destroyed their God-given rights, taken them away from them, destroyed a family. And how are they going to go into the eternities and face their Maker under those conditions?

Marriage according to the law of the Church is the most holy and sacred ordinance. It will bring to the husband and the wife, if they abide in their covenants, the fullness of exaltation in the kingdom of God. When that covenant is broken, it will bring **eternal misery** to the guilty party, for we will all have to answer for our deeds done while in the flesh. It is an ordinance that cannot be trifled with, and the covenants made in the temple cannot be broken without dire punishment to the one who is guilty. When a couple are married in the temple, they should try to live in peace and harmony, and if both are faithful members of the Church, this should not be impossible. Young people should try to tolerate each other's weaknesses and overcome them. If they live worthy of exaltation, they will enter the celestial kingdom without the frailties and weaknesses of mortality and will be perfect (President Joseph Fielding Smith, *Doctrines of Salvation,* 2:80-83).

Husbands are commanded "Love your wife—even as Christ also loved the Church and gave himself for it." The scripture says, "Greater love hath no man than to give his life for his friend. Your wife is your friend. You should be willing to go even to the extent of giving your life—I mean your life—for your wife if the need should appear. Would you give your life for her? Ask yourself—Can you love your wife even as Christ loved the Church?" Can you think of how He loved His Church. Its every breath was important to Him. Its every growth, its every individual was precious to Him. He gave to those people all of his energy, all of his power, all of his interest, His life. **When the husband** is ready to treat his household in that manner, that means his wife and children in that manner—not only the wife but all the family will respond to his loving and exemplary leadership. It will be automatic. He won't need to demand it. It will come because she will want to do what is evidently necessary. Certainly if fathers are to be respected, **they must merit respect.** If they are to be loved they must be consistent, lovable, understanding, and kind, and they must honor their priesthood. They must see themselves as **fortunate trustees** of precious spirit children whom God has entrusted to **their care** (President Kimball, "Husbands and Wives," September 12, 1975, to CES).

Marriage in the temple is one of the most beautiful things in all the world. . . . A man who is married in the temple has no right to be looking at young women, whether they are in the choir or in the Relief Society, or . . . doing any of the duties of the Church. You have a covenant to be true to that wife. Brethren, keep it true, be true to it. You have no right to neglect your wives and go and seek the company of others who seem to be more attractive to you because you are thrown with them in daily life, **in your business affairs**, or in Church affairs. The **Spirit of God will not** strive with a man who in any way helps to break up another man's family (President McKay, Conference Report, April, 1969, p. 8).

How severe is the judgment on the man who has committed adultery, even though he apparently is repentant? In the D&C 42:24-26, the Lord has given us the key to this situation. If a person commits adultery and then repents with all his heart, he may be forgiven. If he repeats the offense, he is not to be forgiven, but is to be cast out (excommunicated). As I read it, **the Lord has not provided that, under those circumstances, he can come back again.**

Now this revelation (in Section 42) was given **before the endowment** was made known. Since that time when a man is married in the temple, he takes a solemn covenant before God, angels, and witnesses that he will keep the law of chastity. Then if he violates that covenant it is not easy to receive forgiveness. I call your attention to this statement by the Prophet Joseph Smith: "If a man commit adultery, he cannot receive the celestial kingdom of God. Even if he is saved in any kingdom, it cannot be the celestial kingdom" (DHC, 6:81) (This was gingerly modified by President Kimball in *Miracle of Forgiveness*, p. 347-8, but it is very serious).

We have been taught that adultery is a crime second only to the shedding of innocent blood. We cannot treat it lightly. For a man to destroy another man's home is too serious an offense to be readily forgiven. Such a man should not be permitted to come back in the Church, under any circumstances, at least until years have elapsed. He should be placed on probation for that length of time to see if he can, or will, remain clean. Even then I confess I do not know what disposition the Lord will make of him (President Joseph Fielding Smith, *Doctrines of Salvation*, 2, p. 94).

Those who claim their love is dead should **return home** with all their loyalty, fidelity, honor, cleanliness—and the love which has become embers will flare up with scintillating flame again. If love wanes or dies, it is often **infidelity of thought or act which gave the lethal potion**. I plead with all people, young and old, bound by marriage vows and covenants to make that marriage holy, keep it fresh, express affection meaningfully and sincerely, and often. Thus will one avoid the pitfalls which destroy marriage (*Miracle of Forgiveness*, p. 251).

Sometimes, as we travel throughout the Church, a husband and wife will come to us and ask if, because they are not compatible in their marriage—they having had a temple marriage—it wouldn't be better if they were to free themselves from each other and then seek more congenial partners. To all such we say, whenever a couple who have been married in the temple say they are tiring of each other, **it is evidence that either one or both are not true to their temple covenants. Any couple married in the temple who are true to their covenants will grow dearer to each other, and love will find a deeper meaning on their golden wedding anniversary than on the day they were married in the house of the Lord. Don't you mistake that** (*Teachings of Harold B. Lee*, 1996, Bookcraft, p. 249).

Marriage is the shelter where families are created. That society which puts low value on marriage sows the wind and, in time, will reap the whirlwind—and thereafter, unless they repent, bring upon themselves a holocaust.

I believe in marriage. I believe it to be the ideal pattern for human living. I know it to be ordained of God. The restraints relating to it were designed to protect our happiness.

Marriage is yet safe, with all its sweet fulfillment, with all its joy and love. **In marriage all of the worthy yearnings of the human soul, all that is physical and emotional and spiritual, can be fulfilled.**

Marriage offers fulfillment all the way through life—in youth and young love, the wedding and on the honeymoon, with the coming of little children and the nurturing of them. Then comes the golden years when young ones leave the nest to build one of their own. The cycle then repeats itself, as God has decreed it should (Boyd K. Packer, "That All May Be Edified," pp. 290-294).

Born in the Covenant

Joseph Fielding Smith

Doctrines of Salvation, Vol. 2, pp. 89-92

Death does not separate righteous parents who are joined by decree and authority of the Father, neither does it take from these parents their righteous children, for they are born under the covenant, and therefore, **their parents have claim upon them forever**. President Brigham Young has said: "When a man and woman have received their endowments and sealings, and then had children born to them afterwards, these children are legal heirs to the kingdom and to all its blessings and promises, and they are the only ones that are on this earth" (*Discourses of Brigham Young*, p. 202). This is certainly true; how can children whose parents have not been married by divine authority be heirs of that kingdom?

It may be asked, what is the advantage coming to those born under the covenant? Being heirs they have claims upon the blessings of the gospel **beyond what those not so born are entitled to receive. They may receive a greater guidance, a greater protection, a greater inspiration from the Spirit of the Lord**; and then there is no power that can take them away from their parents. Children, on the other hand, who are born to parents who were married until death separates them, have no claim upon such parents, and such parents have no claim upon the children after the resurrection from the dead.

Those born under the covenant, throughout all eternity, are the children of their parents. Nothing except the unpardonable sin, or sin unto death, can break this tie. If children do not sin as John said, "unto death," the **parents may still feel after them and eventually bring them back near to them again**. On this point President Brigham Young has said: "Let the father and mother, who are members of this church and kingdom, take a righteous course, and strive with all their might never to do a wrong, but to do good all their lives; if they have one child or one hundred children, if they conduct themselves towards them as they should, binding them to the Lord by their faith and prayers, I care not where those children go, **they are bound up to their parents by an everlasting tie, and no power of earth or hell can separate them from their parents in eternity**; they will return again to the fountain from whence they sprang" (Young, op, cit., p. 322).

All children born under the covenant belong to their parents in eternity, but that does not mean that they, because of that birthright, will inherit celestial glory. The faith and faithfulness of fathers and mothers will not save disobedient children. Salvation is an individual matter, and if a person who has been born under the covenant rebels and denies the Lord, he will lose the blessings of exaltation. Every soul will be judged according to his works and the wicked cannot inherit eternal life. We cannot force salvation upon those who do not want it. Even our Father's children had their agency before this life, and one-third of them rebelled.

It is the duty of parents to teach their children so that they will walk uprightly and thus obtain the blessings of their birthright. But children born under the covenant, who drift away, are still the children of their parents; and the parents have a claim upon them; and if the children **have not sinned away all their rights**, the parents may be able to bring them through repentance, into the celestial kingdom, **but not to receive the exaltation**. Of course, **if children sin too grievously, they will have to enter the telestial kingdom, or they may even become sons of perdition.**

When a man and woman are married in the temple for time and all eternity and then separate, **the children will go with the parent who is justified and who has kept the covenants. If neither of them has kept his covenants, the children may be taken away from both of them and given to somebody else, and that would be by virtue of being born under the covenant**. A child is not to be sealed the second time when born under the covenant, but by virtue of that birthright can be transferred (Joseph Fielding Smith, *Doctrines of Salvation*, Vol. 2, pp. 89-92).

Father, Come Home

Elder James E. Faust

General Conference, April 1993, *Ensign*, May 1993, pp. 35-37

The blessings of the priesthood, honored by fathers and husbands and revered by wives and children, can indeed cure the cancer that plagues our society.

At this Easter season, I extend to all who are participating in these services my warmest greetings and prayers for your happiness and well-being. On this day we remember that the risen Lord has charged us with the responsibility to build the kingdom of God on earth. With this charge in mind, I hope to add a few thoughts that may strengthen the most important of all institutions—the family.

In recent times, society has been plagued with a cancer from which few families have escaped. I speak of the disintegration of our homes. Immediate corrective treatment is urgent. In what I have to say, I do not wish to offend anyone. I affirm my profound belief that God's greatest creation is womanhood. I also believe that there is no greater good in all the world than motherhood. The influence of a mother in the lives of her children is beyond calculation. Single parents, most of whom are mothers, perform an especially heroic service.

I hasten to acknowledge that there are too many husbands and fathers who are abusive to their wives and children and from whom the wives and children need protection. Yet modern sociological studies powerfully reaffirm the essential influence of a caring father in the life of a child—boy or girl. In the past twenty years, as homes and families have struggled to stay intact, sociological studies reveal this alarming fact: much of the crime and many of the behavioral disorders in the United States come from homes where the father has abandoned the children. In many societies the world over, child poverty, crime, drug abuse, and family decay can be traced to conditions where the father gives no male nurturing. Sociologically, it is now painfully apparent that fathers are not optional family baggage. We need to honor the position of the father as the primary provider for physical and spiritual support. I state this with no reluctance because the Lord has revealed that this obligation is placed upon husbands. "Women have claim on their husbands for their maintenance, until their husbands are taken" (D&C 83:2). Further, "All children have claim upon their parents for their maintenance until they are of age" (D&C 83:4). In addition, their spiritual welfare should be "brought to pass by the faith and covenant of their fathers" (D&C 84:99). As regards little children, the Lord has promised that "great things may be required at the hands of their fathers" (D&C 29:48).

It is useless to debate which parent is most important. No one would doubt that a mother's influence is paramount with newborns and in the first years of a child's life. The father's influence increases as the child grows older. However, each parent is necessary at various times in a child's development. Both fathers and mothers do many intrinsically different things for their children. Both mothers and fathers are equipped to nurture children, but their approaches are different. Mothers seem to take a dominant role in preparing children to live within their families (present and future). Fathers seem best equipped to prepare children to function in the environment outside the family. One authority states, "Studies show that fathers have a special role to play in building a child's self-respect. They are important, too, in ways we really don't understand, in developing internal limits and controls in children." He continues, "Research also shows that fathers are critical in establishment of gender in children. Interestingly, fatherly involvement produces stronger sexual identity and character in both boys and girls. It is well established that the masculinity of sons and the femininity of daughters are each greater when fathers are active in family life" (Karl Zinsmeister, "Do Children Need Fathers?" Crisis, Oct. 1992).

Parents in any marital situation have a duty to set aside personal differences and encourage each other's righteous influence in the lives of their children.

Is it not possible to give to womankind all of the rights and blessings that come from God and legal authority without diminishing the nobility of God's other grand creation, manhood? Eliza R. Snow stated in 1872, "The status of women is one of the questions of the day. Socially and politically it forces itself upon the attention of the world. Some . . . refuse to concede that woman is entitled to the enjoyment of any rights other than . . . the whims, fancies or justice. . . men may choose to grant her. The reasons which they cannot meet with argument they decry and ridicule; an old refuge for those opposed to correct principles which they are unable to controvert. Others . . . not only recognize that woman's status should be improved, but are so radical in their extreme theories that they would set her in antagonism to man, assume for her a separate and opposing existence; and . . . show how entirely independent she should be." Indeed, she continued, they "would make her adopt the more reprehensible phases of character which men present, and which should be shunned or improved by them instead of being copied by women. These are the two extremes, and between them is the 'golden mean'" (The Woman's Exponent, 15 July 1872, p. 29).

Many people do not understand our belief that God has wisely established a guiding authority for the most important institutions in the world. This guiding authority is called the priesthood. The priesthood is held in trust to be used to bless all of God's children. Priest-hood is not gender; it is blessings from God for all at the hands of the servants He has designated. Within the Church this authority of the priesthood can bless all members through the ministration of home teachers, quorum presidents, bishops, fathers, and all other righteous brethren who are charged with the administration of the affairs of the kingdom of God. Priest-hood is the righteous power and influence by which boys are taught in their youth and throughout their lives to honor chastity, to be honest and industrious, and to develop respect for, and stand in the defense of, womanhood. Priesthood is a restraining influence. Girls are taught that through its influence and power to bless, they can fulfill many of their desires.

Holding the priesthood means following the example of Christ and seeking to emulate his example of fatherhood. It means constant concern and caring for one's own flesh and blood. The man who holds the priesthood is to honor it by eternally cherishing, with absolute fidelity, his wife and the mother of his children. He is to extend lifelong care and concern for his children, and their children. The plea of David for his rebel son is one of the most moving in all of the scriptures, "O my son Absalom, my son, my son Absalom! would God I had died for thee, O Absalom, my son, my son!" (2 Sam. 18:33).

I urge the husbands and fathers of this church to be the kind of a man your wife would not want to be without. I urge the sisters of this church to be patient, loving, and understanding with their husbands. Those who enter into marriage should be fully prepared to establish their marriage as the first priority in their lives.

It is destructive to the feeling essential for a happy marriage for either party to say to the other marriage partner, "I don't need you." This is particularly so because the counsel of the Savior was and is to become one flesh: "For this cause shall a man leave father and mother, and shall cleave to his wife: and they twain shall be one flesh[.]

"Wherefore they are no more twain, but one flesh" (Matt. 19:5-6). It is far more difficult to be of one heart and mind than to be physically one. This unity of heart and mind is manifest in sincere expressions of "I appreciate you" and "I am proud of you." Such domestic harmony results from forgiving and forgetting, essential elements of a maturing marriage relationship. Someone has said that we should keep our eyes wide open before marriage and half shut afterward (Magdeleine de Scudéry, as cited in The International Dictionary of Thoughts, Chicago: J. G. Ferguson Publishing Co., 1969, p. 472). True charity ought to begin in marriage, for it is a relationship that must be rebuilt every day.

I wonder if it is possible for one marriage partner to jettison the other and become completely whole. Either partner who diminishes the divine role of the other in the presence of the children demeans the budding femininity within the daughters and the emerging manhood of the sons. I suppose there are always some honest differences between husband and wife, but let them be settled in private.

The importance of this subject emboldens me to say a word about covenant breaking. It must be recognized that some marriages just fail. To those in that circumstance, I extend understanding because every divorce carries heartache with it. I hope what I say will not be disturbing. In my opinion, any promise between a man and a woman incident to a marriage ceremony rises to the dignity of a covenant. The family relationship of father, mother, and child is the oldest and most enduring institution in the world. It has survived vast differences of geography and culture. This is because marriage between man and woman is a natural state and is ordained of God. It is a moral imperative. Those marriages performed in our temples, meant to be eternal relationships, then, become the most sacred covenants we can make. The sealing power given by God through Elijah is thus invoked, and God becomes a party to the promises.

What, then, might be "just cause" for breaking the covenants of marriage? Over a lifetime of dealing with human problems, I have struggled to understand what might be considered "just cause" for breaking of covenants. I confess I do not claim the wisdom nor authority to definitively state what is "just cause." Only the parties to the marriage can determine this. They must bear the responsibility for the train of consequences which inevitably follow if these covenants are not honored. In my opinion, "just cause" should be nothing less serious than a prolonged and apparently irredeemable relationship which is destructive of a person's dignity as a human being.

At the same time, I have strong feelings about what is not provocation for breaking the sacred covenants of marriage. Surely it is not simply "mental distress," nor "personality differences," nor "having grown apart," nor having "fallen out of love." This is especially so where there are children. Enduring divine counsel comes from Paul: "Husbands, love your wives, even as Christ also loved the church, and gave himself for it" (Eph. 5:25).

"That they may teach the young women to be sober, to love their husbands, [and] to love their children" (Titus 2:4).

In my opinion, members of the Church have the most effective cure for our decaying family life. It is for men, women, and children to honor and respect the divine roles of both fathers and mothers in the home. In so doing, mutual respect and appreciation among the members of the Church will be fostered by the righteousness found there. In this way, the great sealing keys restored by Elijah, spoken of by Malachi, might operate "to turn the hearts of the fathers to the children, and the children to the fathers, lest the whole earth be smitten with a curse" (D&C 110:15; Mal. 4:6).

President Joseph Fielding Smith stated concerning the keys of Elijah: "This sealing power bestowed upon Elijah, is the power which binds husbands and wives, and children to parents for time and eternity. It is the binding power existing in every Gospel ordinance. . . . It was the mission of Elijah to come, and restore it so that the curse of confusion and disorder would not exist in the kingdom of God" (Elijah the Prophet and His Mission, Salt Lake City: Deseret Book Co., 1957, p. 5). Confusion and disorder are all too common in society, but they must not be permitted to destroy our homes.

Perhaps we regard the power bestowed by Elijah as something associated only with formal ordinances performed in sacred places. But these ordinances become dynamic and productive of good only as they reveal themselves in our daily lives. Malachi said that the power of Elijah would turn the hearts of the fathers and the children to each other. The heart is the seat of the emotions and a conduit for revelation (See Mal. 4:5-6). This sealing power thus reveals itself in family relationships, in attributes and virtues developed in a nurturing environment, and in loving service. These are the cords that bind families together, and the priesthood advances their development. In imperceptible but real ways, the "doctrine of the priesthood shall distil upon thy soul [and thy home] as the dews from heaven" (D&C 121:45).

I so testify that the blessings of the priesthood, honored by fathers and husbands and revered by wives and children, can indeed cure the cancer that plagues our society. I plead with you, Fathers, come home. Magnify your priesthood calling; bless your families through this sacred influence, and experience the rewards promised by our Father and God. I say this in the name of Jesus Christ, amen.

Stillborn Children

1. When the fetus is born dead, it is said to be a **stillbirth**. Such an occurrence gives rise to anxiety on the part of mothers, in particular, as to whether the **stillborn baby** had in fact become a living soul, whether the partially or nearly formed body had become the home of a pre-existent spirit, and whether such a body will be resurrected. These are matters not clearly answered in the revelation so far available for the guidance of the saints in this dispensation.

2. However, based on the truths now known by revelation and in harmony with the general knowledge we have of the mercy and justice of that Infinite Being in whose divine economy nothing is ever lost, we may suppose with confident certainty that the eternal spirit enters the body an appreciable time prior to a normal birth, and therefore that stillborn children will be resurrected. [The First Presidency has said] "The body of man enters upon its career as a tiny germ or embryo, which becomes an infant, **quickened at a certain stage by the spirit** whose tabernacle it is, and the child, after being born, develops into a man" (*Man: His Origin and Destiny,* p. 354). This interpretation is in harmony with the general knowledge we have of the mercy and justice of that Infinite Being in whose divine economy nothing is ever lost. It would appear that we can look forward with hope and anticipation for the resurrection of stillborn children.

3. President Young taught, (in *JD* 17:143), that "when the mother feels life come to her infant, it is the spirit entering the body preparatory to the immortal existence"; and President Joseph Fielding Smith gave it as his opinion "that these little ones will receive a resurrection and then belong to us." "Stillborn children should not be reported nor recorded as births and deaths on the records of the Church," he said, "but it is suggested that parents record in their own family records a name of each such stillborn child (*Doctrines of Salvation,* vol. 2, pp. 280-281). (Bruce R. McConkie, *Morman Doctrine,* p. 768).

    Grieving parents whose child dies before birth, require emotional and spiritual support. **Although temple ordinances are not performed for stillborn children, no loss of eternal blessings or family unity is implied.** The family may record the name of a stillborn child on the **family group record** followed by the word **stillborn** in parentheses. Memorial or graveside services may or may not be held as determined by the parents (Church Handbook of Instructions)

4. Luke 1:41. The babe leaped in her womb. In this miraculous event the pattern is seen in which a spirit follows in passing from his pre-existent first estate into mortality. The spirit enters the body at the time of quickening, months prior to the actual normal birth. The value and comfort attending a knowledge of this eternal truth is seen in connection with stillborn children. Since the spirit entered the body before birth, stillborn children will be resurrected and righteous parents shall enjoy their association in immortal glory (Bruce R. McConkie, *DNT Commentary* 1:84-85).

5. "On the morrow come I into the world." The Book of Mormon account of Christ speaking to Nephi the grandson of Helaman and saying, "On the morrow come I into the world" (3 Ne. 1:13), is not intended to

infer that the spirit does not enter the body until the moment of the actual birth. Rather this revelation to the Nephites was itself being conveyed in a miraculous and unusual way. Quite probably the one uttering these words was speaking in the first person as though he were Christ, in accordance with the law enabling others to act and speak for Deity on the principle of divine investiture of authority (*ibid*).

Parents' Concern for Children

Elder Howard W. Hunter of the Quorum of the Twelve Apostles

October Conference 1983, *Ensign*, November, 1983, pp. 63-65

General Authorities have the privilege of meeting and getting acquainted with members of the Church all over the world who have consistently lived good lives and raised their families in the influence of the gospel. These Saints have enjoyed the great blessings and comfort that can come from looking back, as parents, grandparents, and great-grandparents, over long and successful parenting efforts. Surely this is something each of us would like.

However, there are many in the Church and in the world who are living with feelings of guilt and unworthiness because some of their sons and daughters have wandered or strayed from the fold. My remarks today are directed primarily to those mothers and fathers.

At the outset we understand that conscientious parents try their best, yet nearly all have made mistakes. One does not launch into such a project as parenthood without soon realizing that there will be many errors along the way. Surely our Heavenly Father knows, when he entrusts his spirit children into the care of young and inexperienced parents, that there will be mistakes and errors in judgment.

For every set of parents there are many "first-time" experiences that help to build wisdom and understanding, but each such experience results from the plowing of new ground, with the possibility that errors might be made. With the arrival of the first child the parents must make decisions about how to teach and train, how to correct and discipline. Soon there is the first day at school and the first bicycle. Then follows the first date of the first teenager, the first problem with school grades, and possibly, the first request to stay out late or the first request to buy a car.

It is a rare father or mother indeed who travels the difficult path of parenting without making errors along the way, especially at these first-time milestones when experience and understanding are somewhat lacking. Even after the parent has gained experience, the second-time and third-time occurrences of these milestones are sometimes not much easier to handle, nor do they come with much less chance of error.

What more challenging responsibility is there than working effectively with young people? There are numerous variables that determine the character and the personality of a child. It is probably true that parents are, in many or perhaps most cases, the greatest influence in shaping the life of a child, but sometimes there are other influences that also are very significant. No one knows the degree to which heredity influences lives, but certainly brothers and sisters, friends and teachers, neighbors and Scoutmasters have significant effects.

We know, too, that the influences on a child are not restricted to heredity or to people, certainly, things in the physical surroundings will have their effect—such as the house and the playthings, the yard and the neighborhood. Playgrounds and basketballs, dresses and cars—or the lack of these—all have their influence on the child.

One must conclude that—with the multitude of influences and the innumerable decisions, each with so many alternatives to consider and evaluate—even though parents strive to choose wisely, an unwise choice will sometimes be made. It is almost impossible to always say and do the right thing at every point along the way. I think we would agree that as parents we have made mistakes which have had a negative effect on the attitude of the child or on his progress. On the other hand, parents usually do the right thing or make the right decision under the circumstances, yet boys and girls often have negative responses to right or correct decisions.

If a parent has made what could be considered an error—or, on the other hand, has never made a mistake, but still the lamb has wandered from the fold—in either case there are several thoughts I would like to share with you.

First, such a father or mother is not alone. Our first parents knew the pain and suffering of seeing some of their children reject the teachings of eternal life (See Moses 5:27). Centuries later Jacob came to know of the jealousy and ill feelings of his older sons toward his beloved Joseph (See Gen. 37:1-8). The great prophet Alma, who had a son named Alma, prayed at length to the Lord regarding the rebellious attitude of his son and no doubt was overwhelmed with concern and worry about the dissension and the wickedness his son was causing among those who were within the Church (See Mosiah 27:14). Our Father in Heaven has also lost many of his spirit children to the world; he knows the feelings of your heart.

Second, we should remember that errors of judgment are generally less serious than errors of intent.

Third, even if there was a mistake made with full knowledge and understanding, there is the principle of repentance for release and comfort. Rather than constantly dwelling on what we perceive as a mistake or a sin or a failure to the detriment of our progress in the gospel or our association with family and friends, it would be better for us to turn away from it. As with any mistake, we may repent by being sorrowful and by attempting to correct or rectify the consequences, to whatever extent possible. We should look forward with renewed faith.

Fourth, don't give up hope for a boy or a girl who has strayed. Many who have appeared to be completely lost have returned. We must be prayerful and, if possible, let our children know of our love and concern.

Fifth, remember that ours was not the only influence that contributed to the actions of our children, whether those actions were good or bad.

Sixth, know that our Heavenly Father will recognize the love and the sacrifice, the worry and the concern, even though our great effort has been unsuccessful. Parents' hearts are ofttimes broken, yet they must realize that the ultimate responsibility lies with the child after parents have taught correct principles.

Seventh, whatever the sorrow, whatever the concern, whatever the pain and anguish, look for a way to turn it to beneficial use—perhaps in helping others to avoid the same problems, or perhaps by developing a greater insight into the feelings of others who are struggling in a similar way. Surely we will have a deeper understanding of the love of our Heavenly Father when, through prayer, we finally come to know that he understands and wants us to look forward.

The eighth and final point of reminder is that everyone is different. Each of us is unique. Each child is unique. Just as each of us starts at a different point in the race of life, and just as each of us has different strengths and weaknesses and talents, so each child is blessed with his own special set of characteristics. We must not assume that the Lord will judge the success of one in precisely the same way as another. As parents we often assume that, if our child doesn't become an over-achiever in every way, we have failed. We should be careful in our judgments.

Let us not misunderstand. The responsibilities of parenthood are of the greatest importance. The results of our efforts will have eternal consequences for us and the boys and girls we raise. Anyone who becomes a parent is under strict obligation to protect and love his children and assist them to return to their Heavenly Father. All parents should understand that the Lord will not hold guiltless those who neglect these responsibilities.

After the Exodus and while Israel was in the wilderness, Moses, in teaching his people, instructed them that the commandments of the Lord should be taught by parents to their children in the home. He said to them:

"And these words, which I command thee this day, shall be in thine heart:

"And thou shalt teach them diligently unto thy children, and shalt talk of them when thou sittest in thine house, and when thou walkest by the way, and when thou liest down, and when thou risest up" (Deut. 6:6-7).

We should never let Satan fool us into thinking that all is lost. Let us take pride in the good and right things we have done; reject and cast out of our lives those things that are wrong; look to the Lord for forgiveness, strength, and comfort; and then move onward.

A successful parent is one who has loved, one who has sacrificed, and one who has cared for, taught, and ministered to the needs of a child. If you have done all of these and your child is still wayward or troublesome or worldly, it could well be that you are, nevertheless, a successful parent. Perhaps there are children who have come into the world that would challenge any set of parents under any set of circumstances. Likewise, perhaps there are others who would bless the lives of, and be a joy to, almost any father or mother.

My concern today is that there are parents who may be pronouncing harsh judgments upon themselves and may be allowing these feelings to destroy their lives, when in fact they have done their best and should continue in faith. That all who are parents might find joy in their efforts with their children is my prayer, in the name of Jesus Christ, amen.

Daddy, Donna, and Nephi

Jeffrey R. Holland

Ensign, September 1976, pp. 7-11

So they read in the book in the law of God distinctly, and gave the sense, and caused them to understand the reading (Neh. 8:8). The key to reading any book is staying awake. That means, of course, that you will try to keep your eyes open and some reasonable portion of your blood circulating. But for *real* reading it means much more than that. Reading which will give you any return on your investment will be an exercise—Walt Whitman called it a gymnastic struggle[1] —in which your mental and spiritual muscles are stretched and strengthened forever. This kind of reading means staying alert, attentive, and actively involved as you recreate the book in your own mind, page by page. Writing a good book is very hard work: reading it well is not an easy thing either.

Perhaps that is one of the reasons we are commanded to read "the best books" (D&C 88:118). Anything less is usually not worth the effort. Low-level reading offers what President John Taylor once called "fried froth"—something on which you chew and chew but which finally leaves nothing to swallow—or worse yet, leaves something to swallow which weakens or defiles.[2]

Surely the best of the "best books" are the scriptures, and it is not simply linguistic chance that the divine injunction is to "ponder" them. That word, in its English form, comes from a Latin root meaning weight—and the scriptures are the weightiest books we have. To ponder them suggests a slow and deliberate examination: indeed, there is no way to read the scriptures whimsically or superficially or quickly. They demand time, prayer, and honest meditation.

One of the things that strikes us as we begin to carefully ponder the Book of Mormon is the realization that it is, in the very best sense, exactly that—a book. Technically a book can be anything with a binding and two covers—blank sheets of paper, nonsense syllables, a collection of unrelated essays, or whatever—but we have been agreeing with Aristotle ever since he said it that a good book must have a calculated structure and development which gives a unified impact from beginning to end.[3] By this standard the Book of Mormon is not only a "good book," it is a classic. In spite of the fact that it is written by a series of prophets who had different styles and different experiences, in spite of the fact that it has some unabridged materials mixed with others that have been greatly condensed, in spite of the fact that it has unique and irregular chronological sequences, it is a classic book—Aristotle's kind of book: unified, whole, verses fitting with verses, chapters fitting with chapters, books fitting with books. It has these ideal qualities because it is the clear, compelling word of God, revealed through his chosen prophets.

---

[1] Walt Whitman, "Democratic Vistas," *Leaves of Grass and Selected Prose* (New York: Modern Library, 1950), p. 515).

[2] John Taylor, *The Gospel Kingdom* (Salt Lake City: Bookcraft, 1964, p. 78).

[3] Richard McKeon, ed., *The Basic Works of Aristotle* (New York: Random House, 1941). See "Metaphysics," especially Book X, pp. 834-50 *passim* and "Poetics" p. 1463.

Let's take the first chapter of the first book of Nephi. This is probably the most familiar material in the book to most of us; and yet if we are not alert, we will miss much of its meaning, for it was very carefully written and must be read that way.

Let's assume that a father is helping his twelve-year-old daughter get started in this first chapter. She is a delightful, fun-loving girl who has tried reading the Book of Mormon a few times but hasn't been able to get too interested. We might overhear a conversation something like this:

Dad: O.K., sweetheart, let's read the first chapter of the first book of Nephi. It's only twenty verses long, less than two pages of print. Think about it as you read. Ask yourself questions.

Donna: What kind of questions?

Dad: Oh, questions like "Why should this be the first chapter of the book?" or "What does this verse have to do with that one?"

Donna: Well, I don't know anything about those things but I do want to know why we don't start off reading about those Jaredites. They were here first.

Dad: That's *exactly* the kind of question to ask—and here you've waited at least a minute and a half to ask it. Now—when you begin to find the answers to questions like that—

Donna: Daddy! Surely you're going to tell me the answers if I can finally think up the questions!

Dad: Tut, tut, Impatience. When *you* begin to find the answers to questions like that, the whole Book of Mormon will open up to you. You'll find out why the Book of Ether should come exactly where it does when you read it *very* carefully. We'll talk about that when we get to it, which is nearly the very end of the book. Now, let's start reading.

Donna: Whatever you say, Dad. (*Donna begins reading, silently. With a furrowed brow or two she makes it to the end of the first chapter*). O. K., I've read it.

Dad: Good. What do you think it says?

Donna: Daddy, I said I *read* it. I didn't say I knew what it meant.

Dad: Well, then we have to read it again, only a little slower this time. And out loud. We'll talk as we go.

Donna: Whatever you say, Dad. (*Reading aloud*) "I, Nephi, having been born of goodly parents. . . ."

Dad: Now why do you think Nephi starts his book like that?

Donna: Maybe he's a nice man.

Dad: Maybe. What else?

Donna: Maybe it's going to be about his family.

Dad: Maybe. What else?

Donna: Maybe he wants us to know who is telling the story.

Dad: Maybe. What else?

Donna: Daddy! This could go on all night and I have school tomorrow. If I read this slowly in class my teacher would bean me. Now let me read it clear through and don't stop me unless I ask you something. O.K.?

Dad:O.K. (*Donna reads the chapter aloud. Slowly. With one eye on her father.*)

Dad: Good. Now. What does that chapter say?

Donna: (*With a wry smile because she had known he was going to ask her that question*). It's about a man named Lehi who has a vision and warns his people about their destruction. But they don't like him.

Dad : (*With a wry smile because he had known she was going to read more thoughtfully*). Terrific! What do we call a man like Lehi?

Donna: A prophet.

Dad: What did he do that brought the vision?

Donna: I don't know. It doesn't say.

Dad: Yes it does. Look. In verse 5.

Donna: (*Reading*) Oh. He prayed. I didn't notice that. I guess I turned the page too fast.

Dad: That's O.K., honey. You're not the only one moving too fast to remember to get the prayer worked in.

Donna: What?

Dad: Nothing. Now exactly what did Lehi see in his vision?

Donna: He saw that Jerusalem was going to be destroyed.

Dad: Hold on! You're going too fast. *How* did he see that Jerusalem was going to be destroyed?

Donna: (*Rereading*) Well, some heavenly messengers brought him a book and he read it.

Dad: Can you tell who the heavenly messengers are?

Donna: I think one of them sounds like Jesus.

Dad: I think he does, too. Now you said that when Lehi tries to tell the people about Jerusalem being destroyed, they don't like it. What do they do?

Donna: (*Rereading*) They get mad and make fun of him.

Dad: How mad do they get?

Donna: Well, finally they try to kill him.

Dad: Let's just put down on paper a little outline of this chapter. I think it would look something like this:

a prophet prays

has a vision

sees heavenly messengers (apparently including Jesus)

receives a book

is rejected by most of the people

Now that's a rough outline of the story you described in chapter 1. Does it look at all familiar to you?

Donna: I don't believe so.

Dad: Think about it.

Donna: Well, it does sort of sound like Joseph Smith's experience. Hey! It sounds a *lot* like Joseph Smith's experience. That's neat. What is that, Daddy?

Dad: Terrific comments! It seems to me one possible answer to your question is that all prophets usually have some very similar experiences. In any case one thing we *know* they have in common is receiving revelation from the Lord. Joseph Smith once said that revelation is the rock on which the Church of Jesus Christ will always be built and there would never be any salvation without it.[4] I think we're going to find, Donna, that this whole book will be one long revelation about revelation. And Jesus is going to be at the center of it all. These first 20 verses tell an awfully lot about what is to follow. You can't do much better than that in an opening chapter.

And maybe there's another reason for having the Book of Mormon begin like this. Maybe it helps in its own way to teach that if we accept Lehi and the Book of Mormon, we surely have to accept Joseph Smith as a prophet of God. On the other hand, when we accept Joseph Smith as a prophet, we must accept and faithfully live by the teachings of this book which he helped bring forth.

In a way, Donna, this record is not only the testimony of Nephi and Alma and Mormon and Moroni, but it is also the testimony of Joseph Smith and Brigham Young and Harold B. Lee and Spencer W. Kimball. Maybe that's why the Church wasn't even organized until the Book of Mormon was completely translated and published. The Prophet Joseph Smith once called it "the keystone of our religion,"[5] and I think most of us do not yet understand how essential the Book of Mormon was to everything that would happen after Moroni handed those plates over to the seventeen-year-old Prophet. When I think of what the Church has become since Joseph's first vision and the delivery of this book I want to shout with Lehi in verse 14: "Great and marvelous are thy works, O Lord God Almighty." Donna, I love this book with all my heart and I know it's the word of God.

Donna: Daddy, I've never heard you talk like this before.

Dad: Well, I've never had my twelve-year-old daughter read the Book of Mormon to me before.

Donna: Whillikers! It's past 10:00! We've been talking more than forty-five minutes on one little chapter. I've got to get to bed. You're going to bean me.

Dad: I doubt it. But then I might. Scurry. Abish.

---

[4] *Teachings of the Prophet Joseph Smith* (Deseret Book Co., 1970), p. 274.

[5] *History of the Church of Jesus Christ of Latter-day Saints,* (Deseret Book Co., 1974), 4:461.

Donna: Abish? Who's Abish?

Dad: Just someone I read about once. Scoot! Now! Pronto!

With a kiss and a hug for her dad, Donna dashes off to bed, more assuredly on her way to a testimony of the truthfulness of the Book of Mormon and the reality of the restoration than she realizes.

Of course, what Donna's father knows—and what she is about to find out—is that every chapter is charged with meaning, often many meanings, and always meanings that illuminate and inspire. As Donna drops deeply into sleep let's stay a bit longer with her dad, who sits thinking, not wishing to have this special experience end.

With the idea of revelation so clearly suggested in the first chapter, it is not startling to find it bubbling to the surface on virtually every page of the first book of Nephi. Chapter 2 begins, "The Lord spake unto my father, yea, even in a dream, and said. . . ." In verse two the message is reinforced—"The Lord commanded my father"—and by verses 16 and 19, the circle has widened to include Nephi: "The Lord . . . did visit me" and "the Lord spake unto me," he says.

More revelation comes in the chapters which follow. Lehi tells his son, "I have dreamed a dream, in the which the Lord hath commanded me that thou and thy brethren shall return to Jerusalem" (I Ne. 3:2). When fulfilling this commandment presents some difficulties for the brothers, "an angel of the Lord came and stood before them, and he spake unto them" (I Ne. 3:29). Going into Jerusalem alone, Nephi is "led by the Spirit," and in his most difficult hour he records, "I was constrained by the Spirit" (I Ne. 4:6, 10). Ultimately a man is killed before Nephi can obtain the object of his quest—the written revelations of God. In so chilling a way, Nephi and his readers are taught the absolute necessity—even the life-and-death necessity—of holy scripture. Without it, entire nations would dwindle and perish in unbelief.

So five chapters conclude: dreams, prophecies, records, the voice of God, visions, angels, spiritual promptings—revelation heaped upon revelation, verse after verse. In these first few pages any serious reader must come to grips with the fundamental issue of man's ability to receive divine direction from God. In this book that proposition comes forcefully and *it comes first.* To one who is not willing to believe that a heavenly father directs the affairs of his children here on earth, the Book of Mormon will simply have nothing more to say. Of course when the reader is willing to go on, he is then led to some of the most magnificent revelations ever recorded, including Lehi's vision of the Tree of Life (which tree is successfully reached only by clinging to the word of God) and Nephi's own remarkable vision of events from the birth of Christ to the end of the world. As the first book of Nephi closes, Jehovah asks through Isaiah, "Can a woman forget her sucking child, that she should not have compassion on the son of her womb? Yea, they may forget, yet will I not forget thee, O house of Israel. Behold I have graven thee upon the palms of my hands" (I Ne. 21:15-16). The Book of Mormon teaches, both by what it is and what it says, that Jehovah will never forget us.

I think it is also important to note that through these chapters we are repeatedly taught *our* role in the process of revelation. Starting with Lehi's first prayer and moving through Nephi's later pondering, we are led to some of the most detailed scriptural accounts we have of how revelation may be received. For example, in chapters 11-15 Nephi is continually commanded by the Spirit of the Lord of an angel to "Look!" "Look," the Spirit invites, and Nephi sees the same symbols as his father saw in vision. "Look," the Spirit directs, and he learns the meaning of those things. "Look," the Spirit cries, and Nephi sees the fate of a nation and the end of the world. "Look," the Spirit commands nearly a dozen times in less than half as many pages. Could it be that this short imperative is also crucial to what will—or won't—happen as we read the rest of the book? "Look," the angels of heaven seem to be declaring to us. "Use your eyes and save your souls. Read the revelations of God. Open your understanding to see a world of dreams, visions, prophecies, and promptings." Surely the only thing more tragic than not reading the scriptures is not wanting to. Jesus wept over those who had eyes and yet would not see (Matt. 13:9-17).

Something else seems to be happening in these opening chapters of Donna's Book of Mormon, something which suggests not only that chapters are linked within books but that books are linked to other books to make a unified whole. Somewhere along the way we realize that there is, in this first book of Nephi, a repeated series of confrontations and alternatives. Nephi is one kind of son; Laman is another. Lehi is one kind of local leader; his relative Laban is another, and so on. Our twelve-year-old may think this looks like an advertisement for a boxing match or the table of contents in a legal textbook but a list of these alternatives might include:

Nephi, Sam	vs.	Laman, Lemuel
Lehi	vs.	Laban
New Jerusalem	vs.	Old Babylon
Tree of Life	vs.	Depths of Hell
Virgin Mother of Christ	vs.	Harlot Mother of Abomination
The Church of the Lamb of God	vs.	The Church of the Devil

Of course, the contest that we ultimately see is:

Christ	vs.	Satan

And Satan is eventually conquered, bound "for the space of many years" (I Ne. 11:26). Along such a path of choices and alternatives Nephi comes, prayerfully, and with some difficulty, through the wilderness of mortal life. He and his little band of faithful followers seem reconciled to the fact that there will probably be opposition to every good effort they make.

"Opposition in all things." That has a familiar ring to it. And we start reading in the second book of Nephi one of the greatest scriptural discourses of which we have record on "opposition in all things," dramatized in the fall of Adam, the atonement of Christ, and the fundamental issue of free agency which involves us in the effect of both (See 2 Ne. 2:11).

I am sure Lehi could have given a mighty sermon (or a patriarchal blessing) on opposition and agency somewhere back in the first book of Nephi, but how much more powerful it is for his sons—and readers—to have lived through fifty pages of such confrontations and alternatives before they hear it. The faithful few in this little group have had about as much "opposition in all things" as they can stand, but it has taught them something about themselves, a fallen world, the plan of God, and the exercise of choice. It has surely taught them a great deal about the Messiah who would come, withstand all opposition from the beginning to the end of the world, and give "liberty and eternal life" to any who wish freedom from the galling chains of hell.

It seems, then, that all the hardships of the first book of Nephi have had the purpose of pointing us toward the second book of Nephi and the figure of Christ which entirely dominates that book. Those thirty-three chapters testify of Christ's role in our mortal journey, drawing heavily on Isaiah's prophecies of the Messiah and the events surrounding the coming forth of our latter-day witness of his divinity, the Book of Mormon. The second book of Nephi then concludes with Nephi's majestic "doctrine of Christ" sermon, his final testimony to generations yet unborn. At Nephi's death Jacob enters to warn against sins which take us away from Christ—pride, riches, sexual immorality, even the direct influence of an anti-Christ such as Sherem. And so the book goes on.

Why does Alma 31, a chapter on the self-righteous "prayerful" Zoramites, follow Alma 30, a chapter on Korihor, the most unrighteous, unprayerful anti-Christ in the book? What do either of these chapters—or rather both of them—have to do with Alma 32, that masterful lesson of faith? Why is a peculiar little chapter like Alma 33, an unknown sermon from Zenos, inserted between two masterpieces like Alma 32 and Alma 34? Is it also a masterpiece, linking the other two? And what do all of these (Alma 30 through 34) have to do with the "strictness of the word" in Alma 3 5 and Alma's intensely personal counsel to his sons in Alma 36 through 42?

Or what contribution does 3 Nephi 11 make to the Book of Mormon's "Sermon on the Mount" (3 Nephi 12, 13, 14)? In what sense does "building on a rock" provide the brackets to that whole sermon? Why does a lesson on the sacrament (3 Nephi 18) follow that special experience Christ has with little children in 3 Nephi 17? And what does the great need for the Holy Ghost (3 Nephi 19) have to do with either of those preceding chapters?

Before we know it, dawn peeks out of the east on Dad and his book, though it seems to have been a night without darkness. Words charged with meaning. Doctrines of salvation. Lengthy prophetic segments constructed like works of art. Book after book controlled and condensed into the "most correct book on earth," a book with just one message, that Jesus is the Christ and there is no other way. It is by every worthy standard a great book, a classic book, a book of books. It is the word of God and the keystone of our religion. We ought to drink constantly at its fountain like the thirsty children we are.

P.S. Why *is* the Book of Ether positioned exactly where it is?

Tithing

Elder Boyd K. Packer

Excerpts from Conference Report, October, 1974, pp. 126-127

Several years ago I presided over one of our missions. Two of our missionaries were teaching a fine family, and they had expressed a desire to be baptized, and then they suddenly cooled off. The father had learned about tithing and canceled all further meetings with the missionaries.

Two sad elders reported to the branch president, who himself was a recent convert, that he would not have this fine family in his branch.

A few days later the branch president persuaded the elders to join him in another visit to the family.

"I understand," he told the father "that you have decided not to join the Church."

"That is correct," he answered.

"The elders tell me that you are disturbed about tithing."

"Yes," said the father. "They had not told us about it; and when I learned of it, I said, 'Now that's too much to ask. Our church has never asked anything like that.' We think that's just too much, and we will not join."

"Did they tell you about fast offering?" he asked.

"No," said the man. "What is that?"

"In the Church we fast for two meals each month and give the value of the meals for the help of the poor."

"They did not tell us that," the man said.

"Did they mention the building fund?"

"No, what is that?"

"In the Church we all contribute toward building chapels. If you joined the Church, you would want to participate both in labor and with money. Incidentally, we are building a new chapel here," he told him.

"Strange," he said, "that they didn't mention it."

"Did they explain the welfare program to you?"

"No," said the father. "What is that?"

"Well, we believe in helping one another. If someone is in need or ill or out of work or in trouble, we are organized to assist, and you would be expected to help.

"Did they also tell you that we have no professional clergy? All of us contribute our time, our talents, our means, and travel—all to help the work. And we're not paid for it in money."

"They didn't tell us any of that," said the father.

"Well," said the branch president, "if you are turned away by a little thing like tithing, it is obvious you're not ready for this Church. Perhaps you have made the right decision and you should not join."

As they departed, almost as an afterthought, he turned and said, "Have you ever wondered why people will do all of these things willingly? I have never received a bill for tithing. No one has ever called to collect it. But we pay it—and all of the rest—and count it a great privilege.

"If you could discover **why**, you would be within reach of the pearl of great price, which the Lord said the merchant man was willing to sell all that he had that he might obtain it.

"But," said the branch president. "It is **your** decision. I only hope you will pray about it."

A few days later the man appeared at the branch president's home. No, he did not want to reschedule the missionaries. That would not be necessary. He wanted to schedule the baptism of his family. They had been praying, fervently praying.

This happens every day with individuals and entire families attracted by the high standards, not repelled by them.

What Spending Money Reveals about You

How you feel about money in terms of spending it, using it, etc., tells much about you and your personality—particularly in marriage. The way a couple acts together in money situations reveals how they feel and relate to each other in other areas of the marriage. Here are some symbolic meanings of $$.

1. **Money is knowledge, culture and expertise**. If you have money you are successful, happy, and able to enjoy all the wonders of the world. You have arrived!

2. **Money is an antidote to loneliness, self-rejection, and depression**. Some people believe that money will give them self-esteem as well as an ability to relate successfully to others. People believe that money symbolizes the end of misery and the beginning of happiness. When it brings neither, the believer sometimes feels that he or she simply must get more money.

3. **Money means friendships with important people**. Those who feel this way will display their money in expensive dress and possessions in an attempt to impress others.

4. **Money brings power, prestige and status**. "Showing off" with the aim of impressing others is often an attempt to hide underlying feelings of inferiority. Some people throw money around by overtipping or overspending just to show themselves and others that they "have arrived." These people are often shocked when they realize that money, however much they acquire, does not really change basic feelings of worth, nor does it confer real self-confidence.

5. **Money is like blood**. As a result, spending money is like hemorrhaging or giving away vital pieces of one's self. People who feel this way are stingy people. They can't spend money unless they are convinced they are getting the best deal possible. "Being taken," or getting the worst end of a bargain, can bring on terrible feelings of despair, even an urge to commit suicide. Usually people who can't spend money (assuming they have it to spend) can't spend emotions, either.

6. **Money is mastery over others, a manipulative tool to gain love or control other people**. I have known parents who can't understand why their children do not love them even though they have *given their children so much money*. For these parents money equals love; they feel that the money-love they have given is as good as emotional love. Some women, to whom money equals love, will see their husbands' failure to love his family enough. In effect, these women are saying to their husbands, "If you loved me you would go out and earn more money for me."

7. **Money is a medium of exchange in a marriage.** The wife is dependent on her husband for her spending money which creates a dependency relationship in which he feels mastery and she feels weak and protected. The husband may complain that his wife refuses to learn how to care for money, and the wife may complain that her husband won't treat her like an adult, but neither will take responsibility for changing until they examine their emotional outlook toward themselves and each other. Or they may exchange money, homes, cars, prestige, nice things—for sex.

8. **Money is things**—innumerable things—cars, clothes, appliances, houses, lawns—things that, if possessed, will replace a missing self and sense of belonging.

9. **Money is freedom from drudgery**. It makes work unnecessary and permits its possessor to spend his/her time as he/she wishes.

Ten Common Sense Rules for Financial Independence

1. **Pay tithing and fast offerings**. Be charitable. The Lord will inspire more on how to use the 90 percent than you can do by yourself.

2. **Spend less than you make**. This sounds incredibly basic, but unfortunately most people can't manage to live within their means. Obviously, you cannot become financially independent if your spending regularly exceeds your income . . . unless you marry or inherit wealth.

3. **Use payroll deductions for savings**. The most effective method is to have the money you plan to invest come straight out of your paycheck or bank account.

4. **Pay the Lord and then yourself**. You can't spend what you don't see. By establishing a routine of automatically diverting some of your paycheck into savings each month, you become accustomed to making ends meet with less income than before. The money you save goes into building a portfolio that can be used for a retirement nest egg.

5. **Buying a house is a good investment**. Though real estate values will probably not be repeated as they have been earlier, it is a wise thing to do. The only way to get interest that is deductible on income taxes is to have a 2nd mortgage.

6. **Aim to save at least 10 percent of your net income**. That's the money left over after you've paid federal, state and local taxes. Saving 1/10th may seem like an impossible undertaking, but if you do for a couple of months you will get by.

7. **Use tax shelters to increase the amount of money you can invest**. The law allows you to put aside money before taxes are taken out—for retirement or long-range savings. This way you have all of the money being used in the investment rather than after-tax monies.

8. **In general, do not buy individual stocks**—but invest in a carefully selected mutual fund, where you buy into a diversified portfolio of stocks and gain access to a professional money manager.

9. **Your biggest enemy is procrastination**. The earlier you start investing, and reaping the benefits of compound interest, the better . . . and it's never too late to start. Find a few good mutual funds, leave your money in there and forget about it. You'll be astounded at how much your money will grow over the years.

10. **Make financial decisions together as a companionship**. Too many husbands do things on the side or even on the sly. If a stock goes under, you both need to know about it. If you do well together, you will feel better about your success.

"If there is any one thing that will bring peace and contentment into the human heart, and into the family, it is to live within [one's] means. And if there is any one thing that is grinding and discouraging and disheartening, it is to have debts and obligations that one cannot meet" (Heber J. Grant, *Gospel Standards,* p. 111).

Constancy Amid Change

President N. Eldon Tanner

Ensign, November 1979, pp. 80-82

As a young man getting started in life, I experienced personal depression. I have experienced a national and international depression, as well as periods of recession and inflation. I have watched so-called solutions come and go with each change in the economic cycle. These experiences have led me to the same conviction as Robert Frost, who once said:

> Most of the change we think we see in life
> Is due to truths being in and out of favor.
> ("The Black Cottage," in The Poetry of Robert Frost, ed. Edward Connery Latham, New York: Holt, Rinehart and Winston, 1969, p. 58).

What I would like to share with you today are my observations about the constant and fundamental principles which, if followed, will bring financial security and peace of mind under any economic circumstances.

First, I would like to build a foundation and establish a perspective within which these economic principles must be applied.

One day a grandson of mine said to me:

> I have observed you and other successful men, and I have made up my mind that
> I want to be a success in my life. I want to interview as many successful people as I
> can to determine what made them successful. So looking back over your experience,
> grandpa, what do you believe is the most important element of success?

I told him that the Lord gave the greatest success formula that I know of: "Seek ye first the kingdom of God, and his righteousness; and all these things shall be added unto you (Matt. 6:33).

Some argue that some men prosper financially who do not seek the kingdom first. This is true. But the Lord is not promising us just material wealth if we seek first the kingdom. From my own experience I know this is not the case. In the words of Henrik Ibsen:

> Money may be the husk of many things, but not the kernel. It brings you food,
> but not appetite; medicine, but not health; acquaintances, but not friends; servants, but
> not faithfulness; days of joy, but not peace or happiness (In The Forbes Scrapbook of
> Thoughts on the Business of Life, New York: Forbes, Inc., 1968, p. 88).

Material blessings are a part of the gospel if they are achieved in the proper way and for the right purpose. I am reminded of an experience of President Hugh B. Brown. As a young soldier in World War I, he was visiting an elderly friend in the hospital. This friend was a millionaire several times over who, at the age of eighty, was lying at death's door. Neither his divorced wife nor any of his five children cared enough to come to the hospital to see him. As President Brown thought of the things his friend "had lost which money could not buy and noted his tragic situation and the depth of his misery," he asked his friend how he would change the course of his life if he had it to live over again.

The old gentleman, who died a few days later, said:

> As I think back over life the most important and valuable asset which I might have had but which I lost in the process of accumulating my millions, was the simple faith my mother had in God and in the immortality of the soul.
>
> . . . You asked me what is the most valuable thing in life. I cannot answer you in better words than those used by the poet.

He asked President Brown to get a little book out of his briefcase from which he read a poem entitled "I'm an Alien."

> I'm an alien, to the faith my mother
>   taught me.
> I'm a stranger to the God that heard
>   my mother when she cried.
> I'm an alien to the comfort that,
>   "Now I lay me," brought me.
> To the everlasting arms that held my
>   father when he died.
> When the great world came and
>   called me, I deserted all to follow.
> Never noting in my blindness I had
>   slipped my hand from His.
> Never dreaming in my dazedness that
>   the bubble fame is hollow.
> That the wealth of gold is tinsel, as I
>   since have learned it is.
> I have spent a lifetime seeking things
>   I spurned when I found them,
> I have fought and been rewarded in
>   many a winning cause,
> But I'd give it all, fame and fortune
>   and the pleasures that surround them,
> If I only had the faith that made my
>   mother what she was.

That was the dying testimony of a man who was born in the Church but had drifted far from it. That was the brokenhearted cry of a lonely man who could have anything money could buy, but who had lost the most important things of life in order to accumulate this world's goods (*Continuing the Quest*, Salt Lake City: Deseret Book Co., 1961, pp. 32-35).

In the Book of Mormon, the prophet Jacob gives us some important counsel on this matter:

> But before ye seek for riches, seek ye for the kingdom of God.
>
> And after ye have obtained a hope in Christ ye shall obtain riches, if ye seek them; and ye will seek them for the intent to do good—to clothe the naked, and to feed the hungry, and to liberate the captive, and administer relief to the sick and the afflicted (Jacob 2:18-19).

The foundation and perspective then are these: We must first seek the kingdom, work and plan and spend wisely, plan for the future, and use what wealth we are blessed with to help build up that kingdom.

When guided by this eternal perspective and by building on this firm foundation, we can pursue with confidence our daily tasks and our life's work, which must be carefully planned and diligently pursued.

It is within this framework that I would like to explain five principles of economic constancy.

Constancy #1: Pay an honest tithing. I often wonder if we realize that paying our tithing does not represent giving gifts to the Lord and the Church. Paying tithing is discharging a debt to the Lord. The Lord is the source of all our blessings, including life itself.

The payment of tithing is a commandment, a commandment with a promise. If we obey this commandment, we are promised that we will "prosper in the land." This prosperity consists of more than material goods—it may include enjoying good health and vigor of mind. It includes family solidarity and spiritual increase. I hope those of you not presently paying your full tithe will seek the faith and strength to do so. As you discharge this obligation to your Maker, you will find great, great happiness, the like of which is known only by those who are faithful to this commandment.

Constancy #2: Live on less than you earn. I have discovered that there is no way that you can ever earn more than you can spend. I am convinced that it is not the amount of money an individual earns that brings peace of mind as much as it is having control of his money. Money can be an obedient servant but a harsh taskmaster. Those who structure their standard of living to allow a little surplus, control their circumstances. Those who spend a little more than they earn are controlled by their circumstances. They are in bondage. President Grant once said:

> If there is any one thing that will bring peace and contentment into the human heart, and into the family, it is to live within our means. And if there is any one thing that is grinding and discouraging and disheartening, it is to have debts and obligations that one cannot meet (*Gospel Standards*, Salt Lake City: Improvement Era, 1941, p. 111).

The key to spending less than we earn is simple—it is called discipline. Whether early in life or late, we must all eventually learn to discipline ourselves, our appetites, and our economic desires. How blessed is he who learns to spend less than he earns and puts something away for a rainy day.

Constancy #3: Learn to distinguish between needs and wants. Consumer appetites are man-made. Our competitive free enterprise system produces unlimited goods and services to stimulate our desire to want more convenience and luxuries. I do not criticize the system or the availability of these goods or services. I am only concerned about our people using sound judgment in their purchases. We must learn that sacrifice is a vital part of our eternal discipline.

In this and many other countries, any parents and children born since World War II have known only prosperous conditions. Many have been conditioned to instant gratification. There have been ample job opportunities for all who are capable of working. Yesterday's luxuries for most are considered today's necessities.

This is typified by young couples who expect to furnish their homes and provide themselves with luxuries as they begin their marriages which their parents have managed to acquire only after many years of struggle and sacrifice. By wanting too much too soon, young couples may succumb to easy credit plans, thereby plunging themselves into debt. This would keep them from having the financial means necessary to do as the Church suggests in the matter of food storage and other security programs.

Overindulgence and poor money management place a heavy strain on marriage relationships. Most marital problems, it seems, originate from economic roots—either insufficient income to sustain the family or mismanagement of the income as earned.

One young father came to his bishop for financial counseling and told an all-too-frequent story: "Bishop, I have been well trained as an engineer, and I earn a good salary. It seems that all through school I was taught how to make money, but no one taught me how to manage money."

While we believe it is desirable for every student to take classes in consumer education, the primary training rests with the parents. Parents cannot leave this vital training to chance or transfer the responsibility entirely to our public schools and universities.

An important part of this training should be to explain debt. For most of us there are two kinds of financial debt—consumer debt and investment or business debt. Consumer debt refers to buying on credit those things we use or consume in daily living. Examples would include installment buying of clothes, appliances, furniture, etc. Consumer debt is secured by mortgaging our future earnings. This can be very dangerous. If we are laid off work, disabled, or encounter serious emergencies, we have difficulties meeting our obligations. Installment buying is the most expensive way to purchase. To the cost of the goods we buy must be added heavy interest and handling charges.

I realize that young families find it necessary at times to purchase on credit. But we caution you not to buy more than is truly necessary and to pay off your debts as quickly as possible. When money is tight, avoid the extra burden of additional interest charges.

Investment debt should be fully secured so as not to encumber a family's security. Don't invest in speculative ventures. The spirit of speculation can become intoxicating. Many fortunes have been wiped out by the uncontrolled appetite to accumulate more and more. Let us learn from the sorrows of the past and avoid enslaving our time, energy, and general health to a gluttonous appetite to acquire increased material goods.

President Kimball has given this thought-provoking counsel:

> The Lord has blessed us as a people with a prosperity unequaled in times past. The resources that have been placed in our power are good and necessary to our work here on the earth. But I am afraid that many of us have been surfeited with flocks and herds and acres and barns and wealth and have begun to worship them as false gods, and they have power over us. Do we have more of these good things than our faith can stand? Many people spend most of their time working in the service of a self-image that includes sufficient money, stocks, bonds, investment portfolios, property, credit cards, furnishings, automobiles, and the like to guarantee carnal security throughout, it is hoped, a long and happy life. Forgotten is the fact that our assignment is to use these many resources in our families and quorums to build up the kingdom of God" (*Ensign*, June 1976, p. 4).

By way of testimony, may I add this to President Kimball's statement. I know of no situation where happiness and peace of mind have increased with the amassing of property beyond the reasonable wants and needs of the family.

Constancy #4: Develop and live within a budget. A friend of mine has a daughter who went overseas with a BYU study-abroad program for a semester. She was constantly writing home for more money. His concern was such that he called her long-distance and questioned her about the need for the additional funds. At one point in the conversation the daughter explained, "But dad, I can tell you where every penny you have sent me has been spent.

He replied, "You don't seem to get the point. I'm interested in a budget—a plan for spending—not in a diary of where the money has gone."

Perhaps parents should be more like the father of the college boy who wired home, "No mon, no fun, your son." His father wired back, "How sad, too bad, your dad."

It has been my observation in interviewing many people through the years that far too many people do not have a workable budget and have not disciplined themselves to abide by its provisions. Many people think a budget robs them of their freedom. On the contrary, successful people have learned that a budget makes real economic freedom possible.

Budgeting and financial management need not be overly complicated or time-consuming. The story is told of an immigrant father who kept his accounts payable in a shoe box, his accounts receivable on a spindle, and his cash in the cash register.

"I don't see how you can run your business this way," said his son. "How do you know what your profit is?"

"Son," replied the businessman

> when I got off the boat, I had only the pants I was wearing. Today your sister is an art teacher, your brother is a doctor, and you're an accountant. I have a car, a home, and a good business. Everything is paid for. So you add it all up, subtract the pants, and there's my profit.

Wise financial counselors teach that there are four different elements to any good budget. Provision should be made first for basic operating needs such as food, clothing, etc.; second, for home equity; third, for emergency needs such as savings, health insurance, and life insurance; and, fourth, for wise investment and a storage program for the future.

May I comment on two of these elements. Nothing seems so certain as the unexpected in our lives. *So true!* With rising medical costs, health insurance is the only way most families can meet serious accident, illness, or maternity costs, particularly those for premature births. Life insurance provides income continuation when the provider prematurely dies. Every family should make provision for proper health and life insurance.

After these basics are met, we should by frugal management regularly save to create funds for investment. It has been my observation that few people have been successful with investments who have not first developed the habit of saving regularly This requires discipline and discriminating judgment. There are many ways to invest. My only advice is to choose wisely your investment counselors. Be sure they merit your confidence by maintaining a successful investment record.

Constancy #5: Be honest in all your financial affairs. The ideal of integrity will never go out of style. It applies to all we do. As leaders and members of the Church, we should be the epitome of integrity.

Brothers and sisters, through these five principles, I have tried to sketch what might be characterized as the true pattern of financial and resource management.

I hope that each of us may benefit from their application. I bear my witness that they are true and that this Church and the work we are engaged in are true. In the name of Jesus Christ, amen.

Stewardship

Following **is a statement** by President David O. McKay to a group of brethren in the church offices.

Let me assure you, Brethren, that some day you will have a personal priesthood interview with the Savior himself. If you are interested, I will tell you the order in which he will ask you to account for your earthly responsibilities:

First, He will request an accountability report about your relationship with your wife. Have you actively been engaged in making her happy and ensuring that her needs have been met as an individual?

Second, He will want an accountability report about each of your children individually, information about your relationship to each and every child.

Third, He will want to know what you personally have done with the talents you were given in the premortal life.

Fourth, He will want a summary of your activity in your church assignments. He will not necessarily be interested in *what* assignments you have had, for in his eyes the home teacher and a mission president are probably equals, but He will request a summary of how you have been of service to your fellow men in your Church assignments.

Fifth, He will have no interest in how you earned your living, but if you were honest in all your dealings.

Sixth, He will ask for an accountability on what you have done to contribute in a positive manner to your community, state, country, and the world (Fred Baker reporting on the interview with President McKay).

Some Reflections on Marriage & Family Relations

Douglas Brinley

"The most popular—and the roughest—contact sport in the country is not professional football; it is marriage. Consider the statistics: Over 90 percent of us try our hand at it, either ignoring the dangers or simply hoping for the best. A third of us, however, sustain so many injuries that we are willing to suffer the humiliation of divorce to get off the field. Yet the promise, the attractiveness, is so great that 80 percent of those divorced put themselves back into the marriage (game)—most of them within three years. Clearly, the problem is not how to make matrimony more popular; it's how to make it less hazardous" (*Couples,* p. 13).

General Principles

1. *You can be no better spouse/parent than you are as a person.* If you are dishonest, break promises, are mentally (or physically) immoral, have a low self-esteem, use temper to manipulate others, or have other character problems, (1) these characteristics will negatively affect your family relations now and (2) will be passed on to your posterity in the future.

2. *Happiness in this life is based on the quality of your marriage and family relations.* We often think it is things—money, whether BYU wins or loses, TV, gardening, boating, but—no. They may give satisfaction, but they don't compare to the primary joy that comes from a solid marriage and family.

3. *As the marriage goes, so goes the family.* In general, this is true. Each spouse must work consciously to build and keep a strong, solid, marriage. A very wise man once said, "A happy wife is worth 100 books on child development." There are marital termites that can eat away at marital happiness, so never relax.

4. *All couples and families have adjustments to make—no one ever sailed off into the sunset and lived "happily ever after."* We all marry someone we know little about, but we commit ourselves to accept the weaknesses as well as the strengths we discover in our spouse. We ought to be getting better each year we are together. It is the worst form of being a traitor to defect, to flirt, to allow romance to develop with others after bearing children, varicose veins, sagging bellies, or hair loss! TV may portray affairs as glamorous—but—in the clinic it is a disaster. The real world shows it to be heartbreak, tears, anger, and hostility—besides divorce. "Every wife has grounds for divorce. Every husband has grounds for divorce," but we don't.

5. *Greet your spouse with love and enthusiasm when either one of you comes home.* Embrace often and renew your love briefly before tackling the problems that have developed during the day. Treat your husband at least as good as the dog! Jump up on him and give him a hug and a kiss.

6. *Take time to get off alone together*—just the two of you; and take time to be together as a family. Children remember trips the best! Don't be so cheap that you don't escape occasionally. You need dates, trips, outings.

7. *Seek feedback from each other*—*both spouse and children.* We often fail to seek help from those who can do something about our concerns, or who know best how things could be improved. Check in with the children to see how they view your discipline methods, marriage, allowance system, etc.

8. *Trust is very fragile*—*never take it for granted.* Your marital commitment must be a solemn, eternal pledge. If it is broken it is very difficult to repair. Be a therapist in the family. Be sensitive to feelings, hurt, disappointment, ups and downs. Never use sex as a weapon or punishment. Intimacy is to renew commitment, to strengthen, to reinforce love feelings. It is not to be used as a threat for compliance or non-compliance. Your intimacy should be something private between you two.

9. *Learn to express love in the daylight*—*frequently*—*with both your spouse and children.* Expressions of love are indispensable in strong family relations. We die emotionally and spiritually without them. Increase the non-sexual affection, love, romance, and sexual affection! Touch is crucial in marriage and a very important form of communication. Hold hands. Hug.

10. *Learn to express positives and stay away from negatives.* If you need to "teach" something to your spouse, find a time when you are not emotional about it—and ask for a time to visit. "Honey, there is something that I need to visit with you about." Be positive and constructive, and charitable.

11. *Develop decent, moral attributes that makes human relations run smoothly:* kindness, patience, love, charity, long-suffering, meekness, humility, gentleness, forgiveness, turning the other cheek, a repenting spirit;

Marriage Evaluation

On another sheet write down these items. Give several responses. After completing the items, sit together and share your answers.

1. How do I let my spouse know that I love him/her?

2. How does my spouse let me know that he/she loves me?

3. How would I like my spouse to show love to me?

4. What things do I appreciate most about my companion?

5. What areas can we talk about easily? Are there some we avoid? What?

6. What are the major strengths in your children?

Parenting

1. *You cannot positively influence your children (or anyone else for that matter) unless you first build a relationship with them.* That will take (1) time; (2) positive love and praise; (3) personal sharing sessions; (4) listening; (5) caring; and (6) bearing your own soul. "Behavioral problems are relationship problems."

2. *You must parent as partners.* It took both of you to get them into this world, and it takes both of you to properly raise them. Children need fathers desperately. As the father functions, so will go the family.

3. *Teach your children what you want them to know and become.* Teach your children both gospel principles and "preparation for life." We have too many boarding houses and not enough "families." Children need limits, rules. They need to know something about life and what they will face in the future. They need a philosophy of living and parents are often negligent in teaching principles before the crisis hits. The most important variable: "The amount of conversation time between parents and children."

4. *Mothering is the most important and difficult job in the world today.* It is the husband's task to help his wife feel loved, appreciated, and secure in her marriage so that she can give of her divine love and attributes to her children, and to her husband. No one can replace mother—no one.

5. *Build traditions:* service projects, giving, sharing, risking, singing, working together, playing, worshiping together. Selfishness is the curse of the day. Treat your own children at least as good as the neighbors!

The Family Profile

Bernie Boswell

Cottage Program for Families in Focus, *Famileer*, pp. 8-9

1	2	3	4	5
Almost Never	Once in a While	Sometimes	Frequently	Almost Always

Describe your family the way it actually is:

_____ 1. We enjoy doing things together.

_____ 2. We all help make the decisions in our family

_____ 3. We are proud of our family.

_____ 4. We think the same things are important.

_____ 5. We compliment each other.

_____ 6. We can say what we really feel.

_____ 7. We know we can handle the problems that come up.

_____ 8. We share interests and hobbies.

_____ 9. When there is a problem, children's suggestions are followed.

_____ 10. We respect one another.

_____ 11. We have similar values and beliefs.

_____ 12. We do nice things for each other.

_____ 13. We really listen to each other.

_____ 14. We can count on each other.

_____ 15. Our family often does fun things together.

_____ 16. Children have a say in the rules and discipline.

_____ 17. We stick together as a family.

_____ 18. We agree about what is right and wrong.

_____ 19. We express love for each other.

_____ 20. We believe it's important to understand others' feelings.

_____ 21. Things usually work out for the best in our family.

_____ 22. Togetherness is very important in our family.

_____ 23. Chores are divided up fairly in our family.

_____ 24. We have traditions that we carry on.

_____ 25. We agree about what really matters in life.

_____26. We feel very close to each other.

_____27. We can talk about things without arguing.

_____28. We have friends and relatives we can count on.

_____29. It is easy for us to think of things to do together.

_____30. Our family discusses problems until we find a solution that's good for everyone.

_____31. We are proud of our family's history.

_____32. It's important to do what is right in our family.

_____33. We care about how others in the family feel.

_____34. We enjoy talking about things together.

_____35. We look forward to what the future will bring.

There are seven areas evaluated on this exercise:

Family Fun — Items 1, 8, 15, 22, 29

Family decision-making — Items 2, 9, 16, 23, 30

Family pride — Items 3, 10, 17, 24, 31

Family values — Items 4, 11, 18, 25, 32

Family communication — Items 5, 12, 19, 26, 33

Family feelings — Items 6, 13, 20, 27, 34

Family confidence — Items 7, 14, 21, 28, 35

Maximum would be 25 per category.
So, add up the entire score for each category
Divide this score by the possible—to get the % that your family is functioning near its potential.
Discuss those areas where you or the children have less than 4s—and decide what you can do to
    improve.

Believing Christ:
A Practical Approach to the Atonement

Stephen E. Robinson

BYU Devotional, 29 May 1990

The greatest dichotomy, the greatest problem in the entire universe, consists of two facts. The first we can read in Doctrine and Covenants 1:31: "For I the Lord cannot look upon sin with the least degree of allowance." That means he can't stand it, he can't tolerate it, he can't blink, or look the other way, or sweep it under the rug. He can't tolerate sin in the least degree. The other side of the dichotomy is very simply put: I sin, and so do you. If that were all there were to the equation the conclusion would be inescapable that we, as sinful beings, cannot be tolerated in the presence of God.

But that is not all there is to the equation. This morning I would like to talk to you about the Atonement of Christ, that glorious plan by which this dichotomy can be resolved. I would like to share with you incidents from my own life that illustrate how the Atonement works in a practical, everyday setting.

Believing Christ

First is a story about my son, Michael, who did something wrong when he was six or seven years old. He's my only son, and I'm hard on him. I want him to be better than his dad was, even as a boy, and so I lean on him and expect a great deal. Well, he had done something I thought was incredibly vile, and I let him know how terrible it was. I sent him to his room with the instructions, "Don't you dare come out until I come and get you."

And then I forgot. It was some hours later, as I was watching television, that I heard his door open and heard the tentative footsteps coming down the hall. I said, " Oh, my gosh," and ran to my end of the hall to see him standing with swollen eyes and tears on his cheeks at the other end. He looked up at me—he wasn't quite sure he should have come out and said, "Dad, can't we ever be friends again?" Well, I melted, ran to him, and hugged him. He's my boy, and I love him.

Like Michael, we all do things that disappoint our Father, that separate us from his presence and spirit. There are times when we get sent to our rooms spiritually. There are sins that maim; there are sins that wound our spirits. Some of you know what it is like to do something that makes you feel as if you just drank raw sewage. You can wash, but you can never get clean. When that happens, sometimes we ask the Lord as we lift up our eyes, "O Father, can't we ever be friends again?"

The answer that can be found in all the scriptures is a resounding "Yes, through the Atonement of Christ." I particularly like the way it is put in Isaiah 1:18.

Come now, and let us reason together, saith the Lord: though your sins be as scarlet, they shall be as white as snow; though they be red like crimson, they shall be as wool.

I like to paraphrase that for my students. What the Lord is saying is "I don't care what you did. It doesn't matter what you did. I can erase it. I can make you pure and worthy and innocent and celestial. "

Brothers and sisters, to have faith in Jesus Christ is not merely to believe that he is who he says he is, to believe in Christ. Sometimes, to have faith in Christ is also to believe Christ. Both as a bishop and as a teacher in the Church, I have learned there are many that believe Jesus is the Son of God and that he is the

Savior of the World, but that he cannot save them. They believe in his identity, but not in his power to cleanse and to purify and to save. To have faith in his identity is only half the process. To have faith in his ability, in his power to cleanse and to save, that is the other half. We must not only believe in Christ, we must believe Christ when he says, "I can cleanse you and make you celestial."

When I was a bishop, I used to hear several variations on a theme. Sometimes it was, "Bishop, I've punched my ticket wrong. I've just made mistakes that have gotten me off on the wrong track, and you can't get there from here." I've heard those who say, "Bishop, I've sinned too horribly. I can't have the full blessings of the gospel because I did this, or I did that. I'll come to Church, and I'll be active, and I'm hoping for a pretty good reward, but I couldn't receive the full blessings of exaltation in the celestial kingdom after what I've done." There are those members who say, "Bishop, I'm just an average Saint. I'm weak and imperfect, I and I don't have all the talents that Sister So-and-So does, or Brother So-and-So does. I'll never be in the bishopric, or I'll never be the Relief Society president. I'm just average. I hope for a place a little further down." All of these are variations of the same theme: "I do not believe Christ can do what he claims. I have no faith in his ability to exalt me."

My favorite is a fellow who said to me once, "Bishop, I'm just not celestial material." Well, I'd had enough, so I said back to him, "Why don't you admit your problem? You're not celestial material? Welcome to the club. None of us are! None of us qualify on the terms of perfection required for the presence of God by ourselves. Why don't you just admit that you don't have faith in the ability of Christ to do what he says he can do?"

He got angry. He had always believed in Christ. He said, "I have a testimony of Jesus. I believe in Christ."

I said, "Yes, you believe in Christ. You simply do not believe Christ, because he says even though you are not celestial material, he can make you celestial material."

Why He Is Called the Savior

Sometimes the weight of the demand for perfection drives us to despair. Sometimes we fail to believe that most choice portion of the gospel that says he can change us and bring us into his kingdom. Let me share an experience that happened about ten years ago. My wife and I were living in Pennsylvania. Things were going pretty well; I'd been promoted. It was a good year for us, though a trying year for Janet. That year she had our fourth child, graduated from college, passed the CPA exam, and was made Relief Society president. We had temple recommends, we had family home evening. I was in the bishopric. I thought we were headed for "LDS yuppiehood." Then one night the lights went out. Something happened in my wife that I can only describe as "dying spiritually." She wouldn't talk about it; she wouldn't tell me what was wrong. That was the worst part. For a couple of weeks she did not wish to participate in spiritual things. She asked to be released from her callings, and she would not open up and tell me what was wrong.

Finally, after about two weeks, one night I made her mad and it came out. She said, "All right. You want to know what's wrong? I'll tell you what's wrong. I can't do it anymore. I can't lift it. I can't get up at 5:30 in the morning and bake bread and sew clothes and help my kids with their homework and do my own homework and do my Relief Society stuff and get my genealogy done and write the congressman and go to the PTA meetings and write the missionaries . . ." And she just started naming one brick after another that had been laid on her, explaining all the things she could not do. She said, "I don't have the talent that Sister Morrell has. I can't do what Sister Childs does. I try not to yell at the kids, but I lose control, and I do. I'm just not perfect, and I'm not ever going to be perfect. I'm not going to make it to the celestial kingdom, and I've finally admitted that to myself. You and the kids can go, but I can't lift it. I'm not 'Molly Mormon,' and I'm not ever going to be perfect, so I've given up."

"Why break my back?"

Well, we started to talk, and it was a long night. I asked her, "Janet, do you have a testimony?"

She said, "Of course I do! That's what's so terrible. I know it's true. I just can't do it."

"Have you kept the covenants you made when you were baptized?"

She said, "I've tried and I've tried, but I cannot keep all the commandments all the time."

Then I rejoiced because I knew what was wrong, and I could see the light at the end of the tunnel. It wasn't any of those horrible things I thought it might be. Who would have thought after eight years of marriage, after all the lessons we'd given and heard, and after all we had read and done in the Church, who would have thought that Janet did not know the gospel of Jesus Christ? You see, she was trying to save herself. She knew why Jesus is a coach, a cheerleader, an advisor, a teacher. She knew why he is an example, the head of the Church, the Elder Brother, or even God. She knew all of that, but she did not understand why he is called the Savior.

Janet was trying to save herself with Jesus as an advisor. Brothers and sisters, we can't. No one can. No one is perfect—not even the Brethren. Please turn to Ether 3:2. This is about one of the greatest prophets that ever lived, the brother of Jared. His faith is so great that he is about to pierce the veil and see the spiritual body of Christ. As he begins to pray, he says,

> Now behold, O Lord, and do not be angry with thy servant because of his weakness before thee; [One of the greatest prophets who ever lived, and he starts his prayer with an apology as an imperfect being for approaching a perfect God.] for we know that thou art holy and dwellest in the heavens, and that we are unworthy before thee, because of the fall our natures have become evil continually; nevertheless, O Lord, thou hast given us a commandment that we must call upon thee, that from thee we may receive according to our desires.

Of course we fail at the celestial level. That's why we need a savior, and we are commanded to approach God and to call upon him so we may receive according to our desires. In the New Testament the Savior says, "Blessed are they which do hunger and thirst after righteousness: for they shall be filled" (Matthew 5:6). We misinterpret that frequently. We think that means blessed are the righteous. It does not. When are you hungry? When are you thirsty? When you don't have the object of your desire. Blessed are those who hunger and thirst after the righteousness that God has, after the righteousness of the celestial kingdom, because as that is the desire of their heart, they can achieve it—they will be filled. We may receive "according to our desires."

Becoming One

Perfection comes through the Atonement of Christ. We become one with him, with a perfect being. And as we become one, there is a merger. Some of my students are studying business, and they understand it better if I talk in business terms. You take a small bankrupt firm that's about ready to go under and merge it with a corporate giant. What happens? Their assets and liabilities flow together, and the new entity that is created is solvent.

It's like when Janet and I got married. I was overdrawn; Janet had money in the bank. By virtue of making that commitment, of entering into that covenant relationship of marriage with my wife, we became a joint account. No longer was there an I, and no longer a she—now it was we. My liabilities and her assets flowed into each other, and for the first time in months I was in the black.

Spiritually, this is what happens when we enter into the covenant relationship with our Savior. We have liabilities, he has assets. He proposes to us a covenant relationship. I use the word "propose" on purpose because it is a marriage of a spiritual sort that is being proposed. That is why he is called the Bridegroom. This covenant relationship is so intimate that it can be described as a marriage. I become one with Christ, and as partners we work together for my salvation and my exaltation. My liabilities and his assets flow into each other. I do all that I can do, and he does what I cannot yet do. The two of us together are perfect.

This is why the Savior says in Matthew 11:28 "Come unto me, all ye that labour and are heavy laden, and I will give you rest." What heavier load is there than the demand for perfection, that you must do it all, that you must make yourself perfect in this life before you can have any hope in the next? What heavier burden is there than that? That is the yoke of the law.

Come unto me, all ye that labour and are heavy laden, and I will give you rest.

Take my yoke upon you, and learn of me; for I am meek and lowly in heart: and ye shall find rest unto your souls.

For my yoke is easy, and my burden is light (Matthew 11:28-30).

"Trust Me"

Turn, if you will, to 2 Nephi 4:17-19. You know the prophet Nephi. He was one of the great prophets, yet he had a sense of his need for the Savior and his reliance upon the Savior. He says,

O wretched man that I am! Yea, my heart sorroweth because of my flesh my soul grieveth because of mine iniquities.

I am encompassed about, because of the temptations and the sins which do so easily beset me.

And when I desire to rejoice, my heart groaneth because of my sins.

Did Nephi have an appreciation for his mortal condition, for his need of the Savior to be saved from his sins? Oh yes, and the key is what comes next, "nevertheless, I know in whom I have trusted." All right, I'm imperfect. My sins bother me. I'm not celestial yet, but I know in whom I have trusted. Nephi trusted in the power of Jesus Christ to cleanse him of his sins and to bring him into the kingdom of God.

I had a friend who used to say quite frequently, "Well, I figure my life is half over, and I'm halfway to the celestial kingdom, so I'm right on schedule."

One day I asked her, "Judy, what happens if you die tomorrow?" It was the first time that thought had ever occurred to her.

"Let's see, halfway to the celestial kingdom is . . . mid-terrestrial! That's not good enough!"

We need to know that in this covenant relationship we have with the Savior, if we should die tomorrow, we have hope of the celestial kingdom. That hope is one of the promised blessings of the covenant relationship. Yet many of us do not understand it or take advantage of it.

When our twin daughters were small, we decided to take them to the public pool and teach them how to swim. I remember starting with Rebekah. As I went down into the water with Rebekah, I thought, "I'm going to teach her how to swim." But as we went down into the water, in her mind was the thought, "My dad is going to drown me. I'm going to die!" The water was only three and a half feet deep, but Becky was only three feet deep. She was so petrified that she began to scream and cry and kick and scratch and was unteachable.

Finally, I just had to grab her. I threw my arms around her, and I just held her, and I said, "Becky, I've got you. I'm your dad. I love you. I'm not going to let anything bad happen to you. Now relax." Bless her heart, she trusted me. She relaxed, and I put my arms under her and said, "Okay, now kick your legs." And we began to learn how to swim.

Spiritually there are some of us who are similarly petrified by the questions "Am I celestial? Am I going to make it? Was I good enough today?" We're so terrified of whether we're going to live or die, or whether we've made it to the kingdom or not, that we cannot make any progress. It's at those times when the Savior grabs us and throws his arms around us and says, "I've got you. I love you. I'm not going to let you die. Now relax and trust me." If we can relax and trust him and believe him, as well as believe in him, then together we can begin to learn to live the gospel. Then he puts his arms under us and says, "Okay, now pay tithing. Very good. Now pay a full tithing" And so we begin to make progress.

Turn to Alma 34:14-16.

And behold, this is the whole meaning of the law, every whit pointing to that great and last sacrifice; and that great and last sacrifice will be the Son of God, yea, infinite and eternal.

And thus he shall bring salvation to all those who shall believe on his name, this being the intent of this last sacrifice, to bring about the bowels of mercy, which overpowereth justice, and bringeth about means unto men that they may have faith unto repentance.

And thus mercy can satisfy the demands of justice, and encircles them in the arms of safety.

"The arms of safety"—that is my favorite phrase from the Book of Mormon.

Brothers and sisters, do Mormons believe in being saved? If I ask my classes that question with just the right twang in my voice, "Do we believe in being saved?" I can generally get about a third of my students to shake their heads and say, " Oh no, no! Those other guys believe in that." What a tragedy! Brothers and sisters, we believe in being saved. That's why Jesus is called the Savior. What good is it to have a savior if no one is saved? It's like having a lifeguard that won't get out of the chair. "There goes another one down. Try the backstroke! Oh, too bad, he didn't make it." We have a savior who can save us from ourselves, from what we lack, from our imperfections, from the carnal individual within us.

Turn to Doctrine and Covenants 76:68-69. In Joseph's vision of the celestial kingdom, he describes those who are there in these terms:

These are they whose names are written in heaven, where God and Christ are the judge of all.

These are they who are just men made perfect through Jesus the mediator of the new covenant. Just men and women, good men and women, those who hunger and thirst after righteousness, made perfect through Jesus, the mediator of the new covenant.

Give Him All That We Have

As my wife and I talked about her feeling of inadequacy and her feeling that she couldn't do it and that she couldn't make it, I had a hard time reaching her until finally I hit upon something that had happened in our family just a couple of months earlier. In our home it is now called the parable of the bicycle.

After I had come home from school one day, I was sitting in a chair reading the newspaper My daughter Sarah, who was seven years old, came in and said, "Dad, can I have a bike? I'm the only kid on the block who doesn't have a bike."

Well, I didn't have enough money to buy her a bike, so I stalled her and said, "Sure, Sarah."

She said, "How? When?"

I said, "You save all your pennies, and pretty soon you'll have enough for a bike." And she went away.

A couple of weeks later as I was sitting in the same chair, I was aware of Sarah doing something for her mother and getting paid. She went into the other room and I heard "clink, clink." I asked, "Sarah, what are you doing?"

She came out and she had a little jar all cleaned up with a slit cut in the lid and a bunch of pennies in the bottom. She looked at me and said, "You promised me that if I saved all my pennies, pretty soon I'd have enough for a bike. And, Daddy, I've saved every single one of them."

She's my daughter, and I love her. My heart melted. She was doing everything in her power to follow my instructions. I hadn't actually lied to her. If she saved all of her pennies, she would eventually have enough for a bike, but by then she would want a car. But her needs weren't being met. Because I love her, I said, "Let's go downtown and look at bikes."

We went to every store in Williamsport, Pennsylvania. Finally we found it—the perfect bicycle, the one she knew in the premortal existence. She got up on that bike; she was thrilled. She then saw the price tag, reached down, and turned it over. When she saw how much it cost, her face fell and she started to cry. She said, "Oh Dad, I'll never have enough for a bicycle."

So I said, "Sarah, how much do you have?"

She answered, "Sixty-one cents."

"I'll tell you what. You give me everything you've got and a hug and a kiss, and the bike is yours." Well, she's never been stupid. She gave me a hug and a kiss. She gave me the sixty-one cents. Then I had to drive home very slowly because she wouldn't get off the bike. She rode home on the sidewalk, and as I drove along slowly beside her it occurred to me that this was a parable for the Atonement of Christ.

We all want something desperately—it isn't a bicycle. We want the celestial kingdom. We want to be with our Father in Heaven. And no matter how hard we try, we come up short. At some point we realize, "I can't do this!" That was the point my wife had reached. It is at that point that the sweetness of the gospel covenant comes to our taste as the Savior proposes, "I'll tell you what. All right, you're not perfect. How much do you have? What can you do? Where are you now? Give me all you've got, and I'll pay the rest. Give me a hug and a kiss; enter into a personal relationship with me, and I will do what remains undone."

There is good news and bad news here. The bad news is that he still requires our best effort. We must try, we must work—we must do all that we can. But the good news is that having done all we can, it is enough for now. Together we'll make progress in the eternities, and eventually we will become perfect—but in the meantime, we are perfect only in a partnership, in a covenant relationship with him. Only by tapping his perfection can we hope to qualify.

When I explained to Janet how it worked, finally I broke through and she understood. She bloomed. I remember her saying through her tears, "I've always believed he is the Son of God. I have always believed that he suffered and died for me. But now I know that he can save me from myself, from my sins, from my weakness, inadequacy, and lack of talent."

Oh, brothers and sisters, how many of us forget the words of 2 Nephi 2:8:

There is no flesh that can dwell in the presence of God, save it be through the merits, and mercy, and grace of the Holy Messiah. There is no other way. Many of us are trying to save ourselves, holding the Atonement of Jesus Christ at arm's distance and saying, "When I've done it, when I've perfected myself, when I've made myself worthy, then I'll be worthy of the Atonement. Then I will allow him in. " We cannot do it. That's like saying, "When I am well, I'll take the medicine. I'll be worthy of it then." That's not how it was designed to work.

There is a hym—it is one of my favorites—that says, "Dearly, dearly has he loved! And we must love him too, And trust in his redeeming blood, And try his works to do" ("There Is a Green Hill Far Away," Hymns, 1985, no. 194). I think one of the reasons why I love that hymn so much is because it expresses both sides of that covenant relationship. We must try his works to do with all that is in us. We must do all that we can, and having done all, then we must trust in his redeeming blood and in his ability to do for us what we cannot yet do.

Elder McConkie used to call this being in the gospel harness. When we are in the gospel harness, when we are pulling for the kingdom with our eyes on that goal, although we are not yet there, we can have confidence that just as that is our goal in life, so it will be our goal in eternity. Through the Atonement of Christ we can have hope of achieving and an expectation of receiving that goal.

I bear testimony to you that this is true. I have learned this lesson in my life. My family has learned this lesson in our collective life. I bear testimony that Jesus Christ is the Son of God, that he is the Savior of the World, that he is our individual Savior, if we will only enter into that glorious covenant relationship with him and give him all that we have. Whether it be sixty-one cents or a dollar and a half or two cents, hold nothing back, give it all, and then have faith and trust in his ability to do for us what we cannot yet accomplish, to make up what we yet lack of perfection.

I bear testimony of him. I love him. I love his gospel dearly, and I say these things in the name of Jesus Christ. Amen.

God's Love for Us Transcends Our Transgressions

Elder Ronald E. Poelman

General Conference, April 1982, *Ensign*, May 1982, pp. 27-29

The Galilean fisherman Simon Peter, upon recognizing for the first time the divine power of Jesus, exclaimed, "Depart from me; for I am a sinful man, O Lord" (Luke 5:8).

Each one of us, at times, may feel as Peter, conscious of our failings and uncomfortable at the thought of approaching the Lord. Transgression causes us to feel estranged from our Father in Heaven, and we feel unworthy of his love and fearful of his disapproval.

Yet, having transgressed his laws or disobeyed his commandments, we need the strengthening influence of our Father to help us overcome our weakness, to repent and become reconciled with him. Unrepentant sin tends to become habitual and is frequently accompanied by a deepening sense of guilt which may make repentance increasingly difficult. This feeling of estrangement from the Lord becomes, itself, an impediment to repentance and reconciliation with him.

Knowing we have offended our Father in Heaven, we are afraid to ask his help, feeling that we don't deserve it. Paradoxically, when we are most in need of the Lord's influence we deserve it least. Nevertheless, in such circumstances he says to us, as Jesus said to the trembling Peter, "Fear not" (Luke 5: 10).

My message today might best be illustrated through the experiences of a young couple whom I will call John and Gayle.

John was a thoughtful, kind young man, affectionate, with a frank and open manner. He sincerely tried to obey the Lord's commandments and found honest contentment in the joys of family life. Gayle, his wife, was young, attractive, high-spirited, but inclined toward more worldly interests and activities. The society in which they lived was, in general, one of affluence and materialism. People seemed preoccupied with temporal gain, social status, entertainment, and self-gratification. Religious leaders were concerned about the apparent breakdown in family life and moral standards.

In the early years of their marriage, John and Gayle were blessed with children, first a boy and then a girl; but Gayle seemed uninterested in her domestic responsibilities. She longed for glamour and excitement in her life and was frequently away from home at parties and entertainments, not always with her husband. In her vanity, Gayle encouraged and responded to the attentions of other men until eventually she was unfaithful to her marriage vows.

Throughout, John encouraged Gayle to appreciate the joys of family life and experience the rewards of observing the laws of God. He was patient and kind, but to no avail. Shortly after the birth of a third child, a son, Gayle deserted her husband and children and joined her worldly friends in a life of self-indulgence and immorality. John, thus rejected was humiliated and brokenhearted.

Soon, however, the glamour and excitement that had attracted Gayle turned to ashes. Her so-called friends tired of her and abandoned her. Then each successive step was downward, her life becoming more and more degraded. Eventually she recognized her mistakes and realized what she had lost, but could see no way back. Certainly John could not possibly love her still. She felt completely unworthy of his love and undeserving of her home and family.

Then one day, passing through the streets, John recognized Gayle. Surely he would have been justified in turning away, but he didn't. As he observed the effect of her recent life, all too evident, a feeling of compassion came over him—a desire to reach out to her. Learning that Gayle had incurred substantial debts, John repaid them and then took her home.

Soon John realized, at first with amazement, that he still loved Gayle. Out of his love for her and her willingness to change and begin anew, there grew in John's heart a feeling of merciful forgiveness, a desire to help Gayle overcome her past and to accept her again fully as his wife.

Through his personal experience there arose in John another profound awareness, a realization of the nature of God's love for us, his children. Though we disregard his counsel, break his commandments, and reject him, when we recognize our mistakes and desire to repent, he wants us to seek him out and he will accept us.

John had been prepared, through his personal experiences, for a divine mission. Though I have taken some literary license in telling the story, it is the account, perhaps allegorical, of Hosea, prophet of the Old Testament, and his wife, Gomer.

Portraying God to ancient Israel as a loving, forgiving father, Hosea foreshadowed, more than most Old Testament prophets, the spirit and message of the New Testament, the Book of Mormon, and modern revelation.

In these latter days the Lord has said:

> For I the Lord cannot look upon sin with the least degree of allowance;
> Nevertheless, he that repents and does the commandments of the Lord shall be
> forgiven (D&C 1:31-32).

By disobeying the laws of God and breaking his commandments, we do offend him, we do estrange ourselves from him, and we don't deserve his help and inspiration and strength. But God's love for us transcends our transgressions.

When we disobey the laws of God, justice requires that compensation be made a requirement which we are incapable of fulfilling. But out of his divine love for us, our Father has provided a plan and a Savior, Jesus Christ, whose redeeming sacrifice satisfies the demands of justice for us and makes possible repentance, forgiveness, and reconciliation with our Father. For indeed, "God so loved the world, that he gave his only begotten Son, that whosoever believeth in him should not perish, but have everlasting life" (John 3:16).

We may accept this great gift through faith in Jesus Christ and repentance, followed by a covenant made with him through baptism of the water and of the Spirit. Then, each week, as we receive the sacrament, we renew our covenant that we will "always remember him and keep his commandments." The promise attached to that covenant is that we "may always have his Spirit to be with [us]" (D&C 20:77).

Hosea's ancient message is repeated and elaborated throughout the scriptures. Through Isaiah, another Old Testament prophet, the Lord said to his people:

> Wash you, make you clean; put away the evil of your doings from before mine
> eyes; cease to do evil;
> Learn to do well . . .
> Come now, and let us reason together, saith the Lord: though your sins be as scarlet,
> they shall be as white as snow; though they be red like crimson, they shall be as wool
> (Isaiah 1:16-18).

The Lord, speaking to Alma, the Nephite prophet, says:

> Whosoever transgresseth against me, him shall ye judge according to the sins
> which he has committed; and if he confess his sins before thee and me, and repenteth
> in the sincerity of his heart, him shall ye forgive, and I will forgive him also.
> Yea, and as often as my people repent will I forgive them their trespasses against me
> (Mosiah 26:29-30).

Too often we make repentance more difficult for each other by our failure to forgive one another. However, we are admonished in modern revelation that

> ye ought to forgive one another; for he that forgiveth not his brother his trespasses standeth condemned before the Lord; for there remaineth in him the greater sin.
>
> I, the Lord, will forgive whom I will forgive, but of you it is required to forgive all men (D&C 64:9-10).

Also from modern revelation comes one of the most comforting, hopeful pronouncements ever spoken: "He who has repented of his sins, the same is forgiven, and I, the Lord, remember them no more" (D&C 58:42).

God is our father; he loves us; his love is infinite and unconditional. His sorrow is great when we disobey his commandments and break his laws. He cannot condone our transgressions, but he loves us and wants us to return to him.

I know of no greater inducement to repentance and reconciliation with our Father in Heaven than an awareness of his love for us personally and individually. That such awareness may increase within each of us is my prayer, to which I add my personal witness to you individually that Jesus of Nazareth is the Son of God, the Savior of all mankind, and the Redeemer of each of us individually, in the sacred name of Jesus Christ, amen.

Within the Clasp of Your Arms

President Jeffrey R. Holland

Priesthood Meeting, April 1983, *Ensign*, May 1983, pp. 36-38

Brethren, it is impossible to express the overwhelming sense of responsibility I feel tonight. Like the mule who entered the Kentucky Derby, I know I probably shouldn't be here, but I surely like the company it lets me keep. Tonight I include in that special company my son Matt, whom I love with all my heart. I pray earnestly for the Spirit of the Lord to be with us in our assignment.

Brethren, a recent study conducted by the Church has forcefully confirmed statistically what we have been told again and again. That is, if loving, inspired instruction and example are not provided at home, then our related efforts for success in and around Church programs are severely limited. It is increasingly clear that we must teach the gospel to our families personally, live those teachings in our homes, or run the risk of discovering too late that a Primary teacher or priesthood adviser or seminary instructor could not do for our children what we would not do for them.

May I offer just this much encouragement regarding such a great responsibility? What I cherish in my relationship with Matt is that he is, along with his mother and sister and brother, my closest, dearest friend. I would rather be here at this priesthood meeting tonight with my son than with any other male companion in this world. I love to be with him. We talk a lot. We laugh a lot. We play one-on-one basketball; we play tennis and racquetball, though I do refuse to play golf with him (that's a private joke). We discuss problems. I am the president of a small university, and he is the president of a large high school class. We compare notes and offer suggestions and share each other's challenges. I pray for him and have cried with him, and I'm immensely proud of him. We've talked long into the night lying on his water bed, a twentieth century aberration which I know, as part of the punishment of the last days, will one day burst and wash the Hollands helplessly into the streets of Provo (that's another private joke).

I feel I can talk to Matt about how he is enjoying seminary because I try to talk to him about all of his classes at school. We often imagine together what his mission will be like because he knows how much my mission meant to me. And he asks me about temple marriage because he knows I am absolutely crazy about his mother. He wants his future wife to be like her and for them to have what we have.

Now, even as I speak, I know that there are fathers and sons in this meeting tonight who feel they do not have any portion of what is here described. I know there are fathers who would give virtually their very lives to be close again to a struggling son. I know there are sons in our meeting who wish their dads were at their side, tonight or any night. I have wondered how to speak on this assigned topic without sounding self-righteous on the one hand or offending already tender hearts on the other. In answer to that, I simply say to us all, young and old, never give up. Keep trying, keep reaching, keep talking, keep praying but never give up. Above all never pull away from each other.

May I share a brief but painful moment from my own inadequate efforts as a father?

Early in our married life my young family and I were laboring through graduate school at a university in New England. Pat was the Relief Society president in our ward, and I was serving in our stake presidency. I was going to school full-time and teaching half-time. We had two small children then, with little money and lots of pressures. In fact, our life was about like yours.

One evening I came home from long hours at school, feeling the proverbial weight of the world on my shoulders. Everything seemed to be especially demanding and discouraging and dark. I wondered if the dawn would ever come. Then, as I walked into our small student apartment, there was an unusual silence in the room.

"What's the trouble?" I asked. "Matthew has something he wants to tell you," Pat said. "Matt, what do you have to tell me?" He was quietly playing with his toys in the corner of the room, trying very hard not to hear me. "Matt," I said a little louder, "do you have something to tell me?"

He stopped playing, but for a moment didn't look up. Then these two enormous, tear-filled brown eyes turned toward me, and with the pain only a five-year-old can know, he said, "I didn't mind Mommy tonight, and I spoke back to her." With that he burst into tears, and his entire little body shook with grief. A childish indiscretion had been noted, a painful confession had been offered, the growth of a five-year-old was continuing, and loving reconciliation could have been wonderfully underway.

Everything might have been just terrific—except for me. If you can imagine such an idiotic thing, I lost my temper. It wasn't that I lost it with Matt—it was with a hundred and one other things on my mind; but he didn't know that, and I wasn't disciplined enough to admit it. He got the whole load of bricks.

I told him how disappointed I was and how much more I thought I could have expected from him. I sounded like the parental pygmy I was. Then I did what I had never done before in his life—I told him that he was to go straight to bed and that I would not be in to say his prayers with him or to tell him a bedtime story. Muffling his sobs, he obediently went to his bedside, where he knelt—alone—to say his prayers. Then he stained his little pillow with tears his father should have been wiping away.

If you think the silence upon my arrival was heavy, you should have felt it now. Pat did not say a word. She didn't have to. I felt terrible!

Later, as we knelt by our own bed, my feeble prayer for blessings upon my family fell back on my ears with a horrible, hollow ring. I wanted to get up off my knees right then and go to Matt and ask his forgiveness, but he was long since peacefully asleep.

My relief was not so soon coming; but finally I fell asleep and began to dream, which I seldom do. I dreamed Matt and I were packing two cars for a move. For some reason his mother and baby sister were not present. As we finished I turned to him and said, "Okay, Matt, you drive one car and I'll drive the other."

This five-year-old very obediently crawled up on the seat and tried to grasp the massive steering wheel. I walked over to the other car and started the motor. As I began to pull away, I looked to see how my son was doing. He was trying—oh, how he was trying. He tried to reach the pedals, but he couldn't. He was also turning knobs and pushing buttons, trying to start the motor. He could scarcely be seen over the dashboard, but there staring out at me again were those same immense, tear-filled, beautiful brown eyes. As I pulled away, he cried out, "Daddy, don't leave me. I don't know how to do it. I am too little." And I drove away.

A short time later, driving down that desert road in my dream, I suddenly realized in one stark, horrifying moment what I had done. I slammed my car to a stop, threw open the door, and started to run as fast as I could. I left car, keys, belongings, and all—and I ran. The pavement was so hot it burned my feet, and tears blinded my straining effort to see this child somewhere on the horizon. I kept running, praying, pleading to be forgiven and to find my boy safe and secure.

As I rounded a curve nearly ready to drop from physical and emotional exhaustion, I saw the unfamiliar car I had left Matt to drive. It was pulled carefully off to the side of the road, and he was laughing and playing nearby. An older man was with him, playing and responding to his games. Matt saw me and cried out something like, "Hi, Dad. We're having fun." Obviously he had already forgiven and forgotten my terrible transgression against him.

But I dreaded the older man's gaze, which followed my every move. I tried to say "Thank you," but his eyes were filled with sorrow and disappointment. I muttered an awkward apology and the stranger said simply, "You should not have left him alone to do this difficult thing. It would not have been asked of you."

With that, the dream ended, and I shot upright in bed. My pillow was now stained, whether with perspiration or tears I do not know. I threw off the covers and ran to the little metal camp cot that was my son's bed. There on my knees and through my tears I cradled him in my arms and spoke to him while he slept. I told him that every dad makes mistakes but that they don't mean to. I told him it wasn't his fault I had had a bad day. I told him that when boys are five or fifteen, dads sometimes forget and think they are fifty. I told him that I wanted him to be a small boy for a long, long time, because all too soon he would grow up and be a man and wouldn't be playing on the floor with his toys when I came home. I told him that I loved him and his mother and his sister more than anything in the world and that whatever challenges we had in life we would face them together. I told him that never again would I withhold my affection or my forgiveness from him, and never, I prayed, would he withhold them from me. I told him I was honored to be his father and that I would try with all my heart to be worthy of such a great responsibility.

Well, I have not proven to be the perfect father I vowed to be that night and a thousand nights before and since. But I still want to be, and I believe this wise counsel from President Joseph F. Smith:

> Brethren, . . . If you will keep your [children] close to your heart, within the clasp of your arms; if you will make them . . . feel that you love them . . . and keep them near to you, they will not go very far from you, and they will not commit any very great sin. But it is when you turn them out of the home, turn them out of your affection . . . that [is what] drives them from you. . . .
>
> Fathers, if you wish your children to be taught in the principles of the gospel, if you wish them to love the truth and understand it, if you wish them to be obedient to and united with you, love them! and prove . . . that you do love them by your every word and act to[ward] them (Gospel Doctrine, 5th ed., Salt Lake City: Deseret Book Co., 1966, pp. 282, 316).

Brethren, we all know fatherhood is not an easy assignment, but it ranks among the most imperative ever given, in time or eternity. We must not pull away from our children. We must keep trying, keep reaching, keep praying, keep listening. We must keep them "within the clasp of our arms." That is what friends are for. Of this I bear witness in the name of Jesus Christ, amen.

The Doer of Our Deeds and the Speaker of Our Words

M. Catherine Thomas

BYU Devotional, December 7, 1993

My subject this morning concerns the pursuit of self-esteem. I'm going to resist defining self-esteem and simply use the term to circumscribe a number of ways of viewing the self. I would like to explore the nature of the self and the conditions under which it flourishes. In particular, I want to ask this question: What is the eternal value of the pursuit of self-esteem?

Whatever the valid uses of the term *self-esteem* are, however much good is intended, I wonder if self-esteem isn't a red herring. The term *red herring* comes from the practice of dragging this smelly fish across a trail to destroy the original scent. Thus a red herring is a diversion intended to distract attention from the real issue. I suggest that the issue of self-esteem is a diversion to distract us from the real issue of our existence.

We might be justified in telling people to fix their self-esteem in order to solve their most basic problems if we knew nothing of man's premortal life, or the spiritual purpose of his earthly probation, or his glorious destiny. But the fullness of the gospel of Jesus Christ teaches the true nature and true needs of the self. There are two major human conditions that the self is subject to that may have led to the idea that the pursuit of self-esteem was important: man's vulnerability, or even pain, incident to the fall of man; and the conflict and insecurity, or pain, created by personal sin.

First, the pain incident to fallenness: Like our Savior, though to a lesser degree, we condescended to come to a fallen world, having agreed to submit to a considerable reduction in our premortal powers. As we came to earth, separated from the presence of heavenly parents, we died spiritually (see Helaman 14:16) and, in a sense, we were "orphaned." And now, with memory veiled, and much reduced from our premortal estate—somewhat as aliens in a world that is inimical to our spiritual natures—we may carry an insecurity, a self-pain that pervades much of our emotional life. Like Adam and Eve, we feel our self-consciousness or spiritual nakedness. The scriptures teach about this nakedness as a feeling of guilt or shame (see 2 Nephi 9:14, Mormon 9:5). Do we have a sense of loss from deeply buried memories of who we once were in contrast with who we are now? But here is my main question: Is it possible that in our efforts to find security, we have fallen into a number of errors? Is it possible that we have created the whole issue of self-esteem in an attempt to soothe this fallen, homesick self?

But there is a better way. Our Savior, who felt all this pain himself (Alma 7:11-13), would not send us to earth without compensation for the distresses he knew we would feel, separated from him. He would not leave us comfortless. You recall the passages in John in which the Savior has told the twelve that he will be with them only a little while (John 13:33). Peter responds with, "Lord, why cannot I follow thee now? I will lay down my life for thy sake" (John 13:37). Jesus senses their pain, almost their desperation, at his leaving them. He promises, "I will not leave you comfortless: I will come to you" (John 14:18). The English word *comfortless* translates the Greek word for "orphans": "I will not leave you orphaned." The Savior continued,

> If a man love me, he will keep my words: and my Father will love him, and we
> will come unto him, and make our abode with him . . . .

. . . my peace I give unto you: not as the world giveth, give I unto you. Let not your heart be troubled, neither let it be afraid (John 14:23, 27).

Here we grasp the stunning insight that the Lord Jesus Christ himself is that consolation, that compensation, designed from the foundation of the world to comfort the human pain of fallenness, to compensate men and women for their earthly reductions and sacrifices. Only the Atonement, or more expressly, the *At-one-ment*, can heal the pain of the Fall.

Now to the second source of pain: The Lord explained, speaking to Adam: "When [thy children] begin to grow up, sin conceiveth in their hearts, and they taste the bitter (Moses 6:55). What is this bitterness? The Lord says it is the conception of sin in our hearts. The pain of fallenness, then, is compounded by the bitterness of sin.

To understand why sin produces bitterness in the human soul, we remember that each individual spirit was begotten by glorious heavenly parents and thereby inherits a nature that is at its very core light, truth, intelligence, and glory (D&C 93:23, 29, 36). "Knowest thou not," the Prophet John Taylor wrote, "that thou art a spark of Deity, struck from the fire of his eternal blaze, and brought forth in the midst of eternal burnings?" ("Origin, Object and Destiny of Women," *The Mormon* 3 (28): 3, 29 August 1857). Christ says, "I am the true light that is in you, and that you are in me; otherwise ye could not abound" (D&C 88:50). Christ is the life and the light of every person (John 1:4, 9). King Benjamin teaches similarly that God preserves us from day to day, lending us breath, that we may live and move—even supporting us from one moment to another (see Mosiah 2:21), and that all we have and are come from him (see Mosiah 4:21).

I ask, if we live and move and have our being in him (see Acts 17:28), where is self-esteem? How do I even separate my self out from the abundant grace that makes my life and even my intellect go forward in some marvelous symbiosis with my Creator?

Is it not obvious that we, created out of the very stuff of truth and permeated by his power, cannot live against our own natures of light and truth and intelligence without setting up conflict and spiritual disease within ourselves? The quality of our emotional and spiritual existence is absolutely governed by divine law, and whether or not we know about these laws, or observe them, we are continually and profoundly affected by them. I suggest that at the base of much low self-esteem lies not only spiritual conflict but a deep self-disapproval, whether conscious or not, over neglect of the spiritual laws that govern happiness and freedom.

So here we have a challenging situation: a person, whose primeval nature is truth and light and purity, begins, under the influence of a fallen environment and a fallen body, to act against his spiritual nature. His sins of ignorance or choice produce bitterness, and he begins to suffer—but usually he doesn't know what the real source of his unhappiness is. He thinks it has something to do with the people around him, or he thinks it has to do with his circumstances. But Elder Neal A. Maxwell observes: "The heaviest load we feel is often from the weight of our unkept promises and our unresolved sins, which press down relentlessly upon us" (*CR*, October 1989, p. 106; also, "Murmur Not," *Ensign,* November 1989, p. 85).

Resistance to our spiritual natures manifests itself as guilt, despair, resentment, self-pity, fear, depression, feelings of victimization, fear over the scarcity of needed things, and other forms of distress. These are all functions of the fallen self, and we all necessarily experience them. But the pursuit of self-esteem will not solve the problems of the self that is in conflict because of sin. It will not even solve the problems of those who suffer from others' sins against them.

King Benjamin called this fallen self the natural man:

> For the natural man is an enemy to God, and has been from the fall of Adam, and will be, forever and ever, unless he yields to the enticings of the Holy Spirit, and putteth off the natural man and becometh a saint through the atonement of Christ the Lord, and becometh as a child, submissive, meek, humble, patient, full of love, willing to submit to all things which the Lord seeth fit to inflict upon him, even as a child doth submit to his father (Mosiah 3:19).

Could this putting off of the natural man through the Lord Jesus Christ actually be a recovery of our true, premortal self?

We have this account of King Benjamin's people, who, upon hearing the word of God, became painfully conscious of their carnal state. They cried out, "O have mercy, and apply the atoning blood of Christ that we may receive forgiveness of our sins" (Mosiah 4:2). Whereupon their sensitive souls were cleansed by the Holy Spirit, top to bottom, of all their accumulations of willfulness and disobedience; into that vacuum rushed the sublime love of God. They received "peace of conscience, because of the[ir] exceeding faith . . . in Jesus Christ" (Mosiah 4:3). They probably had not realized just how spiritually sluggish they were until that Mighty Power consumed in love all their sins and their pain and their sickness and their infirmity. They became acquainted with God's goodness and tasted his love.

King Benjamin, seeing their joy, taught them how to retain it:

> I would that ye should remember, and always retain in remembrance, the greatness of God, and your own nothingness, and his goodness and longsuffering towards you. . . .
> . . . if ye do this ye shall always rejoice, and be filled with the love of God, and always retain a remission of your sins (Mosiah 4:11-12).

What does the Lord mean by the nothingness of man? We recoil at nothingness because we try so hard to overcome our feelings of unimportance. But nothingness refers to man's state in this mortal sphere (see Mosiah 4:5). Nothingness describes not man's lack of value, but rather his powerlessness during his mortal probation and, especially, his all-encompassing need for the Lord. Nothingness reminds us of the reductions we voluntarily subscribed to before the foundations of this world in order to come to earth and learn how to be taught from on high.

Elder Richard G. Scott recently told of a sacred experience when strong impressions came to him during a period when he struggled to do a work the Lord had given him far beyond his personal capacity to fulfill. The Lord said to him, "Testify to instruct, edify, and lead others to full obedience, not to demonstrate anything of self. All who are puffed up shall be cut off." And then the Lord said to him, "You are nothing in and of yourself, Richard." That was followed with some specific counsel on how to be a better servant ("Acquiring Spiritual Knowledge," *BYU 1992-93 Devotional and Fireside Speeches,* Provo, Utah: Brigham Young University, 1993, p. 155).

You remember Ammon, who joyfully described his own nothingness:

> I do not boast in my own strength, nor in my own wisdom; but behold, my joy is full, yea, my heart is brim with joy, and I will rejoice in my God.
> Yea, I know that I am nothing; as to my strength I am weak; therefore I will not boast of myself, but I will boast of my God, for in his strength I can do all things (Alma 26:11-12).

For Ammon, it seems, the whole concept of self-esteem was irrelevant. Being filled with the love of God was of far greater worth than any sense of self-confidence. If one grand objective of earth life is to gain access to the grace of Jesus Christ for our trials and divine development, then we will immediately realize that self-confidence is a puny substitute for God-confidence.

With respect to confidence, the Lord says, "Let thy bowels also be full of charity towards all men, . . . let virtue garnish thy thoughts unceasingly; then shall thy confidence wax strong in the presence of God" (D&C 121:45).

The Lord identifies love and virtue as the essential ingredients in feelings of confidence and security. By these we dwell safely in the Holy One of Israel (see I Nephi 22:28).

Indeed, might the pursuit of self-confidence actually pull us away from the connection the Lord is trying to make? Might it merely produce "carnal security" (2 Nephi 28:2 1)?

Have you noticed that the pursuit of self-esteem seems to produce anxiety, whereas increasing humility and faith in the Lord produces consolation and rest? Mormon describes Church members who, waxing "stronger and stronger in their humility, and firmer and firmer in the faith of Christ," are filled with joy and consolation (Helaman 3:35). Alma instructs his son to teach the people to humble themselves and "to be meek and lowly in heart; for such shall find rest to their souls" (Alma 37:34).

Some may not like the dichotomy between the pursuit of self-esteem and faith in the Lord Jesus Christ. Some may say that you can pursue and have both. But I do not find this idea of both pursuits in the scriptures. It seems to me that King Benjamin finds these two incompatible. He said to remember your own nothingness and God's goodness. In trying to have both, is there a possible double-mindedness? James says that a double-minded man is "unstable in all his ways" (James 1:8). Nephi says of self-promotion:

> Priestcrafts are that men preach and set themselves up for a light unto the world, that they may get gain and praise of the world; but they seek not the welfare of Zion.
> Behold, the Lord hath forbidden this thing; wherefore, the Lord God hath given a commandment that all men should have charity, which charity is love. And except they should have charity they were nothing (2 Nephi 26:29-30).

Nephi seems to view setting oneself up for a light to the world in order to get praise as directly antithetical to having the pure love of Christ. One apparently can't do both. The Savior says, "Therefore, hold up your light that it may shine unto the world. Behold I am the light which ye shall hold up" (3 Nephi 18:24). In Doctrine and Covenants 88, verse 67, again he says that if our eye be single to his glory, our whole bodies will be filled with light: "Therefore, sanctify yourselves that your minds become single to God, and the days will come that you shall see him" (D&C 88:68). It seems as though the less attention we can give to self-esteem, the more light we can have.

Low self-esteem is often associated with feelings of incapacity, or a sense of victimization, or the realization that we can't make happen the opportunities, the approval, the feelings, etc., that we feel we need. But our relief comes when we realize that God made us powerless so that as we cleaved unto him, he could work his mighty miracles in our lives. Indeed, Moroni teaches that hopelessness and despair come of that iniquity which is lack of faith in one's access to the Lord Jesus Christ (see Moroni 10:22-23).

We may think that we or some other mortal opens the necessary doors to our future, but this conclusion is an error: We ourselves do not open these doors; only the Lord does. We give him our obedience, our diligence, our cooperation, but he opens and closes the doors. We can only make right choices; he controls the consequences of our choices.

Often doors have closed before us that seemed to lead to the opportunities we thought we had to have. We assumed that the closed door was a reflection of some inadequacy in ourselves. But perhaps the closed door had nothing to do with whether we were good or bad or capable or incompetent. Rather, a loving Father shapes, even now, our path according to a prearranged, premortal covenant (see Abraham 2:8). The opening or the closing of these various doors is absolutely dependent on the Lord's perfect perception of our developmental needs. All the elements that we really need for our individual experience here, he puts onto our path. The most important things that will happen to us in this life will come to us often by no initiative of our own, but they come because he is piloting the plan. He says that he does nothing save it·be for our benefit (see 2 Nephi 26:24); he has promised that all things work together to our good in order that we may be conformed to the image of his Son (see Romans 8:28-29).

Therefore, one does not need to fear that one's future lies in the fact that an authority over us plays favorites, or that one's employer isn't well-disposed toward him. Under such a belief, one might be tempted to think that only self-promotion, or image manipulation, or compromising of what one really believes will open the doors one needs to open. But even though someone in authority thinks he opens doors, there is really only one Keeper of the Gate (see 2 Nephi 9:41). "No weapon that is formed against thee shall prosper," he says, "This is the heritage of the servants of the Lord" (3 Nephi 22:17).

Now, I ask you, as various doors open and close, as the Lord Jesus Christ orchestrates even the details of our lives, where is the need to pursue self-esteem? We don't need it. Faith in the Lord Jesus Christ will take us farther.

Christ himself is our model where the self is concerned. Hear the manner in which he presents himself. He says,

1. "The Son can do nothing of himself, but what he seeth the Father do: for what things soever he doeth, these also doeth the Son likewise" (John 5:19).

2. "I do nothing of myself; but as my Father hath taught me, I speak these things" (John 8:28).

3. "The words that I speak unto you I speak not of myself but the Father that dwelleth in me, he doeth the works" (John 14:10).

You remember that Moroni wrote that the resurrected, perfected Christ spoke to him in "plain humility" (Ether 12:39). Elder Maxwell observed that "The Savior—the brightest individual ever to walk this planet—never sought to 'prosper' or to 'conquer' 'according to his genius' and 'strength'!" (See Alma 30:17). ("Out of the Best Faculty," BYU Annual University Conference, 23-26 August 1993, p. 37). Alma identified the precept that man prospers by his own resources as the doctrine of the antichrist (see Alma 30:17).

It seems to me that the self may actually be an interloper in most of what we do and that we can find relief from the stresses and strains of self-promotion by saying, in effect, "Get thee behind me, Self." I wonder if this is what the Savior means when he says, "He who seeketh to save his life shall lose it: and he that loseth his life for my sake shall find it" (JST Matthew 10:39). The self seems to be a constant intruder as we strive for selflessness. But President Benson pointed out that "Christ removed self as the force in His perfect life. It was not *my* will, but *thine* be done" (CR, 5 April 1986, p. 6; also, "Cleansing the Inner Vessel," *Ensign,* May 1986, p. 6; emphasis in original).

I have become aware of how demanding of attention the self is. What a lot of prayer and deliberate living it will take for me to remove my self as the force in my life. I have become aware that all my sins rise out of the self-absorption of my heart—impulses rising like the ticking of a clock in their persistent quest for self-gratification. It seems as though a change is needed at the very fountain of my heart out of which all thought and emotion rise. Could I actually come to the point where I could act without calculating my own self-interest all the time? Could I really live my daily life so that I was constantly searching out the Lord's will and drawing down his grace to accomplish it? And when the Lord in his mercy meshes his power with my agency and my effort and brings forth some measure of success, I ask, where is self-esteem? I feel as though I just want to say instead, "Oh, Lord, increase my faith."

How then does one appropriately think about oneself. I offer you Elder Enzio Busche's remarks. He said,

> A disciple of Christ is . . . constantly, even in the midst of all regular activities, striving all day long through silent prayer and contemplation to be in the depth of self-awareness to keep him in the state of meekness and lowliness of heart ("Truth Is the Issue," *Ensign,* November 1993, p. 25).

It seems appropriate as well to be conscious of our preciousness to our Father and at the same time to feel meek and lowly before his sacrifices on our behalf, his reverence for us, and his continuing graciousness to us. Again, Elder Busche spoke of the point at which we realize the Lord's love:

> This is the place where we suddenly see the heavens open as we feel the full impact of the love of our Heavenly Father, which fills us with indescribable joy. With this fulfillment of love in our hearts, we will never be happy anymore just by being ourselves or living our own lives. We will not be satisfied until we have surrendered our lives into the arms of the loving Christ, and until He has become the doer of all our deeds and He has become the speaker of all our words (Busche, "Truth," p. 26).

When Christ is the doer of all our deeds and the speaker of all our words, I have to ask, where is self-esteem? Where is the need of self-esteem? I propose that self-esteem becomes a nonissue for the person who is perfecting his faith in the Lord Jesus Christ.

If I decide to give up some of the attention my self-demands, what will I replace it with? The Lord answers, "Look unto me in every thought; doubt not, fear not" (D&C 6:36). The self is so demanding that perhaps one can only let go of the pursuit of self-promotion as one cleaves to the Lord Jesus Christ (see Omni 1:26). Like Peter walking on the water, it may be our sudden self-consciousness that will cause us to fall (see Matthew 14:30).

The world speaks of self-image, but Alma spoke of receiving the image of God in our countenances (see Alma 5:14). In fact, as the *Lectures on Faith* inform us,

> All those who keep his commandments shall grow up from grace to grace, and become . . . joint heirs with Jesus Christ; possessing the same mind, being transformed into the same image. . . . even the express image of him who fills all in all; being filled with the fullness of his glory, and become one in him, even as the Father, Son and Holy Spirit are one (Lectures on Faith 5:2).

It seems as though the perception of the self as an entity separate from God will, under the right conditions, just get thinner and thinner.

President Benson has pressed us to be changed for Christ, captained by Christ, and consumed in Christ (see "Born of God," *Ensign,* July 1989, p. 5). We might ask, what is it that must be consumed? Maybe it is our old concept of self, the one we have learned from the precepts of men. Is it possible that the pursuit of self-esteem might delay this mighty change? Indeed, what if one ceased defining self-esteem or justifying one's pursuit of it, and just ignored it? What if, instead, one just began to obey whatever divine instruction he was not obeying, to sacrifice whatever needed sacrificing, and to consecrate whatever he was holding back? What if he just set out to "seek this Jesus" (Ether 12:4 1)?

So many issues that revolve around the subject of self fade like the dew in the sun as one cultivates faith in the Savior. Without him, nothing else matters. No amount of self-esteem or anything else can adequately fill the void.

I'll close with some thoughts of Robert Browning, quoted by President David O. McKay:

> There is an answer to the passionate longings of the heart for fullness . . . : Live in all things outside yourself by love, and you will have joy. That is the life of God; it ought to be our life. In him it is accomplished and perfect; but in all created things it is a lesson learned slowly and through difficulty (David O. McKay, *Cherished Experiences,* comp. Clare Middlemiss, Salt Lake City: Deseret Book Company, 1976, p. 161).

One who practices faith in the Lord Jesus Christ will find relief from the stresses and anxieties of the pursuit of self-esteem. In the name of the Lord Jesus Christ. Amen.

The Gospel----The Foundation for Our Career

Elder Boyd K. Packer

Conference Report, April 1982, pp. 121-125

There is a recurring theme in the revelations having to do with learning. And, from the beginning, Church leaders have counseled us to get all of the education we can as a preparation for and as an improvement of our careers. For example:

Dignity and Worth in Honest Work

Seek ye diligently and teach one another words of wisdom; yea, seek ye out of the best books words of wisdom; seek learning, even by *study* and also by *faith* (D&C 88:118; italics added. See also D&C 90:15; 109:7).

Learning is to be accompanied by faith, and as the Book of Mormon teaches us, learning "is good if [we] hearken unto the counsels of God" (2 Ne. 9:29).

There is one thought that must come at the very beginning of a discussion on occupations and careers in order to establish it as preeminent, and it is this:

Do not ever belittle anyone, including yourself, nor count them, or you, a failure, if your livelihood has been modest. Do not ever look down on those who labor in occupations of lower income. There is great dignity and worth in any honest occupation. Do not use the word menial for any labor that improves the world or the people who live in it.

There is no shame in any honorable work, and the principle of faith, which the Lord connected with learning, is precious above the technologies of man.

There will be many who struggle through life with small ownership and low income who discover, because they have been decent, the meaning of the scripture, "He that is greatest among you," let him be "the least and the servant of all" (Matt. 23:11; D&C 50:26).

Elisha and Naaman

While *schooling* and *education* generally go together, there are kinds of wisdom which are not usually taught in school classrooms.

To illustrate, I begin with the Old Testament record of Naaman who, as the commander of the armies of Syria, had "given deliverance" to his country. He became a leper and the king of Syria feared he would die.

An Israelite slave girl who served Naaman's wife spoke of prophets in Israel who had the power to heal.

The king of Syria sent a message to the king of Israel saying, "I have sent Naaman my servant to thee, that thou mayest recover him of his leprosy." The king of Israel suspected a plot and complained, "He seeketh a quarrel against me. . . . Am I God, to kill and to make alive, that this man doth send unto me to recover a man of his leprosy?"

Elisha, the prophet, heard of the king's distress. And "he sent to the king, saying, . . . let him come now to me." Elisha would heal Naaman, and he told why: that "he shall know that there is a prophet in Israel."

When Naaman was near, Elisha sent a messenger to him, saying, "Go and wash in Jordan seven times, . . . and thou shalt be clean." Naaman was angry. There were rivers aplenty in Syria, as good, he thought, as the Jordan. He had expected Elisha to perform some impressive ceremony like clapping his hands upon him. And he "turned . . . away in a rage."

But one of his servants (it seems there is always a servant) courageously chastised the general and said, "If the prophet had bid thee do some *great* thing, wouldest thou not have done it?"

Humbled by his servant, Naaman "went . . . down, and dipped himself seven times in Jordan, according to the saying of the man of God: and he was clean" (2 Kings, 5:1-14; italics added).

Self-reliance

Human nature hasn't changed over the years. Even today some of us expect to be bidden to do some "great things" in order to receive the blessings of the Lord. When we receive ordinary counsel on ordinary things, there is disappointment, and, like Naaman, we turn away.

Let me give you a modern-day example. President Kimball has been president of the Church for eight years. In virtually every conference sermon he has included at least a sentence telling us to clean up, paint up, and fix up our property. Many of us have paid little attention to the counsel.

Question: Why would a prophet tell us to do that? Has he no great prophecies to utter?

But, is that not a form of prophecy? For has he not said to us over and over again, "Take good care of your material possessions, for the day will come when they will be difficult, if not impossible, to replace."

Already there is a fulfillment. Families who might have afforded a home when first he spoke now despair of getting one.

For some reason, we expect to hear, particularly in welfare sessions, some ominous great predictions of calamities to come. Instead, we hear quiet counsel on ordinary things which, if followed, will protect us in times of great calamity.

It was Alma the prophet who said, "By small and simple things are great things brought to pass; and small means in many instances doth confound the wise" (Alma 37:6).

Now, all of this was to prepare you for the fact that the counsel I will give may seem ordinary, even trivial to some of you. But it will be consistent with the doctrines and principles announced by the First Presidency when the welfare program was first introduced:

> Our primary purpose [is] to set up, in so far as it might be possible, a system under which the curse of idleness would be done away with, the evils of a dole abolished, and independence, industry, thrift and self-respect be once more established amongst our people. The aim of the Church is to help the people to help themselves. Work is to be re-enthroned as the ruling principle of the lives of our Church membership (In Conference Report, October 1936, p. 3).

That emphasis, on self-reliance, suggests something about education. We cannot expect the Church to assume responsibility for the schooling of all of us.

Direction, Counsel, Encouragement, Vision

One of the questions most often asked of General Authorities as we travel usually begins in this way: "Why doesn't the Church . . . ?" And then there follows a description of some worthy project that would, if it should succeed, bring credit to the Church and benefit many people.

For example, why doesn't the Church establish schools to prepare members for financial security?

Some years ago I was near our front gate splitting rails for a fence. A young man came to make a delivery. He had recently returned from over-seas combat duty. He had falsified his age and left school to join the Marines. When I asked about his future plans, he didn't know. Jobs were scarce; he had no skills to offer.

I counseled him to go back to high school and get his diploma. He thought he couldn't do that; he was too old now. "If you do it," I told him, "you probably will not exactly fit in. And the students will call you the 'old man' or 'grandpa.' But you faced an enemy in combat; surely you've got the courage to face that."

The lesson is this. I only spent ten minutes with him, sitting on a log by our front gate. I did not build a school nor ask the Church to build one. I did not pay his tuition or prepare his lessons. What he needed was some direction, some counsel, some encouragement, and some vision. In this case he took the counsel and returned to school. Now he has a family and an occupation.

I only gave him vision and encouragement. It does not take additional Church budget to do that. That is the responsible role of every priesthood leader in counseling members on careers. We must help people to *help themselves*.

Several years ago a certain country was emerging from a long period of political and economic distress, and there was a need for skilled workers of many kinds. Some of our local leaders, sensing the need, conceived the idea of establishing vocational schools in our chapels to train the brethren in their skills. They could then upgrade themselves in their employment. It was a very appealing idea.

They pointed out that the money expended would be justified on the basis that these brethren would return in tithes more than the cost of the program. They were greatly disappointed when the Brethren did not approve their idea.

There were several things they'd not considered. The most important was that vocational training was already available to those who really looked for it. Classes to train new employees, and to upgrade the experienced ones, were offered by business and industry, and by their government.

What our brethren needed most was counsel and encouragement to take advantage of opportunities that were already available.

We ourselves are responsible to seek out and take advantage of every opportunity to improve ourselves.

Teach Moral and Spiritual Values

Now, there are some things that the Church must do, for we are commanded to do them. We must preach the gospel. We must build temples. We must perfect the Saints. These things others cannot do. The many other good things (which are not central to the mission of the Church) must take second place. For we do not have the resources to do all that is worth doing, however worthy it may be.

While we cannot build schools for everyone, there is a most important contribution the Church can make to our careers, one that is central to the mission of the Church. And that is to teach moral and spiritual values. There are ordinary virtues which influence our careers even more than technical training; among them are these:

Integrity
Dependability
Courtesy
Respect for others
Respect for property

Let me illustrate one or two of these.

It is likely that our children, and yours, for the first part of their married life at least, will live in rented apartments.

I had a conversation with a stake president who owns a large number of apartments which he rents to middle-income families. As he showed them to me, he described the abuse of his property, not just the normal wear and tear, but outright abuse bordering on vandalism.

Such conduct is unworthy of a Latter-day Saint! We should know better than that. We should be willing to drive a nail or set a screw in a hinge, if it's needed.

Our people should regard an apartment as their home and keep it inviting and clean and in good repair. Has not the prophet told us to do it? When they leave an apartment, it should be clean and essentially ready for the next tenant.

Transfer Learning from Home to Work

Now, what has this got to do with a career? Surely you can see the transfer of learning from our homes to our work.

Years ago my father, as a young married man with several children, went nervously into the bank in Brigham City to ask for a loan to start in business. He was asked about collateral. He had none beyond his willingness to work and some mechanical aptitude.

The banker, in turning down his request, happened to ask father where he lived. "In the old box house on First West," was the answer. The banker passed that corner on the way to work. He'd watched the transformation in the yard. He'd wondered who lived there, and admired what they were doing.

Father got the loan to start in business on the strength of the flowers that mother had planted in the yard of a very modest adobe house they were renting.

We have raised a large family on a very modest income, and it's likely that our children are going to have the same privilege. In order to prepare them, we've trained them to do ordinary, necessary things as preparation for their careers.

For instance, we have maintained an area (sometimes it's the corner of a basement room) where there is a work bench, where projects could be left. There can be some paint or a little sawdust on the floor, without a problem. In spite of continuous cleanup, this area is perpetually untidy, but with a purpose.

We have followed another practice. Each Christmas, at least one of the presents for the boys has been a hand tool. When they were old enough, a good metal toolbox was included. When each has left home, he has had his own set of tools and some knowledge of how to use them. He can tune up a car, or drive a nail, or turn a screw, or replace a plug or a faucet washer.

The girls, in turn, have learned to cook and to sew, and each has left home with a sewing machine. This training is doubly important—first, in frugal living at home, and then in their value as an employee. They would, we hoped, be not only good, but good for something.

Be Really Willing to Work

Now, I have an idea that some soul will be very upset with us for not providing our boys with a sewing machine and our girls a box of tools as well.

So I hasten to explain that our boys can cook enough to survive a mission and they can sew on a button. The girls in turn can change a faucet washer and drive a nail, and both of them can type and even change a tire on a car.

While many, many occupations suit a man or a woman equally well, I, for one, have grave concern over the growing trend for both men and women to choose careers which in some respects are against their very natures.

We have tried to prepare our boys for manly work and our girls for work that would suit the opportunities that womanhood will bring them. In defense of our doing that, I can only observe that in this Church we are not exempt from using common sense.

There are so few nowadays who are really willing to work. We must train our children and ourselves to give, in work, the equivalent of the pay we receive and perhaps just a little extra. There are so few who will come a bit early to get organized for the day, or stay a minute after to tidy up the work bench or the desk for tomorrow's work.

The attitude that demands compensation and benefits in excess of the value of labor has come near destroying the economy of the world. Now, however, many workers quite willingly accept reductions in pay just to keep their jobs. That spirit of doing a little extra would have prevented the crisis had it been evident earlier.

The Gospel----Formula for Success

Family responsibilities and tight budgets sometimes prevent us from obtaining all the schooling we desire.

We can, however, improve ourselves. The only tuition required is the time it takes, the work required, and the desire to build into our lives the ordinary virtues so much in demand and so short in supply.

I hope you have not been too disappointed that I have not presented some "great thing" for you to do, some elaborate formula for career planning, rather than such ordinary things so obvious, so close to us, that they are often overlooked.

There is a formula. The Lord said,

> Verily I say unto you, that every man who is obliged to provide for his own family, let him provide, and he shall in nowise lose his crown; *and let him labor in the church* (D&C 75:28; italics added).

The gospel of Jesus Christ is the formula for success. Every principle of the gospel, when lived, has a positive influence over your choice of an occupation and on what you will achieve. The counsel to labor in the Church has great value. Living the gospel will give you a perspective and an inspiration that will see you successful however ordinary your work may be or however ordinary your life may seem to others.

God bless the members of this Church, that you can be happy with who you are and where you are, that you can improve yourselves. We pray that God will bless those who are struggling now with unemployment, with the loss of their employment, with the fear of that loss. May he bless us that we can build into our lives those principles of reliance and integrity that have been part of the gospel from the very beginning, for the gospel is true. Of this I bear witness, in the name of Jesus Christ, amen.

The Power of the Word

President Ezra Taft Benson

Priesthood Leadership Meeting, April 4, 1986

My **dear brethren** what a thrilling sight it is to look out over this body of priesthood leadership and to know how many thousands of Saints you serve and how much dedication and faithfulness you collectively represent! There is no other body anywhere in the world today that meets for the same righteous purpose as does this group, nor is there any other group—political, religious, or military—that holds the power that you do here tonight.

We live in a day of great challenge. We live in that time of which the Lord spoke when he said, "Peace shall be taken from the earth, and the devil shall have power over his own dominion" (D&C 1:35). We live in the day which John the Revelator foresaw when "the dragon was wroth with the woman, and went to make war with the remnant of her seed, which keep the commandments of God, and have the testimony of Jesus Christ" (Rev. 12:17). The dragon is waging war against the members of the Church of Jesus Christ. Satan is waging war against the members of the Church who have testimonies and are trying to keep the commandments. And while many of our members are remaining faithful and strong, some are wavering. Some are falling. Some are fulfilling John's prophecy that in the war with Satan, some Saints would be overcome (See Rev. 13:7).

The prophet Lehi also saw our day in his great visionary dream of the tree of life. He saw that many people would wander blindly in the mists of darkness, which symbolized the temptations of the devil (See 1 Ne. 12:17). He saw some fall away in "forbidden paths," others drown in rivers of filthiness, and still others wander in "strange roads" (1 Ne. 8:28, 32). When we read of the spreading curse of drugs, or read of the pernicious flood of pornography and immorality, do any of us doubt that these are the forbidden paths and rivers of filthiness Lehi described?

Not all of those Lehi saw perishing were of the world. Some had come to the tree and partaken of the fruit. In other words, some members of the Church today are among those souls Lehi saw which were lost.

The Apostle Paul also saw our day. He described it as a time when such things as blasphemy, dishonesty, cruelty, unnatural affection, pride, and pleasure seeking would abound (See 2 Tim. 3:1-7). He also warned that "evil men and seducers shall wax worse and worse, deceiving, and being deceived" (2 Tim. 3:13).

Such grim predictions by prophets of old would be cause for great fear and discouragement if those same prophets had not, at the same time, offered the solution. In their inspired counsel we can find the answer to the spiritual crises of our age.

In his dream, Lehi saw an iron rod which led through the mists of darkness. He saw that if people would hold fast to that rod, they could avoid the rivers of filthiness, stay away from the forbidden paths, stop from wandering in the strange roads that lead to destruction. Later his son Nephi clearly explained the symbolism of the iron rod. When Laman and Lemuel asked, "What meaneth the rod of iron?" Nephi answered, "It was the word of God; and [note this promise] whoso would hearken unto the word of God, and would hold fast unto it, they would never perish; neither could the temptations and fiery darts of the adversary overpower them unto blindness, to lead them away to destruction" (1 Ne. 15:23-24). Not only will the word of

God lead us to the fruit which is desirable above all others, but in the word of God and through it we can find the power to resist temptation, the power to thwart the work of Satan and his emissaries.

Paul's message is the same as Lehi's. After portraying the terrible wickedness of future times—future to him, but present to us!—he said to Timothy: "But continue thou in the things which thou hast learned. . . .

"From a child thou hast known the holy scriptures, which are able to make thee wise unto salvation" (2 Tim. 3:14-15).

My dear brethren, this is an answer to the great challenge of our time. The word of God, as found in the scriptures, in the words of the living prophets, and in personal revelation, has the power to fortify the Saints and arm them with the Spirit so they can resist evil, hold fast to the good, and find joy in this life.

Now to you priesthood leaders we say, look to the prophetic counsel of Lehi and Paul and others like them. In that counsel you will find the solution to the challenges you have in keeping your flocks safe from the "ravening wolves" that surround them (See Matt. 7:15; Acts 20:29). We know that you too have great anxiety for the members of your wards and stakes and expend great time and effort in their behalf. There is much that we ask of you who have been chosen for leadership. We place many loads upon your shoulders. You are asked to run the programs of the Church, interview and counsel with the members, see that the financial affairs of the stakes and wards are properly handled, manage welfare projects, build buildings, and engage in a host of other time-consuming activities.

While none of those activities can be ignored and laid aside, they are not the most important thing you can do for those you serve. In recent years, time and again we have counseled you that certain activities bring greater spiritual returns than other. As early as 1970, President Harold B. Lee told the regional representatives:

> We are convinced that our members are hungry for the gospel, undiluted, with its abundant truths and insights. . . . There are those who have seemed to forget that the most powerful weapons the Lord has given us against all that is evil are His own declarations, the plain simple doctrines of salvation as found in the scriptures (In Regional Representatives seminar, Oct 1, 1970, p. 6).

In a First Presidency message in 1976, President Kimball said:

> I am convinced that each of us, at least some time in our lives, must discover the scriptures for ourselves—and not just discover them once, but rediscover them again and again. . . .
>
> The Lord is not trifling with us when he gives us these things, for "unto whom much is given, of him shall be much required" (Luke 12:48). Access to these things means responsibility for them. We must study the scriptures according to the Lord's commandment (see 3 Ne. 23:1-5); and we must let them govern our lives (*Ensign*, Sept. 1976, pp. 4-5).

In April 1982, Elder Bruce R. McConkie spoke to the regional representatives about the priority the scriptures should take in our labors. He said:

> We are so wound up in programs and statistics and trends, in properties, lands and mammon, and in achieving goals that will highlight the excellence of our work, that we have "omitted the weightier matters of the law." . . . However talented men may be in administrative matters; however eloquent they may be in expressing their views; however learned they may be in the worldly things—they will be denied the sweet whisperings of the Spirit that might have been theirs unless they pay the price of studying, pondering, and praying about the scriptures (In Regional Representatives' seminar, April 2, 1982, pp. 1-2).

That same day, Elder Boyd K. Packer spoke to the stake presidents and regional representatives. He said:

> Buildings and budgets, and reports and programs and procedures are very important. But, by themselves, they do not carry that essential spiritual nourishment and will not accomplish what the Lord has given us to do. . . . The right things, those with true spiritual nourishment, are centered in the scriptures (In Meeting with Stake Presidents and Regional Representatives, April 2, 1982, pp. 1-2).

I add my voice to these wise and inspired brethren and say to you that one of the most important things you can do as priesthood leaders is to immerse yourself in the scriptures. Search them diligently. Feast upon the words of Christ. Learn the doctrine. Master the principles that are found therein. There are few other efforts that will bring greater dividends to your calling. There are few other ways to gain greater inspiration as you serve.

But that alone, as valuable as it is, is not enough, You must also bend your efforts and your activities to stimulating meaningful scripture study among the members of the Church. Often we spend great effort in trying to increase the activity levels in our stakes. We work diligently to raise the percentages of those attending sacrament meetings. We labor to get a higher percentage of our young men on missions. We strive to improve the numbers of those marrying in the temple. All of these are commendable efforts and important to the growth of the kingdom. But when individual members and families immerse themselves in the scriptures regularly and consistently, these other area of activity will automatically come. Testimonies will increase. Commitment will be strengthened. Families will be fortified. Personal revelation will flow.

The Prophet Joseph Smith said that "the Book of Mormon was the most correct of any book on earth, and the keystone of our religion, and a man would get nearer to God by abiding by its precepts, than by any other book" (Book of Mormon, Introduction). Isn't that what we want for the members of our wards and stakes? Aren't we desirous that they get nearer to God? Then encourage them in every way possible to immerse themselves in this marvelous latter-day witness of Christ.

You must help the Saints see that studying and searching the scriptures is not a burden laid upon them by the Lord, but a marvelous blessing and opportunity. Note what the Lord himself has said about the benefits of studying his word. To the great prophet-leader Joshua, He said:

> This book of the law shall not depart out of thy mouth; but thou shalt meditate therein day and night, that thou mayest observe to do according to all that is written therein: for then thou shalt make they way prosperous, and then thou shalt have good success (Josh. 1:8)

The Lord was not promising Joshua material wealth and fame, but that his life would prosper in righteousness and that he would have success in that which matters most in life, namely the quest to find true joy (See 2 Ne. 2:25).

Do you have members in your stakes whose lives are shattered by sin or tragedy, who are in despair and without hope? Have you longed for some way to reach out and heal their wounds, soothe their troubled souls? The prophet Jacob offers just that with this remarkable promise: "They have come up hither to hear the pleasing word of God, yea, the word which healeth the wounded soul" (Jacob 2:8).

Today the world is full of alluring and attractive ideas that can lead even the best of our members into error and deception. Students at universities are sometimes so filled with the doctrines of the world they begin to question the doctrines of the gospel. How do you as a priesthood leader help fortify your membership against such deceptive teachings? The Savior gave the answer in His great discourse on the Mount of Olives when He promised, "And whoso treasureth up my word, shall not be deceived" (JS-M 1:37).

The scriptures are replete with similar promises about the value of the word. Do you have members who long for direction and guidance in their lives? The Psalms tell us, "Thy word is a lamp unto my feet, and a light unto my path' (Ps. 119:105), and Nephi promises that feasting upon the words of Christ "will tell you all things what you should do" (2 Ne. 32:3).

Are there members of your flock who are deep in sin and need to pull themselves back? Helaman"s promise is for them: "Yea, we see that whosoever will may lay hold upon the word of God, which is quick and powerful, which shall divide asunder all the cunning and the snares and the wiles of the devil" (Hel. 3:29).

Success in righteousness, the power to avoid deception and resist temptation, guidance in our daily lives, healing of the soul—these are but a few of the promises the Lord has given to those who will come to His word. Does the Lord promise and not fulfill? Surely if He tells us that these things will come to us if we lay hold upon His word, then the blessings can be ours. And if we do not, then the blessings may be lost. However diligent we may be in other areas, certain blessings are to be found only in the scriptures, only in coming to the word of the Lord and holding fast to it as we make our may through the mists of darkness to the tree of life.

And if we ignore what the Lord has given us, we may lose the very power and blessings which we seek. In a solemn warning to the early Saints, the Lord said this of the book of Mormon:

> Your minds in times past have been darkened because of unbelief, and because you have treated lightly the things you have received—Which vanity and unbelief have brought the whole church under condemnation. And this condemnation resteth upon the children of Zion, even all. And they shall remain under condemnation until they repent and remember the new covenant, even the Book of Mormon (D&C 84:54-57).

Oh, my brethren, let us not treat lightly the great things we have received from the hand of the Lord! His word is one of the most valuable gifts He has given us. I urge you to recommit yourselves to a study of the scriptures. Immerse yourselves in them daily so you will have the power of the Spirit to attend you in your callings. Read them in your families and teach your children to love and treasure them. Then prayerfully and in counsel with others, seek every way possible to encourage the members of the Church to follow your example. If you do so, you will find as Alma did, that "the word [has] a great tendency to lead people to do that which [is] just—yea, it has more powerful effect upon the minds of the people than the sword, or anything else, which [has] happened to them" (Alma 31:5).

Like Alma, I say unto you, "It [is] expedient that [you] should try the virtues of the word of God" (Alma 31:5), in the name of Jesus Christ, amen.

Same-Gender Attraction

Elder Dallin H. Oaks

The Ensign, October 1995, pp. 7-14

Every Latter-day Saint knows that God has forbidden all sexual relations outside the bonds of marriage. Most are also aware of the Savior's teaching that it is sinful for a man to look upon and lust after a woman (see Matt. 5:28; D&C 42:24; 63:16).

Attraction between man and woman was instilled by the Creator to ensure the perpetuation of mortal life and to draw husband and wife together in the family setting he prescribed, including the raising of children. In contrast, deviations from God's commandments in the use of procreative powers are grave sins. President Joseph F. Smith taught:

> Sexual union is lawful in wedlock, and if participated in with right intent is honorable and sanctifying. But without the bonds of marriage, sexual indulgence is a debasing sin, abominable in the sight of Deity.[1]

Some Latter-day Saints face the confusion and pain that result when a man or a woman engages in sexual behavior with a person of the same sex, or even when a person has erotic feelings that could lead toward such behavior. How should Church leaders, parents, and other members of the Church react when faced with the religious, emotional, and family challenges that accompany such behavior or feelings? What do we say to a young person who reports that he or she is attracted toward or has erotic thoughts or feelings about persons of the same sex? How should we respond when a person announces that he is a homosexual or she is a lesbian and that scientific evidence "proves" he or she was "born that way"? How do we react when persons who do not share our beliefs accuse us of being intolerant or unmerciful when we insist that erotic feelings toward a person of the same sex are irregular and that any sexual behavior of that nature is sinful?

Gospel Doctrines

Our attitudes toward these questions are dictated by gospel doctrines we know to be true.

1. God created us "male and female" (D&C 20:18; Moses 2:27; Gen. 1:27). What we call gender was an essential characteristic of our existence prior to our birth.[2]

2. The purpose of mortal life and the mission of The Church of Jesus Christ of Latter-day Saints is to prepare the sons and daughters of God for their destiny—to become like our heavenly parents.

3. Our eternal destiny—exaltation in the celestial kingdom is made possible only through the atonement of Jesus Christ (through which we became and can remain "innocent before God" [D&C 93:38]) and is only available to a man and a woman who have entered into and been faithful to the covenants of an eternal marriage in a temple of God (See D&C 13:14; 132).

4. Through the merciful plan of our Father in Heaven, persons who desire to do what is right but through no fault of their own are unable to have an eternal marriage in mortal life will have an

336

opportunity to qualify for eternal life in a period following mortality if they keep the commandments of God and are true to their baptismal and other covenants.[3]

5. In addition to the cleansing effect of the Atonement, God has given us agency—the power to choose between good (the path of life) and evil (the path of spiritual death and destruction [See 2 Ne. 2:27; Moses 4:3]). Although the conditions of mortality can limit our freedom (such as by restricting our mobility or our power to act on certain options), when we have reached the age or condition of accountability (see Moro. 8:5-12; D&C 68:27; 101:78) no mortal or spiritual power can deprive us of our agency.

6. To accomplish one of the purposes of mortal life, it is essential that we be tested against opposition to see if we will keep the commandments of God (See 2 Ne. 2:11; Abr. 3:25-26). To provide that opposition, Satan and his followers are permitted to tempt us to use our agency and our freedom to choose evil and to commit sin.

7. Because Satan desires that "all men might be miserable like unto himself" (2 Ne. 2:27), his most strenuous efforts are directed at encouraging those choices and actions that will thwart God's plan for his children. He seeks to undermine the principle of individual accountability, to persuade us to misuse our sacred powers of procreation, to discourage marriage and childbearing by worthy men and women, and to confuse what it means to be male or female.

8. In all of this, the devil, who has no body, seeks to persuade mortals to corrupt their bodies by

> choos[ing] eternal death, according to the will of the flesh . . . . which giveth the spirit of the devil power to captivate, to bring [them] down to hell, that he may reign over [them] in his own kingdom (2 Ne. 2:29).

9. The First Presidency has declared that "there is a distinction between [1] immoral thoughts and feelings and [2] participating in either immoral heterosexual or any homosexual behavior."[4] Although immoral thoughts are less serious than immoral behavior, such thoughts also need to be resisted and repented of because we know that "our thoughts will also condemn us" (Alma 12:14). Immoral thoughts (and the less serious feelings that lead to them) can bring about behavior that is sinful.

10. Because of God's great love for his children, even the worst sinners (or almost all of them) will ultimately be rewarded with assignment to a kingdom of glory.[5] Persons who have lived good lives and received most of the ordinances of salvation but have failed to qualify for exaltation through eternal marriage will be saved in a lesser place in the celestial kingdom where there is no eternal increase (See D&C 131:1-4).

11. In the midst of the challenges and choices of mortal life, we are all under the Savior's commandment to "love one another" (John 15:12, 17). As the First Presidency said in a recent message:

> We are asked to be kinder with one another, more gentle and forgiving. We are asked to be slower to anger and more prompt to help. We are asked to extend the hand of friendship and resist the hand of retribution. We are called upon to be true disciples of Christ, to love one another with genuine compassion, for that is the way Christ loved us.[6]

Kindness, compassion, and love are powerful instruments in strengthening us to carry heavy burdens imposed without any fault of our own and to do what we know to be right.

Application of Doctrines and Responsibilities

These doctrines, commandments, and responsibilities guide us in answering the questions posed earlier in this article.

Our doctrines obviously condemn those who engage in so-called "gay bashing"—physical or verbal attacks on persons thought to be involved in homosexual or lesbian behavior.

We should extend compassion to persons who suffer from ill health, including those who are infected with HIV or who are ill with AIDS (who may or may not have acquired their condition from sexual relations). We should encourage such persons to participate in the activities of the Church.

Applying the First Presidency's distinction to the question of same-sex relationships, we should distinguish between (1) homosexual (or lesbian) "thoughts and feelings" (which should be resisted and redirected), and (2) "homosexual behavior" (which is a serious sin).

We should note that the words *homosexual, lesbian,* and *gay* are adjectives to describe particular thoughts, feelings, or behaviors. We should refrain from using these words as nouns to identify particular conditions or specific persons. Our religious doctrine dictates this usage. It is wrong to use these words to denote a *condition,* because this implies that a person is consigned by birth to a circumstance in which he or she has no choice in respect to the critically important matter of sexual *behavior.*

Feelings are another matter. Some kinds of feelings seem to be inborn. Others are traceable to mortal experiences. Still other feelings seem to be acquired from a complex interaction of "nature and nurture." All of us have some feelings we did not choose, but the gospel of Jesus Christ teaches us that we still have the power to resist and reform our feelings (as needed) and to assure that they do not lead us to entertain inappropriate thoughts or to engage in sinful behavior.

Different persons have different physical characteristics and different susceptibilities to the various physical and emotional pressures we may encounter in our childhood and adult environments. We did not choose these personal susceptibilities either, but we do choose and will be accountable for the attitudes, priorities, behavior, and "lifestyle" we engraft upon them.

Essential to our doctrinal position on these matters is the difference between our freedom and our agency. Our freedom can be limited by various conditions of mortality, but God's gift of agency cannot be limited by outside forces, because it is the basis for our accountability to him. The contrast between freedom and agency can be illustrated in the context of a hypothetical progression from feelings to thoughts to behavior to addiction. This progressions can be seen on a variety of matters, such as gambling and the use of tobacco and alcohol.

Just as some people have different feelings than others, some people seem to be unusually susceptible to particular actions, reactions, or addictions. Perhaps such susceptibilities are inborn or acquired without personal choice or fault, like the unnamed ailment the Apostle Paul called "a thorn in the flesh, the messenger of Satan to buffet me, lest I should be exalted above measure" (2 Cor. 12:7). One person may have feelings that draw him toward gambling but unlike those who only dabble, he becomes a compulsive gambler. Another person may have a taste for tobacco and a susceptibility to its addiction. Still another may have an unusual attraction to alcohol and the vulnerability to be readily propelled into alcoholism. Other examples may include a hot temper, a contentious manner, a covetous attitude, and so on.

In each case (and in other examples that could be given) the feelings or other characteristics that increase susceptibility to certain behavior may have some relationship to inheritance. But the relationship is probably very complex. The inherited element may be nothing more than an increased likelihood that an individual will acquire certain feelings if he or she encounters particular influences during the developmental years. But regardless of our different susceptibilities or vulnerabilities, which represent only variations on our mortal freedom (in mortality we are only "free according to the flesh" [2 Ne. 2:27]), we remain responsible for the exercise of our agency in the thoughts we entertain and the behavior we choose. I discussed this contrast in a talk I gave at Brigham Young University several years ago:

> Most of us are born with [or develop] thorns in the flesh, some more visible,
> some more serious than others. We all seem to have susceptibilities to one disorder or

another, but whatever our susceptibilities, we have the will and the power to control our thoughts and our actions. This must be so. God has said that he holds us accountable for what we do and what we think, so our thoughts and actions must be controllable by our agency. Once we have reached the age or condition of accountability, the claim 'I was born that way' does not excuse actions or thoughts that fail to conform to the commandments of God. We need to learn how to live so that a weakness that is mortal will not prevent us from achieving the goal that is eternal.

God has promised that he will consecrate our afflictions for our gain (See 2 Ne. 2:2). The efforts we expand in overcoming any inherited [or developed] weakness build a spiritual strength that will serve us throughout eternity. Thus, when Paul prayed thrice that his 'thorn in the flesh' would depart from him, the Lord replied, "My grace is sufficient for thee: for my strength is made perfect in weakness." Obedient, Paul concluded:

"Most gladly therefore will I rather glory in my infirmities, that the power of Christ may rest upon me.

"Therefore I take pleasure in infirmities, in reproaches, in necessities, in persecutions, in distresses for Christ's sake: for when I am weak, then am I strong" (2 Cor. 12:9-10).

Whatever our susceptibilities or tendencies [feelings], they cannot subject us to eternal consequences unless we exercise our free agency to do or think the things forbidden by the commandments of God. For example, a susceptibility to alcoholism impairs its victim's freedom to partake without addiction, but his free agency allows him to abstain and thus escape the physical debilitation of alcohol and the spiritual deterioration of addiction.

. . . Beware the argument that because a person has strong drives toward a particular act, he has no power of choice and therefore no responsibility for his actions. This contention runs counter to the most fundamental premises of the gospel of Jesus Christ.

Satan would like us to believe that we are not responsible in this life. That is the result he tried to achieve by his contest in the pre-existence. A person who insists that he is not responsible for the exercise of his free agency because he was 'born that way' is trying to ignore the outcome of the War in Heaven. We *are* responsible, and if we argue otherwise, our efforts become part of the propaganda effort of the Adversary.

Individual responsibility is a law of life. It applies in the law of man and the law of God. Society holds people responsible to control their impulses so we can live in a civilized society. God holds his children responsible to control their impulses in order that they can keep his commandments and realize their eternal destiny. The law does not excuse the short-tempered man who surrenders to his impulse to pull a trigger on his tormentor, or the greedy man who surrenders to his impulse to steal, or the pedophile who surrenders to his impulse to satisfy his sexual urges with children. . . .

There is much we do not know about the extent of freedom we have in view of the various thorns in the flesh that afflict us in mortality. But this much we do know; we all have our free agency and God holds us accountable for the way we use it in thought and deed. That is fundamental.[7]

The Insights of Science

In contrast to our doctrinal approach, many persons approach the problems of same-sex attraction solely from the standpoint of current science. While I am not qualified as a scientist, with the aid of scientific literature and with the advice of qualified scientists and practitioners, I will attempt to refute the claim of some that scientific discoveries demonstrate that avowed homosexuals and lesbians were "born that way."

We live in a time of accelerating scientific discoveries about the human body. We know that our inheritance explains many of our physical characteristics. At the same time, we also know that our behavior is profoundly influenced by psychosocial factors such as parental and sibling relationships (especially during the formative years) and the culture in which we live. The debate over whether, or the extent to which, specific behavior is attributable to "nature" or to "nurture" is centuries old. Its application to the subject of same-sex feelings and behaviors is only one manifestation of a highly complex subject on which scientific knowledge is still in its infancy.

Some scientists deny that behavior is genetically influenced.[8] Others are advocates of evidence or theories suggesting that "there is substantial evidence for genetic influence on sexual orientation."[9]

We are, of course, aware of evidence that inheritance explains some susceptibilities to certain diseases like some cancers and some other illnesses like diabetes mellitus. There are also theories and some evidence that inheritance is a factor in susceptibilities to various behavior-related disorders like aggression, alcoholism, and obesity. It is easy to hypothesize that inheritance plays a role in sexual orientation. However, it is important to remember, as conceded by two advocates of this approach, that

> the concept of substantial heritability should not be confused with the concept of inevitable heritability. . . . Most mechanisms probably involve interactions between constitutional predispositions and environmental events.[10]

Wherever they fall along the spectrum between outright rejection and total acceptance of biological determinism of sexual orientation, most scientists concede that the current evidence is insufficient and that firm conclusions must await many additional scientific studies.

A study of fifty-six pairs of identical male twins in which one twin classified himself as "gay" reported that 52 percent of the co-twins also classified themselves as gay.[11] A similar study of female identical twins yielded approximately the same proportion of co-twins who classified themselves as gay (thirty-four of seventy-one pairs, 48 percent).[12] If these studies show some inherited influence on whatever causes a man or woman to classify himself or herself as homosexual or lesbian, it is clear that this influence is not determinative. As a prominent scientist observed, "Even the identical twin of a gay man has a 50 percent or more chance of being heterosexual—even though he has the exact same genes and is reared by the same parents."[13] We should also note that the results of these studies (and others described below) are based on the subjects' self-classifications, a shaky foundation for scientific conclusions when "there is still no universally accepted definition of homosexuality among clinicians and behavioral scientists—let alone a consensus regarding its origins."[14]

In any emerging area of knowledge, a new source of evidence is most welcome. In July 1993, Dr. Dean Hamer made worldwide headlines when he announced that he had found

> a statistically significant correlation between the inheritance of genetic markers [an identifiable strip of DNA] on chromosomal region Xq28 and sexual orientation in a selected group of. . . homosexual men and their relatives over age 18.

In other words, "it appears that Xq28 contains a gene that contributes to homosexual orientation in males."[15] Putting the most positive interpretation on his discovery, Dr. Hamer's subsequent book concludes:

> We can make only educated guesses about the importance of Xq28 in the population at large. On the high side, the region couldn't possibly influence more than 67 percent of gay men, the proportion 'linked' to this region in our highly selected group of gay siblings. On the low side, if much of homosexuality is caused by the environmental factors, or by a large number of interacting genes, Xq28 could account for as little as a few percent of the variation in male sexual orientation. The median range, taken from our linkage data and from the available twin and family studies, suggests that Xq28 plays some role in about 5 to 30 percent of gay men. The broad range of these estimates is proof that much more work remains to be done.[16]

"Some role in about 5 to 30 percent" of self-classified "gay" men surely falls far short of justifying the claim that science has shown that "homosexuality" is "caused by" genetic inheritance. One eminent scientist identified two of the uncertainties:

> What evidence exists thus far of innate biological traits underlying homosexuality is flawed. . . . Confirmation of genetic research purporting to show that homosexuality is heritable makes clear neither what is inherited nor how it influences sexual orientation.[17]

In their impressive reappraisal of biologic theories of human sexual orientation, Drs. Byne and Parsons of Columbia University's Department of Psychiatry offer these important cautions and suggestions:

> It is imperative that clinicians and behavioral scientists begin to appreciate the complexities of sexual orientation and resist the urge to search for simplistic explanations, either psychosocial or biologic.
> Conspicuously absent from most theorizing on the origins of sexual orientation is an active role of the individual in constructing his or her identity. . . . We propose an interactional model in which genes or hormones do not specify sexual orientation per se, but instead bias particular personality traits and thereby influence the mariner in which an individual and his or her environment interact as sexual orientation and other personality characteristics unfold developmentally.[18]

This observation, but one of many suggestions from scientists, is particularly persuasive because it takes account of the vital element of individual choice that we know to be a true principle of our mortal condition.

The Responsibilities of Church Officers and Members

In their 14 November 1991 letter concerning the importance of the law of chastity, the First Presidency declared:

> Sexual relations are proper only between husband and wife appropriately expressed within the bonds of marriage. Any other sexual contact, including fornication, adultery, and homosexual and lesbian behavior, is sinful.

Consistent with that direction, Church officers are responsible to call transgressors to repentance and to remind them of the principle the prophet Samuel taught the wicked Nephites:

> Ye have sought all the days of your lives for that which ye could not obtain; and ye have sought for happiness in doing iniquity, which thing is contrary to the nature of that righteousness which is in our great and Eternal Head (Hel. 13:38).

Persons cannot continue to engage in serious sin and remain members of the Church. And discipline can be given for encouraging sin by others. There is no Church discipline for improper thoughts or feelings (though there is encouragement to improve them), but there are consequences for behavior. In the same sermon in which he taught that men should not be "cast out," the Savior commanded his servants that "ye shall not suffer any one knowingly to partake of my flesh and blood unworthily . . . ; therefore if ye know that a man is unworthy . . . ye shall forbid him" (3 Ne. 18:28-29). The Savior also commanded, "But if he repent not he shall not be numbered among my people, that he may not destroy my people" (v. 31; see also Mosiah 26:36; Alma 5:56-61). Consequently, if transgressors do not respond to calls to repentance, the shepherds of the Church flock must take disciplinary action in fulfillment of their God-given responsibilities.

At the same time, we should always distinguish between sinful *acts* and inappropriate *feelings* or potentially dangerous *susceptibilities*. We should reach out lovingly to those who are struggling to resist temptation. The First Presidency did this in their 14 November 1991 letter. After reaffirming the sinful nature of "fornication, adultery, and homosexual and lesbian behavior," the Presidency added:

> Individuals and their families desiring help with these matters should seek counsel from their bishop, branch president, stake or district president. We encourage Church leaders and members to reach out with love and understanding to those struggling with these issues. Many will respond to Christlike love and inspired counsel as they receive an invitation to come back and apply the atoning and healing power of the Savior (See Isaiah 53:45; Mosiah 4:23).

Similarly in a conference address on this same subject, President Gordon B. Hinckley said:

> I desire now to say with emphasis that our concern for the bitter fruit of sin is coupled with Christlike sympathy for its victims, innocent or culpable. We advocate the example of the Lord, who condemned the sin, yet loved the sinner. We should reach out with kindness and comfort to the afflicted, ministering to their needs and assisting them with their problems.[19]

Despite such invitations and assurances, the Church and its members continue to experience misunderstandings about our positions on these matters. Last fall in an interview with a television reporter, one of our Church officials was asked, "What is being done in the Church to try to stop the atmosphere of hate towards homosexuals?" Nine years ago, during a television interview on this subject, I was questioned about reports that the Church taught or implied "that these people are somehow pariahs . . . and these people hate themselves and that this is an attitude brought forth by the Church."

More significantly, we also receive such questions from faithful members. A recent letter is illustrative:

> Another concern we have is the way in which our sons and daughters are classified as people who practice deviant and lascivious behavior. Perhaps some do, but most do not. These young men and women want only to survive, have a spiritual life, and stay close to their families and the Church. It is especially damaging when these negative references are spoken from the pulpit. We believe such talks only create more depression and a tremendous amount of guilt, shame, and lack of self-worth, which they have endured throughout their entire lives. There is sometimes a real lack of the pure love of Christ expressed to help them through their ordeals. We will all appreciate anything you can do to help with the plight of these much misunderstood children of our Father in Heaven. If some of the General Authorities could express more sensitivity to this problem, it would surely help to avoid suicides and schisms that are caused within families. Many simply cannot tolerate the fact that Church members judge them as 'evil people,' and they, therefore, find solace in gay-oriented lifestyles.[20]

These communications surely show the need for improvement in our communications with brothers and sisters who are struggling with problems—all types of problems. Each member of Christ's church has a clear-cut doctrinal responsibility to show forth love and to extend help and understanding. Sinners, as well as those who are struggling to resist inappropriate feelings, are not people to be cast out but people to be loved and helped (See 3) Ne. 18:22-23, 30, 32). At the same time, Church leaders and members cannot avoid their responsibility to teach correct principles and righteous behavior (on all subjects), even if this causes discomfort to some.

Church leaders are sometimes asked whether there is any place in The Church of Jesus Christ of Latter-day Saints for persons with homosexual or lesbian susceptibilities or feelings. Of course there is. The degree of difficulty and the pattern necessary to forgo behavior and to control thoughts will be different with different individuals, but the message of hope and the hand of fellowship offered by the Church is the same for all who strive.

I tried to describe the crucial distinctions in my answer to the television reporter who implied that the Church taught that "these people are somehow pariahs." I said:

> The person that's working [to resist] those tendencies ought not to feel himself to be a pariah. Now, quite a different thing is sexual relations outside of marriage. A person engaging in that kind of behavior should well feel guilt. They should well feel themselves estranged from God, who has given commandments against that kind of behavior. It's not surprising to me that they would feel estranged from their church. What surprises me is that they would feel that the Church can revoke God's commandments. . . . To the woman taken in adultery (which is a pretty good precedent for us), . . . [the Savior] was merciful and loving . . . , but he said, 'Go thy way and sin no more.' He loved the sinner; he condemned the sin. I think the Church does the same thing, imperfectly perhaps, but that's what we teach our members: love the sinner, condemn the sin.[21]

The struggles of those who are troubled by same-sex attraction are not unique. There are many kinds of temptations, sexual and otherwise. The duty to resist sin applies to all of them.

The most important help the Church can offer to persons who have surrendered 'to sin or to those who are struggling to resist it is to fulfill its divine mission to teach true doctrine and administer the divine ordinances of the restored gospel. The gospel applies on the same basis to everyone. Its central truth is our Savior's atonement and resurrection, that we might have immortality and eternal life. To achieve that destiny, an eternal marriage is the divine and prescribed goal for every child of God, in this life or in the life to come. Nevertheless, this sacred goal must come about in the Lord's way. For example, President Gordon B. Hinckley has declared that "marriage should not be viewed as a therapeutic step to solve problems such as homosexual inclinations or practices."[22]

Through Christ and his church, those who struggle can obtain help. This help comes through fasting and prayer, through the truths of the gospel, through church attendance and service, through the counsel of inspired leaders, and, where necessary, through professional assistance with problems that require such help. Another important source of help is the strengthening influence of loving brothers and sisters. All should understand that persons (and their family members) struggling with the burden of same-sex attraction are in special need of the love and encouragement that is a clear responsibility of Church members, who have signified by covenant their willingness "to bear one another's burdens" (Mosiah 18:8) "and so fulfil the law of Christ" (Gal. 6:2).

The first principle of the gospel is faith in the Lord Jesus Christ, who gives us the light and the strength to overcome the obstacles of mortality and to use our God-given agency to choose the behavior that will lead us to our divine destiny. We are promised:

> There hath no temptation taken you but such is as common to man: but God is faithful, who will not suffer you to be tempted above that ye are able; but will with the temptation also make a way to escape, that ye may be able to bear it (I Cor. 10:13).

Conclusion

The differing perspectives of scientific evidence and religious doctrine can be likened to the difference between studying about an automobile by observing its operation and disassembling and analyzing its various parts or by reading the operator's manual written by the manufacturer. Much can be learned by observation and analysis, but that method will yield only partial knowledge of the function and potential of a machine. The best and most complete knowledge about the operation and potential of a machine will be revealed by studying the manual written by its manufacturer. The operator's manual for our bodies and souls is the scriptures, written by the God who created us and interpreted by his prophets. These are the best sources of knowledge about the purpose of life and the behavior and thoughts we should cultivate in order to live in happiness and to achieve our divine destiny.

All who struggle with the challenges of mortality can identify with the lament in the psalm of Nephi:

> O wretched man that I am! Yea, my heart sorroweth because of my flesh; my soul grieveth because of mine iniquities.
>
> I am encompassed about, because of the temptations and the sins which do so easily beset me (2 Ne. 4:17-18).

To have the will and strength to resist sin, we must trust in God and pray for his help. Nephi rejoiced in the Lord, who had supported him and led him through his afflictions (see v. 20). "Why should I yield to sin, because of my flesh?" Nephi asked (v. 27), adding a prayer that the Lord would redeem his soul and make me that I may shake at the appearance of sin" (v. 3 1).

Nephi concludes with words that apply directly to those who seek to find their way through the difficulties discussed in this article:

> O Lord, I have trusted in thee, and I will trust in thee forever. I will not put my trust in the arm of flesh; for I know that cursed is he that putteth his trust in the arm of flesh. Yea, cursed is he that putteth his trust in man or maketh flesh his arm.
>
> Yea, I know that God will give liberally to him that asketh (vs. 34-35).

He who has commanded us to be perfect has shed his blood to provide us the opportunity to achieve our divine destiny. His confidence in our ability to achieve eternal life is manifest in his incredible invitation "What manner of men ought ye to be? Verily I say unto you, even as I am" (3 Ne. 27:27).

Notes

1. *Gospel Doctrine,* 5th ed. (Salt Lake City: Deseret Book Co., 1939), p. 309.
2. Statement of the First Presidency, 31 Jan. 1912; printed in *Improvement Era,* Mar. 1912, p. 417; see also *Millennial Star,* 24 Aug. 1922, p. 539.
3. Lorenzo Snow, *Millennial Star,* 31 Aug. 1899, p. 547; discussed in Dallin H. Oaks, *Pure in Heart* (Salt Lake City: Bookcraft, 1988).
4. Letter of the First Presidency, 14. Nov. 1991.
5. See D&C 76; discussed in Dallin H. Oaks, "Apostasy and Restoration," *The Ensign,* May 1995, pp. 86-87.
6. "An Easter Greeting from the First Presidency," *Church News,* 15 Apr. 1995, p. 1.
7. "Free Agency and Freedom," *Brigham Young University 1987-88 Devotional and Fireside Speeches,* (Provo: BYU Publications 1988), pp. 46-47; the edited version printed here is found in Monte S. Nyman and Charles D. Tate, Jr., eds., *The Book of Mormon: Second Nephi, The Doctrinal Structure,* (Provo: BYU Religious Studies Center, 1989), pp. 13-15.
8. R. C. Lewontin and others, *Not in Our Genes,* (New York: Pantheon Books, 1984); R. Hubbard and E. Wald, *Exploding the Gene Myth,* (Boston: Beacon Press, 1993).
9. R. C. Friedman and J. Downey, "Neurobiology and Sexual Orientation: Current Relationships," *Journal of Neuropsychiatry* 50 (1993):149.
10. *Ibid.*
11. J. M. Bailey and R. C. Pillard, "A Genetic Study of Male Sexual Orientation," *Archives of General Psychiatry* 48, (1991):1089-96.
12. J. M. Bailey, R. C. Pillard, and others, "Heritable Factors Influence Sexual Orientation in Women," *Archives of General Psychiatry* 50 (1993):228.
13. D. Hamer and P. Copeland, *The Science of Desire* (New York: Simon & Schuster 1994), p. 218.
14. W. Byne and B. Parsons, "Human Sexual Orientation: The Biologic Theories Reappraised," *Archives of General Psychiatry* 50 (1993):228.

15. Dean Hamer and others, "A Linkage Between DNA Markers on the X Chromosome and Male Sexual Orientation," *Science* 261 (16 July 1993): 321-27.

16. *The Science of Desire*, pp. 145-46.

17. W. Byne, "The Biological Evidence Challenged," *Scientific American,* May 1994, pp. 50, 55.

18. Byne and Parsons, "'Human Sexual Orientation," pp. 236-37.

19. Gordon B. Hinckley, "Reverence and Morality," *The Ensign,* May 1987, p. 47.

20. Letter to Dallin H. Oaks, 3 Sept. 1994.

21. Television interview with Elder Dallin H. Oaks, 3 Dec. 1986; answer not telecast; excerpts printed in "Apostle Reaffirms Church's Position on Homosexuality," *Church News,* 14 Feb. 1987, pp. 10, 12.

22. Gordon B. Hinckley, "Reverence and Morality," p. 47.

Four Simple Things to Help Our Families and Our Nations

President Gordon B. Hinckley

The Ensign, September 1996, pp. 2-8

I have a profound feeling of gratitude for life in this remarkable age. What great technical progress has been made in communications, in travel, in medicine, in conveniences for home and work. I stand in respect, almost reverence, for the men and women of science who have made life better for each of us.

When I was born, the life expectancy in the United States was 50 years. Today, it is 75 years. Is it not a thing of wonder that 25 years have been added to the average life span during this time? The same is happening in other areas of the world. I was 30 years of age when penicillin was discovered, followed by a variety of other miracle drugs.

You are familiar with these things. I simply remind us of them as an expression of gratitude. We have achieved technical miracles, but tragically we are experiencing a moral and ethical disaster. May I take you who are older back in memory to the homes of your childhood. I think that in many cases there was prayer in those homes; families knelt together in the morning and invoked the watchful care of God. At night they joined again in prayer. Something wonderful came of this. It is difficult to describe, but it did something for children. The very act of expressing gratitude to God, our Eternal Father, brought with it a feeling of respect, reverence, and appreciation. The sick were remembered in those prayers, as were the poor and the needy. The leaders in the government were remembered in those prayers. This cultivated a spirit of respect for those in public office. Where is that respect today?

There was no uncouth or profane language heard in those homes. Civility and altruism were also taught in those days. A man recently sent me a recording of a talk given some years ago by Abner Howell who lived in my neighborhood. Belonging to a minority race, he had worked hard to achieve an education. He served as sergeant at arms for the Utah State Legislature. In that talk he expressed appreciation for the time when he was a boy in school and my mother helped him with his work and defended him against those who were taunting him. We were taught in our home that all of the people of the earth are sons and daughters of God. The color of their skin may be different, but their hearts and emotions are the same.

I would also like to say that it was unthinkable for us to go to school in sloppy attire. The first pair of long trousers I wore was for graduation from junior high school. Prior to that, like my friends, I wore short pants and long, black cotton socks. But they were neat and they were tidy. The mending of socks was a great chore, but it was an important chore.

We attended the public schools. My elementary school was named after American statesman Alexander Hamilton. My junior high school was named for United States president Theodore Roosevelt. We learned about these men. On February 12 we had a holiday for President Abraham Lincoln's birthday. On February 22 we had another holiday to honor President George Washington. Just before these holidays we had school programs in which we learned about "Honest Abe" and the boy George who admitted to chopping down his father's cherry tree. Maybe there was little historical substance to some of those stories, but there was something of substance that came into our lives. We developed an appreciation for the principle of honesty. Today we have Presidents' Day in the United States, but for many it has become primarily a play day.

We were taught respect for girls. We played games with them in the neighborhood. We had parties in our homes with boys and girls. Even as we grew older and went on dates, there was a certain wholesomeness about it and respect for the girls with whom we associated. Yes, society has made a lot of technical progress since those days, but we have also lost a tremendous reservoir of values.

Today there are fancier cars, yet we worry about car jacking and drive-by shootings. We have television and cable and all of their related paraphernalia, where entertainment, coarse in its nature, profane and obscene in its language, is poured into our living rooms. We dare not walk the streets of many cities at night. Crime has been listed as the most serious problem in our day. Using the United States only as an example, it is estimated that there are six million serious crimes a year committed in the land. Per capita crime increased 371 percent between 1960 and 1992. That is only 32 years. There were 23,760 murders in 1992, almost half the number of Americans killed during the entire Vietnam War.

Children killing children has become one of the tragic elements of society. Murder is the second-highest cause of death among youth. More money is constantly sought to hire more policemen and to build more prisons. I do not doubt that they are necessary. But I am rather confident they would not substantially alter the picture, because that is not getting at the roots of the problem.

Of course, these concerns are not peculiar to our nation. The same problems are being felt across the world. Yes, we are the beneficiaries of a technological revolution. There has been more of scientific discovery during my lifetime than during all of the centuries that preceded it. But in so many other areas, we are slipping into the jungle in terms of real civilization—at least in larger urban areas.

Now, I know that societies have always had crime and that they always will, have crime, some of it, of course. Societies have had and will have pornography, immorality, and other problems. But we cannot continue the trend that we are presently experiencing without some kind of catastrophe overtaking us. We have, for instance, always had illegitimate births in society, and we likely always will have them. But we cannot tolerate an increase in this ugly social phenomenon without paying a terrible price. All of society pays for situations where there are fatherless children.

I am more concerned about the moral deficit in our nations than I am about their budget deficits, though that, too, is a most serious matter. Do societies need more policemen? I do not dispute it. Do societies need more prisons? I suppose so. But what they need, above all else, is a strengthening of the homes of the people. Every child is a product of a home. Societies are having terrible youth problems, but I am convinced that they have a greater parent problem. I am grateful that we of the Church have for a long time taught and are teaching and spending a substantial part of our resources to fortify the homes of our people.

I am glad for the conveniences of the modem home, but I am distressed by what is going on in our homes. It was recently reported that there are 800,000 or more violent incidents within families each year in the United States alone. The terrible divorce rate says something about the stability of a society's homes. A troubled home inevitably leads to a generation of troubled children.

What can be done? We cannot effect a turnaround in a day or a month or a year. But I am satisfied that with enough effort we can begin a turnaround within a generation and accomplish wonders within two generations. That is not very long in the history of man. There is nothing any of us can do that will have greater long-time benefit than to rekindle wherever possible the spirit of the kind of homes in which goodness can flourish.

When I was a boy, we lived in the city during the school term and lived on a farm in the summer. On that farm we had an apple orchard and a peach orchard and various other trees. When we were in our early teens, my brother and I were taught the art of pruning trees. Every Saturday in February and March while snow was still on the ground, we would go out to the farm. We attended demonstrations put on by the agricultural college. I think we learned something about pruning as it was taught in those days. We learned, for instance, that you could prune a peach tree in February and in large measure determine the kind of fruit you would pick in September. The idea was to prune in such a way that the developing fruit would be exposed to air and sunlight, uncrowded as it occupied its place on the branch of the tree.

The same principle applies to children. There is an old and true proverb which says, "As the twig is bent, so the tree is inclined." May I repeat a story I have told in general conference. Not long after we were married, we built our first home. We had little money, and I did a lot of the work. The landscaping was entirely my responsibility. The first of many trees that I planted was a thornless honey locust, and I envisioned the day when its shade would assist in cooling the house in the summer. I put it in a place at the corner where the wind from the canyon to the east blew the hardest. I dug a hole, put in the bare root, put soil around it, poured on water, and largely forgot it. It was only a wisp of a tree, perhaps three-quarters of an inch in diameter. It was so supple that I could bend it with ease in any direction. I paid little attention to it as the years passed. Then one winter day when the tree was barren of leaves, I chanced to look out the window at it. I noted that it was leaning to the west, misshapen and out of balance. I could scarcely believe it. I went out and braced myself against it as if to push it upright. But the trunk was now nearly a foot in diameter. My strength was as nothing against it. I took from my toolshed a block and tackle, attaching one end to the tree and the other to a well-set post. I pulled the rope. The pulleys moved just a little, and the trunk of the tree trembled slightly. But that was all. It seemed to say to me, "You can't straighten me. It's too late. I've grown this way because of your neglect, and I will not bend."

Finally in desperation I took my saw and cut off the great heavy branch on the west side. I stepped back and surveyed what I had done. I had cut off a major part of the tree, leaving a huge scar about eight inches across and only one small branch growing skyward.

More than half a century has passed since I planted that tree. My daughter and her family now live there. I recently looked again at the tree. It is large, its shape is better, and it is a great asset to the home. But how serious was the trauma of its youth and how painful the treatment I had used to straighten it. When the tree was first planted, a piece of string would have held it against the forces of the wind. I could have and should have supplied that string with ever so little effort, but I did not. And it bent to the forces that came against it.

Children are like trees. When they are young, their lives can be shaped and directed, usually with ever so little effort. Said the writer of Proverbs, "Train up a child in the way he should go: and when he is old, he will not depart from it" (22:6). That training finds it roots in the home. There will be little of help from other sources. Do not depend on government to help in this darkening situation. Barbara Bush, wife of former United States president George Bush, spoke wisely when in Wellesley Massachusetts, in 1990 she addressed the Wellesley College graduating class and said, "Your success as a family, our success as society, depends not on what happens at the White House, but on what happens inside your house."

Religion can help and will do wonders. Religion is the great conservator of values and teacher of standards. Its message on values has been consistent through the ages. From the days of Sinai to the present, the voice of the Lord has been an imperative voice concerning right and wrong. In modern revelation, that voice has declared, "I have commanded you to bring up your children in light and truth" (D&C 93:40).

What, you may ask, can be done? The observance of four simple things on the part of parents would in a generation or two turn our societies around in terms of their moral values.

They are simply these: Let parents and children (1) teach and learn goodness together, (2) work together, (3) read good books together, and (4) pray together.

To the parents of young families I suggest:

1. Teach your children goodness. Teach them civility toward others. We have witnessed a situation beyond understanding as Yugoslavia dismembered itself into hateful groups killing one another. There seemed to be no sense of mercy; the innocent were gunned down without consideration. Why all of this? I believe it comes of the fact that for generations in the homes of that area, hatred has been communicated, hatred for those of ethnic roots other than one's own. The terrible situation in that area is the bitter fruit of seeds of hatred sown in the hearts of children by the previous generation.

There is no need in any land for conflict between diverse groups of any kind. Let there be taught in the homes of people that we are all children of God, our Eternal Father, and that as surely as there is fatherhood, there can and must be brotherhood. Let there be taught respect for womanhood and manhood. Let every husband speak with respect, kindness, and appreciation for his wife. Let every wife look for and speak of the virtues of her husband. President David O. McKay was wont to say that a man could do no greater thing for his children than to let them see that he loves their mother.

Is this old-fashioned? Of course if it. It is as old as truth itself. Quarreling families are only an expression of the sophistry of the devil.

Let parents teach their children the sanctity of sex, that the gift of creating life is sacred, that the impulses that burn within us can be and must be disciplined and restrained if there is to be happiness, peace, and goodness. Let there be instilled in the mind of every young man the great salient fact that every young woman is a daughter of our Eternal Father and that in offending her he not only demonstrates his own weakness but also offends his God. Let him understand that to sire a child brings a responsibility that will last as long as he lives.

Let the truth be taught by example and precept—that to steal is evil, that to cheat is wrong, that to lie is a reproach to anyone who indulges in it. If we are to put civility back into civilization, the process must begin in the home with parents, while children are very young. It will not happen otherwise.

2. Work together. I do not know how many generations or centuries ago someone first said, "An idle mind is the devil's workshop." Children need to work with their parents, to wash dishes with them, to mop floors with them, to mow lawns, to prune trees and shrubbery, to paint and fix up, to clean up, and to do a hundred other things in which they will learn that labor is the price of cleanliness, progress, and prosperity. There are too many youth who are growing up with the idea that the way to get something is to steal it.

Graffiti would soon disappear if those who spray it on had to clean it off. I still remember an experience during my first year in high school. I was eating lunch with some other boys. I peeled a banana and threw the peeling on the ground. Just at that moment the principal walked by. He asked me to pick up the banana peeling. I say he asked —here was a certain steely firmness in his voice. I got off the bench on which I was sitting and picked up the banana peeling. I put it in the trash can. There was other litter around the can. He told me that while I was picking up my own trash, I could pick up the trash of others. I did it. I have never thrown another banana peeling on the ground.

3. Read good books together. I regard television as perhaps the greatest tool yet created to teach and educate people in large numbers. But I decry the filth, the rot, the violence, and the profanity that spew from television screens into our homes. It is a sad commentary on our societies. The fact that the television set is on six or seven hours every day in many homes says something of tremendous importance. I feel sorry for those who are addicted to the tube. I believe it is an addiction. It becomes a habit as pernicious as many other bad habits. I feel sorry for parents who do not read to their young children. I feel sorry for children who do not learn the wonders to be found in good books, or how stimulating an experience it is to get into the mind of a great thinker as that person expresses himself or herself, with language cultivated and polished, concerning great and important issues.

I read once that United States president Thomas Jefferson grew up on the magnificent phrases of the King James Bible. As we continually study the scriptures, what an opportunity it is not only to walk with great people, even to walk with the Lord Himself, but also to read and savor the majestic language of the prophets of old as that language was translated into words and phrases that are beautiful and powerful and moving.

If we could follow a slogan that says, "Turn off the TV and open a good book," we would do something of substance in strengthening another generation. Do not misunderstand: There are so very many things of value that come over television, but we must be selective and not be as dumb, driven slaves to the trash of many writers and producers.

Recently, a man sent me a book. He is a doctor of philosophy in a great university. He told me that reading that book had become a significant experience in his life. I read it. It is the story of a boy in Paris who, in an accident, was blinded at the age of eight. It is an account of how when darkness surrounded him, there came a new light into his life. When he was 16 or 17, the Germans conquered France and German soldiers marched into Paris. This blind boy, a brilliant student, organized a resistance group. He and his associates ran an operation for getting information and circularizing it with a little newspaper they printed on a duplicator. The effort grew until they were distributing more than 250,000 copies an issue. Then he was betrayed by a member of the group, arrested, and sent to Buchenwald. There in the filth and despair he lived with similar victims. He could not see, but there was light within him that rose above the tragedy of his circumstances. He survived as a leader among those in that foul camp. The little newspaper he started became a great newspaper. I read that book and was lifted and strengthened by the story of that remarkable young man. If you cannot find good heroes and heroines for your children on television help your children find them in good books.

4. Finally, pray together. Is prayer such a difficult thing? Would it be so hard to encourage fathers and mothers to get on their knees with their little children and address the throne of Deity to express gratitude for blessings, to pray for those in distress as well as for themselves, and then to ask it in the name of the Savior and Redeemer of the world? How mighty a thing is prayer. Of that I can testify and to that you can testify. How tragic the loss for any family that fails to take advantage of this precious and simple practice.

These are vital issues concerning parents and children. Let us teach and learn goodness together, work together, read good books together, pray together. These things can be done notwithstanding the frenetic pressures of our lives. They can be done with children and particularly when children are small. Sometimes it may seem too late when they are in their teens. Yet, remember my thornless locust tree. Surgery and suffering brought about something beautiful, whose later life has provided welcome shade from the heat of the day.

I encourage you as one who has been ordained to the holy apostleship and to the calling I now hold. That sacred office is not given as a bestowal of honor. It is given with the responsibility to bless, encourage, strengthen, and build faith in things good and things divine. In the authority of that priesthood, my brethren and sisters, I bless you, that each of you, each of us, feeble as our efforts may seem to be, may become a factor for good in capturing the spirit of goodness in our homes and in recapturing it for our nations.

Visits by Former Church Leaders to Present Church Leaders

Now I will give you a little of my experience in this line. Joseph Smith visited me a great deal after his death, and taught me many important principles. On one occasion **he and his brother Hyrum visited me while I was in a storm at sea**. . . .The night following [the storm at sea] Joseph and Hyrum visited me, and the **Prophet laid before me a great many things.** Among other things he told me to get the Spirit of God; that all of us needed it. . .

Joseph Smith continued visiting myself and others up to a certain time, and then it stopped. The last time I saw him. . . [he] came to me and spoke to me. He said he could not stop to talk with me because he was in a hurry. The next man I met was Father Smith; he could not talk with me because he was in a hurry. **I met half a dozen brethren who had held high positions on earth, and none of them could stop to talk with me because they were in a hurry**. I was much astonished. By and by I saw the Prophet again and I got the privilege of asking him a question.

"Now," said I, "**I want to know why you are in a hurry**. I have been in a hurry all my life; but I expected my hurry would be over when I got into the kingdom of heaven, if I ever did."

Joseph said: "I will tell you, Brother Woodruff. **Every dispensation that has had the priesthood on the earth and has gone into the celestial kingdom has had a certain amount of work to do to prepare to go to the earth with the Savior when he goes to reign on the earth. Each dispensation has had ample time to do this work. We have not. We are the last dispensation, and so much work has to be done, and we need to be in a hurry in order to accomplish it.**" Of course, that was satisfactory, but it was a new doctrine to me (*Deseret Weekly* 53:642-643, October 19, 1896).

An Interview with Brigham Young

I believe the eyes of the heavenly hosts are over this people; I believe they are watching the elders of Israel, the prophets and apostles and men who are called to bear off this kingdom. I believe they watch over us all with great interest. . . . I have had many interviews with Brother Joseph until the last fifteen or twenty years of my life; I have not seen him for that length of time. But during my travels in the southern country last winter I had many interviews with President Young, and with Heber C. Kimball, and George A. Smith, and Jedediah M. Grant, and many others who are dead. They attended our conference, they attended our meetings. And on one occasion, I saw Brother Brigham and Brother Heber ride in [a] carriage ahead of the carriage in which I rode when I was on my way to attend conference; and they were dressed in the most priestly robes. When we arrived at our destination I asked President Young if he would preach to us. He said, "No, I have finished my testimony in the flesh. I shall not talk to this people any more." "But," said he, "I have come to see you; I have come to watch over you, and to see what the people are doing." Then, said he, "**I want you to teach the people—and I want you to follow this counsel yourself**—that they must labor and so live as to obtain the Holy Spirit, for without this you cannot build up the kingdom; without the spirit of God you are in danger of walking in the dark, and in danger of failing to accomplish your calling as apostles and as elders in the church and kingdom of God." And, said he, "Brother Joseph taught me this principle."

And I will here say, I have heard him refer to that while he was living. But what I was going to say is this: the thought came to me that Brother Joseph had left the work of watching over this Church and kingdom to others, and that he had gone ahead, and that he had left this work to men who have lived and labored with us since he left us. This idea manifested itself to me, that such men advance in the spirit world. And I believe myself that these men who have died and gone into the spirit world had this mission left with them; that is, a certain portion of them, to watch over the Latter-day Saints (*Journal of Discourses* 21:317-318, Oct. 10, 1880) (Both of these quotes are found in *The Discourses of Wilford Woodruff*, G. Homer Durham, ed., Bookcraft, 1946:287-290).

President Ezra Taft Benson

Now this dear, venerable prophet has entered in, there to rejoice with his beloved Flora and to speak of their wonderful family, there to rejoice with Joseph and Brigham and John and Wilford and the others.

The prophets who preceded him, ancient and modern, have on occasion communed with the servants of the Lord on this earth. So it well may be that we have not seen the last of this great prophet of God.

I testify that the veil between this mortal realm and the spirit world opens to such revelation and visitation as the needs of the church and kingdom of God on earth may require. I bear witness that he was a prophet of God, that Jesus is the Christ, the Son of God, that the gospel of Jesus Christ is true; and that this true servant now takes His hand and enters in, in the name of Jesus Christ, amen (Boyd K. Packer, funeral sermon for Pres. Benson, *Ensign,* July, 1994, p. 34).

As I said in the beginning, you are young and I am not. And yet in the eternal scheme of things, I am just as young as you are. Maybe a little closer to the final curtain on Act II, **but I know, for I have seen a little behind the curtain into Act III** *and bear personal witness that the gospel is true, and bear witness of Jesus Christ* (Boyd K. Packer, "The Plan and the Plan," Fireside for Young Adults, CES, Kirkland Washington, 7 May 1995).